WHY DO
SHEPHERDS
NEED A
BUSH?

WHY DO
SHEPHERDS
NEED A
BUSH?

LONDON'S UNDERGROUND HISTORY
OF TUBE STATION NAMES

DAVID HILLIAM

The
History
Press

First published 2010

The History Press
The Mill, Brimscombe Port
Stroud, Gloucestershire, GL5 2QG
www.thehistorypress.co.uk

Reprinted 2011
This paperback edition printed 2015, 2016

British Library Cataloguing in Publication Data.
A catalogue record for this book is available from the British Library.

ISBN 978 0 7509 6303 9

Typesetting and origination by The History Press
Printed in Great Britain.

CONTENTS

INTRODUCTION

The names of the 300 or so London Underground stations are so familiar to us as we strap-hang our way across the capital that we take them utterly for granted. We hardly ever question their meanings or origins – yet these well-known names are almost always linked with fascinating stories of bygone times.

Until the mid-nineteenth century, London was unbelievably rural, with names belonging to a countryside that we would neither recognise nor could imagine today. The old fields and turnpikes, market gardens and trees and bushes have completely disappeared, but their names still remain – given extra permanence as they are now forever enshrined as parts of our Underground network.

But who, in the twenty-first century, thinks of a real flesh and blood shepherd lolling back on a specially trimmed hawthorn bush, when travelling through Shepherd's Bush Underground Station? Who nowadays thinks of the original gigantic Fairlop Oak at the far end of the Central Line? And who, travelling through Totteridge and Whetstone on the Northern Line, imagines medieval soldiers sharpening their swords and daggers at the aptly named Whetstone just before engaging in the appallingly bloody battle of Barnet?

What about all those fifth- and sixth-century Saxon chieftains all bringing their families and followers to settle into what was dangerous new territory for them on a foreign island? Padda and Tota, Brihtsige and Wemba – none of them have any memorial, except that we unconsciously use their names as we speak of Paddington, Tottenham, Brixton and Wembley.

This book is not about the Underground itself, but about the names to be found on the network lines. It is hoped that both hardened old commuters and fresh-eyed new visitors to London will find this collection of origins an intriguing pathway into the rich, half-hidden history of England's capital...

... and as an extra, the second part of this book contains a short selection of other well-known London place-names with particularly interesting derivations.

David Hilliam

A BRIEF TIMELINE

The history of the various London Underground lines is complicated, as they were gradually formed bit by bit through the amalgamation of different railway companies.

The present well-known names of the London Underground lines – and indeed the very word 'line' itself – did not come into being until the formation of the London Passenger Transport Board on 1 July 1933. Until that time, several separate railway companies owned and managed different parts of the underground network. Strictly speaking, using the present names of the 'lines' before 1933 is anachronistic.

However, it must be stressed that this book is <u>not</u> a history of the underground, but an account of the derivations of station names. There are many books on the history of the London Underground, and the facts can also easily be found on Wikipedia. As this book is aimed at the general reader, it has seemed unnecessary to insist on the niceties of how these lines came into being. Nevertheless, for the record:

Bakerloo Line began life as the Baker Street and Waterloo Railway.
Central Line began as the Central London Railway (early on, it was popularly known as 'The Twopenny Tube'!).
Circle Line began as parts of the Metropolitan Railway with other parts belonging to the Metropolitan District Railway.
District Line began as the Metropolitan District Railway.
Metropolitan Line began as the Metropolitan Railway.
Northern Line evolved from the City and South London Railway, and also from the Charing Cross, Euston and Hampstead Railway.
Piccadilly Line began as the Great Northern, Piccadilly and Brompton Railway, which had been formed from the merger of

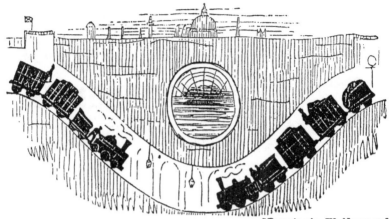

[*Drawing by W. Newman.*]

A PROPHETIC VIEW OF THE SUBTERRANEAN RAILWAYS.

A cartoon in *Punch*, 26 September 1846, when the London underground railway was first proposed. The very idea was considered to be ludicrous.

the Great Northern and Strand Railway and the Brompton and Piccadilly Circus Railway.

Given below is a much-abbreviated timeline, which is cheerfully brief and, though anachronistic, is perhaps more instantly meaningful to the ordinary passenger scrambling for place on the 'tube'.

1863	9 January	Metropolitan Line opens: Paddington to Farringdon
1864	13 June	Hammersmith and City Line opens
1868	1 October	District Line opens: High Street Kensington to Gloucester Road
1884	6 October	Circle Line completed
1890	November	Northern Line opens
1898	11 July	Waterloo and City Line opens
1900	27 June	Central Line opens
1906	10 March	Bakerloo Line opens
1906	15 December	Piccadilly Line opens
1969	7 March	Victoria Line officially opened: Warren Street to Victoria
1979	1 May	Jubilee Line opens
1987	31 August	Docklands Light Railway opens: Tower Gateway and Stratford to Island Gardens

ACKNOWLEDGEMENTS

Most of the illustrations are taken from *Old and New London* by Walter Thornbury and Edward Walford, published in 1897 by Cassell and Company Ltd. The exceptions are: the cartoon 'A Prophetic View of the Subterranean Railways', which appeared in *Punch* on 16 September 1846; the illustrations of Old Charing Cross, Swiss Cottage and the Fairlop Oak, which were taken from *London Stories* by 'John O' London'; and the drawing of the bull's head at Hornchurch, which was drawn by the author.

A–Z OF TUBE STATION NAMES

ACTON TOWN W3
District and Piccadilly
Originally opened on 1 July 1879 as MILL HILL PARK
Name changed to ACTON TOWN on 1 March 1910

'Acton' means 'farm among the oak-trees' – coming from two Saxon words: *ac*, 'oak-tree' and *tun*, 'farm' or 'settlement'. Most English place names beginning with 'Ac' derive from the once plentiful crop of oak trees that grew there. There are over twenty other 'Acton' place names in the British Isles.

ALDGATE EC3
Circle and Metropolitan
Opened on 18 November 1876

'Old Gate'. One of the six gates built by the Romans in London's city wall. From here the road from London led to the Roman capital of Britain – Colchester. The gate was already old when the Saxons came here in the fifth century, so they called it Ealdgate. Pulled down in 1761, its name still lives on as an Underground station.

The original Aldgate, demolished in 1761.

ALDGATE EAST E1
Hammersmith & City, District
Opened on 6 October 1884
Re-sited on 31 October 1938

Obviously the name is borrowed from Aldgate, the Underground station that had been opened eight years earlier. It had been proposed to call it Commercial Road, but in the end the name Aldgate East won the day, despite the fact that it is not sited particularly close to the original London gate. See ALDGATE.

ALDWYCH WC2
A 'lost' station on the Piccadilly Line
Opened as STRAND on 30 November 1907
Name changed to ALDWYCH on 9 May 1915
Closed on 30 September 1994

Old Underground maps show Aldwych at the end of a branch-line from Holborn. Although now no longer in use, the name is too interesting to forget. When the Saxon King Alfred (871–899) defeated the invading Danes, he generously allowed some of them to live on in this area, under his rule. At that time it was well outside the city walls.

This Danish settlement was known by the Saxons as *Aldwic* – the 'old village' and the Church of St Clement Danes is said to be on the site of the old Danish burial ground. Drury Lane was known as *Via de Aldwych* in the Middle Ages, and the name was revived when this part of London, together with an Underground station, was modernised in the early twentieth century.

Sadly, Aldwych Underground Station was closed on 30 September 1994. It is one of more than forty London Underground stations that have closed or been re-sited over the years.

ALL SAINTS E14
Docklands
Opened on 31 August 1987

Named after All Saints' church in East India Dock Road, which was built in the years 1821–23. The parish of Poplar was created in 1821 and the parishioners raised over £30,000 – a very considerable sum in those days – to build their parish church. Designed by Charles Hollis, the church was consecrated in 1823.

ALPERTON MIDDLESEX
Piccadilly
Opened as PERIVALE-ALPERTON on 28 June 1903
Name changed to ALPERTON on 7 October 1910

The name comes from a Saxon chief named Ealhbeart. It is Ealhbeart's *tun*, or 'settlement'.

AMERSHAM BUCKINGHAMSHIRE
The terminus of the Metropolitan Line
Opened on 1 September 1892

Named after a Saxon landowner called Ealgmund. It is Ealgmund's *ham*, or 'homestead'.

ANGEL N1
Northern
Opened on 17 November 1901

The Angel was, for centuries, one of the most important inns in England, as it was the nearest staging post to London on the Great North Road (nowadays upstaged by the M1 motorway). The Angel was mentioned by Charles Dickens in *Oliver Twist* and it remained an inn until 1899. It later became a Lyons' Corner House. The site has now been taken over by a bank. The Underground station serves to remind us of the famous inn that once stood here.

ARCHWAY N19
Northern
Opened as HIGHGATE on 22 June 1907
Name changed to ARCHWAY (HIGHGATE) on 11 June 1939
Name changed to HIGHGATE (ARCHWAY) on 19 January 1941
Changed finally to ARCHWAY in December 1947

The Underground station and the North London district of Archway take their name from Archway Road, first built in 1813 with an impressive viaduct designed by John Nash (1752–1835) in the style of a Roman aqueduct, 36 feet high (11 metres) and 18 feet wide (5.48 metres). The present viaduct used by the road was designed and built in 1897 by Sir Alexander Binnie (1839–1917).

Archway is near the spot where Dick Whittington famously heard the bells of London telling him to 'Turn again, Whittington … thrice Mayor of London!'

ARNOS GROVE N11
Piccadilly
Opened on 19 September 1932

Arnos Grove was the former name of a large country house built
on the site of a medieval religious house known as Arnholt Wood in
the fourteenth century. It is now a beautiful retirement home called
Southgate Beaumont – but its original name is preserved in the name
of the Underground station, opened in 1932.

ARSENAL N5
Piccadilly
Opened as GILLESPIE ROAD on 15 December 1906
Name changed to ARSENAL (HIGHBURY HILL) on 31 October 1932
Use of HIGHBURY HILL gradually dropped over the years

Arsenal Football Club was founded in 1886, with its first football ground
in Woolwich. Arsenal Underground Station is named after this ground.
However, Arsenal Football Club moved to its Highbury Stadium in 1913.

There was an establishment here for making and testing arms
dating from Tudor times, and was granted the title Royal Arsenal by
George III in 1805. During the Second World War it employed 40,000
workers making armaments. However, Royal Arsenal ceased to be a
military establishment in 1994 and has now been developed for housing.

BAKER STREET NW1
Bakerloo, Circle, Hammersmith & City, Jubilee and Metropolitan
Opened on 10 January for the Metropolitan Railway
Opened on 10 March 1906 for the Baker Street and Waterloo Railway
*   (later to be named the Bakerloo Line)*
Opened on 1 May 1979 for the Jubilee Line

Baker Street itself is not named after any bread maker. The Baker
after whom the street is named was William Baker, a builder in the
mid-eighteenth century who originally laid out the road. Opened
on 10 January 1863, this station saw the first underground journey
in the world.

Within walking distance: London Planetarium
                              Madame Tussaud's
                              Regent's Park
                              Royal Academy of Music
                              London Zoo

SHERLOCK HOLMES IN BAKER STREET

Baker Street is famous throughout the English-speaking world as the street where the detective Sherlock Holmes lived.

The house on which Sir Arthur Conan Doyle based his fiction was actually No. 21, the home of his friend Dr Malcolm Morris. In 1866 Conan Doyle thoroughly examined the house and based his 'No. 221A' on it. He made one alteration, however, to disguise it from the prying public: he gave his imaginary house only two front windows instead of three.

221B Baker Street is now the Sherlock Holmes Museum.

BALHAM SW12
Northern
Opened on 6 December 1926

The name Balham was first recorded in AD 957 as Bælgenham – which possibly meant that it was a 'smooth or rounded enclosure'. A more likely explanation is that it was the *ham*, or 'homestead', of a Saxon chief named Bealga.

BANK EC2
Central, Docklands, Northern, Waterloo & City
Waterloo & City opened as CITY on 8 August 1898
Northern Line opened as BANK on 25 February 1900
Central Line opened as BANK on 30 July 1900
Waterloo & City renamed BANK on 26 October 1940
Docklands Line opened as BANK on 29 July 1991

Bank gets its name because it is so near the Bank of England, founded in 1694. The actual Bank of England building however, designed by Sir John Soane, dates from 1788.

The word 'bank' comes from the Italian word *banco*, meaning a 'bench' – this particular bench would have been that on which money changers would display their money.

Within walking distance: Bank of England Museum
Guildhall
Mansion House
Stock Exchange
Merchant Taylors' Hall
St Margaret Lothbury
St Stephen Walbrook

BARBICAN EC2
Circle, Hammersmith & City, Metropolitan
Opened as ALDERSGATE STREET on 23 December 1865
Name changed to ALDERSGATE & BARBICAN in 1923
Changed finally to BARBICAN on 1 December 1968

The development of this area since the Second World War, with the new Guildhall School of Music and Drama and its theatre and concert hall, has given the name Barbican a totally new meaning for Londoners. In fact, it's easy to forget just what a barbican originally was.

During the castle-building days of the Middle Ages, a 'barbican' was an outer fortification or watchtower outside the main walls. Here in London, the Barbican was some sort of extra defence work constructed outside the main wall. Unfortunately, we can't be certain what it looked like as it was pulled down by Henry III in 1267 after his civil war with the barons.

Aldersgate itself was one of the six gates in the city wall originally built by the Romans. The origin of the word 'barbican' is uncertain – but it has been suggested that it derives from an Arab or Persian term *barbar khanah*, meaning 'house on the wall'.

Within walking distance: Barbican Centre
Guildhall School of Music and Drama

London Wall
Museum of London
St Bartholomew the Great

BAKERLOO – A 'GUTTER TITLE'!

Hundreds of thousands of people travel on the Bakerloo Line every day – and no one is in the least bothered about its name.

However, when the line first opened in 1906, many Londoners were quite disgusted by this brand new name, coined by the *Evening News*.

It was the first Underground line to run from north to south in London, linking Baker Street and Waterloo, so it seemed quite natural to invent this rather chirpy name for it.

However, in *The Railway Magazine*, an outraged reader called Bakerloo a 'gutter title' and complained that such a name 'is not what we expect from a railway company. English railway officers have more dignity than to act in this manner.'

What a horror! But then, this was Edwardian England!

BARKING ESSEX
District, Hammersmith & City (see BARKINGSIDE)
Opened by the London, Tilbury & Southend Railway on 13 April 1854
First used by Underground trains on 2 June 1902

BARKINGSIDE ESSEX
Central
Opened by the Great Eastern Railway on 1 May 1903
First used by Underground trains on 31 May 1948

'Berica's people'. Like so many English place names, Barking comes from the name of a Saxon leader – in this case, Berica – who came here and settled with his family and friends. The Old Saxon word *ingas* meant 'family' or 'followers', so place names containing 'ing' almost always point to a Saxon chief and his group of followers. Other examples include Tooting, Paddington and Kensington.

BARONS COURT W14
District, Piccadilly
Opened on 9 October 1905

This is not an ancient name. In fact it was invented in the late nineteenth century by Sir William Palliser for his housing development to the west of North End Road. He probably intended it as a sort of companion piece to the name Earls Court, but there is no connection between the two. As with so many place names, it became firmly established when it was adopted by the Underground system as a station name.

BAYSWATER W2
Circle, District
Opened on 1 October 1868

Bayswater has a fascinating derivation. According to an old medieval legend, Charlemagne (747–814), the great king of the Franks, gave a magical horse to four brothers. When only one of these brothers

The Bayswater Conduit in 1798: 'a watering-place for horses'.

was mounted, the horse was of normal size, but if all four brothers mounted it, the horse would miraculously lengthen itself to seat them all!

The name of this extraordinary steed was Bayard, and the story was so famous throughout Europe in medieval times that the very name Bayard came to mean a horse.

It seems a far cry from Charlemagne to Bayswater, but in fact the name Bayswater is derived from a drinking place for horses – a 'Bayards' Watering'.

The point is that there are natural springs nearby, which once provided refreshment for many generations of 'bayards'.

BECKTON E6
BECKTON PARK E6
Docklands
Both stations opened on 28 March 1994

So many London names are derived from Saxon chieftains that it may come as a surprise to learn that the district known as Beckton comes from the name of a nineteenth-century producer of coal gas – Simon Adams Beck. He was the governor of the Gas Light and Coke Co., which bought a site in East Ham and was particularly successful in bringing the benefits of cheap gas lighting to London.

BECONTREE ESSEX
District
*Opened as GALE STREET by the London Midland & Scottish Railway on
    28 June 1926*
Name changed to BECONTREE on 18 July 1932
First used by Underground trains on 12 September 1932

'Beohha's tree'. In early Saxon times, trees were often used as landmarks for meetings and assemblies. The Saxon chief Beohha must have used this easily recognisable tree to serve as a rallying point.

Belsize House in 1800, demolished in 1854.

BELSIZE PARK NW3
Northern
Opened on 22 June 1907

The name is a reminder of Belsize Manor, an important manor house that existed in one form or another from the fourteenth century until it was pulled down in 1854.

The house and grounds were large and beautiful – Samuel Pepys thought the gardens were the most noble he had ever seen. Its very name – Belsize – came from two Norman French words: *bel assis*, meaning 'beautifully situated'.

BERMONDSEY SE1
Jubilee
Opened on 17 September 1999

'Beormund's island'. This isn't really an island, but the name refers to an original Saxon settlement here on slightly higher land among the watery marshes. Beormund was the Saxon chief who lived here with his followers.

BETHNAL GREEN E1
Central
Opened on 4 December 1946

Bethnal is another Saxon name. The second part of the word means 'corner', but it is not known whether the first part refers to a stream or a person. 'Bethnal' could have meant a corner or bend in a river, or else a 'place where Blytha lives'.

Within walking distance: Victoria & Albert Museum of
Childhood

THE BLITZ AND 'BOMBERS' MOONS'

During the Blitz in the Second World War, seventy-nine Underground stations were used regularly as air-raid shelters. It has been estimated that 177,000 people used them. The Liverpool Street extension had not been completed at that time, so no trains were running along that stretch of line under the East End. The result was that many people literally lived there for weeks at a time.

The parts of London worst affected by the Blitz were Holborn, the City, Westminster, Shoreditch, Southwark and Stepney. The Thames was a perfect navigation aid for the German bombers, especially when there was a full moon. Londoners came to call these 'bombers' moons'.

BLACKFRIARS SE1
Circle, District
Opened on 30 May 1870

In 1221 a monastery was founded in Chancery Lane for Dominican monks. Dominicans, by tradition, always wore black habits, so the monastery became known for its 'black friars'.

The monastery was closed down in 1538 by Henry VIII, but it had been a place of great importance. Parliaments had met there, and a court sitting there heard the divorce case against Catherine of Aragon, Henry VIII's first wife.

The black-robed monks are remembered in the names of Blackfriars Road, Blackfriars Bridge and other places in this area. The only piece of the original monastery left today is a part of a wall in Ireland Yard. In 1613 William Shakespeare bought a house nearby for £140 – but did not live in it himself.

Within walking distance: Dr Johnson's House

                                     St Bride's church

BLACKHORSE ROAD E17
Victoria
Opened on 1 September 1968

Blackhorse Road was built on Blackhorse Fields, and both road and fields took their name from the Blackhorse Inn in Evelyn Street. Black horses still feature in the attractive artwork decorating this station. Despite this, however, a conflicting fact exists – the Blackhorse Road was called Black House Lane in the early nineteenth century – so are the horses simply the result of mispronunciation? We will never know.

BLACKWALL E14
Docklands
Opened on 28 March 1994

The name Blackwall comes from the black artificial bank constructed here to enable building to take place along the marshy banks of the Thames. The area was used for making and repairing ships and was also a place of arrival and departure. The Virginia Settlers under Captain John Smith set off from here in 1606 to found the first permanent colony in America.

BOND STREET W1
Central, Jubilee
Opened on 24 September 1900

Sir Thomas Bond, a seventeenth-century speculator, developed this area when he bought the land in 1664, hence, Bond Street.

It quickly became a fashionable shopping area, and over the years many famous people have taken lodgings above the shops: Jonathan Swift, Edward Gibbon, William Pitt the Elder, Lawrence Sterne, James Boswell, Admiral Nelson and his mistress Lady Hamilton.

'Prinny' – the Prince of Wales who later became George IV – had a bet with Charles James Fox, the liberal statesman, as to how many cats they would see on either side of Bond Street as they took a stroll there. Fox easily won the bet – thirteen cats to none – as he had cunningly chosen the sunny side!

Within walking distance: The Wallace Collection

BOROUGH SEI
Northern
Opened on 18 December 1890

The borough here is the Borough of Southwark, famous for being the setting off point for Chaucer's Canterbury pilgrims.

The Tabard Inn, where the pilgrims gathered, is no longer here, but the site is now occupied by Talbot Yard, Borough High Street.

The importance of Borough High Street can easily be imagined, as it was once the main road to London Bridge from the south. As London Bridge was the *only* bridge across the Thames until 1750, every coach load of travellers had to come this way. Furthermore, as London Bridge itself was too narrow for coaches, Borough High Street became the inevitable terminus. It was a flourishing, bustling area, with vast numbers of inns and a pillory, which stood in the middle of the street until 1620.

Shakespeare would have known this area well, as the original Globe Theatre was nearby – and today the modern reconstructed Globe still pulls in the crowds.

BOSTON MANOR MIDDLESEX
Piccadilly
Opened as BOSTON ROAD on 1 May 1883
Name changed to BOSTON MANOR on 11 December 1911

Named after the beautiful Jacobean manor house, Boston Manor, built in 1623, which can now be visited free of charge, is 'one of West London's lesser-known gems'. The house is about half a mile (0.8 kilometres) from the Underground station. The name Boston itself was derived in this instance from Bordeston – the *tun*, or 'farm', of someone named Bords who lived here in the Middle Ages.

BOUNDS GREEN N11
Piccadilly
Opened on 19 September 1932

'A green area belonging to the family of le Bonde'. A John le Bonde is recorded as being the tenant in 1294. Remarkably, his name still flourishes here more than seven centuries later.

BOW CHURCH E3
Docklands   (see BOW ROAD)
Opened on 31 August 1987

Named after the local church, the full name of which is St Mary Bow Church.

BOW ROAD E3
District, Hammersmith & City
Opened on 11 June 1902

Queen Matilda (1080–1118), wife of Henry I and daughter of Malcolm, King of Scotland (he appears in Shakespeare's *Macbeth*), had an accident while fording the River Lea near here. She got herself 'well washed' and only just escaped drowning. Indeed, some of her attendants did lose their lives in the river.

To give thanks, and to avoid a repetition of the accident, she had a bridge built here. It was the first arched bridge in England, and was called a 'bow' bridge.

This in turn gave its name to the road leading to it – Bow Road – and also to the whole district, Stratford-le-Bow.

Bow Bridge – the first arched bridge in England.

BRENT CROSS NW4
Northern
Opened as BRENT on 19 November 1923
Name changed to BRENT CROSS on 20 July 1976

The name Brent is Celtic – that is, it goes back to prehistoric times even before the Romans or Saxons came to England. The river Brent has been thought to mean 'holy one'.

When this Underground station opened in 1923 it was named simply Brent, but this was changed to Brent Cross in 1976, when the nearby Brent Cross Shopping Centre was opened. 'Cross' refers to the fact that it is the centre of three major trunk roads.

BRIXTON SW2
Victoria
Opened on 23 July 1971

In 1062, just before the Norman Conquest, this name was recorded as Brixges stane – the stone of a Saxon chieftain called Brihtsige. Such a stone would have been used as a landmark meeting place in early Saxon times, like the tree in Becontree.

BROMLEY-BY-BOW E3
District, Hammersmith & City
Opened as BROMLEY by the London, Tilbury & Southend Railway on 31 March 1858
First used by Underground trains on 2 June 1902
Name changed to BROMLEY-BY-BOW on 18 May 1968

'The wood near Bow where the broom or brambles grow'.
(See BOW ROAD)

BUCKHURST HILL ESSEX
Central
Opened by the Eastern Counties Railway on 22 August 1856
First used by Underground trains on 21 November 1948

'Buckhurst' derives from two Saxon words: *boc hyrst*, meaning 'beech grove'.

Interestingly, our word 'book' also comes from this Saxon word for a beech tree.

Even before books as we know them were invented, wooden writing tablets were made of thin slices of beech wood, on which letters known as runes could be scratched. These, of course, were pieces of *boc*.

BURNT OAK MIDDLESEX
Northern
Opened on 27 October 1924

The Romans used to mark boundaries by burning a conspicuous tree. Perhaps this name refers to some such noteworthy landmark – literally a burned oak tree, either branded deliberately or else struck by lightning. In Prehistoric and early Saxon times, trees and stones were used as meeting points. See BECONTREE, BRIXTON and FAIRLOP.

CALEDONIAN ROAD N1
Piccadilly
Opened on 15 December 1906

When the Caledonian Road was first built in 1826 it was known as Chalk Road, because of the chalky soil in that area. However, its name was changed to Caledonian Road after an orphanage, the Caledonian Asylum, was built there.

The orphanage was built specially for Scottish boys whose fathers had been killed on war service, or whose parents were too poor to look after them. In 1846 it took in girls as well as boys. The orphanage moved to Bushey, Hertfordshire, in 1903 and the building in Caledonian Road was demolished. However, the name for the road remained, and when the Underground station opened here in 1906, it seemed only natural to call it 'Caledonian Road'.

Caledonia was the ancient Roman name for Scotland, deriving from Caledones, the term for the inhabitants of north-west Scotland.

CAMDEN TOWN NW1
Northern
Opened on 22 June 1907

The name Camden Town has an extremely roundabout origin ultimately connected with the name of William Camden (1551–1623), a famous Elizabethan schoolmaster, historian and writer. However, Camden would have been astonished if he had been told that a large area to the north of London would bear his name long after his death. After all, this part of modern London was completely open countryside in his day – and in any case, he had no connection whatever with the area.

Camden had a house in Surrey, which was later bought by a family named Pratt. Much later, in 1765, a Charles Pratt became Attorney General and was created a baron. He decided to take the title Baron Camden – naming himself after his house, the former home of old William Camden. This Baron Camden was further ennobled to become an earl, becoming very rich and buying up many acres of fields in north London.

In 1791 Lord Camden decided to lease this land for the building of 1,400 new houses, and the newly built-up area became known as Camden Town.

The Underground station was opened here in 1907 – nearly three centuries after the death of the old schoolmaster, William Camden.

Within walking distance: London Zoo
                            Regent's Park

CANADA WATER SE16
Jubilee, East London
Opened on 17 September 1999

The whole of the former docklands area has now been transformed. Canada Water is now a lake and wildlife refuge in Rotherhithe. The lake is named after Canada Dock, which used to be on this site and was principally used by ships importing and exporting goods from Canada.

CANARY WHARF E14
Docklands, Jubilee
Opened on 17 September 1999

Canary Wharf was built in 1936, largely for the importing of fruits and produce from the Canary Islands.

Interestingly, the Canary Islands themselves were named because of the large wild dogs that the ancient Romans found there – *canis* being the Latin word for 'dog'.

Word history has some curious twists – in this case from ancient dogs to a modern railway station!

CANNING TOWN E16
Docklands, Jubilee
Opened on 28 March 1999

This area of London was first developed in the early nineteenth century, and some believe that it was named in honour of Charles

John Canning (1812–62), an English statesman and first Viceroy of India. A more likely alternative suggestion however, is that it was named after a firm whose premises once stood in the area.

CANNON STREET EC4
Circle, District, Docklands
Opened on 6 October 1884

It would be easy to imagine that Cannon Street and Cannon Street Station get their names in some way from military cannons. However, somewhat surprisingly, the word 'cannon' in these names is a reference to all the candle makers who used to live and work there. The present name is a corruption of the original Candlewick Street.

Within walking distance: St Stephen Walbrook

CANONS PARK MIDDLESEX
Jubilee
Opened as CANONS PARK (EDGWARE) on 10 December 1932
  (becoming simply CANONS PARK sometime in 1933)

The 'Canons' in this name derive from the fact that the Augustinian Canons of St Bartholomew's, Smithfield, held the land here back in the fourteenth century. The land came to be known as Canons – so when the 1st Duke of Chandos built a large country house here in the eighteenth century, he took up the name and called it Canons.

Unfortunately, his son, the 2nd Duke, had to demolish the house to pay off his enormous debts – nevertheless, the name Canons Park still clung to the grounds of the old house, and of course it was perpetuated even more firmly when the Underground station opened in 1932.

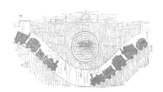

CHALFONT (CHALFONT & LATIMER) BUCKINGHAMSHIRE
Metropolitan

Opened as CHALFONT ROAD on 8 July 1889
Name changed to CHALFONT & LATIMER on 20 November 1915

A tenth-century manuscript refers to this place as Caedeles funta, which means 'Caedel's spring or fountain'. By the time of the Domesday Book in 1086, this had turned to Celfunta, and this version gradually developed into the present Chalfont. (See LATIMER).

CHALK FARM NW3
Northern

Opened on 22 June 1907

There's nothing at all chalky about Chalk Farm! The name goes back to Saxon times, when it was known as Chaldecote, meaning 'cold cottages'!

Old Chalk Farm in 1720. It became a favourite spot where duels took place – often resulting in deaths.

In the seventeenth century there was an Upper Chalcot Farm in this area, and this form of the name is still perpetuated in Chalcot Crescent, Chalcot Gardens, Chalcot Road and Chalcot Square.

There was also a Lower Chalcot Farm, which became a tavern in the nineteenth century and was known as Chalk Farm Tavern. Chalk Farm then became firmly established when the Northern Line arrived here in 1907.

CHANCERY LANE WC2
Central (NB – closed on Sundays)
Opened on 30 July 1900

In the Middle Ages this lane was known as New Street, but in 1377 – in the time of Chaucer – the Keeper of the Rolls of Chancery was given his office here, and so the name changed to Chancellor's Lane. Successive Keepers of the Rolls of Chancery had their office here until 1896. The site is now occupied by the Maughan Library – the largest library of King's College London.

The very words 'chancery' and 'chancellor' have a curious and fascinating derivation. They come from the Latin word *cancelli* – the bars or rails that surrounded the Roman judgement seat. Curiously, in churches the word 'chancel' also comes from the same Latin word – and in churches the *cancelli* refers to the bars of the communion rail.

Within walking distance: The Charles Dickens Museum
                                 Dr Johnson's House
                                 Inns of Court and Temple

CHARING CROSS WC2
Bakerloo, Northern
The history of this station is complicated as it is an amalgamation of two former, separate stations. However, this book is about name-derivations rather than history.
Bakerloo Line opened as TRAFALGAR SQUARE on 10 March 1906
Northern Line opened as CHARING CROSS on 22 June 1907
After various other variant names, the combined stations opened as
  CHARING CROSS on 1 May 1979

The original thirteenth-century Charing Cross, which stood at the top of Whitehall on the spot now taken by the statue of Charles I on horseback.

The royal and romantic story behind this name goes back over 700 years to the year 1290. King Edward I (reigned 1272–1307) was just about to launch a savage attack on Scotland, and his queen, Eleanor of Castile, was travelling north to join him. However, on her journey north, she died quite unexpectedly in the little village of Harby in Nottinghamshire, aged only forty-six.

Edward was devastated, and immediately rushed back south – but alas, he could do nothing but make arrangements for her funeral.

Eleanor had to be taken back to Westminster in stages, and Edward ordered a beautiful memorial cross to be erected in each of the stopping places. In all, there were twelve: at Lincoln, Grantham, Stamford, Geddington, Northampton, Stony Stratford, Woburn, Dunstable, St Albans, Waltham, Cheapside, and – best known of all – the final village just before Westminster itself – Charing.

Inevitably, the village became known by the name of the memorial: Charing Cross.

Today, in the forecourt of Charing Cross Railway Station, surrounded by parked cars and taxis, there is a tall stone monument – a memorial to Eleanor – the 'Charing Cross'. Somewhat disappointingly it is a Victorian replacement of the original cross, which stood at the top of Whitehall on the site now occupied by the statue of Charles I on horseback.

Within walking distance:	Cleopatra's Needle
	The National Gallery
	The National Portrait Gallery
	St Martin-in-the-Fields
	Savoy Hotel
	Strand
	Trafalgar Square

CHESHAM BUCKINGHAMSHIRE
Metropolitan
Opened on 8 July 1889

Chesham derives from the Old English word *ceaster*, 'a heap of stones', and *hamm*, 'a water meadow'. In the Domesday Book it is called Cestreham – a clearing or homestead near a pile of rubble. Although Chesham lies on the river Chess, the river is named from the town and not *vice versa*.

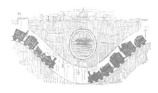

CHIGWELL ESSEX
Central
Opened by the Great Eastern Railway on 1 May 1903
First used by Underground trains on 21 November 1948

There are two possible derivations. Chigwell may be named after a Saxon called Cica or Cicca who once lived here by a well or spring.

Alternatively, Chigwell may be derived from the Old English word *ceacge*, meaning 'gorse', in which case the name means 'a well surrounded by gorse bushes'.

CHISWICK PARK W4
District
Opened as ACTON GREEN on 1 July 1879
Name changed to CHISWICK PARK & ACTON GREEN in March 1887
Finally changed simply to CHISWICK PARK on 1 March 1910

'Chiswick' means 'cheese farm'. The Old English word *wic* refers to a specialised farm, and was often linked to the name of the produce of that farm. Keswick in the Lake District is a variation of the same name, also indicating a cheese farm. Butterwick obviously produced butter; Smethwick had its smithy; and Gatwick, site of today's busy airport, had its goats.

CHORLEYWOOD HERTFORDSHIRE
Metropolitan
Opened as CHORLEY WOOD on 8 July 1889
Name changed to CHORLEYWOOD & CHENIES on 1 November 1915
Changed back to CHORLEYWOOD in 1934
Finally, the one-word version CHORLEYWOOD appeared c.1964

Chorley derives from two Saxon words: *ceorla*, 'peasants' and *leah*, 'woodland clearing' or 'glade'. 'Chorleywood' means 'clearing in the peasants' wood'.

A 'churl' (deriving from *ceorla*) is a forgotten word today, but it was formerly used to mean a free peasant or countryman. Although we have lost the word 'churl', we still retain the adjective 'churlish' to mean surly or ill mannered. Linguistically speaking then, the inhabitants of Chorleywood may be said to be churlish!

CLAPHAM COMMON SW4
Northern
Opened on 3 June 1900

CLAPHAM NORTH SW4
Northern
Opened as CLAPHAM ROAD on 3 June 1900
Name changed to CLAPHAM NORTH on 13 September 1926

CLAPHAM SOUTH SW4
Northern
Opened on 13 September 1926

The Domesday Book spells Clapham as *Clopeham*, which means 'village or homestead on the hill'.

COCKFOSTERS HERTFORDSHIRE
Piccadilly
Opened on 31 July 1933

Cockfosters Station is the northern terminus of the Piccadilly Line, near the ancient and royal forest of Enfield Chase.

The Chief Forester of Enfield Chase had a house on the edge of this forest. It is now a hotel called West Lodge Park. However, before its present name, this house was known as Cockfosters – the home of the 'Cock' or 'Chief' Forester. The name could easily have been lost – but when the station was opened in 1933, it became firmly and permanently established.

A possible alternative explanation is that the word derives from the personal name of a family living in the area.

COLINDALE NW9
Northern
Opened on 18 August 1924

'Collin's valley'. The name is derived from a family called Colin, who are known to have lived hereabouts in the sixteenth century. An earlier version of the name, in 1550, was Collyndene. 'Dene' was an old English word for 'valley'.

COLLIERS WOOD SW19
Northern
Opened on 13 September 1926

'Woodland occupied by charcoal burners'. Charcoal used for fuel gave this area its name. Charcoal burners are known to have worked here in the sixteenth century.

COVENT GARDEN WC2
Piccadilly
Opened on 11 April 1907

This land was once the herb and vegetable garden belonging to the Convent of St Peter at Westminster – better known today as Westminster Abbey. This 'convent garden' supplied the monks with their vegetables, and surplus produce was sold off to the local inhabitants.

When the monasteries were destroyed by Henry VIII, the land passed to the Duke of Somerset, and then to John Russell, the 1st Earl of Bedford.

In 1631, the 4th Earl of Bedford began to create the square and develop the area. He commissioned Inigo Jones to design a new piazza and the Church of St Paul. Then, in 1670, the 5th Earl of Bedford

Covent Garden market in about 1820. St Paul's church is seen at the back of the picture.

obtained a licence to hold a flower, fruit and vegetable market in the square, thus continuing the tradition begun by the earlier convent garden.

The square at Covent Garden has been compared with the square at Leghorn in Italy and the Place des Vosges in Paris. It was so popular that it became a town-planning trendsetter and inspired the numerous other London squares which were laid out in succeeding decades.

Within walking distance: Courtauld Institute Galleries
(Somerset House)
Covent Garden piazza
The Royal Opera House
St Paul's, Covent Garden (wall
tablets commemorating many actors)
London Transport Museum

CROSSHARBOUR E14
Docklands
Opened on 13 August 1987

This station is built in the right-angled cross formed by Millwall Inner Dock and the two docks at either end running at right-angles to it – the Main Section Dock and the Millwall Outer Dock

CROXLEY HERTFORDSHIRE
Metropolitan
Opened as CROXLEY GREEN on 2 November 1925
Name changed to CROXLEY on 23 May 1949

This name derives from two Old English words: *crocs*, 'a clearing' and *leah*, 'a forest'. So, 'Croxley' means 'a clearing in the forest'.

CUSTOM HOUSE E16
Docklands
The station opened in 1855 for the Great Eastern Railway's North Woolwich branch.
Used by the Docklands Light Railway from 28 March 1994

The area known as Custom House is named after the custom house which was situated on the north side of the Victoria Dock. It was an area developed for housing from about 1880, but was very badly damaged in the Blitz during the Second World War. The Docklands Light Railway Station is named after this area.

CUTTY SARK SE10
Docklands
Opened on 3 December 1999

The station is named after the historic merchant clipper the *Cutty Sark*, launched in 1869 and now on permanent exhibition in Greenwich. It was used in the Australian tea trade and made some very fast return journeys from Australia to the UK – seventy-three days in 1885 and sixty-nine days in 1888.

In modern English, we would refer to a *Cutty Sark* as a 'mini-skirt'! The ship got its name from the witch in Robert Burns' poem 'Tam o' Shanter' (1791), which was written in a Scottish idiom. The witch wore just a 'cutty sark' – a short shift or smock. Burns described it in the poem as 'in longitude tho' sorely scanty'. She must have been a deliciously tempting sight for sailors!

Within walking distance: Greenwich
                                  The National Maritime Museum
                                  The Queen's House
                                  The Royal Observatory

CYPRUS E16
Docklands
Opened on 28 March 1994

Britain acquired Cyprus as a colony in 1878 (since 1960 it has been an independent republic within the British Commonwealth). Three years after this acquisition, in 1881, a housing estate known as the Cyprus Estate was built near here for workers at the Royal Albert Dock. The Docklands station Cyprus is named after the Cyprus Estate.

DAGENHAM EAST ESSEX
District
Opened as DAGENHAM by the London, Tilbury & Southend Railway on
   1 May 1885
First used by Underground trains on 12 September 1932
Name changed to DAGENHAM EAST on 1 May 1949

DAGENHAM HEATHWAY ESSEX
District
Opened as HEATHWAY on 12 September 1932
Name changed to DAGENHAM HEATHWAY on May 1949

'Daecca's village or homestead'. Daecca was one of the many early Saxon chieftains whose name has been perpetuated in the place where he set up his home.

DEBDEN ESSEX
Central

*Opened as CHIGWELL ROAD by the Great Eastern Railway on
    24 April 1865*
Name changed to CHIGWELL LANE on 1 December 1865
*Finally changed to DEBDEN and first used by Underground trains on
    25 September 1949*

'Debden' means 'deep valley', and derives from two Old English
words: *deb*, 'deep' and *den*, 'valley'.

DEPTFORD BRIDGE SE8
Docklands

Opened on 20 November 1999

Deptford is the 'deep ford' that once existed to cross the little
River Ravensbourne – a tributary of the Thames. Chaucer called
it Depeford.

DEVONS ROAD E3
Docklands

Opened on 31 August 1987

Devons Road passes over this Docklands Light Railway station with
a bridge at the northern end. Clearly, the station name derives from
the road, and the road itself probably got its name from a Thomas
Devon who once owned land in this area.

DOLLIS HILL NW2
Jubilee

Opened on 1 October 1909 on the Metropolitan Railway
First used by the Bakerloo Line at 20 November 1939
Transferred to the Jubilee Line in 1979

In the sixteenth century this area was called Daleson Hill, probably
after a local resident. Later, it became Dolly's Hill, but in 1909, when
the Metropolitan Railway Station was built there, Dollis Hill became
the final version.

EALING BROADWAY W5
District, Central
District Line opened on 1 July 1879
Central Line opened on 3 August 1920

EALING COMMON
District, Piccadilly
Opened on 1 July 1879

The name Ealing is Saxon and tells us that this was 'the place where Gilla's people live'.

EARLS COURT SW5
District, Piccadilly
Opened on 30 October 1871 on the Metropolitan Railway
Opened on 15 December 1906 for the Great Northern, Piccadilly &
  Brompton Railway

The earls of Oxford were lords of a manor house or 'court' here until the sixteenth century. The house stood on the site between the present Barkston Gardens and Bramham Gardens. The hamlet that grew up round the 'court' naturally became known as Earl's Court.

'BUMPER HARRIS' AND HIS WOODEN LEG

The first railway escalator was installed at Earls Court Underground Station in 1911. Nervous passengers were so suspicious of this new-fangled device that the station authorities employed a man with a wooden leg – nicknamed 'Bumper' Harris – to travel up and down the escalator all day long, just to show everyone how safe it was!

EAST ACTON W3
Central   (see ACTON)
Opened on 3 August 1920

EASTCOTE MID
Metropolitan, Piccadilly
Opened on 26 May 1906

Former meanings of 'cot' included a cottage or a shelter for sheep and other animals. 'Eastcote', therefore, means 'shelter in the east'.

EAST FINCHLEY N2
Northern   (see FINCHLEY)
Opened as a train station called EAST END, FINCHLEY on 22 August 1867
Name changed to EAST FINCHLEY on 1 February 1887
First used by Underground trains on 3 July 1939

EAST HAM E6
District, Hammersmith & City
Opened by London, Tilbury & Southend Railway on 31 March 1858
First used by Underground trains on 2 June 1902

East Ham was an ancient parish that existed long before it became engulfed in the spreading housing development of London. The Old English word *hamm* meant 'a low-lying water-meadow', so this village gained its name from the marshy lands some distance from West Ham.

EAST INDIA E14
Docklands
Opened on 28 March 1994

This station takes its name from the East India Dock, which in turn was named because it was used by the large ships of the East India Company, which was founded in 1600 to trade with the Far East. The famous clipper *Cutty Sark*, launched in 1869, used to berth in the East India Dock, which finally closed in 1967.

EAST PUTNEY SW15
District   (see PUTNEY BRIDGE)
Opened by the Metropolitan District Railway on 3 June 1889

EDGWARE ROAD W2
Bakerloo   (see EDGWARE)
Opened on 15 June 1907

EDGWARE ROAD W2
Circle, District, Hammersmith & City   (see EDGWARE)
Opened on 1 October 1863

EDGWARE MIDDLESEX
Northern
Opened on 18 August 1924

Somewhat confusingly, there are two quite separate Underground stations both named Edgware Road and both with entrances on the Edgware Road. They are only about 150 metres apart – but they are on different Underground lines.

Then, quite separately from these, there is *another* station, simply called Edgware, at the end of the Northern Line in Middlesex. The actual Edgware Road gets its name because it leads to the town of Edgware.

As a name, Edgware has an interesting derivation, coming from the name of a Saxon farmer called Ecgi who must have built – or at least possessed – a weir. The place is named after Ecgi's weir, which was probably a fishing enclosure in the local stream.

ELEPHANT AND CASTLE SE1
Bakerloo, Northern
Northern Line opened on 18 December 1890
Bakerloo Line opened on 5 August 1906

The Underground station is named after the pub that stands near the meeting point of the roads to Kennington, Walworth and Lambeth.

Originally, the site was occupied by a smithy, but this was converted to a tavern around the year 1760, and it then became a well-known terminus for stagecoaches in the eighteenth and nineteenth centuries.

The odd name probably comes from the figure found on the sign of the Cutlers' Company, which used ivory in its manufacture of knife handles. The sign depicted a traditional medieval picture of an elephant with a castle on its back – presumably to show how huge and strong this extraordinary foreign beast was.

It has been suggested that the origin of Elephant and Castle is a badly pronounced version of 'Infanta of Castile', but this is false folk etymology.

The gaudy gilt model of an elephant with a castle on its back which once adorned the old pub, is now to be seen inside the Elephant and Castle Shopping Centre, opened in 1965.

Within walking distance: Imperial War Museum

ELM PARK ESSEX
District
Opened on 13 May 1935

The name speaks for itself. There are many streets named after trees in this neighbourhood.

ELVERSON ROAD SE8
Docklands
Opened on 20 November 1999

Elverson Road is named after one of the roads nearby, but the origin of the name is obscure, possibly deriving from a local person.

EMBANKMENT WC2
Bakerloo, Circle, District, Northern
District Line opened as CHARING CROSS on 30 May 1870
(See below for comment on subsequent name)

Sir Joseph Bazalgette, Chief Engineer of the Metropolitan Board of Works, constructed the Victoria, Albert and Chelsea embankments between 1868 and 1874, thus for the first time in London's history providing the banks of the Thames with a firm protective wall. It was an immense undertaking, with a total of 3½ miles (5.63 kilometres) of embankment, reclaiming 32 acres of swampy riverside mud.

Today we take this neat river edge for granted, and hardly give it a second thought, but until the embankments were built, London was a very different place – the Thames sprawled its muddy edges right up to the Strand.

Charles Dickens, who died in 1870, could never have seen the completed Embankments, and all his descriptions of London refer to the muddy squalor that existed before Bazalgette tidied up the riverbanks.

When Embankment Underground Station opened in May 1870 it was named Charing Cross. The Victoria Embankment itself was declared open just a few weeks later, in July of that year. Over the next century, the name of the Underground station has changed several times, and it wasn't until 12 September 1976 that it finally settled on its present name – Embankment.

EPPING ESSEX
Central
Opened by the Great Eastern Railway on 24 April 1865
First used by Underground trains on 25 September 1949

The name is derived from the Saxon word *yppe*, meaning 'raised place' or 'look-out point', and *ing*, meaning 'people'. It is thought that the 'raised place' may refer to the Iron Age hill fort known as Ambersbury Banks in Epping Forest, where Boadicea (Boudicca) fought her last battle against the Romans.

EUSTON NW1
Northern, Victoria   (see EUSTON SQUARE)
Opened on 12 May 1907 by the City and South London Railway

EUSTON SQUARE NW1
Circle, Hammersmith & City, Metropolitan
Opened as GOWER STREET on 10 January 1863
Name changed to EUSTON SQUARE on 1 November 1909

The village of Euston, a few miles south of Thetford in Suffolk, indirectly gives its name to Euston Road, Euston Square and

Euston Station, the earliest of London's main-line railway termini – which opened on 20 July 1837, exactly a month after Victoria became queen.

The Fitzroy family (descended from one of Charles II's many illegitimate sons by Barbara Palmer, Duchess of Cleveland) were titled the Dukes of Grafton and Earls of Euston – in fact, the 11th Duke still lives in Euston Hall near Thetford, which is, at times, open to the public.

In the eighteenth century the Euston family owned much of this area in London. It's difficult to imagine it now, but in those days flocks of sheep and herds of cattle were constantly being driven along Oxford Street to Smithfield Market. The animals became such a nuisance that in 1756 the then Duke of Grafton had the bright idea of constructing an alternative road parallel to Oxford Street to the north, to take this farming traffic. At first this was called New Road, but it was officially renamed Euston Road in 1857, because by then Euston Station and Euston Square had been built, and Euston Road seemed a more appropriate name for a road that was no longer 'new'.

EUSTON SQUARE – THE BEGINNING OF IT ALL!

Euston Square has the distinction of being the site of the very first shaft to be sunk in the ground anywhere in the world in order to build an underground railway. This momentous event took place in January 1860, and was the first stage in constructing the Metropolitan Railway from Paddington to Farringdon.

No one could have guessed at the time just how important underground railways would become.

It is estimated that 1,000 slum homes were demolished in order to cut the first 4-mile (6.43-kilometre) stretch of the Metropolitan Line, linking Paddington, Euston Square, St Pancras, King's Cross and Farringdon. About 12,000 people had to be displaced.

The original Euston Square Station, which opened for overground trains in 1837.

FAIRLOP ESSEX
Central
Opened by the Great Eastern Railway on 1 May 1903
First used by Underground trains on 31 May 1948

A gigantic tree once grew here known as the Fairlop Oak and a popular annual fair used to take place around it every July. The word 'lop' refers to a lopped tree. This famous oak tree, associated with the fair, measured 48½ feet (14.78 metres) round its trunk and was reputed to be almost 1,000 years old. Sadly, it was cut down in 1820, but a part of it still remains, as the pulpit in St Pancras' church, which is carved from a portion of its boughs.

Other Underground 'tree names' include Becontree and Burnt Oak. The trees may have gone, but their names live on.

FARRINGDON EC1
Circle, Hammersmith & City, Metropolitan
Opened as FARRINGDON STREET on 10 January 1863
Name changed to FARRINGDON & HIGH HOLBORN on 26 January 1922
Finally became simply FARRINGTON on 21 April 1936

When this station opened on 10 January 1863 (an important date – see below) it was named Farringdon Street, a road that was built in 1845–46 and still exists. The road was named after

Farringdon Ward, which in turn was named after two aldermen of the City of London, William and Nicholas de Farndon, who lived in the thirteenth century.

FARRINGDON STREET TO PADDINGTON – THE WORLD'S FIRST UNDERGROUND JOURNEY

At 6 am on 10 January 1863, the world's very first underground train took passengers along its 4-mile journey (6.43-kilometre) from Farringdon Street Station to Paddington. There were seven stations, including the two termini, in this first stretch of the Metropolitan Line.

The steam-driven locomotive pulled its passengers along in first-, second- and third-class carriages – lit with gas so that 'newspapers might be read with ease'.

Naming a new invention is always an interesting task, and the chosen word, 'Metropolitan' comes from two ancient Greek words meaning 'mother city', referring, of course, to London.

The venture was so successful, and the 'Metropolitan' gained such fame and prestige that it became the standard name for underground railways in other countries as they took up the idea.

Both the Paris Metro and the Russian Metro take their name from this pioneering first Underground line in London.

FINCHLEY CENTRAL N3
Northern   (see FINCHLEY ROAD)

Opened by the Great Northern Railway as FINCHEY & HENDON on 22 August 1867
Name changed to FINCHLEY (CHURCH END) on 1 February 1894
Finally changed to FINCHLEY CENTRAL on 1 April 1940
First used by Underground trains on 14 April 1940

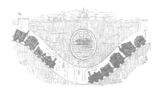

Entrance to Clerkenwell tunnel from Farringdon Street.

FINCHLEY ROAD NW2
Jubilee, Metropolitan
Opened on 30 June 1879

'Finchley' is a reminder of those days when this was a completely
rural area. Its Saxon name means 'wood where finches are to
be found'.

FINSBURY PARK N4
Piccadilly, Victoria
Opened by the Great Northern Railway as SEVEN SISTERS ROAD on 1 July 1861
Name changed to FINSBURY PARK in 1869
First used by Underground trains on 15 December 1906

'Finsbury' means 'settlement belonging to Finn' – one of the innumerable Saxon chiefs who have left their memorial within the name of the place where they settled.

Finsbury Park used to be called Stroud Green, *stroud* being an Old English word meaning 'marshy land overgrown with brushwood'.

It was not until 1869 that Finsbury Park came into existence. It was named after the district of Finsbury, whose inhabitants wanted an open space or park. It was specially purchased for recreational use, and Finsbury Park became one of the first municipal parks in the country.

FULHAM BROADWAY SW6
District
Opened as WALHAM GREEN on 1 March 1880
Name changed to FULHAM BROADWAY on 2 March 1952

The place where a Saxon chief called Fulla settled with his family and friends. The 'hamm' part of the name means low-lying land in the bend of a river.

GALLIONS REACH E16
Docklands
Opened on 28 March 1994

Gallions Reach Station is named after a stretch of the Thames between Woolwich and Barking Creek – Gallions Point, at the entrance to the King George V Dock. The name is derived from the Galyons, a fourteenth-century family who owned property on this shoreline.

GANTS HILL ESSEX
Central
Opened on 14 December 1947

Named after Richard le Gant, or perhaps one of his relations.
He lived here in the late thirteenth century. The area was called
Gantesgrave in 1291 and Gauntes Hethe in 1545.

GLOUCESTER ROAD SW7
Circle, District, Piccadilly
Opened as BROMPTON (GLOUCESTER ROAD) on 1 October 1868
Name changed to GLOUCESTER ROAD in 1907

Gloucester Road itself was built in 1826, and was named after Maria,
Duchess of Gloucester, who secretly married a brother of King
George III. She had bought a house, Orford Lodge, on the site of
what is now Stanhope Gardens. The road was named soon after the
Duchess died. Formerly, it had been just a track called Hogmore
Lane.

The very first trial trip on the London underground in 1863.

GOLDERS GREEN NW11
Northern
Opened on 22 June 1907

The name comes from a local landowner, and was first recorded as Golders Greene in 1612. At that time it was just a green field in Middlesex, and it remained totally undeveloped until the coming of the underground railway in the early twentieth century.

GOLDHAWK ROAD W6
Hammersmith & City
Opened on 1 April 1914

Named after fourteenth-century farmer John Goldhawk of Sands End, whose family continued to hold several plots of land in this area for many generations.

GOODGE STREET W1
Northern
Opened as TOTTENHAM COURT ROAD on 22 June 1907
Name changed to GOODGE STREET on 9 March 1908

In the eighteenth century this land was called Crab Tree Field and Walnut Tree Field. It belonged to a carpenter called John Goodge. On his death in 1748, his nephews Francis and William Goodge developed the land for building.

GRANGE HILL ESSEX
Central
Opened by the Great Eastern Railway on 1 May 1903
First used by Underground trains on 21 November 1948

In the Middle Ages a 'grange' meant an outlying farm, often belonging to a monastery or nearby religious community. In this case, the 'grange' belonged to Tilty Priory, but after Henry VIII's dissolution of the monasteries it ultimately became a part of Brentwood Grammar School. It was finally demolished in the late nineteenth century. The 'hill' leads down to the front of the station.

GREAT PORTLAND STREET W1
Circle, Hammersmith & City, Metropolitan
Opened as PORTLAND ROAD on 10 January 1863
Name changed to PORTLAND STREET on 1 March 1917

Great Portland Street was built in the eighteenth century, and given its name because it was on land owned by the second Duke of Portland.

GREENFORD MIDDLESEX
Central
Opened by the Great Western Railway on 1 October 1904
First used, in a new station, by Underground trains on 30 June 1947

A place by a 'green ford' – a useful crossing-place through the river Brent. The name goes back to Saxon times and was recorded as Greneforde in 1066.

GREEN PARK SW1
Jubilee, Piccadilly, Victoria
Opened as DOVER STREET on 15 December 1906
Name changed to GREEN PARK on 18 September 1933

Green Park itself, after which the Underground station is called, consists of 53 acres of green lawns and green trees, so it is appropriately named. It is believed to have been the burial place of the lepers who used to live in the former Hospital of St James's, the site of which was used by Henry VIII to build St James's Palace.

The name *Green* Park was given because no flowers are planted there, the reason for this being that it was a burial area. In the eighteenth century it was a favourite place for duelling, and it was also a haunt of highwaymen.

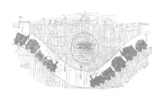

Within walking distance: Buckingham Palace
                              Royal Mews
                              Queen's Gallery
                              Royal Academy of Arts
                              St James's Piccadilly
                              St James's Palace
                              Spencer House

GREENWICH SE10
Docklands
Opened on 11 November 1994

Greenwich, with its palace and its observatory, has played an immensely important role in English history and has witnessed many extraordinary events from Saxon times onwards. The name means 'green port' or 'landing place'. The Old English word *wic* in this name means 'harbour'.

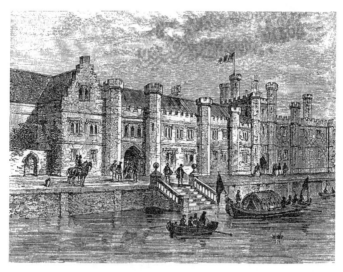

The old palace of Greenwich in 1630. It was a favourite Tudor royal residence, and Elizabeth I was born there.

GUNNERSBURY MIDDLESEX
District
Opened by the London & South Western Railway as BRENTFORD ROAD on
   1 January 1869
Name changed to GUNNERSBURY on 1 November 1871
First used by Underground trains on 1 June 1877

Gunnersbury House and Gunnersbury Park, which give this station
its name, are possibly derived from Gunhilda, a niece of King
Canute (reigned 1016–35) who lived in a manor house here until
she was banished from England in 1044. 'Gunnersbury' means 'the
manor of Gunhilda'.

HAINAULT ESSEX
Central
Opened by the Great Eastern Railway on 1 May 1903
First used by Underground trains on 31 May 1948

The name of this part of the Royal Forest of Essex means 'wood
belonging to a monastic community' – from the Old English *higna*,
'household', and *holt*, 'wood' – and the community referred to was
that of Barking Abbey.

   Despite the apparent link with Edward III's queen – Philippa of
Hainault – there is no connection at all with this Flemish name.

HAMMERSMITH W6
District, Hammersmith & City, Piccadilly
Hammersmith & City Line opened on 13 June 1864
Metropolitan District Railway opened on 9 September 1874
Great Northern, Piccadilly & Brompton Railway opened on 15 December
   1906

The first record of this name – as Hammersmyth – was in 1294. There
must have been a smithy here with a good, resounding hammer. The
words are so fundamental to that basic tool and trade that they have
remained unchanged for well over 700 years.

HAMPSTEAD NW3
Northern
Opened on 22 June 1907

Hampstead is simply a Saxon word meaning 'homestead'. Its first recorded use was in AD 959, as Hemstede. It is the deepest Underground station in London – at 192 feet (58.5 metres) below ground level.

HANGER LANE W5
Central
Opened on 30 June 1947

Hanger was a Saxon word for a slope – often a wooded slope. It is quite a common part of English place names such as Clayhanger in Cheshire, Oakhanger in Hampshire and Hartanger (stag slope) in Kent.

HARLESDEN NW10
Bakerloo
Opened by the London & North Western Railway on 15 June 1912
First used by Underground trains on 16 April 1917

This name ultimately comes from the Old English *Herewulf's tun*. Herewulf must have been a Saxon chief, and his *tun* was a farm or settlement.

HARROW & WEALDSTONE MIDDLESEX
Bakerloo
Opened by the London & Birmingham Railway as HARROW on 20 July 1837
Name changed to HARROW & WEALDSTONE on 1 May 1897
First used by Underground trains on 16 April 1917

The 'Harrow' in this name comes from a Saxon word *hearg*, meaning 'shrine' or 'temple'. The earliest record of this name dates back to

AD 767, when it was known as *Gumeninga hergae*, or 'temples of the Gumeningas', the name of an early tribe of settlers.

There is no relic from this original shrine but the lovely Church of St Mary in Harrow-on-the-Hill may well stand on the site, as Christian missionaries were urged to turn heathen temples into churches by Pope Gregory the Great.

Wealdstone refers to the Harrow Weald boundary stone – a boundary mark separating Harrow Weald from the parish of Harrow itself. 'Weald' means 'forest' or 'woodland'.

HARROW-ON-THE HILL MIDDLESEX
Metropolitan   (see HARROW & WEALDSTONE)
Opened as HARROW on 2 August 1880
Name changed to HARROW-ON-THE-HILL on 1 June 1894

HATTON CROSS MIDDLESEX
Piccadilly
Opened on 19 July 1975

There are many places called Hatton in Britain. It is a Saxon name meaning a *tun*, or 'settlement on the heath'. The 'cross' refers to a road junction there.

HEATHROW MIDDLESEX
Piccadilly
Terminals 1, 2, 3 opened as HEATHROW CENTRAL on 16 December 1977
Name changed to HEATHROW CENTRAL TERMINALS 1, 2, 3 on
*   3 October 1983*
Changed again to HEATHROW (Terminals 1, 2, 3) on 12 April 1986
HEATHROW TERMINAL 4 opened on 12 April 1986
HEATHROW TERMINAL 5 opened on 27 March 2008

Today this name is inseparable from the airport, one of the busiest in the world. Originally, it simply meant a row of dwellings near a heath – in this case, Hounslow Heath. Gatwick, the airport further away from London, has an equally rural meaning –'goat farm'.

HENDON CENTRAL NW4
Northern
Opened on 19 November 1923

'High hill' stems from the Saxon words *haeh dune*, a 'high dun' or 'hill'.

HERON QUAYS E14
Docklands
Opened on 31 August 1987

The name refers to herons – long-necked wading birds – which used to nest on the buildings here, and which can sometimes still be seen in this dockland area.

HIGH BARNET HERTFORDSHIRE
Northern
Opened by the Great Northern Railway on 1 April 1872
First used by Underground trains on 14 April 1940

The Saxon word *baernet* meant a 'burning' – in other words, a clearing in the forest made by burning the trees and undergrowth.

THE BLOODY BATTLE OF BARNET

It was on Easter Sunday, 14 April 1471, that the bloody Battle of Barnet took place between the opposing forces of the Yorkists and the Lancastrians in one of the final clashes in the Wars of the Roses. At that time there were two rival kings of England – Henry VI and Edward IV.

Henry VI – a Lancastrian – had been taken prisoner by Edward IV, and was taken captive to Barnet to watch his supporters, led by the Earl of Warwick, being butchered by Edward's Yorkist troops. Much of the fighting took place in dense fog, adding greatly to the confusion.

The Earl of Warwick and his brother were both slain, and their bodies were taken back to London to be publicly displayed outside Old St Paul's Cathedral. Henry VI was taken back to the Tower of London to be murdered. And Edward IV went on to win another battle shortly afterwards at Tewkesbury, killing Henry VI's son, the then Prince of Wales, after which he settled himself firmly on the throne without any fear of further opposition.

The three-hour battle was fought on Hadley Green, a little to the north of High Barnet.

HIGHBURY & ISLINGTON N5
Victoria
Opened as HIGHBURY on 28 June 1904
Named changed to HIGHBURY & ISLINGTON on 20 July 1922

'Highbury' means 'high manor' – so called because it was built on higher ground than its two neighbouring manors, Canonbury and Barnsbury.

'Islington' means 'Gisla's hill' – Gisla is the personal name of some Saxon chief, with the addition of dune ('hill') as a suffix.

HIGHGATE N6
Northern
Opened by the Great Northern Railway on 22 August 1867
The underground station was opened in an incomplete state on 19 January 1941

This area once belonged to the bishops of London. In the fourteenth century one of the bishops allowed a road to be built over the hill, but he made a profit for himself by erecting toll gates along it. Highgate gets its name from the toll gate which stood at the top of the hill.

Tradition has it that Dick Whittington rested at the bottom of Highgate Hill and heard Bow Bells ring out the famous message:

<blockquote>
Turn again, Whittington,
Thrice Lord Mayor of London Town.
</blockquote>

HIGH STREET KENSINGTON W8
Circle, District   (see KENSINGTON (OLYMPIA))
Opened on 1 October 1868

Within walking distance: Kensington Gardens
                            Kensington Palace

HILLINGDON MIDDLESEX
Piccadilly, Metropolitan
Opened on 10 December 1923

This is a Saxon name meaning the *dun*, or 'hill', where a man with a
name something like Hilla, Hildric or Hildwulf lived.

HOLBORN WC2
Central, Piccadilly
Piccadilly Line opened on 15 December 1906
Central Line platforms opened on 25 September 1933

The upper part of the Fleet river used to be called the *Hole-bourne*,
or 'stream in the hollow'.

A rustic view of Highgate as it was in 1745.

Nowadays, somewhat ignominiously, this stream is diverted into the Thames in an underground pipe, and few people are aware of the rivulet that gives this part of London its name.

Within walking distance: The British Museum
                             The Courtauld Gallery
                             (Somerset House)
                             Inns of Court
                             Sir John Soane's Museum
                             The Old Curiosity Shop

HOLLAND PARK W11
Central
Opened on 30 July 1900

This Underground station is named after Holland House, a large and beautiful Jacobean house in Kensington, with adjoining grounds called Holland Park. It was owned by Henry Rich, who became Earl of Holland in 1624.

The widow of the third Earl of Holland married the writer Joseph Addison, who wrote many of his essays for the *Spectator* in Holland House. In the long gallery there, Addison composed his writings by walking up and down and placing a bottle of wine at each end, so that he could refresh his mind at regular intervals.

Sadly, the house was largely destroyed by bombing during the Second World War.

HOLLOWAY ROAD N7
Piccadilly
Opened on 15 December 1906

In former times the name holloway referred to the fact that the road was low-lying and boggy – the 'hollow way'.

"... A TERROR TO EVIL DOERS"

The famous Holloway Prison was opened in 1852 for both men and women, and originally known as The City House of Correction. Since 1902 it has been used exclusively for women. Mrs Emmeline Pankhurst, leader of the Suffragettes' campaigning for women's rights, was imprisoned here, together with fellow female campaigners.

Although the buildings have been redesigned, the original glass foundation stone remains, with its formidable inscription: 'May God preserve the City of London and make this place a terror to evil doers'.

HORNCHURCH ESSEX
District
Opened by the London, Tilbury & Southend Railway on 1 May 1885
First used by Underground trains on 2 June 1902

The origin of this name is obscure. A fourteenth-century manuscript gives the name as Hornedecherche, so it has been suggested that this 'horned church' meant 'church with the horn-like gables'.

This odd carving of a bull's head is on the exterior of St Andrew's, Hornchurch, and gives the town its name.

On the eastern gable end of St Andrew's church in Hornchurch is a wooden carving of a bull's head with a pair of magnificent copper-plated horns. It was placed there in the eighteenth century but there must have been an earlier tradition of horns attached to this 'horned church'. Could it be an association with some pre-Christian cult? It is an odd mystery.

HOUNSLOW CENTRAL MIDDLESEX
Piccadilly
Opened as HESTON HOUNSLOW on 1 April 1886
Name changed to HOUNSLOW CENTRAL on 1 December 1925

HOUNSLOW EAST MIDDLESEX
Piccadilly   (see HOUNSLOW CENTRAL)
Opened as HOUNSLOW on 1 May 1883
Name changed to HOUNSLOW TOWN in 1884 (closed 1886)
New station opened on 2 May 1909
Finally named HOUNSLOW EAST on 1 December 1925

HOUNSLOW WEST MIDDLESEX
Piccadilly   (see HOUNSLOW CENTRAL)
Opened as HOUNSLOW BARRACKS on 21 July 1884
Name changed to HOUNSLOW WEST on 1 December 1925
New station opened on 11 December 1926

In Old English, a *lawe* was a piece of rising land or a barrow, so the earlier form of Hounslow was Hundeslawe, a hill where a man named Hund may have lived – though it has been suggested (incorrectly) that it was a place where dogs (hounds) were to be found.

The first mention of the name of the town of Hounslow appears in the year of Magna Carta, 1215, when, after the signing of the charter, the barons held a celebration in the form of a tournament in Staines Wood, and at Hounslow itself.

HYDE PARK CORNER SW1
Piccadilly
Opened on 15 December 1906

Shortly after the Norman Conquest in 1066, Geoffrey de Mandeville bequeathed three extensive properties, Ebury, Neate and Hyde, to the monks of Westminster.

Almost six centuries later, when Henry VIII destroyed all the monasteries, he sold the first two, but kept the manor and lands of Hyde for himself as a hunting ground.

It's difficult to imagine that deer, wild boar and wild bulls were to be found here, but deer were still being hunted here in the park as late as 1768.

The name Hyde is interesting, as it was an area of land that could support a single family – i.e. between 60 and 120 acres (24–49 hectares) depending on the quality of the land – and it is linked with the Old English word *hiw*, 'family' or 'household'. It is likely that the original property consisted of just one 'hyde'.

Within walking distance: Apsley House (Wellington Museum)
                             Buckingham Palace
                             Constitution Arch
                             Hyde Park
                             The Queen's Gallery
                             Royal Mews
                             Wellington Monument

ICKENHAM MIDDLESEX
Metropolitan, Piccadilly
Opened as ICKENHAM HALT on 25 September 1905

'Ticca's village'. This name has lost its first letter 't', probably because of the phrase 'at Ticca's ham' (village). Said quickly, the two 't's merge together and over time it became simply 'at Icca's ham' – hence, 'Ickenham'. Ticca was another of those innumerable Saxon chieftains whose existence is inferred only by a place name.

ISLAND GARDENS E14
Docklands
Opened on 31 August 1987

The island referred to is the Isle of Dogs. This is not a proper island, but is the peninsula within the big bend in the river Thames opposite Greenwich. The origin of the name has never been finally explained – but it may be that it is derived from the fact that Edward III (reigned 1327–77) kept his royal kennels here. Another explanation is that it is a corruption of Isle of Ducks – a reference to the wildfowl that once inhabited the marshes here. Alternatively, it may have been just a rude term of contempt.

More directly, Island Gardens is a reference to a park named Island Garden, opened here in 1895 by the London County Council.

KENNINGTON SE11
Northern
Opened on 18 December 1890

'Kennington' probably derives from the name of a Saxon chief known as Cœna and means 'the farm or estate of Cœna's people'.

A placid scene in rural Kennington, in 1780.

Alternatively, there is a possibility that it may derive from the Old English *kynig-tun*, or 'king's town', for it was once a royal manor. The Black Prince (1330–78), son of Edward III – given his strange nickname because of his black armour – had a palace in this area, which was used as a royal residence until the reign of Henry VII. This association with the Black Prince is kept alive in the name of Black Prince Road, running from the Embankment to Kennington Road.

Charles I (reigned 1625–49) lived for a while in a house built on the site of the Black Prince's palace. No trace of these old buildings now remain, but a part of the former grounds of the palace is now taken up by the Oval Cricket Ground, which is within walking distance of this station.

KENSAL GREEN NW10
Bakerloo
Opened on 1 October 1916

'Kensal' is derived from the Old English word *Kingisholt*, meaning 'King's wood' – so 'Kensal Green' means 'clearing in the King's forest'.

KENSINGTON (OLYMPIA) W6
District
Opened by the West London Railway as KENSINGTON on 27 May 1844
Site moved on 2 June 1862
Name changed to KENSINGTON (ADDISON ROAD) in 1868
Name finally changed to KENSINGTON (OLYMPIA) on 19 December 1946

Kensington is derived from Cynesige's *tun*, or 'farm'. In 1086 the Domesday Book referred to it as Cheninton. For Olympia, see below.

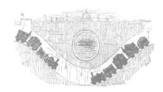

'OLYMPIA' – 10 YEARS BEFORE THE FIRST OLYMPIC GAMES!

London had its 'Olympia' here ten years before the first modern Olympic Games took place in 1896.

Olympia on the Hammersmith Road was built on the site of a large former nursery garden, and was originally called The National Agricultural Hall.

When the Paris Hippodrome circus came to perform here in 1886, with 400 animals, a chariot race and a stag hunt, it was felt that the venue needed a more exciting name – so Olympia was proposed and adopted – with reference to the famous Greek games of antiquity.

It has been the scene of circuses, shows and exhibitions ever since.

KENTISH TOWN NW5
Northern
Opened on 22 June 1907

The obvious meaning might seem to be that this is a town where Kentish people settled – but this would be wrong. Here, the name is probably derived from a farm or estate belonging to someone called Le Kentish. It was recorded as Kentisston in 1208.

Coach and horses approaching an old pub in Kentish Town in 1820.

KENTON MIDDLESEX
Bakerloo
Opened by the London & North Western Railway on 15 June 1912
First used by Underground trains on 16 April 1917

There is a similarity between Kenton and Kennington in that both places are derived from the name of a Saxon leader named Coena, and *tun* refers to the farm or homestead where he lived. Whether they were one and the same person is impossible to tell after this length of time.

KEW GARDENS SURREY
District
Opened by the London & South Western Railway on 1 January 1869
First used by Underground trains on 1 June 1877

Kew gets its name from its situation on the Thames. It means 'quay' or 'wharf'.

The 'Gardens' part of the name refers to the Royal Botanic Gardens, now a world famous scientific centre and popular pleasure garden, which attracts many thousands of visitors annually.

The gardens were the grounds of a small palace – or 'wonderful country house' as Prince Charles calls it – renovated and re-opened to the public in 2006. It was a favourite residence of King George III (reigned 1760–1820) and also of Queen Adelaide, consort of William IV. The house and gardens were given to the nation by Queen Victoria in 1841, as she had taken up residence in her new home in Buckingham Palace.

Within walking distance: Royal Botanic Gardens

KILBURN NW6
Jubilee
Opened as KILBURN & BRONDESBURY on 24 November 1879
Name changed to KILBURN on 25 September 1950

Kilburn may be derived from the Saxon *cylenburne*, meaning 'stream by a kiln', or alternatively 'place near a stream where cattle graze'.

KILBURN PARK NW6
Bakerloo   (see KILBURN)
Opened on 31 January 1915

KING GEORGE V SE9
Docklands
Opened on 2 December 2005

This station is named after King George V Dock, the third of the royal docks. King George V himself (reigned 1910–35) officially opened this dock in 1921. It was built to enhance and extend the trade that was passing through the two other royal docks – the Royal Victoria and the Royal Albert. The King George V Dock was closed in 1981.

KINGSBURY NW9
Jubilee
Opened on 10 December 1932

'The king's burg'. This is an old name, dating from Saxon times, before the Norman Conquest. It was recorded as *Kynges byrig* in 1046. A *burg* was a fortified place, stronghold or manor. The Saxon king, Edward the Confessor (reigned 1042–66) gave this Kingsbury to the monks of Westminster Abbey in 1044.

The antiquity of this name contrasts greatly with that of Queensbury, the next station along the Jubilee Line to Stanmore. (See QUEENSBURY)

KING'S CROSS ST PANCRAS NW1
Circle, Hammersmith & City, Metropolitan, Northern, Piccadilly, Victoria
Metropolitan Line opened as KING'S CROSS on 10 January 1863
Piccadilly Line opened on 15 December 1906
Northern Line opened on 12 May 1907
Name changed to KING'S CROSS & ST PANCRAS in 1925
Name changed imperceptibly to KING'S CROSS for ST PANCRAS in 1927
Name changed sensibly to KING'S CROSS ST PANCRAS in 1933

After much reconstruction to include the Victoria Line, the present station opened on 1 December 1968

King's Cross is a comparatively recent name, compared with, say, Charing Cross. The king referred to is George IV (reigned 1820–30). Six years after his death, a 60-feet (18.29-metre) high monument was erected at the junction of Euston, Pentonville, St Pancras and Gray's Inn roads. On top of this was a statue of George IV. This odd-looking monument was used first as a police station and then as a public house.

The whole monstrosity was so unpopular that the king's statue was removed after only six years and the monument itself was demolished in 1845.

However, the name King's Cross hung around in people's memories, and became used for the railway station, which was built a few years later, in 1851–52. (See ST PANCRAS)

The strange monument which carried a statue of George IV on top – thus giving the name 'King's Cross' to the area.

KNIGHTSBRIDGE SW1
Piccadilly
Opened on 15 December 1906

The name is so famous and so frequently used that few people ever question what it means or take it literally as the 'knights' bridge'.

Legend has it that two knights fought here on a bridge that spanned the river Westbourne. According to this old story, the two knights both fell into the river and were drowned. Since then, so it is said, the bridge and the former village nearby took the name of Knightsbridge. How true this is, no one will ever know – but it is an intriguing old tale. The name was recorded as Cnihtebricge during the reign of King Edward the Confessor (reigned 1042–66).

The river Westbourne was 'tamed' in the eighteenth century to form the Serpentine in Hyde Park. From there it is now taken, somewhat ignominiously, down to the Thames in a large conduit. En route, the conduit can be seen crossing the lines and above the trains at Sloane Square Underground Station.

Within walking distance: Harrods
                             Hyde Park

LADBROKE GROVE W10
Hammersmith & City
Opened as NOTTING HILL on 13 June 1864
Name changed to NOTTING HILL & LADBROKE GROVE in 1880
Name changed again to LADBROKE GROVE (NORTH KENSINGTON) on
*   1 June 1919*
Finally simplified to LADBROKE GROVE in 1938

All the Ladbroke names in this area refer to Richard Ladbroke, who owned two farms north of Notting Hill in the seventeenth century. The streets were laid out in the nineteenth century, when the area was sold by later generations of Ladbrokes for housing development.

LAMBETH NORTH SE1
Bakerloo
Opened as KENNINGTON ROAD on 10 March 1906
Name changed to WESTMINSTER BRIDGE ROAD on 5 August 1906
Finally changed to LAMBETH NORTH on 15 April 1917

There are many hythes, or wharves, along the banks of the Thames, which are named after the goods that were once predominantly shipped there. Lambeth gets its name from being a 'lamb hythe' – the wharf where lambs were shipped.

Within walking distance: Imperial War Museum

LANCASTER GATE W2
Central
Opened on 30 July 1900

Named in honour of the Duchy of Lancaster. One of Queen Victoria's titles was Duchess of Lancaster, and she had been born in Kensington Palace in 1819. The beautiful Lancaster Gate itself was designed in 1857 by the architect Sancton Wood, and is situated on the north side of Kensington Gardens. All the places of interest in these gardens are easily accessible from Lancaster Gate.

Within walking distance: Hyde Park
                              Diana, Princess of Wales
                                 Memorial Fountain
                              Kensington Gardens
                              Kensington Palace
                              Serpentine Gallery

LANGDON PARK E14
Docklands
Opened on 9 December 2007

Opened in December 2007, Langdon Park is one of the very latest
stations on the Docklands Light Railway. It can be found only on
the most up-to-date maps of the London Underground system. It is
situated between All Saints and Devons Road.

When in the planning stage, this station was provisionally called
Carmen Street but then it was changed to Langdon Park, named
after a local park and an adjacent secondary school, which were
themselves named after the Revd C.G. Langdon, vicar of All Angels,
Bromley-by-Bow between 1913 and 1925.

LATIMER ROAD W12
Hammersmith & City
Opened on 16 December 1868

Latimer Road takes it name from Edward Latymer (1557–1627), a
wealthy London merchant whose bequest to educate and feed 'eight
poore boies' has resulted in one of London's most prestgious co-edu-
cational independent schools – Latymer Upper School, now situated
between King Street and the Thames.

Leicester Square in about 1750.

LEICESTER SQUARE WC2
Northern, Piccadilly

Opened on 15 December 1906

Robert Sidney, a nephew of the famous Elizabethan poet Sir Philip Sidney, acquired the land here in the 1630s. He was the 2nd Earl of Leicester, so the house he built for himself between 1631 and 1635 on this spot naturally became known as Leicester House. Leicester Square was laid out in 1670, in front of the earl's house.

Leicester House was demolished in 1790, and its nineteenth-century replacement burnt down in 1865.

Within walking distance: National Gallery
National Portrait Gallery
St Martin-in-the-Fields
Trafalgar Square

LEWISHAM SE13
Docklands

Opened on 11 November 1999

'Leofsa's village'. In other words, the *ham*, or 'homestead', of a Saxon chief with this name.

LEYTON E10
Central

Opened as LOW LEYTON by the Eastern Counties Railway on 22 August 1856
Name changed to LEYTON on 1 January 1868
First used by Underground trains on 5 May 1947

'Farm on the river Lea' – a Saxon name.

LEYTONSTONE E11
Central
Opened as LEYTONSTONE by the Eastern Counties Railway on 22 August 1856
First used by Underground trains on 5 May 1947

This station is north of Leyton (see above) and the name means 'Leyton by the stone'. Local tradition has it that the 'stone' in this name was in fact a Roman milestone, but in any case it signifies a boundary stone of some sort.

LIMEHOUSE E14
Docklands
Opened on 31 August 1987

The lime kilns, or 'oasts', around this dockland area gave Limehouse its name – for the 'house' part is a corruption of the Old English word *ast*, meaning 'kiln'. Supplies of chalk were brought up from Kent from at least the fourteenth century onwards.

LIVERPOOL STREET EC2
Central, Circle, Hammersmith & City, Metropolitan
Opened by the Metropolitan Line as BISHOPSGATE on 12 July 1875
Name changed to LIVERPOOL STREET on 1 November 1909
Central Line opened on 28 July 1912

A twisting old street named Old Bethlem was built over in 1829 to form Liverpool Street, named in honour of Lord Liverpool, Prime Minister 1812–27. Liverpool Street Station, opened in 1874, was named after this newly built and renamed street.

SHEER BEDLAM!

The former name of Liverpool Street – Old Bethlem – referred to the Bethlem Hospital, which used to stand on the site of the present day Liverpool Street Station.

Our word 'bedlam' derives from the name of this hospital, because many of its patients were mentally deranged. It became a crude but fashionable sport among the gentry in the eighteenth century to go and watch the pathetic antics of these unfortunate inmates – all crowded together in an appalling rabble. This, indeed, was 'bedlam'.

In the final image of *The Rake's Progress*, the artist William Hogarth (1697–1764) depicts Tom Rakewell ending his wretched life in 'Bethlehem Hospital madhouse'.

LONDON BRIDGE SE1
Northern, Jubilee
Opened on 25 February 1900

The first London Bridge was built by the Romans during their occupation of Britain between AD 100 and AD 400. The Roman name for the settlement here was recorded as Londinium in *c.* AD 115 – but the origin is 'tantalizingly obscure' and is probably pre-Celtic.

Many bridges have been built over the Thames since then, but the one on this site is *the* London Bridge. Its importance can best be understood when it is remembered that until Westminster Bridge was opened in 1750, London Bridge was the *only* bridge across the Thames in London. In fact, apart from a wooden structure constructed at Putney in 1727–29, the next bridge upstream from London Bridge was the one at Kingston upon Thames, a distance of about 12 miles (20 kilometres).

One reason for the lack of bridges was the sturdy hostility of the huge number of Thames watermen, who carried passengers across and up and down the river. It is estimated that in the seventeenth century about 40,000 watermen earned their living on the river. Obviously, any bridge building was a threat to their livelihood.

The present bridge was built in 1967–72, and its immediate predecessor, built by Sir John Rennie and opened in 1831 by King William IV and Queen Adelaide, was shipped across the Atlantic in pieces and re-erected at Lake Havasu City, Arizona.

Old London Bridge as it was in 1756 – an illustration made just before the demolition of the houses built on it.

Before Rennie's bridge, many other picturesque versions of London Bridge existed, with houses and chapels along the entire length, making it impossible for traffic to pass with any ease.

Within walking distance: Clink Prison Museum
                             Design Museum
                             HMS *Belfast*
                             The London Dungeon
                             Southwark Cathedral
                             Tower Bridge

LOUGHTON ESSEX
Central
Opened originally by the Eastern Counties Railway on 22 August 1856
A new station opened on 28 April 1940
First used by Underground trains on 21 November 1948

The name of Loughton derives from the fact that it was the *tun*, or 'dwelling place', of Luca, a Saxon landowner.

MAIDA VALE W9
Bakerloo
Opened on 6 June 1915

The name of this district north of Paddington commemorates the almost forgotten Battle of Maida, fought in 1806 on the southern tip of Italy, in which the British, led by General Sir John Stuart, defeated the French.

'Maida' (deriving from the Italian town of San Pietro di Maida, near where this battle was fought) first came to the area soon after the victory was won, in the name of a pub on the Edgware Road called Hero of Maida. Gradually, the name of the pub was transferred to the road itself: first as Maida Hill, and then as Maida Vale.

MANOR HOUSE N4
Piccadilly
Opened on 19 September 1932

Manor House is the name of a nearby pub – and this gives the station its name.

MANSION HOUSE EC2
Circle, District
Opened on 3 July 1871

The Mansion House was specially built to be the official residence of the Lord Mayor of London, where he must reside during his year of office.

In 1735 many famous architects were asked to produce plans, but it was George Dance, Clerk of the City Works at that time, whose design was chosen. The Mansion House itself was completed in 1752.

Within walking distance: Guildhall
                            Shakespeare's Globe Theatre

MARBLE ARCH W1
Central
Opened on 30 July 1900

Marble Arch, constructed out of Carrara marble and one of the most famous landmarks in London, is rather oddly sited. John Nash, the architect who designed it, based it on the Arch of Constantine in Rome. Originally, in 1827, it was set up in front of Buckingham Palace, during the reign of George IV (reigned 1810–30). However, it did not find favour with Queen Victoria (reigned 1837–1901) and so it was moved to its present site in 1851.

George IV's intention was to have an equestrian statue of himself on top of Marble Arch, but this was never done, and the statue that was to have been used can now be seen in the north-east corner of Trafalgar Square.

Officially, only senior members of the Royal Family and the King's Troop Royal Horse Artillery are allowed to pass through it.

Within walking distance: Diana, Princess of Wales
Memorial Fountain
Hyde Park
Oxford Street shopping
Serpentine Gallery

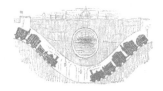

TYBURN GALLOWS

Marble Arch stands very near the site of the most notorious place of public execution in London – Tyburn gallows. It has been estimated that about 50,000 criminals were hanged there between the twelfth century and 1783, the year when the gallows were moved to Newgate Prison. This averages a rate of about seven a month. Important 'hanging days' were public holidays as the authorities considered that the sight of people being hanged would act as a deterrent to crime.

Tyburn gallows were triangular in shape with three upright posts supporting three strong horizontal wooden beams from which the malefactors were hanged. The method of hanging was crude and brutal. A seventeenth-century visitor to London described how the hangman brought his victim under the gallows on a horse-drawn cart, then with the criminal still on the cart, tied an end of his rope around one of the crossbeams 'while the other went round the wretch's neck. This done, he gives the horse a lash with his whip, away goes the cart and there swings my gentleman, kicking in the air'.

MARYLEBONE WI
Bakerloo
Opened as GREAT CENTRAL on 27 March 1907
Name changed to MARYLEBONE on 15 April 1917

In the Middle Ages this district was known as Tyburn, named after the river Tyburn, meaning 'boundary stream'. The little Church of St Mary stood by this river and gave the village its name; various forms of it were St Mary-at-Bourne, Marybourne, Mary-by-the-Bourne, Mary-le-bone and finally the present form: Marylebone. Literally, then, it means 'St Mary's church by the boundary river'.

The rural area around present-day Marble Arch, which was the setting of Tyburn Gallows, where hundreds of criminals were hanged.

Lord Ferrers being hanged at Tyburn. He was the last member of the House of Lords to be hanged there. As he was a lord, a silken noose was used for his noble neck.

MILE END E1
Central, District, Hammersmith & City
Opened on 2 June 1902

'Mile End' means exactly what it says – it is 1 mile from the City of London – or, more accurately, from Aldgate. A medieval hamlet existed here just about where Mile End meets Globe Road.

MILL HILL EAST NW7
Northern
Opened as MILL HILL by the Great Northern Railway on 22 August 1867
Name changed to MILL HILL EAST on 1 March 1928
First used by Underground trains on 18 May 1941

'Hill on which a windmill stands' – recorded as Myllehill in 1547.

MONUMENT EC3
Circle, District
Opened as EASTCHEAP on 6 October 1884
Name changed to MONUMENT on 1 November 1884

The Monument is a tall column designed by Sir Christopher Wren in memory of the Great Fire of London in 1666. It is 202 feet high (61.57 metres), the exact distance between its position and the bakery in Pudding Lane where the fire started.

Wren originally wanted to put a statue of King Charles II on top, but the king objected to this, reasoning that he was not responsible for the fire! Charles II was, however, closely involved with dealing with the fire, and he took personal charge of pulling down houses to try to stop the spread of the flames.

Visitors can climb up the Monument at certain times, and there is an interesting view across the Thames. At one time, the Monument was a commanding landmark, but is now dwarfed by the huge modern buildings that surround it.

Within walking distance: London Bridge
                              The Monument
                              Southwark Cathedral

MOORGATE EC2
Circle, Hammersmith & City, Northern, Metropolitan
Opened as MOORGATE STREET on 23 December 1865
Name changed to simply MOORGATE on 24 October 1924
Northern Line opened as MOORGATE on 25 February 1900

In medieval times a moor gate led out to the moors and fens beyond
the city of London. Originally it was a postern gate built in 1415 in
the old city wall but was enlarged over the years. The height of the
gateway was raised so that the London Trained Bands, an early form
of Militia, could march through with their pikes held upright.

The gate was finally demolished in 1762, and the street, named
Moorgate, was constructed in the 1840s.

Within walking distance: The Museum of London

MOOR PARK HERTS
Metropolitan
Opened as SANDY LODGE on 9 May 1910
Name changed to MOOR PARK & SANDY LODGE on 18 October 1923
Finally changed to MOOR PARK on 25 September 1950

This station was opened in 1910 with the name Sandy Lodge. In
1923 the name was changed to Moor Park and Sandy Lodge – and
then in 1950 it became simply Moor Park.

The original name, Sandy Lodge, is the name of a nearby golf
course. Moor Park is an open public park near the golf course. But
the name la More is recorded as early as *c.* 1180.

MORDEN SURREY
Northern
Opened on 13 September 1926

'Morden' derives from two Old English words: *mor*, meaning 'marsh'
and *dun*, 'hill'. It means a hill surrounded by marshy land.

The original Moor Gate, one of six gates in the city wall, demolished in 1762. Today's underground station preserves its memory.

MORNINGTON CRESCENT NWI
Northern
Opened on 22 June 1907
Closed on 23 October 1992
Re-opened on 27 April 1998

The imposing crescent of dwelling houses that is Mornington Crescent is named after Richard Wellesley, Earl of Mornington, the eldest brother of the Duke of Wellington. He served as foreign secretary from 1809–12. He was appointed lord lieutenant of Ireland in 1821, when the crescent was being built. The Underground station takes its name from this crescent.

MUDCHUTE E14
Docklands
Opened on 31 August 1987
Re-sited on 20 November 1999

This station is named after the nearby Mudchute Park and Farm. This was originally a piece of derelict land created in the nineteenth century from the spoil from the construction of Millwall Dock.

Since the late twentieth century this area has been developed into a remarkable educational and leisure facility, with the Mudchute Equestrian Centre, a café, a shop, an education centre and a large variety of farm animals to see: pigs, cows, goats, sheep, ducks, geese and even llamas.

NEASDEN NW10
Jubilee
Opened as KINGSBURY & NEASDEN on 2 August 1880
Named changed to NEASDEN & KINGSBURY on 1 January 1910
Finally changed to NEASDEN on 1 January 1932

Literally, this name, which is Saxon in origin, means 'nose-shaped hill', '*nese dun*'.

NEWBURY PARK ESSEX
Central
Opened by the Great Eastern Railway on 1 May 1903
First used by Underground trains on 14 December 1947

'The new manor house at the park' – 'new', however, is a relative term, as the name was first recorded in the middle of the fourteenth century. Newbury is derived from two Old English words: *niwe burh*.

NEW CROSS SE14
East London   (see NEW CROSS GATE)
Opened in October 1850
First used by Underground trains on 1 October 1884

NEW CROSS GATE SE14
East London
Opened as NEW CROSS on 5 June 1839
First used by Underground trains on 1 October 1884
Name changed to NEW CROSS GATE in 1923

The 'cross' referred to is the junction of the road to Dartford and the Old Kent Road.

NORTH ACTON NW10
Central   (see ACTON TOWN)
Opened on 5 November 1923

NORTH EALING W5
Piccadilly   (see EALING)
Opened on 23 June 1903

NORTHFIELDS W13
Piccadilly
Opened as NORTHFIELD HALT on 16 April 1908
Name changed to NORTHFIELDS & LITTLE EALING on 11 December 1911
Finally re-sited further east as NORTHFIELDS on 19 May 1932

The name goes back to the fifteenth century and is self-explanatory – the 'fields in the north'.

'TUBE' BABY!

In the 1920s, a baby girl was born on the Bakerloo Line. She was given the name Thelma Ursula Beatrice Eleanor – giving her the initials TUBE – an unforgettable reminder of her link with the London Underground!

NORTH GREENWICH SE10
Jubilee   (see GREENWICH)
Opened on 14 May 1999

NORTH HARROW MIDDLESEX
Metropolitan   (see HARROW)
Opened on 22 March 1915

NORTHOLT MIDDLESEX
Central
Opened on 21 November 1948

'Northern *halhs*'. The meaning of the Saxon word *halh* is not entirely clear. It could mean a corner, a secret place, a cave, recess, or some sort of 'nook'. The name of Southall in Middlesex is similarly derived – the 'Southern *halhs*'.

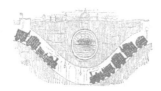

NORTH WEALD ESSEX
Formerly Central – now Epping Ongar Railway

Opened by the Eastern Counties/Great Eastern Railway in 1865
Central Line extended to use this station in 1949
Closed on 30 September 1994

Triumphantly re-opened on 10 October 2004 by the Epping Ongar Railway – the situation throughout the past half-century is so complicated that it cannot be described here. Those interested in following the historical details should consult the official website of the Epping Ongar Railway Volunteer Society (www.eorailway.co.uk) or Wikipedia.

The Saxon word *weald* meant 'woodland'. Here, the name refers to Epping Forest.

NORTH WEMBLEY MIDDLESEX
Bakerloo (see WEMBLEY)

Opened as WEMBLEY CENTRAL by the London & North Western Railway
*   on 15 June 1912*
First used by Underground trains on 16 April 1917

NORTHWICK PARK MIDDLESEX
Metropolitan

Opened as NORTHWICK PARK & KENTON on 28 June 1923
Named changed to NORTHWICK PARK on 15 March 1937

Named after the Northwick family, who owned the manor of Harrow in the late eighteenth century. Today Northwick Park is the home of a popular and prestigious golf course.

NORTHWOOD MIDDLESEX
Metropolitan (see NORTHWOOD HILLS)

Opened on 1 September 1887

NORTHWOOD HILLS MIDDLESEX
Metropolitan
Opened on 13 November 1933

Self-explanatory – the 'northern wood' – in this case the woodland
north of Ruislip. The arrival of the Metropolitan Line gave an
immediate boost to building development, and as a result of
this, the area soon lost most of its woodland. The 'hills' are also
self-explanatory, referring to high ground nearby.

NOTTING HILL GATE W11
Central, Circle, District
Opened on 1 October 1868

The 'gate' in this name is a reminder that here once was a turnpike
gate, built in the eighteenth century by the Uxbridge Turnpike
Trust. The gate was removed in 1864, just four years before the
Underground station opened.

'Notting' may derive from a family surname, the Knottings, in
which case the name would mean 'hill belonging to the Knotting
family'. As long ago as 1358 it was recorded as Knottynghull, and
in 1376 it appears as Knottyngwode. It has been suggested that the
family may have had a connection with the Bedfordshire village
of Knotting.

Within walking distance: Portobello Road Market

OAKWOOD N14
Piccadilly
Opened as ENFIELD WEST on 13 March 1933
Name changed to ENFIELD WEST (OAKWOOD) on 3 May 1934
Finally became simply OAKWOOD on 1 September 1946

The 'oak wood' referred to was once a part of Enfield Chase. The
first syllable of 'Enfield' derives from the name of a Saxon landowner
here – so 'Enfield' means 'Eana's clearing'.

Notting Hill in 1750 – very different from the scene of the Notting Hill festivals in the twenty-first century.

Notting Barn Farm in 1830, near today's Notting Hill Gate underground station.

OLD STREET EC1
Northern
Opened on 17 November 1901

When the Saxons came here, the Roman road out of London leading to Colchester was already several centuries old. According to John Stow, the sixteenth-century historian of London, Old Street got its name 'for that it was the old highway from Aldersgate for the north east parts of England, before Bishopsgate was built'. The name was given further significance when this Underground station opened in 1901.

OSTERLEY MIDDLESEX
Piccadilly
Opened as OSTERLEY & SPRING GROVE on 1 May 1883
Name changed and station re-sited on 25 March 1934

'Woodland clearing with a sheepfold' – the name derives from two Old English words, *eowestre* and *leah*.

OVAL SE11
Northern
Opened on 18 December 1890

Kennington Oval was opened for cricket in 1845. Formerly, it had been a part of a market garden, and before that it had been part of a site on which a royal residence had been built (see **KENNINGTON**). The first Test Match in England against Australia was played here in 1880 – happily, England won by five wickets.

The name is derived from the Latin word *ovum*, meaning 'egg', so it simply means 'egg-shaped'. Perhaps this is appropriate for those cricketers who are 'out for a duck' – which is short for a 'duck's egg' the shape of which is o, or nothing!

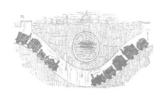

OXFORD CIRCUS W1

Bakerloo, Central, Victoria

Central Line (then Central London Railway) opened 30 July 1900
Bakerloo Line (then Baker Street & Waterloo Railway) opened 10 March
*   1910*
Victoria Line opened 7 March 1969

Oxford Street was once known as Tyburn Road, and the notorious Tyburn gallows stood at its western end, near where Marble Arch stands today. The reason for its present name, which became established in the early eighteenth century, is that much of the land to the north of it was bought by Edward Harley, 2nd Earl of Oxford.

Oxford 'Circus' was a part of John Nash's circular design at the place where his New Street (later to be known as Regent Street) crossed the much older Oxford Street.

The road we now know as Oxford Street has existed in one form or another possibly from as early as Roman times.

Within walking distance: Oxford Street shops
                            Soho

PADDINGTON W2

Bakerloo, Circle, District, Hammersmith & City

Opened as PADDINGTON (BISHOP'S ROAD) by the Hammersmith & City
*   Line on 10 January 1863*
Name changed to PADDINGTON on this line on 10 September 1933
Opened as PADDINGTON (PRAED STREET) by the Circle Line on
*   1 October 1868*
Name changed to PADDINGTON on this line on 11 July 1948
Opened as PADDINGTON by the Bakerloo Line on 1 December 1913

The name Paddington is typical of so many Saxon names. Padda was the name of the Saxon leader who settled here; *ingas* meant 'family' or 'followers' of Padda; and the ending *tun* simply tells us that this was their 'village'.

As an Underground station, Paddington was part of the very first stretch of the Metropolitan Line, which opened in 1863 with Paddington as the western terminus of the world's first underground system.

Paddington village church shown as it was in 1750 and then, after 'improvements', as it was in 1805.

As for the main-line railway station, Paddington began its life as a wooden structure, and opened as early as 1838 – the year of Queen Victoria's coronation. Queen Victoria herself arrived here on her very first railway journey – from Slough – in 1842. She had been somewhat alarmed at the speed, which averaged 44 miles per hour. ('Not so fast next time, Mr Conductor' admonished Prince Albert!)

PADDINGTON BEAR

Paddington Bear, the star of Michael Bond's popular children's stories, was named after Paddington Station. The author and his wife were living nearby when he bought a small teddy bear. The name was an inspired choice! A large Paddington Bear statue is now on permanent view in the main-line station's entrance hall.

It is interesting to imagine what Padda, the Old Saxon chief, would think if he could return and see his ursine namesake!

PARK ROYAL NW10
Piccadilly
Opened as PARK ROYAL & TWYFORD ABBEY on 23 June 1903
Name changed and the station re-sited on 6 July 1931

Although this name may sound ancient and connected with royalty, in fact it is relatively recent. In the late nineteenth century the Royal Agricultural Society obtained a large site here for a permanent exhibition – a 'park' for themselves. It was a scheme that never succeeded, and the area became used for industry. The name, Park Royal, however, remained, and when the Underground station was opened in 1903 it was originally named Park Royal & Twyford Abbey.

PARSONS GREEN SW6
District
Opened on 1 March 1880

A parsonage or rectory, which stood here for centuries, provides the name for this area – it was 'the village green standing by the parson's house'. The parsonage itself was first mentioned in 1391 and was finally demolished in 1882.

PERIVALE MIDDLESEX
Central
Opened as PERIVALE HALT by the Great Western Railway on 2 May 1904
First used by Underground trains on 30 June 1947

'Pear tree valley'. Before the sixteenth century this hamlet was called Little Greenford or Greenford Parva, meaning 'the small village by the green ford'. The next station along the Central Line is Greenford – which is named after Greenford Magna – 'the *large* village by the green ford'.

PICCADILLY CIRCUS W1
Bakerloo, Piccadilly
Opened on 10 March 1906

In the early seventeenth century, a London tailor called Robert Baker made a fortune for himself by selling 'picadils' – a kind of wide stiff collar that was fashionable at that time – from his shop in the Strand.

Out of the profits he bought lands to the north of what is now Piccadilly Circus, on which he built himself a large house. Londoners of the time promptly nicknamed this mansion 'Piccadilly Hall'.

The name Piccadilly has remained attached to this part of London ever since and became even better known when Piccadilly Circus was formed in 1819, at the intersection of Piccadilly with John Nash's newly constructed Regent Street.

Piccadilly Circus as it was in 1875 – just a decade or so after the first Underground trains began to run.

Within walking distance: Burlington House and Burlington Arcade
Piccadilly Circus and the 'Eros' statue
Regent Street
St James's Piccadilly
Soho

EROS AT PICCADILLY

Everyone knows the statue of 'Eros' in the middle of Piccadilly Circus – and everyone knows that Eros is the Greek God of sexual love.

However, when the sculptor Sir Alfred Gilbert (1854–1934), created the statue and designed the fountain, he meant it to represent the Angel of Christian Charity. It was intended to be a memorial to the great public benefactor, Anthony Ashley Cooper, 7th Earl of Shaftesbury (1801–85), who campaigned to reform factories, reduce working hours, and prohibit underground employment of women and children in coal mines.

The statue, made of aluminium, was unveiled in 1893, and the nickname 'Eros' instantly became universal – though who first thought of it will never be known.

PIMLICO SW1
Victoria
Opened on 14 September 1972

The station name Pimlico is something of a mystery. It may be derived from the name of an innkeeper, Ben Pimlico, who lived in Hoxton in the late sixteenth century and was famous for his 'nut-brown ale'. Somehow his name became that of his hostelry and then of the surrounding area. An early version of the word is recorded in 1630 as Pimplico, referring to what was then an almost uninhabited district in Westminster.

Other suggested explanations of 'Pimlico' are that it was the name of some long-forgotten drink, or – perhaps far-fetched – that it is linked with the Pamlico tribe of native Americans, who used to export timber to England in the seventeenth century.

This word has been puzzled over for several centuries.

PINNER MIDDLESEX
Metropolitan
Opened on 25 May 1885

'Pynn's home by the river bank'. Pynn was a Saxon name, and *ora* is Old English for a riverbank. Interestingly, the *ora* part of the name is also found in 'Windsor' – which means 'the river bank where the windlass is' – a curious derivation for the name of the royal house of Windsor. The River Pinn, hereaboits, is named after Pinner, not *vice versa*.

PLAISTOW E13
District, Hammersmith & City
Opened by the London, Tilbury & Southend Railway on 31 March 1858
First used by Underground trains on 2 June 1902

The Old English word *plegstow* means 'playground'. This area was a place of recreation, and the name is first recorded here as long ago as 1414 as Playstowe. There are similar place names in other parts of England, all meaning 'sports area'.

PONTOON DOCK E16
Docklands
Opened on 2 December 2005

Pontoon Dock Station was opened in December 2005 on the King George V branch of the Docklands Light Railway, between West Silverton and London City. The word 'pontoon' – here meaning the floating gate of a dock – is derived from the Latin word *ponto*, 'a punt'.

POPLAR E14
Docklands
Opened on 31 August 1987

The land in this area is very marshy and suited to poplars, the rapidly growing trees of the willow family, which give this district its name. The word comes from the Old French word *poplier*, which in turn was derived from the Latin *populus*, 'a poplar tree'.

POPLAR IN THE BLITZ

A girl in Poplar had a most embarrassing moment in the Blitz on London during the Second World War. She was having a bath when a bomb hit her house. The bomb blast shattered the house and the bath was turned upside down with the girl herself still inside it. Luckily, the bath provided the perfect shelter from the bricks and rubble dropping around her.

After the air raid, she was dug out, frightened, safe, wet and stark naked.

She was lucky. It was been calculated that more than 15,000 people were killed in the London Blitz, and over 3.5 million houses were damaged or destroyed.

PRESTON ROAD MIDDLESEX
Metropolitan
Opened as PRESTON ROAD HALT on 21 May 1908
Name changed to PRESTON ROAD and station re-sited on 22 November 1931

The 'Preston' part of this station name derives from two Old English words: *preosta* and *tun*, meaning 'homestead of the priests'. The name is very widespread, in fact there are more than forty place names in Britain consisting of or containing the word 'preston'.

PRINCE REGENT E16
Docklands
Opened on 28 March 1994

Named in memory of 'Prinny' – the Prince of Wales, son of King George III (reigned 1760–1820), who became Regent of Great Britain for nine years (1811–20) during the period when his father became so mentally ill that he was unable to undertake his royal duties. On the death of his father in 1820, the Prince Regent became crowned as King George IV and reigned until 1830. More precisely, the Docklands station is named after Prince Regent Lane – the road outside.

PUDDING MILL LANE E15
Docklands
Opened on 15 January 1996

Pudding Mill Lane (E15) must not be confused with the Pudding
Lane in the City of London (EC3) where the Great Fire of London
started in 1666.

The word 'pudding', however, is common to both lanes, and it
may come as a surprise to some to learn that in the Middle Ages –
and later – 'pudding' referred to the guts and entrails of slaughtered
animals. We still have a linguistic memory of this meaning in the
name of 'black pudding' – which is made of dried blood.

'Pudding' had to be disposed of, and the rivers and tributaries of
the Thames provided a convenient dumping place.

A windmill stood near here until the early nineteenth century,
when it was demolished, but quite what the connection was between
the 'pudding' and the 'mill' is unclear.

PUTNEY BRIDGE SW6
District
Opened as PUTNEY BRIDGE & FULHAM on 1 March 1880
Name changed to PUTNEY BRIDGE & HURLINGHAM on 1 September 1902
Finally became simply PUTNEY BRIDGE in 1932

A Saxon chieftain called Puttan is remembered in the name of
Putney. Together with the Saxon word *hyp*, 'landing place', the name
means 'Puttan's wharf'.

QUEENSBURY NW9
Jubilee
Opened on 16 December 1934

The name Queensbury has no historical roots. It was the winning
suggestion in a competition run by an estate agent in the 1930s.
The Underground station, opened in 1934, needed a name, and
Queensbury appealed to the judges of the competition because it
complemented the next station along this line – Kingsbury – which
had opened two years earlier, in 1932.

QUEEN'S PARK NW6
Bakerloo

Opened as QUEEN'S PARK (WEST KILBURN) by the London and North
*   Western Railway on 2 June 1879*
This new station was first used by Underground trains as QUEEN'S PARK on
*   11 February 1915*

The park in this area after which the Underground station is named
was laid out by the Corporation of the City of London and opened
in 1887 to honour Queen Victoria in the year of her Golden Jubilee.

QUEENSWAY W2
Central

Opened as QUEEN'S ROAD on 30 July 1900
Name changed to QUEENSWAY on 1 September 1946

Queensway, the road on which this station is built, was once called
Black Lion Lane, named after a pub here called The Black Lion. This
road was renamed Queensway in honour of Queen Victoria shortly
after she came to the throne in 1837, for this was one of the roads
along which she rode as she left her home in Kensington Palace.

The old name of the road is still remembered in Black Lion Gate,
which leads from Queensway into Kensington Gardens.

Within walking distance: Diana, Princess of Wales
                                    Memorial Fountain
                                Kensington Gardens and
                                    Peter Pan statue
                                Kensington Palace
                                Serpentine Gallery

RAVENSCOURT PARK W6
District
Opened as SHAFTESBURY ROAD by the London & South Western Railway
on 1 April 1873
Name changed to RAVENSCOURT PARK on 1 March 1888
First used by Underground trains on 1 June 1877

'Ravenscourt' is a word with a curious history. In 1747, Thomas Corbett, Secretary to the Admiralty, bought the manor here. Its name was Paddenswick and it was an ancient manor house owned in the fourteenth century by Alice Perrers, mistress of King Edward III (reigned 1327–77).

Thomas Corbett was extremely proud of his name, and even had a raven on his coat of arms, because *corbeau* is French for 'raven' and so this was a kind of pun on his name 'Corbett'.

Just to make sure everyone was aware of the *corbeau*/Corbett pun, he went to the length of changing the name of his house: Paddenswick became Ravenscourt.

RAYNERS LANE MIDDLESEX
Metropolitan, Piccadilly
Opened as RAYNERS LANE HALT on 26 May 1906

This station is named after an old shepherd called Daniel Rayner, who lived alone in a cottage near here until about 1905.

The Metropolitan Railway opened its station here in 1906 and gave it the name Rayners Lane – thus giving this old shepherd a permanent memorial.

REDBRIDGE ESSEX
Central
Opened on 14 December 1947

There used to be a red bridge here over the river Roding, which was the boundary between Wanstead and Ilford. The bridge was demolished in 1922, but the name hung about, and was adopted to name the Underground station here when it opened twenty-five years later, in 1947.

REGENT'S PARK NW1
Bakerloo
Opened on 10 March 1906

When King George III became incurably mad in 1810 it was necessary to replace him as king. His eldest son, the Prince of Wales, also a George, took over his duties and for nine years he ruled the country uniquely as 'Regent'.

These were momentous years for the development of London, and the Regent's energetic architect, John Nash, transformed the capital, giving us Regent's Park, Regent Street and the vastly enlarged Buckingham House, which became Buckingham Palace.

Regent's Park was originally known as Marylebone Park, and the well-forested land here was acquired by Henry VIII for use as a hunting area. John Nash planned its development as a town park during the Napoleonic wars, and by 1841 it was opened to the public.

Regent Street, originally known as New Street, was designed specially to run from Regent's Park to Carlton House, the Regent's home in the Mall (now demolished).

Within walking distance: London Zoo

RICHMOND SURREY
District
Opened by the London & South Western Railway on 27 July 1846
First used by District Underground trains on 1 June 1877

Henry VII (reigned 1485–1509) had been Earl of Richmond in Yorkshire before he defeated Richard III at the Battle of Bosworth Field and seized the throne.

When he became king he decided to rebuild the royal palace of Sheen for himself and to rename it Rychmonde – alluding to his former earldom. The Richmond here in Surrey, therefore, is a transplant from Yorkshire.

The name Richmond is pure Norman French – *Richemont*, or 'royal hill'. Originally it was the name of a village in Normandy, and when Count Alan of Brittany, a cousin of William the Conqueror, built his castle in Yorkshire, he gave it this name from Normandy. William the Conqueror created him Earl of Richmond.

Other Richmonds in California, Indiana, New York City and the capital of Virginia show how popular this name has been.

RICKMANSWORTH HERTFORDSHIRE
Metropolitan
Opened on 1 September 1887

The Old English word *worth* means 'homestead'. 'Rickmansworth' is 'Ricmar's homestead'.

RODING VALLEY ESSEX
Central
Opened by the London & North Eastern Railway on 3 February 1936
First used by Underground trains on 21 November 1948

The river Roding used to be called the river Hyle, which gave Ilford its name ('ford on the Hyle').

Roding itself derived its name from the fact that it was once the dwelling of the *ing*, or 'family', of a Saxon leader who had a name something like 'Hroda'.

There are no fewer than nine 'Roding' villages lying on or near this river: Abbess Roding, Aythorpe Roding, Barwick Roding, Beauchamp Roding, Berners Roding, High Roding, Leaden Roding, Margaret Roding and White Roding. All these have interesting derivations, for example, 'Leaden' Roding is so named because of the costly leaden roof that its church possessed.

ROTHERHITHE SE16
East London
Opened by the East London Railway on 7 December 1869
Metropolitan and District Lines began to use this station on 1 October 1884
Metropolitan Line closed on 31 July 1905
District Line closed on 2 December 1906
Metropolitan Line resumed on 31 March 1913

There are a number of place names ending in *hythe*, which is an Old English word for a 'landing place'.

The first part of these names usually denotes what sort of commodity was handled at that particular landing place – in this case it was cattle, the name coming directly from another Old English word – *rother*.

Interestingly, a famous name in London contains a hidden form of the Old English *hythe* – Lambeth – which derives from the fact that it was a 'lambs' *hythe*', or a place where lambs were the main item which was traded.

ROYAL ALBERT E16
Docklands
Opened on 28 March 1994

Named after the Royal Albert Dock, opened in 1880 and one of the Royal Group of Docks (the other two are the Royal Victoria (1855) and the King George V (1921)).

The Royal Albert Dock itself was named after Prince Albert (1819–61), Consort of Queen Victoria.

The Royal Albert Dock and the Royal Victoria Dock lie end to end, separated by the Connaught Bridge, and together they contain 175 acres of water and provide 7 miles of quay. Sadly, they are hardly in use today.

ROYAL OAK W2
Hammersmith & City
Opened on 30 October 1871

Royal Oak is named after an old inn that once stood near where Paddington Station is now situated. The inn no longer exists, but the Underground station, opened in 1871, preserves its name.

Royal Oak pubs exist throughout the British Isles, named after the famous oak tree in which King Charles II hid after his defeat at the Battle of Worcester in 1651. He hid in this tree while the soldiers of Cromwell's army were scouring the woods looking for him. He managed to evade them and a few weeks later escaped to France, where he remained in exile until he was recalled to be crowned in 1660.

ROYAL VICTORIA E16
Docklands
Opened on 28 March 1994

Named after the Royal Victoria Dock, opened in 1855. The
first to be constructed of the group of three 'Royal' docks. (See
ROYAL ALBERT)

RUISLIP MIDDLESEX
Metropolitan, Piccadilly
Opened on 4 July 1904

'Ruislip' is Old English, meaning 'the wet place where the rushes
grow'. The name is derived from two words: *rysc*, meaning 'rush',
and *slaep*, meaning 'wet place'.

An alternative explanation of the second part of this name is that
it derives from *hlype*, meaning 'leap'. If this is so, it would refer to a
point on the river where, if you were athletic enough, you could
'leap' across it – or perhaps your horse could make the jump across.

RUISLIP GARDENS MIDDLESEX
Central   (see RUISLIP)
Opened on 21 November 1948

RUISLIP MANOR MIDDLESEX
Central   (see RUISLIP)
Opened on 5 August 1912

Ruislip Manor takes its name from a Manor Farm, which has been
in this area since the Middle Ages.

RUSSELL SQUARE WC1
Piccadilly
Opened on 15 December 1906

Russell Square is built on land belonging to the Russells – Russell is the family name of the Dukes of Bedford. There are over seventy Bedford/Russell place names in this area of London, showing just how influential this family was in the history of London's development.

Russell Square is the largest of all London's squares, and it was laid out in 1800 by Humphrey Repton (1752–1818) the famous landscape gardener. The Underground station was opened in 1906.

Within walking distance: The British Museum
                             The Charles Dickens Museum

ST JAMES'S PARK W1
Circle, District
Opened on 24 December 1868

St James's Park derives its name from St James's Hospital for leper women, which stood here long before King Henry VIII rebuilt it as St James's Palace after he acquired it in 1532.

According to the sixteenth-century historian John Stow, there was an old hospital here even before the Norman Conquest. It was dedicated to St James the Less because he is the patron saint of lepers.

St James's Palace is still a royal residence, and all foreign ambassadors are still, even today, accredited to the Court of St James. It is from a balcony of this palace that the formal announcement of the death of a sovereign is made – together with the proclamation of the successor: 'The King [Queen] is dead. Long live the King!'

The old leper women would have been astonished if they had known that St James would become the name of a park and then of an Underground station!

Within walking distance: Buckingham Palace
                             Houses of Parliament and Big Ben
                             Jewel Tower
                             Queen's Gallery
                             Royal Mews
                             Westminster Abbey

ST JOHN'S WOOD NW8
Jubilee

An earlier station of this name was opened by the Metropolitan Line on
*   13 April 1868*
It was replaced by a new station, which opened on the Bakerloo Line on
*   20 November 1939*
This was transferred to the Jubilee Line in 1979

This area was formerly owned by the Knights Templar (see TEMPLE), but when the Knights Templar were disbanded in 1312, the land was given to the Knights of St John of Jerusalem. It was thickly wooded throughout the Middle Ages – hence 'St John's Wood'.

The name began in this manner and has remained ever since, although since the Reformation there have been many owners and the land has been divided into separate estates.

ST PANCRAS (KING'S CROSS ST PANCRAS) NW1
Circle, Hammersmith & City, Northern, Victoria
(see KING'S CROSS ST PANCRAS)

For most people, St Pancras is simply a railway station, and it takes an effort of will to remember that the old church of St Pancras, in whose parish the station is built and which gave its name to the station, is dedicated to a fourteen-year-old Roman boy called Pancratius. According to tradition he was converted to Christianity and was put to death for his faith by the Emperor Diocletian in the year 304.

Although he is scarcely remembered today, it is worth noting that when St Augustine brought Christianity to Kent in the year 597, the very first church he consecrated at Canterbury was dedicated to St Pancras.

At St Pancras Old Church in London, a Saxon altar was found, dating from about 600. This means that it is one of the oldest Christian sites in Britain.

It is an odd quirk of history that it took over fifteen centuries and the invention of the railway to make the name of this murdered Roman teenager an everyday household word for thousands of modern commuters.

The village church of St Pancras in 1820.

The little Fleet River meandering gently near St Pancras in 1825. Fleet Street gets its name from this little stream.

ST PAUL'S EC4
Central
Opened as POST OFFICE on 30 July 1900
Name changed to ST PAUL'S on 1 February 1937

Obviously, this station is named after the great cathedral that stands nearby. However, it is interesting to note that the building we see today, designed by Sir Christopher Wren, is the fifth St Paul's to occupy this site – and even before the first cathedral, there had been a Roman Temple to Diana on this spot.

Within walking distance: Globe Theatre
                             Guildhall
                             Museum of London
                             Paternoster Square (incorporating the
                                 old Temple Bar)
                             St Martin-within-Ludgate
                             St Paul's Cathedral

The seven trees planted in memory of seven sisters – as seen in 1830.

THE FIVE ST PAUL'S CATHEDRALS

The first St Paul's Cathedral was built in 604 by Ethelbert, the Saxon King of Kent, who was the first Christian king in England. It was destroyed by fire.

The second St Paul's Cathedral was built between 675 and 685 by Erconwald, the fourth Bishop of London. The Vikings destroyed this building in 961.

A third St Paul's Cathedral was built shortly afterwards, but this was also destroyed by fire in 1087.

The fourth St Paul's Cathedral, which most people know as 'Old St Paul's', was built by Maurice, Bishop of London and Chaplain to William the Conqueror. This beautiful building was one of the largest cathedrals ever built. Its spire was the tallest of any church in the world – 520 feet (158.5 metres). In comparison, Salisbury Cathedral's spire is 404 feet high (121.92 metres), and the London Telecom Tower is 580 feet high (176.78 metres) – only 60 feet more (18.29 metres).

Old St Paul's was destroyed by the Great Fire of London in 1666. The present cathedral, built by Sir Christopher Wren, was begun in 1675 and completed in 1710.

Wren was seventy-eight years old when the cathedral was completed, so his son laid the last stone of all in the lantern at the top.

SEVEN SISTERS N15
Victoria
Opened on 1 September 1968

A story is told that there was once in this area a family of seven sisters, who, when they grew up and decided to go their various ways, planted seven elm trees outside a pub in Tottenham, as a sort of memorial to themselves. Who they were is now forgotten, but their sisterly enterprise has given us the name of the road and also of this Underground station.

SHADWELL E1
Docklands
Opened by the East London Railway on 10 April 1876
Opened by the Docklands Light Railway on 31 August 1987

Shadwell is derived from two words, meaning 'shallow well' or 'shallow stream'.

SHEPHERD'S BUSH W12
Central
Opened on 30 July 1900

In earlier times this area had the picturesque name of Gagglegoose Green. The present name of Shepherd's Bush is another reminder that until comparatively recently many parts of London were still completely rural.

This name derives from the widespread practice among shepherds of clipping and trimming a suitable tree or bush into a sort of upright shelter which was lined with straw so that they could stand, leaning back, to watch their sheep in comfort.

There used to be 'shepherd's bushes' throughout the country, but nowadays the name of this area near West Kensington is virtually the only reminder of this ancient custom.

Within walking distance: Westfield Shopping Centre, opened in
                              2008, Europe's largest in-town
                              shopping centre.

'... A BEAUTIFUL PIECE OF TOPIARY WORK'

From an article in *The Morning Post*, 1910

There are in many parts of the country … shepherd's bushes still in existence, and as they are invariably situated on rolling downs and commons in out-of-the-way haunts of solitude, a short description may not be out of place.

Imagine, then, a stiff thorn-bush with the sharp and slender leaf-stems starting about three feet from the ground. Instead of the bush being left to grow in the ordinary way, all the inner wood has been cut out until an oval cup has been formed by the sprouting outer branches growing densely together to a thickness of about eighteen inches, while the trunk of the bush forms at its top a platform within and a step without.

On the top of this platform are placed and replaced, as required, bundles of clean wheaten straw, so that with a sack thrown over the inside of the cup to shield him from the prickles the shepherd can stand up with his arms resting on the edges of the bowl and look around him far and wide, watching the movements of his flock.

… When such a bush is kept judiciously clipped and trimmed it forms an effective, artistic, and even beautiful piece of topiary work, especially in the months of May and early June, when the hawthorn is in full bloom.

SHEPHERD'S BUSH MARKET W12
Hammersmith & City   (see SHEPHERD'S BUSH)
Opened as SHEPHERD'S BUSH on 1 April 1914
Changed to SHEPHERD'S BUSH MARKET in 2008

SHOREDITCH E1
East London Section (Limited service)
Opened by the East London Railway on 10 April 1876
First used by Underground trains on 31 March 1913

It has been thought that this refers to a ditch near the shore of the Thames, but this is somewhat unlikely, as the Thames is quite a distance from here. The first record of the name appears in a manuscript of 1148, and is given as Scoredich, so it is much more likely to derive from a personal name, being the 'ditch of Sceorf' or 'Scorre'.

Shoreditch Station has been described as 'possibly the least known Underground station in Inner London'.

SLOANE SQUARE SW1
Circle, District
Opened on 24 December 1868

Named after one of the most remarkable men to have lived in London, Sir Hans Sloane (1660–1753). He was born in Ireland, the son of an Ulster Scot, and arrived in London when he was nineteen to study medicine and natural history. After a varied life of study and travel he became President of the College of Physicians, Physician General to the Army and, in 1727, he was appointed Royal Physician. He succeeded Sir Isaac Newton as President of the Royal Society.

He wrote many books on medicine and natural history, and when he died, aged ninety-two, his personal museum and his collection of 50,000 books and 3,560 manuscripts formed the beginning of the British Museum.

He was Lord of the Manor of Chelsea, and this is why in that area there are so many roads named after him: Sloane Square, Sloane Street, Sloane Avenue, Sloane Court, Sloane Gardens, Sloane Terrace – as well as Hans Crescent, Hans Place, Hans Street, Hans Road and, of course, Sloane Square Underground Station.

Within walking distance: National Army Museum

SNARESBROOK E11
Central
Opened as SNAKESBROOK & WANSTEAD by the Eastern Counties
  Railway on 22 August 1856
First used by Underground trains and name changed to SNARESBROOK on
  14 December 1947

'The brook where snares and traps are laid.'

SOUTH EALING W5
Piccadilly   (see EALING)
Opened on 1 May 1883

SOUTHFIELDS SW18
District
Opened on 3 June 1889

Originally this was the site of the 'south fields' of a former manor house, Durnsford Manor.

SOUTHGATE N14
Piccadilly
Opened on 13 March 1933

Southgate station is named after the hamlet that grew up by this entrance to Enfield Chase. It is recorded as Suthgate in 1370, and Le South Gate in 1608. Lord Lawrence, Viceroy of India 1863–69, lived at Southgate House – which later became Minchenden School (now closed).

SOUTH HARROW MIDDLESEX
Piccadilly   (see HARROW & WEALDSTONE)
Opened on 28 June 1903
Re-sited on 5 July 1935

SOUTH KENSINGTON SW7
Circle, District, Piccadilly   (see KENSINGTON (OLYMPIA))
Opened on 24 December 1868

Within walking distance:　　Albert Memorial and Royal Albert Hall
　　　　　　　　　　　　　　Brompton Oratory
　　　　　　　　　　　　　　Hyde Park
　　　　　　　　　　　　　　Kensington Gardens, Diana Memorial,
　　　　　　　　　　　　　　Peter Pan Statue, Serpentine
　　　　　　　　　　　　　　Kensington Palace

Natural History Museum
Royal College of Music
Science Museum
Victoria and Albert Museum

SOUTH KENTON MIDDLESEX
Bakerloo
Opened on 3 July 1933

'The farm or homestead belonging to Cœna' – who was a
Saxon chieftain.

SOUTH QUAY E14
Docklands
Opened on 31 August 1987

The name of this station is clearly a reference to a quay in the
docklands area. This Docklands station is situated between Heron
Quays and Crossharbour, but it is scheduled to close and be relocated
– its proposed name is Millennium Quarter, a reference to the time
of the redevelopment of the whole dockland area.

SOUTH RUISLIP MIDDLESEX
Central   (see RUISLIP)
Opened by the Great Western Railway and Great Central Railway as
  NORTHOLT JUNCTION on 1 May 1908
Name changed to SOUTH RUISLIP & NORTHOLD JUNCTION on
  12 September 1932
Changed again to SOUTH RUISLIP on 30 June 1947

SOUTHWARK SE1
Jubilee
Opened on 20 November 1999

'Buildings on the south bank' or 'southern defensive work'. In early centuries this part of London, south of the Thames and opposite the City, obviously needed to be well fortified in order to deter possible invaders who wished to cross the river at this point.

Within walking distance: Shakespeare's Globe Theatre
                                Tate Modern

SOUTH WIMBLEDON SW19
Northern   (see WIMBLEDON)
Opened on 13 September 1926

SOUTH WOODFORD E18
Central   (see WOODFORD)
*Opened by the Eastern Counties Railway as GEORGE LANE on
    22 August 1856*
Name changed to SOUTH WOODFORD (GEORGE LANE) on 5 July 1937
First used by Underground trains on 14 December 1947
Name finally changed to SOUTH WOODFORD in 1950

STAMFORD BROOK W6
District
Opened on 1 February 1912

'Brook with the stony ford'. The 'ford' itself was on the Great West Road and the 'brook' was one of the tributaries of the Thames, formed by three streams. Stamford Brook itself was turned into a sewer by the end of the nineteenth century. The name of this Underground station is an almost subliminal reminder that the brook ever existed.

STANMORE MIDDLESEX
Jubilee
Opened on 10 December 1932

The name of this station, the last one at the northern end of the
Jubilee Line, means 'stony mere', referring to the 'mere', or pond, on
Stanmore Common, which is locally known as 'Caesar's Pond'.

If legend is to be believed, it was here that the ancient British
leader, Cassivellaunus, and his tribe, the Catuvellauni, fought a
battle with Julius Caesar in 54 BC. There used to be an obelisk on
Stanmore Common, erected in 1750, to commemorate the event,
but this is now in the grounds of the National Orthopaedic Hospital.

Another local tradition holds that it was near here, on Stanmore
Common, that Boudicca (Boadicea) was finally defeated by the
Romans in AD 61 after her ferocious attack on London.

STEPNEY GREEN E1
District, Hammersmith & City
Opened by the Whitechapel and Bow Railway on 23 June 1902
District had begun to use the line three weeks earlier
First used by Metropolitan Line (Hammersmith & City) on 30 March 1936

The 'Stepney' part of this name means 'Stebba's landing-place' – a
Thames-side settlement of a Saxon leader. It can be compared with
Putney. (See PUTNEY)

STOCKWELL SW9
Northern, Victoria
Opened on 18 December 1890

This name was first recorded in 1197, meaning 'the well or spring by
the tree stump'.

STONEBRIDGE PARK NW10
Bakerloo
Opened by the London & North Western Railway on 15 June 1912
First used by Underground trains on 16 April 1917

A stone bridge over the river Brent gave its name to a former farm here, Stonebridge Farm. The farm disappeared when housing development took place in this area in the 1870s and 1880s. This housing development was given the name Stonebridge Park Estate. The Underground station on the Bakerloo Line took up the name when it opened here in 1917.

STRATFORD E15
Central, Docklands, Jubilee
Opened by the Eastern Counties Railway on 20 June 1839
First used by Underground trains on 4 December 1946

The old Roman road (street) to Colchester crossed the river Lea at this spot, where there was a somewhat deep and dangerous ford. It is the 'street ford'. A bridge was ultimately built to avoid the necessity of getting wet braving the ford. (See BOW ROAD)

SUDBURY HILL MIDDLESEX
Piccadilly   (see SUDBURY TOWN)
Opened on 28 June 1903

SUDBURY TOWN MIDDLESEX
Piccadilly
Opened on 28 June 1903

Sudbury means 'Southern manor'.

SURREY QUAYS SE16
East London
Opened as DEPTFORD ROAD by the East London Railway on
    7 December 1869
First used by Underground trains on 1 October 1884
Name changed to SURREY DOCKS on 17 July 1911
After major reconstruction, the name was changed again to SURREY QUAYS
    on 24 October 1989

The present name, Surrey Quays, was given to this station to coincide with the opening of a nearby shopping centre, which had been given this name.

SWISS COTTAGE NW3
Jubilee
Opened by the Metropolitan Railway on 13 April 1868
That station closed on 18 August 1940 and was replaced by another station of the same name on the Bakerloo Line, opening on 20 November 1939
This finally became a part of the Jubilee Line on 1 May 1979

When Finchley Road was first constructed in 1826, a toll gate was established at the southern end to help pay for it, and one of the first buildings to grow up near it on the new road was a picturesque tavern designed in the style of a Swiss alpine chalet.

Swiss Tavern, as it was then known (later Swiss Cottage) has given its name to the station of the Jubilee Line and the whole surrounding area.

The original Swiss Cottage as it was at the beginning of the nineteenth century.

TEMPLE EC4
Circle, District (closed Sundays)
Opened on 30 May 1870

The name 'temple' is found in many places around the meeting point of Fleet Street and the Strand: Temple Bar, Temple Avenue, Middle Temple Lane and of course Temple Church itself, after which Temple Underground Station is named.

The Temple Church has a history going back more than 800 years – see below.

Within walking distance: Courtauld Gallery (Somerset House)
Dr Johnson's House
Royal Courts of Justice
St Dunstan-in-the-West
St Clement Dane
Strand
The Temple and the Inns of Court
Temple Bar Monument

LONDON'S TEMPLE CHURCH...

In 1118, nine French knights formed the beginning of an Order of Chivalry to protect pilgrims on their way to the Holy Land. They became known as Templars, or Knights Templar, because they had their headquarters in Jerusalem on the site of the old Temple of Solomon.

The Templars quickly grew in number and influence, spreading throughout Europe. In England they built a great house and a round church on the banks of the Thames in 1185, and called this church the New Temple. Its circular shape is believed to have been modelled on the Church of the Holy Sepulchre at Jerusalem, built by Constantine over the reputed tomb of Christ. There are five such circular churches in England, including the well-known Round Church in Cambridge.

...AND LONDON'S TEMPLE BAR

Temple Bar, near the Temple Church, marks the boundary between the City of London and the City of Westminster. It sometimes comes as a surprise to visitors to find that today's 'London' consists of *two* cities.

Nowadays, in the middle of Fleet Street, this boundary between the two cities is marked by the Griffin Pillar, erected in 1880. In the Middle Ages there was simply a chain stretched between wooden posts; later, there was a city gate with a prison on top and then, after the Great Fire of London, Sir Christopher Wren rebuilt it and stretched his beautiful Temple Bar across the Strand.

With increasing traffic, Wren's Temple Bar proved to be far too narrow, so it was pulled down in 1870 – the very year in which this Underground station – then called The Temple – was opened. Over the years, it has become, simply, 'Temple'.

Throughout the twentieth century Temple Bar was virtually forgotten by most people. It had been taken down and re-erected in the grounds of Theobald's – a large country house in Hertfordshire.

Triumphantly, however, Temple Bar was carefully taken down again in the early twenty-first century and *re*-re-erected as a pedestrian gateway to the redeveloped Paternoster Square, adjacent to St Paul's Cathedral. It was officially opened in November 2004 by the Mayor of London – a remarkable moment in London's architectural history.

THEYDON BOIS ESSEX
Central

Opened by the Great Eastern Railway as THEYDON on 24 April 1865
Name changed to THEYDON BOIS on 1 December 1865
First used by Underground trains on 25 September 1949

Theydon is an Old English word meaning 'valley where thatch can be obtained' and *Bois* is the French word for a wood.

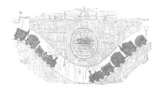

Temple Bar in its original position in Fleet Street in the early eighteenth century. Note the three poles sticking up into the air – they hold aloft the heads of beheaded criminals.

TOOTING BEC SW17
Northern
Opened as TRINITY ROAD on 13 September 1926
Name changed to TOOTING BEC on 1 October 1950

The 'Tooting' part of this station name is Saxon, and means 'place where Tota's followers live' and 'Bec' refers to the fact that in medieval times the land here was owned by the Benedictine Abbey of St Mary of Bec in Normandy.

TOOTING BROADWAY SW12
Northern   (see TOOTING BEC)
Opened on 13 September 1926

The Broadway was formerly a large open space near the station – it is now just a small triangular area.

TOTTENHAM COURT ROAD W1
Central, Northern

Opened by the Central London Railway on 30 July 1900
An adjacent station was opened by the Charing Cross & Hampstead
   Railway as OXFORD STREET on 22 June 1907
Name of this adjacent station renamed TOTTENHAM COURT ROAD on
   9 March 1908
The first Tottenham Court Road station was then (9 March 1908) renamed
   Goodge Street

Although 'Tottenham' appears in both Tottenham Court Road and
Tottenham Hale, it is thought that they may be derived from the names of
two separate Old Saxon chiefs both known by the name Totta. 'Tottenham
Hale' means 'Totta's corner of land' (from the Old English *healh*, 'a corner
of land'), and 'Tottenham' means 'Totta's village'. As the names were so
similar, they eventually became identical in form. If Tottenham had not
existed, it is probable that Tottenham Hale would have become Totnal –
but Tottenham was the eventual form of the name.

TOTTENHAM HALE N17
Victoria   (see TOTTENHAM COURT ROAD)

Opened on 1 September 1968

TOTTERIDGE (TOTTERIDGE & WHETSTONE) MIDDLESEX
Northern

Opened by the Great Northern Railway as TOTTERIDGE on 1 April 1872
Name changed to TOTTERIDGE & WHETSTONE on 1 April 1874
First used by Underground trains on 14 April 1940

'Totta's ridge' – referring to a Saxon settler there. (See also
WHETSTONE)

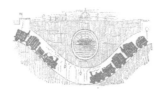

TOWER GATEWAY EC3
Docklands (Bank Branch)
Opened on 31 August 1987

This is situated near Tower Bridge Approach, so it is a 'gateway' to this important bridge.

Although Tower Bridge is one of the most memorable landmarks in London, it is only just over a century old. It was opened in 1894 by Edward, Prince of Wales, son of Queen Victoria and later King Edward VII (reigned 1901–10).

TOWER HILL EC3
District, Circle
Opened as MARK LANE on 6 October 1884
Name changed to TOWER HILL on 1 September 1946
Re-sited on 5 February 1967

The road Tower Hill, running beside the Tower of London, has the dubious distinction of having been one of the principal places of execution in London. Famous victims include Sir Thomas More, Thomas Cromwell, the Duke of Somerset, John Dudley, the Earl of Strafford, Archbishop Laud and the Duke of Monmouth.

The last executions took place there as late as 1780, and there is a stone in Trinity Square to indicate the exact spot where the executions took place.

The name Tower Hill is self-explanatory. The Tower of London itself was begun by William the Conqueror (reigned 1066–87) and has been at the centre of English history ever since – even holding important enemy prisoners during the Second World War.

Within walking distance: All Hallows-by-the-Tower
                             Design Museum
                             HMS *Belfast*
                             London Wall
                             St Katharine Docks
                             St Olave
                             Tower Bridge
                             Tower Hill Scaffold Memorial
                             The Tower of London

TUFNELL PARK N7
Northern
Opened on 22 June 1907

Named after the owner of the land in the mid-eighteenth century, William Tufnell. He was a brewer's son who had the luck to become rich by inheriting money from wealthy relations, and so became the lord of the manor of Barnsbury. He inherited this estate from his godfather on condition that he changed his name to Joliffe – so he called himself William Tufnell Joliffe to comply with this somewhat curious request.

Tradition has it that Tufnell Park Road is in fact an old Roman road.

TURNHAM GREEN W4
District, Piccadilly
Opened by the London & South Western Railway on 1 January 1869
First used by Underground trains on 1 June 1877
Rebuilt station opened on 3 December 1911

'Green place near the village of Turnham'. The 'ham' element means either a 'homestead' or else 'riverside pasture' and 'turn' refers to 'the land within a bend in a river'.

THE BATTLE OF TURNHAM GREEN

Turnham Green is a peaceful enough suburban area today – but it witnessed a crucial moment in the Civil War, when the Royalist forces, commanded by King Charles I were intercepted by the Parliamentarian army under the command of the Earl of Essex.

The battle took place in November 1642, three weeks after the Battle of Edgehill, in which the Royalists had won a narrow victory. The king withdrew to Oxford, where he made the mistake of delaying too long before marching south to take London. The delay led to disaster. When he did turn towards London, the Parliamentarians were ready to meet him in force, and the encounter at Turnham Green was an unequal one, with the Parliamentarians having an army of about 24,000 men and the Royalists having between 7,000 and 12,000.

It was more of a standoff than a battle. Charles decided not to engage his troops in a major battle and withdrew, retreating back to Oxford. Only a few shots were made, and there were hardly any casualties or losses. Yet the encounter – not worth the name of a battle – was a crucial factor in Charles's ultimate defeat, because he could not win the war without capturing London – and the opportunity such as he might have had at Turnham Green, never came to him again.

Think of poor King Charles I as you travel into London from Turnham Green on the District or Piccadilly Line.

TURNPIKE LANE N8
Piccadilly
Opened on 19 September 1932

'Lane beside a toll-gate'. Turnpike gates gained their name because they were constructed with large vertical spikes – thus making it difficult or impossible for horses to jump over them.

A TOLLGATE STILL IN USE!

The last major turnpike in England was that at Mile End Road, which was pulled down as late as 1866. However, quite astonishingly, a tollgate is still functioning in the twenty-first century in the College Road, Dulwich.

The original tollgate was constructed in 1789 by John Morgan, who built a road from the top of the hill down to some fields that he rented from Dulwich College. After his death, the College continued to charge people – and animals – to pass through their property. In 1983 the charge for cars was 5p, but in 2005 this had gone up to 50p.

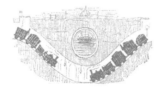

UPMINSTER ESSEX
District
Opened by the London, Tilbury & Southend Railway on 1 May 1885
First used by Underground trains on 2 June 1902

'Upminster' means 'a large church on rising ground' or 'upper church'. In this case, the present Church of St Lawrence goes back to the eleventh or twelfth century, but there may have been a church here previously at Chafford (the original name) as early as the seventh century.

UPMINSTER BRIDGE ESSEX
District   (see UPMINSTER)
Opened on 12 September 1934

This station gets its name because it is situated near a small iron road bridge called Upminster Bridge, over the little river Ingrebourne.

UPNEY ESSEX
District
Opened on 12 September 1932

'Upney' means 'up on an island' – indicating that it is slightly higher and drier land which is raised above the surrounding marshes.

UPTON PARK E7
District, Hammersmith & City
Opened by the London, Tilbury & Southend Railway in 1877
First used by Underground trains on 2 June 1902

'The upper estate'. Over the years the manor of this estate has had various names: first as Rooke Hall then as Upton House and then Ham House.

UXBRIDGE MIDDLESEX
Metropolitan, Piccadilly
Opened on 4 July 1904
Re-sited on 4 December 1938

A Saxon family called the Wixan are believed to have built themselves a bridge across the Colne river here, so this became known as the Wyxebrigge, or Wixan-bridge.

VAUXHALL SW8
Victoria
Opened on 23 July 1971

The origin of the name Vauxhall goes back to the reign of King John (reigned 1199–1216), when the Norman baron Falkes de Breauté, built himself a house here. It became known as Fulke's Hall. There were many variant spellings, such as Faukeshall, or Foxhall – but eventually it settled into 'Vauxhall', which has remained.

What we now call Vauxhall Bridge, which opened in 1816, was originally called Regent's Bridge after the Prince of Wales, who later became George IV (reigned 1820–30), but who was at that time acting as Regent for his father, George III.

Within walking distance: Tate Britain

The old village of Vauxhall in 1825.

The 'Italian Walk' in the once-famous Vauxhall pleasure gardens.

VICTORIA SW1
Circle, District, Victoria
Opened on 24 December 1868

Named after Queen Victoria, whose reign (1837–1901) was the longest of all British monarchs.

Victoria Street, which leads to Victoria Station, was opened in 1851, cutting through what were then the slums of Westminster, and providing a vista of Westminster Abbey and the then newly built Houses of Parliament.

The main-line terminus, Victoria Station, was opened in 1860 at the west end of Victoria Street. The station took its name from the street, and subsequently the whole area came to be known simply as 'Victoria'.

Within walking distance: Buckingham Palace
Queen's Gallery
Royal Mews
Westminster Cathedral

WALTHAMSTOW CENTRAL E17
Victoria
Opened as WALTHAMSTOW (HOE STREET) by the Great Eastern Railway
on 26 April 1870
Name changed to WALTHAMSTOW CENTRAL on 6 May 1968
The station's present name was given only when the Victoria Line arrived

'Walthamstow' means holy place (*stow*) of the Abbess Wilcume. Wilcume was an abbess who lived here some time before the Norman Conquest. In 1067 its name is recorded as Wilcumestuue.

WANSTEAD E11
Central
Opened on 14 December 1947

'Homestead by a small hill'. Alternatively the 'wan' part may refer to a wagon or *wain* – as in John Constable's painting, *The Haywain*. Unfortunately, the exact meaning of this name is not clear.

WAPPING E1
East London Line
Opened by the East London Railway as WAPPING & SHADWELL on
7 December 1869
Name changed to WAPPING on 10 April 1876
First used by Underground trains on 1 October 1884
After much rebuilding, Second World War bombing and subsequent
rebuilding, station was finally finished in 1982

Like almost all names ending in 'ing', Wapping tells us that a Saxon leader, probably called something like Waeppa, settled here with his family and followers. 'Wapping' means 'place where Waeppa's people live'.

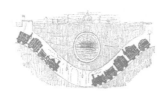

WARREN STREET W1
Northern, Victoria
Opened as EUSTON ROAD on 22 June 1907
Name changed to WARREN STREET on 7 June 1908

Warren Street, built in 1790–91, is named after Sir Peter Warren, a well-known and important eighteenth-century vice-admiral. Few people remember him now, but he has a monument in Westminster Abbey. His son-in-law, Charles Fitzroy, 1st Baron Southampton, owned the land, and named the street after his wife, Anne Warren, and his famous father-in-law, Sir Peter. The Underground station is named after the street.

WARWICK AVENUE W2
Bakerloo
Opened on 31 January 1915

Warwick Avenue is named after Jane Warwick, an heiress who married Sir John Morshead. Her family once lived in this area, in Paddington Manor.

WATERLOO SE1
Bakerloo, Northern, Waterloo & City, Jubilee
Waterloo & City Line opened on 8 August 1898
Bakerloo Line opened on 10 March 1906
Northern Line opened on 13 August 1926

The name 'Waterloo' commemorates the historic battle of 1815 in which Napoleon was finally defeated.

At the time of the battle a new bridge was being constructed across the Thames at the eastern end of the Strand. It was begun in 1811 and was to have been called the Strand Bridge. However, after Wellington's great victory, an Act of Parliament changed its name to Waterloo 'in remembrance of great and glorious achievements'.

The Prince Regent opened the bridge on 18 of June 1817 – the second anniversary of the battle. Inevitably, the new southern approach road was given the name Waterloo Road.

Trains had not been invented at that time, but thirty years later, in 1848, the new railway station built nearby naturally assumed the name 'Waterloo'.

The present bridge over the Thames is a replacement of the original, which began to show signs of collapse in 1923. The present bridge was constructed between 1937 and 1942.

Within walking distance: London Eye
London Aquarium
Houses of Parliament and Big Ben
Tate Britain
Westminster Abbey
Whitehall

WATFORD HERTFORDSHIRE
Metropolitan
Opened on 2 November 1925

'Watford' means 'the hunter's ford' – deriving from the Old English word *wath*, meaning 'hunting'. The ford in this case crosses the river Colne.

WEMBLEY CENTRAL MIDDLESEX
Bakerloo
Opened by the London & Birmingham Railway as SUDBURY in 1842
Name changed to SUDBURY & WEMBLEY on 1 May 1882
Name changed again to WEMBLEY FOR SUDBURY on 1 November 1910
First used by Underground trains on 16 April 1917
Name finally changed to WEMBLEY CENTRAL on 5 July 1948

In the ninth century this area was referred to as *Wemba Lea*, or 'the meadows where Wemba lived'. Wemba was another long-forgotten Saxon chieftain.

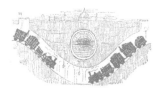

WEMBLEY PARK MIDDLESEX
Jubilee, Metropolitan   (see WEMBLEY CENTRAL)
Opened on 12 May 1894

The site of the original 'Park' is now taken by Wembley Stadium exhibition and entertainment centre.

WEST ACTON W3
Central   (see ACTON)
Opened on 5 November 1923

WESTBOURNE PARK W2
Hammersmith & City
Opened on 1 February 1866

'Westbourne' derives from the two Saxon words, *westan*, 'west', and *burnam*, 'place', and was evidently referring to a 'place west of ...' something. The 'something' was in fact a little stream, which took its name from the district, becoming known as the Westbourne. In other words, the area gave the name to the stream – rather than vice versa. There used to be a Westbourne Farm here, and in much earlier times the river was called Knightsbridge Brook, or Bayswater Rivulet.

Westbourne Park, Westbourne Grove, Westbourne Terrace: all these and other 'Westbourne' places are associated with this early beginning.

No one ever sees the river Westbourne nowadays, but its waters are still here, dammed up and forming the Serpentine in Hyde Park. It was the idea of Queen Caroline, the wife of George II (reigned 1727–60) to create the Serpentine in 1730.

The word 'serpentine' means 'like a snake' and refers to the gently winding contours of its design. It was the height of fashion in those years to make lakes and paths 'serpentine' in contrast to the French preference for geometrical patterns and straight lines, as in the gardens of Versailles.

Nowadays the Westbourne river leaves the Serpentine in the Ranalagh Sewer on its way to the Thames. In former years, the bridge across it gave us the name of Knightsbridge. (See KNIGHTSBRIDGE)

WEST BROMPTON SW10
District
Opened on 12 April 1869

'Western part of the farm or area where broom grows'.

WESTFERRY E14
Docklands
Opened on 31 August 1987

There are several 'Westferry' names in this area, reminding us of the ferries which were once so necessary to cross the Thames. West Ferry Road was once known as the Deptford and Greenwich Ferry Road.

Although the ferries are no longer here, the name of this Docklands station is now a memorial to them like Horseferry Road near the Houses of Parliament, which led down to the Thames to ferry horses across to Lambeth.

WEST FINCHLEY N12
Northern   (see FINCHLEY CENTRAL)
Opened by the London & North Eastern Railway on 1 March 1933
First used by Underground trains on 14 April 1940

WEST HAM E7
District, Hammersmith & City, Jubilee
(see EAST HAM)
Opened by the London Tilbury & Southend Railway on 1 February 1901
First used by Underground trains on 2 June 1902

'Western part of the riverside pasture'.

WEST HAMPSTEAD NW6
Jubilee   (see HAMPSTEAD)
Opened on 30 June 1879

WEST HARROW MIDDLESEX
Metropolitan   (see HARROW-ON-THE-HILL)
Opened on 17 November 1913

WEST INDIA QUAY E14
Docklands
Opened on 31 August 1987

Named after the West India Docks, which opened in 1802 and closed in 1980. These docks were originally built for trade with the West Indies but later used for India and the Far East.

WEST KENSINGTON W14
District   (see KENSINGTON (OLYMPIA))
Opened as NORTH END (FULHAM) on 9 September 1874
Name changed to WEST KENSINGTON on 1 March 1877

WESTMINSTER SW1
Circle, District, Jubilee
Opened as WESTMINSTER BRIDGE on 24 December 1868
Name changed to WESTMINSTER in 1907

It must have been a Londoner who first named Westminster – for it means 'the monastery in the west'. Its very name implies that it is to the west of a London that already existed.

Within walking distance: Banqueting House
Cabinet War Rooms
Cenotaph
Downing Street
Horse Guards
Houses of Parliament and Big Ben
London Eye
Royal Festival Hall
St Margaret's
Westminster Abbey
Westminster Cathedral

THE CITY AND PALACE OF WESTMINSTER: LEGACY OF A SAXON KING AND SAINT

It was the Saxon King and Saint, Edward the Confessor (reigned 1042–66) who first began to build a palace at Westminster, when he was rebuilding an ancient monastery here – now known as Westminster Abbey.

Three centuries earlier, King Offa of Mercia (d. 796) had founded a small monastery here on Thorney Island (Isle of Brambles) in the triangle formed where the Tyburn river forked near the present St James's Park Underground Station, reaching the Thames in two separate streams.

Edward the Confessor's decision to settle here and move away from London had an immensely profound effect on London's history, separating the seat of government at Westminster from the centre of commercial activity in the City of London.

Visitors to London do not always realise that Westminster and London are two separate cities. The boundaries as you pass (almost imperceptibly) from one to the other are marked by statues of griffins – the unofficial badge of the City of London.

Strictly speaking, these are dragons, but are usually referred to as 'griffins'.

Perhaps the easiest one to find is in the middle of the road marking where Temple Bar used to be, as the Strand leads into Fleet Street. There is another on the pavement almost opposite Cleopatra's Needle on the north side of the road. (See also the entry on WESTMINSTER ABBEY on page 162)

WEST RUISLIP MIDDLESEX
Central (see RUISLIP)
The main-line station was opened as RUISLIP & ICKENHAM by the Great Western & Great Central Joint Committee on 2 April 1906
Name changed to WEST RUISLIP on 30 June 1947
Underground station opened on 21 November 1948

WEST SILVERTOWN E16

Docklands

Opened on 2 December 2005

'Silvertown' is named after the rubber and telegraph works of S.W. Silver and Co., who had their factory here in the mid-nineteenth century. As it developed, this area took on the name of this large firm.

THE SILVERTOWN EXPLOSION

The area around West Silvertown Docklands Station, now situated in a rapidly developing part of London, was the scene of a terrifying explosion in January 1917, during the First World War. It was the largest single explosion to have taken place in Britain at that time.

To help the war effort, a munitions factory had been set up here – dangerously, in the middle of a highly populated area – to produce the chemical explosive Trinitrotoluene (TNT). Safety standards were not strict, and a fatal fire started, which ignited 50 tons of TNT, killing 73 people and injuring over 400. The blast was so great that it is said to have been heard 100 miles away – even at Sandringham in Norfolk. Seventy thousand properties were damaged and thousands of people were left homeless.

Casualty numbers could have been far higher, but fortuitously the explosion happened on a Friday evening when few workers were present on the factory site. Nevertheless the cost to the surrounding buildings was estimated at £2.5 million.

The event is now in memory only, but inside the entrance to the factory location on North Woolwich Road there is a memorial to those who lost their lives in the First and Second World Wars – and in the Silvertown Explosion.

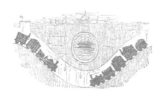

WHITECHAPEL E1
District, Hammersmith & City, East London Line
Opened by the East London Railway on 10 April 1876

Built around 1250, a chapel dedicated to St Mary was built here in white stone. The road to this chapel became known as Whitechapel Road and the whole area has been named from the original chapel, rebuilt three times over the centuries but finally destroyed in 1952.

WHITE CITY W12
Central
Opened by the Hammersmith & City Line as WOOD LANE on
*   1 May 1908*
Opened by the Central Line as WOOD LANE on 14 May 1908
Name changed to WHITE CITY and Central Line and re-sited on
*   23 November 1947*
Hammersmith & City Line closed on 25 October 1959

In 1908, 140 acres were taken here for the Franco-British Exhibition, which was the largest exhibition that had been held in Britain up to that date. Forty acres of gleaming white buildings gave this exhibition centre its name. The 4th Olympic games took place here in the same year.

The centre was commandeered by the government during the First World War and then left derelict afterwards until 1927, when greyhound racing was introduced. The stadium was demolished in 1985 to make way for the BBC White City building.

WILLESDEN GREEN NW10
Jubilee
Opened on 24 November 1879

'Hill with a well or spring' – deriving from the Old English *weill*, 'a spring', and *dun*, 'a hill'.

WILLESDEN JUNCTION NW10
Bakerloo

Opened by the London & North Western Railway on 1 September 1866
First used by Underground trains on 10 May 1915

Named because of the railway junction here.

WIMBLEDON SW19
District

Opened by the London & Southampton Railway on 21 May 1838
First used by Underground trains on 3 June 1889

The *dun*, or 'hill', of a Saxon settler called Winebeald or some similar name.

WIMBLEDON PARK SW19
District   (see WIMBLEDON)

Opened by the London and South Western Railway on 3 June 1889

WOODFORD ESSEX
Central

Opened by the Eastern Counties Railway on 22 August 1856
First used by Underground trains on 14 December 1947

The obvious meaning is that this is a place where there existed a ford in a wooded area. The original ford must have been replaced by a bridge some time in the thirteenth century, for it is referred to as *Wudeforde* in 1225 but *Ponte de Woodford* ('Bridge of Woodford') by 1285. By 1429 it was known as *Woodfordbrigge*.

The ford was situated at the point where a Roman road out of London had to cross the river Roding.

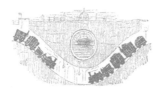

WOOD GREEN N22
Piccadilly
Opened on 19 September 1932

The original hamlet here was situated at a 'green place near the wood'. Here, the wood referred to is Enfield Chase.

WOOD LANE W12
Hammersmith & City
Opened 12 October 2008

Three stations here have been either replaced, renamed or demolished – the first one opening 1 May 1908. The present station, opened in 2008, is a splendid new creation serving the area and especially useful for access to the Westfield London retail and leisure centre.

Wood Lane is a self-explanatory and truly rural name dating back to the early nineteenth century or even earlier. Clearly it tells us of a time when this was a wooded area with a path running through it. In no way can this name be applicable to the area in this twenty-first century, but nevertheless Wood Lane has a thoroughly comfortable and traditional feel to it, despite its anachronism.

WOODSIDE PARK N12
Northern
Opened by the Great Northern Railway as TORRINGTON PARK on 1 April 1872
Name changed to WOODSIDE PARK on 1 May 1882
First used by Underground trains on 14 April 1940

'Park beside a wood' – in this case the wood referred to is Finchley Wood. (See FINCHLEY)

WOOLWICH ARSENAL SE18

Docklands   (see ARSENAL)

Opened on 10 January 2009

According to Boris Johnson, who opened the station in his capacity as Mayor of London: 'People in this part of London will now be just a 24-minute hop, skip and a jump away from the Olympic site.'

SADLY...

... Charles Pearson, the man who in 1845 had first proposed the construction of a London underground railway, and who had worked so hard to make it possible, died just four months before the first journey was made on 10 January 1863. He never lived to see the results of his hard work and far-sighted imagination.

The Fairlop Oak - the gigantic ancient tree that gave its name to Fairlop.
(see FAIRLOP, page 50.)

CAPITAL WORDS

A Selection of Famous London Names

ALBERT HALL SW7

Everyone knows that this great hall is named after Prince Albert, the consort of Queen Victoria. He died in 1861, aged forty-one, and Victoria spent the remaining forty years of her life in perpetual mourning for him. Ten years earlier, in 1851, Prince Albert had organised The Great Exhibition, and the cluster of museums in South Kensington and the Albert Hall itself were paid for out of the profits of that event.

What is less well known is that Queen Victoria herself named the hall – startling spectators at the ceremony for the laying of the foundation stone by suddenly announcing the name it was to bear.

Originally, it was to be known simply as The Hall of Arts and Sciences – but as she laid the foundation stone the Queen surprised the assembly by declaring that 'Royal Albert' would be added to the proposed name. Today no one uses the phrase 'Arts and Sciences' in its name – it has become, simply, the Royal Albert Hall.

Nearest Underground station:
South Kensington   *Circle, District, Piccadilly*

BERKELEY SQUARE W1

Named after Lord Berkeley of Stratton (d. 1678), who was an ambassador to Sweden and a vigorous commander of part of the Royalist forces during the Civil War. After the Restoration in 1660 he had a palatial mansion built in this area, which is no longer in existence. His name, however, lives on in Berkeley Square, Berkeley Street and the Berkeley Hotel.

Nearest Underground station:
Green Park   *Jubilee, Piccadilly, Victoria*

BIRDCAGE WALK SW1

This road, along the south side of St James's Park, is on the site of James I's Royal Menagerie and Aviary, which was enlarged later by Charles II. There were many cages of rare birds there. In 1661 Samuel Pepys wrote in his diary that he walked 'in St James's Park, and saw great variety of fowl which I never saw before'.

A few years later, in 1665, John Evelyn described his own visit there: '… I saw various animals, and examined the throat of ye "Onocratylus", or Pelican, a fowle between a Stork and a Swan, a melancholy waterfowl brought from Astracan by the Russian Ambassador; it was diverting to see how he would toss up and turn a flat fish, plaice or flounder, to get it right into its gullet…'

Although the cages are no longer there, St James's Park is still the home of many interesting species of bird.

Nearest Underground stations:
Westminster   *Circle, District*
St James's Park   *Circle, District*

BUCKINGHAM PALACE

Named after John Sheffield (1648–1721) who was Lord Chamberlain to James II and a cabinet councillor under William III. Queen Anne created him Duke of Buckingham in 1703. He was a man of importance during these reigns, and as well as being prominent in politics, he was also a poet and playwright and a friend of John Dryden and Alexander Pope. However, on the death of Queen Anne he fell out of favour and intrigued to bring the Stuarts back to the throne.

Nowadays, he is little remembered, but his name is perpetuated due to the fact that in 1702–05 he built a grand house for himself, called Buckingham House, on the site of what is now Buckingham Palace.

George III bought Buckingham House in 1762, and it became known as The Queen's House. Then, when George IV (reigned 1820–30) came to the throne, he enlarged the house to such an extent that it became Buckingham Palace. He never lived in it himself, and it was left to his niece Queen Victoria (reigned 1837–1901) to be the first monarch to take up residence there.

Nearest Underground stations:

St James's Park	*Circle, District*
Victoria	*Circle, District, Victoria*
Green Park	*Jubilee, Piccadilly, VictoriA*
Hyde Park Corner	*Piccadilly*

BURLINGTON HOUSE, PICCADILLY W1

Burlington House is famed today for its major art exhibitions, visitors to which have the added pleasure of visiting the last remaining example of the great mansions built by wealthy noblemen in the Piccadilly area shortly after the Restoration in 1660.

It is named after Richard Boyle, 1st Earl of Burlington (1612–97), a statesman who supported the Royalists during the Civil War and was an active politician supporting William and Mary at the time of the 'Glorious Revolution' of 1688.

Nearest Underground station:

Piccadilly Circus   *Bakerloo, Piccadilly*

CARNABY STREET W1

Famous, especially in the '60s, for its colourful clothing shops for the trendy hippie generation – even entering the Oxford English Dictionary to mean 'fashionable clothing for young people'. In 1683, Richard Tyler, a bricklayer and developer, built himself a house in this road, which he named Karnaby House – but no one knows why. The street is named after this.

Nearest Underground station:

Oxford Circus   *Bakerloo, Central, Victoria*

CENOTAPH SW1

The Cenotaph in Whitehall is so much a part of the London scene that its somewhat curious name is rarely questioned. It means 'empty tomb' from the two Greek words *kenos*, 'empty' and *taphos*, 'tomb'.

Designed in 1919 by Sir Edwin Lutyens to commemorate those killed in the First World War, it has an interesting shape – although it looks geometrically regular, in fact there is no single straight line in its design. If you were to continue the almost imperceptible curves of the sides, they would meet at a point about 1,000 feet (304.8 metres) from their starting points.

Unlike the Tomb of the Unknown Warrior, it contains no body and there is no religious symbolism. It is decorated simply with the flags of the three services and the Merchant Navy.

Nearest Underground station:
Westminster   *Circle, District, Jubilee*

CLARENCE HOUSE SW1

Clarence House has been the home of many members of the Royal Family since it was completed in 1828. It was built for William, Duke of Clarence and heir to the throne, who became William IV in 1830 on the death of his brother, George IV.

George IV had greatly transformed and enlarged Buckingham House into Buckingham Palace, to make it fit for British monarchs – but he did not live to occupy it himself. William hated it and proposed it should be turned into a new Houses of Parliament when the old building was burnt down in 1834. Instead, William continued to live at his own 'Clarence House' – the name by which it has always been called.

Nearest Underground stations:
Green Park   *Jubilee, Piccadilly, Victoria*
St James's Park   *Circle, District*

'COCKNEY'

The word 'cockney' is known worldwide as a name given to Londoners and 'cockney rhyming slang' as the extraordinary and unique vocabulary that they often use.

The strange origin of 'cockney' goes back to the Middle Ages when country people used the word to refer to people who lived in towns. It was a term of contempt, deriving from *cockeney*, or 'cock's egg' – a small, misshapen, deformed egg supposedly laid by a cockerel. The point was that town people were no good for anything, as they were considered ignorant of country skills and, perhaps, as living 'softer' lives.

Eventually, the word has come to refer exclusively to Londoners – especially those who are born within the sound of 'Bow Bells', that is, the bells of St Mary-le-Bow in Cheapside. This church was destroyed by bombs in 1941 but was re-built 1956–62.

Traditionally, cockneys have a very sharp wit, and are often chirpily disrespectful of authority or members of the 'posh' upper classes who take themselves too seriously.

DUKE OF YORK COLUMN SW1

This somewhat pretentious and unnecessary column is named after Frederick, Duke of York (1763–1827), the second son of George III He was made Commander-in-Chief of the British Army from 1798 to 1809, but his military career was rather less than spectacular, as described in the children's nursery rhyme:

> The Grand Old Duke of York,
> He had ten thousand men;
> He marched them all to the top of the hill,
> And marched them down again.

The rhyme refers to an abortive operation led by the Duke against the French forces in Flanders in 1794. To put the record straight, however, the 'old' duke was only twenty-nine at the time, he had 30,000 men, and there was no hill.

The column is 124 feet high (37.8 metres) and was completed in 1833, some years after the Duke's death, and was paid for mainly by stopping one day's pay for every soldier in the army – an imposition that did not endear him, posthumously, to his former troops. They suggested that the height of the column was such as to enable the debt-ridden Duke to keep out of the clutches of his creditors (he owed £2,000,000).

Second sons of British monarchs are traditionally given the title of Duke of York. Notably, New York is named after James, Duke of York (1633–1701), who was the second son of Charles I.

Nearest Underground station:
St James's Park   *Circle, District*
Piccadilly Circus   *Bakerloo, Piccadilly*

FLEET STREET EC4

Fleet Street is (or was) synonymous with the world of newspapers, and the term 'Fleet Street' is still used to refer to the 'tittle-tattle' of the press. However, with modern techniques of newspaper production, much of the trade has now departed from Fleet Street itself.

The name itself is taken from the Fleet river – one of the many tributaries flowing into the Thames. In former times these were fair-sized rivers, but they are now 'tamed' and run underground in pipes and sewers.

'Fleet' is derived from the Old English word *fleot*, meaning 'flowing water', and is linked with the modern English words 'float' and 'flood'. It could also mean a 'tidal inlet'. The almost invisible Fleet river rises at Hampstead and flows into the Thames at Blackfriars Bridge.

Nearest Underground station:
Blackfriars   *Circle, District*
Temple   *Circle, District*

GROSVENOR SQUARE W1

Grosvenor Square, Grosvenor Hill, Grosvenor Place, Grosvenor Street, Grosvenor Road: all these names and several more are associated with the enormously wealthy Grosvenor family, who for three centuries have owned vast areas in Mayfair, Belgravia and Pimlico.

The first Grosvenor to become involved in all these London estates was a young Baronet from Cheshire, Sir Thomas Grosvenor, who gained his fortune by marrying a wealthy heiress, Mary Davies – aged only twelve – in St Clement Danes in 1677.

The Grosvenor family name goes back to Norman times, when it must have been something of a nickname: '*le gros veneur*' which means 'the fat huntsman'.

Queen Victoria gave the title Duke of Westminster to Hugh Lupus Grosvenor in 1874. The present Duke, who is the 6th Duke of Westminster, is the 3rd richest person in Great Britain.

Nearest Underground stations:

Bond Street   *Central, Jubilee*

Green Park   *Jubilee, Piccadilly, Victoria*

HAYMARKET SW1

For several centuries, from Tudor times onward, the royal stables were kept on the site now occupied by Trafalgar Square. Horses need hay and straw, so it was convenient to have a thriving hay market nearby.

It was not until 1830 that the last bundle of hay was sold here, when the market itself moved to Cumberland Market, just north of Regent's Park.

Nearest Underground station:

Piccadilly Circus   *Bakerloo, Piccadilly*

HORSEFERRY ROAD SW1

Like the Haymarket, Horseferry Road gained its name by being literally what it says it is.

The road led to what used to be the only horse ferry allowed to ply its trade in, or near, London. The ferry was situated between the present Westminster Bridge, opened in 1750, and Lambeth Bridge, opened a century later in 1861.

The ferry was still in use even in the nineteenth century, and the profitable tolls belonged to the Archbishops of Canterbury, whose palace at Lambeth is situated nearly opposite Horseferry Road on the south bank of the Thames.

Almost unbelievably, London Bridge was the *only* bridge over the Thames until 1750, so when Westminster Bridge was built it was a disaster for the Thames watermen, who for centuries had vigorously opposed the building of any other bridge over the river.

They were given £25,000 in compensation, an enormous sum in those days, and the Archbishop, who owned the ferry, was given £21,025.

Nearest Underground station:
Westminster   *Circle, District, Jubilee*

LORD'S CRICKET GROUND NW8

This world-famous cricket ground has no connection with the House of Lords or any English lord but is in fact named after a London wine merchant, Thomas Lord (1755–1832).

He was passionately keen on cricket, and was encouraged by wealthy friends to establish a new cricket ground for Middlesex Cricket Club. In 1787 he took possession of what was then little more than an open field, 'Mary-le-bone Field', which was used for a variety of sporting activities including pigeon shooting and 'hopping matches'. He moved from this to another field in 1810, but soon found that a part of this was to be used for the new Regent's Canal. Finally, he moved, in 1814, to the present site in St John's Wood Road.

Thomas Lord retired in 1825 after thirty-eight years of association with the MCC – but his name is forever used by the cricketing world whenever a prestigious match is to be played. His portrait by George Morland still hangs in the pavilion at the present-day Lord's.

Nearest Underground station:
Warwick Avenue   *Bakerloo*
St John's Wood   *Jubilee*

THE MALL and PALL MALL SW1

The interesting origin of the name The Mall is that it comes from the Italian word for a game similar to croquet, involving hitting a ball (*palla*) through an iron ring with a mallet (*maglio*).

The game of 'pall mall' was popular in the seventeenth century, and was played in an alley where the present road, Pall Mall, is situated. When this alley was made into a road, a new course for the game was created in about 1660, very shortly after Charles II came to the throne – and this course came to be known as The Mall.

The game lost its popularity in the eighteenth century, and

The Mall became a place where it was fashionable for ladies and gentlemen to promenade. It was only after the death of Queen Victoria in 1901 that, in her memory, a 'New Mall' was created as a wide and impressive route from Admiralty Arch to the Queen Victoria Memorial in front of Buckingham Palace.

Nearest Underground station:
St James's Park   *Circle, District*
Piccadilly Circus   *Bakerloo, Piccadilly*

PATERNOSTER ROW and PATERNOSTER SQUARE EC4

Pater noster is, of course, the Latin for 'Our Father' – the beginning of the Lord's Prayer.

According to John Stow (1525–1605), the famous London historian who wrote his great *Survey of London and Westminster* in 1598, Paternoster Row gained its name because in medieval times bead makers lived in this road, making rosaries. The prayers recited with the use of these rosaries prompted the name Paternoster.

Stow may be right in thinking this – but an alternative explanation may simply be that the clergy of St Paul's could often have been heard praying aloud in the neighbourhood of their cathedral, which lay nearby.

Nearest Underground station:
St Paul's   *Central*

PETTICOAT LANE E1

This Sunday street market near Liverpool Street Station is officially called Middlesex Street, but such is its huge popularity that the traditional name, Petticoat Lane, has never been allowed to be forgotten. In the Middle Ages it was called Hog's Lane, but this had changed to Petticoat Lane by the end of the seventeenth century – named for the selling of old clothes there. But, as everyone knows, there is an enormous range of goods on sale here today, with stalls spreading all around the neighbouring area.

Nearest Underground station:
Aldgate   *Circle, Metropolitan*
Liverpool Street   *Central, Circle, Hammersmith & City, Metropolitan*

PORTOBELLO ROAD W11

It may seem far-fetched to say that Christopher Columbus named Portobello Road, but in fact the history of this foreign sounding word shows that he did – although admittedly in an indirect way.

When Columbus discovered a small bay in Panama, Central America, he admired it so much that he called it 'Porto Bello' – beautiful port. The Spanish founded a town here in 1597 and developed it as a port, but its strategic and commercial importance led to constant attacks by the British.

The English naval commander Admiral Vernon (1684–1757) captured Porto Bello from the Spanish in 1739 – a victory which was greeted with great delight in Britain, leading to a number of places being re-named Portobello, including a farm in this area – which was then open countryside west of London.

In the eighteenth century, the road we know today as Portobello Road was just a farm track leading to this Porto Bello Farm. Then, in the nineteenth century, the Saturday street market started to become popular, at first as a centre for horse dealing.

Nearest Underground station:
Grove   *Hammersmith & City*

HAVE YOU EVER FELT 'GROGGY'?

The eighteenth-century British admiral mentioned above – Edward Vernon – became known as 'Old Grog' because of the coat of 'grogram' that he wore – a coarse-grained cloth which derived its name from the French *gros grain*, or 'coarse thread'.

He was the much-feared naval Commander-in-Chief West Indies, who in 1740 ordered watered-down rum to be served to both officers and men. Naturally, this made him very unpopular and the mixture itself was nicknamed 'grog'.

If you take too much 'grog' or more generally nowadays if you are feeling unsteady or unwell, you say you are feeling 'groggy'. So, whenever you do feel groggy – spare a thought for Admiral Vernon, the celebrated man who captured Porto Bello.

PUDDING LANE EC3

The Great Fire of London started in this lane, in Farryner's bakery, on 2 September 1666. The Monument was built to commemorate this crucial event in London's history. (See MONUMENT on page 85)

Alas, this 'lane' is now the scene of massive modern buildings and is totally different from the picturesque place you might hope to see, judging from its name.

The name itself, Pudding Lane, is perhaps deceptive, probably conjuring up images of delicious sweet desserts. However, the original meaning of 'pudding' was 'guts' and 'entrails'. Pudding Lane almost certainly got its name from filthy droppings from carts taking unwanted offal from the butchers in Eastcheap down to the river Thames.

This original meaning of 'pudding' is perpetuated in the dish known as 'black pudding' – made largely with blood.

Nearest Underground station:
Monument   *Circle, District*

RITZ HOTEL W1

Opened in 1906, the Ritz Hotel is named after its first owner, César Ritz (1850–1918), who built its exterior to resemble the Rue de Rivoli in Paris.

César Ritz was the thirteenth child of a poor Swiss Alpine shepherd. Very few people have been so successful in moving from rags to riches as Monsieur Ritz – in fact his very name has passed into the English language as 'ritzy', meaning glitteringly and ostentatiously smart and luxurious.

Nearest Underground station:
Piccadilly   *Bakerloo, Piccadilly*

ROTTEN ROW SW7

Rotten Row is a sandy track almost a mile in length, which runs along the south side of Hyde Park adjacent to South Carriage Drive. It was laid out by William III (reigned 1689–1702) as a route through Hyde Park along which to ride between St James's Palace and Kensington Palace, where he had set up his court.

It was known as the *Route du Roi* – the 'King's Road' – and, over time, people used the name 'Rotten Row' as a garbled version of this French phrase.

It is still used by the Household Cavalry, who exercise their horses here – and members of the public may also use it for riding lessons and practice.

William III needed to feel safe at night as he travelled along this track – so he had it lit with 300 oil lamps in 1690 – the first artificially lit highway in Britain.

Nearest Underground station:
Knightsbridge   *Piccadilly*
Hyde Park Corner   *Piccadilly*

SADLER'S WELLS E1

In the Middle Ages the Priory of St John's at Clerkenwell had a holy well here, but this was covered over at the time of the Reformation and became quite forgotten.

In 1683 the owner of the land, a Mr Thomas Sadler, re-discovered the well, and the waters were considered to be so health-giving that for a while the well made a good profit as a medicinal spa. As a side attraction, Thomas Sadler built a 'musick house' here.

Since this time, music, pantomime and dance have been features of the succession of theatres built here on the site of Mr Sadler's original popular well – which can still be seen under a trap door at the back of the present theatre's stalls.

Nearest Underground station:
Angel   *Northern Line City Branch*

ST BARTHOLOMEW'S HOSPITAL   EC1

St Bartholomew's – popularly known as 'Bart's' – is the oldest hospital in London, founded in 1123, but why it was founded and how its got its name belongs, literally, to the world of dreams.

According to tradition, Rahere, a courtier of Henry I (reigned 1100–45) had gone on a pilgrimage to Rome and had suffered a fever on his way there. He made a vow that if he recovered he would build a hospital in London when he got back home. The legend tells how St Bartholomew appeared to Rahere in a dream and said: 'I have chosen a place in a suburb of London at Smoothfield where, in my name, thou shalt found a church.'

The prediction came true. When Rahere did return, Henry I granted him a strip of land just outside the city wall, at Smithfield ('Smoothfield') and this was where he built a hospital and a priory.

Rahere's vow has now helped the sick for almost 1,000 years. Among its patients was Wat Tyler, who was taken there after he was stabbed by the Lord Mayor of London during the Peasants' Revolt in 1381.

Nearest Underground stations:

Barbican	*Circle, Hammersmith & City, Metropolitan*
Farringdon	*Circle, Hammersmith & City, Metropolitan*
St Paul's	*Central*

SAVILE ROW W1

Named after Lady Dorothy Savile, the wife of the 3rd Earl of Burlington. Today the street is associated with fine tailoring, but it was a fashionable residential street in the eighteenth century, when it was originally laid out.

Richard Sheridan the dramatist (1751–1816) lived and died here at No. 14.

Nearest Underground station:

Oxford Circus *Bakerloo, Central, Victoria*

SAVOY HOTEL WC2

The Savoy Hotel, famous as one of London's most luxurious hotels, is built on land on which the former Savoy Palace stood. This belonged to Peter, Count of Savoy and uncle to Queen Eleanor of Provence, the French wife of Henry III (reigned 1216–72).

Henry III gave the palace to Peter of Savoy for an annual rental of three barbed arrows. It was one of many enormous medieval palaces built along the banks of the Thames. It had a long and fascinating history: John of Gaunt owned it in the fourteenth century and Geoffrey Chaucer was married in its chapel. In 1510 it became a hospital for the poor.

The Savoy Hotel opened in 1889, with César Ritz as its first manager (see RITZ HOTEL) and Auguste Escoffier as its first chef. It was one of the first London hotels to have electric light and electric lifts. It also had a high ratio of bathrooms to bedrooms – a novel level of hygiene in those days!

Nearest Underground station:
Embankment   *Bakerloo, Circle, District, Northern*

SCOTLAND YARD SW1

The phrase 'Scotland Yard' – or even just 'the Yard' is of course synonymous with the Metropolitan Police Force, which now has its headquarters on Broadway and Victoria Street.

Its official name is now New Scotland Yard, which reminds us that its previous premises were in Great Scotland Yard – a part of the complex of buildings of the old Whitehall Palace – the name 'Scotland' has been linked to that location for over 1,000 years.

The Scottish association began when the Saxon King Edgar (reigned 959–75) gave land near the bank of the Thames to Kenneth III of Scotland (reigned 997–1005) so that Scottish kings could build a palace there for their use when in London. The last Scottish sovereign to live there was Margaret, sister of Henry VIII (reigned 1509–47), who came there after her husband James IV of Scotland was killed on Flodden Field in 1513.

Nearest Underground station (to both Great Scotland Yard and New Scotland Yard):
Westminster   *Circle, District, Jubilee*

THE SERPENTINE W2

The artificial lake in Hyde Park known as The Serpentine was created in the 1730s by Queen Caroline, wife of George II (reigned 1727–60). She was a keen gardener, and followed the fashion, then prevalent, of shaping paths and lakes in a winding, tortuous manner. This growing fashion of landscape gardening emphasised the difference between the English 'natural' style and the more formal geometrical lines preferred by the French King Louis XIV in his gardens at Versailles.

The Serpentine lake was formed by damming the river Westbourne – which followed a markedly winding course here like a twisting snake – 'serpent-like' – hence 'Serpentine'.

Nearest Underground stations:

Knightsbridge	*Piccadilly*
Lancaster Gate	*Central*

SOHO W1

Soho, the area famous for its restaurants and vibrant nightlife, derives its name from the hunting-cry 'So Ho' – especially used when a hare has been started. It is the equivalent of 'Tally-ho', the cry used by fox hunters when a fox breaks cover.

Today it's almost impossible to imagine this part of London being farmland and open countryside with fields and woods, but until the seventeenth century this was an area often used for hunting.

One of the first residents here was the Duke of Monmouth (1649–85), the illegitimate son of Charles II, who led the rebellion against his uncle James II in 1685. It is said that at the battle of Sedgemoor the Duke's forces used 'Soho' as a password and a rallying-cry.

Nearest Underground stations:

Oxford Circus	*Bakerloo, Central, Victoria*
Piccadilly Circus	*Bakerloo, Piccadilly*
Tottenham Court Road	*Central, Northern*

SOMERSET HOUSE WC2

When Henry VIII died in 1547, he was succeeded by his young son Edward, who was only nine years old. Obviously a regent had to be appointed, so before he died Henry appointed Edward's uncle, the Duke of Somerset, to be 'Lord Protector'.

For five years, until his execution in 1552, the Duke of Somerset was virtually king of England, and on taking office one of his first acts was to build himself a large palace on the banks of the Thames – Somerset House.

This Somerset House was the residence of royalty for almost two centuries but when Queen Charlotte decided that she preferred to live in Buckingham House, Somerset House was demolished. If only she had chosen to live here, perhaps present British kings and queens would still be living in that gracious Thames-side palace.

The present Somerset House was built on the site of the old one, designed by William Chambers and completed by others after his death. It has recently been given a complete makeover and now houses art galleries and museums and has become a home for arts and learning, with an ice rink for open-air skating in the main courtyard in the winter.

Nearest Underground stations:

Embankment	*Bakerloo, Circle, District, Northern*
Temple	*Circle, District*
Waterloo	*Bakerloo, Northern, Waterloo & City, Jubilee*

STRAND WC2

The name of this important street, leading from Charing Cross to the Law Courts, reminds us that in previous centuries, before the Victoria Embankment was built, (1864–70) the buildings here had access right down to the edge of the river. In fact, it was originally a bridle path along the bank of the Thames.

The word 'strand', meaning 'landing place', is hardly used nowadays, but we still speak of being 'stranded', which literally means 'to be driven on shore'.

Nearest Underground stations:

Covent Garden	*Piccadilly*
Embankment	*Bakerloo, Circle, District, Northern*

THAMES

Julius Caesar found that the ancient Britons had given this river a name, and he wrote it down as Tamesis. It is believed that this Celtic word simply meant 'river' – or alternatively, perhaps, 'the dark one'.

Whatever the ultimate derivation, the Thames is the second oldest recorded place name in England. The oldest is Kent – recorded as Kantion by the Greek explorer Pytheas in the fourth century BC.

TRAFALGAR SQUARE SW1

Unlike the sites of land battles, the places where naval engagements have taken place are not the haunt of modern tourists. The result of this is that comparatively few people can pinpoint exactly where Cape Trafalgar is.

It is a quirk of fate that the name of this insignificant little promontory on the south coast of Spain – south-east of Cadiz and west-north-west of the Strait of Gibraltar – should now be known throughout the world, associated with Horatio Nelson and the greatest naval victory in English history. And in modern times, Trafalgar Square is also now forever linked with demonstrations, pigeons, Norwegian Christmas trees and boozy New Year celebrations.

The battle took place on 21 October 1805 but it wasn't until 1829–41 that Trafalgar Square, commemorating the event, was laid out, and it wasn't until 1868 that the four bronze lions by Sir Edwin Landseer were put in place.

In the Middle Ages this area was the site of the Royal Mews where the royal hawks were kept and falconers had their lodgings. Among his many other duties, Geoffrey Chaucer held the post of Clerk of Mews. In later centuries the site was used for the royal stables.

The actual name Trafalgar is derived from Arabic, and may mean 'end of the west' or 'end of the column', which could refer to the Pillars of Hercules.

Nearest Underground station:

Charing Cross   *Bakerloo, Circle, District, Northern*

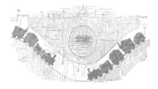

WESTMINSTER ABBEY –
AN EXTRAORDINARY
'ROYAL PECULIAR'

It was the Saxon King and Saint, Edward the Confessor (reigned 1042–66) who first began to rebuild an ancient monastery here – now famous throughout the world as Westminster Abbey.

Three centuries earlier, King Offa of Mercia (d. 796) had founded a small monastery here on Thorney Island (Isle of Brambles), in the triangle formed where the Tyburn river forked near the present St James's Park Underground Station, reaching the Thames in two separate streams.

Edward the Confessor's new abbey here was specially built to be the crowning place of English kings – and it is a proud boast that every reigning English monarch has been crowned in Westminster Abbey since 1066. King Harold, defeated by William the Conqueror at the Battle of Hastings in October 1066, had been the first king to be crowned here, just ten months earlier, in the preceding January.

Importantly, Edward the Confessor himself – who for centuries was England's patron saint – is buried here, and throughout the Middle Ages his shrine in Westminster Abbey was considered one of the holiest places in the country, attracting huge numbers of pilgrims hoping for cures and spiritual blessing.

However, all English abbeys were ruthlessly abolished by Henry VIII in the 1530s, and most of them were severely damaged or destroyed altogether. Westminster Abbey was no exception. The holy shrine of Edward the Confessor was moved and broken up, and the abbot and all of the monks were forced out of office. They surrendered everything to the king at a miserable little ceremony in the Chapter House on 16 January 1540.

For almost a year, the former abbey lay abandoned, but then, in December of that year, Henry VIII decided to 'promote' it into a cathedral with a bishop, dean and prebendaries (canons). So, for almost ten years, Westminster Abbey became Westminster Cathedral, but then, in 1550, under Henry's Protestant son Edward VI, it was absorbed into the diocese of London, so that the Bishop of London had in fact *two* cathedrals.

It was a curious position. But further changes were to take place. When the Catholic Queen Mary came to the throne in 1553, she turned the cathedral back into an abbey complete with new monks, and the shrine of Edward the Confessor was mended and restored to its former importance.

Even then, still further changes were to come – for when the Protestant Queen Elizabeth I came to the throne, the 'abbey' was yet *again* dissolved, on 10 July 1559.

So what exactly is Westminster Abbey today?

Interestingly, Westminster Abbey is one of a very small group of churches known as a 'Royal Peculiar' – in other words it is totally independent of any bishop or even archbishop. It is a free chapel of the Sovereign, and directly under the sole authority of whichever king or queen happens to be on the throne.

Nearest Underground stations:

St James's Park   *Circle, District*
Westminster   *Circle, District, Jubilee*

(For a comment on the word 'Westminster' see WESTMINSTER Underground Station, p. 138).

... AND FINALLY ... WHAT ABOUT MIDDLESEX? DOES IT EXIST?

Well, officially, No! But popularly and non-officially, Yes!!

The London Government Act of 1965 abolished it as a county. Nevertheless, as a name it had existed in one form or another since early Saxon times. It literally means the 'middle Saxons' – as opposed to the west Saxons of Wessex, the east Saxons of Essex, and the south Saxons of Sussex. These tribes of Saxons had poured into the country just after the Romans left Britain in about AD 410.

After the London Government Act, Middlesex still existed for several years as a 'postal county' – but sadly it was stripped even of that title in 2000.

Luckily, names take a long time to die. The county of Rutland refuses to go under the government sledge-hammer and still thrives. The name of Middlesex as used in this book may be mildly anachronistic, but everyone still recognises it as an old friend and long may it continue to be remembered!

RECOMMENDED FURTHER READING

Ekwall, Eilert, *The Concise Oxford Dictionary of English Place Names*,
    Oxford University Press, 1936
Fairfield, Sheila, *The Streets of London*, Macmillan, 1983
Field, John, *Place-Names of Greater London*, B.T. Batsford Ltd, 1980
Glover, John, *London's Underground*, Ian Allan Publishing, 1996
Halliday, Stephen, *Underground to Everywhere*, Sutton Publishing, 2001
Harris, Cyril M., *What's in a name?*, Capital History, 1977
Leboff, David, *London Underground Stations*, Ian Allan Publishing, 1994
Weinreb, Ben & Christopher Hibbert, *The London Encyclopaedia*,
    Book Club Associates (Macmillan), 1983

Visit our website and discover thousands of
other History Press books.

www.thehistorypress.co.uk

Contents – Text

Contents – Maps

MAP LEGEND   see back page

The Authors

Chris Rowthorn

Chris was born in England and grew up in the USA. He lived in Kyoto from 1992 to 2000, where he worked first as an English teacher and then as a writer for *The Japan Times*. He considers Kyoto his second home and still returns there whenever he gets the chance. He's worked on a total of 11 books for Lonely Planet, including *Tokyo*, *Malaysia, Singapore & Brunei*, *Japan*, *Hiking in Japan* and *Read This First: Asia & India.* Chris currently lives in Bondi, Sydney, where he bodysurfs and writes.

Mason Florence

Mason relocated from Colorado to Japan in 1990. Now a photojournalist based in Kyoto, he spends half the year on the road in South-East Asia, and free moments in Japan in rural Shikoku. As well as writing the 1st edition of *Kyoto*, some of his other books for LP include *South-East Asia*, *Vietnam*, *Hanoi*, *Japan*, *Hiking in Japan* and *Rocky Mountain States*.

FROM THE AUTHOR
From Chris

I would like to thank Inuishi Tomoko and the entire staff of the Kyoto TIC. I would also like to thank Ishiura Hisayo, Hashimoto Keiji, Araki Yasko, John Ashburne, Chiyoma Izumi, Noda Kaoru, Neelu Kaur, Gordon Maclaren, Numata Maki, Hayashi Chinami, John Benson and Mason Florence. Big thanks are also due to the readers of the 1st edition who sent in letters about the book and the city. Thanks also to Cameron Hay and Sarah Downs for providing a great place to live during the writing of this guide, as well as sharing their considerable knowledge of Kyoto. And most importantly, I would also like to thank all the people of Kyoto who made my stay unforgettable.

This Book

The 1st edition of Kyoto was written by Mason Florence. Chris Rowthorn has built on the work of Mason to produce this 2nd edition.

FROM THE PUBLISHER

The production of this edition of Kyoto was coordinated by Nick Stebbing (cartography and design) and Kyla Gillzan (editing). Nick was assisted with mapping by Meredith Mail, Chris Love and Chris Thomas. Kyla was assisted by Michael Day, Anastasia Safioleas and Janine Eberle.

The Language chapter was written by Quentin Frayne with the assistance of Yoshi Abe and Emma Koch. Matt King coordinated illustrations. Mark Germanchis assisted with tricky layout issues.

The illustrations were drawn by Clint Curé, Kelli Hamblet, Martin Harris, Jenny Bowman, Margaret Jung and Mick Weldon. Lonely Planet Publications provided other illustrations. Cover design was by Jenny Jones.

The whole process was overseen by Meredith Mail and Jack Gavran (cartography and design) and Jocelyn Harewood (editorial).

THANKS

Lonely Planet would like to thank the following readers for sending us their anecdotes, suggestions and recommendations:

Devo Alibegic, Jeroen Bok, Tom Booij, Joel Baumgardner, Rosie Chin, Holly Crisson, Elisabeth M Dalen, Ian Fenwick, Del Ford, Andrew Goodwille, David Greig, Juli Gudehus, Benjamin Hedrick, Clifton Hood, Jessica Jacob, Michelle Kelner, David Mason, Mike Mcgee, Ian Moseley, Joe Poconto, Yves Prescott, Tee and Marty Ravell, Fitzcarl Reid, Dan Rempel, Vincent Shields, Beverly Suderman, Hans van der Veen, Liz Wade, Mark Watson, Brian Wopershall, Gary David Yngve, Kim Yonsk

Foreword

ABOUT LONELY PLANET GUIDEBOOKS

The story begins with a classic travel adventure: Tony and Maureen Wheeler's 1972 journey across Europe and Asia to Australia. Useful information about the overland trail did not exist at that time, so Tony and Maureen published the first Lonely Planet guidebook to meet a growing need.

From a kitchen table, then from a tiny office in Melbourne (Australia), Lonely Planet has become the largest independent travel publisher in the world, an international company with offices in Melbourne, Oakland (USA), London (UK) and Paris (France).

Today Lonely Planet guidebooks cover the globe. There is an ever-growing list of books and there's information in a variety of forms and media. Some things haven't changed. The main aim is still to help make it possible for adventurous travellers to get out there – to explore and better understand the world.

At Lonely Planet we believe travellers can make a positive contribution to the countries they visit – if they respect their host communities and spend their money wisely. Since 1986 a percentage of the income from each book has been donated to aid projects and human rights campaigns.

Updates Lonely Planet thoroughly updates each guidebook as often as possible. This usually means there are around two years between editions, although for more unusual or more stable destinations the gap can be longer. Check the imprint page (following the colour map at the beginning of the book) for publication dates.

Between editions up-to-date information is available in two free newsletters – the paper *Planet Talk* and email *Comet* (to subscribe, contact any Lonely Planet office) – and on our Web site at www.lonelyplanet.com. The *Upgrades* section of the Web site covers a number of important and volatile destinations and is regularly updated by Lonely Planet authors. *Scoop* covers news and current affairs relevant to travellers. And, lastly, the *Thorn Tree* bulletin board and *Postcards* section of the site carry unverified, but fascinating, reports from travellers.

Correspondence The process of creating new editions begins with the letters, postcards and emails received from travellers. This correspondence often includes suggestions, criticisms and comments about the current editions. Interesting excerpts are immediately passed on via newsletters and the Web site, and everything goes to our authors to be verified when they're researching on the road. We're keen to get more feedback from organisations or individuals who represent communities visited by travellers.

Lonely Planet gathers information for everyone who's curious about the planet – and especially for those who explore it first-hand. Through guidebooks, phrasebooks, activity guides, maps, literature, newsletters, image library, TV series and Web site we act as an information exchange for a worldwide community of travellers.

Research Authors aim to gather sufficient practical information to enable travellers to make informed choices and to make the mechanics of a journey run smoothly. They also research historical and cultural background to help enrich the travel experience and allow travellers to understand and respond appropriately to cultural and environmental issues.

Authors don't stay in every hotel because that would mean spending a couple of months in each medium-sized city and, no, they don't eat at every restaurant because that would mean stretching belts beyond capacity. They do visit hotels and restaurants to check standards and prices, but feedback based on readers' direct experiences can be very helpful.

Many of our authors work undercover, others aren't so secretive. None of them accept freebies in exchange for positive write-ups. And none of our guidebooks contain any advertising.

Production Authors submit their raw manuscripts and maps to offices in Australia, USA, UK or France. Editors and cartographers – all experienced travellers themselves – then begin the process of assembling the pieces. When the book finally hits the shops, some things are already out of date, we start getting feedback from readers and the process begins again ...

WARNING & REQUEST

Things change – prices go up, schedules change, good places go bad and bad places go bankrupt – nothing stays the same. So, if you find things better or worse, recently opened or long since closed, please tell us and help make the next edition even more accurate and useful. We genuinely value all the feedback we receive. A well travelled team reads and acknowledges every letter, postcard and email and ensures that every morsel of information finds its way to the appropriate authors, editors and cartographers for verification.

Everyone who writes to us will find their name in the next edition of the appropriate guidebook. They will also receive the latest issue of *Planet Talk*, our quarterly printed newsletter, or *Comet*, our monthly email newsletter. Subscriptions to both newsletters are free. The very best contributions will be rewarded with a free guidebook.

Excerpts from your correspondence may appear in new editions of Lonely Planet guidebooks, the Lonely Planet Web site, *Planet Talk* or *Comet*, so please let us know if you *don't* want your letter published or your name acknowledged.

Send all correspondence to the Lonely Planet office closest to you:

Australia: Locked Bag 1, Footscray, Victoria 3011
USA: 150 Linden St, Oakland, CA 94607
UK: 10A Spring Place, London NW5 3BH
France: 1 rue du Dahomey, 75011 Paris

Or email us at: talk2us@lonelyplanet.com.au

For news, views and updates see our Web site: www.lonelyplanet.com

HOW TO USE A LONELY PLANET GUIDEBOOK

The best way to use a Lonely Planet guidebook is any way you choose. At Lonely Planet we believe the most memorable travel experiences are often those that are unexpected, and the finest discoveries are those you make yourself. Guidebooks are not intended to be used as if they provide a detailed set of infallible instructions!

Contents All Lonely Planet guidebooks follow roughly the same format. The Facts about the Destination chapters or sections give background information ranging from history to weather. Facts for the Visitor gives practical information on issues like visas and health. Getting There & Away gives a brief starting point for researching travel to and from the destination. Getting Around gives an overview of the transport options when you arrive.

The peculiar demands of each destination determine how subsequent chapters are broken up, but some things remain constant. We always start with background, then proceed to sights, places to stay, places to eat, entertainment, getting there and away, and getting around information – in that order.

Heading Hierarchy Lonely Planet headings are used in a strict hierarchical structure that can be visualised as a set of Russian dolls. Each heading (and its following text) is encompassed by any preceding heading that is higher on the hierarchical ladder.

Entry Points We do not assume guidebooks will be read from beginning to end, but that people will dip into them. The traditional entry points are the list of contents and the index. In addition, however, some books have a complete list of maps and an index map illustrating map coverage.

There may also be a colour map that shows highlights. These highlights are dealt with in greater detail in the Facts for the Visitor chapter, along with planning questions and suggested itineraries. Each chapter covering a geographical region usually begins with a locator map and another list of highlights. Once you find something of interest in a list of highlights, turn to the index.

Maps Maps play a crucial role in Lonely Planet guidebooks and include a huge amount of information. A legend is printed on the back page. We seek to have complete consistency between maps and text, and to have every important place in the text captured on a map. Map key numbers usually start in the top left corner.

Although inclusion in a guidebook usually implies a recommendation we cannot list every good place. Exclusion does not necessarily imply criticism. In fact there are a number of reasons why we might exclude a place – sometimes it is simply inappropriate to encourage an influx of travellers.

Introduction

With an astonishing 1600 Buddhist temples, 400 Shintō shrines, a trio of palaces, and dozens of gardens and museums, Kyoto is Japan's cultural treasure house. Perhaps more impressive, 17 of Kyoto's ancient structures and gardens have been declared Unesco World Heritage Sites, making Kyoto one of the world's most culturally rich cities.

But there is far more to this 1200-year-old city than the sights proudly paraded in tourist brochures. Spared the onslaught of the American bombs that levelled Tokyo and nearby Osaka during WWII, Kyoto ironically suffers from deep cultural and aesthetic wounds that have been largely self-inflicted. During the past few decades much of the city's facade has been swept away in a euphoric rush to modernise. As Kyoto struggles to reconcile development with historical preservation, this living museum seems to hang in the balance.

Filled with 'old Japan' anticipation, many flinch at their first sights of Kyoto – the eye-smartingly ugly expanse of grey concrete that surrounds Kyoto station. Yet hidden among all those concrete boxes, sharp eyes can pick out the soaring pagoda of Tō-ji and the gentle curves of Higashi Hongan-ji, two of Kyoto's lovely ancient temples. These serve as welcome reassurances that something of the old city survives under the current wave of concrete.

Heartened by these first glimpses, the determined visitor can venture out into the city and find endless pockets of beauty: ancient teahouses sit sandwiched between high-rise apartment buildings; sacred shrines are tucked neatly into modern shopping arcades; and exquisite *kaiseki* restaurants competing for customers with a growing legion of fast food restaurants.

Indeed, Kyoto, perhaps more than any other city in the world, rewards the determined explorer. Whether you've been in the city for two days, two years or two decades, you can still take a short stroll and make new discoveries, often right around the corner. We believe that this is Kyoto's most endearing quality – the feeling that the closer you look, the more there is to see.

And make no mistake: Kyoto is far more than hoary old buildings and quiet Zen gardens. In Kyoto, you can sample all the wonders of Japanese cuisine, drink to the early hours in a perfect little bar and then soak you cares away in some of Japan's best baths. And once you've done all that, you can lay your head to rest in an atmospheric old ryokan, the pinnacle of Japanese hospitality.

Thus, all told, we believe that Kyoto is *the* city to visit in Japan and one of the world's great destinations. Indeed, we are inclined to repeat what was once said about another great city: If you don't love Kyoto, you don't love life.

Facts about Kyoto

HISTORY
Early History
Though the origins of the Japanese race remain unclear, anthropologists believe humans first arrived on the islands via the land bridges that once connected Japan to Siberia and Korea, and by sea from the islands of the South Pacific. The first recorded evidence of civilisation in Japan is pottery fragments with cord marks (*jōmon*) produced in the Neolithic period, about 10,000 BC. During this Jōmon period, people lived a primitive existence as independent fishers, hunters and food-gatherers.

This Stone Age period was gradually superseded by the Yayoi era, dating roughly from 300 BC. The Yayoi people are considered to have had a strong connection with Korea and their most important developments were the wet cultivation of rice and the use of bronze and iron implements. The Yayoi period witnessed the progressive development of communities represented in more than 100 independent family clusters dotting the archipelago.

As more and more of these settlements banded together to defend their land, regional groups became larger and by AD 300, the Yamato kingdom had emerged in the region of present-day Nara. Forces were loosely united around the imperial clan of the Yamato court, whose leaders claimed descent from the sun goddess, Amaterasu, and who introduced the title of emperor (*tennō*). The Yamato kingdom established Japan's first fixed capital in Nara, eventually unifying the regional groups into a single state. By the end of the 4th century, official relations with the Korean peninsula were initiated and Japan steadily began to introduce arts and industries such as shipbuilding, leather-tanning, weaving and metalwork.

The Yamato period is also referred to as the Kofun period by archaeologists, who discovered thousands of ancient burial mounds (*kofun*), mainly in western Japan.

These massive tombs contained various artefacts including tools, weapons and *haniwa*, clay figurines of people and animals which had been ceremonially buried with people of nobility. With the arrival of Buddhism, this labour-intensive custom was abandoned in favour of cremation.

Buddhism & the Nara Period
When Buddhism drifted onto the shores of Japan, Kyoto was barely more than a vast, fertile valley. First introduced from China in 538 via the Korean kingdom of Paekche, Buddhism was pivotal in the evolution of the Japanese nation. It brought with it a flood of culture, in literature, arts, architecture, and a distinctive system of writing in Chinese characters, *kanji*. Buddhism eventually received the endorsement of the nobility and emperors, who authorised widespread temple construction and in 588, as recorded in the 8th century *Chronicle of Japan* (Nihon Shoki), Japan's first great temple complex, Asuka-dera, was completed.

Gradually, the wealth and power of the temples began to pose a threat to the governing Yamato court, prompting reforms from Prince Shōtoku (574–622), regent for first Empress Suiko. He set up the Constitution of 17 Articles and laid the guidelines for a centralised state headed by a single ruler. He also instituted Buddhism as a state religion and ordered the construction of more temples, including Nara's eminent Hōryū-ji, the world's oldest surviving wooden structure.

Despite family feuds and coups d'etat, subsequent rulers continued to reform the country's administration and laws. Previously, it had been the custom to avoid the pollution of imperial death by changing the site of the capital for each successive emperor, but in 710 this custom was altered and the capital, known as Heijō-kyō, was shifted to Nara, where it remained for 75 years.

Historical Periods

historical periods	date
Palaeolithic	pre-10,000 BC
Jōmon	10,000–300 BC
Yayoi	300 BC–AD 300
Yamato (Kofun)	300–710
Nara	710–94
Heian	794–1185
Kamakura	1185–1333
Muromachi	1333–1576
Azuchi-Momoyama	1576–1600
Edo (Tokugawa)	1600–1867
Meiji	1868–1912
Taishō	1912–26
Shōwa	1926–89
Heisei	1989 to present

Establishment of Heian-kyō

The Kyoto basin was first settled in the 7th century when the region was known as Yamashiro-no-kuni. The original inhabitants were immigrants from Korea, the Hata clan, who established Koryū-ji in 603 as their family temple in what is today the Uzumasa district.

By the end of the 8th century the Buddhist clergy in Nara had become so meddlesome that Emperor Kammu decided to insulate the court from their influence by moving the capital. The first move occurred in 784, to Nagaoka (a suburb of Kyoto), and a decade later the capital was shifted to present-day Kyoto, where it was to remain until 1868.

The new capital was given the name Heian-kyō; literally, the capital of peace *(hei)* and tranquillity *(an)*. As with the previous capital in Nara, the city was laid out in accordance with Chinese geomancy in a grid pattern adopted from the Tang dynasty (618–907) capital, Chang'an (present-day Xi'an). The rectangle-shaped precincts were established west of where the Kamogawa flows today. Originally measuring 4.5km east to west and 5.3km north to south, the city was about one-third the size of its Chinese prototype. Running through the centre was Suzaku-ōji, an 85m-wide,

willow-lined thoroughfare dividing the eastern (Sakyō-ku) part of the city from the west (Ukyō-ku). The northern tip of the promenade was the site of the ornate Imperial Palace and to the far south stood the 23m-high, two storey Rajō-mon, over 35m wide and 10m deep.

The ensuing Heian period (794–1185) effectively lived up to its name. Over four centuries, the city went beyond its role as a political hub to become the country's commercial and cultural centre. Toward the end of the 9th century contact with China became increasingly sporadic, providing an opportunity for Japan to cultivate its native culture. This produced a great flowering in literature, the arts and religious thinking, as the Japanese adapted ideas and institutions imported from China.

The development of *hiragana* (Japanese native characters) led to a popular literary trend best recalled by Murasaki Shikibu's legendary saga, *The Tale of Genji* (Genji Monogatari). This period in Kyoto's history conjures up romantic visions of riverside moon-gazing parties where literati drew calligraphy and composed poetry while the aristocracy frolicked in their self-imposed seclusion.

Rivalry between Buddhism and Shintō, the traditional religion of Japan, was reduced by presenting Shintō deities as manifestations of Buddha. Religion was separated from politics, and Japanese monks returning from China established two new sects, Tendai and Shingon, that became the mainstays of Japanese Buddhism. Soon other sects were springing up and temples were being enthusiastically built.

The Heian period is considered the apogee of Japanese courtly elegance, but in the provinces a new power was on the rise – the *samurai* or warrior class (see the boxed text 'Samurai' later in this chapter), which built up its armed forces to defend its autonomy. Samurai families moved into Kyoto, where they muscled in on the court, and subsequent conflicts between rival military clans led to civil wars and strife. This was the beginning of a long period of feudal rule by successive samurai families *(shōgun-ates)*. This feudal system effectively lingered on for seven centuries until imperial power was restored in 1868.

From Aristocracy to Military Rule

Although Kyoto served as home to the Japanese imperial family from 794 to 1868, it was not always the focus of Japanese political power. During the Kamakura period (1185–1333) Kamakura (near present-day Tokyo) was the national capital, and during the Edo period (1600–1867) the Tokugawa Shōgunate ruled Japan from Edo (present-day Tokyo). Still, despite the decline in influence of the imperial court, the city flourished commercially as townspeople continued their age-old manufacturing traditions.

By the 12th century the imperial family had become increasingly isolated from the mechanics of political power. By the time the corrupt Fujiwara Shōgunate was eclipsed by the Taira clan, who ruled briefly before being ousted by the Minamoto family (also known as the Genji) in the epic battle of Dannoura (Shimonoseki) in 1185, the name 'Kyoto' had emerged as the common title of the city.

Minamoto Yoritomo set up his headquarters in Kamakura in 1192, while the emperor remained nominal ruler in Kyoto. Yoritomo purged members of his own family who stood in his way, but after his death in 1199 his wife's family, the Hōjō, eliminated all of his potential successors and in 1213 became the true wielders of power behind the figureheads of shōguns and warrior lords.

During this era, the popularity of Buddhism spread to all levels of society. From the late 12th century, Japanese monks returning from China introduced a new sect, Zen, the austerity of which appealed particularly to the samurai class.

Meanwhile, as the spiritual fervour grew, Japanese merchants prospered in increased trade dealings with China.

Forces beyond the sea undermined the stability of the Kamakura regime. The Mongols, under Kublai Khan, reached Korea in 1259 and sent envoys to Japan seeking Japanese submission. The envoys were expelled and the Mongols sent an invasion fleet which arrived near present-day Fukuoka in 1274. This first attack was only barely repulsed, with the aid of a typhoon, and further envoys were beheaded as a sign that the government of Japan was not interested in paying homage to the Mongols.

In 1281, the Mongols dispatched an army of over 100,000 soldiers to Japan. After an initial success, the Mongol fleet was almost completely destroyed by yet another typhoon. Ever since, this lucky typhoon has been known to the Japanese as *kamikaze* (divine wind) – a name later given to the suicide pilots of WWII.

Although the Kamakura government emerged victorious, it was unable to pay its soldiers and lost the support of the warrior class. Emperor Go-Daigo led an unsuccessful rebellion against the government and was exiled to the Oki Islands near Matsue. A year later, he toppled the government, ushering in a return of political authority to Kyoto.

Country at War

After completing his takeover, Emperor Go-Daigo had refused to reward his warriors, favouring the aristocracy and priesthood instead. In the early 14th century this led to a revolt by the warrior, Ashikaga Takauji, who had previously supported Go-Daigo. Ashikaga defeated the emperor in Kyoto, then installed a new emperor and appointed himself shōgun, initiating the Muromachi period (1333–1576). Go-Daigo escaped to set up a rival court at Yoshino in a mountainous region near Nara. Rivalry between the two courts continued for 60 years until the Ashikaga made a promise (which was not kept) that the imperial lines would alternate.

Kyoto gradually recovered its position of political significance, and within the sanctuary of the art-loving Ashikaga enjoyed an epoch of cultural and artistic fruition. Talents now considered typically Japanese flourished, including such arts as landscape painting, classical nō drama, flower arranging *(ikebana)* and tea ceremony *(chanoyu)*.

Samurai

However difficult it is to envision today, legendary samurai warriors once waged bloody battles on Kyoto's streets. In the Museum of Kyoto you can see painted scrolls *(e-maki)* depicting courageous sword fights and bands of costumed crusaders proudly parading along Sanjō-dōri displaying the freshly severed heads of traitors for all to heed.

The prime duty of a samurai was to give faithful service to his feudal lord. In fact, the origin of the term samurai is closely linked to a word meaning 'to serve', and this can be seen in the *kanji* (Chinese script) character for the word. Over the centuries, the samurai established a code of conduct which came to be known as *bushidō* (the way of the warrior). This code was drawn from Confucianism, Shintō and Buddhism.

Confucianism required the samurai to show absolute loyalty to his lord; toward the oppressed he was expected to show benevolence and exercise justice. Subterfuge was to be despised, as were all commercial and financial transactions. A real samurai had endless endurance, exhibited total self-control, spoke only the truth and displayed no emotion. Since his honour was his life, disgrace and shame were to be avoided above all else and all insults were to be avenged.

From Buddhism, the samurai learnt the lesson that life is impermanent, enabling him to face death with serenity. Shintō provided the samurai with patriotic beliefs in the divine status both of the emperor and of Japan, the abode of the gods.

Ritual suicide *(seppuku* or *harakiri)*, to which Japanese Buddhism conveniently turned a blind eye, was an accepted means of avoiding dishonour. This grisly procedure required the samurai to ritually disembowel himself before a helpful aide, who then drew his sword and lopped off the samurai's head. One reason for this ritual was the requirement that a samurai should never surrender but always go down fighting. Since surrender was considered a disgrace, prisoners received scant mercy.

During WWII this attitude was reflected in Japanese treatment of prisoners of war – still a source of bitter memories for those involved.

The samurai's standard battle dress or armour (usually made of leather or lacquered steel) consisted of a breastplate, a similar covering for his back, a steel helmet with a visor, and more body armour for his shoulders and lower body. Samurai weaponry – his pride and joy – included a bow and arrows (in a quiver), swords and a dagger, and he wasn't complete without his trusty steed.

The classic samurai battle took the form of duelling between individuals rather than the clashing of massed armies. In slack moments when he wasn't fighting, the samurai dressed simply but was easily recognisable by his triangular *eboshi*, a hat made from rigid black cloth.

Not all samurai were good warriors adhering to their code of conduct: portrayals of samurai indulging in double-crossing, subterfuge or outright cowardice became popular themes in Japanese theatre.

UNBEATEN TRACKS IN JAPAN, F.J. BISHOP

Many of Kyoto's famous gardens date from this period, as do such monuments as Kinkaku-ji (Golden Pavilion) and Ginkaku-ji (Silver Temple). Eventually, formal trade relations were reopened with Ming China and Korea, although Japanese piracy remained a bone of contention with both.

The Ashikaga ruled, however, with diminishing effectiveness in a land slipping steadily into civil war and chaos. By the 15th century Kyoto had become increasingly divided as *daimyō* (domain lords) and local barons fought for power in bitter territorial disputes that were to last for a century. In 1467, the matter of succession to the shōgun between two feudal lords, Yamana and Hosokawa, ignited the most devastating battle in Kyoto's history. With Yamana's army of 90,000 camped in the south-west and Hosokawa's force of 100,000 quartered in the north of the city, Kyoto became a battlefield. The resulting Ōnin War (Ōnin-no-ran; 1467–77) wreaked untold havoc on the city; the Imperial Palace and most of the city was destroyed in fighting and subsequent fires and the populace left in ruin.

The war marked the rapid decline of the Ashikaga family and the beginning of the Warring States period (Sengoku-jidai) which lasted until the start of the Momoyama period in 1576.

Return to Unity
In 1568 Oda Nobunaga, the son of a daimyō, seized power from the imperial court in Kyoto and used his military genius to initiate a process of pacification and unification in central Japan. This manoeuvre marked the start of the short-lived Azuchi-Momoyama period (1576–1600). In 1582, Nobunaga's efforts were cut short when he was betrayed by his own general, Akechi Mitsuhide. Under attack from Mitsuhide and seeing all was lost, Nobunaga disembowelled himself in Kyoto's Honnō-ji.

Nobunaga was succeeded by his ablest commander, Toyotomi Hideyoshi, who was reputedly the son of a farmer, although his origins are not clear. His diminutive size and pop-eyed features earned him the nickname Saru-san (Mr Monkey). Hideyoshi worked on extending unification so that by 1590 the whole country was under his rule and he developed grandiose schemes to invade China and Korea. The first invasion was repulsed in 1593 and the second was aborted on Hideyoshi's death in 1598.

By the late 16th century, Kyoto's population had swelled to 500,000 and Hideyoshi was fascinated with redesigning and rebuilding the city. He transformed Kyoto into a castle town and greatly altered the cityscape by ordering major construction projects including bridges, gates and the Odoi, a phenomenal earthen rampart designed to isolate and fortify the perimeter of the city, and to provide a measure of flood control.

The rebuilding of Kyoto is usually credited to the influence of the city's merchant class, which led a citizens' revival that gradually shifted power back into the hands of the townspeople. Centred in Shimogyō, the commercial and industrial district, these enterprising people founded a self-governing body *(machi-shū)*, which contributed greatly to temple reconstruction. Over time, temples of different sects were consolidated in one quarter of the city, creating the miniature 'city of temples' *(tera-machi)*, a part of Kyoto that still exists.

The Momoyama period has been referred to as the 'Japanese Renaissance' as the arts further flourished. Artisans of the era are noted for boisterous use of colour and gold-leaf embellishment, while Zen-influenced tea ceremony was developed to perfection under Master Sen no Rikyū. The performing arts also matured, along with skill in ceramics, lacquerware and fabric-dyeing. There was also a vogue for building castles and palaces on a flamboyant scale; the most impressive examples were Osaka-jō, which reputedly required three years of labour by up to 100,000 men, and the extraordinary Ninomaru Palace in Kyoto's Nijō-jō.

Peace & Seclusion
The supporters of Hideyoshi's young heir, Toyotomi Hideyori, were defeated in 1600 by his former ally, Tokugawa Ieyasu, at the

battle of Sekigahara. Ieyasu set up his field headquarters *(bakufu)* at Edo, marking the start of the Edo (Tokugawa) period (1600–1868). Meanwhile the emperor and court exercised purely nominal authority in Kyoto.

The Tokugawa family retained large estates and took control of major cities, ports and mines; the remainder of the country was allocated to autonomous daimyō. Tokugawa society was strictly hierarchical. In descending order of importance were: the nobility, who had nominal power; the daimyō and their warriors (samurai); farmers; and, at the bottom, artisans and merchants. Mobility from one class to another was blocked; social standing was determined by birth.

To ensure political security, the daimyō were required to make ceremonial visits to Edo every alternate year, and their wives and children were kept in permanent residence in Edo as virtual hostages of the government. At the lower end of society, farmers were subject to a severe system of rules which dictated in minutest detail their food, clothing and housing.

There emerged a pressing fear of religious intrusion (seen as a siphoning of loyalty to the shōgun) and Ieyasu set out to stabilise society and the national economy. Japan entered a period of national seclusion *(sakoku)* during which Japanese were forbidden on pain of death to travel to (or return from) overseas, or to trade abroad. As efforts to 'expel the barbarians and protect the throne' spread, only Dutch, Chinese and Koreans were allowed to remain and they were placed under strict supervision.

One effect of this strict rule was to create an atmosphere of relative peace and isolation in which the native arts excelled. There were great advances in *haiku* poetry, *bunraku* puppet plays and *kabuki* theatre. Crafts such as wood-block printing, weaving, pottery, ceramics and lacquerware became famous for their refined quality. Furthermore, the rigid emphasis of these times on submitting unquestioningly to rules of obedience and loyalty has lasted to the present day.

By the turn of the 19th century, the Tokugawa government was facing stagnation and corruption. Famines and poverty among the peasants and samurai further weakened the system. Foreign ships started to probe Japan's isolation with increasing insistence and the Japanese soon realised that their outmoded defences were ineffectual. Russian contacts in the north were followed by British and American visits. In 1853, Commodore Matthew Perry of the US Navy arrived with a squadron of 'black ships' to demand the opening of Japan to trade. Other countries also moved in with similar demands.

Despite being far inland, Kyoto felt the foreign pressure, which helped bring to a head the growing power struggle between the shōgun and emperor, eventually pushing Japan back into a state of internal conflict. A surge of antigovernment feeling among the Japanese followed and Kyoto became a hotbed of controversy. The Tokugawa government was accused of failing to defend Japan against foreigners, and of neglecting the national reconstruction necessary for Japan to meet the West on equal terms. In 1867 the ruling shōgun, Keiki, resigned and Emperor Meiji resumed control of state affairs.

Kyoto flourished under Emperor Meiji, who ruled from 1868 to 1912.

Emergence from Isolation

Prior to the Meiji era (1868–1912) Kyoto was under the jurisdiction of the prefectural government. With the Meiji Restoration in 1868, political power was again restored in Kyoto, but the following year the capital was transferred to Edo along with the imperial court. Many great merchants and scholars of the era followed the emperor. After more than a millennium as capital, the sudden changes came as a major blow to Kyoto as the population dropped dramatically and the city entered a state of bitter depression.

Kyoto quickly set its sights on revival, taking steps to secure self-autonomy and rebuild its infrastructure. It again flourished as a cultural, religious and economic centre, with progressive industrial development. By the late 1800s Kyoto led the country in education reforms by establishing Japan's first kindergarten, elementary and junior high schools and public library. In the same period the city introduced Japan's first electricity system, water system and fully functioning transportation network. In 1885, work began on the monumental Lake Biwa Canal, which in just five years made Kyoto the first Japanese city to harness hydroelectric power.

A city government system was finally formed in 1889, a factor which further strengthened Kyoto's industries. As traditional industry pushed on, research developed in the sciences, in particular physics and chemistry. Modern industries like precision machinery also grew, as did the introduction of foreign technologies like the automated weaving loom; Western architectural techniques are reflected in many of the city's Meiji-era brick and stonework buildings. In 1895, to celebrate the 1100th anniversary of the city's founding, Kyoto hosted the 4th National Industrial Exhibition Fair and established the country's first streetcar system (fuelled by the Keage Hydroelectric Plant). The same year saw the construction of the Heian-jingū (actually a five-to-eight scale replica of Daigokuden, the emperor's Great Hall of State), and the birth of the Jidai Matsuri (Festival of the Ages).

The initial stages of this restoration were resisted in a state of virtual civil war. The abolition of the shōgunate was followed by the surrender of the daimyō, whose lands were divided into the prefectures that exist today. With the transfer of the capital to Edo, now renamed Tokyo (Eastern Capital), the government was recentralised and Western-style ministries were appointed for specific tasks. A series of revolts by the samurai against the erosion of their status culminated in the Saigō Uprising, when they were finally beaten and stripped of their power.

Despite nationalist support for the emperor under the slogan of *sonnō-jōi* (revere the emperor, repel the barbarians), the new government soon realised it would have to meet the West on its own terms. Promising *fukoku kyōhei* (rich country, strong military), the economy underwent a crash course in Westernisation and industrialisation. An influx of Western experts was encouraged to provide assistance, and Japanese students were sent abroad to acquire expertise in modern technologies. In 1889, Japan created a Western-style constitution.

By the 1890s, government leaders were concerned at the spread of liberal Western ideas and encouraged a swing back to nationalism and traditional values. Japan's growing confidence was demonstrated by the abolition of foreign treaty rights and by the ease with which it trounced China in the Sino-Japanese War (1894–95). The subsequent treaty nominally recognised Korean independence from China's sphere of influence and ceded Taiwan to Japan. Friction with Russia led to the Russo-Japanese War (1904–05), in which the Japanese navy stunned the Russians by inflicting a crushing defeat on their Baltic fleet at the battle of Tsu-shima. For the first time, the Japanese commanded the respect of the Western powers.

The Pursuit of Empire

On his death in 1912, Emperor Meiji was succeeded by his son, Yoshihito, whose period of rule was named the Taishō era. When WWI broke out, Japan sided against Germany but did not become deeply involved

Portable karaoke, a bicycle-mounted system for easy entertaining.

Looking cute in school uniform

A crowd of visitors burning incense as an offering at a Nara temple.

A worker in traditional dress.

Squeezing in a few more passengers – Kyoto morning rush hour

FRANK CARTER

FRANK CARTER

MARTIN MOOS

IZZET KERIBAR

Behind the closed doors of the exclusive teahouses and restaurants dotting the backstreets of Kyoto, kimono-clad women of exquisite grace and refinement entertain gentlemen of considerable means. Geisha are versed in an array of visual and performing arts.

in the conflict. While the Allies were occupied with war, the Japanese took the opportunity to expand their economy at top speed.

The Shōwa period commenced when Emperor Hirohito ascended to the throne in 1926. A rising tide of nationalism was quickened by the world economic depression that began in 1930. Popular unrest was marked by political assassinations and plots to overthrow the government. This led to a significant increase in the power of the militarists, who approved the invasion of Manchuria in 1931 and the installation of a Japanese puppet regime, Manchukuo. In 1933, Japan withdrew from the League of Nations and in 1937 entered into full-scale hostilities against China.

As the leader of a new order for Asia, Japan signed a tripartite pact with Germany and Italy in 1940. The Japanese military leaders saw their main opponents as the USA. When diplomatic attempts to gain US neutrality failed, the Japanese drew the USA into WWII with a surprise attack on Pearl Harbor on 7 December 1941.

At first, Japan scored rapid successes, pushing its battle fronts across to India, down to the fringes of Australia and out into the mid-Pacific. But eventually the Battle of Midway turned the tide of the war against Japan. Exhausted by submarine blockades and aerial bombing, by 1945 Japan had been driven back on all fronts. In August, the declaration of war by the Soviet Union and the atomic bombs dropped by the USA on Hiroshima and Nagasaki were the final straws: Emperor Hirohito announced unconditional surrender.

What Really Saved Kyoto?

Kyoto's good fortune in escaping US bombing during WWII is a well-publicised fact. Still, while it may be a source of pride for some Americans to hear that the city was consciously spared out of US goodwill and reverence for Kyoto's cultural heritage, not everyone agrees with the prevailing story.

The common belief is that Kyoto was rescued through the efforts of American scholar Langdon Warner (1881–1955). Warner sat on a committee during the latter half of the war which endeavoured to save artistic and historical treasures in war-torn regions. Now, more than a half-century later, Warner is a household name in Japan and is still alluded to in discussions on the future preservation of Kyoto. He is said to have urged a desperate plea through to top US military authorities to spare the cities of Kyoto, Nara, Kamakura and Kanazawa.

Despite this popular account, other theories have surfaced, along with some documentation pointing to an elaborate *X-Files*-style conspiracy aimed at quelling anti-American sentiment in occupied Japan. The evidence has fuelled a debate as to whether or not it was in fact a well-planned public relations stunt scripted by US intelligence officials to gain the trust of a nation that had been taught to fear and hate the American enemy.

Some historians have suggested that in fact both Kyoto and Nara were on a list of some 180 cities earmarked for air raids. Kyoto, with a population of over one million people, was a prime target (along with Hiroshima and Nagasaki) for atomic annihilation and many avow the choice could easily have been Kyoto. Nara, it has been suggested, escaped merely due to having a population under 60,000, which kept it far down enough on the list not to be reached before the unconditional surrender of Japan in September 1945.

Whether the preservation of Kyoto was an act of philanthropy or a simple twist of fate, the efforts of Warner and his intellectual contemporaries are etched into the pages of history and even taught in Japanese schools. Warner's near-mythical status was ensured when he was posthumously honoured by the Japanese government, which bestowed upon him the esteemed Order of the Sacred Treasure in recognition of his invaluable contribution to the Japanese nation. Today, Japanese who wish to honour Warner's memory can visit a monument to him in the precincts of Nara's Hōryū-ji.

Despite avoiding air raids (see the boxed text 'What really saved Kyoto?'), Kyoto suffered a great drain of people and resources during the war. To prevent the spread of fires, hundreds of magnificent wooden shops and houses were torn down, and even great temple bells and statues were melted down into artillery, but thankfully most of its cultural treasures survived.

Postwar Reconstruction & Revival

Japan was occupied by Allied forces until 1952 under the command of General Douglas MacArthur. The chief aim was a major reform of Japanese government through demilitarisation, the trial of war criminals and the weeding out of militarists and ultrana-tionalists from the government. A new constitution was introduced which dismantled the political power of the emperor, who completely stunned his subjects by publicly renouncing any claim to divine origins. This left him with the status of mere figurehead.

At the end of the war, the Japanese economy was in ruins and inflation was running rampant. A program of recovery provided loans, restricted imports and encouraged capital investment and personal saving. In 1945, the Kyoto Revival Plan was drafted and again, as had happened repeatedly in its history, Kyoto was set for rebuilding. By 1949 Kyoto University had already produced its first in a long line of Nobel Prize winners and the city went on to become a primary educational centre.

Kyō-machiya

Topping the list of Kyoto's endangered species are its priceless *kyō-machiya* (wooden townhouses), with their delicate latticework exteriors, exquisite inner gardens and soaring kitchen/entryways.

Like machiya in other parts of Japan, kyō-machiya were designed with the scorching heat of the Japanese summer in mind (the reasoning being that it is a lot easier to bundle up in winter than cool down in summer). The latticework exteriors and removable *shōji* (sliding rice-paper screens) take advantage of even the slightest breeze to cool the house. Likewise, gossamer building materials, like paper and wood, allow heat to escape easily from the house.

In the case of the kyō-machiya, form is wedded to function in a most pleasing manner, and where they remain in significant numbers, these houses form some of Kyoto's most lovely scenery.

Unfortunately, since the end of WWII, it is estimated that some 40,000 of these irreplaceable treasures have been razed. Perhaps even more dreadful, though, is the sea of mundane concrete slabs and parking lots that has replaced them. Tragically, the Kyoto cityscape continues to slip into a uniform façade matching most other Japanese cities. Stay in Kyoto just a short time, and you will no doubt see demolition crews at work and trucks hauling loads of history away down the narrow streets.

The causes of the destruction are complex. It is partly to do with strict inheritance tax laws that make it cheaper to tear down an old building and replace it with an office or apartment building than to pass it on to descendants. There is also the general desire to live in less cramped, brighter spaces as well as widespread apathy among homeowners.

Despite the losses, however, more and more people realise how much has disappeared and are starting to take action. In recent years the number of citizens' groups fighting to preserve what's left of traditional Kyoto has increased.

At the forefront of the preservation movement is Kyoto Mitate, an organisation working to promote ways for the city to integrate its rich cultural heritage with development. Among its recent projects is an intriguing program called 'Art in Machiya', which urges kyō-machiya owners to open their homes for art installations and related events, helping to foster a growing appreciation for these buildings.

Visit the Kyoto Mitate Web site at W www.mitate.org to learn more about the organisation, and how you can help.

By the late 1950s, trade was flourishing and the Japanese economy continued to experience rapid growth. From textiles and the manufacture of labour-intensive goods such as cameras, the Japanese 'economic miracle' had branched out into virtually every sector of society and Kyoto increasingly became an international hub of business and culture.

In 1956 Japan's first public orchestra was founded in Kyoto and two years later the city established its first sister-city relationship, with Paris. Japan was now looking seriously toward tourism as a source of income and foreign visitors were steadily arriving on tours for both business and pleasure. By this time Kyoto had further developed as a major university centre, and during the 'Woodstock era' of the late 1960s anti-war movements and Japanese flower power mirrored that of the West and brought student activism out into the streets.

In the 1970s, Japan faced recession, inflation surfacing in 1974 and again in 1980, mostly as a result of steep price hikes for imported oil, on which Japan is still gravely dependent. By the early '80s, however, Japan had fully emerged as an economic superpower and Kyoto's high-tech companies were among those dominating fields such as electronics, robotics and computer technology. The notorious 'bubble economy' that followed led to an unprecedented era of free spending by Japan's nouveau riche. Shortly after the 1989 death of Emperor Shōwa and the start of the Heisei period (with the accession of the current emperor, Akihito) the miracle bubble burst, launching Japan into a critical economic downfall from which many contend it may never fully recover.

Kyoto Today & Tomorrow

The battles in Kyoto today are being fought not with swords, but with pens, as preservationists desperately struggle to save the city from a coalition of local government forces and commercial interests who seem bent on the heedless modernisation of the city at the expense of its traditional architecture (see

Kyoto's Sister Cities	
sister city (shimai toshi)	chronological order of affiliation
Paris, France	1958
Boston, USA	1959
Cologne, Germany	1963
Florence, Italy	1965
Kiev, Ukraine	1971
Xi'an, China	1974
Guadalajara, Mexico	1980
Zagreb, Croatia	1981
Prague, Czech Republic	1996

The official sister 'province' of Kyoto-fu is Oklahoma State, USA.

the boxed text 'Kyō-machiya'). While there have been a handful of tenuous victories in the efforts to protect Kyoto's surviving heritage, such triumphs are few and far between.

Marking the 1200th anniversary of the founding of Kyoto, 1994 was a monumental year. Developers capitalised on this proud milestone by further exploiting the city. Controversy swelled over the blatant bending of city construction ordinances which allowed projects such as the Kyoto Hotel and new Kyoto station to be built higher than previous legal limits, setting a frightful precedent for the future.

Fuelling the rush to develop Kyoto is the knowledge that the city can no longer depend on tourist revenue as its main source of income. Thus, the city is desperately trying to shift its economic focus from tourist-related service industries to manufacturing and research. Unfortunately, efforts by the city fathers to increase the city's industrial base (see the Economy section later in this chapter) have met with only limited success.

Still, the city remains an important cultural and educational centre. Today over 60 museums and 37 universities and colleges are scattered throughout the city, and it houses more than 200 of Japan's National Treasures and nearly 1700 important Cultural Properties.

The city also continues to expand its infrastructure. In 1997 two transportation milestones were reached: the new Tōzai subway line was opened and the giant new Kyoto station building was unveiled.

At the dawn of the new millennium, Kyoto hangs in a limbo, torn between the desire to preserve its heritage and the need to develop its economy. The real challenge for Kyoto is to find ways to survive in the modern world without sacrificing its cultural and architectural heritage.

GEOGRAPHY

Landlocked and surrounded by mountains to the north, east and west, the city of Kyoto sits in the south-east of Kyoto-fu (Kyoto prefecture) at 135° east longitude and 35° north latitude. About 370km west of Tokyo and 45km north-east of Osaka, present-day Kyoto occupies what was once a massive lake bed. When the city was first established it occupied just 30 sq km, but over the centuries it has spread outward, incorporating several surrounding towns and villages. Today Kyoto-shi (Kyoto City) covers more than 600 sq km and is divided into 11 wards, extending some 50km north to south and 25km east to west.

The mountains which surround the city are the Kitayama (Northern Mountains), the Higashiyama (Eastern Mountains) and the Arashiyama (Stormy Mountains). Only the south side of the city is free of mountains, and is consequently one of the city's most heavily developed areas. Kyoto basin itself is relatively flat, with only a few hills cropping up here and there.

Kyoto has two major rivers flowing north to south, the Kamo-gawa and Katsura-gawa. Traditionally these rivers and their tributaries played a crucial role in the lives of the people, both as a means of transportation and as a vital source of water for drinking and irrigation. The purity of the water was highly praised for the production of Fushimi sake and also for use in traditional fabric-dyeing. In times of heavy rains, however, the rivers frequently wreaked havoc when major floods struck the city.

Today the problem has been solved primarily by concrete reinforcement of the river banks and improved drainage.

Unesco World Heritage Sites

In 1994, 13 of Kyoto's Buddhist temples, three Shintō shrines and one castle met the criteria to be designated World Heritage sites by the United Nations. Each of the 17 sites has buildings or gardens of immeasurable historical value and all are open for public viewing.

Kamigamo-jinja
Shimogamo-jinja
Ujigami-jinja
Tō-ji
Kiyomizu-dera
Enryaku-ji
Daigo-ji
Ninna-ji
Byōdō-in
Kōzan-ji
Saihō-ji
Tenryū-ji
Kinkaku-ji
Ginkaku-ji
Ryōan-ji
Nishi Hongan-ji
Nijō-jō

CLIMATE

Japan is renowned for the changing scenery of its four distinct seasons, and perhaps in no place else on the archipelago are the cycles of nature more clearly visible than in Kyoto. References to Kyoto's fickle weather, due in part to its valley location, have appeared in countless poems and works of literature, and consequently provide material for a large share of the daily conversation of Kyoto residents.

Kyoto's summers and winters can be unpleasant. Temperatures in the humid summers (July to September) can reach over 40°C. In winter (December to March) the temperature does occasionally fall below 0°C, though it usually hovers somewhere in the single digits. Snow falls in the city about

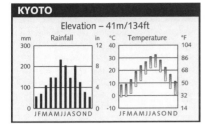

two or three times each winter, but it rarely stays on the ground; cold rain is much more common.

Even within the city, weather patterns can vary greatly. Locals cite the fork in the Kamo-gawa at Imadegawa-dōri as a barrier beyond which the bitter northern winter seldom descends. In summer, Kyotoites take advantage of the cooler northern temperatures, fleeing the often unbearable heat of the city to take refuge in cool mountain valleys like Kurama and Kibune.

The average yearly rainfall is around 140cm, much of which arrives during the rainy season in June. The end of the rainy season usually signals the arrival of the scorching heat of summer, which usually lasts into early to mid-September.

In contrast to the summer and winter, spring (March to May) and autumn (September to November) weather tends to be delightful. Clear skies and warm temperatures are the rule. Occasional typhoons do roll in during the late summer and early autumn, but Kyoto is far enough inland to be spared most of their destructive effects.

ECOLOGY & ENVIRONMENT

In general, there is a low level of concern in Japan about environmental issues, particularly when it comes to activities which do not have an effect on life within Japan itself.

One example of this lack of environmental concern (which every visitor will soon be aware of) is the Japanese penchant for overpackaging. At a time when most Western nations are trying to cut back on packaging, in Japan it's full speed ahead to wrap things in the most layers of paper, plastic and cardboard possible, all tied together

with string and bows. Likewise, Japan's vast number of restaurants almost all provide their customers with disposable chopsticks *(waribashi)*.

Recycling is two-sided in Japan. On one hand, many household disposables, such as glass bottles, are efficiently recycled. On the other, Japan is the throwaway society *par excellence*. The severe *shaken* vehicle inspection system encourages car owners to constantly update their vehicles; cars more than a few years old are a rare sight on Japanese roads. There's little demand for second-hand goods and appliances, and consumer items are quickly replaced by the latest model. Stories abound of resident foreigners completely furnishing their homes from Japanese throwaways. Around almost any big city railway station there will be tangled heaps of perfectly good, but abandoned, bicycles.

In recent years there has been a steadily growing environmental awareness, even bordering on 'chic' among some young Japanese. Kyoto has a long history of grassroots activism and the large student population helps make it one of the country's ecocentres. Even the city government has jumped on the bandwagon, hosting an international summit on global warming in 1997 and passing a law to curb littering. Still, the law only applies to certain 'beautification enforcement areas' in the city, mostly around major sightseeing venues, and enforcement is variable at best.

Kyoto's environmental organisations have made great efforts to focus attention on issues like recycling, reducing construction of incinerators in residential areas, and on the country's nuclear future (Japan's greatest concentration of nuclear power plants runs along the Sea of Japan coast north of Kyoto). Another controversial issue is urban construction, which can be environmentally unsound and obstruct views of the surrounding mountains. The 'stop idling' campaign is targeting the nationwide problem of people sleeping in parked cars with their engines idling to heat or air-condition their cars (taxi and truck drivers seem to specialise in this practice).

Up in (Toxic) Flames

Japan likes to burn things. It is estimated that 70% of the world's incinerators are located in this country and indeed the smokestacks seem to be everywhere: running up the sides of university buildings, on the playgrounds of schools, behind hospitals, towering over the outskirts of cities.

Trash is burned rather than buried because most of Japan is covered with mountains. There have been attempts to dump garbage on artificial islands near port cities such as Kōbe and Yokohama, but these sites are of limited capacity. Despite a decreasing population and scientific warnings of the potential dangers of toxic emissions from large-scale incinerators, Japan continues to burn.

In 1997 city officials in Kyoto decided to construct a supermodern incinerator in the village of Ichihara, a few kilometres north of the city centre in the Kitayama mountains. Though Kyoto already has five large-scale, ageing incinerators, they claimed a new one was needed to fill the gap when the old ones were shut down for repairs.

Local residents argued that a new incinerator would not be needed if recycling efforts were boosted. They found fault with the city's environmental assessment surveys for the area and even conducted their own weather balloon tests to back up their claim that gases from the proposed incinerator could become dangerously trapped in the valley. Despite an agreement with local residents to proceed only after mutual, step-by-step consensus, the city broke its promise and began construction of the incinerator in the middle of the night.

Despite continuing protests from Ichihara residents, the plant came on line in April 2000. Although city officials argue that the plant adheres to the strictest European emissions standards, residents are unconvinced. Unfortunately for them, there seems little they can do now that the plant plays a major role in Kyoto's garbage disposal scheme.

Luckily, there is some good news on the environmental front: In 1997 a national container law was passed to put more pressure on industry to recycle PET plastic bottles and packaging materials. It is now possible to recycle PET bottles at many of Kyoto's convenience stores and supermarkets – look for the specially marked bins.

Though it is Kyoto's residents who ultimately need to take responsibility for the environment of their city, even short-term visitors can have an impact. Shoppers willing to do without fancy wrapping can use the simple phrase *'Fukuro wa iranai desu'* to decline a bag. Carrying your own chopsticks is also a good way to save a tree and let others get the idea (you can buy a very nice pair of chopsticks with their own case for around ¥500). Several local groups organise events like river clean-ups and regular hikes in and around Kyoto, great ways to meet local residents and find your way into nature (see 'The Great Outdoors' boxed text in the Things to See & Do chapter).

FLORA & FAUNA
Flora
Kyoto's valley locale, ample water supply and extreme yearly temperature fluctuations give rise to diverse vegetation. The city boasts an abundance of foliage throughout the year, particularly on the fringes, in the Imperial Palace Park and at the Kyoto Botanical Gardens. Camellias *(tsubaki)* in winter, spring cherry blossoms *(sakura)* and lotuses *(hasu)* in summer, plus maples *(momiji)* – whose changing autumn leaves or *kōyō* are the highlight of autumn – are just a few of the hundreds of species of colourful plants which flourish around the city.

When Kyoto was originally being developed, the locations for temples and shrines were carefully chosen to take into account the existing foliage, proximity to streams and waterfalls and the potential for autumn moon viewing. These sacred places best highlight the changing of the seasons and offer endless spots to take in Kyoto's extensive array of flora.

Flower Viewing in Kyoto

flower	Japanese	season in bloom	places
Azaleas	*tsutsuji*	late April to late June	Shōren-in, Manshu-in, Shōden-ji, Chishaku-in, Shisen-dō, banks of the Hozu-gawa
Hydrangeas	*ajisai*	late May to mid-July	Sanzen-in, Fujinomori-jinja, Tō-ji, Shisen-dō, Jakkō-in, Nison-in
Water lilies	*suiren*	early June to early July	Ryōan-ji, Kanshū-ji, Heian-jingū, Ōharano-jinja, Tōfuku-ji
Wisteria and irises	*fuji* and *ayame* or *shōbu*	late May to mid-June	Heian-jingū, Byōdō-in, Umemiya-taisha, Hokongo-in, Shisen-dō
Lotuses	*hasu*	mid-July	Hokongo-in, Heian-jingū, Kajū-ji
Bush clover	*hagi*	mid- to late September	Nanzen-ji, Heian-jingū, Nashinoki-jinja
Chrysanthemum	*kiku*	October and November	Kyoto Botanical Gardens, Arashiyama area, Daikaku-ji, Fushimi Momoyama-jō

What you see today as you travel around Kyoto is not what Japanese saw hundreds of years ago. Japan's natural landscape has succumbed to modern urban culture, and much of its flora is not indigenous. It is thought that some 200 to 500 plant species have been introduced into Japan since the Meiji period, mainly from Europe but increasingly from the USA in recent years. In Kyoto, however, many of the gardens were laid out in the Edo period or earlier and represent a great opportunity to see native Japanese flora.

Much of the region was once heavily forested and modern Kyoto is still a world of magnificent trees. Small forests surround many temples and shrines, great bamboo groves shade the walking paths of the Sagano area, and exhaustively cultivated forests of cedar (*sugi*) blanket the northern hills.

There are also several places to see fantastic old-growth trees like the 800-year-old camphors at Shōren-in, gigantic pines in the precincts of Nanzen-ji and Shōkoku-ji, and in the Tadasu-no-mori Forest leading into Shimogamo-jinja. For anyone willing to embark on a substantial hiking route, the immense protected forest reserve in Ashiū, Miyama-chō, about an hour's drive north of Kyoto city, provides an excellent area to explore virgin forest terrain (see the Miyama-chō section in the Excursions chapter).

Fauna

Japan's one-time connection with the Asian mainland led to a migration of animals from Korea and China, and its fauna has much in common with these regions. The hills surrounding the city are home to a small population of deer (*shika*), a large number of monkeys (*saru*) and a few of Japan's beloved raccoon dogs (*tanuki*), all of which can occasionally be spotted, especially in the north.

Perhaps the region's most popular animal is the Japanese macaque (*nihon-zaru*), a medium-sized monkey inhabiting Honshū, Shikoku and Kyūshū. It averages around 60cm in length and has a short tail. If you don't have the time to spend romping the hills in search of the wily critters, you can see their antics at the Iwatayama Monkey Park (see the Arashiyama-Sagano district section in the Things to See & Do chapter).

Other wildlife roaming the Kyoto hills includes rabbits (*usagi*), foxes (*kitsune*), weasels *(itachi)* and the rare serow *(kamoshika)*, Japan's indigenous mountain goat. Hunting season for several regional species lasts from mid-November to mid-February, and hikers venturing beyond well-travelled trails should take care not to be mistaken for possible game; eg, wear bright-coloured clothing, although the actual danger of being fired upon or attacked by any animal is slim.

Deep into Kyoto's northern mountains is a large population of wild boar *(inoshishi)*, and on occasion they have even found their way into the city. Boar meat is widely enjoyed in winter stew *(botan-nabe)*, but the hunter faces a risky occupation; the rounded tusks on these ferocious beasts can inflict fatal damage. Though sightings are relatively infrequent, if you do come across a boar in the forest, try not to face it from a downhill slope – you are far less vulnerable if positioned above the creature.

An equally dangerous, but ever rarer sight are bears. Hunting and rural development have contributed to their dwindling numbers. According to a recent study conducted by Kyoto prefecture, there are approximately 400 brown bears living in the mountain region between Kyoto and the Sea of Japan. Smaller than Hokkaidō's *higuma* (brown bear), the *tsuki-no-wa-guma* (Asiatic brown bear) on Honshū is named for its white collar breast-mane resembling the moon. These bears average a height of 1.4m and weight of 200kg, and getting off on the wrong foot with them could be perilous. On the remote chance you should end up face-to-face with one, it is advisable *not* to run away, but to stand your ground and even create noise to try and frighten it away.

Kyoto is a prime locale for birdwatching, especially from late spring to early autumn. Japan's vital position on the trans-Asian and trans-Pacific flyways means feathered friends swoop in from as far south as Tasmania, west from South-East Asia and north from Siberia, Alaska and the Arctic tundra. More than 100 species of birds are found in the Kyoto region including pheasant, flycatchers, kingfishers and owls.

Some of the best areas to spot birds are the bird sanctuary at Midori-ga-ike Pond (Map 3) in the far north-east of Kyoto, the Arashiyama area, the Imperial Palace Park, Kyoto Botanical Gardens and the many small forests surrounding temples and shrines. The rivers flowing into Kyoto are home to a variety of fish such as the Japanese trout *(ayu)*, and a stroll along the banks of the Kamo-gawa often provides the chance to see graceful egret *(sagi)* bathing and hunting for fish.

Some of the most popular creatures in Japan are insects *(mushi)*, and bug-lovers in Kyoto can encounter a wide array of beetles *(kabuto-mushi)*, butterflies *(cho-cho)* and dragonflies *(tonbo)*. During summer, people relish the chance to be serenaded by orchestras of cicada *(semi)*, whose high-pitched chirping fills the air.

GOVERNMENT & POLITICS

The Kyoto city council is made up of 72 members elected by majority vote. Council members serve a four-year term, and elections are held every two years. Despite its post as prefectural capital, the city assembly is completely autonomous from the Kyoto prefectural assembly, which handles prefectural issues and is set up like a state government with an elected governor.

The Kyoto city assembly is dominated by the Liberal Democratic Party (LDP). The conservative LDP has strong ties to Osaka-based construction and utility companies, through which much of the money for electing Kyoto LDP members is funnelled.

Kyoto is also well known as a stronghold of the Japan Communist Party (JCP). As the second-largest party in the city council, it has the ability to check the LDP's power and initiatives. The JCP is known for its straight-talking politicians, an emphasis on social welfare programs and a lack of scandals and corruption. The JCP has a long history in Kyoto and many young people still see it as the best alternative to the LDP.

Voter frustration at the failure of the LDP and the JCP to halt Kyoto's economic slide resulted in a victory for independent candidate Masumoto Yorikane in the 1996

Three Beloved Trees

The Japanese are almost obsessed with the changing of the seasons. From haiku to *han-ga* (woodblock prints), the changing seasons are a central motif in much of Japanese art. Indeed, no well-educated Japanese person would think of starting a letter without a brief reference to the present season. Among all the seasonal markers which so entrance the Japanese, none are more beloved than plum, cherry and maple trees. Viewing the plum and cherry blossoms is *the* ritual of springtime in Japan, while viewing the blazing colours of the maple is almost a national mania. From jam-packed temples to secluded mountain paths, Kyoto is packed with places to join the Japanese in celebrating these fabulous seasonal spectacles.

Japanese Plum The arrival in late February of the fragrant pink flowers on Kyoto's plum trees *(ume)* is one of nature's most eloquent signs that spring is just around the corner.

Plum trees are believed to have arrived from China in the 8th century and were warmly adopted in Japan as protective charms against evil. These trees are typically found near the north-east corner of gardens, the direction from which evil is believed to come. Another daily measure for preventing misfortune involves eating the super-sour pickled version of the Japanese plum *(ume-boshi)* with breakfast (if you can survive the biting, tart flavour, you should be able to endure anything!).

One of the best places to see plum trees in bloom is during the 25 February Baika-sai Festival at Kitano-Tenman-gū (see the boxed text 'Festivals' in the Facts for the Visitor chapter). Other popular viewing spots are the Imperial Palace Park, Zuishin-in, Nijō-jō and Seiryō-ji.

Cherry Tree With the beginning of April comes cherry blossom *(sakura)* season, when the telltale pink and white flowers of Japan's indigenous cherry trees bloom throughout the city. Triumphant messengers of spring, the blossoms relieve the lingering chill of winter. Sweets shops celebrate their coming by preparing bean-filled *sakura-mochi*, exquisite pink-coloured rice cakes carefully wrapped in the leaves from neighbourhood cherry trees.

Thousands flock daily to stare in awe at the tremendous branches of Kyoto's most beloved cherry tree, the Gion shidare-zakura, in Maruyama-kōen, the site of the city's largest cherry blossom viewing *(hanami)* parties.

Groves of sakura can also be viewed in the Imperial Palace Park, along the Tetsugaku-no-michi (Path of Philosophy), the banks of the Kamo-gawa, at Nijō-jō, the Arashiyama area, Heian-jingū, and Ninna-ji, Kiyomizu-dera, Daikaku-ji and Daigo-ji.

Japanese Maple Chances are most Westerners have never tasted a tempura-fried red maple leaf, but autumn visitors with a yen for culinary adventure should not pass up the opportunity. When the first frigid breezes of late autumn sweep down into the valley from the north, *kōyō* (the changing of the autumn foliage) transforms Kyoto's countless Japanese maples *(momiji)* into a breathtaking spectrum of vibrant colour.

Momiji season is an ideal time for walking the mountain trails of Kyoto, as nearly every place you reach will be teeming with maples. Popular kōyō viewing spots include the Arashiyama/Sagano area, the Takaōarea, the Kurama/Kibune area, Ōhara and Yoshida-yama, as well as Kiyomizu-dera, Eikan-dō, Nanzen-ji and Tōfuku-ji.

FRANK CARTER

The fairyland wonder of a giant cherry blossom tree lit up at night.

mayoral election. Promising to halt wasteful construction projects and revitalise the city's economy, the centrist Masumoto won by a narrow 0.9%. Re-elected by a more comfortable margin in 2000, Masumoto is now focusing his energies on improving the city's educational system (he used to be head of the Kyoto Board of Education).

ECONOMY

Because of Kyoto's role as the historical and cultural centre of Japan, much of the city's economy is dependent on tourism. Its tourism and related retail and service industries presently employ about 65% of the workforce, down from about 70% in 1988. A large number of tourists continue to pass through Kyoto, but the strong yen has hurt international tourism and the number of overseas visitors has dropped by half in the last 15 years. With the construction of the enormous Kyoto International Conference Hall (Map 2) in the far north-east of the city, Kyoto has had some success in drawing international conventions and continues to enthusiastically promote itself as 'Conference City Kyoto'.

Recent economic trends show that Kyoto is continuing to lose business to Osaka, especially in low-tech industries. In manufacturing, the Kyoto economy is heavily dependent on the textile and machinery industries, which account for almost half its wholesale industry. In 1998, the gross economic product of Kyoto-fu was estimated at ¥9.9 trillion. Per-capita income in the prefecture was just over ¥3 million (around US$25,000).

While many of Kyoto's traditional industries such as silk weaving, fabric dyeing and cabinet making have been in steady decline, several of its high-tech companies are thriving, including international camera giant Kyocera and video game trailblazer Nintendo.

Kyoto's business and civic leaders today face a dilemma: how to keep tourism and the traditional industries an integral part of the economy while modernising to remain competitive. Some effort is under way to preserve parts of traditional Kyoto (perhaps those most profitable to tourism) and as part of its plan to boost local infrastructure, the city has invested heavily in both creating world-class science facilities and in joint private-public ventures, such as Kyoto Research Park, Kyoto Science City, and Kansai Science City on the border of Kyoto and Nara prefectures.

POPULATION & PEOPLE

Kyoto has a population of about 1.47 million people, making it the fifth-largest city in Japan behind Tokyo, Yokohama, Osaka and Nagoya. Over the past 50 years, the city's birth rate and population have declined by about 20%. Although Kyoto is home to one of the largest concentrations of colleges and universities in Japan, the majority of students leave after graduation for the bigger economic centres of Tokyo and nearby Osaka. Consequently, many traditional industries are dying out for lack of younger apprentices, who are unwilling to undergo years of training and hard work for relatively little pay.

Kyoto is famous for its aesthetic beauty and refined culture, but not for the kindness of its people, who often are said to be cold, unnecessarily formal and snobbish to outsiders. While short-term tourists are made to feel welcome, many who live long-term in the city receive a very different reception – one of strained patience.

The Kyoto dialect itself (Kyoto-ben) can be extremely vague, allowing people to mask their true feelings behind a smokescreen of veiled smiles and nebulous wording. Needless to say this *tatemae* mode of communication can easily confuse the visitor. Perhaps the best example of this is the expression for guests, *'Ochazuke demo dō desu ka?'*, literally 'Won't you have a cup of tea?' (actually, tea poured over rice), which is in fact a signal that the guest's visiting time is up.

Such manners and phrases are often not understood even by other Japanese, and Tokyo and Osaka businesspeople agree that Kyotoites are the most difficult to do business with, being notoriously ambiguous. Kyoto people are also known for their finicky sense of style. An old Japanese proverb says an Osaka merchant will spend time and money on eating, whereas a Kyotoite will spend time and money on nice clothes. In general, Kyoto

The Current Emperor

For over 1000 years, Kyoto was home to the emperor and imperial family. With the opening up of Japan, the decline of the *shōgun* and the restoration to national prominence of the Meiji emperor in 1868, the imperial family relocated to Edo (now Tokyo). Although the clan will not be moving back to Kyoto any time soon, there are local citizens' groups who still occasionally issue public calls for returning the throne to Kyoto.

The current emperor, Akihito, is the great-grandson of the Meiji emperor. Akihito formally ascended the throne in 1990, about 18 months after the death of his father, Emperor Hirohito (known posthumously as the Emperor Shōwa). Hirohito's reign is known as the Shōwa era, while Akihito's is called the Heisei era. Born on 23 December 1933, Akihito is the first emperor to ascend the Chrysanthemum Throne under Japan's postwar, American-drafted constitution.

Unlike his father, who Japanese were taught was a living god, Akihito's functions are purely ceremonial. He bestows formal authority on a newly chosen prime minister, as well as on the chief judge of the Supreme Court. Newly appointed ambassadors present their credentials to him, and he receives formal visitors of state, occasionally at one of the imperial properties in Kyoto. The constitution also provides him with the role of convening the Diet, dissolving the House of Representatives, and attesting to the appointment and dismissal of government ministers. All of this is done with the advice and approval of the Cabinet.

In Kyoto, the Imperial Household Agency (a collection of descendants of aristocrats whose functions are extremely secretive) owns and maintains four properties: the Imperial Palace (Gosho), the Sentō Gosho within the palace grounds, and the Katsura Rikyū and Shūgaku-in Rikyū imperial villas. It is interesting to note that when the emperor or other members of his family visit Kyoto, they do not stay at any of these ancient properties, but opt for the modern amenities of one of Kyoto's finer hotels.

Akihito is head of an imperial family which includes Empress Michiko, Crown Prince Naruhito and Crown Princess Masako (a former diplomat), second son Prince Akishinomiya and his wife Princess Kiko (and their two daughters Mako and Kako), and Princess Sayako, the emperor's youngest daughter. Crown Prince Naruhito is to ascend the throne upon the death of his father.

The comings and goings of the imperial family are tightly controlled by the Imperial Household Agency. The Japanese media treats the family very carefully, censoring stories at the request of the agency, out of fear of violent attacks from right-wing thugs, and to avoid the displeasure of those senior business and political leaders who support the current system. In fact, this fear of offending the wrong people led to a major embarrassment in 1993, when the Japanese press promised the agency it would not publish news of Naruhito's engagement to Owada Masako until the 'proper time'. The news, however, leaked to a Tokyo correspondent for the *Washington Post* and the story broke first in the USA.

Today's Japanese have differing opinions about the imperial system. Akihito is not nearly as controversial as his father, who led Japan to war and later renounced his divine status in defeat. Newspaper polls show many Japanese simply don't care about the imperial family, and there is no serious debate about whether the family should modernise along the lines of Europe's monarchies. Some feminists have been disappointed with Princess Masako's virtual silence since tying the knot and her complete lack of initiative in trying to open up the system. Meanwhile, media coverage focuses on when Masako will produce an heir to the throne and recent reports of her pregnancy made headlines across Japan. Although empresses occasionally ruled Japan in its early history, men have commanded the throne for over a millennium.

people prefer small and refined over large and flashy. Many exhibit a passion for the culture and fashions of Paris and Italy.

While sometimes held in contempt by other Japanese, Kyotoites are, at the same time, admired for their struggle to retain their city's traditional values. Many younger Japanese tourists who visit Kyoto see it as a kind of vast amusement park, full of temples and other peculiar attractions not seen in everyday life. Kyoto also offers a sense of comfort to many older Japanese, who find remnants of a prewar Japan.

But Kyoto is not all Japanese. An estimated 33,000 Japanese-Koreans have made their homes here, especially in the neighbourhoods south of Kyoto station. Many are children or grandchildren of Koreans who were brought to Japan as slave labourers following Japan's annexation of Korea in 1905.

Though born and raised in Japan, these *zai-nichi-kankoku-jin* (resident Koreans) were only recently released from the obligation to carry fingerprinted ID cards at all times. They still face severe job discrimination, especially when applying to public universities or for civil service positions. 'Prestigious' Japanese companies often refuse to hire them. While working-class Japanese are more accepting, middle and upper-middle class Kyotoites are known to hire detectives from special agencies to ensure that potential marriage partners are not of Korean heritage.

Another 'hidden' group in Japan is the *burakumin* class (Japanese whose ancestors worked in trades such as leather tanning, grave digging, or other professions deemed 'unclean'). Many burakumin reside in south Kyoto and, although their situation has vastly improved over the last 20 years, they still face conspicuous discrimination, from schools to the workplace.

Kyoto is also home to a large number of foreign artists, musicians, teachers, scholars, writers and people 'just passing through'. A large percentage of these, including some former hippies who came over in the 1960s and never left, live in old wooden houses that most Japanese don't want to live in today. A bohemian atmosphere still prevails among the Western members of Kyoto's foreign population. This population co-exists happily with Kyoto's local bohemian class, former Japanese student activists who now run offbeat coffee shops, restaurants, bars and other establishments in the city.

SOCIETY & CONDUCT
Traditional Culture
The Japanese live in a society governed by an almost infinite number of unwritten and highly complex rules. These rules, which evolved during Japan's rigidly hierarchical feudal period, are concerned with ideas of debt, obligation and social standing.

As the cultural capital of Japan, Kyoto is where this complex social system is at its most refined. Indeed, Kyoto has developed a breed of conservatism that takes the rigours of Japanese protocol to uncontested heights.

Kyoto is also one of the last places in the country where age-old traditions are still practised. For example, one classic custom still common today in Kyoto is the morning ritual of *kadohaki* (sweeping) and *mizumaki* (spreading water). Like clockwork, every morning Kyotoites can be seen purifying the ground in front of their homes and shops by sweeping the sidewalk and spreading water to create a clean, shiny surface. Ryokans and high-class restaurants may do this several times a day, and some scrub their walkways with tea leaves to create an agreeable patina on their cobblestones.

Of course, Kyoto is not immune to the rush of time, and like many of its old buildings, the old ways of Kyoto are slowly being replaced by the efficient and homogenous ways of modern consumer society. One of the bittersweet joys of visiting Kyoto today is seeing the last glimpses of Japan as it used to be.

The Group
One of the most cherished ideas about the Japanese is that the group is more important than the individual. The image of loyal company workers bellowing out the company anthem and attending collective exercise sessions is synonymous with Japan Inc – itself a corporate metaphor.

Urban Anthropology

Visitors to Japan expecting to find a nation of suit-wearing conformists are often shocked at the sheer variety they discover. Indeed, in places like Kyoto's Shijō-Kawaramachi crossing and Kiyamachi-dōri, ordinary pedestrian traffic on a weekend night approaches a kind of gaudy street theatre. The people-watching in such places is often half the fun of being there. Keep your eyes peeled for some of the following types.

Salarymen Just what you'd expect: businessmen, always clad in suits, right down to the matching company lapel pins. Observe the metamorphosis after they've kicked back a few *mizu-wari* (whisky and water).

Office Ladies Also known as OLs, these women may be secretaries, but may equally be women who do the same work as their male bosses for half the pay. OLs usually travel in small groups wearing matching uniforms of skirt, white blouse and vest.

Ojō-sans These are young women, usually college students or graduates, middle-class and headed for marriage to young salarymen. Ojō-sans dress conservatively, with the exception of the occasional miniskirt.

MW

Yanquis Pronounced 'yankees', these men prefer brown or blond hair, sport flashy clothes and have a cellular phone permanently glued to their ear. Yanquis often work in the construction industry, where their taste for loud clothes is expressed in brightly coloured *nikka-bokka* pants (from the English word knickerbockers).

Chimpira These are often yanquis who've taken rebellion a step further. They hope to attract the attention of *yakuza* (mafia) gangsters and be asked to join the gang, becoming another type – junior yakuza.

Bosozoku These motorcycle gangs offer more dyed hair and flashy clothes. A typical night is spent loudly revving motorcycle engines and speeding off tailed by the police, who never catch them. Like chimpira, some of the wilder bosozoku go on to become yakuza.

Yakuza This is the real thing. They used to stand out, with tight 'punch-perms' and loud suits, but modern yakuza are hardly noticeable, except perhaps for the swagger and black Mercedes with tinted windows.

Ike-Ike Onna Literally, go-go girl; these young women sport day-glo miniskirts, dyed brown hair, dark suntans and expensive handbags. Many ike-ike onna work in hostess bars, massage parlours and the like; hence they are sometimes referred to as *o-mizu*, as in 'mizu-shōbai', the so-called 'water trade'.

Ko Gyaru The name derives from *kōko*, the Japanese word for high school, and *gyaru*, from the English word 'girl' or 'gal': a high school girl who dresses like an ike-ike onna, often seen talking on a cellular phone.

Chanelah A young woman who leans strongly toward Chanel goods, particularly expensive handbags with gold chains – perhaps the world's most dedicated shoppers.

Yamamba These girls in their late teens get their name from a witch-like figure with long white hair who appears in Japanese *mukashi-banashi* (fairy tales). Not only is their hair white, but they also wear white lipstick and eyeshadow, which contrasts vividly with their dark, salon-tanned faces, giving the appearance of a raccoon. While this type is more common in Tokyo, you'll find a few brave yamamba tottering around Kyoto on towering high-heeled boots.

MW

It's easy to start seeing Japan's business-suited workers as members of a collectivised society that rigorously suppresses individual tendencies. But remember that the Japanese are no less individual than their Western counterparts: they experience the same frustrations and joys as Westerners do, and are just as likely to complain about their work conditions, the way their boss treats them and so on. The difference is that while these individual concerns have a place, they are less likely to be seen as defining.

The tension between group and individual interests has been a rich source of inspiration for Japanese art. Traditional values emphasise conflict between *honne* (the individual's personal views) and *tatemae* (the views that are demanded by the individual's position in the group). The same conflict is expressed in the terms *ninjō* (human feelings) and *giri* (social obligations). Salaried workers who spend long hours at the office away from the families they love are giving priority to giri over ninjō.

All this is deeply rooted in Japanese history. Until very recently, almost all Japanese lived in small villages, many of them engaged in rice farming. In order to live in harmony and produce a successful harvest, a high degree of cooperation was vital – there was little room for free-thinking individualists. Perhaps more importantly, with so many people packed into so little space, the Japanese learned long ago that the only way to live together was to put the needs of the group before those of the individual.

Men & Women

Traditional Japanese society restricted the woman's role to the home, where as housekeeper she wielded considerable power, overseeing all financial matters, monitoring the children's education and, in some ways, acting as the head of the household. Even in the early Meiji period, however, the ideal was rarely matched by reality: labour shortfalls often resulted in women taking on factory work. Even before that, women often worked side by side with men in the fields.

As might be expected, the contemporary situation is complex. There are, of course, those who stick to established roles. They tend to opt for shorter college courses, often at women's colleges, and see education as an asset in the marriage market. Once married, they leave the role of breadwinner to their husbands.

Increasingly, however, Japanese women are choosing to forgo or delay marriage in favour of pursuing their own career ambitions. Of course, changing aspirations do not necessarily translate into changing realities, and Japanese women are still significantly under-represented in upper-management and political positions, but over-represented as office fodder, such as OLs (office ladies).

Part of the reason for this is the prevalence of gender discrimination and sexual harassment in Japanese companies. Societal expectations, however, also play a role: Japanese women are forced to choose between having a career and having a family. Not only do most companies refuse to hire women for career-track positions, the majority of Japanese men are simply not interested in having a career woman as a spouse. This makes it very intimidating for a Japanese woman to step out of her traditional gender role and follow a career path.

The visitor to Kyoto is likely to encounter women working in *ryokan* (traditional inns), restaurants, tourist information offices and many other tourism-related positions. Indeed, it's very easy to conclude that the face Kyoto shows to the visitor is overwhelmingly female.

The Japanese & Gaijin

As a foreign visitor to Japan, you are a *gaijin*, literally, an 'outside person'. Some foreigners insist (correctly in fact) that the term *gaikokujin* (literally, 'outside country person') is more polite than the contraction gaijin, but the latter is so widely used that you will be knocking your head against a brick wall if you try to change it.

Away from the big cities it's not unusual to hear whispered exclamations of *gaijin da* (it's a foreigner!). Luckily, Kyoto has long been a favourite destination of foreign travellers and has a relatively large foreign community, so you can expect little in the way of outright scrutiny while in the city. Of course, Kyotoites are famous for treating even other Japanese as outsiders. As a foreigner, you are the ultimate outsider, so you might occasionally meet a certain coolness from Kyotoites, particularly in some of the city's haughtier traditional establishments.

Fortunately, most visitors to the city come away with miracle stories of kindness from city residents. If you approach the people you meet with an open mind and a smile on your face, it's almost certain that you too will have some heart-warming memories as souvenirs of your trip.

Etiquette

One of the most enduring Western notions about Japan is that of Japanese courtesy and rigid social etiquette. However, with a little sensitivity, there is almost no chance of offending anyone, and the visitor to Kyoto should rest easy in the knowledge that the Japanese are very forgiving when it comes to the little slip-ups of foreign visitors.

To be sure, many things are different: the Japanese bow and indulge in a ritualised exchange of *meishi* (business cards) when they meet; they exchange their shoes for slippers before entering the home; and social occasions involve sitting on the floor in positions that will put the legs of a foreigner to sleep within five minutes. But, overall, most of the complex aspects of Japanese social interaction are functions of the language and only pose problems for the advanced student who's trying to get as close to the culture as possible.

Sitting When visiting a Japanese home or eating in certain types of restaurants, you will be expected to sit on the floor. In very formal situations, this is done by tucking your legs directly beneath you in what is known as the seza position. However, in ordinary situations, it is perfectly acceptable to sit in whatever manner is comfortable, as long as you don't point your feet at anyone. Indeed, the Japanese themselves are unlikely to sit in seza pose for very long and

are quick to adopt a more comfortable position. If you are unsure of what to do, simply imitate your Japanese hosts.

Bowing & Shaking Hands There is a distinct etiquette to bowing. The general rule is that the deepness of a bow depends on the status (relative to oneself) of the person to whom one is bowing. Fortunately, no-one expects foreigners to understand this and the polite thing to do when meeting Japanese is to incline your head slightly and perhaps bow very slightly from the waist. Nowadays, of course, many Japanese have taken to shaking hands. Since the practice is still a little unusual, it's probably better not to offer your hand – let the other party take the lead.

Business Cards If you intend to find work in Japan, make sure you get some business cards printed. All introductions and meetings in Japan involve an exchange of business cards – handing out yours to the right people can make things happen. Cards should be exchanged and accepted with some ceremony, studied carefully and referred to often. It's polite to accept a card with two hands. Do not simply stuff a proffered card into your pocket. Also, never write anything on a card you are given.

Gift Giving The exchange of gifts, the return of one kindness with another, is an important part of Japanese social life. If you visit somebody at their home, you should bring them a gift. It needn't be anything big – chocolates, flowers or other items similar to those given as gifts in the West will do. Ideally, bring something from your own country. If you haven't got anything from home, Kyotoites are usually very happy with some carefully wrapped green tea (see Japanese Tea in the Shopping chapter) or a bouquet of flowers.

As a foreigner, it's quite likely that you will sometimes be given gifts 'for your travels'. You may not be able to reciprocate in these situations. The polite thing to do is to refuse a couple of times when the gift is offered. The other party will probably keep pushing as long as you keep refusing. A couple of refusals should be enough to ensure that you will not seem too grasping if you finally make off with the spoils.

Flattery What passes for flattery in the West is often perceived as quite natural in Japan. The Japanese rarely pass up the opportunity to praise each other in company. The foreigner who has made an effort to learn a few sentences of Japanese or to get

Omiyage

Gifts are the grease that keeps the wheels of Japanese society turning. A gift can serve as a token of appreciation, a sign of respect, a guarantee of continued favour or even a bribe (look at Japanese politics).

Perhaps the most troublesome and time-consuming gift of all is the *omiyage* – a souvenir given to friends, family and co-workers upon return from travel. In most Japanese companies, leaving for a vacation naturally entails a sense of shame, of letting down the team. To make up for this betrayal, an armful of omiyage is required. Of course, shopping for all these gifts can eat up an entire vacation (particularly a Japanese vacation, which usually lasts only a few days anyway).

Ever resourceful, the Japanese have come up with a unique solution to this problem – the train station regional speciality store. These stores are located in the passageways around big-city train stations. In the space of a few hundred metres you can pick up crab from Hokkaidō, dolls from Kyūshū and pickled vegetables from Shikoku. Even if everybody knows that their souvenir was picked up at the local train station, the obligation is fulfilled and everybody is happy.

People have also thought of new ways to make use of goods purchased at these stores. Apparently, gifts purchased at train station speciality stores are commonly used as alibis – after a weekend spent at the local love hotel with a secretary, a gift purchased at a regional speciality store is proof that a wayward husband was actually on a business trip.

by with chopsticks is likely to receive regular dollops of praise. The correct response to praise is to decline it with something like *'Sono koto wa arimasen'* ('Not at all'). Try to reciprocate if you can.

Needless to say, Kyotoites are masters of the flattery game. One of the best ways to handle this flattery is to reciprocate in kind – praising the beauty of the city is always a good way to win points with your host.

Directness Japanese do not make a virtue of being direct. Indeed, directness is seen as vulgar. The Japanese prefer to feel their way through a situation when dealing with others. There is an expression for this that translates as 'stomach talk' – where both sides tentatively edge around an issue, feeling out the other's point of view until it is clear which direction negotiations can go. This can often result in what for many Westerners is a seemingly interminable to-ing and fro-ing that only ever seems to yield ambiguous results. But don't be deceived – the Japanese can usually read the situation just as clearly as if both sides were clearly stating their interests.

Try to avoid direct statements that may be seen as confrontational. If someone ventures an opinion, however stupid it may seem, try not to crush it with a statement like 'No, I disagree completely'. And remember, silence has a very distinct meaning in Japan and it almost never signifies agreement.

Calls of Nature It's not unusual to find men urinating in crowded streets; on the other hand, the public use of handkerchiefs for blowing your nose is definitely frowned upon. The polite thing to do if you have a cold in public is to keep sniffing until you can get to a private place to have a good honk!

Avoiding Offence Japanese are tolerant of foreigners' customs for the most part; there's little chance of committing any grave faux pas. But there are certain situations where it is important to follow the Japanese example.

continued on page 51

ARTS

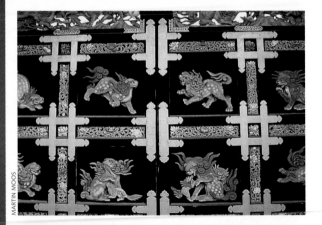

MARTIN MOOS

FRANK CARTER

STUART WASSERMAN

Title Page: A kabuki poster outside Kyoto's Minami-za theatre. Performed exclusively by men, kabuki is based on stylisation and formulised beauty (Photograph by Frank Carter).

Top: Decorated Kara-mon gate doors displaying intricate ornamental carvings and metal work.

Middle: Daruma dolls are thought to bring exceptionally good luck as they always return to their original position even when knocked over.

Bottom: Japan's theatre scene is a vital interplay of tradition and innovation, and Kyoto is Japan's theatre capital.

FRANK CARTER

Until the last century, the main influences on Japanese art came from China and Korea, from where Buddhism had passed on from India in the 6th century AD. However, the Japanese have always added something of their own to their art. There is a fascination with the ephemeral, with the unadorned, with forms that echo the randomness of nature. Perhaps more importantly, there is a tremendous respect for the materials themselves. A gift for caricature is also present, from early Zen ink paintings right up to contemporary *manga* (comics). An interest in the grotesque or the bizarre is also often visible, from Buddhist scrolls depicting the horrors of hell to the highly stylised depictions of body parts in *ukiyo-e* wood-block prints of the Edo period.

When asked to define their aesthetic principles, Japanese reach for words like *wabi*, *sabi* and *shibui*, words which have no real English-language equivalents. Together they refer to a kind of rustic simplicity and to a restrained, quiet and cultivated sense of beauty. These ideals can be seen in the measured proceedings of the tea ceremony or in the spare beauty of a haiku. They are by no means, though, the final say on a long and vibrant artistic tradition that continues to seek new inspirations and produce new forms.

Art Periods

The Jōmon period (10,000–300 BC) takes its name from the decorative 'coiled rope' pottery produced by early hunters and gatherers. Similarly, the Yayoi period (300 BC–AD 300), which saw the introduction of wet-rice farming and bronze and iron use, has left many examples of simple earthenware and clay figurines. The Kofun period (AD 300–710) is named after the keyhole-shaped burial mounds of the earliest emperors. *Haniwa* (clay ring) earthenware cylinders and sculptures, some as tall as 1.5m, surrounded these burial mounds.

The Asuka (552–645) and Hakuhō (645–710) periods mark an important turning point. The arrival of Mahayana (Greater Vehicle) Buddhism introduced religious themes that would inspire Japanese art for over five hundred years. The earliest works of sculpture were produced by Korean artisans – notable examples can be seen at Kōryū-ji in Kyoto and Hōryū-ji in Nara – but by the Nara period (710–94) a golden age of Japanese sculpture had arrived, producing such masterpieces as the Yakushi Nyorai (Healing Buddha) at Shin-Yakushi-ji in southern Nara.

By the early Heian period (794–1185), as Japan distanced itself from China, a truly native culture began to emerge. The imperial capital moved from Nara to Heian-kyō (modern-day Kyoto), and the break with Chinese tradition can be seen in the development of the 31-syllable *waka* poem, precursor to the 17-syllable *haiku*, and in narrative epics like *Genji Monogatari* (The Tale of Genji) by Murasaki Shikibu. In the visual arts, *yamato-e* (Japanese painting) broke with

Chinese landscape tradition by depicting court scenes on folding panels. The graceful lines of Uji's Byōdō-in south of Kyoto are testament to the beauty of Heian architecture.

The early art of the Kamakura period (1185–1333), when power moved away from Kyoto, was filled with a wild energy, later becoming more subdued under the influence of a military government. During this period, Zen became popular in Japan. Its disavowal of Buddha images gave rise to a new tradition of human portraits and statues, and marked the beginning of a secularisation of art.

In 1336 the centre of power moved back to Kyoto. During the Muromachi period (1333–1576), Zen had an enormous impact on the arts, exemplified by the ink paintings of Sesshū, the tea ceremony of Sen no Rikyū and the garden at Kyoto's Ginkaku-ji. However, in 1467, the Ōnin War broke out, which essentially destroyed Kyoto. This 'brush with the void' left a deep impact on Japan, and the idea of wabi, or stark simplicity, was born.

Eventually, the powerful shōgun Toyotomi Hideyoshi took control and the new elite encouraged artists to produce elaborate works to decorate their palaces. This Momoyama period (1576–1600) was typified by huge gardens, gilded screen paintings and brilliant textile work. The first Westerners arrived, bringing with them technology and treasures unlike anything seen before in Japan.

During the Edo period (1600–1867), Japan shut itself off from the world and its arts coalesced into the forms they are known by today. With the rise of the merchant class, art was no longer the province of emperors and nobles, and Japanese artists could now sell their work to a much wider audience. The most important development was the ukiyo-e wood-block print depicting the 'floating world' of Edo courtesans and *kabuki* actors.

From the Meiji Restoration, Japan's arts have been revolutionised by contact with the West, with Japanese artists moving swiftly from imitation to innovation.

Performing Arts

The two most famous Japanese theatrical traditions are kabuki and nō. Both forms work well as spectacle and some theatres have programs with an English synopsis, or even headphones for an English commentary.

Other forms of theatre include the comic drama of *kyōgen;* the puppet theatre known as *bunraku; rakugo,* which employs comic narrative; and *manzai,* a style of comic narrative.

See the Entertainment chapter for details on where you can see performances of some of these arts.

Kabuki The origins of kabuki lie in the early 17th century when a maiden of a shrine led a troupe of women dancers to raise funds for the shrine. Soon prostitutes were performing the lead roles until the Tokugawa government banned women from the kabuki stage; they were replaced with attractive young men, and finally by older men. This had a profound effect on kabuki, as these older male actors required greater artistry to credibly perform their roles. Thus, while remaining a popular art form, kabuki also became a serious art form.

Kabuki employs opulent sets, a boom-crash orchestra and a ramp through the audience to allow important actors to get the most out of their melodramatic entrances and exits. Kabuki mostly deals with feudal tragedies, of the struggle between duty and inner feelings; the latter has produced a large body of work on the theme of love suicides.

Unlike the theatre of the West, the playwright is not the applauded champion of kabuki; the play is merely a vehicle for the genius of the actor.

Nō An older form of theatre, nō dates back some 600 years. It seems to have evolved as a cross-pollination between indigenous Shintō-related dance and mime traditions, and dance forms that originated elsewhere in Asia. It was adopted as a courtly performing art and underwent numerous refinements, becoming an essentially religious theatre whose aesthetic codes were defined by the minimalism of Zen. The power of nō lies in understatement. Its use of masks as a mode of expression and the bleak emptiness of its sets direct all attention to the performers.

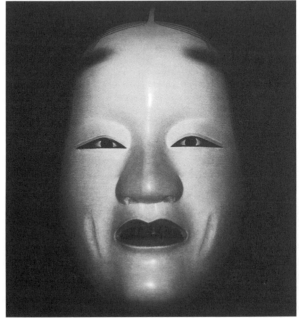

Right: In *nō* theatre masks are an integral part of the character's role. Although at first glance the masks seem expressionless, emotions can be expressed by a slight change in the angle of the mask when worn, reflections of light, chanting and musical accompaniment.

STUART WASSERMAN

Kyōgen A comic drama that originally served as a light interlude within a nō play, kyōgen is now more often performed separately between two different nō plays. Kyōgen draws on the real world for its subject matter and actors use colloquial Japanese. The subjects of its satire are often samurai, depraved priests and faithless women – the performers are without masks and a chorus often accompanies the drama.

Bunraku Like kabuki, bunraku developed in the Edo period. It is Japan's professional puppet theatre, using puppets that are a half to two-thirds life-size and hand-held, controlled by three puppeteers dressed in black robes and usually hooded. On a raised dais near the stage, a narrator *(tayū)* tells the story and provides the voices for individual characters, while musical accompaniment is provided by the three-stringed *shamisen*.

Rakugo The Chinese characters for rakugo literally mean 'the dropped word', and this art of comic narrative is thought to have emerged from the warlord practice of including comic storytellers in retinues for light amusement. It is delivered by a solitary kimono-clad performer, most commonly a middle-aged man, seated on a cushion in the centre of a propless stage. Performers are unaccompanied except for a brief musical flourish of shamisen, flute and drums which announces their entrance and exit. Vocal mimicry and facial contortions are used to comic and dramatic effect throughout the storytelling. The entertainers typically keep a traditional paper fan in the fold in their kimono which is repeatedly drawn and replaced during their routine.

Rakugo has a contemporary cousin called *manzai*, also highly popular in the Kansai region. This freewheeling comedy style is based on a call and response between the clever one *(tsukome)* and the fool *(boke)*. Manzai language reaches its peak of humour when neighbourly conversation turns quarrelsome. The largest manzai troupe is the Osaka-based Yoshimoto school, which produces countless comedy duos in its distinctive style.

There are frequent performances of rakugo and manzai, primarily in Osaka, and both regularly appear on TV (a better bet for foreigners, as the racy dialogue is virtually impossible to understand).

Butō This is Japanese experimental or avant-garde dance which was born in the 1960s. Butō dancers perform nearly nude except for loincloths and their bodies are painted. Movement is drawn-out and occasionally grotesque. The exaggerated expressions are intended to express the emotions of the dancers and choreographer in the most direct way possible, making it more accessible than other types of Japanese performance art.

Unfortunately for those interested in seeing butō performed, most troupes are small and their dances underground affairs.

Right: *Koto* (plucked zither) players at a kabuki performance.

MASON FLORENCE

Music

Ancient Music *Gagaku* is the 'elegant' music of the Japanese imperial court. It flourished in the 8th to 12th centuries, and became part of a revived interest in national traditions during the Meiji period.

The repertoire of an orchestra included *kangen* (instrumental) pieces and *bugaku* (dance) pieces. Nowadays, a gagaku ensemble usually consists of 16 players performing on drums and kettle drums, string instruments such as the *biwa* (lute) and *koto* (plucked zither), and wind instruments such as the *hichiriki* (Japanese oboe) and various types of flute.

Traditional Instruments Several traditional instruments continue to play a part in Japanese life. The three-stringed shamisen resembles a banjo with an extended neck. It was very popular during the Edo period and is still used as formal accompaniment in kabuki and bunraku. The ability to perform on the shamisen remains one of the essential skills of a geisha.

The *koto* is a type of plucked zither with 13 strings, adapted from a Chinese instrument before the 8th century. A bass koto, with 17 strings, has been created this century. The *biwa*, which resembles a lute, was also derived from a Chinese instrument. It was played by travelling musicians, often blind, to accompany recitations of Buddhist *sutras* (collections of dialogues and discourses). Most recently, the composer Takemitsu Tōru has found a niche for the biwa amongst Western orchestras.

The *shakuhachi* is a wind instrument that was popularised by wandering Komusō monks in the 16th and 17th centuries, who played it as a means to enlightenment.

Taiko refers to any of a number of large Japanese drums often played at festivals or in parades. The drummers train year-round to endure the rigours of playing these enormous drums.

A Word Is Worth a Thousand Pictures

Bashō Matsuo, considered the father of haiku poetry (though the form originated in the 15th century), wielded the sword before picking up the pen. Born in Ueno, Mie Prefecture, in 1644 to a samurai family, the young Bashō studied the art of war in preparation for becoming a samurai. He swore loyalty to a local lord and would have gone on to become a regular fighting man, if not for two unforeseen events. First, the lord to whom Bashō had sworn loyalty was something of an aesthete who took to instructing his protege in the art of poetry. Second, the lord passed away while Bashō was only 22. Instead of finding another master, Bashō set out for Kyoto in search of culture and excitement.

After some time spent among the literati of the capital, Bashō moved to Edo (now Tokyo), where he refined his poetry and gained enough recognition to support himself as a teacher of haiku. In the fall of 1684, Bashō embarked on a voyage westward, hoping to quell an inner restlessness which had plagued him in the city. This was the first of the major voyages which would become the hallmark of his poetic life.

Back in Edo, Bashō studied Zen under a teacher by the name of Butchō. Zen philosophy had a deep impact on his work, and many comparisons have been made between his haiku and Zen *koan* (short riddles intended to bring about a sudden flash of insight in the listener). Indeed, the best of Bashō's haiku have the effect of a koan on the listener – a rare case of a word being worth a thousand pictures.

Bashō was also influenced by the natural philosophy of the Chinese Taoist sage Chuangzi, from whom he learned a way of looking at nature uncritically – seeing the 'just-so-ness' of each object. Later, he developed his own poetic principle by drawing on the concept of *sabi*, usually translated as a kind of spare, lonely beauty. This lonely beauty is perhaps better experienced than explained, a good example being a haiku he wrote in Arano:

on a withered branch
a crow is perched
an autumn evening

Bashō embarked on three more poetic pilgrimages in his life and was in the midst of a fourth when he fell sick and died in Osaka in 1694. His ceaseless peregrination certainly qualifies Bashō as the poet laureate of the traveller, to whom he addressed this haiku:

traveller's heart
never settled long in one place
like a portable fire

After his death, Bashō's disciples went on to popularise the art of haiku, and today haiku is the best known of Japan's literary arts. For those who would like to delve deeper into Bashō's poetry, the most comprehensive books on the subject are *Bashō's Haiku, Volumes I and II* by Oseko Toshiharu.

Literature

Japan's first real literature, the *Kojiki* (Record of Ancient Matters) and *Nihon Shoki* (Chronicle of Japan), were written in the 8th century in emulation of Chinese historical accounts. Later, Japanese literature developed its own voice; interestingly, much of the early literature was written by women. One reason for this was that men wrote in imported Chinese characters, while women were relegated to writing in Japanese script *(hiragana)*. Thus, while the men were busy copying Chinese styles and texts, women were inadvertently producing the first authentic Japanese literature. Among these early female authors is Murasaki Shikibu, who wrote Japan's all-time classic *Genji Monogatari* (The Tale of Genji), documenting the intrigues and romances of early Japanese court life.

The Narrow Road to the Deep North is a travel classic by the revered Japanese poet Bashō Matsuo. *Kokoro*, by Sōseki Natsume, is a modern classic depicting the conflict between old and new Japan in the mind and heart of an aged scholar. The modern and the traditional also clash in the lives of two couples in *Some Prefer Nettles* by Tanizaki Junichirō. *The Makioka Sisters*, also by Tanizaki, is a family chronicle that has been likened to a modern-day *Monogatari*. Ibuse Masuji's *Black Rain* is a response to Japan's defeat in WWII.

Mishima Yukio's *The Golden Pavilion* reconstructs the life of a novice monk who burned down Kyoto's Kinkaku-ji in 1950. Mishima is probably the most controversial of Japan's modern writers and is considered unrepresentative of Japanese culture by many Japanese – his work makes for interesting reading.

Not all Japanese fiction can be classified as literature. Murakami Ryū's *Almost Transparent Blue* is strictly sex and drugs, and was a blockbuster in the 70s. Murakami has written another provocative bestseller for the '90s in *Coin Locker Babies*. Murakami Haruki is another bestselling author; novels available in English include *A Wild Sheep Chase* and *Dance, Dance, Dance* – both touch on sheep and Hokkaidō. Banana Yoshimoto has had unaccountable international success for her poorly translated novel *Kitchen*.

Ōe Kenzaburō is Japan's Nobel laureate. Look for *Pluck the Buds, Shoot the Kids* – which must rate alongside Mishima's *The Sailor Who Fell from Grace with the Sea* as one of the best titles in modern Japanese fiction – and his semi-autobiographical *A Personal Matter*, about how the birth of a brain-damaged child affects the father.

Film

Motion pictures were first imported in 1896 during the Meiji Restoration and, in characteristic fashion, the Japanese were making their own by 1899. Until the advent of talkies, dialogue and general explanation of what was going on was provided by the *benshi*, a live commentator, who became as important a part of the cinematic experience as the film itself.

In the early 1900s, Kyoto became the centre of Japan's motion picture industry, earning itself the designation of 'the Hollywood of Japan', having at one time 15 movie studios (only two remain). In the 1920s, a split developed between period films *(jidaigeki)* and new films *(gendaigeki)* which followed modern themes. The more realistic story-lines of gendaigeki soon reflected on traditional films with the introduction of *shin jidaigeki*, or 'new period films'.

During this era, samurai themes became an enduring staple of Japanese cinema. After WWII, feudal films with their emphasis on blind loyalty and martial ability were banned by the Allied authorities, but cinematic energy soon turned to new pursuits, including animated films, monster movies and comedies.

The '50s are generally considered the golden age of Japanese cinema. Director Kurosawa Akira gained international success when his *Rashōmon* (1950) took the top prize at the 1951 Venice Film Festival. His *Shichinin-no-Samurai* (Seven Samurai; 1954) gained the ultimate accolade when it was shamelessly ripped off by the Hollywood blockbuster *The Magnificent Seven*. Other Kurosawa classics include *Yōjimbō* (1961), the tale of a masterless samurai who single-handedly cleans up a small town bedevilled by two warring gangs, and *Ran* (1985), an epic historical film.

In the '70s and '80s, Japanese cinema retreated before the onslaught of international movie-making, in part because of a failure to develop new independent film-making companies. Nonetheless, Itami Jūzō's *Tampopo* (1985) is a wonderful comedy weaving vignettes on the themes of food and sex into a story about a Japanese noodle restaurant. From the same director came *Marusa-no-Onna* (A Taxing Woman; 1988), an amusing insight into taxation, Japanese style. It was so popular in Japan that it spawned the equally amusing *A Taxing Woman 2*. Harada Masato's 1995 film *Kamikaze Taxi* had some art-house success in the West. Shohei Imamura's film *Unagi* (The Eel), a delightful tale of sin and redemption, set in a Japanese barber shop, was joint winner of the Palm d'Or at Cannes in 1997, and has only recently been released in the USA.

Scenes from movies and TV shows are occasionally shot at Kyoto's Tōei Uzumasa Eiga Mura (Movie Village), now also a popular theme park, and the city is frequently used as a location for shooting both period and contemporary films.

Fine Arts

Painting By the end of the Heian period the emphasis on religious themes painted according to Chinese conventions gave way to a purely Japanese style, known as yamato-e. Ink paintings *(suiboku-ga* or *sumi-e)* by Chinese Zen artists were introduced during the Muromachi period and copied by Japanese artists, who produced hanging pictures *(kakemono)*, scrolls *(e-maki)*, and decorated screens and sliding doors *(fusuma-e)*. During the Momoyama period, Japan's daimyō commissioned artists who painted in flamboyant colours and embellished with copious gold leaf.

Western techniques, including the use of oils, were introduced during the 16th century by the Jesuits, and the ensuing Edo period was marked by the enthusiastic patronage of a wide range of painting styles. The Kanō school was in demand for the depiction of subjects connected with Confucianism, mythical Chinese creatures or scenes from nature, while the Tosa school, whose members followed the yamato-e style, were commissioned by the nobility to paint scenes from the classics of Japanese literature.

The Rimpa school not only absorbed the style of these other schools but progressed to produce a strikingly original decorative style. The works produced by Tawaraya Sōtatsu, Honami Kōetsu and Ogata Kōrin of this school rank among the finest of the period.

Calligraphy Shodō (the way of writing) is one of Japan's most valued arts, cultivated by nobles, priests and samurai alike, and studied by Japanese schoolchildren today as shūji. It was imported from China, but in the Heian period a more fluid and cursive style evolved called wayō. The Chinese style (karayō) remained popular in Japan, even after the Heian period, among Zen priests and the literati.

In both Chinese and Japanese shodō there are three important styles. Most common is kaisho, or block-style script. Due to its clarity, this style is favoured in the media and in applications where readability is a must. Gyōsho, or running hand, is semicursive, and often used in informal correspondence. Sōsho, or grass hand, is a truly cursive style. Sōsho abbreviates and links the characters together to create a flowing, graceful effect; it is popular for calligraphy.

LPP

Ukiyo-e The term ukiyo-e, or wood-block print, comes from ukiyo, a Buddhist metaphor for the transient world of fleeting pleasures. The subjects chosen by artists were from the 'floating world' of the entertainment quarters in Kyoto's Gion, of Osaka and Edo.

The floating world was an inversion of all the usual social hierarchies held in place by the power of the Tokugawa shōgunate. Here, money counted for more than rank, actors and artists were the arbiters of style, and prostitutes elevated their art to such a level that their social and artistic accomplishments matched those of the ladies of noble families.

Right: An example of calligraphy by one of the great Zen masters, Sengai Gibon (1750–1837).

Added to this was an element of spectacle. The vivid colours, novel composition and flowing lines of ukiyo-e caused great excitement in the West, sparking a vogue which a French art critic dubbed 'Japonisme'. Ukiyo-e became a key influence on impressionist (eg, Toulouse-Lautrec,

Manet and Degas) and postimpressionist artists. But among the Japanese, the prints were hardly given more than passing consideration – millions were produced annually in Edo. For many years, the Japanese were perplexed by the keen interest foreigners took in this art form, which they considered of ephemeral value.

The first prints of ukiyo-e were made in black and white in the early 17th century; the technique for colour printing was only developed in the middle of the 18th century. The first stage of production required the artist *(eshi)* to draw a design on transparent paper and indicate the colouring needed. The engraver *(horishi)* then pasted the design face down on a block of cherry wood and carved out the lines of the design in relief. The printer *(surishi)* inked the block and took a proof. Each colour required a separate block; it was up to the printer to obtain accurate alignment and subtle colour effects that depended on the colour mixture and pressure applied.

The reputed founder of ukiyo-e was Iwa Matabei. The genre was later developed by Hishikawa Moronobu, whose wood-block prints of scenes from the entertainment district of Yoshiwara in Edo introduced the theme of *bijin-e* (paintings of beautiful women). Early themes also covered scenes from the theatre (including the actors) and erotic prints known as *shunga*. Kitagawa Utamarō is famed for his bijin-e which emphasise the erotic and sensual beauty of his subjects. All that is known about the painting prodigy Tōshūsai Sharaku is that he produced 145 superb portraits of kabuki actors between 1794 and 1795.

Toward the end of the Edo period, two painters produced outstanding works in this genre. Hokusai Katsushika was a prolific artist who observed his fellow Edo inhabitants with a keen sense of humour. His most famous works include manga, *Fugaku Sanjūrokkei* (Thirty-Six Views of Mt Fuji) and *Fugaku Hyakkei* (One Hundred Views of Mt Fuji).

Hiroshige Andō followed Hokusai, specialising in landscapes, although he also created splendid prints of plants and birds. His most celebrated works include *Tōkaidō Gojūsan-tsugi* (Fifty-Three Stations of the Tōkaidō) and *Omi Hakkei* (Eight Views of Omi) – Omi is now known as Biwa-ko.

Left: Wood block prints taken from *Ehon Sakae-Gusa* (The Illustrated Book of Family Prosperity), Katsukawa (Shuncho), 1790.

Crafts

Craftworkers in Japan have always enjoyed the same esteem accorded artists, and crafts are prized as highly as works of fine art. Since the 8th century, Kyoto's workshops have produced the full spectrum of Japanese crafts; there are still many craftspeople maintaining these traditions in Kyoto. For information on where to see craftspeople at work or take courses in traditional crafts, see the Activities section of the Things to See & Do chapter.

Pottery & Ceramics Ceramic art *(tōjiki)* progressed greatly around the 13th century with the introduction of Chinese techniques and the founding of a kiln in 1242 at Seto in Aichi. One Japanese term for pottery and porcelain, *setomono* (literally, things from Seto), clearly derives from this still-thriving ceramics centre.

The popularity of the tea ceremony in the 16th century stimulated developments in ceramics. The great tea masters, Furuta Oribe and Sen no Rikyū, promoted production of exquisite Oribe and Shino wares in Gifu. Toyotomi Hideyoshi encouraged the master potter Chōjiro to create works of art from clay found near his palace. Chōjiro was allowed to embellish the tea bowls he created with the character *raku* (enjoyment). This was the beginning of Kyoto's famous *raku-yaki* style of pottery. Tea bowls soon became highly prized; today's connoisseurs will pay as much as US$30,000 for just the right tea bowl.

Evidence of the first Kyoto wares *(kyō-yaki)* dates to the reign of Emperor Shōmu in the early 8th century. By the mid-1600s there were more than 10 different kilns active in and around the city; of these, only Kiyomizu-yaki remains today. This kiln first gained prominence through the workmanship of potter Nonomura Ninsei (1596–1660), who developed here an innovative method of applying enamel overglaze to porcelain. This technique was further cultivated by adding decorative features such as transparent glaze *(sometsuke)* and incorporating designs in red paint *(aka-e)* and celadon *(seiji)*.

Kiyomizu-yaki is still actively produced in Kyoto and remains popular with devotees of tea ceremony.

During the Edo period, many daimyō encouraged the founding of kilns and the production of superbly designed ceramic articles. The climbing kiln *(noborigama)* was widely used, and a fine example can be seen at the home of famed Kyoto potter Kawai Kanjirō.

Constructed on a slope, the climbing kiln had as many as 20 chambers and it could reach temperatures as high as 1400°C.

LPP

During the Meiji period, ceramics waned in popularity, but were later part of a general revival in *mingei-hin* (folk arts). This movement was led by Yanagi Sōetsu, who encouraged famous potters such as Kawai, Tomimoto Kenkichi and Hamada Shōji. The English potter Bernard Leach studied in Japan under Hamada and contributed to the folk-art revival. On his return to England, Leach promoted the appreciation of Japanese ceramics in the West.

There are now over 100 pottery centres in Japan, with a large number of artisans producing everything from exclusive tea utensils to souvenir badges *(tanuki)*. Department stores regularly organise exhibitions of ceramics. The TIC's useful *Ceramic Art & Crafts in Japan* leaflet provides full details of kilns, pottery centres and pottery fairs in Japan.

Lacquerware The Japanese have been using lacquer to protect and enhance wood since the Jōmon period. In the Meiji era, lacquerware became very popular abroad and remains one of Japan's best-known products. Today, Kyoto lacquerware *(kyō-shikki)* is highly regarded for its elegance and sound construction.

Lacquerware *(shikki* or *nurimono)* is made using the sap from the lacquer tree *(urushi)*. Once lacquer hardens it becomes inert and extraordinarily durable. The most common colour of lacquer is an amber or brown, but additives are used to produce black, violet, blue, yellow and even white. In the better pieces, multiple layers of lacquer are painstakingly applied and left to dry, and finally polished to a luxurious shine.

Japanese artisans have devised various ways to further enhance the beauty of lacquer. The most common method is *maki-e*, which involves the sprinkling of silver and gold powders onto liquid lacquer to form a picture. After the lacquer dries, another coat seals the picture. The final effect is often dazzling and several of the better examples of maki-e lacquerware are now National Treasures.

FRANK CARTER

Left: A deceptively simple *maki-e* wave design on a laquer box, Sanzen-in.

Right: Decorated fabrics.
Such beautiful fabrics are
worn by many Kyotoites
at important festivals.

Textiles An important role has always been played in Japanese society by textiles: the fabric used in a kimono was an indication of class status. Until the introduction of cotton in the 16th century, Japanese textiles were made mostly of bast fibres or silk. Of all Japanese textiles, intricately embroidered brocades have always been the most highly prized, but sumptuary laws imposed on the merchant class in the Edo period prohibited the wearing of such kimonos.

To circumvent these laws, new techniques of kimono decoration were devised, the most important being the elaborate and ingenious technique of *yūzen*. Yūzen is best represented by Kyoto's renowned *kyō-yūzen*, a method of silk-dyeing *(senshoku)* developed to perfection in the 17th century by fan painter Miyazaki Yūzen. Kyō-yūzen designs typically feature simple circular flowers *(maru-tsukushi)*, birds and landscapes, and stand out for their use of brightly coloured dyes. The technique demands great dexterity in tracing designs by hand *(tegaki)* before rice paste is applied to fabric like a stencil to prevent colours from bleeding into other areas of the fabric. By repeatedly changing the pattern of the rice paste, very complex designs can be achieved.

Traditionally, when the dyeing process was complete, the material was rinsed in the Kamo-gawa and Katsura-gawa rivers (believed to be particularly effective in fixing the colours) before being hung out to dry. Every year in mid-August this ritual is re-enacted and the fabrics flap in the wind like rows of vibrant banners.

Kyoto is also famed for techniques in stencil-dyeing *(kyō-komon)* and tie-dyeing *(kyō-kanoko shibori)*. Kyō-komon (komon means small crest) gained notoriety in the 16th and 17th centuries, particularly among warriors who ordered the adornment of both their armour and kimono, through the stencilling of highly geometric designs onto fine silk with vibrant colours. Typically the patterns incorporate flowers, leaves and other flora.

ARTS

For those who thought tie-dyeing was invented by T-shirt touting Grateful Dead heads, think again. Kyoto's tie-dyeing is said to date as far back as the 6th century, and numerous allusions to its glamour appear in literature as early as the 17th century. By the early 18th century, tie-dyed kimono were at the height of fashion, sought after for the astonishing detail created out of thousands of tiny sections of cloth, each bit individually plucked to form a motif and tied tightly using silk thread. All tediously set by hand, it could take as long as six months just to complete enough fabric to produce one kimono, yet people still practice the craft and employ new techniques.

At the other end of the refined, courtly spectrum, *aizome* (the technique of dyeing fabrics in vats of fermented indigo plants) gave Japan one of its most distinctive colours. Used traditionally in making hardy work clothes for the fields, Japan's beautiful indigo-blue can still be seen in many modern-day textile goods.

Together with Kyoto-dyed fabrics *(kyō-zome)*, Nishijin weaving *(Nishijin-ori)* is internationally renowned and dates to the founding of the city. Nishijin techniques were originally developed to satisfy the demands of the nobility who favoured the quality of illustrious silk fabrics. Over time new methods were adopted by the Kyoto weavers and they began to experiment with materials such as gauze, brocade, damask, satin and crepe.

During the turbulent civil wars of the 15th century, Kyoto's weavers congregated into a textiles quarter near the Kitano-Tenman-gū shrine called Nishijin (literally, Western Camp). The industry was revamped during the Edo period and the popularity of Nishijin workmanship endured through the Meiji Restoration. In 1915, the Orinasu-kan textile museum was established to display Nishijin's fine silk fabrics and embroidery.

The best known Nishijin style is the exquisite *tsuzure*, a tightly woven tapestry cloth produced with a hand loom *(tebata)*, on which detailed patterns are preset. Kyoto's weavers, however, have continually introduced new styles, such as Japanese brocade *nishiki* (woven on Jacquard looms first imported from France around the turn of the century). Even today, innovative methods are being employed, such as the utilisation of computers, both for creating new designs and to pilot automated looms.

Woodwork If jade is the perfect medium for the expression of the Chinese artistic genius, then wood is the perfect medium for the Japanese. Perhaps nowhere else in the world has the art of joinery been lifted to such levels, and the carpentry and woodwork of Kyoto *(kyō-sashimono)* is among the best in the country.

Once a variety of wood types has been carefully chosen, preparations to properly season them can take up to 10 years. Craftspeople work with superior woods, such as cedar *(sugi)*, cherry *(sakura)*, zelkova *(keyaki)*, mulberry *(kuwa)* and paulownia *(kiri)*. They also work with many types of finish, including oils, wax, lacquer and juices of fruits such as persimmon and lime.

Kyoto produces a plethora of wooden furniture and household goods.

Particularly admired by collectors of Japanese antiques are chests called *tansu*, and the most prized of these is the *kaidan dansu*, so-named because it doubles as a flight of stairs (kaidan means stairs). These are becoming increasingly difficult to find, and increasingly expensive, but determined hunting at flea markets and antique shops may still land the occasional good piece.

Another realm of Kyoto wood products is *sadō-sashimono*, props and utensils employed in tearooms *(cha-shitsu)* and used in tea ceremony. High-quality wooden trays, shelves and delicately shaped water containers are an important part of tea ceremony.

Kyoto is also famous for its superb bamboo crafts *(chikkōhin)*, in particular the tools used in tea ceremony like ladles and whisks (which make interesting souvenirs). Japanese bamboo baskets are among the finest in the world and are remarkable for their complexity and delicacy (as well as their price). Be careful when buying bamboo crafts in Japan, as many are cheap imitations imported from countries such as China and the Philippines.

Dolls Among the finest of Japan's handcrafted dolls *(ningyō)* are Kyoto's *kyō-ningyō*. Elaborate in detail and dressed in fine brocade fabrics, they date from the Heian period and their exquisite costumes reflect the taste and styles of that aristocratic time.

Right: A finely crafted *kyō-ningyō* (traditional Kyoto doll).

MASON FLORENCE

Today, dolls figure prominently in two Japanese festivals: the Hina Matsuri (Doll Festival) held on 3 March, when girls display rows of ornamental *hina-ningyō* on tiered platforms in their homes, and on Children's Day (5 May), when both boys and girls display these special dolls.

Some other common dolls are *daruma* dolls, which are based on the figure of Bodhidharma, the religious sage commonly considered to be the founder of Zen Buddhism; *gosho-ningyō*, chubby plaster dolls sometimes dressed as figures in nō dramas; *kiku-ningyō*, large dolls adorned with real chrysanthemum flowers; and *ishō-ningyō*, which is a general term for elaborately costumed dolls, sometimes based on kabuki characters.

Fans Easily recognisable, the folding fan *(sensu)* is one of the few remaining symbols of traditional Japan still commonly used (it is not unusual to see blue-suited businessmen fanning themselves on the train during the rush-hour heat of summer).

As with many of Japan's traditional crafts, fans were first made in Kyoto and continue to be prolifically produced here. *Kyō-sensu* first found popularity among the early aristocracy, but by the late 12th century had spread to the general populace. Though fans were originally a practical and fashionable tool to keep oneself cool in Japan's sweltering summers, they gradually took on more aesthetic purposes as Japan's arts flourished from the 15th century onwards, from plain fans used in tea ceremony and incense smelling, to elaborate ones used in nō drama and traditional dance. Fans are still commonly used as decorative items and for ceremonial purposes.

Originally made from the leaves of the cypress tree, fans are now primarily made with elaborately painted Japanese paper fixed onto a skeleton of delicate bamboo ribs. The paper can feature decorations from simple geometric designs to courtly scenes from the Heian period and are often sprinkled with gold or silver leaf powder. The meticulous, step-by-step process of making kyō-sensu is fascinating to watch at one of the Kyoto fan-making studios that is open to the public.

MASON FLORENCE

Left: *Kyō-sensu* fans are delicate and meticulously constructed.

Washi Traditional Japanese handmade paper was introduced from China in the 5th century and reached its golden age in the Heian era, when it was highly prized by members of the Kyoto court for their poetry and diaries. Washi continued to be made in large quantities until the introduction of Western paper in the 1870s. After that time, the number of families involved in the craft plummeted. However, there are still a number of traditional papermakers active in Kyoto, as well as in the Yoshino area south of Nara city. Recently, washi has enjoyed something of a revival (there's even washi for computer printers!) and a large variety is available in several of Kyoto's speciality stores (see the Shopping chapter).

Flower Arrangement

Ikebana, the art of flower arranging, was developed in the 15th century and can be grouped into three main styles: *rikka* (standing flowers), *shōka* (living flowers) and free-style techniques such as *nageire* (throwing-in) and *moribana* (heaped flowers). There are several thousand different schools, the top three being Ikenobō, Ōhara and Sōgetsu, but they share one aim: to arrange flowers to represent heaven, earth and humanity. Ikebana displays were originally used as part of tea ceremony, but can now be found in private homes – in the *tokonoma* (alcove for displays) – and even in large hotels.

Apart from its cultural associations, ikebana is also a lucrative business – its schools have millions of students, including many young women who view proficiency in the art as a means to improve their marriage prospects.

Gardens

For garden enthusiasts, look no further. Kyoto is *the* place, home to a vast collection of Japan's foremost gardens encompassing the entire spectrum of styles.

Unlike European gardens, you probably won't find flowers, water fountains and flowing streams in Japanese gardens, and grass rarely makes an appearance. No matter how random a Japanese garden looks – with its mossy rocks, gnarled roots, haphazard paving and meandering paths – it is meticulously planned, right down to the last pebble. In the best Japanese gardens there is an exquisite 'compositional' quality, and no component is without a nuance of meaning. Even features that lie outside the garden may influence the layout – *shakkei*, or borrowed scenery, may make use of distant hills or a river, even the cone of a volcano. One example of this is the garden at Shūgaku-in Rikyū Imperial Villa in northern Kyoto, which incorporates mountains 10km distant.

Japanese gardens fall into four basic types: *funa asobi* (pleasure boat style), *shūyū* (stroll style), *kanshō* (contemplative style) and *kaiyū* (many pleasure style).

The funa asobi garden is centred on a large pond used for pleasure boating. The best views are from the water. In the Heian period, such gardens were often built around noble mansions, the most outstanding remaining example being the garden which surrounds Byōdō-in in Uji.

The shūyū garden is intended to be viewed from a winding path, allowing the garden to unfold and reveal itself in stages and from different vantages. Popular during the Heian, Kamakura and Muromachi periods, shūyū gardens can be found around many noble mansions and temples from those eras. A celebrated example is at Kyoto's Ginkaku-ji.

The kanshō garden should be viewed from one place; Zen rock gardens, the rock and raked gravel spaces that are also known as *karesansui*, or dry mountain stream gardens, are an example of this sort. The kanshō garden is designed to facilitate contemplation: such a garden can be viewed over and over without yielding to any one 'interpretation' of its meaning. The most famous kanshō garden of all is at Ryōan-ji in Kyoto.

Lastly, the kaiyū, or many pleasure garden, features many small gardens surrounding a central pond, often incorporating a teahouse. The structure of this garden, like the stroll garden, lends itself to being explored on foot, and provides the viewer with a variety of changing scenes, many built as miniature landscapes. The most famous kaiyū garden is at the Katsura Rikyū Imperial Villa.

MASON FLORENCE

Left: Winter drizzle accentuates the austere style of the dry landscaped rock garden (*karesansui*).

continued from page 32

For example, shoes should be removed when entering a Japanese home or entering a *tatami* (woven floor matting) room of any kind, even when entering a change room – Japanese will not make allowances for foreign customs in this case.

Bathing in Japan also conforms to fairly strict rules and you should follow them. Whether it's a Japanese-style bath in a private home, a *sentō* (public bath) or an *onsen* (mineral or spa bath), remember that body-washing takes place *before* entering the water. Showers or taps and plastic tubs are provided for this purpose. Baths and onsen are for soaking in *after* you have washed.

As in other parts of Asia, the respectful way to indicate that someone should approach you is to wave your fingers with the palm downwards.

Japanese don't eat food in the street unless there are seats provided for them to sit on while they do so. Ice creams are an exception to this rule. It's up to you whether you want to abide by this custom: no-one's going to be particularly upset if they see you wandering down the street munching on a Big Mac.

Meeting the Japanese

One of the best ways to meet Kyotoites is by checking the listings for local events in *Kansai Time Out*. The Kyoto International Community House (KICH) sponsors a noteworthy homevisit program where, with a day's notice, you can arrange to visit the home of a local Kyoto family. Bringing a small gift, especially from home, is always appreciated. You can apply over the phone by calling ☎ 752 3511. There is also a message board at KICH which can provide some interesting leads on meeting people (for more information on KICH see the Useful Organisations section in the Facts for the Visitor chapter).

Being such a large college town, universities also provide places for meeting people. All schools have a variety of clubs from English Speaking Society (ESS) networks to ecogroups and an ample number of computer nerds (see the Universities section in the Facts for the Visitor chapter). Some universities even have clubs which provide free tour-guide services for foreign visitors, and the TIC should be able to give you leads on how to contact them.

Last, but surely not least, is Kyoto's vast assortment of 'something for everyone' watering holes. Like it or not, these bars are practically a fail-safe facility for finding conversation, and alcohol does have a tendency to take away the shyness (see the Entertainment chapter for a sample of places).

Shyness Perhaps the most difficult aspect of getting to meet the Japanese is their almost chronic shyness. Young Japanese generally have been discouraged from taking individual initiative and consequently, visitors are perhaps more likely to be surrounded by a gaggle of giggling school children chorusing 'Haro!' than having an interesting conversation with a Japanese. Some young Japanese will simply freeze in embarrassed silence if directly addressed by a foreigner. Unfortunately, the same applies to many adults if they have had little experience talking to non-Japanese.

Much of this shyness stems from fear of making a mistake and somehow causing offence. If you need to make casual contact with a Japanese, say, to ask directions, try to appear calm and relaxed and smile as you talk.

RELIGION

Religion in Japan is a complex issue, intimately connected with the culture as a whole. Western commentators inevitably focus on the way the Japanese are able to reconcile being simultaneously Shintō and Buddhist. It is far from the contradiction it may seem: Shintō is not really a religion in the conventional sense. It is more like a cultural framework that defines the essence of Japanese culture. A Japanese cannot escape being Shintō any more than a foreigner would be able to convert to it.

The rituals of both Shintō and Buddhism are used depending on their appropriateness to a particular situation – Shintō tends to be used for joyful events (such as weddings) and Buddhism for more sombre ones (such as funerals). Many young Japanese choose also to have Christian wedding ceremonies.

Shintō

Shintō, the way of the gods, is the indigenous Japanese religion, based on respect and awe of natural phenomena. The most powerful of these – the sun, moon, weather, mountain tops, trees, rivers, even grains of rice – are considered to contain their own gods *(kami)*. Shrines are erected in areas considered particularly sacred.

It is difficult to trace the origins of Shintō, as it has no founder or creed. It encompasses myths of the origin of Japan and the Japanese people, beliefs and practices in local communities and the highly structured rituals associated with the imperial family. Until 1945, Shintō belief dictated that the emperor was a divine being. In fact, according to Shintō, the entire Japanese race is descended from the gods.

The concept of purification is central to Shintō. *Oharai* is the most common purification ritual, performed by a priest waving a *sakaki*, a small construction of wood, paper and leaves. Purification ceremonies are conducted for people, cars, wedding ceremonies – almost anything that requires divine assistance. Also central to Shintō are fertility rituals, and certain festivals use symbolic sex acts to pray for or celebrate a good harvest.

Shintō & Buddhism Shintō received its name in the 6th century in order to distinguish it from Buddhism. The Japanese rationalised their coexistence by considering Buddha to be a deity from China. In the 8th century, Shintō gods were enshrined in Buddhist temples as protectors of the Buddha. It was believed that kami, like human beings, were subject to the suffering of rebirth and similarly in need of Buddhist intercession to achieve liberation. Buddhist temples were built close to Shintō shrines and Buddhist sutras (collections of dialogues and discourses) were recited for the kami.

As Buddhism came to dominate, kami were considered to be incarnations of Bodhisattvas (Buddhas who delay liberation to help others). Buddhist statues were included on Shintō altars and statues of kami were made representing Buddhist priests.

State Shintō There was a revival of interest in Shintō during the Edo period, particularly among neo-Confucian scholars. Their writings called for a return to imperial rule with Shintō as a state religion. Nationalist fervour during the Meiji period resulted in 'State Shintō' becoming the official religion. Buddhism was severely restricted and most religious sites containing both Buddhist and Shintō elements were separated. Shintō doctrines were taught in school and became central to the national ideology. After Japan's WWII defeat, the Allied forces dismantled the mechanisms of State Shintō and forced the emperor to refute his divine status.

Shugendō This somewhat offbeat Buddhist school incorporates ancient shamanistic rites, Shintō beliefs and ascetic Buddhist traditions. The founder was En-no-Gyōja, to whom legendary powers of exorcism and magic are ascribed. He is credited with the enlightenment of kami, converting them to *gongen* (manifestations of Buddhas). Practitioners of Shugendō, called *yamabushi* (mountain priests), train both body and spirit with arduous exercises in the mountains. During the Meiji era, Shugendō was barred as being culturally debased, and today yamabushi are more common in tourist brochures and popular fiction than in the flesh. Shugendō survives, however, on mountains such as Dewa Sanzan and Ōmine-san in Nara prefecture.

Buddhism

The founder of Buddhism was Siddhartha Gautama, the son of King Suddhodana and Queen Mahamaya of the Sakya clan. He was born around 563 BC at Lumbini on the border of present-day Nepal and India. In his 20s, Prince Siddhartha left his wife and newborn son to follow the path of an ascetic. When this didn't work out, Siddhartha tried meditation. During the night of the full moon in May, at the age of 35, he became 'the enlightened' or 'awakened one' – the Buddha (Nyorai in Japanese).

As the number of his followers grew, he founded a monastic community and codified the principles according to which the monks should live. The Buddha continued to preach and travel for 45 years, until his death in 483 BC. Buddhists believe that he is just one of the many Buddhas who have appeared in the past and who will continue to appear in the future.

Approximately 140 years after Buddha's death, the Buddhist community diverged into two schools: Hinayana and Mahayana, known as the Lesser Vehicle and the Greater Vehicle respectively. The distinction was made by the Mahayana, and they could just as easily be defined as the southern and northern schools. The essential difference between the two is that Hinayana supports those who strive for the salvation of the individual, whereas Mahayana supports those who strive for the salvation of all beings. Traditionally, Hinayana prospered in south India and later spread to Sri Lanka, Myanmar (Burma), Thailand, Cambodia, Indonesia and Malaysia. Mahayana spread to inner Asia, as well as Mongolia, Siberia, Japan, China and Tibet.

Buddhism was introduced to Japan from China via Korea in the 6th century. Shōtoku Taishi, acknowledged as the 'father of Japanese Buddhism', drew heavily on Chinese culture to form a centralised state based on Buddhism. Hōryū-ji is the most celebrated temple from this period.

Nara Period The establishment of the first permanent capital at Heijō-kyō (present-day Nara) in 710 also marked the consolidation of Buddhism and Chinese culture in Japan. In 741, Emperor Shōmu issued a decree for construction of a network of state temples *(kokubun-ji)*. The centrepiece of this network was Tōdai-ji.

Nara Buddhism revolved around six schools, these being Ritsu, Jōjitsu, Kusha, Sanron, Hossō and Kegon. They covered the whole range of Buddhist thought as received from China. Three of these schools still exist: Kegon, Hossō and Ritsu.

Heian Period When Kyoto became the capital of Japan in 794 it became central to the development and teaching of Buddhism. A number of new schools were established. During this period, political power drifted away from centralised government into the hands of the aristocracy, a major source of Buddhist support. The new schools, which introduced Mikkyō (esoteric Buddhism) from China, were independently founded on sacred mountains away from the orthodoxy of the Nara schools.

The Tendai school, derived from Tian-tai in China, was founded by Saichō (762–822), also known as Dengyō Daishi, who established a base at Enryaku-ji on Hiei-zan. The school was only officially recognised a few days after his death, but Enryaku-ji developed into one of Japan's key Buddhist centres and was the source of all the later important schools (Jōdo, Zen and Nichiren).

The Shingon school (derived from the Chinese term for mantra) was established by the priest Kūkai (714–835; known posthumously as Kōbō Daishi) at Kongōbu-ji on Koya-san and Tō-ji in Kyoto. Kūkai trained for government service but at the age of 18 decided to switch his studies from Confucianism and Taoism to Buddhism. He travelled as part of a mission to Chang-an in China, where he immersed himself in esoteric Buddhism. On his return, his influence included not only spreading and sponsoring the study of Mikkyō, but also compiling the first Chinese-Japanese dictionary and the *hiragana* syllabary.

During this period there was an eventual collapse of law and order and a general feeling of pessimism in society, encouraging the belief in the Mappō or End of the Law theory, which predicted an age of darkness. This set the stage for subsequent schools to introduce the notion of saviour figures such as Amida.

Kamakura Period In this period (1185–1333), marked by savage clan warfare and the transfer of the capital to Kamakura, three schools emerged from the Tendai tradition. The Jōdo (Pure Land) school was founded by Hōnen (1133–1212) and shunned scholasticism in favour of the Nembutsu, a simple prayer that required the believer to recite *'Namu Amida Butsu'* ('Hail Amida Buddha') as a path to salvation. This 'no-frills' approach was popular with the common folk.

Shinran (1173–1262), a disciple of Hōnen, broke away to form the Jōdo Shinshū (true pure land) school. The core belief of this school considered that Amida had *already* saved everyone and hence to recite the Nembutsu was an expression of gratitude, not a petition for salvation.

The Nichiren school bears the name of its founder, Nichiren (1222–82), a fiery character who spurned traditional teachings to embrace the Lotus Sutra. His followers learned to recite *'Namu Myōhō Rengekyō'*, or 'Hail the Miraculous Law of the Lotus Sutra'. Nichiren's strident demands for the religious reform of government caused antagonism all round and he was frequently booted into exile. Yet the Nichiren school increased its influence in later centuries, and many new religious movements in present-day Japan, such as Sōka Gakkai can be linked to it.

Zen

The word Zen is the Japanese reading of the Chinese *chan*. Legend has it that Bodshidharma, a 6th-century Indian monk, introduced Zen to China. Most historians, however, credit this to Huineng (618–907), a Chinese monk. It took another 200 years for Zen to take root in Japan.

It did so in two major schools: Rinzai and Sōtō. The differences between the schools are not easily explained, but at a simple level Sōtō places more emphasis on seated meditation *(zazen)* and Rinzai on riddles *(kōan)*. The object of meditation for both schools is enlightenment *(satori)*, and Zen emphasises a more direct, intuitive approach rather than rational analysis.

The practice of zazen has its roots in Indian yoga. Its posture is the lotus position: the legs are crossed and tucked beneath the sitter, the back ramrod straight, the breathing rhythmical. The idea is to block out all

sensation and empty the mind of thought. A kōan is a riddle that lacks a rational answer. Most are set pieces that owe their existence to the early evolution of Zen in China. In the course of meditating on these insoluble problems, the mind eventually returns to a form of primal consciousness. The most famous kōan was created by the Japanese monk Hakuin: 'What is the sound of one hand clapping?'

Confucianism

Although Confucianism is essentially a code of ethics pervasive throughout north Asia, it has exerted a strong enough influence to become part of Japanese social norms. Confucianism entered Japan via Korea in the 5th century. To regulate social behaviour, Confucius took the family unit as his starting point and stressed the importance of five relationships: master and subject, father and son, elder brother and younger brother, husband and wife, friend and friend. The strict observance of this social 'pecking order' has over the centuries become central to Japanese society.

Christianity

Portuguese missionaries introduced Christianity to Japan in the 16th century. In 1549, Francis Xavier landed at Kagoshima on Kyūshū. At first, the daimyō seemed eager to convert, although gaining trade advantages for Portugal, then building its empire in Asia, was just as important, if not more so.

The initial tolerance that had been shown by Oda Nobunaga was reversed by his successor, Toyotomi Hideyoshi, who saw the religious missionaries as an insidious colonial threat. Sectarian differences revealed themselves in the fight between the Jesuits and Franciscans over Japanese souls to 'balance the account'. Christianity was banned in 1587, and 26 Christians (both Japanese and foreign) were crucified in Nagasaki 10 years later. After expelling the remaining missionaries in 1614, Japan closed itself to the outside world for several centuries. The Christian faith survived in hiding during this period, mainly on Kyūshū. Christian missionaries were allowed back at the beginning of the Meiji era and built churches, hospitals and schools, many of which still exist.

It is difficult to judge the true extent of Christian influence in contemporary Japan. While many parents send their children, particularly girls, to Christian schools because of the increased exposure to English and international connections they receive there, the students largely consider themselves Buddhist or nonreligious. Mormons are active in Japan and have had relative success. However, many of their converts are simply younger Japanese trying to rebel against their parents, and often their enthusiasm wanes.

New Religions
A number of new religions have appeared since the Meiji period. They cover a wide range of beliefs, from personality cults to faith healing and UFOs. By far the largest of these new religions is Sōka Gakkai (Creative Education Society). Founded in the 1930s, it follows Nichiren's teachings and numbers over 20 million followers.

The millennial Aum Shinrikyō sect became instantly famous worldwide in 1995 with its poison gas attack on the Tokyo subway system. Under the influence of guru Shōkō Asahara, the sect had decided to speed up the apocalypse they are imminently expecting. For some time afterwards, rubbish bins disappeared from subway stations all over Japan. A number of the key Aum Shinrikyō members are still at large and their mug shots can be seen on police posters all over Japan.

Religious Services in English
Churches that conduct religious services in English include:

Kyoto International Chapel (Protestant non-Pentecostal; ☎ 0774-64 0754) at Kyō-Tanabe (south Kyoto); services 10am Sunday.
Kyoto Lutheran Church (Protestant; Map 5; ☎ 781 3903) a few minutes' walk east of the Keihan-line Demachiyanagi station; services 10.30am Sunday.
Kyoto St Agnes Episcopal Church (Interdenominational; Map 5; ☎ 0775-78 8015) only a few minutes' walk north of the Karasuma-line Marutamachi station; services 8.30am Sunday.
Shin-Ai Catholic Kindergarten (Roman Catholic; ☎ 822 8952) next to the Kyoto Royal Hotel near the Sanjō-dōri and Kawaramachi-dōri intersection; services 3pm Sunday.
St Mary's Episcopal Church (Anglican/Episcopal; Map 6; ☎ 771 2581) near the northeast corner of Heian-jingū; services 8am Sunday, followed by breakfast.

Members of the Bahai'i faith can call ☎ 712 0447 for information on local gatherings.

LANGUAGE
See the Language chapter at the back of this book for information about Japanese language and Kyoto dialect.

Facts for the Visitor

WHEN TO GO

Without a doubt, the best times to visit Kyoto are the climatically stable seasons of spring (March to May) and autumn (late September to November).

The highlight of spring is the cherry blossom season, which usually arrives in Kyoto in early April. Bear in mind, though, that the blossoms are notoriously fickle, blooming any time from late March to mid-April. Moreover, when the blossoms do come, their moment of glory is brief, lasting a mere week.

Autumn is an equally good time to travel, with pleasant temperatures and soothing autumn colours. The shrines and temples of Kyoto look stunning against a backdrop of blazing leaves, which usually peak between late October to mid-November.

Of course, the Japanese are well aware that Kyoto is most beautiful at these times, and the main attractions can be packed with local tourists. Likewise, accommodation can be hard to find; if you do come at these times, be sure to book well in advance.

Travelling in either winter or summer is a mixed bag. Mid-winter (December to February) weather can be quite cold (but not prohibitively so), while the sticky summer months (June to August) can turn even the briefest excursion out of the air-conditioning into a soup bath.

June is the month of Japan's brief rainy season, which varies in intensity from year to year; some years there's no rainy season to speak of, other years it rains virtually every day. Whatever the case, if June is the only time you can visit, by all means do so – just be sure to pack an umbrella.

Also keep in mind that peak holiday seasons, particularly 'Golden Week', which takes place in late April to early May, and the mid-summer O-bon (Festival of the Dead) can give you travel problems. Likewise, almost everything in Japan shuts down from 29 December to 3 January because of Shōgatsu (New Year celebrations) and you may find yourself surviving on fast food and convenience store rations if you're not prepared. See the Public Holidays & Special Events later in this chapter for more information.

Planning Your Itinerary

There is no limit to the amount of time you could spend exploring Kyoto. In addition to scores of cultural landmarks, Kyoto is blessed with excellent hiking, great shopping and several worthwhile destinations only a short train ride away.

The absolute minimum stay in Kyoto would be two days, in which you could just scratch the surface of sights around Kyoto station and the Higashiyama area in eastern Kyoto. Five days would give you time to add Arashiyama, western and central Kyoto. Ten days would allow you to cover these areas plus northern, southern and southeastern Kyoto and leave a day or so for places farther afield.

Kyoto is an excellent place to indulge specific cultural interests, whether they be the arts, Buddhism or arts and crafts. The best place to find information on such activities is the Tourist Information Center (TIC). The TIC has details on Zen temples that accept foreigners as students of meditation, specialist museums, Japanese gardens and villas, Japanese cooking, traditional crafts, Japanese drama, tea ceremony and *ikebana* (flower arranging).

Whatever your time limit, try not to overdo the number of sights you visit. Quite apart from the sensory overload, intensive sightseeing entails a heavy outlay on admission fees. If you don't find temples to your liking, don't visit them; there are plenty of other things to do, including shopping, people watching, strolling through the backstreets and picnicking in the parks or by the Kamo-gawa.

Kyoto also makes an excellent base for travel in western Japan and is a logical place to begin (or end) a Japan Rail Pass trip (see

Ten Things You Must Do in Kyoto

What follows is a list of ten things that will almost guarantee you a memorable experience in Kyoto:

1. Pick up a copy of the *Kyoto Visitor's Guide*. This free guide is a key to the city. See the Useful Publications section of the Facts for the Visitor chapter.
2. Get a city bus map. You can pick one up in front of Kyoto station at the main bus information centre as you arrive in the city. Armed with a bus map, you can go just about anywhere.
3. Buy a copy of *Kansai Time Out*. Supplement the information in the *Kyoto Visitor's Guide* with this excellent magazine. The best place to buy a copy is Maruzen bookshop (Map 10).
4. Visit the Kyoto TIC. The capable staff at the TIC (Map 11) can give you all the information you need to get the most out of Kyoto. Pick up maps, a transport guide, the *Kyoto Visitor's Guide* and have a look at the upcoming events board.
5. Take a walk through Nishiki Market. A trip to Nishiki Market (Map 10) should whet your appetite for all the delights that await you in Kyoto's restaurants.
6. Make the trip to Kurama. For many visitors, the half-day trip to Kurama is the highlight of their time in Kyoto. If you've got the energy, do the hike over to Kibune.
7. Go to a *sentō* (public bath). Okay, you might be shy about prancing around naked in a room full of strangers, but the sentō is *the* best way to relax after sightseeing (and it's a 'real Japan' experience to boot). See the Baths section of the Things to See & Do chapter or just ask at your lodgings for the nearest local sentō.
8. Eat at a traditional restaurant. Splash out a little for a special meal at one of Kyoto's traditional restaurants. You might wind up having one of the best meals of your life. See the Places to Eat chapter.
9. Walk down the Tetsugaku-no-michi (Path of Philosophy). Take the path less travelled (okay, extremely frequently travelled). It's one of Kyoto's nicest walks, especially during cherry blossom season.
10. Take a hike. Try one of the five walking tours or three hikes listed in the Things to See & Do chapter of this book. There's no better way to see a lot of Kyoto's most beautiful sights in a short time.

---

the Train section in the Getting There & Away chapter). For exploring the Kansai district, Kyoto is by far the best choice considering its wealth of accommodation and its proximity to renowned destinations such as Nara and Himeji. And for those who want to explore urban Japan, Osaka and Kōbe are within an hour's easy train ride away (see the Excursions chapter).

ORIENTATION

Kyoto sits in the southern part of Kyoto-fu, one of Japan's 47 prefectural regions. The city is commonly divided into five sections designating the central *(raku-chū)*, eastern *(raku-tō)*, northern *(raku-hoku)*, western *(raku-sai)* and southern *(raku-nan)* areas of town, plus *raku-gai*, which refers to the outskirts of the city.

Kyoto has retained a rectangular grid system based on the classical Chinese concept. This system of numbered streets running

east-west and avenues running north-south makes it relatively easy to find your way around. Addresses are indicated with the name of the closest intersection and their location north *(agaru)* or south *(sagaru)* of that intersection. Likewise, east *(higashi-iru)* or west *(nishi-iru)* indicate a cross-town direction.

Kyoto station is in the south of the city, and from there Karasuma-dōri runs north past Higashi Hongan-ji, the commercial centre of town and the Imperial Palace. The dining and nightlife centres are between Shijō-dōri and Oike-dōri (to the south and north of the centre respectively) and between the Gion district and Karasuma-dōri (to the east and west respectively). The less populated northern parts of the city have a far greener feel, and you can still find people tending rice fields that are sandwiched between apartment buildings. Most of the south has been overrun with industry.

Although many of the major sights are in the city centre, the best of Kyoto's sightseeing is on the fringes of the city at the base of the mountains to the north, west and east of the city centre. In fact, it's a general rule in Kyoto that the closer you get to the mountains, the more beautiful the city becomes.

Due north of the city, in the Kitayama mountains, quaint rural villages dot the landscape up to the Sea of Japan and Wakasa-wan bay, while south-west flatlands follow the path of the Yodo-gawa toward Osaka and the Seto Inland Sea. West of town are the Tanba mountains and Hyōgo-ken (prefecture) and east, just over Hiei-zan and the Higashiyama mountains, is Shiga-ken and the city's main source of water, Biwa-ko.

Efficient bus services crisscross the city. The quickest way to travel between the north and south of the city is the Karasuma line subway, while the Tōzai line subway is convenient for moving between east and west and also for reaching Yamashina and Daigo in the south-east of the city.

MAPS

Available free at the Kyoto TIC and all JNTO offices, the *Tourist Map of Kyoto-Nara* fulfils most mapping needs and includes a simplified map of the subway and bus systems. *Walking Tour Courses in Kyoto* details five good walks in and around Kyoto. Also available is the *Kyoto Transportation Guide* map which has detailed information on bus routes in the city and some of the major stops written in both English and Japanese. (Some find that the Japanese-only version, available at major bus stops and the main bus information centre in front of Kyoto station, is more useful, as all names are written in Japanese and it is more detailed.)

Another map intended for long-term foreign residents is the *Guide to Kyoto*, available free at the Kyoto International Community House (KICH; see the Useful Organisations section later in this chapter).

There are many other useful maps for sale at local English-language bookshops, some practical for excursions outside Kyoto. Shōbunsha's *Tourist Map of Kyoto, Nara, Osaka and Kōbe* is the best privately produced map of these cities.

Periplus's *Japan* map is the best English-language map of the whole country. Otherwise, JNTO's *Tourist Map of Japan*, available free at the TIC, is a good map for planning your travels around the country.

Serious hikers should pick up Shōbunsha's *Kyoto Kitayama 1* and *Kyoto Kitayama 2* maps, part of their Yama-to-Kōgen Chizu series. These two maps cover Kyoto's northern Kitayama mountains in exquisite detail, showing all hiking trails and topographical features. Unfortunately, they are written entirely in Japanese. These can be found at most local bookshops.

Kyoto Bus company's *Kyoto Kitayama/Hira-san* map, available free at their Kyoto Demachiyanagi office (next to Eizan-Dentetsu Demachiyanagi station, Map 5) is another good map of Kitayama hikes. Again, it's all in Japanese.

TOURIST OFFICES
Local Tourist Offices

The best source of information on Kyoto, Kansai and Japan is the main Kyoto TIC (Map 11; ☎ 371 5649). It's 100m north of Kyoto station, just past Kyoto Tower, on the west side of Karasuma-dōri. It's open from 9am to 5pm on weekdays, 9am to noon on Saturday, closed Sunday and holidays. It's run by the Japan National Tourism Organization (JNTO) and stocks all JNTO-produced information.

The helpful staff at the TIC have maps, literature and an amazing amount of information at their capable fingertips. Full details on accommodation are available and staff at the Welcome Inn Reservation Center counter (inside the TIC office) can make hotel and *ryokan* (traditional inn) reservations at member inns and hotels. This service is available from 9am to 5pm Monday to Friday only. Volunteer guides can also be arranged through the TIC if you allow the staff a day's notice. While you're in the TIC, be sure to check their upcoming events board to see what's on while you're in town.

The Kyoto City Tourist Information Centre (☎ 343 6656), open daily from 8.30am to 7pm, is inside the new Kyoto station building, on the second floor just across from Cafe du Monde. Though it's geared toward Japanese visitors, English speakers are usually on hand and can be of great assistance when the TIC is closed.

On the 9th floor of the Kyoto station building, the Kyoto Tourism Federation (Map 10; ☎ 371 2226) distributes information on outlying destinations in *Kyoto Prefecture* (it has very little on the city itself). Though most literature is only in Japanese, it's worth stopping by to pick up a free map of Kyoto-fu if you plan a trip to outlying areas of the prefecture. It's open daily from 9.30am to 6pm.

There's a JNTO tourist information centre at Kansai International Airport (KIX; ☎ 0724-56 6025), open daily from 9am to 9pm, on the 1st floor of the international arrivals lobby. Staff here can provide information on Kyoto, Kansai and Japan and have a Welcome Inn Reservation Center counter for hotel and ryokan reservations.

The Japan Travel-Phone (☎ 371 5649; ☎ 0088-22 4800 toll-free anywhere outside Kyoto) is a service providing travel-related information and language assistance in English. The service is available seven days a week, from 9am to 5pm. The Kyoto number can be particularly useful if you arrive between those hours on a day when the TIC is closed.

JNTO Offices Abroad
JNTO offices overseas include:

Australia (☎ 02-9232 4522) Level 33, Chifley Tower, 2 Chifley Square, Sydney, NSW 2000
Canada (☎ 416-366 7140) 165 University Ave, Toronto, Ontario M5H 3B8
China (☎ 2968 5688) Suite 3704-05, 37th floor, Dorset House, Taikoo Place, Quarry Bay, Hong Kong
France (☎ 01 42 96 20 29) 4 rue de Ventadour, 75001 Paris
Germany (☎ 069 20353) Kaiserstrasse 11, 60311 Frankfurt am Main 1
South Korea (☎ 02-732 7525) 10th floor, Press Centre Bldg, 25 Taipyongno 1-ga, Chung-gu, Seoul

Thailand (☎ 02-233 5108) 19th floor, Rama-land Bldg, 952 Rama 4 Rd, Bangkok 10500
UK (☎ 020-7734 9638) Heathcoat House, 20 Savile Row, London W1X 1AE
USA
Chicago: (☎ 312-222 0874) Suite 770, 401 North Michigan Ave, IL 60611
Los Angeles: (☎ 213-623 1952) Suite 1470, 515 South Figueroa St, CA 90017
New York: (☎ 212-757 5640) Suite 1250, One Rockefeller Plaza, NY 10020
San Francisco: (☎ 415-989 7140) Suite 601, 360 Post St, CA 94108

TRAVEL AGENCIES
Kyoto has several good central travel agencies that can arrange discount air tickets, car rental, accommodation and other services. These include H.I.S. Travel (Map 9; ☎ 241 2528), A'cross Travellers' Bureau (Map 9; ☎ 255 3559) and No 1 Travel (Map 9; ☎ 251 6970).

English speakers are available at all of these agencies. When you buy an international air ticket from a Japanese travel agency, they'll often ask that you pick up the ticket at the airport on the day of your departure. There's no need to submit to this absurd practice – simply demand that they issue you the ticket in person a least a week or two before your departure. They'll grumble and roll their eyes, but eventually you'll have your ticket in hand.

DOCUMENTS
Visas
Most visitors who are not planning to engage in any remunerative activities while in Japan are exempt from obtaining visas and will be issued a *tanki-taizai* visa (short-stay visa) on arrival.

Stays of up to six months are permitted for citizens of Austria, Germany, Ireland, Mexico, Switzerland and the UK. Citizens of these countries will almost always be given a 90-day short-stay visa upon arrival, which can usually be extended for another 90 days at immigration bureaus inside Japan (see Visa Extensions later in this chapter).

Citizens of the USA, Australia and New Zealand are granted 90-day short-stay visas, while stays of up to three months are permitted for citizens of Argentina, Belgium, Canada, Denmark, Finland, France, Iceland, Israel, Italy, The Netherlands, Norway, Singapore, Spain, Sweden and a number of other countries.

As well as the information following on visas and regulations, check with your nearest Japanese embassy or go to the Japanese Ministry of Foreign Affairs Web site (W www.mofa.go.jp/), where you can check out the 'Guide to Japanese Visas', read about working-holiday visas and find details on the Japan Exchange & Teaching (JET) program, which sponsors native English-speakers to come to Japan to teach in the public school system.

Working-Holiday Visas Australians, Canadians and New Zealanders between the ages of 18 and 25 (the age limit can be pushed up to 30) can apply for a working-holiday visa. This visa allows a six-month stay and two six-month extensions. It aims to enable young people to travel extensively during their stay, and for this reason employment is supposed to be part time or temporary, although in practice many people work full time.

A working-holiday visa is much easier to obtain than a working visa and is popular with Japanese employers. Single applicants must have the equivalent of A$2500 (C$2005) of funds and a married couple A$5000 (C$4010), and all applicants must have an onward ticket from Japan. For details, inquire at the nearest Japanese embassy or consulate (see Embassies & Consulates later in this chapter).

Working Visas It is not as easy as it once was to get a work visa for Japan. Ever-increasing demand has prompted much stricter work-visa requirements. Arriving in Japan and looking for a job is quite a tough proposition these days, though people still do it. There are legal employment categories for foreigners that specify standards of experience and qualifications.

Once you find an employer in Japan who is willing to sponsor you it is necessary for you to obtain a Certificate of Eligibility.

You must then take this certificate to any Japanese embassy or consulate overseas, not in Japan itself, where the actual visa will be issued. The whole procedure usually takes two to three months.

Visa Extensions With the exception of those nationals whose countries have reciprocal visa exemptions and who can stay for six months, 90 days or three months is the limit for most nationalities. To extend a short-stay visa beyond the standard 90 days or three months, apply at the Kyoto branch of the Osaka Immigration Bureau (Map 6), on the 4th floor of the Dai Ni Chihō Godochosha building, 34-12 Higashi Marutamachi, Kawabata Higashi-iru, Sakyō-ku. You must provide two copies of an Application for Extension of Stay (available at the bureau), a letter stating the reasons for the extension and supporting documentation, as well as your passport. There is a processing fee of ¥4000; be prepared to spend well over an hour to complete the process.

The Kyoto branch is best reached from Marutamachi station on the Keihan line. To get there take the No 4 exit, turn left and continue east past a church to the second traffic light. The bureau is in the five-storey building on your left.

The Osaka Immigration Bureau has an English-language visa information line at its Osaka headquarters (☎ 06-6774 3409), though you can usually have most questions about visas answered in English by calling the Kyoto branch (☎ 752 5997). Both offices are open Monday to Friday from 9am to noon and 1pm to 4pm.

Many long-term visitors to Japan get around the extension problem by briefly leaving the country, usually going to South Korea. Be warned, though, that immigration officials are wise to this practice and many 'tourist visa returnees' are turned back at the entry point.

Alien Registration Card Anyone, and this includes tourists, who stays for more than 90 days is required to obtain an Alien Registration Card (*Gaikokujin Torokushō*). This card can be obtained at the municipal office of the city, town or ward in which you're living but moving to another area requires that you re-register within 14 days.

You must carry your Alien Registration Card at all times as the police can stop you and ask to see the card. If you don't have the card, you may be taken back to the station and will have to wait there until someone fetches it for you.

Travel Insurance
Despite the fact that Japan is one of the safest places in the world to travel, travel insurance to cover theft, property loss, accidents and medical problems is a wise idea. With such a wide variety of policies available, it may be best to consult your travel agent for recommendations. Some policies offer a choice between lower and higher medical expense options; choose the high-cost option for Japan. The international student travel policies handled by STA Travel or other student travel organisations are usually good value.

Driving Licence & Permits
Those planning on driving in Kyoto need their home country's driver's licence and an International Driving Permit. Providing you have these, renting a car is no problem at all – finding somewhere to park is another matter. For motorbikes up to 250cc (including scooters), the same combination will suffice. However, anything over 250cc will require a special motorcycle licence rating and corresponding stamp in the international permit. While in past years the police were fairly ignorant when handling foreign driving documents, recently they've produced a handy book of worldwide licence types (and their restrictions), so think twice before trying to pull one over on the cop who pulls you over.

Hostel Cards
Youth hostel accommodation is popular in Japan and there are over 350 hostels nationwide. If you are planning on hostelling around Japan, it is best to obtain an international youth hostel membership before you leave home.

Foreign nonmembers can stay at any hostel in Japan, but they must pay a ¥600 premium (sometimes ¥1000 – the same as Japanese nonmembers pay) on top of the regular cost. If you collect six stamps from any one hostel or a combination of Japan's hostels (a total cost of ¥3600), this entitles you to a year's Japan Youth Hostels (JYH) membership. If you know, however, that you will be staying at hostels for more than six nights, you can save ¥800 by purchasing a 'guest card' for ¥2800, actually a set of six member stickers, which are good for one night each. International YH cards can only be arranged in Japan if you can prove you have lived in the country for over a year.

The combination of national, prefectural and privately run hostels makes the entire system rather complex and it's further complicated by considerable variations in prices and rules between hostels. For details, contact the JYH Kyoto branch (☎ 462 9185). You can also contact the Tokyo branch (☎ 03-3288 1417). JYH publishes annually a comprehensive map of hostels in Japan, which can be picked up at the TIC, JYH offices or any hostel.

Student & Youth Cards
Japan is one of the few places left in Asia where a student card can be useful. Officially, you should be carrying an ISIC (International Student Identity Card) to qualify for a discount (usually for entry to places of interest), but in practice you will often find that any youth or student card will do the trick.

Seniors' Cards
There are a variety of discounts available in Japan for seniors over the age 65. In almost all cases a passport will be sufficient proof of age, so seniors' cards are rarely worth bringing.

Copies
As with travel anywhere, it is a good idea to keep photocopies of any vital documents (passport data pages, birth certificate, credit cards, airline tickets etc), as well as a record

of travellers cheques serial numbers and an emergency stash of about US$50, in a place separate from your daily valuables. Also leave a copy of all these things (except perhaps the cash) with someone at home. Copies can be made at any of Japan's convenience stores for ¥10.

EMBASSIES & CONSULATES
Japanese Embassies & Consulates

Australia (☎ 02-6273 3244) 112 Empire Circuit, Yarralumla, Canberra, ACT 2600
Consulate in Brisbane: (☎ 07-3221 5188)
Consulate in Melbourne: (☎ 03-9639 3244)
Consulate in Perth: (☎ 08-9321 7816)
Consulate in Sydney: (☎ 02-9231 3455)
Canada (☎ 613-241 8541) 255 Sussex Dr, Ottawa, Ontario K1N 9E6
Consulate in Edmonton: (☎ 403-422 3752)
Consulate in Montreal: (☎ 514-866 3429)
Consulate in Toronto: (☎ 416-363 7038)
Consulate in Vancouver: (☎ 604-684 5868)
France (☎ 01 48 88 62 00) 7 Ave Hoche, 75008 Paris
Germany (☎ 0228 81910) Godesberger Allee 102–104, 53175 Bonn
Hong Kong (☎ 852-2522 1184) 47th floor, One Exchange Square, 8 Connaught Place, Central
Ireland (☎ 01-269 4033) Nutley Bldg, Merrion Centre, Nutley Lane, Dublin 4
Netherlands (☎ 70-346 9544) Tobias Asserlaan 2, 2517 KC, The Hague
New Zealand (☎ 04-473 1540) 7th floor, Norwich Insurance House, 3–11 Hunter St, Wellington 1
Consulate in Auckland: (☎ 09-303 4106)
South Korea (☎ 822-739 7400) 9th floor, Kyobo Bldg, Chongro 1-KA, Chongro-ku, Seoul
Thailand (☎ 02-252 6151) 1674 New Petchburi Rd, Bangkok 10310
UK (☎ 020-7465 6500) 101–104 Piccadilly, London, W1V 9FN
USA (☎ 202-238 6700) 2520 Massachusetts Ave, NW Washington DC 20008-2869
There are several Japanese consulates in the USA (check with the embassy), including:
Consulate in Los Angeles: (☎ 213-617 6700)
Consulate in New York: (☎ 212-371 8222)

Embassies & Consulates in Tokyo

Most countries have embassies in Tokyo (area code ☎ 03), some of which are listed below. Visas are generally substantially more expensive in Japan than in neighbouring countries. It's best to call the consular section first to confirm opening times.

Australia (☎ 5232 4111) 2-1-14 Mita, Minato-ku
Canada (☎ 3408 2101) 7-3-38 Akasaka, Minato-ku
China (☎ 3403 3380) 3-4-33 Moto-Azabu, Minato-ku
France (☎ 5420 8800) 4-11-44 Minami-Azabu, Minato-ku
Germany (☎ 3473 0151) 4-5-10 Minami-Azabu, Minato-ku
India (☎ 3262 2391) 2-2-11 Kudan-Minami, Chiyoda-ku
Indonesia (☎ 3441 4201) 5-2-9 Higashi-Gotanda, Shinagawa-ku
Ireland (☎ 3263 0695) 2-10-7 Koji-machi, Chiyoda-ku
Malaysia (☎ 3476 3840) 20-16 Nanpeidaichō, Shibuya-ku
Netherlands (☎ 5401 0411) 3-6-3 Shiba-kōen, Minato-ku
New Zealand (☎ 3467 2271) 20-40 Kamiya-machō, Shibuya-ku
Philippines (☎ 3496 2731) 11-24 Nanpei-daichō, Shibuya-ku
Russia (☎ 3583 4224) 2-1-1 Azabudai, Minato-ku
Singapore (☎ 3586 9111) 5-12-3 Roppongi, Minato-ku
South Korea (☎ 3452 7611) 1-2-5 Minami-Azabu, Minato-ku
Taiwan (Association of East Asian Relations) (☎ 3280 7811) 5-20-2 Shirogane-dai, Minato-ku
Thailand (☎ 3441 7352) 3-14-6 Kami-Osaki, Shinagawa-ku
UK (☎ 3265 5511) 1 Ichibanchō, Chiyoda-ku
USA (☎ 3224 5000) 1-10-5 Akasaka, Minato-ku

Consulates in Osaka

Several countries also have consulates in Osaka (area code ☎ 06). These include:

Australia (☎ 6941 9271) 2-1-61 Shiromi, Chūō-ku
Canada (☎ 6212 4910) 12F, Dai-san Shoho Bldg, 2-2-3 Nishi-shinsaibashi, Chūō-ku
China (☎ 6445 9473) 3-9-2 Utsubo Honmachi, Nishi-ku, Osaka
France (☎ 6946 6181) 1-2-27 Shiromi, Chūō-ku, Osaka
Germany (☎ 6440 5070) 35F, Umeda Sky Bldg, Tower East, 1-1-88 Ōyodo-naka, Kita-ku
Netherlands (☎ 6944 7272) 33F, Twin 21 Mid-Tower, 2-1-61 Shiromi, Chūō-ku
New Zealand (☎ 6942 9016) 28F, Twin 21 Mid-Tower, 2-1-61 Shiromi, Chūō-ku

Philippines (☎ 6910 7881) 101-301 Advan City
Bldg, 2-3-7 Uchiawajichō, Chūō-ku
Russian Federation (☎ 6848 3452) 2-2, Nishi
Midorigaoka 1-Chome, Toyonaka-shi
Singapore (☎ 6261 5131) 14F, Kokusai Bldg,
2-3-13 Azuchi-machi, Chūō-ku
Thailand (☎ 6243 5563) 4F, Kono-ike East
Bldg, 3-6-9 Kitakyohoji-machi, Chūō-ku
UK (☎ 6281 1616) 19F, Seiko Osaka Bldg, 3-5-
1 Bakuro-machi, Chūō-ku
USA (☎ 6315 5900) 2-11-5 Nishi-Tenma, Kita-ku

CUSTOMS

Customs allowances include the usual tobacco products plus three 760mL bottles of
alcoholic beverages, 57g of perfume, and
gifts and souvenirs up to a value of
¥200,000 or its equivalent. The alcohol and
tobacco allowances are available only for
those who are 20 or older. The penalties for
importing drugs are very severe.

Pornography (magazines, videos etc) in
which pubic hair or genitalia are visible is
illegal in Japan and will be confiscated by
customs officers.

There are no limits on the import of foreign or Japanese currency. The export of
foreign currency is also unlimited but a ¥5
million limit exists for Japanese currency.

MONEY

Because the Japanese postal system has recently linked its ATMs to the international
Cirrus and Plus networks, money is no longer
the issue it once was for travellers to Japan.
Of course, it always makes sense to carry
some foreign cash and some credit cards just
to be on the safe side. For those without credit
cards, it would be a good idea to bring some
travellers cheques as a back up.

Currency

The currency in Japan is the *yen* (¥), and
banknotes and coins are easily identifiable.
There are ¥1, ¥5, ¥10, ¥50, ¥100 and ¥500
coins, and ¥1000, ¥5000 and ¥10,000 banknotes. The ¥1 coin is of lightweight aluminium, and the ¥5 (known to bring good
luck) and ¥50 coins have a hole in the middle. There has also been talk of introducing
a new ¥2000 note; keep your eyes peeled
for them.

Exchange Rates

Currency exchange rates (as of mid-2001):

country	unit		yen
Australia	A$1	=	¥62.43
Canada	C$1	=	¥79.00
euro	€1	=	¥102.21
France	FR1	=	¥15.58
Germany	DM1	=	¥52.26
Hong Kong	HK$1	=	¥15.41
New Zealand	NZ$1	=	¥50.28
Singapore	S$1	=	¥66.47
UK	UK£1	=	¥167.26
USA	US$1	=	¥120.18

Exchanging Money

You can change cash or travellers cheques at
any 'Authorised Foreign Exchange Bank'
(signs will always be displayed in English)
or at some of Kyoto's larger hotels and department stores. Main post offices will also
cash travellers cheques. Rates vary little, if
at all, between banks (even the exchange
counters at the airport offer rates comparable to those offered by downtown banks).

In Kyoto, most major banks are located
near the Shijō-Karasuma intersection (Map
9), two stops north of Kyoto station on the
Karasuma line subway. Of these, Sanwa
Bank (Map 9; ☎ 211 4583) is most convenient for changing money and buying travellers cheques. There's also a branch of
Citibank (Map 5; toll-free ☎ 0120-504 189)
which has an international ATM in its lobby.

Cash Cold hard yen is the way to pay in
Japan. While credit cards are becoming more
common in Japan, cash is still much more
widely used, and travellers cheques are
rarely accepted. *Do not* assume that you can
pay for things with a credit card. *Always
carry sufficient cash.* The only places where
you can count on paying by credit card are
department stores and large hotels.

Travellers Cheques Travellers cheques are
fairly commonplace in Japan nowadays,
though they can only be cashed at banks,
major post offices and some hotels (see the
preceding Exchanging Money section). It is
not possible to use foreign currency travellers

cheques in stores and restaurants. In most cases the exchange rate for travellers cheques is slightly better than cash. In order to cash travellers cheques or make cash advances at banks, you will need to show your passport or a valid Alien Registration Card.

ATMs Automatic teller machines are almost as common as vending machines in Kyoto. Unfortunately, most of these do not accept foreign-issued cards. Even if they display Visa and MasterCard logos, most accept only Japan-issued versions of these cards.

Luckily, there are several international ATMs in town that do accept foreign-issued cards (see Credit Cards, following). Better still, the Japanese postal system has recently linked all of its ATMs to the international Cirrus and Plus cash networks (as well as some credit card networks), making life a breeze for foreign travellers to Japan. You'll find postal ATMs in most large post offices. Most postal ATMs are open 9am to 5pm on weekdays, 9am to noon on Saturday, and closed on Sunday and holidays.

There's an international ATM on the B1 floor of the Kyoto Tower Hotel, very close to the TIC and Kyoto station (Map 10), which is open from 10am to 9pm daily. In the middle of town, you'll find another international ATM (Map 9), open from 7am to 11pm daily, in the Zest underground mall 200m west of the Oike-Kawaramachi intersection, near exit 7. Also in the middle of town, the All Card Plaza (Map 9), in the Teramachi shopping arcade just north of Shijō-dōri, provides card services for most major international banks and credit cards. It is open from 9am to 8pm, but closed 1–3 January. Lastly, Citibank (listed earlier under Exchanging Money) has a 24-hour ATM that accepts most foreign-issued cards. Note that only holders of Japan-issued Citibank cards can use the ATM after hours.

Please pay careful attention to the hours listed for these ATMs. Do not plan on being able to use ATMs after hours – you'll be stuck high and dry without cash.

Credit Cards *Do not* rely on credit cards in Japan. While department stores, top-end hotels and *some* fancy restaurants do accept cards, most businesses in Japan do not. Cash-and-carry is still very much the rule in Japan. Among places that accept credit cards, you'll find VISA most useful, followed by Master-Card and American Express.

For cash advances of amounts up to ¥40,000, any of the above-mentioned ATMs should suffice. For larger amounts, VISA card-holders can also get cash advances at the Sumitomo Bank branch on the 1st floor of the Hankyū department store (Map 9).

Currently there is no representation for international card-holders in Kyoto, and for inquiries it is often best to call the number in your home country on the back of your card, or try the offices in Tokyo. The telephone numbers (area code ☎ 03) and addresses of the Tokyo offices are:

American Express (toll-free ☎ 0120-020 120, 24 hours) American Express Tower, 4-30-16 Ogikubo, Suginami-ku

MasterCard (☎ 00531-11 3886) Dai Tokyo Kasai Shinjuku Bldg, 16F, 3-25-3 Yoyogi, Shibuya-ku

VISA (☎ 03-5251 0633, toll-free ☎ 0120-133 173) Nissho Bldg, 4F, 2-7-9 Kita-Aoyama, Minato-ku

International Transfers To make an international transfer you'll have to find a Japanese bank associated with the bank from which the money will be sent. Start by asking at the central branch of any major Japanese bank. If they don't have a relationship with your bank, they can usually refer you to a bank that does. Once you find a related bank in Japan, you'll have to give your home bank the exact details of where to send the money: the bank, branch and location. Telex or telegraphic transfers are much faster, though more expensive, than mail transfers. A credit-card cash advance is a worthwhile alternative.

Bank & Post Office Accounts Opening a regular bank account is difficult for foreign visitors on a short-stay visa. Most banks ask to see an Alien Registration Card and some may also require a name stamp (*hanko* or *inkan*, available at speciality stores).

continued on page 73

Religion

RICHARD I'ANSON

STUART WASSERMAN

Title Page: New Year good luck charms and best wishes at a temple (Photograph by Frank Carter).

Top: An arched walkway at Fushimi-Inari Taisha. This intriguing shrine was dedicated to the gods of rice and sake in the 8th century. Hundreds of *torii* (gates) from devotees line the path to the shrine.

Bottom: The interiors of Japanese temples and shrines contain intricate detail in everything from paintings to architecture.

FRANK CARTER

Buddhist Temples

Temples *(tera, dera, dō, in* or *ji)* vary widely in style, depending on the type of school and historical era of their construction. From the introduction of Buddhism in the 6th century until the Middle Ages, temples were the most important architectural works in Japan, and hence exerted a strong stylistic influence on all other types of building.

There were three main styles of early temple architecture: *tenjiku yō* (Indian), *karayō* (Chinese) and *wayō* (Japanese). All three styles were in fact introduced to Japan via China. Wayō arrived in the 7th century and gradually acquired local character, becoming the basis of much Japanese wooden architecture. It was named so as to distinguish it from karayō (also known as Zen style), which arrived in the 12th century. A mixture of wayō and karayō known as *setchuyō* eventually came to dominate, and tenjikuyō disappeared altogether.

With their origins in Chinese architecture and emphasis on otherworldly perfection, early temples were monumental and symmetrical in layout. A good example of the Chinese influence can be seen in the famous Phoenix Hall at Byōdō-in in Uji (southern Kyoto), a Tang-style pavilion.

The Japanese affinity for asymmetry eventually affected temple design, leading to the more organic – although equally controlled – planning of later temple complexes. An excellent example in Kyoto is Daitoku-ji, a Rinzai Zen monastery, which is a large complex containing a great many subtemples and gardens.

Gates Temples generally have four gates, oriented to the north, south, east and west. The *nandai-mon* is the south gate, usually the largest one. There is also a central gate, *chū-mon*, which is sometimes incorporated into the cloister. The *niō-mon* houses frightful-looking statues of gods such as Raijin (the god of lightning) and Fū-jin (the god of wind).

The following are some common temple features:

kondō or *hondō*	–	main hall
kōdō	–	meeting hall
kyōzō	–	sutra repository
sobō	–	dormitory
jikidō	–	dining hall

The layout of a temple tends to be a variation on a basic theme of pavilions, pagodas and cloisters, all constructed of wood.

Pagodas The Gojū-no-tō, or five-storey pagoda, is a major component of temple design. These are elegant wooden towers, symbolising Shaka, the Buddha. Their design is a variation of the Indian stupa, a structure originally intended to hold the remains of Shaka (sometimes with an actual tooth or chip of bone, more often represented

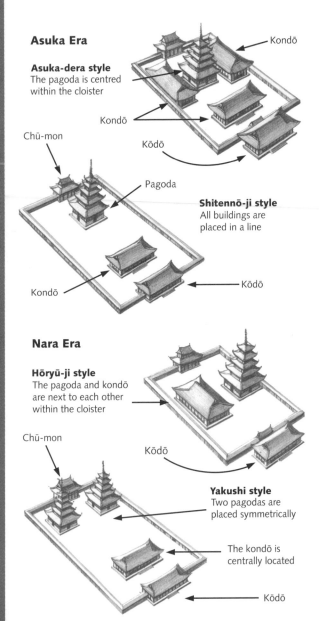

Asuka Era

Asuka-dera style
The pagoda is centred
within the cloister

Kondō

Kondō

Kōdō

Chū-mon

Pagoda

Shitennō-ji style
All buildings are
placed in a line

Kondō

Kōdō

Nara Era

Hōryū-ji style
The pagoda and kondō
are next to each other
within the cloister

Chū-mon

Kōdō

Yakushi style
Two pagodas are
placed symmetrically

The kondō is
centrally located

Kōdō

Left: Various temple
layouts from the Asuka
and Nara eras.

KH

by crystal or amber). The spire on top usually has nine tiers, representing the nine spheres of heaven.

Kyoto contains a number of excellent examples of five-storey pagodas. Tō-ji is the best known and the tallest in Japan. Other impressive pagodas include Yasaka-no-tō, and those at Daigo-ji and Kiyomizu-dera.

Main Hall Known as the *kondō*, *hondō*, *butsu-den*, *miei-dō*, *amida-dō* or *komponchū-dō*, the main hall contains the statue of Buddha, the most holy item in a temple. As the symbol of Shaka, the pagoda was originally given prime position within the temple layout, but as a number of other Buddhas began to gain importance, the kondō became the central structure, as it could contain the images of a variety of Buddhas.

Buddhist Images There are dozens of images in the Japanese Buddhist pantheon, varying from temple to temple, depending on the religious school or period of construction. Four of the most common images are those of Shaka (Sanskrit: Sakyamuni), the Historical Buddha; Amida (Sanskrit: Amitabha), the Buddha of the Western Paradise or of Light; Miroku (Sanskrit: Maitreya), the Buddha of the Future; and Dainichi, the Cosmic Buddha.

Kannon (Sanskrit: Avalokitesvara) is the 'one who hears their cries' and is available in no less than 33 different versions including, as the goddess of mercy, a female form popular with expectant mothers. When Christianity was banned, Japanese believers kept faith with the Holy Virgin by creating a clone 'Maria Kannon'.

Jizō, known formally as O-Jizō-san, is often depicted as a monk with a staff in one hand and a jewel in the other. According to legend, this patron of travellers, children and expectant mothers helps the souls of dead children perform their task of building walls of pebbles on the banks of Sai-no-kawara, the river of the underworld. Believers place stones on or around Jizō statues as additional help.

Right: Buddha images (from top to bottom) Amida (the Buddha of Western Paradise or of Light) & Dainichi (the Cosmic Buddha)

Left: This depiction of Izumo-taisha, the original Shintō shrine, shows the highly influential taisha-zukuri style of shrine architecture. The roof line displays the crisscross elements or the upward extension of the gables known as *chigi*, and the horizontal elements, called *katsuogi*.

Shintō Shrines

Shrines can be called *jinja*, *jingū*, *gū* or *taisha*. The original Shintō shrine is Izumo-taisha in Shimane-ken, which has the largest shrine hall in Japan. It is said to have been modelled on the Emperor's residence, and its style, known as *taisha-zukuri*, was extremely influential on later shrine design. Shrines tend to use simple, unadorned wood construction, and are built raised above the ground on posts. The roof is gabled, not hipped as with temple architecture. The entrance is generally from the end, not the side, again distinguishing it from temple design. The distinctive roof line of shrine architecture is due to an elaboration of the structural elements of the roof. The crisscross elements are called *chigi* and the horizontal elements are called *katsuogi*.

As Buddhism increased its influence over Shintō, it also affected the architecture. The clean lines of the early shrines were replaced with curving eaves and other ornamental details. Worshippers were provided with shelter by extending the roof or even building a separate worship hall. This led to the *nagare* style, the most common type of shrine architecture. Excellent examples in Kyoto can be found at Shimogamo-jinja and Kamigamo-jinja.

The *gongen* style uses an H-shaped plan, connecting two halls with an intersecting gabled roof and hallway called an *ishi no ma*. This element symbolises the connection between the divine and the ordinary worlds. The best example of this style in Kyoto is at Kitano-Tenman-gū.

Shrine Surroundings At the entrance to the shrine is the *torii* (gateway) marking the boundary of the sacred precinct. The most dominant torii in Kyoto is in front of Heian-jingū Shrine, a massive concrete structure a considerable distance south of the shrine.

Fushimi-Inari-taisha, south of Kyoto, has thousands of bright vermilion gates lining paths up the mountain to the shrine itself.

Shimenawa, plaited ropes decorated with strips of white paper (gohei), are strung across the top of the torii. They are also wrapped around sacred rocks or trees or above the actual shrine entrance. A pair of stone lion-like creatures called koma-inu can often be found flanking the main path. One usually has its mouth open in a roar and the other has its mouth closed.

The *kannushi* (chief priest) of the shrine is responsible for religious rites and the administration of the shrine. The priests dress in blue and white; on special occasions they don more ornate clothes and wear an *eboshi* (a black cap with a protruding, folded tip). *Miko* (shrine maidens) dress in vermilion and white. The ceremonial *kagura* dances performed by miko can be traced back to shamanistic trances.

Mythical Creatures A variety of fabulous creatures inhabit Japanese folklore and crop up regularly in shops, festivals and shrines:

Tanuki is often translated as badger, but it bears a closer resemblance to a North American raccoon. Like the fox, the tanuki is thought of as a mischievous creature and is credited with supernatural powers, but is more a figure of fun than the fox. Statues usually depict the tanuki in an upright position with sombrero-like straw headgear and clasping a bottle of sake. Note the enormous testicles.

Kitsune is a fox, but for the Japanese it also has strong connections with the supernatural and is worshipped in Japan at over 30,000 Inari shrines as the messenger of the harvest god. Fushimi-Inari Taisha is the largest of its kind and is crammed with fox statues.

Maneki-neko, the beckoning cat, is a very common sight outside shops or restaurants. The raised left paw attracts customers and their money.

Right: The mythical *tanuki* are mischievous creatures credited with supernatural powers. They usually wear sombrero-like straw headgear and clasp a bottle of sake.

MARTIN MOOS

Tengu are mountain goblins with a capricious nature, sometimes abducting children, sometimes returning those who were missing. Their unmistakable feature is a long nose.

Kappa are amphibious creatures about the size of a 12- or 13-year-old boy and have webbed hands and feet. They have a reputation for mischief, such as dragging horses into rivers or stealing cucumbers (their favourite food). The source of their power is a depression on top of their heads which must always contain water. A crafty method to outwit a kappa is to bow to it. When the kappa – Japanese to the core – bows back, it empties the water from its head and loses its power. The alternatives are not pleasant. Kappa are said to enjoy ripping out their victim's liver through the anus!

Religious Sculpture

Fine art in Japan begins with the introduction of Mahayana Buddhism in the 6th century AD. Existing pottery and metalwork skills were turned to the production of Buddhist images. During the late Heian era, native sculpture techniques flourished and a recognisable Japanese style appeared. A knowledge of the different types of Buddhist sculptures found in Japanese temples is a good step to understanding Buddhism itself. The images fall into four main groups, each of which represents a different level of being in the Buddhist cosmology.

At the head of Japanese Buddhism's hierarchy are *nyorai*, or Buddhas. These are beings who have attained enlightenment *(nirvana)* and freed themselves from the cycle of rebirth. Nyorai images are conspicuous by their simple robes, a lump on the head symbolising wisdom and a head of tight 'snail shell' curls. The major nyorai are: Shaka (the Historical Buddha), one hand raised in a preaching gesture; Yakushi (the Healing Buddha), making the same gesture with one hand while the other clutches a vial of medicine; Amida (the Buddha of Western Paradise or of Light), usually seen sitting with knuckles together in a meditative

CHERYL CONLAN

Left: Giant Buddha on top of Ryokan Kannon, Kyoto

posture; and Dainichi (the Cosmic Buddha), usually portrayed in princely attire, sitting with one hand clasped around a raised finger of the other hand (a sexual gesture indicating the unity of being). Nyorai are usually portrayed with two bodhisattvas in a triad configuration.

After Buddhas, the next most important beings are *bosatsu* (bodhisattvas). These are beings who have put off their own entry into nirvana in order to help others attain enlightenment. Images of bosatsu are more human in appearance than nyorai and most easily distinguished from the latter by a topknot of hair or a crowned headpiece, sometimes with smaller figures built into the crown. The most common bosatsu in Japanese temples is Kannon, the goddess of mercy. Also common, both in temples and around the countryside, are images of Jizō, often depicted carrying children in his arms. The next group of beings are not native to Buddhism, but were borrowed from Hinduism to serve particular purposes in the Buddhist cosmology. These are *ten* (heavenly beings or devas). While some appear as beastly ogres, others are human in appearance. The most common of these are *niō* (guardians), often found in the gates leading up to temples.

Finally, there are the *myō-ō* (kings of wisdom or light). These beings serve as protectors of Buddhism and were introduced to Japan along with esoteric Buddhism in the 9th century. The most common myō-ō image is Fudō Myō-ō, usually depicted clutching an upright sword.

What to Do at Temples & Shrines

There are no steadfast rituals you must follow when visiting temples and shrines, though most Japanese do pray briefly and have a strong penchant for having their fortunes told.

The grounds of many Buddhist temples can be entered free of charge, while others charge an admission fee of ¥300 to ¥600. An additional fee is sometimes necessary to visit a museum of temple treasures, to enter the gardens or main hall, or to drink a cup of tea. Talismans and fortunes are often on sale near the entrance or in one of the halls. An attractive souvenir available for about ¥1000 at many temples is *shūin-chō*, a cloth-covered, pocket-sized booklet with a concertina of folding pages. For a small fee, you can ask a temple monk to give an artistic touch to your booklet by adding calligraphy. As with railway stations and many tourist attractions, temples often provide ink pads and stamps for visitors to print souvenir logos in their booklet.

The central Buddha image, in the main hall, has offerings of incense sticks, food or flowers placed before it. In front of the hall is an offering box *(saisen-bako)*. Visitors stand in front of the hall, toss a coin (or coins) into the box, press their palms together and pray.

Most Shintō shrines have no entrance fee. Before prayer, visitors are expected to rinse their hands and mouth with pure water. In a small pavilion *(temizuya)*, a stone ablution basin *(chōzuya)* and bamboo ladle *(hishaku)* are provided for this purpose. Rinse both hands before pouring water into a cupped hand to rinse the mouth.

Above the offering box hangs a long rope with a bell attached. Visitors toss a coin into the box, then grab and shake the rope to 'wake the gods', bow twice, clap loudly twice, bow again twice (once deeply, once lightly), and then step back and to the side. It is considered improper to turn one's back on the shrine.

Amulets are popular purchases at shrines. *O-mamori*, special talismans, are purchased at shrines to ensure good luck or ward off evil – taxi drivers often have a 'traffic safety' o-mamori dangling from the rear-view mirror. Votive plaques *(ema)* made of wood with a picture on one side and a blank space on the other are also common. On the blank side visitors write a wish, for example success in exams, luck in finding a sweetheart or safe delivery of a healthy child. Dozens of these plaques can be seen attached to boards in shrine precincts.

Fortunes *(o-mikuji)* are selected by drawing a numbered bamboo or steel rod from a box and picking out the associated fortune slip. Luck is classified as *dai-kichi* (great good fortune), *kichi* (good fortune), *shō-kichi* (middling good fortune) and *kyō* (bad luck). If you like the fortune slip you've been given, you can take it home. If you've drawn bad luck, you can tie it to the branch of a tree in the shrine grounds – presumably some other force can then worry about it.

Neighbourhood Shrines

Every neighbourhood in every Japanese town or city has its own tiny shrine to Jizō. Pieces of clothing or red bibs draped around Jizō figures are an attempt to cover the souls of dead children. An annual August children's festival *(Jizō-bon)* features two days of praying and playing around the Jizō shrine by the local children dressed in *yukata* (a light kimono for summer or for bathing in a ryokan).

The shrines are located by *fū-sui* (known in Chinese as feng shui), a specifically Asian form of geomancy. It is impossible (or bad luck) to move them, so they are found almost everywhere, often notched into concrete walls or telephone poles.

These shrines are maintained by the local community, each person contributing a regular small sum of money. The person responsible for the shrine changes on a yearly basis, but everyone in the area will leave offerings for Jizō, usually something they themselves have excess of, such as fruit, chocolate or sake.

continued from page 64

A better option for long-term visitors or those who don't want to bother with changing money all the time is a postal savings account *(yūbin chokin)*. You can open these at any major post office in Japan. With a postal savings account you'll be issued a cash card that enables you to withdraw funds from any post office in Japan (and these are everywhere). You should be able to get things started by using the phrase: *'Yūbin chokin no kōza o hirakitai desu'* ('I would like to open a post office savings account').

Security

In terms of theft, Japan is one of the safest countries in the world. You can safely carry large sums of cash without the fear of being robbed. Of course, it's always possible that you might lose the money. For this reason, we suggest using international ATMs, credit cards and perhaps even a backup of travellers cheques instead of carrying large amounts of cash (see the preceding sections for details on ATMs, credit cards and travellers cheques).

Costs

Japan, as notorious as it is for being prohibitively costly, is often more affordable than many assume – it's just a matter of seeking out the cheaper options. In recent years there has been a noticeable rise in big supermarkets, discount shops and other forms of price-cutting, finally giving consumers more choice in what they pay for goods and services. One area where this rule does not apply is drinking, which is a sure-fire way to get rid of all your yen in a hurry.

For the traveller, compared to other parts of Japan, Kyoto cannot be strictly called expensive or cheap. A skeleton daily budget would be ¥6300. This means taking the cheapest accommodation (¥2800 for a youth hostel or guesthouse dorm bed), eating modestly for another ¥2500 and spending just ¥1000 on local transport. Add at least ¥2500 for extras like snacks, drinks, admission fees and entertainment and you're looking at roughly ¥9000.

More expensive accommodation will cost around ¥5500 to ¥8000 for a budget-range business hotel, and anywhere from ¥14,000 to ¥34,000 for something more luxurious. For stays in traditional surroundings, per person prices range from about ¥4500 per night in one of the cheaper ryokan, to over ¥50,000 in a top-flight ryokan.

Food costs can be kept down by taking set meals. A fixed 'morning service' breakfast *(mōningu sābisu* or *setto)* is available in most coffee shops for around ¥500. Lunchtime set meals *(teishoku)* cost about ¥750. Cheap noodle places, often found at stations, charge around ¥350 for a filling bowl of noodles. Alternatively, you can buy a takeaway *bentō*, or Japanese-style boxed lunch, for around ¥500 from local kiosks, convenience shops or department stores. For an evening meal, there's the option of a set course again or a single order – ¥800 should cover this. An evening meal and a couple of glasses of beer at one of Kyoto's *izakaya* (traditional pubs) will cost around ¥2500. Average prices at youth hostels are ¥450 for a Japanese breakfast and ¥700 for dinner.

Some other costs to consider include: museum admission (¥400–800), movie tickets (¥1600–2000), foreign magazines (¥700), local English newspapers (¥120–140), 36-exposure colour film without processing (¥420), a glass of orange juice at a coffee shop (¥400), a cocktail in an average-priced bar (up to ¥1000), shirt dry-cleaning (¥200) and cigarettes (¥250–300).

Transport costs for trips to the sights around Kyoto can be expensive, but unless you are going to be travelling to other parts of Japan, it probably isn't worth getting a Japan Rail Pass for local excursions. If you want to avoid emptying your wallet at an alarming rate, you should only use taxis as a very last resort. Kyoto has fast, efficient public transport, so it's only on those late-night binges that you need a taxi anyway. For *shinkansen* (bullet train) trips and domestic flights, discounted tickets are available at some discount shops (see the Discount Tickets entry in the Train section of the Getting There & Away chapter for more info on these tickets).

FACTS FOR THE VISITOR

Tipping & Bargaining

The lack of tipping in Japan means that there are no hidden expenses in the sample daily budgets mentioned above. There is no situation, be it for taxi drivers, tour guides, waiters, hotel porters, room service or cleaners, in which it is considered compulsory to tip.

With the exception of antique shops and flea markets, bargaining in Japan is also virtually nonexistent. Possible exceptions are camera and electronic stores (in particular those dealing in used goods). A polite request is all that is required.

Taxes & Refunds

There is a 5% consumption tax on retail purchases in Japan. Visitors on a short-stay visa can, however, avoid this tax on purchases made at major department stores and duty-free stores such as the Kyoto Handicraft Center (Map 6). For a refund on purchases, check first that the department store has a service desk for tax refunds. When you make the purchase the tax will be included; take the purchase, receipt and your passport to the service desk for an immediate refund.

If you eat at expensive restaurants and stay at 1st-class accommodation, you will encounter a service charge, which varies from 10% to 15%. A local tax of 5% is added to restaurant bills exceeding ¥5000 or for hotel bills exceeding ¥10,000. This means it is sometimes cheaper to ask for separate bills.

POST & COMMUNICATIONS
Post

Most local post offices are open Monday to Friday from 9am to 5pm. Kyoto's central post office (Map 10; ☎ 365 2467), on the north side of Kyoto station, is open from 9am to 7pm on weekdays, to 5pm on Saturday and to 12.30pm on Sunday and holidays. Poste restante mail can be collected here. There's an after-hours service counter on the south side of the building open 24 hours a day for air mail, small packages, and special express mail services.

The large Nakagyō post office (Map 9; ☎ 255 1112) at the Nishinotōin-Sanjō crossing is also open until 7pm on weekdays,

but is closed on weekends. There is also a 24-hour service window on the west side of the building.

The airmail rate for postcards is ¥70 to any overseas destination; aerograms cost ¥90. Letters weighing less than 10g cost ¥90 to other countries within Asia, ¥110 to North America, Europe or Oceania (including Australia and New Zealand) and ¥130 to Africa and South America. One peculiarity of the Japanese postal system is that you will be charged extra if your writing runs over onto the address side (the right side) of a postcard.

All post offices offer a reliable international Express Mail Service (EMS); there is also a Kyoto branch of Federal Express (☎ 672 8006, or Tokyo number toll-free ☎ 0120-003 200) in the far south of town. The daily cut-off time to post packages is 5pm; Fed-ex can also provide pick-up service, but requires a full day's notice. For domestic express delivery services 24 hours a day, the services known as *takyūbin* that are handled by most convenience stores are cheap and efficient.

Telephone

The area code for greater Kyoto is ☎ 075; unless otherwise indicated, all numbers in this book fall into this area. Japanese telephone codes consist of an area code plus a local code and number. You do not dial the area code when making a call in that area. When dialling Japan from abroad, the country code is ☎ 81, followed by the area code (drop the 0) and the number. Area codes for some of the main cities are:

Fukuoka/Hakata	☎ 092
Hiroshima	☎ 082
Kōbe	☎ 078
Matsuyama	☎ 0899
Nagasaki	☎ 0958
Nagoya	☎ 052
Nara	☎ 0742
Narita	☎ 0476
Osaka	☎ 06
Sapporo	☎ 011
Sendai	☎ 022
Tokyo	☎ 03
Yokohama	☎ 045

Local Calls The Japanese public telephone system is very well developed. There are a great many public phones and they work almost 100% of the time. Telephone services within Japan are principally handled by NTT (Nippon Telegraph & Telephone Corporation).

Local calls from pay phones cost ¥10 per minute. Long-distance or overseas calls require a handful of coins; unused ¥10 coins are returned after the call is completed but no change is given on ¥100 coins.

In general it's much easier to buy a telephone card *(terefōn kādo)* when you arrive rather than worry about always having coins on hand. Phone cards are sold in ¥500 and ¥1000 denominations (the latter earns you an extra ¥50 in calls) and can be used in most green or grey pay phones. They are available from vending machines and convenience stores, come in a myriad of designs and are also a collectable item.

Directory Assistance For local directory assistance dial ☎ 104 (the call costs ¥30), or for assistance in English ring ☎ 0120-364 463 from 9am to 5pm weekdays. For international directory assistance dial ☎ 0057.

International Calls Due to the proliferation of counterfeit telephone cards, it is no longer possible to make international direct-dial calls from regular green pay phones.

Paid and reverse-charge (collect) overseas calls can be made from grey ISDN phones and green phones that have a gold metal plate around the buttons. These are usually found in phone booths marked 'International & Domestic Card/Coin Phone'. Unfortunately, these are rather rare; try looking in the lobbies of top-end hotels and at airports.

Hotel lobbies also have KDD 'Credit Phones' that allow you to make international calls with credit cards issued outside Japan. In some youth hostels and guesthouses, you will also find pink coin-only phones from which you cannot make international calls (though you can receive them).

Calls are charged by the unit, each of which is six seconds, so if you don't have much to say you could phone home for just ¥100.

You can save money by dialling late at night. Economy rates, with a discount of 20%, apply from 7pm to 11pm weekdays and to 11pm on weekends and holidays. From 11pm to 8am a discount rate brings the price of international calls down by 40%. Note that it is also cheaper to make domestic calls by dialling outside the standard hours.

To place an international call through the operator, dial ☎ 0051 (international operators all seem to speak English). To make the call yourself, dial ☎ 001 (KDD), ☎ 0041 (ITJ) or ☎ 0061 (IDC) – there's very little difference in their rates – then the international country code, the local code and the number.

Another option is to dial ☎ 0039 for home country direct, which takes you straight through to a local operator in the country dialled (your home country direct code can be found in phone books or by calling ☎ 0051). You can then make a reverse-charge call or a credit-card call with a telephone credit card valid in that country.

Another phonecard option is Lonely Planet's eKno Communication Card. It's aimed specifically at independent travellers and provides budget international calls (for local calls, you're usually better off with a local card), a range of message services, free email and travel information. Accessing its Web site is the easiest way to find out more or to join (Ⓦ www.ekno.lonely planet.com). To join by phone from within Japan call Customer Service toll-free on ☎ 00531-21 2039. Once you've joined you can use the phone or the Internet to contact your friends and family and manage your account. You can then check the eKno Web site for access numbers from other countries and updates on super budget local access numbers and new features.

One more option for making international calls is prepaid phone cards, such as the KDD Superworld Card, which provides ¥3200 worth of calls for ¥3000. Unlike conventional phonecards, this one operates via a 'secret' number that lasts as long as the charge remains on the card. There is no need to insert the card into a phone, and you can make international calls from any touch-tone phone. You can purchase these cards in hotels and ryokan that cater to foreigners; otherwise, try a convenience store.

Connecting a Phone Having a home telephone connected is quite simple. Apply at any NTT office (it takes about 15 minutes to complete the paperwork). You must also buy a phone line, which costs about ¥70,000 if you buy it from NTT, but only ¥40,000 to ¥60,000 from someone who no longer wants their line. 'Used' phone lines are advertised at the KICH and in *Kansai Time Out*. For orders and inquiries about phone installation, ring the NTT English Service Section toll-free on ☎ 0120-364 463.

Fax

Most convenience stores in Kyoto have fax machines where you can send and sometimes receive faxes. If you can't understand how to operate the machine, ask the shop assistant for assistance – *'Fakusu o okuritai desu'* ('I want to send a fax'). To receive one ask: *'Koko de fakusu o ukeru koto dekimasu ka?'* ('Can I receive a fax here?'). You can also send and receive faxes at most top-end hotels, although some places only allow paying guests to use their facilities. Lastly, you can send and receive faxes at the KICH (Map 6; see the Useful Organisations section later in this chapter).

Email & Internet Access

If you plan on bringing your laptop with you to Kyoto, first make sure that it is compatible with Japanese current (100V AC; 50Hz in eastern Japan and 60Hz in western Japan, including Kyoto). Most laptops function just fine on Japanese current. Second, check to see if your plug will fit Japanese wall sockets (Japanese plugs are flat two pin, identical to most ungrounded North American plugs). Both transformers and plug adaptors are readily available in electronics districts like Kyoto's Teramachi-dōri (see the Shopping chapter for details on this street).

Modems and phone jacks are similar to those used in the USA (RJ11 phone jacks). Conveniently, many of the grey IDD pay phones in Japan have a standard phone jack and an infrared port so that you can log on to the Internet just about anywhere in the country.

Internet Cafés Kyoto has no shortage of Internet cafés, though rates are much higher than other countries in the region (plan on ¥250 to ¥500 per half hour).

One of the cheaper places in town is the Kyoto Prefectural International Center (Map 10; ☎ 342 5000) on the 9th floor of the Kyoto station building. It is open from 10am to 6pm (closed the second and fourth Tuesday of each month) and Internet access costs ¥250 for 30 minutes. Unfortunately, there are only three terminals here and they're often occupied.

Aspirin (Map 9; ☎ 251 2351) is in the Teramachi shopping arcade on the 3rd floor of the A-Break building, right next to a pachinko parlour. It is open 10am to 9pm and charges ¥500 per hour.

Meix (Map 5; ☎ 221 7511) is located on Karasuma-dōri, a one-minute walk south of the Imperial Palace. Open from 10.30am to 6.30pm (closed Sunday) it charges ¥700 for two hours Note that you must pay a ¥3000 deposit here, ¥2500 of which will be returned on closing your account.

Buttercups (Map 6; ☎ 751 9537) has one terminal available for surfing for ¥250 per 30 minutes. You can send email for ¥50 per batch (typing time free) and also use the café's email (📧 bttrcps@dd.iij4u.or.jp) to receive – your own mail box is created free of charge. The café is open from 10am to 11pm, closed Tuesday.

The KICH charges ¥200 for 30 minutes, see the Useful Organisations section for more details.

If necessary, the Kyoto TIC can recommend additional places to log on.

INTERNET RESOURCES

The World Wide Web is a rich resource for travellers. You can research your trip, hunt down bargain air fares, book hotels, check on weather conditions or chat with locals and other travellers about the best places to visit (or avoid!).

There's no better place to start your Web explorations than the Lonely Planet Web site (**W** www.lonelyplanet.com). Here you'll find succinct summaries on travelling to most places on earth, postcards from other travellers and the Thorn Tree bulletin board, where you can ask questions before you go or dispense advice when you get back. You can also find travel news and updates to many of our most popular guidebooks, and the subWWWay section links you to the most useful travel resources elsewhere on the Web.

Other Web sites with useful Japan and Kyoto information and links include:

Japan National Tourist Organization
  W www.jnto.go.jp
Kansai Time Out Monthly English-language
  magazine for the Kansai area
  W www.kto.co.jp
Kyoto Prefecture Concentrating on the greater
  Kyoto area
  W www.pref.kyoto.jp/index_e.html
Kyoto Visitor's Guide Kyoto-specific
  information
  W www.kyotoguide.com
JR East Information on rail travel in Japan,
  with details on the Japan Rail Pass
  W www.jreast.co.jp/e/index.html

BOOKS

Most books are published in different editions by different publishers in different countries. As a result, a book might be a hardcover rarity in one country while it's readily available in paperback in another country.

Fortunately, bookshops and libraries search by title or author, so your local bookshop or library is best placed to advise you on the availability of the following recommendations. If you can't find these books at home, you should be able to find most of them in Kyoto (see the boxed text 'Kyoto Bookshops'). For books on doing business in Japan and Japanese business practices, see the Doing Business section later in this chapter.

Lonely Planet

For further exploration of the Kansai area and beyond, Lonely Planet's *Japan* (7th edition) is the most complete Japan guide available. LP's *Tokyo* (3rd edition) is an excellent guide to Japan's capital city and surrounding area. Other LP titles include a pocket-size *Japanese phrasebook*, *Japanese audio pack* (including phrasebook and CD or cassette), and *Japan*, a selection from its video series.

Hiking in Japan (1st edition) is a must for anyone wishing to explore Japan's woods and mountains; it includes several hikes in and around Kyoto, as well as farther afield in the Kansai district.

An excellent contemporary nonfiction book on the country is Alex Kerr's *Lost Japan* (1996). Kerr spent 20 years living on the outskirts of Kyoto and shares his candid views of the city and its people in the provocative chapter 'Kyoto Hates Kyoto'.

Guidebooks

The guide you're holding in your hand is the most comprehensive guide available to Kyoto, though there are several other worthwhile books. Perhaps the most detailed guide to Kyoto's cultural attractions is *Kyoto – A Cultural Guide to Japan's Ancient Imperial City* by John & Phyllis Martin.

Exploring Kyoto by long-term Kyoto resident Judith Clancy is an excellent 'on foot' guide with more than 25 well documented walks and hikes throughout the city.

Former Kyoto resident Diane Durston is one of the world's leading experts on Kyoto and its vanishing traditions. Her *Old Kyoto – A Guide to Traditional Shops, Restaurants & Inns* is a must for those in search of specific Kyoto handicrafts. It also provides detailed information on atmospheric old ryokan and restaurants. The material for this book later appeared as *The Living Traditions of Old Kyoto*, a larger coffee-table book. Durston's *Kyoto, Seven Paths to the Heart of the City* is an informative guide for those interested in exploring some of Kyoto's traditional neighbourhoods.

Gouverneur Mosher's classic *Kyoto – A Contemplative Guide* was published in

Kyoto Bookshops

Kyoto has several fine bookshops, the biggest and best of which is Maruzen (Map 10; ☎ 241 2161), on Kawaramachi-dōri between Sanjō-dōri and Shijō-dōri. There is an extensive selection of English-language books, magazines, and maps, as well as a wide selection of Lonely Planet guides. There's also a limited number of French, German and Spanish-language books. This is the place to pick up books about Kyoto and Japan, as well as English teaching materials and fine stationary and writing materials. It's open daily from 10am to 8pm (closed on the third Wednesday of each month).

Kinokuniya (☎ 253 3151), in the Zest underground shopping arcade (Map 9), also has a decent selection of English-language books and magazines. It's open daily from 10.30am to 8.30pm (closed third Wednesday of each month).

On the fifth floor of Kintetsu department store (Map 10) near Kyoto station, the large Asahiya bookshop (☎ 361 1111) has a limited selection of English books and magazines. This is a good spot to pick up Japanese books and maps, including Shōbunsha's excellent hiking map series. It's open from 10am to 8pm.

Book 1st (Map 9; ☎ 253 6700), on Kawaramachi-dōri, is a large Japanese-language bookshop where you can pick up things like hiking maps and Japanese-language books and magazines. It's open from 10am to 9.50pm.

If you want to trade a book you've read, there is a small self-service bookswap at Buttercups cafe (Map 6). Books can also be borrowed (and returned) on an honour system from the YWCA (Map 5). There's also a small lending library for those with long-term visas at the KICH (Map 6).

1964 originally, yet still gives a taste of the amazing scope for exploration possible in Kyoto. Though the transport information is decades out of date, it's well worth a read.

For those anticipating a long stay in Kansai, John Ashburne's *The Best of Kansai* is a great insider's introduction to the region's best restaurants, shops, bars and attractions.

Two books on local architecture worth looking out for are *The Architectural Map of Kyoto*, a painstakingly detailed guide to Kyoto's ancient and modern buildings (written in Japanese, with English footnotes) and *Light in Japanese Architecture* by Henry Plummer, a thoughtfully written and brilliantly illustrated bilingual treatment of both traditional and contemporary Japanese architecture.

The best English guidebook for touring Kyoto's gardens is *A Guide to the Gardens of Kyoto* by Marc Treib and Ron Herman. Also worth a mention are four reasonably priced, compact books from Mitsumura Suiko Shoin: *Invitation to Tea Gardens* by Preston Houser, *Zen Gardens* by Tom Wright and *Invitation to Kyoto Gardens* by Yamamoto Kenzo.

Travel

It seems that anyone who spends more than a few months in Japan feels compelled to write a book-length account of their experiences. These range from the puerile to the sublime. One writer who falls into the latter category is the late Alan Booth, whose *The Roads to Sata* traces a four-month journey on foot from the northern tip of Hokkaidō to Sata, the southern tip of Kyūshū. Booth's *Looking for the Lost – Journeys Through a Vanishing Japan* was his last book, and again recounts walks in rural Japan.

The *Inland Sea* by Donald Richie is another memorable Japanese travelogue, this time about a journey through the little-visited islands between western Honshū and Shikoku.

History & Politics

For general Japanese history, *Japan – Its History & Culture* by W Scott Morton is a worthy read. *Historical Kyoto* by Herbert Plutschow offers perhaps the most detailed history of the city itself.

For a visual perspective on Japan's intriguing past, there are two excellent photo books each featuring numerous images from Kyoto. *Early Japanese Images* by Terry Bennett and *Japan – Caught in Time* by Hugh Cortazzi & Terry Bennett both offer a rare glimpse into old Japan.

Cookbook
Food of Japan by Shirley Booth offers a richly personal but very practical guide to cooking Japanese food. It's also entertaining with chapter headings such as 'Meat – Food of the Hairy Barbarians'.

General
Kyoto Encounters is J Thomas Rimer's provocative collection of reflections on Kyoto in literature, prose and photos, including notables spanning the globe from Bashō to Rudyard Kipling.

In *Introducing Kyoto* Herbert Plutschow provides a basic overview of Kyoto's history, culture and sights illustrated with colour photos. The similar *Kyoto & Nara – The Soul of Japan* by Philip Sandoz, takes in the ancient capital of Nara as well.

The Spirit of Kyoto is another colourful collection of classical Kyoto images shot by noted local photographer Mizuno Katsuhiko.

Arthur Golden's wildly successful *Memoirs of a Geisha* is set mostly in Kyoto and sheds light on the little-known world of geisha and apprentice geisha *(maiko)*. If this book makes you want to know more about geisha, check out two lavishly illustrated books by Aihara Kyoko, *Geisha: A Living Tradition* and *The World of the Geisha*.

NEWSPAPERS & MAGAZINES
There are three English-language daily newspapers in Japan: *The Japan Times*, the *Daily Yomiuri* and the *Asahi*, which recently announced plans to join forces with the *International Herald Tribune* to publish a joint morning paper. All of these can be found at the bookshops listed in the boxed text 'Kyoto Bookshops' in this chapter, at most major hotels and at some newspaper stands in train and subway stations.

Another excellent source of information on Kyoto and the rest of the Kansai area is *Kansai Time Out*, a monthly English-

language what's on magazine (¥300). For short-term visitors, new arrivals and even long-term expats, *Kansai Time Out* is the best investment you'll ever make. Apart from lively articles, it has a large section of announcements and ads for employment, travel agencies, clubs, lonely hearts etc. It's available at Maruzen and Kinokuniya bookshops, or by calling ☎ 078-232 4516 (Kōbe).

Those with more eclectic interests should keep an eye out for the praiseworthy *Kyoto Journal*, which publishes in-depth articles on Asian culture and issues, as well as artwork by Kyoto residents and others. It's also available at local bookshops.

Useful Publications
The monthly *Kyoto Visitor's Guide* is the best source of information on cultural and tourist events. It's available free at the TIC, Maruzen bookshop, the Kyoto International Community House and most major hotels.

Kansai Flea Market is a free monthly publication aimed at foreign residents, with work and housing listings, as well as entertaining personals. It can be picked up at several places in town including bookshops, bars and the TIC.

Life in Kyoto, published by the Kyoto City International Foundation, available at the Kyoto International Community House, is a free monthly journal with Kyoto-related features and useful events listings.

Kansai Scene is a free monthly publication with a few articles, events listings and some handy maps of downtown Kyoto, Osaka and Kōbe. While it's no match for *Kansai Time Out*, it's still fairly useful. You can pick it up at most of the places where you find *Kansai Time Out*.

RADIO & TV
Radio
Kyoto's best station with bilingual broadcasts and decent music is Alpha Station (89.4 FM), but there are several other Kansai stations worth checking out:

76.5 FM COCOLO	(multilingual)
80.2 FM 802	(Japanese/English)
85.1 FM Osaka	(Japanese/English)
89.9 Kiss FM Kōbe	(Japanese/English)

TV

Unless you are fortunate enough to have satellite TV in your hotel room, you won't find any English programming on TV (unless you feel like brushing up your grammar with NHK's (Japan Broadcasting Corporation) televised English lessons). However, it's well worth flipping through the Japanese programs for the window they offer onto Japanese culture.

If you're craving a bit of international news, the KICH and the Kyoto Prefectural International Center play CNN and BBC on their TVs during their opening hours (see the Useful Organisations section later in this chapter).

VIDEO SYSTEM

Japan's video system is the American NTSC standard. If you are using a PAL or SECAM system video camera bring your own video cartridges from home.

PHOTOGRAPHY & VIDEO

Photography is one of Japan's great pastimes. As such, you can be sure that you're never too far from a new roll of film. Colour print film and disposable cameras are found everywhere, from train station kiosks to convenience stores. While most prices are fairly competitive, you're always better off buying a multipack of film at a camera store (these offer substantial savings over purchasing individual rolls).

For amateur and professional supplies including slide film, black and white film and all the latest gadgets, Kyoto's best shop is Medic (Map 9; ☎ 256 6651), on the west side of Kawaramachi-dōri, about 50m north of Sanjō-dōri. It also offers reliable processing services.

Another popular place to have print film developed is at the Yellow Camera chain (with several branches in Kyoto), easy to spot by its all-yellow facade. One-hour processing tends to be slightly more expensive than overnight, but it is offered at many local shops. Japanese labs usually print on what's called *sābisu saizu* (service size), which is about two-thirds of the standard size in most countries (four by six

inches). Unless you're happy with this size, ask to have your photos printed on *hagaki* (postcard) size paper.

For black and white film or slide processing three of Kyoto's best labs are Create (Map 5; ☎ 252 1728), Horiuchi Color (Map 9; ☎ 223 5321), and Kodak Imagica (Map 9; ☎ 252 0577). All offer discounts on large processing orders (usually more than 20 rolls).

Though in Japan it is more often a case of being asked to join in another's snapshot, in general Japanese people are happy to have their photos taken. It never hurts, however, to ask before you shoot. Even the fully dressed *geisha* shuffling through the streets of the entertainment district will often stop to pose if asked politely (just try to make it quick, as they are always hurrying to and from appointments and don't like to wait while you change film or set up your tripod).

If you haven't already experienced the thrill, Kyoto is full of *purika*, self-service miniphoto booths where people cram in to be photographed in front of various backgrounds or with Japanese pop stars. For a

Calendars and Dates

In 1873 the Japanese switched from the lunar calendar to the Gregorian calendar used in the West. As in the rest of Asia, official public holidays are dated according to the Gregorian calendar, while traditional festivals and events still follow the lunar system.

Years are counted in Japan according to two systems: Western and Imperial. The Western system sets the date from the birth of Christ, while the Imperial system calculates the year from the accession of the most recent emperor. The reign of each emperor is assigned a special name; thus the span of the previous emperor, Hirohito (1926–89), is known as the Shōwa (Enlightened Peace) era, meaning 1988 was Shōwa 63. The present emperor, Akihito, who ascended the throne in 1989, reigns in the Heisei (Peace Perfecting) era, so 2001 equals Heisei 13.

An imperial messenger in an oxcart, part of an Aoi Matsuri parade

Costumes at Jidai Matsuri

Giant flaming torches are carried through the streets of Kyoto during the annual Fire Festival.

Jidai Matsuri costume

A giant festival cart in a parade for Kyoto's famous Gion Matsuri.

The arrival of the cherry blossom *(sakura)* marks the beginning of spring and transforms the city into a blaze of pink and white. The Japanese delight in Hanami (Blossom Viewing) from February to April.

FRANK CARTER

few hundred yen you can take home your very own sheet of photo stickers to impress your friends.

TIME

Despite Japan's east-west distance, the country is all in the same time zone, nine hours ahead of Greenwich Mean Time (GMT). Thus, when it is noon in Japan, it is 5pm the previous day in Honolulu, 7pm in San Francisco, 10pm in New York, 3am in London, 11am in Hong Kong, 1pm in Sydney and 3pm in Auckland. Daylight-saving time is not applied in Japan.

Many clocks, in particular those in train and bus stations, operate on a 24-hour clock and most timetables for public transport are based on this system.

ELECTRICITY
Voltages & Cycles

The Japanese electric current is 100V AC, an odd voltage not found elsewhere in the world, though most North American electrical items, designed to run on 117V, will function reasonably well on the Japanese current.

While Tokyo and eastern Japan are on 50 Hz, Kyoto and the rest of western Japan are on a cycle of 60 Hz.

Plugs & Sockets

Identical to North American plugs, Japanese plugs are of the flat, two-pronged variety. Both transformers and plug adaptors are readily available in Kyoto's Teramachi-dōri electronics district (see the Shopping chapter for details on this street).

WEIGHTS & MEASURES

Japan uses the international metric system. One odd exception is the size of rooms, which are often given in *tatami* (woven straw floor matting) measurements known as *jō*.

LAUNDRY

While most youth hostels and some inns are equipped with laundry facilities, most hotels are not. Unless you're prepared to pay for (expensive) hotel laundry services, the next-best option is to find a *koin randorii* (coin laundry). Like most Japanese cities, Kyoto has plenty of these. Costs average from ¥200 to ¥300 per load; dryers run for seven to 10 minutes for ¥100.

Kyoto has plenty of capable dry-cleaners. While most are expensive compared to what you may be used to, one of the better deals is on *Y-shatsu* (white shirts). These are regular cotton button-down business shirts that cost around ¥150 to ¥200 to clean and press.

TOILETS & PUBLIC BATHS
Toilets

To sit or squat...that is the question. In Kyoto you will come across both Western-style and Asian squat toilets. When you are compelled to squat, the correct position is facing the pipes, away from the door. Some squat toilets are equipped with a handlebar fixed to the wall. Also, be sure not to lose the contents of your pockets on the floor, or worse, down the hole.

Public toilets do not always provide toilet paper, so it is a good idea to keep some on hand (you can usually find packets of tissues handed out as advertising on street corners). You will find that most train and subway station toilets are equipped with tissue vending machines (about ¥50 per pack). You can also usually find a toilet in a big hotel or fast-food restaurant if you are in a jam, and in some convenience stores.

Public toilets are free in Japan. The kanji script for 'toilet' is トイレ or お手洗い, for 'men' is 男, and for 'women' is 女.

Lastly, in homes and inns, separate toilet slippers are usually provided just inside the door. These are for use in the toilet only, so remember to change out of them before you exit, or you can expect some horrified looks as you step onto the tatami with them still on.

Public Baths

Kyoto has a large number of *sentō* and a visit to one of these can be a worthwhile experience. Sentō are frequently mistaken with *onsen*. Sentō are simply neighbourhood bath houses that use heated tap water, while onsen are hot spring baths that pipe in natural hot spring water. For more on Japanese bathing etiquette, see the boxed text 'The Japanese Bath' in the Things to See & Do chapter. For a listing of Kyoto sentō, see the Baths section of the Things to See & Do chapter.

Medical Kit Check List

Most of the following items are readily available in Japan. You might want to carry some of them just to be on the safe side.

☐ **Aspirin** or **paracetamol** for pain or fever.
☐ **Antihistamine** (such as Benadryl) – useful as a decongestant for colds, allergies, to ease the itch from insect bites or stings or to help prevent motion sickness.
☐ **Kaolin preparation** (Pepto-Bismol), Imodium or Lomotil – for stomach upsets.
☐ **Antiseptic** and **antibiotic powder** or similar 'dry' spray – to disinfect cuts and grazes.
☐ **Calamine lotion** to ease irritation from bites or stings.
☐ **Bandages** and *Band-Aids* – for minor injuries.
☐ **Scissors, tweezers** and a **thermometer** – mercury thermometers are prohibited by airlines.
☐ **Insect repellent, sunscreen** (can be difficult to find in Japan) and **chapstick**.

If you wear glasses, bring a spare pair and your prescription. If you require a particular medication, take an adequate supply as it may not be available locally. Take the prescription with the generic rather than the brand name, which may be unavailable, as it will make getting replacements easier. Bring the original prescription for any prescription medicine you bring with you to Japan (customs officials can be very strict about unfamiliar medications).

Although oral contraceptives are available from clinics specialising in medical care for foreigners, it is preferable to bring adequate supplies with you. It was only in 1990 that the sale of oral contraceptives was officially authorised in Japan. Condoms are widely available, but bringing some from home is a good idea.

LEFT LUGGAGE

There are coin lockers in larger bus terminals and train stations in Kyoto. Small/medium/large lockers cost ¥300/400/600 for 24 hours. Otherwise, in Kyoto station there is a luggage storage office *(ichiji-nimotsu-azukari)* which charges ¥410 per piece of luggage for up to six days, after which the daily rate increases to ¥820. Luggage can be stored for a total of 15 days and there is a size limit (within two metres across and up to 30kg). The office is on the B1 floor near the centre ticket gate.

HEALTH

Travel health depends on your pre-departure preparations, your day-to-day health care while travelling and how you handle any medical problem or emergency that does develop. However, looking after your health in Japan should pose few problems, since hygiene standards are high and medical facilities are widely available, though expensive. There are very few health risks in Japan to speak of, aside perhaps from an overabundance of secondary smoke.

Travel Health Guides

Lonely Planet produces *Healthy Travel Asia & India*, a handy pocket-size guide packed with useful information including pretrip planning, emergency first aid, immunisation and disease information and what to do if you get sick on the road.

There are a number of other useful guides on travel health:

Staying Healthy in Asia, Africa & Latin America by Dirk Schroeder, Moon Publications, 1994. Probably the best all-round guide to carry; it's compact, detailed and well organised.
Travellers' Health by Dr Richard Dawood, Oxford University Press, 1995. Comprehensive, easy to read, authoritative and highly recommended, although it's rather large to lug around.
Travel with Children by Maureen Wheeler, Lonely Planet Publications, 1995. Includes advice on travel health for younger children.

There are also a number of excellent travel health sites on the Internet. From the Lonely

Planet Web site (**W** www.lonelyplanet.com) there are links to the World Health Organization and the US Centers for Disease Control & Prevention.

Pre-departure Planning

No immunisations are required for Japan though, despite the very low risk factor, you may want to consider vaccinations against Hepatitis A and B. The former is transmitted by contaminated food and drinking water and the latter is spread through contact with infected blood, blood products or body fluids. It is also wise to keep up to date with your tetanus and diphtheria and polio shots (boosters are recommended every 10 years). Tap water is safe to drink and the food is almost uniformly prepared with high standards of hygiene. It is advisable to take out some form of health insurance (see the Documents section earlier in this chapter).

Medical Assistance

Medical care in Japan is relatively expensive. Although the cost of a basic consultation is cheap (about ¥3000) the costs really start to add up with any further examinations, especially with the tendency of Japan's doctors to over-prescribe medicines. If you do need to visit a hospital in Kyoto, it is not usually necessary to have cash in hand; most hospitals will admit people on a pay-later basis. Credit cards are rarely accepted.

Hospitals and clinics have limited walk-in hours and can be contacted for appointments.

For nonemergency medical care in Kyoto, the Japan Baptist Hospital (Map 4; ☎ 781 5191) is popular with foreign residents and has some English-speaking doctors. It's in north-east Kyoto; to get there, take bus No 3 from Shijō Kawaramachi station on the Hankyū line and get off at the Baptist Byōin-mae stop. It's a short walk up the hill. Walk-in hours are from 8.30am to 11am and 1pm to 3.45pm; closed Saturday afternoon, Sunday and holidays.

For an emergency clinic open on Sunday and public holidays, try the Kyoto Holiday Emergency Clinic (Map 5; ☎ 811 5072). For emergency dental problems call the Kyoto Holiday Emergency Dental Clinic (Map 5; ☎ 812 8493) or Igarashi Dental Clinic (Map 2; ☎ 392 0993).

Some other hospitals and clinics around town include:

Hashimoto Pediatric Clinic (☎ 581 0015)
Hirata-chō 24-6, Nagitsuji, Yamashina-ku
Kyoto City Hospital (Map 7; ☎ 311 5311)
Higashi-takada-chō 1-2, Mibu, Nakagyō-ku
Kyoto Prefectural University Hospital (Map 5; ☎ 251 5111) Hirokoji-agaru, Kawaramachi-dōri, Kamigyō-ku
Tomita Maternity Clinic (Map 5; ☎ 221 1202) Sanjō-agaru, Shinmachi-dōri, Nakagyō-ku

For additional hospital recommendations, the TIC has lists of English-speaking doctors and hospitals in Kyoto.

Pharmacies

Pharmacies can be found in any neighbourhood in the city and are easily spotted by their colourful outdoor displays of shampoo and other pharmaceutical products.

Counselling & Advice

Adjusting to life in Japan can be tough but there are several places to turn to for help. KICH (Map 6; see the Useful Organisations section later in this chapter) offers multilingual counselling services, as does the Kyoto Prefectural International Center in Kyoto station (Map 10; see the Useful Organisations section later in this chapter). If you urgently need to speak with someone, try the 24-hour Japan Helpline (toll-free ☎ 0120-461 997).

For professional psychiatric assistance, the private Aoibashi Family Clinic (Map 5; ☎ 431 9150) has foreign staff and offers counselling in English from 10am to 5pm, except Sunday; by appointment only.

WOMEN TRAVELLERS

The major concern, 'Will I be physically safe?' is less of a worry in Japan than many other countries. Statistics show low rates of violent crimes against women, although some Japanese women's organisations and media attribute this to under-reporting.

The biggest hazard for many women travellers is that of adopting a too casual disregard for normal safety precautions while in Japan. Many women, lulled by Japan's reputation for safety, mistakenly assume that nothing can happen to them. This is, unfortunately, false.

Although some expats will assure you that it's safe to walk the streets of any Japanese city alone at night, ignore this and follow your common sense: keep to streets with heavier foot traffic, stay in groups etc. Western women who are alone on foot are easy targets for verbal harassment or worse by passing male motorists. Walking solo along highways in remote rural areas at any time of day and hitchhiking are definitely advised against.

It is the rare (or super streetwise) woman who stays in Japan for any length of time without encountering some type of sexual harassment. Apparently some men find that words are not enough to express how they feel, as flashers and cruder exhibitionists are not uncommon.

Statistics on reported rape are low, but it is estimated that actual rates are significantly higher. If you or someone you know is raped, you should seek immediate medical help and report the matter to the police. Be forewarned, though, that police and medical personnel can be quite unhelpful, even accusatory. Insist on receiving the appropriate medical care (STD tests, antibiotic booster shot, morning after pill) and, as appropriate, filing a police report.

If you do have a problem and find the local police unhelpful, you can call the Human Rights Center Information Line in Tokyo (☎ 03-3581 2303).

See also the Dangers & Annoyances section later in this chapter for general information on safety.

Organisations

There are a variety of helpful contacts and women's services in Kyoto, and the YWCA (see the Useful Organisations section) is a good place to begin. The YWCA offers a free telephone consultation service for foreign women in English, as well as Spanish, Thai, Tagalog and Chinese, on Monday from 3pm to 6pm and Thursday from 3pm to 8pm. You can also arrange long-term accommodation here. There is a useful book of Kansai area contacts for women on display in the lobby.

Recently the Kyoto police launched a women's telephone consultation service staffed by local policewomen. The helpline can be contacted on ☎ 411 0110, Monday to Friday from 9am to 5pm. There are English-speaking staff, and though they're not always on duty, you can arrange a time to call back to speak with one of them (you may have to have a Japanese speaker make the initial call).

Kansai Time Out is a good source to locate women's groups, meetings and activities.

GAY & LESBIAN TRAVELLERS

With the possible exception of Thailand, Japan is Asia's most enlightened nation with regard to the sexual preferences of foreigners. Same-sex couples probably won't encounter many problems travelling in Japan. However, some travellers have reported problems when checking into love hotels with a partner of the same sex; some have been turned away, others have been grossly overcharged. Apart from this, it's unlikely that you'll run into difficulties, but it does pay to be discreet in rural areas.

While there is a sizable gay community in Kyoto and a number of establishments where gays do congregate, they will take a fair amount of digging to find. There is a far more active scene in Osaka, and many of Kyoto's gay residents choose to make the one-hour train trip. If you are in Kyoto on the right day of the month, however, *the* gay event in town is the monthly Non-Hetero-At-The-Metro night at the Metro nightclub (see the Entertainment chapter for details).

Organisations

If you are on your way to the Kansai area, it is worth writing or emailing a group called Out and About, which organises local gay events and outings. Its address is: PM Box 104, Nishigami Bldg, Room 20, Doyama-chō 7-10, Kita-ku, Osaka 530-0027, ⒠ OandA@POBoxes.com.

On the Internet the following organisation may also be of help:

Gay Net Japan Ⓦ www.gnj.or.jp/gaynet/

DISABLED TRAVELLERS

Though Kyoto has made some attempts at making public facilities more accessible, its narrow streets and the terrain of sights such as temples and shrines make it a challenging city for disabled people, especially for those confined to wheelchairs. Both the main Kyoto TIC and the TIC in the Kyoto station building have wheelchairs that can be borrowed free of charge.

If you are going to travel by train and need assistance, ask one of the station workers as you enter the station. Try asking: *'Karada no fujiyuū no kata no tame no sharyō wa arimasu ka?'* ('Are there any train carriages for disabled travellers?').

There are carriages on most lines that have areas set aside for those in wheelchairs. Those with other physical disabilities can use one of the seats set aside near the train exits, called *yūsen-zaseki*. You'll also find these seats near the front of buses; usually they're a different colour from the regular seats.

MK Taxi (☎ 721 2237) can accommodate wheelchairs in many of its cars and is an attractive possibility for anyone interested in touring the city by cab. Facilities for the visually impaired include musical pedestrian lights at many city intersections and raised bumps on railway platforms for guidance.

Organisations

AD-Brain (the same outfit which publishes the monthly *Kyoto Visitor's Guide)* has produced a basic city map for disabled people and senior citizens showing wheelchair access points in town and giving information on public transport access etc. The map is available at the TIC. You might also try contacting the disabled welfare section at Kyoto City Hall (Map 9; ☎ 251 2385), or the Kyoto City Association for Disabled Persons (☎ 822 0770 in Japanese), which publishes the very detailed *Handy Map* guidebook on local facility accessibility, presently in Japanese only.

SENIOR TRAVELLERS

Japan is an excellent place for senior travellers. To qualify for widely available senior discounts, you have to be over 60 or 65, depending upon the place/company.

Japanese domestic airlines (JAS, JAL and ANA) offer senior discounts of about 25% on some flights. For more information, contact the airlines (see the Airline Offices section in the Getting There and Away chapter). JR offers a variety of discounts and special passes, including the 'Full Moon Green Pass', which is good for travel in Green Cars on shinkansen, regular JR trains and sleeper trains. The pass is available to couples whose combined age exceeds 88 years (passports can prove this). A five-day pass, good for two people, costs ¥79,000. Several restrictions apply to these passes, so it's best to inquire at a TIC for details. See also the Getting There & Away chapter for details on the Japan Rail Pass.

In addition to travel discounts, discounts are available on entry fees to many temples, museums and cinemas.

KYOTO FOR CHILDREN

Japan is a great place to travel with children; it's safe, clean and extremely convenient. It's possible to book cots in most proper hotels (as opposed to 'business hotels') and nappy-changing tables are available in the bathrooms of most hotels and in some train stations. Nappies and baby formula are widely available in supermarkets, department stores and convenience stores.

Breastfeeding in public is generally not done in Japan. Child care facilities are usually available in department stores – ask at the information counter when you enter. Otherwise, child care facilities are generally geared to locals only and are hard to access for short-term visitors.

In general, the cost of public transport is half-price for children under 12. Likewise, many of the city's attractions and hotels also offer discounted rates for children.

There are plenty of child-friendly things to see and do in Kyoto. In particular, the western part of town gets high marks with kids: in the Uzumasa area there is Tōei

Uzumasa Eiga Mura (Movie Village; Map 2), Kyoto's answer to a Universal Studios theme park; the entertaining Iwatayama Monkey Park (Map 11) with paddle boats in nearby Arashiyama; and the excitement of shooting the rapids from Kameoka down to Arashiyama on the Hozu-gawa river ride.

Other sights to consider are the Kyoto Municipal Zoo (Map 6), where you can recharge the tots when visiting the Heian-jingū area in Okazaki. For a ride on an authentic steam train, there is the Umekoji Steam Locomotive Museum (Map 7) west of Kyoto station.

Of course, there is always the option of a nature walk around the foothills of the city. If this doesn't do the trick, there are plenty of trademark game centres scattered around town with all the latest in high-tech video games.

You should also consider the surprising number of festivals in Kyoto, as they are not only culturally rich, but often involve kids as participants. Many foreign kids get a kick out of seeing their Japanese counterparts parading down the street dressed in traditional costume. In addition, even at the most 'traditional' of Kyoto's many festivals, there are usually several carnival-like attractions and games to win prizes (see the Festivals section later in this chapter).

Look out for *Japan for Kids* by Diane Wiltshire Kanagawa & Jeane Huey Erickson, an excellent introduction to Japan's highlights from a child's perspective. A useful general guide on taking the kids along is Lonely Planet's *Travelling with Children* by Maureen Wheeler.

USEFUL ORGANISATIONS
Kyoto International Community House (KICH)

The KICH (Map 6; ☎ 752 3010), not far from Nanzen-ji, is an essential stop for those planning a long-term stay in Kyoto and can be quite useful for short-term visitors as well. The office is open from 9am to 9pm but closed Monday (or the following Tuesday if Monday is a national holiday).

Services include typewriter/computer rental, fax (sending and receiving), and a library with maps, books, newspapers and magazines from around the world. Perhaps most useful for residents, however, is the noticeboard, which has messages regarding work, accommodation, rummage sales and so on. They've also just introduced Internet service (¥200 for 30 minutes).

While you're there you can pick up a copy of their excellent *Guide to Kyoto* map and their *Easy Living in Kyoto* book (but please note that both of these are intended for residents). You can also chill out in the lobby and watch CNN news or have a cup of coffee in their café.

If you would like to meet a Japanese family at home, you can also make arrangements through the KICH. Let them know at least one day, preferably two days in advance.

Lastly, see the Activities section for information on cultural demonstrations and classes held at the KICH.

The KICH is in eastern Kyoto about 500m west of Nanzen-ji. You can walk from Sanjō Keihan station in about 20 minutes. Alternately, take the Tōzai subway from downtown and get off at Keage station, from which it's a five-minute walk downhill.

Other Organisations

Another useful resource in the heart of town, a few minutes' walk north of the intersection of Shijō-dōri and Karasuma-dōri, is the Japan Foundation (Map 9; ☎ 211 1312) on the 8th floor of the Yasuda Kasai Kaijō building. It has a well stocked library, message board, monthly lectures and seminars, and screens free Japanese movie classics for foreign visitors on Wednesday at 2pm. The office is open from 10am to 5pm weekdays, closed weekends.

The Kyoto Prefectural International Center (Map 10; ☎ 342 5000) is a multifunction resource centre with information on the Kyoto region. It has a small library of travel literature, English TV news and offers Internet access (¥250 for 30 minutes). The centre is open daily from 10am to 6pm, closed on the second and fourth Tuesday of the month. It's on the 9th floor of the Kyoto station building; take the elevator from inside Isetan department store.

The YWCA (Map 5; ☎ 431 0351), west of the Imperial Palace Park on Muromachi-dōri, offers counselling and long-term accommodation for women. It's open Monday to Friday from 10am to 8pm, Saturday from 11am to 5pm, closed Sunday and public holidays.

Kyoto English Alcoholics Anonymous meets at 11am Sunday and 7pm Thursday at the Kyoto Nishijin Catholic Church (Map 5). Call Bill (☎ 722 0732) for more information.

LIBRARIES

Though there are several public and university libraries in Kyoto, some with reasonable English collections, the best and most accessible books are at the libraries of the KICH and the Japan Foundation (see the previous Useful Organisations section), each with several thousand titles in English.

The Japan Foundation has a particularly strong collection on Japanese history, culture and arts. In addition to a good variety of books on Japan, the KICH also has newspapers and magazines in various languages, and a large collection of travel guides and maps. If there are specific areas of research, the staff at either of these facilities should be able to provide leads on other public or private collections in town.

For travel guides and books on Japan, the Kyoto Prefectural International Center is also worth a look.

UNIVERSITIES

Kyoto is one of Japan's major educational centres. There are 37 universities and junior colleges, whose students account for about 10% of the city's population. The campuses are good areas to meet young Japanese and most have school festivals in autumn worth checking out.

Among the largest schools are:

Bukkyō University (Map 3; Buddhist)
Dōshisha University (Maps 3 & 5; Liberal Arts)
Kyoto Sangyō University (Map 2; Liberal Arts)
Kyoto University (Map 6; Liberal Arts)
Kyoto University of Foreign Studies (Map 2; Foreign Languages)
Ritsumeikan University (Map 2; Liberal Arts)

CULTURAL CENTRES

There are British, French, German and Italian culture centres in Kyoto. Each features libraries and sponsors art exhibitions, lectures and seminars relating to their respective country, and cross-cultural exchange.

British

The British Council (Map 6; ☎ 791 7151) is on Nishimachi-dōri, north-west of the Imadegawa-Shirakawa intersection; open from 10am to 6pm, closed weekends and public holidays.

French

Institut Franco-Japonais du Kansai (Map 6; ☎ 761 2105) is on Higashiōji-dōri, south of Imadegawa-dōri; open from 9.45am to 6.15pm (to 5.45pm Saturday), closed Sunday.

German

Goethe Institute Kyoto (Map 5; ☎ 761 2188) is on Kawabata-dōri, south of Imadegawa-dōri; open from 9am to 5pm, closed weekends and public holidays.

Italian

Instituto Italiano di Cultura di Kansai (Map 6; ☎ 751 1868) is on Higashiōji-dōri, south of Imadegawa-dōri; open from 10am to 6pm, closed weekends and public holidays.

DANGERS & ANNOYANCES

Japan has a reputation as one of the world's safest countries in which to travel. For men, this is indeed the case. Unfortunately, for women, this is not always the case. There have been numerous cases of foreign women being groped, assaulted and even raped. In general, it is best to stay on well travelled, well lit streets at night and remember you will be safer going out in a group of people. For more on this, see the Women Travellers section earlier in this chapter.

Apart from the dangers that face women travellers, the only specific danger spot to be aware of in Kyoto is the west bank of the Kamo-gawa between Sanjō-dōri and Shijō-dōri. This is a popular summer hang-out for couples and Kyoto youth. In recent years, there have been incidents of foreign men being attacked here by gangs of young Japanese males. Luckily, the police have clamped down on the area in the last year or two, but it still pays to be cautious when walking here late at night or alone.

Theft of bicycles can also be a problem, and bicycles should always be locked up (see also the Bicycle section in the Getting Around chapter).

EMERGENCIES

The nationwide number for police *(keisatsu)* is ☎ 110. To summon an ambulance *(kyukyu-sha)* or to report a fire *(kaji)* call ☎ 119. The person answering the phone may not speak good English but if you speak slowly and have your address in hand, you should be able to get your point across.

Police boxes, or *kōban*, are small police stations typically found at city intersections. Most can be recognised by the small, round red lamp outside. They are a logical place to head in an emergency, but remember that the police may not always speak English.

If you need to use English and want help finding the closest suitable service, try the Japan Travel-Phone (☎ 371 5649) or Japan Helpline (☎ 0120-461 997).

There is a local police consultation telephone helpline (☎ 414 0110) with limited English, open Monday to Friday from 9am to 5pm. Another option for women is consulting the YWCA (Map 5; ☎ 431 0351), which can be very helpful with things like locating doctors and assistance for getting to hospitals.

LEGAL MATTERS

Japanese police have extraordinary powers in comparison with their Western counterparts. For starters, Japanese police have the right to detain a suspect without charging them for up to three days, after which a prosecutor can decide to extend this period for another 20 days. Police can also choose whether to allow a suspect to phone his or her embassy or lawyer, though if you find yourself in police custody you should insist that you will not cooperate in any way until allowed to make such a call. Your embassy is the first place you should call if given the chance.

Police will speak almost no English; insist that an interpreter *(tsuyakusha)* be summoned.

Police are legally bound to provide one before proceeding with any questioning. If you do speak Japanese, it's best to deny it and stay with your native language.

For legal advice and contacts for English-speaking lawyers, the best place to turn is the KICH (☎ 752 1187), which also offers free legal counselling to foreigners. Another place to turn for legal help is the Centre for Multicultural Information and Assistance (☎ 06-6973 7506). This Osaka-based agency is staffed by multi-lingual volunteers and offers a free consultation service on Fridays from 6pm to 9pm.

For additional legal counselling in English and some other languages, call the Human Rights Center Information Line in Tokyo (☎ 03-3581 2302) from noon to 5pm on weekdays. The Tokyo Gaikokujin Komarigoto Sōdan (Foreigners' Crisis Consultation, ☎ 03-3503 8484) can provide telephone interpretation with police if necessary.

BUSINESS HOURS

Shops in town are typically open from 10am to 7pm or 8pm. Shopping (or sightseeing for that matter) on Sunday, the only free day for most working Japanese, should be avoided if you've got an aversion to crowds.

Kyoto's six major department stores are open from 10am to 7.30pm and each closes one day a week (though this day varies through the year). If one is closed you stand a good chance of finding another one open close by.

Though most companies technically operate on a 9am to 5pm, five-day work week, many stay in business on Saturday morning as well.

See the earlier Post & Communications section for post office hours.

Banks are open Monday to Friday from 9am to 3pm, and closed on Saturday, Sunday and national holidays.

For those late-night cravings, beer and cigarette vending machines shut down after 11pm, though there are 24-hour convenience stores all over town, some of which stock booze and tobacco.

Festivals

Hatsumōde
1–3 January; first visit of the New Year to a Shintō shrine where you pray to ensure health and good fortune for the year. Kyoto's most-visited shrines are Yasaka-jinja (Map 8) and Heian-jingū (Map 6).

Karuta Hajime
3 January; at Yasaka-jinja (Map 8) from 1pm, pairs of women dressed in Heian-era court costumes play *hyaku-nin-isshu*, an ancient Japanese card game.

Kemari Hajime (Kick Ball Game)
4 January; at Heian-jingū (Map 6) from 2pm, men in elaborate Heian-era court costumes play *kemari*, a traditional court ball game. It's the first of several such events during the year.

Hatsu Ebisu or Tōka Ebisu
8–12 January; at Ebisu-jinja (Map 7) a party is held for Ebisu, patron deity of merchants and one of the beloved Shichi Fuku Jin (Seven Luck Gods); people go to pray for a prosperous year.

Tōshiya (Archery Contest)
15 January; at Sanjūsangen-dō (Map 7) from 8am to 4pm. The largest of Kyoto's three archery events in January, it dates to a 1606 feat by a samurai who shot 51 arrows in rapid succession along the veranda of the temple. Hundreds of kimono-clad archers gather for a competition of accuracy and strength, shooting as many arrows as possible into a 1.5m-diameter target 118m away.

Setsubun
2–4 February; last day of winter by the lunar calendar. People go to temples and bless their homes, driving off demons, sickness and misfortune by scattering roasted soya-beans *(mamemaki)* in and around the house while shouting *'Oni-wa-soto, Fuku-wa-uchi'* ('Out with devils, In with luck'). You can enjoy the revelry at Imamiya-jinja (Map 3) and Yasaka-jinja (Map 8) from 1pm to 3pm.

Yoshida-jinja Setsubun Matsuri
3 or 4 February, check with the TIC; people climb up to Yoshida-jinja (Map 6) in northern Higashiyama to watch a huge bonfire. It's one of Kyoto's more dramatic festivals. The action starts at dusk.

Godai Rikison Ninno-e
23 February; at Daigo-ji (Map 1), participants lift two gigantic rice cakes (150kg for men, 90kg for women!). The winner is the one who keeps it in the air the longest.

Baika-sai
25 February; at Kitano-Tenman-gū (Map 3) this festival features colourful plums and geisha. It's a rare open-air tea ceremony, and provides great photo opportunities (it coincides with the market).

Sagano O-taimatsu
15 March; at Seiryō-ji (Map 11) this commemorates Shaka's (Historical Buddha's) death with Nembutsu Kyōgen (Buddhist Miracle Plays) at 2pm. At 7.30pm torches are lit to divine the new harvest.

Yasurai Matsuri
Second Sunday in April; at Imamiya-jinja (Map 3) from noon to 4pm; a rite against plague, with dancers in demon costumes and flaming red hair. Large parasols are paraded through the streets to collect 'disease-causing spirits', which are taken to the shrine to be exorcised.

Festivals

Kanno-chakai (Flower Viewing Festival)
1–21 April; at Heian-jingū (Map 6), there is tea ceremony (¥600) and cherry blossom viewing.

Taiko Hanami Gyōretsu
Second Sunday in April; at Daigo-ji (Map 1), a parade re-enacts in full period costume a cherry blossom party that Toyotomi Hideyoshi held in 1598. As a result of this party, the temple's abbot was able to secure Hideyoshi's support for the restoration of the dilapidated temple complex.

Mibu Kyōgen
21–29 April; at Mibu-dera (Map 5) from 5.30pm; Buddhist miracle plays are held to teach Buddhist doctrine through pantomime. This has been held every spring for the last 700 years.

Aoi Matsuri (Hollyhock Festival)
15 May; dates to the 6th century and commemorates the successful prayers of the people for the gods to stop calamitous weather. The procession of imperial messengers in oxcarts and 600 people in traditional costume carrying hollyhock leaves departs at 10am from the Imperial Palace (Map 5) to Shimogamo-jinja (Map 3) where ceremonies take place. It leaves again at 2pm and arrives at Kamigamo-jinja (Map 3) at 3.30pm.

Mifune Matsuri
Third Sunday in May; this takes place on boats in the Arashiyama area (Map 11), west of Kyoto. It is one of Kyoto's most colourful festivals and starts at 1pm.

Kibune Matsuri
1 June; at Kibune-jinja (Karuma & Kibune Map) in the mountains north of Kyoto; yet another festival held in the interests of good harvest. *Mikoshi* (portable shrines) are carried along the Kibune-gawa.

Takigi Nō
1 and 2 June; at Heian-jingū (Map 6); a festival of nō drama held by torchlight in the courtyard of the shrine. Tickets cost ¥2500 in advance, ¥3300 on the day (phone ☎ 761-0221 for details).

Takekiri E-shiki
20 June; at Kurama-dera (Kurama & Kibune Map). This bamboo-cutting festival dates back 1000 years when a priest of Kurama-dera defeated two evil serpents with the aid of Bishamon-tei, the Buddhist guardian enshrined at the temple. Today, eight priests in robes and hoods of *yamabushi* (mountain priests) form two teams and race to hack to pieces four lengths of green bamboo symbolising the serpents. The festival begins at 2pm.

Mitoshiro Nō
1 July; at Kamigamo-jinja (Map 3). Nō, kyōgen and dances are offered from 1pm for the protection of rice crops from insects.

Gion Matsuri
17 July; perhaps the most renowned of all Japanese festivals, this month-long fanfare involves a large number of events. Yoi-yama is held on the 16th, when over 200,000 people throng the Shijō-Karasuma area, and reaches a climax on the 17th, when a Yamaboko-junkō parade of over 30 giant floats is held to the accompaniment of flutes, drums and gongs. On the three evenings preceding

the 17th, people gather on Shijō-dōri, many dressed in beautiful light summer kimono, to look at the floats and carouse from one street stall to the next. Events last through July.

Gion Matsuri was initiated in AD 869, when plague had ravished the city. The festival was offered as a prayer of relief to the god Susanō-no-Mikoto (the son of the gods, which according to Japanese mythology gave birth to Japan).

Osuzumi
20 July; at Jōnan-gū (Map 2) people gather from 5pm to enjoy the cooling of the summer heat.

Hiwatari Matsuri
28 July; at Tanuki-dani Fudō-in (Map 2), on the mountain behind Shisen-dō, this festival incorporates a fire walk.

Hassaku
1 August; Geisha and *maiko* (apprentice geisha) make appreciation rounds to teachers and Gion (Map 6) teahouses. Also on 1 August the Nagoshi-no-shinji is held at Shimogamo-jinja (Map 3) to mark the end of the heat of summer (although it always seems to last for at least another month).

Mantō-e
14–16 August; at Higashi Ōtani Cemetery, the graveyard of Higashi Hongan-ji (Map 10), where 10,000 candle-lit lanterns welcome home the dead.

Daimon-ji Gozan Okuribi
16 August; commonly known as Daimon-ji-yaki (literally, burning of Daimon-ji), this is performed to bid farewell to the souls of ancestors. Enormous fires are lit on five mountains in the form of Chinese characters or other shapes. The main fire is the character for *dai*, or great, on Daimonji-yama (Map 1), which is lit first, after which the others are lit at 10-minute intervals, working from left to right. The first fires are lit at 8pm. It is best to watch from the banks of the Kamo-gawa or pay for a rooftop view from a hotel.

Sentō Kuyō
23–24 August; at Adashino-Nembutsu-ji (Map 11) in Sagano. This mass is held in honour of the souls of the dead, each of whom is represented by one of the thousands of *jizō* statues at this temple. Candles are placed at each statue, creating an otherworldly sight. Reserve in advance by post by 15 June. There is a ¥1000 fee (children under 12 free).

Karasu Zumō
9 September; at Kamigamo-jinja (Map 3). This is also called crow wrestling. From 10am young boys compete in bouts of sumō wrestling. The festival is named for a legendary blackbird who came to rest on the arrow of Japan's first emperor, Jimmu.

Tsukimi
Mid-September; moon viewing festivals take place at several places, including Daikaku-ji (Map 11) and Shimogamo-jinja (Map 3). At this time of year *(Jūgoya)*, literally the night of the 15th (full) moon, the Japanese traditionally decorate their verandas, temples and shrines with *susuki* (pampas grass) reeds in a vase, *tsukimi-dango* (rice dumplings), steamed *sato-imo* (taro potatoes) and autumn fruits, all facing the moon as an offering. Tsukimi has its roots in a harvest celebration.

Festivals

Nijū-go Bosatsu Oneri Kuyō
Third Sunday in October; at Sokujō-in (Map 8) from 1pm, a colourful procession of 25 children, wearing elaborate costumes of gold brocade, assume roles of the different Bodhisattvas and parade around the temple.

Jidai Matsuri (Festival of the Ages)
22 October; though one of Kyoto's big three, this festival is of recent origin, dating to 1895. More than 2000 people dressed in costumes ranging from the 8th to the 19th centuries parade from the Imperial Palace (Map 5) to Heian-jingū (Map 6).

Kurama-no-Hi Matsuri (Fire Festival)
22 October; this festival is traced to a rite using fires to guide the gods of the nether world on their tours around this world. Mikoshi are carried through the streets and accompanied by young men in loincloths and with giant flaming torches. The festival climaxes at 10pm at Yuki-jinja in Kurama (Kuamam & Kibune Map).

Yōkō-sai
29 October; at Kitano-Tenman-gū (Map 3); from 2pm in memory of exiled scholar Lord Sugawara Michizane (845–903); people dress in elaborate Heian-era costumes and recite ancient poems.

Arashiyama Momiji Matsuri
Second Sunday in November; in the Arashiyama area (Map 11) a procession of boats moves along the Oi-gawa (a fantastic photo opportunity).

Shichi-go-san
15 November; a nationwide event in which proud parents dress kids aged seven, five and three in colourful kimono, and visit local shrines to pray for their health and happiness. Heian-jingū (Map 6) and Yasaka-jinja (Map 8) are popular places for this event.

Fude Kuyō
23 November; in the grounds of Tōfuku-ji (Map 5), this service is held for used calligraphy brushes.

O-susu-harai
20 December; at Higashi Hongan-ji (Map 10) from 9am to 10.30am. A line of kneeling people beat the tatami with wooden mallets, while monks and devotees of the temple don masks and whisk away the dust with gigantic paper fans, ceremonially cleansing the spirit to mark the end of the year.

Ominugui-shiki
25 December; at Chion-in (Map 6) another temple-cleaning ceremony, this time of a Buddhist statue, has the sensational accompaniment of several hundred monks chanting sutras.

Ōmisoka (New Year's Eve)
31 December; sacred fire-kindling festival *(Okera Mairi)* named for the herb burned in lanterns at Yasaka-jinja (Map 8). It's customary to consume *toshikoshi soba* (buckwheat noodles) before going to the shrine to see off the old year, welcome in the new, and return home with a bit of sacred flame on *kitchō-nawa* rope from the shrine to fend off illness in the new year. Activities continue from about 7pm to 1am, with huge crowds from 11pm.

PUBLIC HOLIDAYS & SPECIAL EVENTS

Japan has 14 national holidays. When a public holiday falls on a Sunday, the following Monday is taken as a holiday. Banks and post offices are closed on public holidays; most large stores and attractions remain open. You can expect a total sell-out for travel and lodging during the New Year (29 December to 6 January), Golden Week (27 April to 6 May) and the mid-August O-Bon festival.

Public Holidays

Ganjitsu (New Year's Day) 1 January
Seijin-no-hi (Coming-of-Age Day) 2nd Sunday in January
Kenkoku Kinem-bi (National Foundation Day) 11 February
Shumbun-no-hi (Spring Equinox) 20 or 21 March
Midori-no-hi (Green Day) 29 April
Kempō Kinem-bi (Constitution Day) 3 May
Kodomo-no-hi (Children's Day) 5 May
Umi-no-hi (Marine Day) 20 July
Keirō-no-hi (Respect-for-the-Aged Day) 15 September
Shūbun-no-hi (Autumn Equinox) 23 or 24 September
Taiiku-no-hi (Sports Day) 2nd Monday in October
Bunka-no-hi (Culture Day) 3 November
Kinrō Kansha-no-hi (Labour Thanksgiving Day) 23 November
Tennō Tanjōbi (Emperor's Birthday) 23 December

Festivals

Kyoto's colourful, lively festivals *(matsuri)* are the real highlights of the city. With over 500 going on throughout the year, you should be able to catch at least one on your visit. And if you've got the flexibility, it would make sense to try to schedule your visit so that it coincides with one of Kyoto's really special festivals, like the Kurama-no-Hi Matsuri (Kurama Fire Festival) or the huge Gion Matsuri, Japan's most famous festival.

Most of these celebrations have their roots in ancient Buddhist and Shintō rituals, from ceremonies for a bountiful harvest to fertility rites or prayers for success in

business. Today, however, many people attend for the sheer fun and fanfare. Photo opportunities abound with elaborate floats, people dressed in period costume, geisha, tea ceremonies, and traditional drama and dances. At many of the festivals, both participants and spectators dress up in kimono or *yukata* (summer kimono).

These spectacular festivals are testimony to the ancient culture of the city, and some have been celebrated for over 1000 years. Interestingly, even some of the most traditional events incorporate modern features, right down to amusement park games for kids, cotton candy and the ever-popular fried squid-on-a-stick.

Festival time has its advantages and disadvantages. While there are often special openings of temple buildings and treasures, you will often be struggling through the crowd to get a view. While some temples and shrines waive entry fees on festival days, there are sometimes other fees involved (usually for tea ceremony, good luck charms or food). Some matsuri, especially the 'big three' (the Aoi, Gion and Jidai festivals) attract hordes of spectators from out of town, so it is important to book accommodation well in advance.

It's best to arrive early (around an hour or so before the main event) and try to stake out a suitable place to view the spectacle. If you're not sure where to set up camp, look for the always-present pack of Japanese photographers with step ladders and other fancy gadgets – they will probably be positioning themselves in prime photo-taking territory.

There have been several books published on Japanese festivals; perhaps the best and most colourful is the coffee-table *Matsuri* by Gorazd Vilhar & Charlotte Anderson. Helen Kay's exhaustive *Japan Festival Guide* lists some 800 festivals throughout the country.

See the 'Festivals' boxed text in this section for a listing of Kyoto's major festivals (though there are many more worthwhile events). Dates and times can vary from year to year, so check with the TIC, the *Kyoto Visitor's Guide* or *Kansai Time Out* (the latter has festival listings for the entire Kansai region). Also see the Entertainment chapter for details on geisha dances.

Fireworks The Japanese are among the world's biggest fireworks enthusiasts, and during summer in Kyoto a cherished local pastime (especially among young people) is gathering on the banks of the Kamo-gawa to set off low-calibre explosives and twirl sparklers. For those more into the heavy artillery, there are several chances to view major displays in early August – including those on the Uji-gawa, down south in Uji (Map 15) and from the shores of Biwa-ko (Map 1; see also Ōtsu in the Excursions chapter). Check *Kansai Time Out*, *Kyoto Visitor's Guide* or with the TIC for up-to-date details. Before you go, you may want to practise two Japanese exclamations – *sugoi* (wow!) and *kirei* (beautiful!) – holler either of these at the right time and you'll fit right in!

Night Illumination at Temples & Shrines In the evening during the peak foliage times of spring and autumn, several temples and shrines light up their grounds to create an incredible scene of pink cherry blossoms or blazing maples. Dates and places change slightly from year to year, though in spring (from the beginning of April through mid-May) they're typically held at Kiyomizu-dera (Map 8), Kōdai-ji (Map 8) and Hirano-jinja (Map 3); in autumn (from mid-November to late November) at Kiyomizu-dera, Kōdai-ji, Shōren-in (Map 6), Eikan-dō (Map 6), Enkō-ji (Map 4) and Tenryū-ji (Map 11). The illumination is usually from dusk till about 9.30pm; bring a sweater or jacket with you, as the nights can become cool. Also bring a tripod if you have any plans of taking decent photos. The TIC can provide up-to-date details on places and times.

DOING BUSINESS

Although the reigning business centre of Kansai is Osaka, Kyoto is not surviving off tourism revenue alone. In addition to traditional cottage industries such as weaving and handicrafts, several of Japan's leading high-tech firms such as Kyocera, Murata, Nintendo and Omron have their headquarters here. Kyoto also has an array of business-related facilities such as the Kyoto International Conference Hall (Map 2), Kyoto Research Park (Map 7) and Kansai Science City's Keihanna Plaza.

One useful organisation is the Kyoto Convention Bureau (KCB; Map 5), which provides services such as introductions to convention facilities, accommodation and, through selected tour operators worldwide, can arrange incentive package tours. Information can be found through JNTO offices (see the Tourist Offices section earlier in this chapter) worldwide or write to KCB through Kyoto Chamber of Commerce, Ebisugawa, Nakagyō-ku, Kyoto 604-0862, or phone ☎ 212 4110; fax 212 4121. You can also check the Web site (Ⓦ www.kyoto-inet.or.jp/org/hellokcb/).

Another organisation with useful information on the Internet is the Osaka-based Kansai International Public Relations Promotion Office (KIPPO). Its Web site (Ⓦ www.kippo.or.jp) has links to other groups such as the Japan External Trade Organization (JETRO). Their *Kansai On Demand* is one of the most useful business guides available for Kyoto and Kansai, with detailed listings of useful contacts and economic facts about the region.

A useful reference for turning up business contacts is Nippon Telephone & Telegraph Corporation's (NTT) Townpage, an English telephone directory complete with an extensive index of Internet listings. This can be picked up at the KICH or at the TIC.

Business Books

There is a mountain of tomes purporting to unlock the secrets of Japanese business. *The Art of Japanese Management – Applications for American Executives* has been around for a while, but is still a good introduction.

For nuts and bolts information, there's the *Japan Company Handbook* (Toyo Keizai) detailing listed companies. *Nippon 1997* (JETRO) is an annual statistical publication. Other annual publications include

Survey of Japanese Corporations Overseas (Toyo Keizai), *Japan Trade Directory* (JETRO), *Japan Economic Alamanac* (the *Nikkei Weekly*), and *Japan – An International Comparison* (Keizai Kōhō Center, or Japan Institute for Social and Economic Affairs).

More-practical guides include *Setting Up an Office in Japan* (American Chamber of Commerce in Japan, 1993), *Setting Up and Operating a Business in Japan* by Helene Thian (Tuttle, 1990), and *Setting Up Enterprises in Japan – Guidelines on Investment, Taxation and Legal Regulations* (JETRO, 1993). JETRO's *Investment Japan – A Directory of Institutions and Firms Offering Assistance to People Seeking to Set Up a Business in Japan* is a comprehensive listing of useful contacts across all industries.

WORK

Kyoto's popularity makes it one of Japan's most difficult cities in which to find work. Despite this fact and increasingly strict immigration policies, there is a relatively quick turnaround of many resident foreigners, so it is often just a case of being patient until something comes up. If you plan of making a try of it in Kyoto, you'll need to have enough money to survive for three months or so (around US$6000).

Many who would prefer to live in Kyoto end up commuting to jobs in Osaka or other neighbouring cities, at least until they find something closer to home. Aside from the English-teaching racket, other popular jobs include bar hostessing (mainly women), work in restaurants and bars, and carpentry.

Women who intend to work in hostess bars should be aware of two things: 1) there aren't many hostess bars in Kyoto that employ foreign women and 2) hostessing can be very dangerous work and there have been a spate of attacks on foreign hostesses in recent years, including the murder of British-born Lucy Blackman in 2000 outside of Tokyo.

The best place to look for work is in *Kansai Time Out*, followed by the *Kansai Flea Market*, *Kansai Scene* or the jobs listing at the KICH (you can also post messages offering your service as a private tutor at the KICH). The Monday edition of *The Japan Times* also has a small Kansai employment section. Word-of-mouth is also a great way to find work in Kyoto – you could try dropping by the Pig & Whistle pub with a pencil and pad in hand (see the Entertainment chapter for more details).

Getting There & Away

While there is no international or domestic airport in Kyoto, the city is within easy reach of both Osaka's Itami airport (domestic flights) and Kansai international airport (KIX). Of course, there are other ways to get to and from Kyoto, including ferries from Shanghai and trains from other parts of the country.

AIR

Generally, the high season for travel between Japan and Western countries is late December and early January (around Christmas and New Year's), late April to early May (around Japan's Golden Week holiday), and July and August (northern hemisphere summer holidays). Flights during these periods can be booked out months in advance and tickets may be unavailable at almost any price. Be sure to ask about when prices go up and down when purchasing your ticket.

Airports

With the opening of KIX in 1994, Kansai is now the first port of call for many visitors to Japan. Built on an artificial island in Osaka Bay, it handles over 500 flights a week to and from 75 cities worldwide. The airport is a pleasure to use, with a wide variety of shops and restaurants where you can get rid of your remaining yen. Best of all, it doesn't suffer from the overcrowding that plagues Tokyo's Narita airport and almost all flights leave on time.

Itami airport has frequent flights to/from Tokyo (about 70 minutes) but unless you are very lucky with connections you'll probably find it more convenient and cheaper to take the *shinkansen* (bullet train).

The trip between Kansai international airport and Kyoto can be quite expensive and time-consuming; so if you are flying domestically and have a choice of airports, always choose Itami. See the Getting Around chapter for details on transport to and from these airports.

Warning

The information in this chapter is particularly vulnerable to change: prices for international travel are volatile, routes are introduced and cancelled, schedules change, special deals come and go, and rules and visa requirements are amended. Airlines and governments seem to take a perverse pleasure in making price structures and regulations as complicated as possible. You should check directly with the airline or a travel agent to make sure you understand how a fare (and ticket you may buy) works. In addition, the travel industry is highly competitive and there are many lurks and perks.

The upshot of this is that you should get opinions, quotes and advice from as many airlines and travel agents as possible before you part with your hard-earned cash. The details given in this chapter should be regarded as pointers and are not a substitute for your own careful, up-to-date research.

It's sometimes cheaper to fly into Tokyo's Narita airport than into KIX. As a rule, it will cost about ¥15,000 and take around five hours to get from Narita to Kyoto. Thus, you'd have to save at least ¥30,000 and have plenty of time and energy to spare to consider Narita as your gateway to Kansai/Kyoto. Of course, if you're interested in seeing other parts of Japan, Narita might well be the gateway of choice.

Kansai International Airport (KIX)

Most people travelling to Kyoto from abroad arrive at KIX. There are information counters throughout the complex that have English-speaking staff. There is also a JNTO-operated information counter with a Welcome Inn Reservation Center on the first floor of the arrivals terminal (☎ 0724-56 6025), open 9am to 9pm.

After clearing customs, it is a short walk to public transport (straight out the doors for buses and up the escalators or elevators for train connections). KIX offers short-term and long-term baggage storage for ¥350 to ¥1000 per day, depending on the size of the bag. You pay the bill when you pick up your bag.

When departing, remember that most flights out of Japan depart on time, so it is a good idea to allow yourself plenty of time to arrive at the airport. International flights require you to be at the airport two hours prior to departure time; for domestic flights you should allow at least an hour.

For international departures, the KIX terminal has a stunning assortment of shops and restaurants to make sure you won't be bored should you arrive early. There are also shower facilities, costing ¥1200. These are available only to those who have cleared passport control and transit passengers.

For further inquiries about the airport and services call KIX's 24-hour information line (☎ 0724-552 500).

Departure Tax There is an international departure tax of ¥2650 at KIX. It's easiest to pay in cash (yen only) but paying by credit card is also possible.

Buying Tickets in Japan

Air tickets in Japan are not as expensive as you might think. If you find yourself stuck in Kyoto without a ticket out, don't despair – bargains *are* available outside of the Golden Week and year-end high seasons. Unfortunately, you'll also find that one-way tickets out of the country are only marginally cheaper than return tickets (fancy coming back to Japan?). You'll find lots of good deals advertised in the back of *Kansai Time Out* and in the pages of the English-language newspapers. See the Travel Agents section of the Facts for the Visitor chapter for details on some reliable Kyoto travel agents.

USA

From New York, in the low season, you can find discount return fares into KIX for as low as US$650. Carriers to check include United Airlines, Korean Air, Japan Airlines (JAL) and All Nippon Airways (ANA).

From the US west coast, low season discount return fares can start as low as US$450. High-season discount fares will just about double these figures.

San Francisco is the discount ticket capital of America, although some good deals can also be found in Los Angeles, New York and other big cities. The *New York Times*, the *Los Angeles Times*, the *Chicago Tribune* and the *San Francisco Examiner* all produce weekly travel sections in which you will find a good number of travel agency ads.

Some good travel agencies in the USA include: Ticket Planet (W www.ticketplanet .com); Council Travel (☎ 800-226 8624, W www.ciee.org); and STA Travel (☎ 800-777 0112, W www.statravel.com).

San Francisco's Avia Travel (☎ 800-950 2842 or 510-558 2150, W www.aviatravel .com) is a favourite of Japan-based English teachers and can arrange tickets originating in Japan. IACE Travel New York (☎ 212-972 3200, e iace@interport.com) is a travel agency specialising in travel between the USA and Japan and they can often dig up the cheapest fares around.

Canada

Canadian Airlines International, which operates out of Vancouver, often matches or beats the best fares available from the USA. Low-season return fares from Vancouver to Japan (Tokyo) start as low as C$928. Likewise, Air Canada offers some very competitive fares from eastern Canada to Japan (both Tokyo and KIX). Low-season return fares from Ottawa start at around C$1240. Other airlines to try from Canada include JAL, Northwest and United.

Travel Cuts (☎ 800-667 2887, W www .travelcuts.com) offers cheap one-way and return Vancouver-Japan flights (as low as C$800/1000), depending on the season. You'll find more travel agencies listed in the *Globe & Mail*, the *Toronto Star*, the *Montreal Gazette* and the *Vancouver Sun*.

Australia

Garuda, Malaysian Airlines and Cathay Pacific have some good deals for travel between

Air Travel Glossary

Alliances Many of the world's leading airlines are now intimately involved with each other, sharing everything from reservations systems and check-in to aircraft and frequent-flyer schemes. Opponents say that alliances restrict competition. Whatever the arguments, there is no doubt that big alliances are the way of the future.

Courier Fares Businesses often need to send urgent documents or freight securely and quickly. Courier companies hire people to accompany the package through customs and, in return, offer a discount ticket which is sometimes a bargain. However, you may have to surrender all your baggage allowance and take only carry-on luggage.

Fares Airlines traditionally offer 1st class (coded F), business class (coded J) and economy class (coded Y) tickets. These days there are so many promotional and discounted fares available that few passengers pay full fare.

Lost Tickets If you lose your airline ticket, an airline will usually treat it like a travellers cheque and, after inquiries, issue you with another one. Legally, however, an airline is entitled to treat it like cash and if you lose it then it's gone forever. Take very good care of your tickets.

Onward Tickets An entry requirement for many countries is that you have a ticket out of the country. If you're unsure of your next move, the easiest solution is to buy the cheapest onward ticket to a neighbouring country or a ticket from a reliable airline which can later be refunded if you do not use it.

Open-Jaw Tickets These are return tickets where you fly out to one place but return from another. If available, this can save you backtracking to your arrival point.

Overbooking Since every flight has some passengers who fail to show up, airlines often book more passengers than they have seats. Usually excess passengers make up for the no-shows, but occasionally somebody gets 'bumped' onto the next available flight. Guess who it is most likely to be? The passengers who check in late. If you do get 'bumped', you are normally offered some form of compensation.

Reconfirmation Some airlines require you to reconfirm your flight at least 72 hours prior to departure. Check your travel documents to see if this is the case

Restrictions Discounted tickets often have various restrictions on them – such as needing to be paid for in advance and incurring a penalty to be altered or cancelled. Others are restrictions on the minimum and maximum period you must be away.

Round-the-World Tickets RTW tickets give you a limited period (usually a year) in which to circumnavigate the globe. You can go anywhere the carrying airlines go, as long as you don't backtrack. The number of stopovers or total number of separate flights is decided before you set off and they usually cost a bit more than a basic return flight.

Ticketless Travel Airlines are gradually waking up to the realisation that paper tickets are unnecessary encumbrances. On simple one-way or return trips, reservations details can be held on computer and the passenger merely shows ID to claim their seat.

Transferred Tickets Airline tickets cannot be transferred from one person to another. Travellers sometimes try to sell the return half of their ticket, but officials can ask you to prove that you are the person named on the ticket. On an international flight, tickets are compared with passports.

Australia and Japan, but these fares will often have a number of restrictions on them. Return fares start at around A$1200 with Garuda, which allows a stopover in Bali. Direct flights to KIX with airlines including Qantas, Air New Zealand and JAL are more expensive – expect to pay around A$1530 for a return fare.

The best place to look for cheap fares is in the travel sections of weekend newspapers, such as the *Age* in Melbourne and the *Sydney Morning Herald*. Two well-known agencies for cheap fares are STA Travel and Flight Centre. STA Travel (☎ 131 776 Australia-wide, W www.statravel.com.au) has offices in all major cities and on many university campuses. Flight Centre (☎ 131 600 Australia-wide, W www .flight centre.com.au) has dozens of offices throughout Australia.

New Zealand

From New Zealand, Malaysian Airlines, Thai International and Qantas have return fares to Japan from around NZ$1500. Flight Centre (☎ 09-309 6171) has a large central office in Auckland at National Bank Towers (corner Queen and Darby Sts) and many branches throughout the country. STA Travel (☎ 09-309 0458, W www.statravel.co.nz) has its main office at 10 High St, Auckland, and has other offices in Auckland as well as in Hamilton, Palmerston North, Wellington, Christchurch and Dunedin.

The UK

Expect to pay around UK£500 to UK£600 for a one-year open return ticket with a good airline via a fast route. Air France is a reliable choice for flights to Japan (usually Tokyo), but you'll have to change in Paris. ANA and JAL also offer direct flights between London and KIX. For a less convenient trans-Asian route, count on about UK£350.

Popular travel agencies in the UK include STA Travel (☎ 020-7361 6144, W www.sta travel.co.uk), which has offices in London and Manchester; and Usit Campus (☎ 0870-240 1010, W www.usitcampus.co.uk),

which has branches throughout the UK. STA, in particular, can put together round-the-world routes incorporating Japan on the itinerary.

Other recommended travel agencies include: Trailfinders (☎ 020-7938 3939), Bridge the World (☎ 020-7734 7447) and Flightbookers (☎ 020-7757 2000). You'll find others listed in *Time Out* (London) magazine.

Continental Europe

Most direct flights between Europe and Japan fly into Tokyo but there are also some flights into Kansai. Typical low-season return fares from major European cities are as follows: Berlin to Tokyo DM900 (Aeroflot); Rome to Tokyo L1,400,000 (Egypt Air); Paris to Tokyo FR3800 (KLM).

Across Europe many travel agencies have ties with STA Travel, where cheap tickets can be purchased and STA-issued tickets can be altered. Outlets in major cities include:

France: Voyages Wasteels (☎ 08 03 88 70 04 within France, fax 01 43 25 46 25) 11 rue Dupuytren, 756006 Paris
Germany: STA Travel (☎ 030-311 0950, fax 313 0948) Goethestrasse 73, 10625 Berlin
Greece: ISYTS (☎ 01-322 1267, fax 323 3767) 11 Nikis St, Upper Floor, Syntagma Square, Athens
Italy: Passaggi (☎ 06-474 0923, fax 482 7436) Stazione Termini FS, Galleria Di Tesla, Rome

France has a network of student travel agencies that can supply discount tickets to travellers of all ages. OTU Voyages (☎ 01 44 41 38 50, W www.otu.fr) has a central Paris office at 39 Ave Georges Bernanos (5e) and another 42 offices around the country. Acceuil des Jeunes en France (☎ 01 42 77 87 80), 119 rue Saint Martin (4e), is another popular discount travel agent.

General travel agencies in Paris that offer some of the best services and deals include Voyageurs du Monde (☎ 01 42 86 16 00), 55 rue Sainte Anne (2e); and Nouvelles Frontières (☎ 08 03 33 33 33, W www.nou velles-frontieres.com), 5 Ave de l'Opéra (1er).

Belgium, Switzerland, the Netherlands and Greece are also good places for buying discount air tickets. In Belgium, Acotra Student Travel Agency (☎ 02-512 86 07) at rue de la Madeline, Brussels, and WATS Reizen (☎ 03-226 16 26) at de Keyserlei 44, Antwerp, are both well-known agencies. In Switzerland, SSR Voyages (☎ 01-297 11 11, ⓦ www.ssr.ch) specialises in student, youth and budget fares. In Zurich, there is a branch at Leonhardstrasse 10 and there are others in most major Swiss cities. In the Netherlands, NBBS Reizen is the official student travel agency. You can find them in Amsterdam (☎ 020-624 09 89) at Rokin 66 and there are several other agencies around the city. Another recommended travel agent in Amsterdam is Malibu Travel (☎ 020-626 32 30) at Prinsengracht 230.

For flights from Germany, check the Just Travel Web site (ⓦ www.justtravel.de).

Asia

Most Asian nations have regular air links with Japan, the most frequent being with China (Hong Kong), Thailand (Bangkok), Singapore and South Korea (close and inexpensive for a short holiday or to renew an expiring visa). Compared to the early 1990s, fares have dropped dramatically, making the possibility of excursions around the region more viable.

China Of the Asian air links, Hong Kong has the highest frequency of daily flights to KIX. There are several daily flights on Cathay Pacific, as well as on JAL, ANA and JAS. Hong Kong–Osaka return costs US$900. Check with agents like the Hong Kong Student Travel Bureau or Phoenix Travel.

There are also flights to KIX from Beijing, Shanghai, Guangzhou and Dalian on all the Japanese carriers as well as on Air China, China Eastern Airways and China Southern Air. Beijing-KIX costs US$800 return.

South Korea There are daily flights between Seoul and KIX on several airlines including JAL, ANA and Asiana, though Korean Airlines has the most flights (three a day) and usually offers the best fares.

There are also several weekly flights from Chejudo Island, Taegu and Pusan. Seoul-KIX will cost around US$200/380 one-way/return.

Taiwan There are daily departures from Taipei on both Japan Asia Airlines (JAA) and Cathay Pacific, and around four flights weekly on Singapore Airlines. Taipei-Osaka return costs around US$400.

Other Asian Countries There are daily flights from Bangkok to KIX on both Thai Airways and ANA with fares costing about US$450 return in the low season. From Singapore (on Singapore Airlines, JAL or ANA) tickets are about US$600 return; from Jakarta or Denpasar in Indonesia (on Garuda, Continental or Japan Asia Airlines), a return flight will cost around US$800.

From the Philippines (Manila) a return flight to KIX is around US$600 and from Malaysia (Kuala Lumpur) it's around US$700 return. From Vietnam (Ho Chi Minh City) a return flight costs US$660.

Other Asian countries with limited weekly flights to Japan include India, Nepal and Myanmar (Burma).

Domestic Air Services

All larger airports in Japan have regular flights to/from Osaka. Bear in mind that Tokyo is serviced by two different airports; Haneda is closer and more convenient to the city centre, while Narita is best for connecting to international flights. For most cities in Honshū (the main island of Japan), including Tokyo, Nagoya and Hiroshima, it is usually faster, cheaper and more convenient to travel by *shinkansen* (bullet train; see the Train section later in this chapter).

Domestic airfares can be rather expensive and tend to vary little between carriers. ANA and JAL offer tickets at up to 50% off if you purchase a month or more in advance, with smaller discounts for purchases made one to three weeks in advance (see the following Airlines section for ANA and JAL offices in Kyoto). Many local travel agents offer packages for short excursions to places such as Nagasaki – prices typically include airfare and a few nights accommodation for around the same as the airlines charge for a return fare.

The following are typical one-way prices for flights between Osaka (Itami or KIX) and several major cities in Japan:

Fukuoka	¥15,800
Kagoshima	¥19,650
Kōchi	¥12,100
Kumamoto	¥16,650
Matsuyama	¥11,900
Nagasaki	¥18,800
Naha	¥25,000
Niigata	¥16,400
Sapporo	¥30,850
Sendai	¥22,800
Tokyo	¥16,250

Airline Offices

Major airline offices in Kyoto include (☎ 0120 numbers are toll-free):

All Nippon Airways (ANA; Map 9; ☎ 211 5471 or 0120-029 333) near the Oike-Kararamachi crossing
Japan Airlines (JAL; Map 10; ☎ 0120-255 931) Kyoto station building
Japan Air System (JAS; ☎ 371 0933 or 0120-711 283) near the Bukkōji-Karasuma crossing

Most foreign airlines have offices in Osaka, including the following (☎ 0120 numbers are toll-free):

Air France (☎ 06-6641 1411)
Air New Zealand (☎ 0120-300 747)
Alitalia (☎ 06-6341 3951)
American Airlines (☎ 0120-000 860)
Ansett Australia (☎ 06-6346 2556)
Canadian Airlines International (☎ 06-6252 4227)
Cathay Pacific Airways (☎ 0120-355 747)
Delta Air Lines (☎ 0120-333 742)
Garuda Indonesia (☎ 06-6445 6985)
KLM-Royal Dutch Airlines (☎ 0120-868 862)
Korean Air (☎ 06-6264 3311)
Lufthansa Airlines (☎ 06-6341 4966)
Northwest Airlines (☎ 0120-120 747)
Qantas Airways (☎ 0120-207 020)
Scandinavian Airlines (☎ 0120-678 101)
Swissair (☎ 0120-667 788)
Thai Airways International (☎ 06-6202 5161)
United Airlines (☎ 0120-114 466)

BUS

The JR Dream Bus runs nightly between Kyoto station and Tokyo (either the Yaesu-guchi long-distance bus stop, which is next to Tokyo station, or to Shinjuku long-distance bus terminal, which is on the west side of Shinjuku station). The trip takes about eight hours. There are nightly departures in both directions at 10pm and 11pm, arriving at 6am and 7am respectively; from Kyoto, these depart from the northern side of Kyoto station, adjacent to the city bus terminal. Tickets are ¥8180 one way; if you're returning within one week a return ticket works out cheaper at ¥14,480.

You just might be able to grab some sleep in the reclining seats; if you find dozing off a bit of a struggle, console yourself with the thought that you are saving on accommodation and will be arriving at the crack of dawn to make good use of the day.

Though it is often possible to just show up and get a seat, reservations and advance purchase are recommended. Contact JR buses on ☎ 341 0489 or go to the ticket counters in most JR stations or the main bus information centre in front of Kyoto station. Most local travel agents can also issue these tickets in a few minutes for a nominal fee.

Other JR bus possibilities to/from Kyoto include (one-way/return) Kanazawa (¥4060/ 7310, four hours), Tottori (¥3870/6970, four hours), Hiroshima (¥6620/ 11,720, 7¾ hours), Nagasaki (¥11,310/ 20,380, 11 hours) and Kumamoto (¥10,800/ 19,440, 11 hours).

For buses to/from the airports, see the Getting Around chapter.

TRAIN

Japan's extensive and highly efficient railway system makes train travel the ideal way to get around the country. Kyoto is reached from most places in Japan by JR (Japan's main train company), but there are also several private lines connecting Kyoto with Nagoya, Nara, Osaka and Kōbe. Where they exist, private lines are always cheaper than JR.

The fastest and best-known train services in Japan are JR's *shinkansen* (bullet trains).

Kyoto station is on the JR Tōkaidō line (one of four major shinkansen routes), which runs between Tokyo and Osaka and continues west to Kyūshū as the Sanyō line. Three types of trains run on this route: the *kodama* (echo), which makes stops at all local shinkansen stations, *hikari* (light), which makes limited stops, and the ultrafast *nozomi* (hope), which reaches speeds of over 300km per hour and stops at very few stations.

All trains are well equipped with facilities including coffee shops, pay phones and mobile food cart services. If you don't share the Japanese passion for cigarettes, there are plenty of nonsmoking cars *(kin-en-sha)* which can be requested when booking. Unreserved carriages are sometimes packed and without a reserved seat during peak travel times you may find yourself standing for the entire trip. Green Car (1st class) carriages offer slightly more spacious seating.

Other Parts of Japan

Kyoto is easily reached by train from Tokyo, Osaka, Nagoya, Fukuoka and other cities in Japan.

Tokyo The JR shinkansen is the fastest and most frequent rail link; the hikari super-express (¥13,220 one way, two hours and 50 minutes) goes to/from Tokyo station.

Travelling by regular express trains (¥7980, around eight hours) involves at least two (often three or four) changes along the way. Get the staff at the ticket counter to write down the exact details of each transfer when you buy your ticket.

Nagoya The shinkansen (¥5340, 44 minutes) goes to/from Nagoya. You can save around half the cost by taking regular express trains, but you will need to change trains at least once and can expect the trip to take about three hours.

Osaka Other than the shinkansen, the fastest way between Osaka station and Kyoto station is a JR *shinkaisoku* (special rapid train; ¥540, 29 minutes).

There is also the cheaper private Hankyū line, which runs between Umeda station in

downtown Osaka and Kawaramachi (¥390, 40 minutes limited express), Karasuma and Ōmiya stations in Kyoto.

Alternately, you can take the Keihan line between Yodoyabashi station in Osaka and Demachiyanagi, Marutamachi, Sanjō (¥400, 45 minutes limited express), Shijō or Shichijō stations in Kyoto.

If you arrive in Osaka at the Osaka-kō or Nan-kō ferry ports, you will find convenient subway connections to JR Osaka station, Keihan Yodoyabashi station or the Hankyū Umeda station. From these stations there are convenient rail connections onward to Kyoto.

From Osaka's Itami airport, take the Osaka monorail to Minami Ibaraki (¥380, 30 minutes) and connect to the Hankyū Kyoto line for Kawaramachi (¥310, about 30 minutes). Of course, it's much easier to take a bus from Itami to Kyoto (see the To/From the Airports section in the Getting Around chapter for details).

Nara Unless you have a Japan Rail Pass, the best option is the Kintetsu line (sometimes written in English as the Kinki Nippon railway), which links Nara (Kintetsu Nara station) and Kyoto (Kintetsu Kyoto station). There are direct limited express trains (¥1110, 35 minutes) and ordinary express trains (¥610, 45 minutes), which may require a change at Saidai-ji.

The JR Nara line also connects JR Nara station with Kyoto station. Your best bet between the two cities is a *kaisoku* (rapid train; ¥690, 46 minutes) but departures are often few and far between.

Kōbe Kobe's Sannomiya station is on the JR Tōkaidō/Sanyō line as well as the private Hankyū line, both of which connect it to Kyoto.

The fastest way between Kōbe and Kyoto station is a JR shinkaisoku (¥1050, 48 minutes).

The Hankyū line, which stops at Kyoto's Kawaramachi (¥590, one hour limited express), Karasuma and Ōmiya stations, is cheaper but less convenient; change at Osaka's Jūsō or Umeda stations.

JR Rail Pass holders should also note that Shin-Kōbe station is on the Tōkaidō/Sanyō shinkansen line.

Kyūshū Kyoto is on the JR Tōkaidō/Sanyō shinkansen line, which runs to Hakata station in Fukuoka, northern Kyūshū (¥15,210, just under four hours). Other places to pick up the train along this route include Shimonoseki (¥13,960, three hours), Hiroshima (¥10,790, 1¾ hours) and Okayama (¥7330, one hour).

The North Kyoto can be reached from the northern cities of Kanazawa and Fukui by the JR Hokuriku and Kosei lines, which run along the west coast of Biwa-ko. From Sea of Japan cities such as Obama and Maizuru, you can take the JR Obama line to Ayabe and then change to the San-in line coming from Kinosaki. In order to reach central Kyoto, it is best to get off at JR Nijō station, which is the last express stop before Kyoto station, and connect to the Tōzai line (see the Subways section in the Getting Around chapter).

Train Passes

Japan Rail Pass One of Japan's few real travel bargains is the Japan Rail Pass. The pass lets you use any JR service for seven days for ¥28,300, 14 days for ¥45,100 or 21 days for ¥57,700. Green Car (1st class) passes are ¥37,800, ¥61,200 and ¥79,600 respectively. The pass cannot be used for the new super-express Nozomi shinkansen service, but is valid for everything else. The only surcharge levied on the Japan Rail Pass is for overnight sleepers. Since a reserved seat Tokyo-Kyoto shinkansen ticket costs ¥13,220, you only have to travel Tokyo-Kyoto-Tokyo once to make a seven-day pass come close to paying off.

The pass can only be bought overseas at JAL and ANA offices and major travel agencies. It can only be used by those with a short-stay visa (you'll need to show your passport), which means it *cannot* be used by foreign residents of Japan.

The clock starts to tick on the pass as soon as you validate it, which can be done at JR Travel Service Centres located in most major train stations and at Narita and Kansai airports if you're intending to jump on a JR train immediately. Don't validate it if you're just going into Tokyo or Kyoto and intend to hang around the city for a few days. The pass is valid *only* on JR services; you will still have to pay for private train services.

For more details on the pass and overseas purchase locations, visit the JR East Web site at [W] www.jreast.co.jp.

JR-West Kansai Pass A great deal for those who only want to explore the Kansai area, this pass covers unlimited travel on JR lines between most major Kansai cities, such as Himeji, Kōbe, Osaka, Kyoto and Nara. It also covers JR trains to/from Kansai airport but does not cover any shinkansen lines. A one-day pass costs ¥2000 and a four-day pass costs ¥6000 (children are half-price). These can be purchased at major train stations inside Japan and also entitle you to discounts on station rent-a-car offices. Note that only those on short-stay visas can buy the pass (thus, resident foreigners on longer-term visas cannot).

Seishun Jūhachi Kippu If you don't have a Japan Rail Pass, one of the best deals going is a five-day Seishun Jūhachi Kippu, literally a 'Youth 18 Ticket'. These can be used by anyone of any age but are only valid during university vacation periods (2 February to 20 April, 20 July to 10 September, 10 December to 20 January). Basically, for ¥11,500 you get five one-day tickets valid for travel anywhere in Japan on JR lines. The only catches are that you can't travel on tokkyū or shinkansen trains and each ticket must be used within 24 hours. However, even if you only have to make a return trip, say, between Tokyo and Kyoto, you'll be saving a lot of money. If you don't want to buy the whole book of five tickets, you can sometimes purchase separate tickets at discount ticket shops around train stations (see the following section).

Discount Ticket Shops

Known as *kakuyasu-kippu-uriba* in Japanese, these stores deal in discounted tickets for trains, buses, domestic plane flights, ferries and a host of other things like cutrate stamps and phone cards. Typical savings on shinkansen tickets are between 5% and 10%, which is good news for longterm residents who are not eligible for Japan Rail Passes. Discount ticket agencies are found around train stations in medium and large cities. The best way to find one is to ask at the *kōban* (police box) outside the station.

In Kyoto, you'll find Tōkai discount ticket shops on the north side of Kyoto station (Map 10; ☎ 344 0330), open from 9.30am to 7.30pm Monday to Friday, from 10am to 7pm Saturday, Sunday and holidays; and on the south side of the station (Map 10; ☎ 662 6640), open from 10am to 7.30pm Monday to Friday, from 10am to 7pm Saturday, Sunday and holidays. In the Excursions chapter of this book, discount ticket shops are listed on the maps of Himeji, Osaka and Kōbe.

CAR & MOTORCYCLE

The Meishin Expressway runs between Nagoya and Kōbe. The best access to Kyoto is from the Kyoto-Minami off-ramp (it will leave you on Rte 1, a few kilometres south of the city centre). Kyoto is also accessible from Osaka on Rte 1, Nishinomiya (Kōbe area) on Rte 171, from the western hills on Rte 9, or from the north (Sea of Japan) on the Shūzan Kaidō (Rte 162).

See the Getting Around chapter for information on car and motorcycle rental.

BICYCLE

Kyoto is accessible from all directions by bike and there are some lovely rides into the city, especially from the north (Sea of Japan and Kitayama regions), east (via Hiei-zan and Biwa-ko in Shiga Prefecture) and the mountains north-west of the city. For more details on cycling in Japan, pick up a copy of *Cycling Japan* (Kodansha, 1993), edited by Brian Harrell, a long-time Japan resident.

HITCHING

Hitching is never entirely safe in any country in the world, and we don't recommend it. Travellers who decide to hitch should understand that they are taking a small but potentially serious risk. In particular, Japan is a very dangerous place for solitary female hitchhikers; there have been countless cases of solitary female hitchers being attacked, molested and raped. People who do choose to hitch will be safer if they travel in pairs and let someone know where they are planning to go.

That said, hitching *can* be an amusing and money-saving way to travel around Japan, in particular to areas where trains and buses don't run. Whether on the highway or by local roads, there are a number of feasible routes for thumbing in and out of Kyoto.

For long-distance hitching, the best bet is to head for the Kyoto-Minami interchange of the Meishin Expressway, which is about 4km south of Kyoto station. Take the Toku No 19 bus – make sure the *kanji* (Chinese character) for 'special' *(toku)* precedes the number – from Kyoto station and get off when you reach the Meishin Expressway signs.

From here you can hitch east toward Tokyo or west to southern Japan. It is a good idea before heading out to make signs in kanji of intended destinations; these can prove very helpful in a country where many still stare in bewilderment at hitchhikers, wondering what in the world could be wrong with the person's thumb!

For more on hitching in Japan pick up a copy of the excellent *Hitchhiker's Guide to Japan* (Tuttle) by Will Ferguson. In addition to lots of general advice, this book details suggested routes and places to stay on the road. It's just about invaluable for anyone contemplating a long hitch around Japan.

BOAT
Domestic Ferries

Domestic overnight ferries are an excellent way to save time and one night's accommodation costs.

Osaka and Kōbe are the main ports for ferries between Kansai and Shikoku, Kyūshū and Okinawa. Sample fares to/from Osaka/Kōbe include:

Beppu (Kyūshū)	¥7030
Imabari (Shikoku)	¥4170
Kōchi (Shikoku)	¥4610
Matsuyama (Shikoku)	¥5000
Naha (Okinawa)	¥15,750*
Shin-Moji (Kyūshū)	¥5700
Takamatsu (Shikoku)	¥1320

* From Naha there are ferries onward to Taiwan (¥15,750, 19 hours).

From the cities north of Kyoto on the Sea of Japan you can also catch ferries as far north as Hokkaidō. Two popular routes, with daily departures, are Maizuru to Otaru (¥6710, 29 hours) and Tsuruga to Otaru (¥7420, 36 hours).

The TIC can provide detailed information on various routes and up-to-date schedules.

International Ferries

There are regular ferry runs between Kansai and Korea and China. There is no international departure tax when leaving Japan by boat.

South Korea The closest country to Japan, South Korea is a popular visa-renewal point. Many people who are teaching English in Japan illegally (ie, without a work visa) travel to Korea when their visa expires and then re-enter on a new visa to continue working. If you choose to follow their example, you can expect to have your passport and your story checked very carefully as immigration officials are now wise to this scheme.

Pusan-Shimonoseki The Kampu Ferry Service operates the Shimonoseki-Pusan ferry service. There are daily departures of the *Hamayū* or the *Pukwan* at 6pm from Shimonoseki and Pusan, arriving at the other end at 8.30am. One-way fares start from ¥6800 for students and continue up through ¥8500 for an open, tatami-mat area, ¥10,500 (six-berth cabin), ¥12,000 (four-berth cabin) and ¥14,000 (two-berth cabin). There is a 10% discount on return fares.

Pusan-Fukuoka Fukuoka has an international high-speed hydrofoil service connecting the city with Pusan in Korea (¥13,000/¥24,000 one-way/return, three hours, daily). The Camelia line also runs a ferry service to Pusan (¥9000/¥17,100 one-way/return, around 15 hours).

China The Japan-China International Ferry service connects Shanghai and Osaka/Kōbe. The number of departures varies with the seasons. During the off-season it's nearly empty, but can become crowded during summer. A 2nd-class ticket is around US$180. For further information in Japan about Shanghai-bound ferries you can ring the Nitchū Kokusai Ferry company (☎ 06-6536 6541, in Japanese).

Ships from Kōbe to Tanggu (near Tianjin) leave from Kōbe every Thursday at noon, arriving in Tanggu the next day. Economy/1st-class tickets cost US$200/300. The food on this boat gets poor reviews so bring a few emergency munchies. Tickets can be bought in Tianjin from the shipping office (☎ 22-31 2243) at 89 Munan Dao, Heping District. In Kōbe, the office is at the port (☎ 078-321 5791).

Getting Around

TO/FROM THE AIRPORTS
Kansai International Airport (KIX)
Train The fastest, most convenient way between KIX and Kyoto is the special JR *haruka* airport express, which makes the trip in about 75 minutes for ¥3490. Most seats are reserved on this train, but there are usually two cars with unreserved seats which cost ¥2990. Unreserved seats are almost always available, so you don't usually need to purchase tickets in advance. First and last departures from KIX to Kyoto are 6.29am and 10.18pm; first and last departures from Kyoto to KIX are 5.45am and 8.16pm.

If you have time to spare, you can save some money by taking the *kankū kaisoku* (Kansai airport express) between the airport and Osaka station and taking a regular *shinkaisoku* (special rapid train) to/from Kyoto. The total journey by this route takes about 90 minutes with good connections and costs ¥1800. The downside is that you will have to lug your baggage from one train to another in Osaka station.

For those travelling on Japanese airlines (JAL and ANA), there is an advance check-in counter inside the JR ticket office in Kyoto station (Map 10). This service allows you to check in with your luggage at the station, a real boon for those with heavy bags.

Limousine Bus There are direct limousine buses (☎ 682 4400) between Kyoto and KIX (¥2300/1150 adult/child, 105 minutes). There are pick-up/drop-off points on the south side of Kyoto station (in front of Avanti department store, Map 10), ANA Hotel (Map 5) and Keihan Sanjō station (Map 9). At KIX, the buses leave from the curb outside the international arrivals hall.

This is only marginally cheaper than an unreserved seat on the *haruka* and there's always the possibility of a delay in traffic, so we don't really recommend this route when you're leaving Kyoto.

Taxi Another convenient, though expensive, option is the MK Taxi *Sky Gate Shuttle* limousine van service (☎ 702 5489), which will pick you up from anywhere in Kyoto city and deliver you to KIX for ¥3500. Call at least two days in advance to reserve. The advantage of this route is that you are delivered from door to door and you don't have to lug your baggage through the train station.

Osaka Itami Airport
This airport is the main terminal for domestic flights in and out of Kansai, and there are frequent airport limousine buses (¥1370, one hour) to/from Kyoto station and some hotels around town. The Kyoto station stop is in front of Avanti department store (Map 10) and the Itami stop is outside the arrivals hall (buy your tickets from the machine near the bus stop). Be sure to allow extra time in case of traffic.

BUS
Kyoto has an intricate network of bus routes providing an efficient way of getting around at moderate cost. Many of the routes used by visitors have announcements in English. The core timetable for buses is between 7am and 9pm, though a few run earlier or later.

The main bus terminals are Kyoto station on the JR and Kintetsu lines, Sanjō station on the Keihan line, Karasuma-Shijō station on the Hankyū and Karasuma lines, and Kitaōji station on the Karasuma line. The bus terminal at Kyoto station is on the north side and has three main departure bays (departure points are indicated by the letter of the bay and number of the stop within that bay)

The TIC's *Kyoto Transportation Guide* is a good map of the city's main bus lines with a detailed explanation of the routes and a Japanese/English communication guide on the reverse side. Since this map is intended for tourists it is not exhaustive. If you can read a little Japanese, pick up a copy of the regular (and more detailed

Japanese bus map available at major bus terminals throughout the city.

Bus stops usually display a map of destinations from that stop on the top section. On the bottom section there's a timetable for the buses serving that stop. Unfortunately, all of this information is in Japanese, and nonspeakers will simply have to ask locals for help.

Entry to the bus is usually through the back door and exit is via the front door. Inner-city buses charge a flat fare (¥220), which you drop into the clear plastic receptacle on top of the machine next to the driver on your way out. A separate machine gives change for ¥100 and ¥500 coins or ¥1000 notes.

On buses serving the outer areas, you take a numbered ticket *(seiri-ken)* when entering. When you leave, an electronic board above the driver displays the fare corresponding to your ticket number (drop the seiri-ken into the ticket box with your fare).

To save time and money, you can buy a *kaisū-ken* (book of five tickets) for ¥1000. There's also a one-day card *(shi-basu senyō ichinichi jōshaken cādo)* valid for unlimited travel on city buses and subways that costs ¥700. A similar pass *(ichinichi jōsha-ken)* that allows unlimited use of the bus *and* subway costs ¥1200. A two-day bus/subway pass *(futsuka jōshā-ken)* costs ¥2000. Kaisū-ken can be purchased directly from bus drivers. The other passes and cards can be purchased at major bus terminals and at the main bus information centre (Map 10).

The main bus information centre is located in front of Kyoto station. Here, you can pick up bus maps, purchase bus tickets and passes (on all lines, including highway buses), and get additional information. Nearby, there's an English/Japanese bus information computer terminal; just enter your intended destination and it will tell you the correct bus and bus stop.

Three-digit numbers written against a red background denote loop lines: bus No 204 runs around the northern part of the city and Nos 205 and 206 circle the city via Kyoto station. Buses with route numbers on a blue background take other routes (usually north/south).

When heading for locations outside the city centre, be careful which bus you board. Kyoto city buses are green, Kyoto buses are tan and Keihan buses are red and white.

TRAIN

There are several quick and efficient options for getting around Kyoto by train.

For heading out to Yamashina, excursions into Shiga-ken, or into south-western Kyoto you can use the JR Tōkaidō line. The JR San-in main line runs from Kyoto station into western Kyoto via Nijō station, and the JR Nara line makes stops in southern Kyoto en route to Nara. On a similar course from Kyoto station, the Kintetsu Kyoto line also makes its way to Nara and on to Nagoya.

The Hankyū Kyoto line runs across town under Shijō-dōri from Kawaramachi to Saiin station (en route to Osaka) and also from Katsura station to the Arashiyama area on the Hankyū Arashiyama line. Keifuku trains also go to Arashiyama, running west from Shijō-Ōmiya station on the Keifuku Arashiyama line.

In the southern and eastern parts of town, the Keihan main line makes underground stops along the Kamo-gawa, terminating in the north at Demachiyanagi station. Here you can connect to the Eizan Dentetsu line for access to Shū-gakuin, Kurama, Kibune and Yase-yūen (near Ōhara). Note that the line splits in two at Takaraga-ike; be sure you board the right train for your destination.

The subway is also a good way to move around the city fast (see the Subway section later in this chapter).

Train Stations

With the exception of the gigantic Kyoto station complex, most station facilities are limited to toilets and a kiosk (newsstand). Several of the larger stations like Hankyū Kawaramachi and Keihan Sanjō have coin lockers and vendors selling *ekiben* (boxed lunches). Stations can have up to 25 numbered exits to cause you confusion; in most cases, especially from underground stations, it is quicker to just pick an exit and surface to the street before trying to get your bearings.

GETTING AROUND

Train Vocabulary

Train Types

shinkansen	新幹線	bullet train
tokkyū	特急	limited express
shin-kaisoku	新快速	JR special rapid train
kyūkō	特急	express
kaisoku	快速	JR rapid or express
futsū	普通	local
kaku-eki-teisha	各駅停車	local

Other Useful Words

jiyū-seki	自由席	unreserved seat
shitei-seki	指定席	reserved seat
green-sha	グリーン車	first-class car
ōfuku	往復	round trip
katamichi	片道	one-way
kin'en-sha	禁煙車	nonsmoking car
kitsuen-sha	喫煙車	smoking car

Buying a Ticket

All stations are equipped with automatic ticket machines, which are simple to operate. Destinations and fares are all posted above the machines in both Japanese and English and once you've figured out the fare to your destination, just insert your money and press the yen amount. Most of these machines accept paper currency in addition to coins (usually just ¥1000 notes). If you've made a mistake, press the red *torikeshi* (cancel) button. There's also a help button to summon assistance.

Train Passes & Discount Tickets

If you plan to do a lot of train travel in the Kansai region, it might make sense to buy a JR-West Kansai Pass. Even if you only plan a single trip out of the city, you can save money by buying your tickets at a discount ticket shop. See the Train section in the Getting There & Away chapter for more details on these.

Subway

Kyoto has two efficient subway lines, which operate from 5.30am to 11.30pm. The minimum fare is ¥200 (children ¥100).

The quickest way to travel between the north and south of the city is the Karasuma line subway. The line has 15 stops and runs from Takeda (Map 2) in the far south, via Kyoto station, to the Kyoto International Conference Hall (Map 2; Kokusai-kaikan station) in the north.

The east/west Tōzai line traverses Kyoto from JR Nijō station (Map 5) in the west, meeting the Karasuma line at Karasuma-Oike station (Map 9), and continuing east to Sanjō Keihan, Yamashina (Map 1) and Daigo (Map 1), in the east and south-east.

CAR & MOTORCYCLE

Kyoto's heavy traffic and narrow roads make city driving difficult and stressful. You will almost always do better on a bicycle or public transport. Unless you have specific needs, don't even entertain the idea of renting a car to tour the city – it's far more cost and headache than any traveller needs (plus parking ticket fines start at ¥15,000!).

However, it does make sense to rent a car if you plan to explore certain rural areas that aren't serviced by train lines. One such place is Miyama-chō (see the Excursions chapter).

There are several car rental agencies in Kyoto. You will need to produce an International Driving Permit (see the Documents section in the Facts for the Visitor chapter) and if you cannot find a local to assist you with the paperwork, speaking a little Japanese will help greatly.

Nissan Rent-a-Car (Map 10) has an office directly in front of Kyoto station. Matsuda Rent-a-Car (Map 7; ☎ 361 0201) is close to the intersection of Kawaramachi-dōri and Gojō-dōri. Nippō Rent-a-Car (Map 9; ☎ 251 7072) has an outlet on Karasuma-dōri, about 100m north of Shijō-dōri.

Rates vary greatly and it's a good idea to shop around, but expect to spend at least ¥6500 per day for an ultracompact sedan, or around ¥10,000 for a regular sedan. Daily rates decrease if you rent for several days.

Motorcycles are a quick (and dangerous) way to get around town or do a bit of countryside touring. Sakaguchi Shōkai (Map 1; ☎ 791 6338) in the Iwakura area (northern Kyoto) rents a variety of bikes ranging from 50cc scooters (¥3200 per day) to 400cc 'ninja' speed machines (¥14,600).

Remember, driving is on the left-hand side in Japan and petrol costs between ¥115 and ¥150 per litre.

TAXI

For just getting from place to place about town, taxis are a convenient, though expensive, way to go. A taxi can usually be flagged down within minutes in most parts of the city at any time. There are also a large number of taxi stands (*takushi noriba*) in town, outside most train/subway stations, department stores etc. Remember, there is no need to touch the back doors of the cars at all – the opening/closing mechanism is controlled by the driver.

Fares start at ¥630 for the first 2km. The exception is MK Taxi (☎ 721 2237) with fares starting at ¥580. If you have a choice, always take an MK taxi – in addition to being cheaper, the drivers are scrupulously polite and can often speak a bit of English. Regardless of which taxi company you use, there's a 20% surcharge for rides between midnight and 6am.

MK Taxi also provides tours of the city with English-speaking drivers. For a group of up to four people, prices start at ¥13,280 for three hours.

Two other companies that offer a similar tour service, English-speaking drivers and competitive prices are Kyōren Taxi Service (☎ 672 5111) and the Keihan Taxi Service (☎ 602 8162).

BICYCLE

Kyoto is a great city to explore on a bicycle; with the exception of outlying areas it's mostly flat and there is a new bike path running the length of the Kamo-gawa.

Unfortunately, Kyoto must rank near the top in having the world's worst public facilities for bike parking (hence the number of bikes you see haphazardly locked up around the city) and many bikes end up stolen or impounded during regular sweeps of the city (in particular near entrances to train/subway stations). If your bike does disappear, check for a poster in the vicinity (in both Japanese and English) indicating the time of seizure and the inconvenient place you'll have to go to pay a ¥2000 fine and retrieve your bike.

For hardcore cyclists touring Japan, or looking for equipment or a professional tune-up, drop by Takenaka (Map 5; ☎ 256 4863), a small, but first-rate bike shop near the south-eastern corner of the Imperial Palace Park. The friendly owner speaks English and is happy to share his wide knowledge of the region's best cycling routes. He also organises regular Sunday road rides, usually day-long outings into the nearby countryside, and welcomes any riders with a helmet.

For more details on cycling in Japan, pick up a copy of *Cycling Japan* (Kodansha, 1993), edited by Brian Harrell, a long-time Japan resident.

Bicycle Rentals

Near Sanjō station on the Keihan line, Kitazawa Bicycle Shop (Map 9; ☎ 771 2272) rents out bicycles for ¥200 per hour and ¥1000 per day, with discounts for rentals over three days. It's a 200m walk north of the station next to the river on the east side. It's open daily from 8am to 5pm.

Nearby on Kawabata-dōri, north of Sanjō-dōri, Rental Cycle Yasumoto (Map 9;

☎ 751 0595), open from 9am to 5pm, offers a similar deal.

Arashiyama has several places for bicycle rental (see the Arashiyama-Sagano District section in the Things to See & Do chapter) and the Higashiyama (Map 6) and Utano (Map 2) youth hostels offer bicycle rental for ¥800 per day (there's a ¥3000 deposit). Staying guests can rent bicycles at discounted rates.

Most rental outfits require you to leave ID such as a passport or driver's licence.

Bicycle Purchase

If you plan on spending more than a week or so exploring Kyoto by bicycle, it might make sense to purchase a used bicycle. One reader wrote:

I just returned from about five weeks in Kyoto...I would recommend that if someone is going to spend a considerable length of time in Kyoto (maybe a couple of weeks or so), then they should consider buying a bicycle. The cost of a bike is less than the cost of taking a train everywhere for that length of time. I purchased one for around US$70 on the second day after I arrived and I used it everyday and rode it everywhere. Kyoto is a great place to ride a bicycle. The day before I left, I sold it back to the same store for about US$50. I highly recommend a bicycle in Kyoto.

James Embry

A simple *mama chari* (shopping bike) can be had for as little as ¥3000. Try the used cycle shop Ei Rin (Map 6; ☎ 752 0292) on Imadegawa-dōri near Kyoto University. Otherwise, you'll find a good selection of used bikes advertised for sale on the message board of the Kyoto International Community House (Map 6).

WALKING

Walking is often the best way to explore the city, taking away the cost and concerns of traffic and parking and allowing you the chance to wander through narrow backstreets where you're far more likely to catch a glimpse of old Kyoto.

There are several excellent walking tours and easily accessible hikes outlined in the Things to See & Do chapter. You may also want to pick up a copy of JNTO's *Walking*

Tour Courses in Kyoto at the Kyoto TIC (Map 10); it details several worthwhile walks in the city. For a more serious exploration of the city on foot, pick up a copy of Judith Clancy's excellent *Exploring Kyoto*, which details 25 walks through some of Kyoto's most beautiful areas.

When walking, take caution – the streets are very narrow and taxis and oversized 4WD recreational vehicles often don't slow down for pedestrians.

For an excellent guided walking tour see the following Organised Tours section.

ORGANISED TOURS

Some visitors to Kyoto who are on a tight schedule find it convenient to join an organised tour of the city. Tours allow you to see a lot of major sites in a short time without the need for arranging your own transport. You'll also be accompanied by a guide who can provide insights into the things you see.

Bus tours are particularly appealing in the sweltering heat of summer or the cold of winter, when walking the city sights can take its toll. Special off-season summer tours *(natsu-no-tabi)* and winter tours *(kyō-no-furu)*, with a variety of themes such as *uruwashi* (beauty), *ajiwai* (taste) and *miyabi* (elegance), are organised by the Kyoto city (see the TIC for information) and are reasonably priced at around ¥9500 (fees included). Although there are no English-language tours, these provide a great opportunity to see places slightly off the beaten track, some of which are often not open for public viewing.

JTB Sunrise Tours (☎ 341 1413, Ⓦ www .jtb.co.jp/sunrisetour/kyoto) offers morning, afternoon and all-day bus tours year-round with English-speaking guides. Morning and afternoon tours cost ¥5300, while all-day tours with a buffet lunch included are ¥11,200. Pick ups are available at all of Kyoto's larger hotels.

For people with very little time and lots of money, another convenient and time-efficient tour option to consider is a chartered taxi (see the Taxi section earlier in this chapter).

One of the greatest ways to acclimatise to Kyoto is to spend a few hours with the popular 'Johnnie Hillwalker', an English-speaking tour guide with 34 years experience as a guide with the Japan Travel Bureau (JTB). Three days each week (Monday, Wednesday and Friday) from 2 March to 30 November, Hirooka Hajime (his Japanese name) leads an intimate, four-hour English-language tour. The tour provides an excellent overview of Kyoto and insights you definitely won't get on a standard city bus tour.

The course, starting from the northern side of Kyoto station, covers some lesser-visited sights in central and eastern Kyoto. The per-person price is ¥2000 (¥1000 for children 13 to 15 years of age). This price includes all fees, and payment is in cash only. You can call ☎ 622 6803 for details, but reservations aren't necessary; just show up at the Sunken Garden (Map 10) in front of Kyoto station between 10am and 10.15am on the days the tour is given.

Things to See & Do

Exploring Kyoto is a fascinating and potentially endless pursuit. As well as the wealth of beautiful temples and shrines that dot the city and its outskirts, there are the imperial palace and villas, the fascinating traditional geisha quarters and teahouses of the Gion district, the bustling department stores and markets downtown, and plenty of museums to keep the visitor occupied.

Add to this the myriad of hikes that can be done in the hills surrounding the city, and the excellent opportunities to view and learn Kyoto's famous crafts, and you will find that Kyoto can keep you happily occupied not only for days, but weeks and even months.

With so much to do it can be hard to choose, especially if you're only in the city for a short time. To help with your planning, we've included a Kyoto Highlights box at the start of this chapter. You might also have a look at the boxed text 'Ten Things You Must Do in Kyoto' in the Facts for the Visitor chapter for some additional hints.

This chapter groups Kyoto's sights under geographical areas of the city to facilitate sightseeing and walking in particular districts. Toward the end of the chapter we have included a complete list of courses in crafts and other activities.

Note that the directions we give to most sights assume you're starting out from Kyoto station. Of course it's usually possible to access these sights from other parts of the city as well; arm yourself with a bus map and a sense of adventure. See the Getting Around chapter for more details on moving around the city.

KYOTO STATION AREA
京都駅付近 **(MAP 10)**

The area around Kyoto station, south of the city centre, is a fairly drab part of town. The main sights are a pair of giant temples, Higashi Hongan-ji and Nishi Hongan-ji. And, of course, there's always Kyoto station itself!

Common Japanese Suffixes

As you read through this book, over and over you'll come across the same suffixes used in place names. We've listed the most common ones and their meanings here. Master a few of these and you'll really start to feel like a Kyoto insider!

Buddhist temples usually end with -*ji*, -*dera*, -*in* or -*dō*, all of which mean temple or hall, eg, Kiyomizu-dera, Ginkaku-ji, Sanjūsangen-dō etc.

In the case of Shintō shrines, the suffix is usually -*jinja*, -*jingū* or -*taisha*, eg, Yasaka-jinja, Heian-jingū, Fushimi Inari-taisha etc.

There are two words used for museum: *hakubutsukan* (museum) or *bijutsukan* (art museum); so the Kyoto National Museum is the Kyoto Kokuritsu Hakubutsukan, and the Nomura Museum is the Nomura Bijutsukan.

Parks end with -*kōen*, eg, Maruyama-kōen. Gardens usually with -*en*, eg, Shōsei-en.

Even when speaking in English, it is common (and much easier) to refer to temples and shrines etc by their Japanese name.

For more on common Japanese words, and to see how the words listed in this section are written in Japanese, see the Glossary of Useful Terms in the Language chapter at the back of this book.

Kyoto Station

Kyoto's new station building is a striking steel and glass structure – a kind of futuristic cathedral for the transportation age. Unveiled in September 1997, the building has met with some decidedly mixed reviews. Some critics assail the building as out of keeping with the traditional architecture of Kyoto; others love its wide-open spaces and dramatic lines.

Whatever the case, we're sure that you'll be impressed by the tremendous space that arches above you as you enter the main concourse. Moreover, you'll probably enjoy a brief exploration of the many levels of the station, all the way up to the 15th-floor observation level. And be sure to take the escalator from the 7th floor on the east side of the building up to the 11th-floor glass corridor that runs high above the main concourse – not a good spot for those with fear of heights!

In the station building you'll find several food courts (see the Places to Eat chapter), Isetan department store, the Kyoto Prefectural International Center, the Kyoto Tourism Federation, a Joypolis game centre and an outdoor performance space.

There is a small tourist information office on the second level of the west side of the station (take the escalator on your right as you enter the station); across the way is the station information counter.

Kyoto Tower

Directly north of the station is one of the city's greatest architectural blunders – the 131m-high Kyoto Tower (☎ 361 3210; ¥770; open 9am-9pm). The tower is said to represent a 'forever-burning candle', but it looks more like a misguided space rocket. Many cite the construction of the tower in 1964 as the beginning of the end of Kyoto's once-graceful skyline.

The tower's observation deck offers a panoramic 360° view of the city (on a clear day you can see all the way to Osaka). If you don't feel like shelling out the entry fee, you might opt for a slightly less dramatic but free vista from the top of the Kyoto station building.

Nishi Hongan-ji

Nishi Hongan-ji (☎ 371 5181; free; 5.30am-5pm, open later in summer) was originally built in 1272 in the Higashiyama mountains by the priestess Kakushin, daughter of Shinran, founder of the Buddhist Jōdo Shinshū (true pure land) school. The temple complex was relocated to its present site in 1591, onto land provided by Toyotomi Hideyoshi. By then the Jōdo Shin-shū had accumulated immense power, and the temple became its headquarters. Tokugawa Ieyasu sought to weaken the power of Jōdo Shin-shū by encouraging a breakaway

---

Six Great Views of Kyoto

Surrounded by mountains on three sides, Kyoto is an attractive city when viewed from up high. The following are some great spots to put it all into perspective:

Daimonji-yama (Map 1; free entry) northern Higashiyama

Kyoto station rooftop observatory (Map 10; free entry) Kyoto station building

Kyoto Tower (Map 10; ¥770) Kyoto station area

Kiyomizu-dera (Map 8; ¥300) southern Higashiyama

Iwatayama Monkey Park (Map 11; ¥500) Arashiyama

Hiei-zan (Map 1; cable car fee ¥840, free entry) north-eastern Kyoto

---

faction to found Higashi Hongan-ji (higashi means east; see next entry) in 1602. The original Hongan-ji then became known as Nishi Hongan-ji (nishi means west). It is now the headquarters of the Hongan-ji branch of Jōdo Shin-shū, which has over 10,000 temples and 12 million followers worldwide.

The temple contains five buildings featuring some of the finest examples of the architectural and artistic achievement of the Momoyama period. Unfortunately, the main hall (Goe-dō) is presently being restored and will be 'under wraps' until 2010. The Daisho-in hall has sumptuous paintings, carvings and metal ornamentation. A small garden and Japan's oldest nō stages are connected with the hall. The dazzling Chinese-style Kara-mon gate displays intricate ornamental carvings and metalwork. The gate has also been dubbed Higurashi-mon (Sunset Gate), purporting that its beauty can distract one from noticing the setting sun. Both Daisho-in and Kara-mon were transported here from Fushimi-jō castle in the south of the city.

The Goe-dō dates from 1636 and contains a seated statue of Shinran, which he is said to have carved at the age of 71. The

THINGS TO SEE & DO

Kyoto Highlights

site	location	description
temples		
Nanzen-ji	eastern Kyoto	wonderful open grounds; rock garden
Kurama-dera	Kurama (northern Kyoto)	fabulous mountain location
Sanjūsangen-dō	eastern Kyoto	1001 Kannon (Buddhist goddess of mercy) statues
Higashi & Nishi Hongan-ji	central Kyoto	enormous wooden structures
Tō-ji	south-central Kyoto	tallest pagoda in Japan; two monthly markets
Sanzen-in	Ōhara (northern Kyoto)	picturesque garden of Yūsei-en; autumn foliage
Byōdō-in	Uji (southern Kyoto)	11th-century Phoenix Hall
Mampuku-ji	Uji (southern Kyoto)	Ming-dynasty Chinese-style buildings
Ginkaku-ji	eastern Kyoto	15th-century shōgun's Silver Pavilion
shrines		
Fushimi-Inari-taisha	southern Kyoto	paths with thousands of vermilion *torii* (Shintō shrine gates)
Yasaka-jinja	eastern Kyoto	colourful torri overlooking Shijō-dōri
Heian-jingū	eastern Kyoto	replica of 8th-century imperial palace
Kitano Tenman-gū	north-western Kyoto	lively flea market held on 25th of each month
Shimogamo-jinja	north-central Kyoto	pleasant, wooded Tadasu-no-mori entry path
Kamigamo-jinja	north-western Kyoto	striking conical sand mounds in peaceful setting

elaborate *hondō* (main hall), last reconstructed in 1760, houses a priceless collection of painted sliding screens adorned with phoenixes and peacocks.

If you'd like to join a tour of the temple, call the temple office (telephone number above) or arrange one through the TIC (Tourist Information Centre; see the Facts for the Visitor chapter). The tours, which are in Japanese, cover some but not all of the buildings and are conducted from Monday to Friday at 10am, 11am, 1.30pm and 2.30pm. On Saturday the tours are at 10am and 11am. The temple is a 12-minute walk north-west of JR Kyoto station.

Higashi Hongan-ji

In 1602, when Tokugawa Ieyasu engineered the rift in the Jōdo Shin-shū school, he founded this temple (☎ 371 9181; free;

open 5.50am-5.20pm, open later in summer) as a competitor to Nishi Hongan-ji (see previous entry). Rebuilt in 1895 after a series of fires destroyed all the original structures, it is certainly monumental but less impressive artistically than its rival. The temple is now the headquarters of the Ōtani branch of Jōdo Shin-shū.

The two-storey Taishidō-mon gate stands 27m high and features giant doors fashioned out of a single slab of wood. Wade through the sea of pigeons to the hondō – place your shoes in one of the plastic bags and carry them with you so you can exit from the neighbouring building. This hall enshrines a 13th-century statue of Amida Nyorai (Buddha of the Western Paradise).

In the corridor between the two main buildings you'll find a curious item encased

Kyoto Highlights

site	location	description
villas		
Shūgaku-in Rikyū	north-eastern Kyoto	sprawling imperial estate at the foot of Hiei-zan
Katsura Rikyū	south-western Kyoto	delightful stroll through garden and buildings
gardens		
Ryōan-ji	north-western Kyoto	classic Zen rock garden
Taizō-in	north-western Kyoto	at Myōshin-ji, some consider it the finest garden in Kyoto
Daitoku-ji	north-western Kyoto	numerous subtemples with Zen gardens
Nijō-jō	central Kyoto	lovely Ninomaru Palace garden
Kōdai-ji	eastern Kyoto	delicate landscape with mountain back drop
Tenryū-ji	western Kyoto	14th-century Zen garden
Saihō-ji	south-western Kyoto	heart-shaped moss garden
museums		
Kyoto National Museum	eastern Kyoto	superb collection of temple treasures
Kawai Kanjirō Memorial Hall	eastern Kyoto	pottery studio in rustic old home
other		
Tetsugaku-no-michi	eastern Kyoto	wonderful canal-side walk
Nishiki market	central Kyoto	Kyoto's best food market
Kamo-gawa river	central Kyoto	one long riverside park
Kyoto Imperial Palace Park	central Kyoto	Kyoto's Central Park

in glass: a tremendous coil of rope made from human hair. Following the destruction of the temple in the 1880s, an eager group of female temple devotees donated their locks to make the ropes that hauled the massive timbers used for reconstruction.

The enormous *taishi-dō* (founder's hall) is one of the world's largest wooden structures, standing 38m high, 76m long and 58m wide. The centrepiece is a self-carved likeness of Jōdo Shin-shū founder Shinran.

It only takes a few minutes to wander through the buildings and you can ask at the information office just inside the main gate for an English leaflet. It's a short stroll north of Kyoto station.

About five minutes' walk east of the temple, the garden **Shōsei-en** *(☎ 371 9181; free; open 9am-3.30pm)* is worth a look. The lovely grounds, incorporating the

Kikoku-tei villa, were completed in 1657. Bring a picnic (and some bread to feed the carp) or just stroll around the beautiful Ingetsu-ike pond. Just when you're caught up in the 'old-Kyoto' moment, note the two love hotels looming in the background outside the wall (modern 'borrowed scenery').

Period Costume Museum
The Period Costume Museum *(Fūzoku Hakubutsukan; ☎ 342 5345; ¥400; open 9am-5pm, closed Sun, public holidays, 16 Dec-6 Jan & 1-19 Jun)* is a museum of wax figures wearing costumes representative of different periods in Japanese history; these include samurai warriors, merchants and fire fighters – not a must-see but worth a peek on a rainy day. From the north-east corner of Nishi Hongan-ji, it's just across Horikawa-dōri.

THINGS TO SEE & DO

AROUND KYOTO STATION
京都駅周辺 **(MAP 7)**
The highlight in this part of town is the temple Tō-ji, with its breathtaking pagoda.

Sumiya Pleasure House
Shimabara, a district north-west of Kyoto station, was Kyoto's original pleasure quarters. At its peak during the Edo period (1600–1867) the area flourished, with over 20 enormous *ageya* – magnificent banquet halls where artists, writers and statesmen gathered in a 'floating world' ambience of conversation, art and fornication. Geisha were often sent from their quarters *(okiya)* to entertain patrons at these restaurant-cum-brothels. By the start of the Meiji period, however, such activities had drifted north to the Gion district and Shimabara had lost its prominence.

Though the traditional air of the district has dissipated, a few old structures remain. The tremendous **Shimabara-no-Ō-mon** gate, which marked the passage into the quarter, still stands, as does the **Sumiya pleasure house** (☎ *351 0024 for Japanese-language tours; ¥1000, tours ¥800 extra; open 10am-4pm, closed Mon, Aug & 16 Dec-31 Jan)* the last remaining ageya, now designated a National Cultural Asset. Built in 1641, this

---

What's Free in Kyoto

A quick glance through the pages of this chapter might convince you that sightseeing in Kyoto is going to require taking a second mortgage on your home. Luckily there are plenty of free things you can do. Indeed, you could fill at least a week with activities that are absolutely free. Here are just a few:

Temples There is no charge to enter the grounds of many of Kyoto's temples, including Nanzen-ji, Chion-in, Hōnen-in and Tōfuku-ji.

Shrines Almost all shrines in Japan can be entered free of charge. A few good ones include Fushimi-Inari-taisha, Heian-jingū, Shimogamo-jinja and Yasaka-jinja.

Kyoto Imperial Palace Park Kyoto's Central Park is a treasure that many visitors to the city overlook.

Kamo-gawa Like the Imperial Palace Park, this is a great place to spend a relaxing afternoon strolling and picnicking. In the summer you'll be treated to free fireworks shows as local youths hold impromptu hanabi-taikai (fireworks festivals).

Nishiki Market It costs nothing to wander through this wonderful market. Of course, you might find something that you just have to buy…

Department Stores Have a look at the fabulous variety of goods for sale in Kyoto's department stores. While you're there, stop by the food floor and snag some free food samples.

Kyoto Station Kyoto's new station building is pretty impressive, and the view from the rooftop observatory is the best you'll get – short of paying to ascend Kyoto Tower or expending the energy to climb Daimonji-yama.

Festivals There's nothing like a colourful Kyoto festival, and they're always free. If you're lucky, you might even be asked to participate.

Hikes It doesn't cost anything to enjoy Kyoto's natural beauty. There are myriad hikes in the mountains that surround the city.

Kyoto Imperial Palace, Shūgaku-in Rikyū Imperial Villa & Katsura Rikyū Imperial Villa These three imperial properties can all be toured free of charge.

stately two-storey, 20-room structure allows a rare glimpse into Edo-era nirvana. With a delicate lattice-work exterior, Sumiya has a huge open kitchen and an extensive series of rooms (including one extravagantly decorated with mother-of-pearl inlay).

Special tours (requiring advance reservations) allow access to the 2nd storey and are conducted daily. An English pamphlet is provided, but you might consider arranging a volunteer guide through the TIC.

It is about 15 minutes' walk west of Nishi Hongan-ji, or 10 minutes north-west of the Umekōji-kōen-mae bus stop (bus No 205).

Umekōji Steam Locomotive Museum

A hit with steam train buffs and kids, this museum *(☎ 314 2996; entry adult/child ¥400/100; train ride adult/child ¥200/100; open 9.30am-5pm, closed Mon)* features 18 vintage steam locomotives (dating from 1914 to 1948) and related displays. It is in the former JR Nijō station building, which was recently relocated here and thoughtfully reconstructed. You can take a 10-minute ride on one of the smoke-spewing choo-choos (departures 11am, 1.30pm & 3.30pm).

From Kyoto station, take bus No 33, 205 or 208 to the Umekōji-kōen-mae stop (make sure you take a west-bound bus).

Tō-ji

This temple *(☎ 691 3325; ¥500; open 9am-4.30pm)* was established in 794 by imperial decree to protect the city. In 823, the emperor handed it over to Kūkai (known posthumously as Kōbō Daishi), the founder of the Shingon school. Many of the temple buildings were destroyed by fire or fighting during the 15th century and most of the remaining buildings were destroyed in the Momoyama period (1576–1600).

The main gate (Nandai-mon) was moved here in 1894 from Sanjūsangen-dō in the southern Higashiyama area. The *kōdō* (lecture hall) dates from the 1600s and contains 21 images representing a Mikkyō (esoteric Buddhist) mandala. The *kondō* (main hall), rebuilt in 1606, combines Chinese, Indian and Japanese architectural styles and contains statues depicting the Yakushi (Healing Buddha) trinity. In the southern part of the garden stands the five-storey Gojū-no-tō pagoda which, despite having burnt down five times, was doggedly rebuilt in 1643. It is now the highest (57m) pagoda in Japan.

The **Kōbō-san** market fair is held here on the 21st of each month. There is also a regular market on the first Sunday of each month. The temple is a 15-minute walk south-west of Kyoto station.

Kodai Yūzen-en Gallery

This building *(☎ 823 0500; ¥500; open 9am-5pm)* is devoted to Kyoto's traditional Yūzen fabric dyeing, created in the 17th century by painter Miyazaki Yūzen. It houses the Yūzen Art Museum, displaying an impressive collection of antique kimono, paintings, scrolls, dyeing patterns and tools. There is a film shown in English about the Yūzen dyeing process and, of course, a shop selling Yūzen dyed goods. On the top floor you can catch a glimpse of fabric artists at work and even stencil-dye your own handkerchief (see the Activities section later in this chapter for details).

From Kyoto station take bus No 9 to the Horikawa-Matsubara stop and walk for two minutes west on Takatsuji-dōri; or walk eight minutes south-east from Ōmiya station on the Hankyū Kyoto line.

A similar facility, the **Yūzen Cultural Hall (Map 2)** *(Kyoto Yūzen Bunka Kaikan; ☎ 311 0025; ¥400; open 9am-4pm, closed Sun)* has a museum dedicated to the craft; it's a five-minute walk east of Nishikyō-goku station on the Hankyū Kyoto line.

CENTRAL KYOTO
京都市中心部 (MAP 5)

In the 16th century, Toyotomi Hideyoshi ordered a defensive wall to be built around the city, and the area within was called *raku-chū*, or central district. Though the exact boundary is hard to define today, it refers to the area in and around the central business district. Once Kyoto's artistic and cultural centre, the area now bristles with office buildings, department stores, banks, restaurants and bars. While most of raku-chū resembles any other Japanese city, there are several major sights in the area, such as the Imperial Palace, Nijō-jō and numerous museums.

Kyoto Imperial Palace Park

The Imperial Palace is surrounded by a spacious park with a welcome landscape of trees and open lawn. It's perfect for picnics, strolls and just about any sport that doesn't require retrieving balls over walls. Best of all, it's free. Take some time to visit the pond at the park's southern end, with its ever-gaping carp. The park is most beautiful in the plum and cherry blossom seasons (early March and early April, respectively). It is bounded by Teramachi-dōri and Karasuma-dōri on the east and west sides, and by Imadegawa-dōri and Marutamachi-dōri on the north and south.

Kyoto Imperial Palace

The original Imperial Palace (Kyoto Gosho) was built in 794 and has undergone numerous rebirths after destruction by fires. The present building, on a different site and smaller than the original, was constructed in 1855. Ceremonies related to the enthronement of a new emperor and other state functions are still held here.

The tour guide (see the next entry, Reservations & Admission) will elaborate on the details in English while you are led for about one hour past the Shishin-den (ceremonial hall), Ko Gosho (small palace), Tsune Gosho (regular palace) and Oike-niwa (pond garden). Regrettably, it is forbidden to enter any of these buildings.

The Shinsen-den is an outstanding, single-storey structure thatched with a cypress-bark roof. Covered walkways connect it to the surrounding buildings. From outside, you can see a throne (takamikura) where the emperor sat on formal occasions. It is covered with a silk canopy, and on each side are stands to hold treasures such as swords, jewels and other imperial regalia. Just in front of the throne are two wooden koma-inu statues, mythical animals believed to ward off evil spirits. The palace is full of other treasures, including priceless sliding screens adorned with Tosa school paintings. Though the hall initially was used as living quarters for the emperor, it was later set aside for ceremonial use only.

Foreigners are given preferential access to the palace and can obtain permission to enter in a few hours or days, while Japanese visitors (unless acting as an 'interpreter' to a foreigner) may have to wait months. Twice-yearly, in spring and autumn, the palace grounds are chock-full when the inner sanctum is opened to the public for several days.

Reservations & Admission Entry is controlled by the Imperial Household Agency office (Kunaichō; ☎ 211 1215; 8.45am-noon, 1pm-4pm Mon-Fri) **Map 5**, a short walk south-east of Imadegawa station on the Karasuma line, on the Karasuma line, or the Karasuma-Imadegawa bus stop. The office is inside the walled park surrounding the palace.

To make a reservation you must fill out an application form in person and show your passport. Children must be accompanied by an adult over 20 years of age. Permission to tour the Imperial Palace is usually granted the same day. Guided tours in English are given at 10am and 2pm from Monday to Friday and at 10am on the third Saturday of the month (except during April, May, October and November); once permission has been granted, you should arrive no later than 20 minutes before the tour time at the Seisho-mon gate. Allow extra time to find your way. Admission is free.

The agency's office is also the place to make reservations to see the Sentō Gosho palace (see next entry) and the Katsura Rikyū and Shūgaku-in Rikyū imperial villas (see entries later in this chapter). As there is limited space for each tour of these three places, you may need to work around their schedules. To arrange reservations from abroad or from outside of Kyoto, the application forms are available from JNTO offices. For an office in your country, see the Facts for the Visitor chapter (and remember to include return postage or international reply coupons).

Sentō Gosho

A few hundred metres south-east of the Imperial Palace in the park is the Sentō Gosho. It was originally constructed in 1630 during the reign of Emperor Go-Mizunō as a residence for retired emperors. The palace was repeatedly destroyed by fire and reconstructed but served its purpose until a final blaze in 1854 (it was never rebuilt). Today only two structures, the Seika-tei and Yūshin-tei teahouses, remain. The magnificent gardens, laid out in 1630 by renowned landscape designer Kobori Enshū, are the main attraction.

Visitors must obtain advance permission from the Imperial Household Agency (see the previous entry) and be over 20 years old. One-hour tours (in Japanese) start daily at 11am and 1.30pm.

Horino Memorial Museum

A few minutes' walk south of the Imperial Palace Park is the Horino Memorial Museum (*Horino Kinenkan;* ☎ *223 2073; ¥300; open 11am-9pm, closed Mon*), an 18th-century sake brewery housed in a vintage *kyō-machiya* (wooden townhouse). Though the original Kinshi Masamune brewery moved south to Fushimi in the 1880s, spring water (a key ingredient in sake brewing) continues to flow from the Momo-no-I well in the courtyard, where it has been since 1781.

Much of the old architecture remains well preserved, including a fine warehouse *(kura)* open for viewing. There are interesting displays on traditional sake brewing methods. Don't miss the cosy cafe serving tasters of the house sake, micro-brewed beer and light meals. For a unique souvenir, you can pick up a bottle of sake and put your own artistic touch on the label.

Nijō-jō

This castle (☎ *841 0096; ¥600; open 8.45am-4pm, gates close 5pm, closed 26 Dec-4 Jan*) was built in 1603 as the official residence of Tokugawa Ieyasu. The ostentatious style was intended as a demonstration of Ieyasu's prestige and to signal the demise of the emperor's power. To safeguard against treachery, Ieyasu had the interior

fitted with 'nightingale' floors (intruders were detected by the squeaking boards) and concealed chambers where bodyguards could keep watch and spring out at a moment's notice. Fans of ninja movies will recognise the features immediately.

The Momoyama-era (1576–1600) Karamon gate, originally part of Hideyoshi's Fushimi-jō castle, features lavish, masterful woodcarving and metalwork. After passing through the gate, you enter the **Ninomaru palace,** which is divided into five buildings with numerous chambers. Access to the buildings used to depend on rank – only those of highest rank were permitted into the inner buildings.

The Ōhiroma Yon-no-Ma (fourth chamber) has spectacular screen paintings. Also, don't miss **Ninomaru garden**, designed by Kobori Enshū. The vast garden is composed of three separate islets spanned by stone bridges, and is meticulously kept. The Ninomaru palace and garden take about an hour to walk through. A detailed fact sheet in English is provided.

The neighbouring **Honmaru Palace** dates from the mid-19th century. After the Meiji Restoration in 1868, the castle became a detached palace of the imperial household and in 1939 was given to Kyoto city. It's only open for a special autumn viewing.

While you're in the neighbourhood, you might want to take a look at **Shinsen-en** *(free)* just south of the castle outside the walls. This forlorn garden, with its small shrines and pond, is all that remains of the original 8th-century Imperial Palace, abandoned in 1227.

To reach the castle, take bus No 9, 12, 50, 61 or 67 to the Nijō-jō-mae stop. Alternatively, you can take the Tōzai line to Nijō-jō-mae station and walk about two minutes.

Nijō Jinya

A few minutes walk south of Nijō-jō, Nijō Jinya (☎ *841 0972; ¥1000, reservations necessary, in Japanese; 10am-11am, 2pm-3pm, closed Wed*) is one of Kyoto's hidden gems. Seldom seen by short-term visitors, this former merchant's home was built in the mid-1600s and served as an inn for provincial feudal lords visiting the capital. What appears to be an average Edo-period mansion, however, is no ordinary dwelling.

The house contains fire-resistant earthen walls and a warren of 24 rooms, which was ingeniously designed to protect the *daimyō* (domain lords) against possible surprise attacks. Here you'll find hidden staircases, secret passageways and an array of counter-espionage devices. The ceiling skylight of the main room is fitted with a trap door from where samurai could pounce on intruders, and sliding doors feature alternate panels of translucent paper to expose the shadows of eavesdroppers.

One-hour tours are conducted several times daily (in Japanese). An English leaflet is provided, but you might consider arranging a volunteer guide through the TIC.

Mibu-dera

Mibu-dera *(☎ 841 3381; free; 8.30am-4.30pm)* was founded in 991 and belongs to the Risshū school. In the late Edo period, it became a training centre for samurai. Mibu-dera houses tombs of pro-shōgunate Shinsen-gumi members, who fought bloody street battles resisting the forces that succeeded in restoring the emperor in 1868. Except for an unusual stupa covered in Jizō statues, visually the temple is of limited interest. It is, however, definitely worth visiting during Mibu Kyōgen performances in late April, or the Setsubun celebrations in early February (see the 'Festivals' boxed text in the Facts for the Visitor chapter).

The temple is a five-minute walk southwest of Ōmiya station on the Hankyū Kyoto line.

DOWNTOWN KYOTO
京都市下町 **(MAP 9)**

Kyoto's downtown area, which is centred on Kiyamachi-dōri and Kawaramachi-dōri, is packed with great restaurants, bars and shops. Without a doubt, this is the place for a night out in Kyoto.

Museum of Kyoto

Housed in and behind the former Bank of Japan, a classic brick Meiji-period building, this museum *(☎ 222-0888; ¥500, extra for special exhibits; open 10am-7.30pm, closed third Wed each month)* is probably only worth visiting if a special exhibit is on. The regular exhibits consist of models of ancient Kyoto, audiovisual presentations and a small gallery dedicated to Kyoto's film industry. On the 1st floor, the Roji Tempō is a reconstructed Edo-period merchant area showing 10 types of exterior lattice work (this section can be entered for free; some of the shops sell souvenirs and serve local dishes).

The museum has English-speaking volunteer tour guides available. The entrance is on Takakura-dōri, just north of Sanjō-dōri.

The museum is a three-minute walk south-east of the Karasuma-Oike stop on the Karasuma and Tōzai lines.

Ponto-chō

Once the city's red-light district, Ponto-chō is a traditional centre for dining and nighttime entertainment in a narrow street running between the Kamo-gawa and Kiyamachi-dōri. It's a pleasant place to take a stroll if you want to observe Japanese nightlife. Many of the restaurants and teahouses can be difficult to enter, but a number of reasonably priced, accessible places can be found (see the Places to Eat chapter). The geisha teahouses *(ocha-ya)* usually control admittance of foreigners, with a policy of introductions from Japanese persons only and astronomical charges.

Ponto-chō is a great place to spot geisha and apprentice geisha *(maiko)* making their way between appointments, especially on weekend evenings at the Shijō-dōri end of the street.

Nishiki Market

If you're interested in seeing all the weird and wonderful foods required for cooking in Kyoto, wander through Nishiki market. It's on Nishiki-kōji, in the centre of town, one block north of (and parallel to) Shijō-dōri. This is a great place to visit on a rainy day or as a break from temple-hopping. The variety of different foods on display is staggering and the frequent cries of '*Irasshia-mase!*' ('Welcome!') are heartwarming.

EASTERN KYOTO 京都市東部

The eastern part of Kyoto, *raku-tō*, notably the Higashiyama (Eastern Mountains) district (Map 8), merits top priority for its fine temples, peaceful walks and the traditional ambience of the Gion district (Map 6). It is a long, narrow area sandwiched between the Kamo-gawa and the eastern hills, stretching north-south, and an ideal area for touring on foot.

The following descriptions of places to see in eastern Kyoto begin with sights in the southern Higashiyama area (Map 8); the sights in the northern area begin with the Okazaki-kōen Area section (Map 6). Allow at least a full day to cover the sights in the southern section and another full day for those in the north.

Much of the area is covered in the TIC's *Walking Tour Courses in Kyoto* pamphlet, as well as in four of the walking tours contained in this chapter.

Southern Higashiyama Area
東山南部 **(Map 8)**

Sanjūsangen-dō The original temple, called Rengeō-in, was built in 1164 at the request of the retired Emperor Go-shirakawa. After it burnt to the ground in 1249 a faithful copy (☎ 525 0033; ¥600; open 8am-5pm in summer, 9am-4pm in winter) was constructed in 1266.

The temple's name refers to the 33 *sanjūsan* (bays) between the pillars of this long, narrow building. The building houses 1001 wooden statues of Kannon (the Buddhist goddess of mercy); the chief image, the 100-armed Senjū-Kannon, was carved by the celebrated sculptor Tankei in 1254. It is flanked on either side by 500 smaller Kannon images, neatly lined in rows.

There are an awful lot of arms, but if you are picky and think the 1000-armed statues don't have the required number, you should remember to calculate according to the nifty Buddhist mathematical formula, which holds that 40 arms are the equivalent of 1000 because each saves 25 worlds.

At the back of the hall are 28 guardian statues in a great variety of expressive poses. The gallery at the western side of the hall is famous for the annual Tōshi-ya festival, held on 15 January, when archers shoot arrows the length of the hall. The ceremony dates from the Edo period, when an annual contest was held to see how many arrows could be shot from the southern to the northern end in 24 hours. The all-time record was set in 1686, when an archer successfully landed over 8000 arrows at the northern end.

The temple is a 15-minute walk east of Kyoto station, or you can take bus No 206 or 208 and get off at the Sanjūsangen-dō-mae stop. It's also very close to Keihan Shichijō station (Map 10), from which you walk east up Shichijō-dōri.

Kyoto National Museum The Kyoto National Museum (☎ 531 7509; ¥420, extra for special exhibitions; open 9am-4pm, closed Mon) was founded in 1895 as an imperial repository for art and treasures from local temples and shrines. It is housed in two buildings opposite Sanjūsangen-dō temple. There are 17 rooms with displays of over 1000 artworks, historical artefacts and handicrafts. The fine arts collection is especially highly rated, holding some 230 items that have been classified as National Treasures or Important Cultural Properties.

See the preceding Sanjūsangen-dō section for transport details.

Chishaku-in (Map 8) An early Edo-period temple, Chishaku-in (☎ 541 5363; ¥350; open 9am-4pm) was built on the ruins of Shōun-ji by Toyotomi Hideyoshi to enshrine his deceased eldest son. The gardens on the east side of the temple are notable, particularly in May when the azaleas are in full bloom. The Shūzōko hall houses Momoyama-era paintings from the Tōhaku Hasegawa school; these include the famed *Sakura-zu* (cherry tree) and *Kaede-zu* (maple tree).

From Sanjūsangen-dō (Map 7) the temple is a five-minute walk east.

Kawai Kanjirō Memorial Hall (Map 8) This museum (☎ 561 3585; ¥900; open 10am-4.30pm, closed Mon, 10-20 Aug & 24 Dec-7 Jan) was once the self-designed home

Southern Higashiyama Walking Tour (Maps 6 & 8)

Time: Half-day
Distance: About 5km
Major Sights: Kiyomizu-dera, Kōdai-ji, Yasaka-jinja

One of the most enjoyable strolls around the backstreets and temples of Kyoto follows a winding route between Kiyomizu-dera (Map 8) and Maruyama-kōen (Map 6). For a detailed map of this route, see the TIC's *Walking Tour Courses in Kyoto*.

The walk begins near the Gojō-zaka slope. Start your walk after a look at the pottery shops on the slope, at the corner of Gojō-dōri and Higashiōji-dōri. Head uphill (between a pharmacy and an old noodle shop) until you reach the first fork in the road; bear right and continue up Chawan-zaka (teapot lane) to **Kiyomizu-dera** (you'll see a pagoda at the top of the hill). When you reach the top, the temple entrance will be on your left; but take a short detour uphill to the right for an amazing view of the neighbouring cemetery before heading toward the temple.

After touring Kiyomizu-dera, exit down **Kiyomizu-zaka**, the steep approach to the temple. It is lined with shops selling Kyoto handicrafts (notably *Kiyomizu-yaki*– a distinctive local pottery), snacks and souvenirs. After about 200m, you'll come to a four-way intersection; take a right down the stone-paved steps. This is **Sannen-zaka**, lined with old wooden houses and traditional shops and restaurants. There are also pleasant teahouses with gardens – it's a good place to relax over a bowl of steaming noodles.

Halfway down Sannen-zaka, the road takes a sharp left. Follow it a short distance, then go right down a flight of steps into **Ninen-zaka**, another street lined with historic houses, shops and teahouses. At the end of Ninen-zaka zigzag left then right, and continue north for five minutes, where you will reach the entrance of **Kōdai-ji** on the right up a long flight of stairs. Just before this entrance you can detour into **Ishibei-kōji** on your left – perhaps the most beautiful street in Kyoto, though it's actually a cobbled alley lined on both sides with elegant, traditional Japanese inns and restaurants.

Exit Kōdai-ji the way you came and walk to the 'T' in the road; turn right here and zigzag right and left into **Maruyama-kōen**, a pleasant spot to take a rest. In the centre of the park, you'll the giant Gion shidare-zakura, Kyoto's most famous cherry tree. Opposite the tree there's a bridge that leads across a carp pond to the lovely upper reaches of the park.

From the park, you can head west into the grounds of **Yasaka-jinja**. You can descend from the shrine to Shijō-dōri and Gion. If you've got the energy, however, it's best to return back through the park and head north to tour the grounds of the impressive **Chion-in**. From here it's a quick walk to **Shōren-in**, famous for its enormous camphor trees. From Shōren-in descend to Sanjō-dōri (you'll see the giant *torii* – shrine gate – of Heian-jingū in the distance). By going left on Sanjō-dōri, you'll soon come to a bus stop where you can catch bus No 5 to Kyoto station.

and workshop of one of Japan's most famous potters, Kawai Kanjirō (1890–1966). The 1937 house is built in rural style and contains examples of his work, his collection of folk art and ceramics, and his workshop and kiln.

Despite the steep cost, most come away satisfied. The museum is a 10-minute walk north of the Kyoto National Museum, or you can take bus No 206 or 207 from Kyoto station and get off at the Uma-machi stop. The museum is near the intersection of Gojō-dōri and Higashiōji-dōri.

Rokuharamitsu-ji (Map 7) An important Buddhist pilgrimage stop, this temple (☎ 561 6980; *admission to treasure house ¥500; open 8am-4.30pm*) was founded in 963 by Kūya Shōnin, who carved an image of an 11-headed Kannon and installed it in the temple in the hope of stopping a plague which was ravaging Kyoto at the time.

The temple itself is unremarkable but the treasure house at the rear contains a rare collection of 15 fantastic statues; the most intriguing is a standing likeness of Kūya, staff in hand and prayer gong draped around his neck, with a string of tiny figurines parading from his gums. Legend holds that while praying one day, these manifestations of the Buddha suddenly ambled out of his mouth.

The temple is about seven minutes' walk north of the Kawai Kanjirō Memorial Hall.

Kiyomizu-dera (Map 8) This temple (☎ 551 1234; ¥300; open 6am-6pm) was first built in 798 and devoted to Jūichi-men, an 11-headed Kannon. The present buildings – built under order of Iemitsu, the third Tokugawa shōgun – are reconstructions dating from 1633. As an affiliate of the Hossō school, which originated in Nara, the temple has survived through the centuries the many intrigues of Kyoto Buddhist schools and is now one of the most famous landmarks of the city. This, unfortunately, makes it a prime target for busloads of Japanese tourists, particularly during cherry blossom season. Some travellers are also put off by the rather mercantile air of the temple – endless stalls selling good luck charms, fortunes and all manner of souvenirs. If you find this bothersome, head to some of the quieter temples further north.

The main hall has a huge veranda which juts out over the hillside, supported by 139 15m-high wooden pillars. The terrace commands an excellent view over the city centre.

Just below this hall is the **Otowa-no-taki waterfall**, where visitors drink the sacred waters, which are believed to have therapeutic properties (and also to improve school test results). South of the main hall is **Koyasu-no-tō**, a three-storey pagoda housing a statue of the goddess responsible for the safe delivery of babies (which explains the frequent visits by pregnant women). At the **Jishu-jinja**, north of the main hall, visitors try to ensure success in love by closing their eyes and walking

about 18m between a pair of stones – if you miss the stone, your desire for love won't be fulfilled!

To get there from Kyoto station take bus No 206 and get off at either the Kiyomizu-michi or Gojō-zaka stops. Plod up the hill for 10 minutes to reach the temple.

Kōdai-ji (Map 8) This temple (☎ 561 9966; ¥500; open 9am-4.30pm, until 4pm Nov-Mar) was founded in 1605 by Kita-no-Mandokoro in memory of her late husband, Toyotomi Hideyoshi. The extensive grounds include gardens designed by Kobori Enshū, teahouses designed by the renowned master of tea ceremony, Sen no Rikyū, and a lovely little grove of bamboo trees.

The temple is a 15-minute walk north of Kiyomizu-dera or five minutes south of Maruyama-kōen (next entry).

Maruyama-kōen (Map 6) This park is a favourite of locals and visitors alike. It's a place to escape the bustle of the city centre and amble around gardens, ponds, souvenir shops and restaurants. Peaceful paths meander through the trees and carp glide through the waters of a small pond in the centre of the park.

For two weeks in early April, when the park's cherry trees come into bloom, the calm atmosphere of the park is shattered by hordes of drunken revellers having *hanami* (cherry viewing) parties under the trees. The centrepiece is a massive *shidare-zakura* cherry tree – one of the most beautiful sights in Kyoto, particularly when lit up from below at night. For those who don't mind crowds, this is a good place to observe the Japanese at their most uninhibited. The best advice is to arrive early and claim a good spot high on the east side of the park from where you can safely peer down on the mayhem below.

See the following Yasaka-jinja section for transport details.

Yasaka-jinja (Map 6) This colourful shrine (*free; open 24-hours*) is down the hill from Maruyama-kōen. It's considered the guardian shrine of neighbouring Gion. The present buildings, with the exception of the older, two-storey west gate, date from 1654. The granite torii on the south side was erected in 1666 and stands 9.5m high, making it one of the largest in Japan. The roof of the main shrine is covered with cypress shingles. Among the treasures here are a pair of carved wooden *koma-inu*, mythological animals, attributed to the renowned sculptor Unkei.

This shrine is particularly popular as a spot for *hatsu-mōde*, the first shrine visit of the new year. If you don't mind a stampede, come here around midnight on New Year's Eve or any of the following days. Surviving the crush is proof that you're blessed by the gods! Yasaka-jinja also sponsors Kyoto's biggest festival, Gion Matsuri.

Take bus No 206, get off at Gion and walk through the orange torii into the shrine. Alternatively, you can easily walk to the shrine from Keihan Shijō and Hankyū Kawaramachi stations.

Chion-in (Map 6) A grand temple (☎ *531 2111; entry to grounds free, entry to inner buildings and garden ¥400; open 9am-4.30pm Mar-Nov, until 4pm Dec-Feb),* Chion-in was built by the monk Genchi in 1234 on the site where his mentor, Hōnen, had taught and eventually fasted to death. Today it is still the headquarters of the Jōdo school, which was founded by Hōnen, and it's a hive of religious activity. For visitors with a taste for the grand and glorious, this temple is sure to satisfy.

The oldest of the present buildings date from the 17th century. The two-storey San-mon gate at the main entrance is the largest in Japan, and prepares the visitor for the massive scale of the temple. The immense main hall contains an image of Hōnen and is connected with the Dai Hōjō hall by a nightingale floor.

After visiting the main hall, with its fantastic gold altar, you can walk around the back of the same building to see the temple's gardens. On the way, you'll pass a darkened hall with a small statue of Amida Buddha on display, glowing eerily in the darkness. It makes a nice contrast to the splendour of the main hall.

The Daishōrō belfry houses a bell cast in 1633, measuring 2.7m in diameter and weighing almost 80 tonnes – the largest in Japan. The combined muscle power of 17 monks is required to make the bell budge for a ceremony held here to ring in the new year.

The temple is near the north-eastern corner of Maruyama-kōen. From Kyoto station take bus No 206 and get off at the Chion-in-mae stop, or walk 15 minutes east from the Keihan-line Sanjō or Shijō stations.

Shōren-in (Map 6) This temple (☎ *561 2345; ¥500; open 9am-4.30pm)* is hard to miss, with its giant camphor trees growing just outside the walls. Shōren-in, commonly called Awata Palace after the road it faces, was originally the residence of the chief abbot of the Tendai school. Founded in 1150, the present building dates from 1895 but the main hall has sliding screens with paintings from the 16th and 17th centuries. Often overlooked by the crowds who descend on other Higashiyama area temples, this is a pleasant place to sit and think while gazing out over one of Kyoto's finest landscape gardens.

The temple is a five-minute walk north of Chion-in.

Gion District (Map 6) Gion is the famous entertainment and geisha quarter on the eastern bank of the Kamo-gawa. While Gion's true origins were in teahouses catering to weary visitors to Yasaka-jinja shrine, by the mid-18th century the area was Kyoto's largest pleasure district. Despite the looming modern architecture, congested traffic and contemporary nightlife establishments which have cut a swathe through its historical beauty, there are still some places left in Gion for an enjoyable walk (see the Night Walk through the Floating World boxed text).

Hanami-kōji runs north to south and bisects Shijō-dōri. The southern section is lined with 17th-century, traditional restaurants and teahouses, many of which are exclusive establishments for geisha entertainment. At the south end you reach **Gion Corner** and next door **Gion Kōbu Kaburen-jō**

Night Walk through the Floating World (Maps 6 & 9)

Time: Two hours
Distance: About 2km
Major Sights: Traditional entertainment districts, classic architecture, contemporary nightlife

The traditional entertainment areas of Gion and Ponto-chō make for an excellent evening stroll. Begin your walk on the steps of the main gate into **Yasaka-jinja** (Map 6), beautifully lit at night. Cross west on the southern side of Shijō-dōri and, just after passing the Gion Hotel, turn left. Wind through the narrow alleys of *ryōtei* restaurants and teahouses, finally working your way out to **Hanami-kōji**.

Heading north on Hanami-kōji, cross Shijō-dōri and go west (left) for about 20m before turning right on to Kiri-dōshi (Map 9); continue north until you cross the small Tatsumi-bashi bridge. This is the lovely and well-preserved **Shinbashi district**, which features some of Kyoto's finest traditional architecture.

At the fork in the road by the small **Tatsumi shrine**, you can go up the left fork or the right (or better yet make a loop) and see a charming group of exclusive teahouses and traditional shops. From this area, work your way out to the neon lights of **Nawate-dōri** (note the gangster-types in black Mercedes with dark-tinted windows!). Continue north to Sanjō-dōri and cross the bridge west.

Just after you've reached the other side of the Sanjō bridge, turn left and soon the road veers to the right. After a few steps veer left into **Ponto-chō**. This narrow alley is pleasantly void of motor traffic and full of restaurants, bars and ancient teahouses; from here it's a leisurely 500m stroll south back to Shijō-dōri. Keep your eyes (and ears) open for geisha and their maiko apprentices in elegant kimono and tall click-clacking wooden sandals (*pokkuri*).

When you reach the southern end of Ponto-chō at Shijō-dōri, turn right. In about 20m you'll hit bustling **Kiyamachi-dōri**. Turn right here to soak up a bit of Kyoto's modern 'floating world'. There are endless bars and restaurants and packs of young Japanese out on the town.

Theatre (for details on these two places, see the Entertainment chapter).

If you walk down from Shijō-dōri along the northern section of Hanami-kōji, you will reach **Shinbashi-dōri** and its traditional restaurants. A bit further north are **Shinmonzen-dōri** and **Furumonzen-dōri**, running east to west. Wander in either direction along these streets, which are packed with old houses, art galleries and shops specialising in antiques – but don't expect flea-market prices here.

For more historic buildings in a beautiful waterside setting, wander down **Shirakawa Minami-dōri**, which is roughly parallel with, and one block south of, the western section of Shinmonzen-dōri.

Kennin-ji (Map 7) Tucked in the heart of Gion, this temple (☎ 561 0190; ¥500; open 10am-4pm) belongs to the Rinzai school. Founded in 1202 by the priest Eisai after returning from China, Kennin-ji holds the distinction of being Kyoto's first Zen temple. With the exception of Chokushi-mon gate, all the original structures were destroyed by fire. The temple is famed for its 17th-century paintings by Tawaraya Sōtatsu depicting the gods of wind and thunder.

Also on the grounds, **Ryōsoku-in** (☎ 561 3216) is known for its garden with springs and ponds – but a visit here usually requires an advance reservation (you may get in without prior reservation if things are quiet though).

THINGS TO SEE & DO

Geisha & Maiko

Of all the stereotypical images one associates with Kyoto and traditional Japan, perhaps the most endearing is that of the kimono-clad *geisha*. Although their numbers are decreasing, geisha (*geiko* in the Kyoto dialect) and *maiko* (apprentice geisha) can still be seen in some parts of Kyoto, especially after dusk.

They cater to the wealthy behind the closed doors of the exclusive teahouses and restaurants that dot the backstreets between the Kamo-gawa and Yasaka-jinja and along the narrow Ponto-chō alley.

A true geisha is well versed in an array of visual and performing arts, including playing the three stringed *shamisen*, singing old teahouse ballads and traditional dancing.

With the exception of public performances at annual festivals or dance presentations, geisha and maiko perform only for select customers. It is virtually impossible to enter a Gion teahouse and witness a performance without the introduction of an established patron.

An evening in a Gion teahouse begins with an exquisite *kaiseki* dinner (see the Cuisine special section in the Places to Eat chapter). While the customers eat, the geisha or maiko enter the room and give a short self-introduction in Kyoto dialect.

A shamisen performance, followed by a traditional fan dance, is often given, and all the while the geisha and maiko pour drinks, light cigarettes and engage in charming banter.

To answer the most frequent question, *no*, geisha are not prostitutes. Some geisha, once they retire at 50 or so and decide to open their own teahouse, do get financial backing from a well-to-do client (with whom they may or may not be intimately involved). The patron has to be wealthy, as an evening with two or three geisha or maiko may cost upward of US$3000.

Although their exact number is something of a mystery, knowledgeable sources estimate that there are perhaps 80 maiko and just over 100 geisha in Kyoto. Geisha and maiko can also be found in other parts of the country, most notably Tokyo. However, it is thought that less than 1000 geisha and maiko remain in all Japan.

Few foreigners have explored the world of maiko and geisha as thoroughly as Kyoto resident Peter MacIntosh. MacIntosh, a Canadian-born photographer, has spent the last several years photographing geisha and maiko and is one of the only foreigners in Kyoto to hold accounts at several of Kyoto's venerable teahouses. If you're intent on an evening with a geisha or maiko (or several) he is the man to call. He can be reached at ☎ 090-8573 8220 or via email at [e] kyoto pmac@hotmail.com. You can also visit his site at [w] www.petermacintosh.com to see a selection of his photographs of Kyoto geisha and maiko.

For those who may wonder how they might appear as a maiko, you can live out your fantasy at one of the numerous Kyoto studios that dress up tourists for the occasion. See the Activities section in this chapter for details.

MJ

Northern Higashiyama Area
東山北部 **(Map 6)**
Okazaki-kōen Area This is the open expanse of parks, canals and museums that lies between Niōmon-dōri and Heian-jingū.

The **National Museum of Modern Art** (☎ 761 4111; ¥420; open 9.30am-5pm, closed Mon) is renowned for its Japanese ceramics and paintings. There is an excellent permanent collection, including many pottery pieces by Kawai Kanjirō.

The **Kyoto Municipal Museum of Art** (☎ 771 4107; admission varies by exhibition; open 9am-4.30pm, closed Mon) organises several major exhibitions a year.

For an interesting break from temple gazing, pop into the **Fureai-kan Kyoto Museum of Traditional Crafts** (☎ 762 2670; free; open 10am-6pm, closed Mon). Exhibits cover things like woodblock prints, lacquerware, bamboo goods and gold-leaf work. It's in the basement of the Miyako Messe (Kyoto International Exhibition Hall).

Another nearby museum of limited interest is the **Lake Biwa Aqueduct** (☎ 752 2530; free; open 9am-4.30pm, closed Mon) dedicated in 1989 to mark the 100th anniversary of the building of the canal.

Finally, those with children might want to stop by the **Kyoto Municipal Zoo** (Kyotoshi Dōbutsu-en). The zoo (☎ 771 0210; adult/child ¥500/200; open 9am-5pm, closed Mon) is home to about 1000 animals, and has some decent gardens and groves of cherry trees.

Heian-jingū This shrine (☎ 761 0221; shrine precincts free, garden ¥600; open 8.30am-5.30pm 15 Mar-31 Aug, until 4.30pm other times) was built in 1895 to commemorate the 1100th anniversary of the founding of Kyoto. The shrine buildings are gaudy replicas, reduced to a two-thirds scale, of the Imperial Court Palace of the Heian period (794–1185).

The spacious garden, with its large pond and Chinese-inspired bridge, is also meant to represent gardens popular in the Heian period. It is well known for its wisteria, irises and weeping cherry trees. About 500m in front of the shrine is a massive steel torii. Although it appears to be entirely separate, this is actually considered the main entrance to the shrine itself.

Two major events, Jidai Matsuri (22 October) and Takigi Nō (1–2 June), are held here. Take bus No 5 from Kyoto station or Keihan Sanjō station and get off at the Jingū-michi stop, or walk up from Keihan Sanjō station; alternatively, walk 10 minutes north from the Tōzai line's Higashiyama station.

Murin-an Villa An elegant villa (☎ 771 3909; ¥350; open 9am-4.30pm) this was the home of prominent statesman Yamagata Aritomo (1838–1922) and the site of a pivotal 1902 political conference as Japan was heading into the Russo-Japanese War.

Built in 1896, the grounds contain well-preserved wooden buildings including a fine Japanese tearoom. The Western-style annex is characteristic of Meiji-period architecture and the serene garden features small streams which draw water from the Biwa-ko Sosui canal. For ¥300 you can savour a bowl of frothy matcha (green powdered tea) while viewing the 'borrowed scenery' backdrop of the Higashiyama mountains.

Nanzen-ji This temple (☎ 771 0365; admission to grounds free, admission to inner buildings/garden ¥400; open 8.40am-4.30pm) is one of the most pleasant in Kyoto, with its expansive grounds and numerous subtemples. It began as a retirement villa for Emperor Kameyama but was dedicated as a Zen temple on his death in 1291. Civil war in the 15th century destroyed most of the temple; the present buildings date from the 17th century. It operates now as the headquarters of the Rinzai school.

At the entrance to the temple stands the massive San-mon gate (1628), its ceiling adorned with Tosa and Kanō school murals of birds and angels. Steps lead up to the 2nd storey (entry ¥300), which has a fine view over the city. Beyond the gate is the hōjō (abbot's) hall with impressive screens painted with a vivid depiction of tigers.

THINGS TO SEE & DO

Northern Higashiyama Walking Tour (Map 6)

Time: Half day
Distance: About 6km
Major Sights: Heian-jingū, Nanzen-ji, Tetsugaku-no-michi (Path of Philosophy), Ginkaku-ji

The walk described here is a great way to see some of the most important temples in Kyoto, along with some wonderful natural scenery. Start at the top (east end) of Sanjō-dōri, where it meets Shirakawa-dōri (this point is easily reached by taking the Tōzai line to Keage station). Walk up the hill and take a left under the old funicular tracks (you'll see a pedestrian tunnel). This leads to a narrow street that winds toward **Konchi-in**, passing some lovely maple trees (fabulous in Autumn).

Just past Konchi-in (enter if you'd like to see its famous rock garden), take a right on the main road and walk up through the gate into **Nanzen-ji**. After touring the grounds of the temple, go to the aqueduct in front of **Nanzen-in** and follow it up the hill. You'll come first to the lovely **Nanzen-ji Oku-no-in** subtemple. Beyond this, the trail enters the woods. Follow it up to the secluded **Kōtoku-an**, a tiny shrine built around a waterfall. It's one of Kyoto's most entrancing spots.

Return the way you came and exit the north side of Nanzen-ji, following the road through a gate. You'll soon come to **Eikan-dō**, a large temple famous for its artworks and pagoda. At the corner just beyond Eikan-dō, there is a sign in English and Japanese pointing up the hill (right) to the **Tetsugaku-no-michi** (Path of Philosophy). At the top of the hill, turn left onto the path.

Follow the quiet, cherry tree-lined canal – a nice break spot for *matcha* (green powdered tea) is **Kanō Shōju-an** teahouse – and after about 15 minutes make a small detour east to the serene **Hōnen-in**. From here, follow the narrow side streets north to **Ginkaku-ji**, the famed Silver Pavilion. If you are still feeling energetic, make the praiseworthy hike up **Daimonji-yama** to view a gorgeous sunset and one of the best views of the city (see the boxed text 'Daimonji-yama Climb' a little further on in this chapter). Otherwise, follow Ginkaku-ji Michi (along the canal) down to Shirakawa-dōri, where you can catch buses to most parts of Kyoto.

Within the precincts of the same building, the **Leaping Tiger Garden** is a classic Zen garden well worth a look. While you're in the hōjō, you can enjoy a cup of tea while sitting on tatami mats gazing at a small waterfall (¥400; ask at the reception desk).

Perhaps the best part of Nanzen-ji is overlooked by most visitors: **Kōtoku-an**, a small shrine hidden in a forested hollow behind the main precinct. To get there, walk up to the red-brick aqueduct in front of Nanzen-in. Follow the road that runs parallel to the aqueduct up into the hills, past Nanzen-ji Oku-no-in on your left. Continue into the woods, past several brightly coloured torii until you reach a waterfall in a beautiful mountain glen. Here, pilgrims pray while standing under the

waterfall, sometimes in the dead of winter. Hiking trails lead off in all directions from this point; by going due north, you'll eventually arrive at the top of Daimonji-yama (two hours; see boxed text 'Daimonji-yama Climb'), go east and you'll get to the town of Yamashina (also about two hours).

Nanzen-ji is a 10-minute walk south-east of Heian-jingū; from Kyoto station, or Keihan Sanjō station, take bus No 5 and get off at the Eikan-dō-mae stop.

Dotted around the grounds of Nanzen-ji are several subtemples that are often skipped by the crowds and consequently easier to enjoy.

Nanzen-in This subtemple (☎ 771 0365; *¥350; same hours as Nanzen-ji*) is on your

Latticework on the exterior of Sumiya, the last remaining *ageya* (traditional banquet hall), built 1641

A 'bullet train' pulls into Kyoto Station.

The Kyoto National Museum, founded in 1895

Traditional signs are displayed outside Minami-za theatre, where regular *kabuki* performances are held.

An Imperial Palace replica at Heian-jingū

Stone lantern in Gion, Kyoto's old pleasure area

This giant *torii* spans a wide road, and is the entrance point to the Shintō shrine Heian-jingū.

Kurodani to Yoshida-jinja Walking Tour (Map 6)

Time: Two to three hours
Distance: About 4km
Major Sights: Kurodani Temple, Shinnyo-dō, Yoshida-jinja

This fine walk is a good way to escape the crowds that flock to the northern Higashiyama area's better-known sights. You might try doing it in the late afternoon or evening, but time it so that you don't get stuck here after dark, as the cemeteries around here can be distinctly spooky once the sun goes down.

The walk starts at an alley a few metres west of the Hotel Sunflower Kyoto at **Okazaki-jinja**. Walk up the alley, climb the steps and continue straight on for 75 metres to the base of the Kurodani cemetery. Climb to the **pagoda** at the top of the steps for a good view over Kyoto.

Return to the bottom of the steps, cross the stone bridge and take a right up the steps to the main precinct of **Kurodani Temple**. Looking south from the wide-open plaza in front of the main hall of the temple, you'll see the impressive *san-mon* entry gate. Then, facing the main hall, go left and then quickly right out of the grounds of Kurodani (passing a statue of the seated Buddha).

Next, you'll pass another cemetery on the right and several subtemples. After going straight for about 200 metres go through a wooden gate and continue on for another 100 metres to the entrance to **Shinnyo-dō** on your right. After exploring this temple, retrace your steps and walk straight west to a stone torii at the base of a hill. Climb the steps here to **Sōchu-jinja**. From here, go right through another stone torii and ascend through a procession of orange torii to **Takenaka-Inari-sha**, a small shrine near the top of Yoshida-yama.

From here, take the steps that lead west over the crest of the hill, then descend through a small park down to the left. Take the first trail down the hill on the right, bearing west (downhill). A few zig-zags down the fall line brings you to the back of **Yoshida-jinja**. After exploring the shrine, you can descend the main stone steps of the shrine to the west and walk out to Higashiōji-dōri where you can catch buses to all parts of Kyoto.

cc

---

right when facing the hōjō – follow the path under the aqueduct. It has an attractive garden designed around a heart-shaped pond. This garden is best seen in the morning or around noon, when sunlight shines directly into the pond and illuminates the colourful carp.

Tenju-an This temple *(☎ 771 0365; ¥300; hours same as Nanzen-ji)* stands at the side of San-mon, a four-minute walk west of Nanzen-in. Constructed in 1337, Tenju-an has a splendid garden and a great collection of carp in its pond.

Konchi-in When leaving Tenju-an, turn left and continue for 100m – Konchi-in *(☎ 771 3511; ¥400; open 8.30am-5pm*
Mar-Nov, until 4.30pm other times) is down a small side street on the left. The stylish gardens fashioned by Kobori Enshū are the main attraction.

Nomura Museum This museum *(☎ 751 0374; ¥700; open 10am-4.30pm, closed Mon)* is a 10-minute walk north of Nanzen-ji. Exhibits include scrolls, paintings, tea ceremony implements and ceramics that were bequeathed by business magnate Nomura Tokushiki.

Eikan-dō Also known as Zenrin-ji, this temple *(☎ 761 0007; ¥500; open 9am-4pm)* is made interesting by its varied architecture, its gardens and works of art. One of Kyoto's best spots for viewing the autumn colours, the temple was founded in 855 by the priest Shinshō, but the name was changed to Eikan-dō in the 11th century to honour the philanthropic priest Eikan.

The best approach is to follow the arrows and wander slowly along the covered walkways connecting the halls and gardens.

In the Amida-dō hall at the southern end of the complex is a famous statue of Mikaeri Amida (Buddha glancing backwards).

From Amida-dō, head north to the end of the curving covered walkway (garyūrō). Change into the sandals provided, then climb the steep steps up the mountainside to the **Tahō-tō pagoda**, from where there's a fine view across the city.

From Kyoto station, or Keihan Sanjō station, take bus No 5 and get off at the Eikandō-mae stop.

Tetsugaku-no-michi The name translates as the 'path of philosophy'. It has been a favourite with contemplative strollers since noted 20th-century philosopher

Nishida Kitarō is said to have meandered along the path 'lost in thought'. Follow the traffic-free route along a canal lined with cherry trees which come into spectacular bloom in April. It only takes 30 minutes to do the walk, which starts at Nyakuōji-bashi, above Eikan-dō, and leads to Ginkaku-ji. During the day you should be prepared for crowds; a night stroll will definitely be quieter.

Hōnen-in This temple (☎ 771 2400; free; open 7am-4pm) was founded in 1680 to honour the priest Hōnen. This is a lovely, secluded temple with carefully raked gardens set back in the woods. The temple buildings include a small gallery where frequent exhibitions featuring local and international artists are held.

Hōnen-in is a 12-minute walk from Ginkaku-ji, on a side street just east of the Tetsugaku-no-michi. Cross the bridge over the canal and follow the road uphill through the bamboo groves.

Daimonji-yama Climb

Time: two hours (round trip)
Distance: about 5km
Major Sights: nature, site of the main Daimonji Gozan Okuribi bonfire, panoramic view over Kyoto

Directly behind Ginkaku-ji, **Daimonji-yama (Map 6)** is the main site of the momentous **Daimonji Gozan Okuribi fire festival**. From almost anywhere in town the Chinese character for great (dai) is visible in the middle of a bare patch on the face of this mountain. Every year on 16 August, this character is set ablaze to guide the spirits of the dead on their journey home. The view of Kyoto from the top is unparalleled.

Take bus No 5 to the Ginkakuji-michi stop and walk up to **Ginkaku-ji**. Here you have the option of visiting the temple or starting the hike immediately. To find the trailhead, turn left just in front of the temple and head north for about 50m toward a stone torii. Just before the torii, turn right up the hill.

The trail proper starts just after a small parking lot on the right with a barn where horses are kept. It's a broad avenue through the trees. A few minutes walking brings you to a red banner hanging over the trail (warning of forest fire danger). Soon after this you must cross a bridge to the right, then continue up a smaller, switchback trail. When the trail reaches a saddle not far from the top, go to the left. You'll climb a long flight of steps (and see the pulley system used for transporting wood for the bonfire) before coming out in the middle of the bald patch. The sunset from here is great, but bring a torch (flashlight) for the way down.

CC

Ginkaku-ji One of Kyoto's most breathtaking temples, Ginkaku-ji (☎ 771 5725; ¥500; open 8.30am-5pm 15 Mar-30 Nov, 9am-4.30pm other times) is definitely worth seeing; unfortunately it is usually swamped with busloads of visitors jamming the narrow pathways. Also known as Jishō-ji, the temple belongs to the Shōkokuji school of the Rinzai school.

In 1482, shōgun Ashikaga Yoshimasa constructed a villa here, which he used as a genteel retreat from the turmoil of civil war. Although its name translates as Silver Pavilion, the scheme to completely cover the building in silver leaf was never carried out. After Yoshimasa's death, it was converted to a temple.

The approach to the main gate runs between tall hedges before turning sharply into the extensive grounds. Walkways lead through the gardens laid out by painter and garden designer Sōami. The gardens include meticulously raked cones of white sand (kōgetsudai) designed to reflect moonlight and enhance the beauty of the garden at night.

In addition to the Buddha image in the main hall, the Tōgudō (residence of Yoshimasa) houses an effigy of Yoshimasa dressed in monk's garb. The tiny tearoom here is said to be the oldest in Japan (closed to the public).

From Kyoto station or Keihan Sanjō station, take bus No 5 and get off at the Ginkakuji-michi stop. From Keihan Demachiyanagi station or Keihan Shijō station, take bus No 203 to the same stop.

NORTHERN & NORTH-EASTERN KYOTO 京都市北部／京都市北東部

The area north of Imadegawa-dōri, rakuhoku, provides scope for exploration of rural valleys and mountainous regions. Kitayama-dōri, Kyoto's answer to Madison Avenue, is lined with boutiques, chic restaurants and galleries. It is an excellent area to get a taste for some of the city's modern architecture.

Several worthwhile sights lie on the 'island' between the Kamo-gawa and the Takano-gawa. These include the ancient sister shrines of Shimogamo-jinja and Kamigamo-jinja, and the sprawling Botanical Gardens.

In the far north-eastern region are the Shūgaku-in Rikyū Imperial Villa (Map 4) and several secluded temples; further afield (Map 1) you can head up Hiei-zan and wander through the temple Enryaku-ji's vast precincts.

Shisen-dō (Map 4)

Its name meaning 'house of poet-hermits', Shisen-dō (☎ 781 2954; ¥500; open 9am-5pm) was built in 1641 by Ishikawa Jōzan, a scholar of Chinese classics and a landscape architect who wanted a place to retire to. Formerly a samurai, Jōzan abandoned his warrior status after a rift with Tokugawa Ieyasu and became a recluse here until his death in 1672 at the age of 90.

The hermitage is noted for its display of poems and portraits of 36 ancient Chinese poets, which are found in the Shisen-no-ma room. The karesansui (waterless pond) white-sand garden is lined with azaleas, which are said to represent islands in the sea. The garden also reflects Jōzan's distinct taste for Chinese aesthetics. It's a tranquil place to relax.

Water flows from a small waterfall to the shishi-odoshi, or sōzu, a device designed to scare away wild boar and deer. It's made from a bamboo pipe into which water slowly trickles, fills up and swings down to empty. On the upswing to its original position, the bamboo strikes a stone with a 'thwack' – just loud enough to interrupt your snooze – before starting to refill.

It's a five-minute walk from the Ichijōji-sagarimatsu-mae bus stop on the No 5 route.

Manshu-in (Map 2)

About 30 minutes' walk north of Shisen-dō you'll reach the stately gate of Manshu-in (☎ 781 5010; ¥500; open 9am-4.30pm), a popular retreat of former emperors and a great escape from the crowds. This temple was originally founded by Saichō on Hiei-zan, but was relocated here at the beginning of the Edo period by Ryōshōhō, the son of Prince Hachijōnomiya Tomohito (who built Katsura Rikyū).

The graceful temple architecture is often compared with Katsura Rikyū for its detailed

Kyoto's Contemporary Architecture

Kyoto is deservedly famous for its wealth of traditional buildings. The city also abounds with dramatic examples of contemporary architecture, and although modern architecture is anathema to preservationists, such buildings are not wholly out of place in a city that has been the most progressive and innovative in Japanese history.

A tour should begin on **Kitayama-dōri (Map 3)**, the northern edge of the city proper. Originally developed by overenthusiastic investors during the 'bubble economy' years of the late 1980s, Kitayama-dōri's boutiques are hardly bustling. Yet the street does contain some of the stranger architectural sights in town.

Coming out of the Karasuma-line Kitayama subway exit, interesting buildings are only a minute's walk in every direction. To the south is the **Kyoto Concert Hall (Map 3)** by Isozaki Arata, a leading light in contemporary Japanese architecture. It's a stylish combination of old and new that doesn't resort to historical pastiche. The spiral ramp in the lobby is worth a look, a space entirely devoid of colour – just nuanced shades of grey. Its elegant restraint is very Kyoto, very *shibui*. If you have time (and money) for a concert, the acoustics are superb.

To the north-east of the subway exit, you can't miss the **Syntax building (Map 3)** by Takamatsu Shin. Takamatsu is Kyoto's local architectural star, with projects all over Japan, offices in Europe and even appearances in TV commercials. Inside, Syntax is just a collection of expensive shops, but outside it is typical, inimitable Takamatsu: concrete monumentality articulated in robotic stone and steel. Directly opposite is **Ining '23 (Map 3)**, another Takamatsu work, of similar ilk to Syntax.

A few minutes' walk west, past the entrance to the Kyoto Botanical Gardens and on the north side of Kitayama-dōri, is a work by noted architect Andō Tadaō, a small collection of boutiques called **B-Lock (Map 3)**. It's a good example of Andō's interest in the juxtaposition of pure geometric forms and the play of natural light, all executed in unadorned concrete. A little further along is Takamatsu's **WEEK building (Map 3)**, a collage in concrete and steel housing a collection of small boutiques.

Back in the centre of town, you'll find Andō's much celebrated **TIME'S building (Map 9)** on the corner of Sanjō-dōri and Kiyamachi-dōri. It's a long concrete box with a barrel-vaulted roof and

---

woodwork and rare works of art like sliding *fusuma-e* doors painted by Kanō Eitoku, a famed artist of the Momoyama era. The karesansui garden by Kobori Enshū features a sea of gravel intended to symbolise the flow of a waterfall, and stone islands representing cranes and turtles.

Shūgaku-in Rikyū Imperial Villa (Map 2)

Lying at the foot of Hiei-zan, this villa (☎ 211 1215; free; see further on for visiting hours), or detached palace, was begun in the 1650s by Emperor Go-Mizunō following his abdication; work was continued after his death in 1680 by his daughter Akenomiya. It was designed as a lavish summer retreat for the imperial family.

The villa grounds are divided into three enormous garden areas on a hillside –

lower, middle and upper. Each has superb tea ceremony houses; the upper, **Kami-no-chaya** and lower, **Shimo-no-chaya**, were completed in 1659, and the middle teahouse, **Naka-no-chaya**, was completed in 1682. The gardens' reputation rests on its ponds, pathways and impressive use of 'borrowed scenery' in the form of the surrounding hills. The view from the Rinun-tei teahouse in Kami-no-chaya is particularly impressive.

One-hour tours (in Japanese) start at 9am, 10am, 11am, 1.30pm and 3pm; try to arrive early. A basic leaflet in English is provided and more detailed literature is on sale in the tour waiting room.

You must make reservations through the Imperial Household Agency – usually several weeks in advance (see the earlier Kyoto Imperial Palace section for details).

Kyoto's Contemporary Architecture

a beautiful little plaza facing onto the narrow canal beside it (one of the few outdoor public spaces in the city centre). The neighbouring cherry trees are brilliant in April. A one-minute walk south on Kiyamachi-dōri is Takamatsu's **Cella building (Map 9)**, a black stone cylindrical tower of karaoke rooms.

Across the river is Gion, Kyoto's traditional entertainment district; home to unsurpassed clashes between old and new and the city's most extreme architectural indulgences. Unfortunately, little of it is very good; just a mishmash of mediocre buildings trying to out-weird one another. The highlights are a couple of Takamatsu's, and several buildings by another local architect, Wakabayashi Hiroyuki. One is memorably named **Gion Freak (Map 10)**.

Gion is certainly fun to wander around, especially by night (see the boxed text 'Night Walk through the Floating World') – buildings are at their best when covered in luminous neon. During the day, make sure you visit the **Shinbashi District (Map 9)**, with two of Kyoto's best preserved historic streets. While there, step into the **Nexus building**, where you'll discover that a tiny traditional exterior conceals a large, three-storey bar and restaurant.

If you're heading down to Uji (see the Uji section, later in this chapter), you can broaden your contemporary architectural tour at a couple of stops along the way. Right next to Momoyama-Minamiguchi station, on the Keihan Uji line, is Takamatsu Shin's infamous **Ark dental clinic (Map 2)**. All chimneys and portholes, it resembles a train. Further along the line, near Mimurodo station, you'll find architect Umebayashi Katsu's **Organ building**. It's an office that seems to be growing like an enormous aluminium plant!

Finally, love it or hate it, you can't avoid Hara Hiroshi's **Kyoto station building (Map 10)**. The outcome of an international architectural design competition several years ago, the station is hyper-modern, a big chunk of city compressed into a single building. It's fantastically out of scale in Kyoto, although it does handle admirably the huge volume of people flowing in and out.

See the Books section in the Facts for the Visitor chapter for information on a couple of books detailing Kyoto's contemporary architecture.

From Kyoto station or Keihan Sanjō station, take bus No 5 and get off at the Shūgaku-in Rikyū-michi stop. The trip takes about an hour. From the bus stop (or from Manshu-in) it's a 15-minute walk to the villa. You can also take the Eizan Dentetsu Eizan line from Demachiyanagi station to the Shūgaku-in stop and walk east for about 25 minutes toward the mountains.

Hiei-zan & Enryaku-ji (Map 1)

A visit to 848m-high Hiei-zan and the vast Enryaku-ji complex (☎ 077-578 0001; ¥550; 8.30am-4.30pm, earlier in winter) is a good way to spend half a day hiking, poking around temples and enjoying the atmosphere of a key site in Japanese history.

Enryaku-ji was founded in 788 by Saichō, also known as Dengyō-daishi, the priest who established the Tenzai school.

This school did not receive imperial recognition until 1823, after Saichō's death. But from the 8th century the temple grew in power; at its height it possessed some 3000 buildings and an army of thousands of sōhei, or warrior monks. In 1571, Oda Nobunaga saw the temple's power as a threat to his aims to unify the nation and he destroyed most of the buildings, along with the monks inside. Today only three pagodas and 120 minor temples remain.

The complex is divided into three sections – Tōtō, Saitō and Yokawa. The **Tōtō** (Eastern Pagoda section) contains the Kompon Chū-dō (primary central hall), which is the most important building in the complex. The flames on the three Dharma (wheel of the law, in Sanskrit) lamps in front of the altar have been kept lit for over 1200 years. The Daikō-dō (great lecture hall) displays life-size wooden statues of the founders of various Buddhist schools. This part of the temple is heavily geared to group access, with large expanses of asphalt for parking.

The **Saitō** (western pagoda section) contains the Shaka-dō, which dates from 1595 and houses a rare Buddha sculpture of the Shaka Nyorai (Historical Buddha). The Saitō, with its stone paths winding through forests of tall trees, temples shrouded in mist and the sound of distant gongs, is the most atmospheric part of the temple. Hold onto your ticket from the Tōtō section, as you may need to show it here.

The **Yokawa** is of minimal interest and a 4km bus ride away from the Saitō area. The Chū-dō (central hall) here was originally built in 848. It was destroyed by fire several times and has undergone repeated reconstruction (the most recent in 1971). If you plan to visit this area as well as Tōtō and Saitō, allow a full day for in-depth exploration.

Getting There & Away You can reach Hiei-zan and Enryaku-ji by either train or bus. The most interesting way is the train/cable-car/ropeway route described below. If you're in a hurry or would like to save money, the best way is a direct bus from Sanjō Keihan or Kyoto stations.

By train, take the Keihan line north to the last stop, Demachiyanagi, and change to the Yase-yūen/Hiei-bound Eizan Dentetsu Eizan-line train (be careful not to board the Kurama-bound train which sometimes leaves from the same platform). At the last stop, Yase-yūen (¥260), board the cable car (¥530, nine minutes) and then the ropeway (¥310, three minutes) to the peak, from which you can walk down to the temples.

By bus, take Kyoto bus (not Kyoto city bus) No 17 or 18, which run from Kyoto station to the Yase-yūen stop (¥390, about 50 minutes). From there it's a short walk to the cable car station.

Alternately, if you want to save money (by avoiding the cable car and ropeway), there are direct Kyoto buses from Kyoto and Keihan Sanjō stations to Enryaku-ji, which take about 70 and 50 minutes respectively (both cost ¥800).

Takara-ga-ike-kōen (Map 4)

This expansive park is an excellent place for a stroll or picnic in natural surroundings. Far from the throngs in the city centre, it is a popular place for birdwatching and has spacious gardens. It runs a 1.8km loop around the main pond, where rowing boats can be hired for ¥1000 per hour.

In the north-east of the park, the **Kyoto International Conference Hall (Map 2)** is an unfortunate attempt at replicating Japan's traditional thatched roof *gasshō zukuri* style in concrete. Behind the conference hall, the **Hosho-an Teahouse** (designed by Soshitsu Sen, Grand Tea Master XV of the Urasenke school) is worth a look.

The park is best reached by taking the Tōzai line to the last stop, Kokusai-kaikan.

Entsū-ji (Map 2)

Emperor Reigen built this remote temple (☎ 781 1875; ¥500; open 10am-4pm) in 1678 on the ruins of Emperor Go-Mizunō's villa. The picturesque garden, with some 40 carefully arranged rocks, is bordered by a manicured hedge of sananqua trees; there are fantastic views of Hiei-zan from here. In an effort to keep the place quiet, no photography, children or tour guides are permitted.

Take Kyoto bus No 45 from Kyoto station (¥340, 40 minutes), get off at the Entsūji-michi stop and walk 10 minutes west.

Kamigamo-jinja (Map 3)

Kamigamo-jinja (☎ 781 0011; free; open 8am-4pm) is one of Japan's oldest shrines and predates the founding of Kyoto. Established in 679, it is dedicated to Raijin, the god of thunder, and is one of Kyoto's 17 Unesco World Heritage sites. The present buildings (over 40 in all), including the impressive Haiden hall, are exact reproductions of the originals, dating from the 17th to 19th century. The shrine is entered from a long approach through two torii. The two large conical white-sand mounds in front of Hosodono hall are said to represent mountains sculpted for gods to descend upon.

From Kyoto station take bus No 9 and get off at the Kamigamo/Miso-no-bashi stop (40 minutes).

Kamigamo-Yamabata-sen (Map 3)

This street, which runs along a canal from Kamigamo-jinja to **Ōta-jinja**, is one of Kyoto's most picturesque. It's lined with traditional Japanese homes, each of which has its own private bridge over the canal. You can do this walk after visiting Kamigamo-jinja, finishing with lunch at the charming Azekura restaurant (see the Places to Eat chapter for details).

Kyoto Botanical Gardens (Map 3)

This vast garden (☎ 701 0141; ¥200, greenhouse ¥200 extra; open 9am-4pm), opened in 1914, occupies 240,000 sq metres and features 12,000 plants, flowers and trees. It is pleasant to stroll through the rose, cherry and herb gardens or see the rows of camphor trees and the large tropical greenhouse. The gardens are just west of the Karasuma-line Kitayama station.

Shimogamo-jinja (Map 3)

Shimogamo-jinja (☎ 781 0010; free; open dawn to dusk) dates from the 8th century and is a Unesco World Heritage site. It is nestled in the fork of the Kamo-gawa and Takanogawa rivers, and is approached along a shady path through the lovely Tadasu-no-mori. This wooded area is said to be a place where lies cannot be concealed and is considered a prime location to sort out disputes.

The shrine is dedicated to the god of harvest. Traditionally, pure water was drawn from the nearby rivers for purification and agricultural ceremonies. The hondō dates from 1863 and, like the Haiden hall at its sister shrine, Kamigamo-jinja, is an excellent example of *nagare*-style shrine architecture.

There is a ¥500 charge to enter the Ōidono, the shrine's national treasure house.

Take bus No 205 from Kyoto station and get off at the Shimogamo-jinja-mae stop.

ŌHARA & KURAMA/KIBUNE
大原、鞍馬・貴船

In the far north of Kyoto, the twin valleys of Kurama and Kibune, and nearby Ōhara make pleasant day trips, providing a feeling of being deep in the country without the necessity of long travel.

A trip to Ōhara could be combined with an excursion to Hiei-zan and Enryaku-ji, or Shūgaku-in Rikyū (see the earlier Northern & North-Eastern Kyoto section for these).

Ōhara (Map 13)

Since ancient times Ōhara, a quiet farming town about 10km north of Kyoto, has been regarded as a holy site by followers of the Jōdo school. The region provides a charming glimpse of rural Japan, along with the picturesque Sanzen-in, Jakkō-in and several other fine temples. It's most popular in autumn, when the maple leaves change colour and the mountain views are spectacular. During the peak foliage season (late October to mid-November) avoid this area on weekends as it will be packed. (For details on hands-on papermaking or wool dyeing in Ōhara, see the Activities section later in this chapter.)

From Kyoto station, Kyoto bus Nos 17 and 18 run to Ōhara. The ride takes about an hour and costs ¥580. From Keihan Sanjō station, take Kyoto bus No 16 or 17 (¥470, 45 minutes). Be careful to board a tan-coloured Kyoto bus, not a green Kyoto city bus of the same number. Allow at least half a day for a visit, possibly combined with an excursion to Hiei-zan and Enryaku-ji (see the earlier Northern & North-Eastern Kyoto section).

Sanzen-in Founded in 784 by the priest Saichō, Sanzen-in (☎ 744 2531; ¥600; open 8.30am-4.30pm Mar-Nov, until 4pm other times) belongs to the Tendai school. Saichō, considered one of the great patriarchs of Buddhism in Japan, also founded Enryaku-ji.

The temple's garden, **Yūsei-en**, is one of the most often-photographed sights in Japan, and rightly so. Take some time to sit on the steps of the Shin-den hall and admire the garden's beauty. Then head off to Ōjō-gokuraku-in hall (temple of rebirth in paradise) to see the impressive Amitabha trinity, a large Amida image flanked by attendants Kannon and Seishi (god of wisdom). After this, walk up to the hydrangea garden at the back of the temple where, in late spring and summer, you can walk among hectares of blooming hydrangea.

To get to Sanzen-in, follow the signs west from Ōhara's main bus stop up the hill past a long arcade of souvenir stalls. The entrance is on your left as you crest the hill. On the way up, pop into **Shibakyū**, a venerable *tsukemono* (Japanese pickle) store. It's located inside an atmospheric old Japanese country house and free samples are available.

A short walk uphill from Sanzen-in, **Raigō-in** *(☎ 744 2161; ¥300; 9am-5pm)* is the place where Shōmyō Buddhist chanting originated (these hypnotic chants are said to have had a profound influence on traditional Japanese folk music, or *minyō*). Each Sunday from 1pm you can come and see the monks chanting here.

If you feel like a short hike after leaving the temple, continue up the hill to see the rather oddly named **Soundless Waterfall** (Oto-nashi-no-taki). Though in fact it sounds like any other waterfall, its resonance is believed to have inspired Shōmyō Buddhist chanting.

Jikkō-in Only about 50m north of Sanzen-in, this small temple *(¥500; open 9am-4.30pm)* is often praised for its lovely garden and *fudan-zakura* cherry tree, which blossoms between October and March.

Shōrin-in This temple *(☎ 744 2537; ¥200; open 9am-5pm)* is worth a look, if only through its admission gate, to admire the thatched roof of the main hall.

Hōsen-in This temple *(¥500; open 9am-5pm)* is just down the path west of Shōrin-in's entry gate. The main tatami room offers a view of a bamboo garden and the surrounding mountains, framed like a painting by the beams and posts of the building. There is also a fantastic 700-year-old pine tree in the garden. The blood-stained Chi Tenjō ceiling boards came from Fushimi-jō castle.

Jakkō-in The history of Jakkō-in *(☎ 744 3341; ¥500; open 9am-5pm)* is exceedingly tragic. The actual founding date of the temple is subject to some debate (somewhere between the 6th and 11th centuries), but it acquired fame as the temple which harboured Kenrei Mon-in, a lady of the Taira clan. In 1185, the Taira were soundly defeated in a sea battle with the Minamoto clan at Dan-no-ura. With the entire Taira clan slaughtered or drowned, Kenrei Mon-in threw herself into the waves with her son Antoku, the infant emperor; she was fished out – the only member of the clan to survive.

She was returned to Kyoto, where she became a nun living in a bare hut until it collapsed during an earthquake. Kenrei Mon-in was accepted into Jakkō-in and stayed there, immersed in prayer and sorrowful memories, until her death 27 years later. Her tomb is located high on the hill behind the temple.

Unfortunately the main building of the temple burned down in 1999. It's estimated that reconstruction won't be finished until at least 2004. For this reason it's best to climb up to the entrance gate and look from there.

Jakkō-in lies to the west of Ōhara. Walk out of the bus station up the road to the traffic lights, then follow the small road to the left. Since it's easy to get lost on the way, we recommend familiarising yourself with the kanji for Jakkō-in (see the key item on Map 13) and following the Japanese signs.

Kurama & Kibune (Map 12)

Only 30 minutes north of Kyoto on the Eizan Dentetsu line, Kurama and Kibune are a pair of tranquil valleys long favoured by Kyotoites as places to escape the crowds and stresses of the city below. Kurama's main attractions are its mountain temple and *onsen* (mineral hot spring). Kibune, over the ridge, is a cluster of *ryokan* (traditional inns) overlooking a mountain river. Kibune is best enjoyed in summer, when the ryokan serve dinner on platforms built over the rushing waters of Kibune-gawa, providing welcome relief from the summer heat.

The two valleys lend themselves to being explored together. In winter, you can start from Kibune, walk 30 minutes over the ridge, visit Kurama-dera, then soak in the onsen before heading back to Kyoto. In summer, the reverse route is best: start from

Kurama, walk up to the temple, then down the other side to Kibune to enjoy a meal suspended above the cool river. If you happen to be in Kyoto on the night of 22 October, be sure not to miss the Kurama-no-himatsuri fire festival. It's one of the most exciting festivals in the Kyoto area.

To get to Kurama and Kibune, take the Eizan Dentetsu's Eizan line from Kyoto's Demachiyanagi station. For Kibune, get off at the second-to-last stop, Kibune Guchi, take a right out of the station and walk about 20 minutes up the hill. For Kurama, go to the last stop, Kurama, and walk straight out of the station. Both destinations are ¥410 and take about 30 minutes to reach.

Kurama-dera In 770 the monk Gantei left Nara's Toshōdai-ji in search of a wilderness sanctuary in which to meditate. Wandering in the hills north of Kyoto, he came across a white horse which led him to the valley known today as Kurama. After seeing a vision of the deity Bishamon-ten, guardian of the northern quarter of the Buddhist heaven, he established Kurama-dera (☎ 741 2003; ¥200; open 9am-4.30pm) just below the peak of Kurama-yama. Originally belonging to the Tendai school of Buddhism, since 1949 Kurama has been independent, describing its own brand of Buddhism as Kurama-kyō.

The entrance to the temple is just up the hill from Kurama station. A tram goes to the top for ¥100, or you can hike up in about 30 minutes (follow the main path past the tram station). The trail is worth taking if it's not too hot, as it winds through a forest of towering old-growth cryptomeria trees, passing Yuki-jinja on the way. Near the peak, there is a courtyard dominated by the *honden* (main hall). Behind the honden a trail leads off to the mountain's peak.

At the top, you can take a brief detour across the ridge to Ōsugi-gongen, a quiet shrine in a grove of trees. Those who want to continue to Kibune can take the trail down the other side. It's a 1.2km, 30-minute hike from the honden to the valley floor of Kibune. On the way down are two mountain shrines, Sōjō-ga-dani Fudō-dō and Okuno-in Maō-den, which make pleasant rest stops.

Kurama Onsen This hot spring resort (☎ 741 2131; open 10am-9pm), one of the few onsen within easy reach of Kyoto, is a great place to relax after a hike. The outdoor bath, with its fine view of Kurama-yama, costs ¥1100. For ¥2300, you get use of the indoor bath as well, but even with a sauna and locker thrown in, it's difficult to imagine why you would opt for the indoor bath. For both baths, buy a ticket from the machine outside the door of the main building (instructions are in Japanese and English).

To get to Kurama Onsen, walk straight out of Kurama station and continue up the main street passing the entrance to Kurama-dera on your left. The onsen is about 10 minutes' walk on the right. There's also a free shuttle bus between the station and the onsen, which meets incoming trains.

Kibune Kibune's main attractions are its river dining platforms, which are open from 1 June to the end of September. In addition to these, all the ryokan in the valley are open year-round and are a romantic escape for travellers willing to pay mid-range to top-end ryokan prices (see the Places to Stay chapter).

Halfway up the valley, **Kibune-jinja** is worth a quick look, particularly if you can ignore the unfortunate plastic horse statue at its entrance. The shrine predates the 8th century founding of Kyoto. It was established to worship the god of water and has been long revered by farmers and sake brewers.

From Kibune you can hike over the mountain to Kurama-dera (see the Kurama section previously); the trail starts halfway up the valley on the east side.

NORTH-WESTERN KYOTO
京都市北西部

The north-western part of Kyoto is predominantly residential, but there are a number of superb temples with tranquil gardens. For Zen fans, visits to Daitoku-ji and Ryōan-ji are a must. The 'Golden Temple' at Kinkaku-ji is one of Japan's most famous sites. The TIC's *Walking Tour Courses in Kyoto* leaflet includes a walk in the area of these temples, but most of the walk is along unremarkable city streets. Closer to the city centre, the Nishijin area still retains a feeling of old Kyoto and is a home to two traditional weaving museums.

Shōkoku-ji (Map 3)

Shōkoku-ji (☎ 231 0301; free; 10am-4pm) the headquarters of the Rinzai Shōkoku-ji school, sits in an ancient pine grove north of Dōshisha University. It was established in 1392 by the third Ashikaga shōgun, Yoshimitsu. The original buildings were almost totally destroyed during the civil wars in the 15th century. Inside the vast compound, the **Jōtenkaku Museum** (☎ 231 0301; ¥600; open 10am-4.30pm) houses treasures from Kinkaku-ji and Ginkaku-ji.

The temple is a five-minute walk northeast of the Karasuma line's Imadegawa - station.

Urasenke Foundation (Map 3)

Anyone interested in tea ceremony should make their first stop at the Urasenke Chadō Research Center (☎ 431 6474). Urasenke is also Japan's largest tea school, and hosts hundreds of students annually who come from branch schools worldwide to further their studies in 'the way of tea'.

The **gallery** (¥800; open 9.30am-4.30pm, closed Mon) on the 1st and 2nd floors holds quarterly exhibitions on tea-related arts; call to see if there is a show being held during your stay. The entrance fee entitles you to a bowl of matcha and a sweet.

The **Konnichi-an library** (☎ 431 6474; free; 10am-4pm, until 3pm Sat; closed Sun & public holidays) here has more than 50,000 books (about 100 in English), plus videos on tea, which can be viewed.

For more information contact Urasenke's **Office of International Affairs** (Kokusai Kyoku; ☎ 431 3111).

Take bus No 9 to the Horikawa-tera-no-uchi stop and walk east for a minute.

Nishijin Textile Center (Map 5)

In the heart of the Nishijin textile district, this centre (☎ 451 9231; free, ¥600 charge for certain kimono displays; open 9am-5pm) is a good place to observe the weaving

of fabrics used in kimono and their ornamental belts (obi). There are also displays of completed fabrics and kimono. It's on the south-west corner of the Horikawa-dōri and Imadegawa-dōri intersection.

Take bus No 9 from Kyoto station to the Horikawa-Imadegawa stop; otherwise walk for 10 minutes west of the Karasuma line's Imadegawa station.

Orinasu-kan (Map 3)

This museum (☎ 431 0020; ¥500; open 10am-4pm, closed Mon) is housed in a Nishijin weaving factory. It has impressive exhibits of Nishijin textiles. The **Susameisha** building (recently restored) next door is also open to the public and worth a look. With advance reservations, traditional weaving workshops can be attended (see the Activities section later in this chapter).

Kitano Tenman-gū (Map 3)

Commonly known as Kitano Tenjin, this shrine (☎ 461 0005; free; open 5.30am-dusk) was established in 947 to honour Sugawara Michizane (845–903), a noted Heian-era statesman and scholar.

It is said that having been defied by his political adversary Fujiwara Tokihira, Sugawara was exiled to Kyūshū for the rest of his life. Following his death in 903, earthquakes and storms struck Kyoto, and the Imperial Palace was repeatedly struck by lightening. Fearing that Sugawara, reincarnated as Raijin, had returned from beyond to avenge his rivals, locals erected and dedicated this shrine to him.

The present buildings were built in 1607 by Toyotomi Hideyori, and the grounds contain an extensive grove of plum and apricot trees (baika), said to have been Sugawara's favourite fruits.

Unless you are trying to avoid crowds, the best time to visit is during the Tenjin-san market fair, held here on the 25th of each month. Those held in December and January are particularly colourful.

From Kyoto station, take bus No 50 or 101 and get off at the Kitano-Tenmangū-mae stop. From Keihan Sanjō station, take bus No 10 to the same stop.

Daitoku-ji (Map 3)

The precincts of this temple, headquarters of the Rinzai Daitoku-ji school, contain an extensive complex of 24 subtemples, three of which are mentioned below, but eight are open to the public. If you want an intensive look at Zen culture, this is the place to visit.

The eponymous Daitoku-ji is on the eastern side of the grounds. It was founded in 1319, burnt down in the next century and rebuilt in the 16th century. The San-mon gate (1589) contains a self-carved statue of its erector, the famous tea master Sen no Rikyū, on the 2nd storey.

Some sources say that Toyotomi Hideyoshi was so angry when he discovered he'd been demeaning himself by walking under Rikyū's effigy that he forced the master to commit *seppuku* (ritual suicide) in 1591.

The temple bus stop is Daitokuji-mae. Convenient buses from Kyoto station are No 205 and 206. It's also not a far walk west of Kitaōji station on the Karasuma line.

Daisen-in The Zen garden masterpiece in this subtemple (☎ 491 8346; ¥400; open 9am-5pm) is an elegant example of 17th-century karesansui style, and ranks with the revered rock garden at Ryōan-ji. Here the trees, rocks and sand are said to represent and express various spectacles of nature, from waterfalls and valleys to mountain lakes.

Kōtō-in This subtemple (☎ 492 0068; ¥400; open 9am-4.30pm) in the western part of the grounds swarms with slightly fewer visitors than Daisen-in. Surrounded by lovely maples and bamboo, the moss garden viewed from the temple veranda is superb.

Zuihō-in Zuihō-in (☎ 491 1454; ¥400; open 8am-5pm) enshrines the 16th-century Christian daimyō, Ōtomo Sōrin. In the early 1960s, a landscape architect named Shigemori Misuzu rearranged the stones in its rock garden into the shape of a crucifix!

Kinkaku-ji (Map 3)

Kinkaku-ji (☎ 461 0013; ¥400; open 9am-5pm), the famed 'Golden Temple', is one of Japan's best-known sights. Also known as Rokuon-ji, it belongs to the Shōkokuji school. The original building was constructed in 1397 as a retirement villa for shōgun Ashikaga Yoshimitsu. His son, complying with father's wishes, converted it into a temple.

The three-storey pavilion is covered in bright gold leaf and features a bronze phoenix on top of the roof. The mirror-like reflection of the temple in the Kyō-ko pond is extremely photogenic, especially when the maples are ablaze in autumn. In 1950, a young monk consummated his obsession with the temple by burning it to the ground. The monk's story is fictionalised in Mishima Yukio's *The Golden Pavilion*.

In 1955, a full reconstruction was completed which exactly followed the original design, but the gold-foil covering was extended to the lower floors. The temple may not be to everyone's taste (the tremendous crowds just about obscure the view anyway), but it is still an impressive feat.

Take bus No 205 or 101 and get off at the Kinkakuji-michi stop; bus No 59 from Keihan Sanjō station also stops close to the temple.

Ryōan-ji (Map 1)

This temple (☎ 463 2216; ¥400; open 8am-5pm, 8.30am-4.30pm Dec-Feb) belongs to the Rinzai school and was founded in 1450.

The main attraction is the garden arranged in the karesansui style. An oblong of sand with an austere collection of 15 carefully placed rocks, apparently adrift in a sea of sand, is enclosed by an earthen wall. The designer, who remains unknown, provided no explanation.

Although many historians believe it was arranged during the Muromachi period (1333–1576) by Sōami, some contend that it is a much later product of the Edo period. It is Japan's most famous *hira-niwa* (a flat garden void of hills or ponds), and reveals the stunning simplicity and harmony of the principles of Zen meditation.

The viewing platform for the garden can become packed solid, but the other parts of the temple grounds are also interesting and less of a target for the crowds. Among these, Kyoyo-chi pond is perhaps the most beautiful, particularly in autumn.

Come as early in the day as possible. From Keihan Sanjō station take bus No 59 and get off at the Ryōanji-mae stop. You can also walk from Kinkaku-ji for about 15 minutes.

Ninna-ji (Map 2)

Ninna-ji (☎ 461 1155; free; open 9am-4.30pm) was built in 888 and is the head temple of the Omuro branch of the Shingon school. Originally there were more than 60 structures; the present temple buildings, including a five-storey pagoda, date from the 17th century. On the extensive grounds you'll find a peculiar grove of short-trunked, multi-petal cherry trees called Omuro-no-Sakura, which draw large crowds in April.

Separate entrance fees (¥500) are charged for the kondō and reihōkan (treasure house), which is only open for the first two weeks of October.

To get there, take bus No 59 from Keihan Sanjō station and get off at the Omuro Ninnaji stop, which is opposite the entrance gate. From Kyoto station take bus No 26 to the same stop.

Myōshin-ji (Map 2)

Myōshin-ji (☎ 461 5226; ¥400; open 9.10am-3.40pm, closed one hour at lunch), a vast complex dating to 1342, belongs to the Rinzai school. There are 47 subtemples, but only a few are open to the public.

From the north gate, follow the broad stone avenue flanked by rows of temples to the southern part of the complex. The ceiling of the hattō (lecture hall) features Tanyū Kanō's unnerving painting Unryūzu (dragon glaring in eight directions).

The north gate of Myōshin-ji is an easy 10-minute walk south of Ninna-ji, or you can take bus No 26 from Kyoto station or No 10 from Keihan Sanjō station to the Myōshinji-kita-mon-mae stop.

Taizō-in This subtemple (☎ 463 2855; ¥400; open 9am-5pm) is in the south-western corner of the grounds of Myōshin-ji. The karesansui garden depicting a waterfall and islands is well worth a visit.

Takagamine Area
京都市北西部 (Map 3)

In the far north-west area of Takagamine there are several interesting, less-visited temples worth exploring.

Kōetsu-ji This temple (☎ 491 1399; ¥300; open 8am-5pm) dates from 1651 and was once the hermitage of Honami Kōetsu, a celebrated Edo-period artisan. After his death the villa was reconstructed as a temple and dedicated to him. The grounds contain seven tea ceremony houses and a notable fence called Kōtsu-gaki, made with slats of interwoven bamboo.

From Kyoto station, take bus No 6 to the Takagamine-genkō-an-mae bus stop (40 minutes) and walk three minutes west.

A short walk north-east of Kōetsu-ji, two other small temples worth a visit are **Genkō-an** (☎ 492 1858; ¥300; open 8am-5pm) and **Joshō-ji** (☎ 492 6775; ¥300; open 8.30am-5pm).

Shōden-ji This temple (☎ 491 3259; ¥300; open 9am-5pm) is approached up a long flight of stone steps through a thick grove of trees. It was founded south of its current location in 1268, but shortly after was destroyed in a fire and was rebuilt in 1282 on the present site. Of interest here are the wooden ceiling boards of the Chi Tenjō (blood ceiling), once flooring a corridor of Fushimi-jō, where 1200 people committed ritual suicide following the surrender of the castle in 1600.

Take bus No 9 from Kyoto station and get off at the Jinkō-in-mae stop, then walk 15 minutes north-east. Near the bus stop, **Jinkō-in** (free entry) is of limited interest, but on the 21st of each month exhibits a rare self-carved statue of 9th century priest Kūkai.

WESTERN KYOTO
京都市西部

Kyoto's western region, raku-sai, is famed for its beautiful natural scenery and tranquility, and holds a place in Kyoto history. Arashiyama (literally, stormy mountains) flourished in the 8th century as a romantic playground for Heian-era emperors, warlords and aristocrats, who built lavish villas and Buddhist temples. Nearby Sagano was the *monzen machi* (town in front of a temple/shrine gate) of Atago-jinja, and the lovely walk between Arashiyama and Sagano's Atago Torii district is one of Kyoto's best (see the 'Arashiyama-Sagano Walking Tour' boxed text in this section).

In Uzumasa stands Kyoto's oldest temple, Kōryū-ji, and the tacky Tōei Uzumasa Movie Village, a theme park that celebrates Japan's movie industry.

Tōei Uzumasa Movie Village (Map 2)

In the Uzumasa area, Tōei Uzumasa Eiga Mura (☎ 864 7716; adults/six to 18s/under six ¥2200/1100/900; open 9am-4.30pm 1 Mar-30 Nov, 9.30am-3.30pm 1 Dec-Feb) is one of Kyoto's most notorious tourist traps. However, it does have some recreations of Edo-period street scenes that give a decent idea of what Kyoto must have looked like before the advent of concrete.

The main conceit of the park is that real movies are actually filmed here. While this may occasionally be the case, more often than not this entails a bunch of bored flunkies being ordered around by an ersatz movie 'director' complete with megaphone and a vintage 1930's-era movie camera. This seems to delight some tourists but left us a little less than convinced.

Aside from this, there are displays relating to various aspects of Japanese movies and regular performances involving Japanese television and movie characters like the Power Rangers. This should entertain the kids – adults will probably be a little bored.

Eiga Mura is a short walk from Uzumasa station on the JR San-in Main (Sagano) line or the Keifuku Arashiyama line.

Kōryū-ji (Map 2)

Kōryū-ji (☎ 861 1461; ¥600; open 9am-5pm, until 4.30pm Dec-Feb), one of the oldest temples in Japan, was founded in 622 to honour Prince Shōtoku, who was an enthusiastic promoter of Buddhism.

The hattō to the right of the main gate houses a magnificent trio of 9th-century statues: Buddha, flanked by manifestations of Kannon. The reihōkan contains numerous fine Buddhist statues, including the Naki Miroku (crying Miroku) and the renowned Miroku Bosatsu, which is extraordinarily expressive. A national upset occurred in 1960 when an enraptured university student embraced the statue in a fit of passion and inadvertently snapped off its little finger.

Take bus No 11 from Keihan Sanjō station, get off at the Ukyō-ku Sogō-chōsha-mae stop and walk north. The temple is also close to Uzumasa station on the Keifuku Arashiyama line.

Arashiyama-Sagano District
嵐山、嵯峨野地域 **(Map 11)**

Tucked into the western hills of Kyoto, Arashiyama and Sagano are both worth visiting if you feel like strolling in pleasant natural surroundings and visiting temples tucked inside bamboo groves. The area makes a nice full-day excursion from central Kyoto. There are bicycle rental shops (¥600 for three hours, ¥1000 for the day) near the stations, but it's more enjoyable to cover the relatively short distances between sights on foot.

Note that this area is wildly popular with Japanese tourists and can be packed, particularly in the cherry blossom and maple leaf seasons. To avoid the crowds, go early on a weekday or head to some of the more offbeat spots. Upon arrival here, you may wonder why the Japanese make such a fuss about this place; it's not very beautiful around the stations, particularly with all the tacky shops and vending machines nearby. The best advice is to head north immediately to the quieter regions of Sagano (see the 'Arashiyama/Sagano Walking Tour' boxed text in this section for details).

Bus No 28 links Kyoto station with Arashiyama (¥240, 40 minutes). Bus No 11 connects Keihan Sanjō station with Arashiyama (¥240, 45 minutes). The best rail connection is the ride from Shijō-Ōmiya station on the Keifuku-Arashiyama line to Arashiyama station (¥230, 20 minutes).

You can also take the JR San-in Main (Sagano) line from Kyoto station (¥230, 20 minutes) or Nijō station (¥190, 12 minutes)

THINGS TO SEE & DO

Arashiyama-Sagano Walking Tour (Map 11)

Time: half day
Distance: about 3km
Major Sights: Temples, shrines, gardens, bamboo forests

There is a detailed map for the walk described here in the TIC's *Walking Tour Courses in Kyoto* leaflet. It begins at **Tenryū-ji**, which is famous for its Zen garden (if you'd like to skip the temple, and save on the entry fee, you can bypass it by walking 200m north of the temple on the main road and taking a left). After checking out the temple, exit via the north gate, take a right and walk down the hill for a few metres to see humble **Nonomiya-jinja**. From the shrine, continue back up the hill, passing through a wonderful grove of bamboo. At the top of the hill, you will see the entrance to **Ōkōchi-sansō villa**, a wonderful stop provided it's not swarming with crowds.

Continuing from Ōkōchi-sansō, you'll cross two sets of train tracks and descend past Okura-ike pond. On the left you'll soon see a set of stone steps that lead up to the pleasant grounds of **Jōjakkō-ji**. A few minutes further brings you to **Rakushisha**, a charming poet's hut. Continuing north-west from here you'll reach **Nison-in**, in an attractive setting on the wooded hillside.

Return to the main road from Nison-in and follow it gradually north-west for a few minutes. This will bring you to the narrow alley that leads up to **Giō-ji** and **Takiguchi-dera**, two wonderfully atmospheric little hillside temples. Returning to the main road, follow it up to **Adashino Nembutsu-ji**. It's worth entering this temple to admire its stone Buddhas. From here it is a short climb past a few of Sagano's remaining thatched-roof houses to the huge orange **Atago Torii**

From here, tired legs can catch a Kyoto bus (No 72) from the Atago Torii bus stop back to Arashiyama (it continues to Kyoto station). If you're still in the mood for temples, head back down the slope and take your first left toward **Seiryō-ji** and **Daikaku-ji**; from here take Kyoto bus No 71 or 81, or city bus No 28, back to Kyoto station from the Daikakuji bus stop.

---

and get off at JR Saga Arashiyama station (be careful to take the local train, as the express does not stop in Arashiyama). Arashiyama is the disembarking point for the Hozu-gawa River ride (see the following section), hands-down the most interesting (and expensive) way to reach the area.

Togetsu-kyō This bridge is the dominant landmark in Arashiyama and just a few minutes on foot from either the Keifuku-line or Hankyū-line Arashiyama stations. The original crossing, constructed in 1606, was about 100m upriver from the present bridge.

On 13 April *jūsan-mairi*, an important rite of passage for local children aged 13, takes place here. Boys and girls (many in kimono), after paying respects at Hōrin-ji and receiving a blessing for wisdom, cross the bridge under strict parental order not to look back toward

the temple until they've reached the northern side of the bridge. Not heeding this instruction is believed to bring bad luck for life!

From July to mid-September, this is a good spot to watch *ukai* (cormorant fishing) in the evening. If you want to get close to the action, you can pay ¥1700 to join a passenger boat. The TIC can provide a leaflet and further details.

Hōrin-ji This temple (*☎ 862 0013; free; open dawn to dusk*) was originally founded in 713 by the priest Gyōki. There are 80 steps up the hondō, where in 829 Dōshō, a disciple of maverick monk Kūkai, installed a large Jizō statue and named the temple Hōrin-ji. Hōrin-ji is renowned for the *jūsan-mairi* ceremony (see the Togetsu-kyō section later in this chapter). The temple is close to the southern end of Togetsu-kyō.

Cormorant Fishing

Ukai (cormorant fishing) is mentioned in Japanese historical documents as early as the 8th century. It is still practised in Gifu and Kyoto prefectures, although it's largely a tourist attraction these days. The cormorants and the crew splash about while the passengers have a fun time drinking and eating.

The season lasts from May to September. The best times for fishing are moonless nights when the fish are more easily attracted to the glare of a fire in a metal basket suspended from the bow of the boat. Fishing trips are cancelled during and after heavy rain.

The cormorants, up to a dozen, sit on the boat attached to long leashes. In the water, a small metal ring at the base of their necks stops them from guzzling down their catch. After filling their gullets with fish, they are hauled on board and forced to disgorge the contents. Each boat usually has a crew of four to handle the birds, the boat and the fire.

The cormorant catch is usually *ayu*, a type of trout much prized by the Japanese. A fine cormorant can catch several dozen fish in a night. After completing their night's work, the cormorants are loaded into bamboo baskets in strictly observed order of seniority – cormorants are very conscious of social ranking and will protest if this is not respected (life expectancy for a cormorant is between 15 and 20 years, so they probably do have a point).

Iwatayama Monkey Park Home to some 200 Japanese monkeys of all sizes and ages, this nature park (☎ *861 1616; adult/child ¥500/¥150; open 9am-5pm 15 Mar-15 Nov, until 4pm winter*) is a joy. Though it is common to spot wild monkeys in the nearby mountains, here you can encounter them at a sensationally close distance and enjoy watching the playful creatures frolic about. It makes for an excellent photo opportunity, not only for the monkeys but for the panoramic view over Kyoto. Refreshingly, it is the animals who are free to roam while the humans who observe them are caged in a box!

There are a few rules to remember:

• Do not feed the monkeys (as the sign reads, 'Please don't show them any food!')
• Do not touch the monkeys (unless you fancy being bitten)
• Do not stare into their eyes (remember *Planet of the Apes*?)

You enter the park near the south side of Togetsu-kyō, through the orange torii of Ichitani-jinja. Reaching the monkeys involves a moderate hike uphill.

Daihikaku Senkō-ji A short walk up the south bank of the river, Daihikaku-Senkō-ji (☎ *861-2913; ¥400; open 9am-5pm*) is a seldom-visited and very pleasant hillside temple with a fine view over Kyoto. It was originally constructed from 1596 to 1615 and was dedicated to the hundreds of people who died working to widen the Ōi-gawa in the 17th century. *Daihi* means compassion or sympathy, and the temple name refers to 'pulling out the pain'. The temple enshrines an impressive statue of the monk Raidō – check out the lifelike eyes.

MARTIN MOOS

The Iwatayama Monkey Park in Kyoto's hills is certain to entertain children.

Kameyama-kōen Just upstream from Togetsu-kyō and behind Tenryū-ji, this park is a nice place to escape the crowds of Arashiyama. It's laced with trails, the best of which leads up to a lookout over Katsuragawa and up into the Arashiyama mountains. It's particularly nice here during cherry blossom and autumn foliage seasons.

Tenryū-ji This temple (☎ 881 1235; ¥500; open 8.30am-5.30pm Apr-Oct, until 5pm other times) is one of the major temples of the Rinzai school. It was built in 1339 on the former site of Emperor Go-Daigo's villa after a priest had dreamt of a dragon rising from the nearby river. The dream was interpreted as a sign that the emperor's spirit was uneasy, and the temple was constructed as appeasement – hence the name tenryū (heavenly dragon). The present buildings date from 1900, but the main attraction is the 14th-century Zen garden.

Tenryū-ji is a popular place to sample Zen vegetarian cuisine (shōjin ryōri) – see the Western Kyoto section in the Places to Eat chapter.

Ōkōchi-sansō Villa This is the lavish home (☎ 872 2233; ¥900 with tea & cake; open 9am-5pm) of Ōkōchi Denjirō, a famous actor in samurai films. The extensive gardens allow fine views over the city and are open to visitors. If you've got the extra cash, it's worth splashing out to enjoy this spot, particularly during the early morning before the crowds arrive.

Jōjakkō-ji This temple (☎ 861 0435; ¥300; open 9am-4.30pm) sits atop a moss-covered knoll, and is famed for its brilliant maples and thatched-roof Niō-mon gate. The hondō was constructed in the 16th century from wood brought from Fushimi-jō.

Rakushisha This building (☎ 881 1953; ¥150; open 9am-5pm) was the hut of Mukai Kyorai, the best-known disciple of illustrious haiku poet Bashō. Literally, 'house of fallen persimmons', legend holds that Kyorai dubbed the house Rakushisha after waking one morning after a storm to find the persimmons he had planned to sell from the garden's trees scattered on the ground.

Nison-in This temple is a popular spot with maple watchers. Nison-in (¥500; open 9am-4pm) was originally built in the 9th century by Emperor Saga. It houses two important Kamakura-era Buddha statues side by side (Shaka on the right and Amida on the left). The temple features lacquered nightingale floors.

Giō-ji This quiet temple (☎ 861 0687; ¥500; open 9am-4.30pm) was named for the Heian-era shirabyōshi (traditional dancer) Giō. Giō, aged 21, committed herself here as a nun after her romance with Taira-no-Kiyomori, the mighty commander of the Heike clan. She was usurped by a fellow entertainer Hotoke Gozen (who later deserted Kiyomori to join Giō at the temple). Enshrined in the main hall are five wooden statues: these are Giō, Hotoke Gozen, Kiyomori, and Giō's mother and sister (who were also nuns at the temple).

Takiguchi-dera The history of this temple (☎ 871 3929; ¥300; open 9am-5pm) reads like a Romeo and Juliet romance. Takiguchi-dera was founded by Heian-era nobleman Takiguchi Nyūdō, who entered the priesthood after being forbidden by his father to marry his peasant consort Yokobue. One day Yokobue came to the temple with her flute to serenade Takiguchi, but was again refused by him; she wrote a farewell love sonnet on a stone (in her own blood) before throwing herself into the river to perish. The stone remains at the temple.

Adashino Nembutsu-ji This rather unusual temple (☎ 861 2221; ¥500; open 9am-4.30pm) is where the abandoned bones of paupers and destitutes without kin were gathered. More than 8000 stone images are crammed into the temple grounds, dedicated to the repose of their spirits. The abandoned souls are remembered with candles each year in the Sentō Kuyō ceremony held here on the evenings of 23 and 24 August.

White paper lanterns decorated with *kanji* at a local Kyoto shop

A boatman poling a pleasure boat. In ancient days river transport into the city was common.

Night view of a serene Japanese garden with shining trails of light left by carp

A bamboo fence; bamboo is also used in the superb craft works that Kyoto is famous for.

The snow-covered Kinkaku-ji (Golden Temple) is reflected in Kyō-ko pond.

The mystical 14th-century gardens of Saihō-ji (Moss Temple) are the temple's namesake.

Seiryū-ji This temple (☎ 861 0343; ¥400; open 9am-4pm) was established in 986 on the site of Seika-kan, the lavish villa of Genji family military commander Minamoto-no-Tōru (the inspiration for the main character in the classic *Genji Monogatari* (Tale of the Genji). The Shaka-dō Hall houses a rare, 10th-century Chinese Buddha statue carved from cherry wood. This life-size sculpture can be viewed by request (and with a donation of ¥1000, which includes a private chant and drumming by a resident monk).

Daikaku-ji Just a 25-minutes walk northeast of Nison-in you will find Daikaku-ji (☎ 871 0071; ¥500; open 9am-4.30pm). It was built in the 9th century as a palace for Emperor Saga, who converted it into a temple. The present buildings date from the 16th century, but are still palatial in style, with some impressive paintings. The large Osawa-no-ike pond was once used by the emperor for boating and is a popular spot for viewing the harvest moon.

Close to the temple entrance are separate terminals for Kyoto city buses (No 28 goes to/from Kyoto station, ¥250, 45 minutes) and Kyoto buses (No 71 goes to/from Kyoto station, ¥250, 50 minutes; No 61 to/from Keihan Sanjō station, ¥250, 50 minutes).

Hozu-gawa River Trip

The Hozu-gawa river ride (☎ 0771-22 5846; per person ¥3900) is a great way to enjoy the beauty of Kyoto's western mountains without any strain on the legs. With long bamboo poles, boatmen steer flat-bottom boats down the Hozu-gawa from Kameoka, 30km west of Kyoto station, through steep forested mountain canyons, before arriving at Arashiyama. Between 10 March and 30 November, there are seven trips (from 9am to 3.30pm) daily. During winter, the number of trips is reduced to four a day and the boats are heated. There are no boat trips from 29 December to 4 January.

The ride lasts two hours and covers 16km through occasional sections of choppy water – a scenic jaunt with minimal danger. The scenery is especially breathtaking during cherry blossom season in April and maple foliage season *(momiji)* in autumn.

The boats depart from a dock eight minutes' walk from Kameoka station. Kameoka is accessible by rail from Kyoto station or Nijō station on the JR San-in main (Sagano) line. The TIC provides an English leaflet and timetable for rail connections. The fare from Kyoto to Kameoka is ¥400 one way by regular train (don't spend the extra for the express, as it makes little difference in travel time).

Takao Area 高雄付近 **(Map 1)**

This is a secluded district tucked far away in the north-western part of Kyoto. It is famed for autumn foliage and a trio of temples: Jingo-ji, Saimyō-ji and Kōzan-ji.

Jingo-ji (☎ 861 1769; ¥400; open 9am-4pm) is the best of the three temples. This mountain temple sits at the top of a long flight of stairs that stretch from the Kiyotaki-gawa to the temple's main gate. The Kondō (Gold Hall) is the most impressive of the temple's structures, located roughly in the middle of the grounds at the top of another flight of stairs.

After visiting the Kondō, head in the opposite direction along a wooded path to an open area overlooking the valley. Here you'll see people tossing small disks over the railing into the chasm below. These are *kawarakenage*, light clay disks that people throw in order to rid themselves of their bad karma. Be careful, it's addictive and at ¥100 for two it can get expensive (you can buy the disks at a nearby stall). The trick is to flick the disks very gently, convex side up, like a Frisbee. When you get it right, they sail all the way down the valley – taking all that bad karma with them (try not to think about the hikers down below).

To reach Jingo-ji, take bus No 8 from Nijō station to the last stop, Takao (¥500, 40 minutes). From Kyoto station, take an hourly JR bus to the Takao stop (¥500, 50 minutes). To get to the temple, walk down to the river and climb the steps on the other side.

If you have time after visiting Jingō-ji, you can walk north from the base of the steps (follow the river upstream) for around

Kiyotaki-gawa Hike (Map 1)

Time: About two hours
Distance: About 5km
Major Sights: Jingo-ji, Kiyotaki-gawa, Hozu-gawa

This is one of the better hikes in the Kyoto area, especially in autumn, when the maples set the hillsides ablaze with colour. Start from **Jingo-ji** (see the Takao Area section of this chapter for transport details). The trail begins at the bottom of the steps leading up to the temple and follows the Kiyotaki-gawa south (downstream).

After about one hour of riverside walking, you'll get to the small hamlet of **Kiyotaki**, with its quaint riverside inns and restaurants. Just before the town there is a trail junction that can be confusing; the trail leaves the riverside for a while and comes to a junction on a hillside. At this spot, head uphill back toward the river, not further into the woods. After passing through the town, cross over a bridge and continue downstream. The trail hugs the river, and passes some excellent, crystal-clear swimming holes – great on a hot summer day.

After another 30 minutes or so you'll come up to a road. Turn right, walk through the tunnel and continue along this road for another 30 minutes to reach Hozukyō station. The riverside below the bridge here is a popular summer picnic and swimming spot – bring a bathing suit and picnic basket and join the fun (but be warned that currents can be treacherous – parents take note). From Hozukyō station you can catch a local train back to Kyoto (¥230, 20 minutes).

cc

---

five minutes to reach **Saimyō-ji** *(free; open 9am-5pm);* walk up onto the main road and in another ten minutes you'll reach **Kōzan-ji** *(entry to grounds free, entry to main hall ¥600; 8.30am-5pm).* Lovely Saimyō-ji is the better of the two, but if you've got the energy, it's also worth exploring the grounds of Kōzan-ji (but don't waste the money to enter the main hall – it's just not worth the steep admission fee).

SOUTH-WESTERN KYOTO
京都市南西部 **(MAP 2)**
Katsura Rikyū Imperial Villa
This villa (☎ *211 1211; free),* considered one of the finest examples of Japanese architecture, was built in 1624 for the emperor's brother, Prince Toshihito. Every conceivable detail of the villa – the teahouses, the large pond with islets and the surrounding garden – has been given meticulous attention.

Tours (in Japanese) start at 10am, 11am, 2pm and 3pm, and last about 40 minutes. You should be there 20 minutes before the start time. An explanatory video is shown in the waiting room and a leaflet is provided in English. You *must* make reservations through the Imperial Household Agency (see the Kyoto Imperial Palace section earlier in this chapter for details), and often several weeks in advance. Visitors must be over 20 years of age.

To get to the villa from Kyoto station, take bus No 33 (¥230, 22 minutes) and get off at the Katsura Rikyū-mae stop, which is a five-minute walk from the villa. The easiest route from the city centre is to take a Hankyū Kyoto-line train from Hankyū Kawaramachi station to Hankyū Katsura station, which is a 15-minute walk from the villa (don't take an express train as they don't stop in Katsura).

Saihō-ji
The main attraction at this temple (☎ *391 3631, 56 Kamigaya-chō, Matsuo, Nishikyō-ku, Kyoto-shi 615-8286; ¥3000; entry as part of tour only)* is the heart-shaped garden, designed in 1339 by Musō Kokushi. The garden is famous for its luxuriant mossy growth – hence the temple's other

name, Koke-dera (moss temple). Visiting the temple is recommended only if you have time and patience to follow the reservation rules. If you don't, visit nearby Jizō-in (see next listing) to get a taste of the atmosphere of Saihō-ji without the expense or fuss.

Reservations Reservations are the only way you can visit. This is to prevent the overwhelming crowds which used to swamp the place (and consequently pulverise the moss) in the days when reservations were not required.

Send a postcard (to the address given above) at least one week before the date you require and include details of your name, number of visitors, address in Japan, occupation, age (you must be over 18) and desired date (a choice of alternative dates is preferred). Enclose a pre-stamped postcard for a reply to your Japanese address. You might find it convenient to buy an *ōfuku-hagaki* (send-and-return postcard set) at any post office.

You should arrive at the time and on the date supplied by the temple office. After paying your 'donation', you spend up to 90 minutes chanting sutras or doing Zen meditation before finally being guided around the garden for 90 minutes.

Take city bus No 28 from Kyoto station to the Matsuo-taisha-mae stop (¥240, 35 minutes) and walk 15 minutes south-west; or from Keihan Sanjō station, take Kyoto bus No 63 to Koke-dera, the last stop (¥270, 50 minutes), and walk two minutes.

Jizō-in

This delightful little temple (☎ 381 3417; ¥400; 9am-5pm) could be called the 'poor man's Saihō-ji'. It's only a few minutes' walk south of Saihō-ji in the same atmospheric bamboo groves. While the temple does not boast any spectacular buildings or treasures, it has a nice moss garden and is almost completely ignored by tourists, making it a great place to sit and contemplate.

For transport details see the earlier Saihō-ji section. From the parking lot near Saihō-ji, there is a small stone staircase that climbs to the road that leads to Jizō-in (it helps to ask someone to point the way as it's not entirely clear).

Matsuo-taisha

Founded in 701, Matsuo Taisha (☎ 871 5016; entry to grounds free, entry to garden and treasure house ¥500; grounds open dawn to dusk, garden and treasure house open 9am-4pm) is one of Kyoto's oldest shrines. It enshrines the deity of water, which sake-brewing families have worshipped since the Muromachi period (hence the large stacks of sake barrels). Pure spring water, designated 'one of the 100 best in Japan', spews from the mouth of the *kame-no-ido* (turtle well) statue here.

Take bus No 28 from Kyoto station to the Matsuo-taisha-mae stop (¥240, 35 minutes).

SOUTHERN KYOTO
京都市南部

The district to the south of Kyoto, *raku-nan*, is a rather unprepossessing industrial suburb, lacking the greenery that makes the more northerly parts of Kyoto so attractive. However, there are some attractions in the area that warrant a visit for those with time. Tōfuku-ji and Fushimi-Inari-taisha (see the 'Fushimi-Inari Hike' boxed text further on in this section) are quite close to downtown Kyoto and rate highly, as does Byōdō-in, further south in the city of Uji. To the southeast, Daigo-ji is in semi-rural surroundings and offers scope for some gentle hiking to complement the area's architectural splendours.

Tōfuku-ji (Map 8)

Founded in 1236 by the priest Enni, Tōfuku-ji (☎ 561 0087; entry to grounds free, entry to main temple ¥400, entry to other sub-temples ¥300; open 9am-4pm) belongs to the Rinzai school. Since this temple was intended to compete with Tōdai-ji and Kōfuku-ji temples in Nara, it was given a name combining characters each of these.

This impressive temple complex is considered one of the five main Zen temples in Kyoto. The huge San-mon gate is the oldest Zen main gate in Japan. Other ancient structures include the *tōsu* (lavatory) and *yokushitsu* (bathroom), dating from the 14th century. The present complex includes 24 subtemples; at one time there were 53.

The hōjō was reconstructed in 1890. The gardens, laid out in 1938, are worth a visit. As you approach the northern gardens, you cross a stream over the Tsūten-kyō (bridge to heaven), which is a pleasant, leafy spot – the foliage is renowned for its autumn colour. The northern garden has stones and moss neatly arranged in a chequerboard pattern. The nearby **Reiun-in** receives few visitors to its attractive garden.

To reach Tōfuku-ji by train, take a *local* train on the Keihan line to Tōfukuji station (it's one stop south of Shichijō station) and

walk east up the hill toward the mountains. Bus No 208 also runs from Kyoto station past Tōfuku-ji. Get off at the Tōfukuji-mae stop.

Fushimi-Inari-taisha (Map 2)

This intriguing shrine (☎ 641 7331; *free, dawn to dusk*) was dedicated to the gods of rice and sake by the Hata family in the 8th century. As the role of agriculture diminished, deities were enrolled to ensure prosperity in business. Nowadays, the shrine is one of Japan's most popular, and is the head shrine for some 40,000 Inari shrines scattered the length and breadth of the country.

The entire complex, consisting of five shrines, sprawls across the wooded slopes of Inari-san. A pathway wanders 4km up

---

Fushimi-Inari Hike (Maps 2, 7 & 8)

Time: About two hours
Distance: About 6km
Major Sights: Fushimi Inari-taisha (Map 2), Tōfuki-ji (Map 8)

The climb up 233m **Inari-san** is one of southern Kyoto's real highlights. The hike described here starts at **Fushimi-Inari-taisha**, wends its way to **Tōfuku-ji** temple, and ends at **Tōfukuji station**. Along the way, you'll pass through thousands of bright red torii.

After checking out the main halls of Fushimi-Inari, climb the stairs behind the shrine and turn to the right where the first colonnade of torii begins. The row of gates splits into two – take either one (they merge again further on). You will then come to a small shrine and another set of torii leading to the left. This path gradually winds its way up the mountain until arriving at a T-junction.

Turn right and continue uphill to a saddle where there are a couple of teahouses and an intersection. Turn right here and follow the ridge over two small peaks of Inari-san. Veering left and dropping into a thickly wooded valley on the north side of the mountain, the path eventually comes to yet another junction. Nearby is an atmospheric grotto with a small waterfall. Take the path on the right and, just before another row of torii, go down the flight of stairs to the right.

The path soon becomes a dirt trail that parallels a small stream. After passing a large vegetable garden and a short flight of steps you will come out to a road. Take the first left and follow the road for about 100m until you get to a tiny playground on the left. Turn left onto the adjacent dirt path and then go right. This path will take you down a small ridge to another road. At the nearby T-junction go right.

Upon reaching a mounted street mirror, turn left and you will soon come to the south gate of **Tōfuku-ji**. After visiting the temple's gardens, leave from the main gate on the west side and take the first road to the right. Passing by some of Tōfuku-ji's subtemples, this road makes a series of turns in a north-westerly direction, eventually bringing you to an overpass. Keihan Tōfukuji and JR Tōfukuji stations (Maps 2 & 7) are situated next to each other, down the hill on the opposite (west) side of the overpass.

the mountain and is lined with hundreds of red torii. There are also dozens of stone foxes. The fox is considered the messenger of Inari, the god of cereals, and the stone foxes, too, are often referred to as Inari. The key often seen in the fox's mouth is for the rice granary. On an incidental note, the Japanese traditionally see the fox as a sacred, somewhat mysterious figure capable of 'possessing' humans – the favoured point of entry is under the fingernails.

The walk around the upper precincts of the shrine is a pleasant day hike. It also makes for a very eerie stroll in the late afternoon and early evening, when the various graveyards and miniature shrines along the path take on a mysterious air. It's best to go with a friend at this time.

On 8 April there's a Sangyō-sai festival with offerings and dances to ensure prosperity for national industry. During the first few days in January, thousands of believers visit this shrine as their hatsu-mōde to pray for good fortune.

Local delicacies sold on the approach streets include barbecued sparrow and *inari-sushi*, which is fried tofu wrapped around sweetened sushi – commonly believed to be the favourite food of the fox.

The Keihan line is the easiest way to get there; take a local train and get off at Fushimi-Inari station. From Kyoto station, you can take a JR Nara-line train to Inari station, but beware that departures are few and far between.

Daigo-ji (Map 1)

Daigo-ji (☎ 571 0002; entry to grounds free, except during cherry blossom and autumn foliage seasons when it's ¥600; 9am-5pm) was founded in 874 by the priest Shobo who gave it the name of Daigo (which means the ultimate essence of milk). This refers to the five periods of Buddha's teaching, which were often compared to the five forms of milk prepared in India – the highest form is called 'daigo' in Japanese.

The temple was expanded into a vast complex on two levels, Shimo Daigo (lower) and Kami Daigo (upper). During the 15th century, those buildings on the

lower level were destroyed, with the sole exception of the five-storey pagoda. Built in 951, this pagoda is treasured as the oldest of its kind in Japan and the oldest existing building in Kyoto.

In the late 16th century, Hideyoshi took a fancy to Daigo-ji and ordered extensive rebuilding. It is now one of the main temples of the Shingon school. To explore Daigo-ji thoroughly and at a leisurely pace, mixing hiking with temple viewing, you will need at least half a day.

Take the Tōzai line from downtown Kyoto to the last stop, Daigo station, and walk 400m east.

Sampō-in This was founded as a subtemple (☎ 571 0002; ¥500; open 9am-5pm) in 1115, but received a total revamp under Hideyoshi's orders in 1598. It is now a fine example of the amazing opulence of that period. The Kanō paintings and the garden are special features.

The garden is jam-packed with about 800 stones – the Japanese mania for stones goes back a long way. The most famous stone here is Fujito-no-ishi, which is linked to deception, death and a fabulous price that was spurned; it's even the subject of a nō play, *Fujito*.

Hōju-in Treasure House This (☎ 571 0002; ¥700; open 9am-5pm) is close to Sampō-in. Despite the steep admission fee, it really should not be missed if you're a fan of traditional Japanese art. The display of sculptures, scrolls, screens, miniature shrines and calligraphy is superb.

Hōkō Hanami Gyōretsu Parade On the second Sunday in April, a parade called Hōkō Hanami Gyōretsu takes place in the temple precincts. This re-enacts in full period costume the cherry-blossom party that Hideyoshi held in 1598. As a result of this party, the temple's abbot was able to secure Hideyoshi's support for restoration of the dilapidated temple complex.

Climb to Daigo-yama From Sampō-in, walk up the large avenue of cherry trees, through Niō-mon gate and past the pagoda. From there you can continue for a pleasant climb through the upper part of Daigo-yama, browsing through temples and shrines on the way. Allow 50 minutes to reach the top.

Fushimi 伏見 (Map 14)

Fushimi, home to 37 sake breweries, is one of Japan's most famous sake-producing regions. Its location on the Uji-gawa made it a perfect location for sake production, as fresh, high-quality rice was readily available from the fields of neighbouring Shiga-ken and the final product could be easily loaded onto boats for export downriver to Osaka.

Despite its fame as a sake producing region, Fushimi is one of Kyoto's least prepossessing areas. It's also a hard area to navigate due to a lack of English signage. It's probably only worth a visit if you've got a real interest in sake and sake production.

To get to Fushimi, take a local or express (not a limited express) on the Keihan line to Chūshojima station (¥260, 20 minutes). Alternatively, you can take the Kintetsu line from Kyoto station to Momoyama-Goryō-mae station (¥250, 11 minutes).

Gekkeikan Sake Ōkura Museum The largest of Fushimi's sake breweries is Gekkeikan, the world's leading producer of sake. Although most of the sake is now made in a modern facility in Osaka, a limited amount of handmade sake is still made in a Meiji-era *kura* (warehouse) here in Fushimi.

The Gekkeikan Ōkura Museum (☎ 623 2056; ¥300; open 9.30am-4.30pm, closed Mon) houses a collection of artefacts and memorabilia tracing the 350 year history of Gekkeikan and the sake brewing process. Giant murals depicting traditional methods of brewing adorn the walls and there is the chance to taste (and of course buy) some of the local brew.

If you are travelling with a tour group larger than 20 people and call two weeks in advance (☎ 623 2001), you can arrange a guided English tour of the brewery.

Otherwise, ask at the TIC about joining a tour given in Japanese.

It's a 10-minute walk north-east of Chūshojima station. You might have to ask a passer-by for directions as the way is poorly marked.

Kizakura Kappa Country A short walk from its competitor Gekkeikan, Kizakura (☎ 611 9919; free; open 10am-5pm, closed Mon) is another sake brewery worth a look while you're in the neighbourhood. The vast complex houses both sake and beer breweries, courtyard gardens and a small gallery dedicated to the mythical (and sneaky) creature, Kappa. The restaurant/bar is an appealing option for a bite to eat or a freshly brewed ale (see the Southern Kyoto section in the Places to Eat chapter).

It's a short walk north of the Ōkura Museum.

Teradaya Inn & Museum Famed as the inn of choice for rebel samurai Sakamoto Ryōma (1834–67), today Teradaya (☎ 611 1223; ¥400; open 10am-4pm) functions as a museum by day and a ryokan by night. Fans of Ryōma faithfully make the pilgrimage here to see the room where he slept.

It's a 10-minute walk north of Chūsho-jima station. You might have to ask a passer-by for directions as the way is poorly marked.

Fushimi Momoyama-jō (Map 2)

Toyotomi Hideyoshi's Fushimi-jō (☎ 611 5121; ¥800; open 9.30am-4.30pm) was completely destroyed during the Sekigahara war in 1600, then reconstructed by Tokugawa Ieyasu, but by 1623 was abandoned. The present buildings are unfortunate modern replicas from the 1960s. Unless you are travelling with kids and fancy visiting the on-site Castle Land (Kasuru-rando) amusement park, you can safely give this place a miss. If you want to visit a proper castle, make the day trip to Himeji or Hikone (see the Excursions chapter).

The castle is a 400m walk uphill from Momoyama station on the JR Nara line (¥250, 11 minutes from Kyoto station).

UJI 宇治 (MAP 15)

Uji is a small city south of Kyoto. Historically rich in Heian-period culture, its main claims to fame are Byōdō-in and Ujigami-jinja (both Unesco World Heritage sites) and tea cultivation. The Uji-bashi Bridge, originally all wood and the oldest of its kind in Japan (it is now constructed of concrete and wood), has been the scene of many bitter clashes in previous centuries, though traffic jams seem to predominate nowadays.

Between 17 June and 31 August, ukai trips are organised in the evening around 7pm on the river near Byōdō-in. Prices start at ¥1800 per person. The TIC has a leaflet with up-to-date information on booking. For more details on ukai, see the Cormorant Fishing boxed text in the Arashiyama-Sagano District section.

There is a small **tourist information office** (☎ 0774-22 8783; open 9am-5pm) on the south side of Uji-bashi that has a decent map of the area.

Uji can be easily reached by rail from Kyoto on the Keihan Uji line (¥460, 30 minutes from Keihan Sanjō station; change at Chūshojima) or JR Nara line (¥210, 20 minutes from Kyoto station).

Byōdō-in

This temple (☎ 0774-21 2861; ¥500; open 8.30am-5pm Mar-Nov, 9am-4pm other times) was converted from a Fujiwara villa into a Buddhist temple in 1052.

The **Phoenix hall** (Hōō-dō), more properly known as the Amida-dō, was built in 1053 and is the only original building remaining. The phoenix was a popular mythical bird in China and was revered by the Japanese as a protector of Buddha. The architecture of the building resembles the shape of the bird, and there are two bronze phoenixes perched opposite each other on the roof. The building was originally intended to represent Amida's heavenly palace in the Pure Land. This building is one of the few extant examples of Heian-period architecture, and its graceful lines make you wish that far more had survived the wars and fires which plagued Kyoto's past. Inside the hall is the famous statue of Amida and 52 Bosatsu (Bodhisattvas) dating from the 11th century and attributed to the priest-sculptor, Jōchō.

The temple, complete with its reflection in a pond, is a major attraction in Japan and draws huge crowds. For a preview without the masses, take a look at the 10 yen coin.

Nearby, the **Hōmotsukan Treasure House** (¥300; open 9am-4pm 1 Apr-31 May & 15 Sept-23 Nov) contains the original temple bell and door paintings, and the original phoenix roof adornments. Allow about an hour to wander through the grounds.

The approach street to the complex is lined with souvenir shops, many of which roast local tea outside. A small packet of the tea is popular as a souvenir or gift.

Uji Tea

On the river bank behind Byōdō-in, is the delightful **Taihō-an** (☎ 0774-23 3334; ¥500; open 10am-4pm; closed 21 Dec-14 Jan). The friendly staff conduct a 30-minute tea ceremony (unless you've got knee trouble, ask for the tatami room). Casual dress is fine here and no reservations are necessary. Buy your tickets at the Uji-shi Kanko centre next door.

Another stop for a taste of Uji's famed green tea is **Tsūen-jaya** (☎ 0774-21 2243; open 9.30am-5.30pm). Japan's oldest surviving tea shop, it has been in the Tsūen family for more than 830 years. The present building, near Uji-bashi, dates from 1672 and is full of interesting antiques. You can try fresh matcha, including a sweet, for ¥530.

Ujigami-jinja

Ujigami-jinja (☎ 0774-21 4634; free; dawn to dusk) holds the distinction of being Japan's oldest shrine (and the least visited of Kyoto's 17 Unesco World Heritage sites). According to ancient records, Uji-no-waki-Iratsuko, a 5th century prince, tragically sacrificed his own life to conclude the matter of whether he or his brother would succeed the imperial throne; needless to say his brother, Emperor Nintoku, won the dispute. The main building was dedicated to the twosome and their father Emperor Ōjin, and enshrines the tombs of the trio.

The shrine is across the river from Byōdō-in and a short walk uphill.

On the way, you'll pass through **Uji-jinja** (*free; dawn to dusk*), which is actually more attractive than its more famous neighbour.

Mampuku-ji (Map 1)

Mampuku-ji (☎ *0774-32 3900; ¥500; open 9am-4pm*) was established as a Zen temple in 1661 by the Chinese priest Ingen. It is a rare example in Japan of a Zen temple built in the pure Chinese style of the Ming dynasty. The temple follows the Ōbaku school, which is linked to the mainstream Rinzai school but incorporates a wide range of esoteric Buddhist practices.

The temple is a short walk east of the two railway stations (JR Nara line and Keihan Uji line) at Ōbaku – about 30 minutes by rail from Kyoto. You can also walk there from Uji-bashi bridge in about 30 minutes.

ACTIVITIES

There's more to Kyoto than just temples, shrines and parks. In addition to shopping, hiking and people-watching, there are several places to get hands-on experience in traditional arts and crafts including tea ceremony, Japanese *washi* paper, textiles, ceramics and calligraphy.

This is only a partial list of what's available in Kyoto. The people at the TIC can help with requests for more specialised activities. You might also check at KICH to see what is being offered on its bulletin boards. *Kansai Time Out* also has extensive listings of meetings, courses and activities.

Tea Ceremony

At **Urasenke Chadō Research Center (Map 3)** (☎ *431 6474; ¥800*), it is possible to view a 20-minute tea making procedure *(temae)* during the Urasenke Foundation's quarterly art exhibitions. Here you can sample a bowl of matcha and a sweet (included in the cost to visit to the centre's gallery).

Another spot offering a casual bowl of tea is **Kanō Shōju-an (Map 6)** (☎ *751 1077; tea & sweet ¥1050; open 10am-4.30pm, closed Wed*) a pleasant teahouse near Eikan-dō.

You might also try the teahouses at the **Miyako Hotel (Map 6)** (☎ *771 7111; ¥1155; open 10am-7pm; no reservations*

MASON FLORENCE

A host prepares tea for the guests while a pot is heated over a brazier.

necessary) near Keage station on the Tōzai line, or the **Kyoto International Community House (Map 6)** (☎ *752 3512; session ¥1000; 2pm Tues & Thurs; call in the morning to reserve*).

Lastly, the **Taihō-an Teahouse (Map 15)** (☎ *0774-23 3334; cost ¥500*) in Uji is possibly the cheapest place in the world to experience an authentic tea ceremony. See the Uji section for details.

Maiko Costume

If you ever wondered how *you* might look as a maiko, Kyoto has numerous outfits in town offering the chance. **Maika (Map 7)** (☎ *551 1661; open 10am-4pm Mon-Fri, 9am-5pm Sat, Sun & holidays*) is in the Gion district. There you can be dressed up to live out your maiko fantasy. Prices begin at ¥6400 for the basic treatment, which includes full make-up and formal kimono (studio photos cost ¥500 per print and you can have stickers made from these). If you don't mind spending some extra yen, it's possible to head out in costume for a stroll through Gion (and be stared at like never before!).

The process takes about an hour. Call to reserve at least one day in advance.

Traditional Crafts

Several of Kyoto's artisans offer introductory classes in traditional Japanese crafts. Few speak English so if you don't speak Japanese, get a Japanese speaker to call to make a reservation. You might also try to convince a Japanese speaker to come along as a translator. If not, be prepared to muddle along with sign language and broken English.

Bamboo Craft Takemata Nakagawa Takezai-ten (Map 5) (☎ 231 3968; ¥3500; sessions 9am & 1pm, except Sun) offers hands-on bamboo craft workshops (minimum three people) where you can learn to weave a small shikai-nami-kago basket (takes about two hours). Reservations in Japanese are required a few days in advance.

Braiding Kyoto's most famed braid maker, Adachi Kumihimo-kan (Map 5) (☎ 432 4113; cost ¥5000/2500; open 8.30am-5.30pm, closed second, third & fourth Sat each month, Sun & holidays) has a gallery of fine items on display. Here you can weave your own braid on wooden hand looms. It takes about two hours, and the cost depends on the length of the class and what you make. Delicately woven kyō-kumihimo (Kyoto-style braidwork) was developed in the Heian period for fastening kimono, but gradually spread to other ornamental applications. Today the braid is again most commonly used as obi-jime (the tie for kimono sashes). Reservations in Japanese are necessary.

Calligraphy Shōhō-in (Map 7) (☎ 811-7768 in Japanese; ☎ 090-3947 4520 in English, ask for Kato-san; free for temple guests) is a great place to try your hand at copying Buddhist scriptures (sutra). In the peaceful surroundings of the temple, you'll be provided with brushes and all the materials necessary to trace or create your own masterpiece. It takes about two hours. The course is only

available to temple guests; see the Shukubō section in the Places to Stay chapter.

Dolls In about four hours at Honke Katsura (Map 9) (☎ 221 6998; cost ¥10,500; open 10am-6pm, closed third Mon each month) you can learn to paint the face on and assemble a handcrafted kyō-ningyō doll. Reservations in Japanese are necessary.

The Great Outdoors

Kyoto is blessed with mountains on three sides, all of which are latticed with a fine network of hiking trails. Many hikes in and around Kyoto can be combined with a visit to a temple or shrine, making hiking the perfect way to experience Kyoto.

In addition to the two excellent hikes listed in this chapter, there are endless hiking possibilities within easy reach of downtown Kyoto. Getting advice on hikes and finding good hiking companions can sometimes prove harder than the hikes themselves. Luckily, there are several groups in the Kansai area that organise outdoor events. Check the Kansai Time Out for current listings, or contact the groups below.

Japan Environmental Exchange (JEE) plans fun monthly hikes in the Kyoto area (a ¥500 donation goes toward the group's activities); call Nakano Shigeru (☎ 771 9764).

The Kansai Ramblers organise hikes throughout the Kansai region on the second Sunday of each month; call Mr Fukunishi (☎ 0729-88 0600).

The International Outdoor Club (IOC) of Kansai organises hiking, cycling, running and weekend trips. Check the Outdoor/Sports section of Kansai Time Out for the latest contact numbers, as they change from time to time.

Serious cyclists can join the all-day Sunday road rides organised by the Takenaka bike shop (☎ 256 4863).

Finally, for beer-guzzling runners, the Osaka Hash House Harriers hold runs in various parts of Kansai. Check the Sports/Pastimes section of Kansai Time Out for the latest contact numbers as they change from time to time. There's also a Kōbe Ladies Hash (check the same section for details).

Ai-zome Dyeing In the Nishijin area, **Aizen-Kōbō (Map 7)** (☎ *441 0355; open 9.30am-5pm*) dyes beautiful indigo-blue *ai-zome* fabrics in a charming *kyō-machiya*. You can observe and try your hand at tie-dyeing a handkerchief (¥2000) or scarf (¥6300) in about an hour. Reservations should be made a few days in advance.

Vegetable Dyeing In the rural Ōhara area, **Ōhara Kōbō (Map 13)** (☎ *744 3138; open 10am-5pm, closed Wed*) offers a chance to dye fabrics using vivid plant and vegetable dyes *(kusaki-zome)*. The time and cost depend on the item; choose from a handkerchief (¥500), scarf (¥3000) or plain woollen yarn (enough to knit one sweater ¥8000); if you bring your own wool to dye, the cost is ¥5000. Advance reservations in Japanese are required, and the process takes from about two to four hours. See the Ōhara entry in the Ōhara & Kurama-Kibune section for transport details.

Yūzen Dyeing At the **Kodai Yūzen-en Gallery (Map 7)** (☎ *823 0500; admission ¥500 museum; open 9am-5pm*) there are facilities to try Yūzen stencil-dyeing in about 40 minutes. You can choose from various items to dye, such as a handkerchief (¥1050) or necktie (¥4200).

Offering similar activities is the **Yūzen Cultural Hall (Map 2)** *(Yūzen Bunka Kaikan;* ☎ *311 0025; admission ¥400 museum; open 9am-5pm, closed Sun)*. In about 20 minutes you can stencil-dye a hankie (¥450 to ¥800) or try hand painting (¥2100). The workshop closes for one hour at lunch (noon to 1pm) and you must arrive by 4pm to begin.

See the Central Kyoto section earlier in this chapter for transport details to these places.

Ikebana (Flower Arrangement) On the second and fourth Friday of each month the Kyoto International Community House (see the Cultural Demonstrations & Classes entry a little later in this section) holds ikebana classes conducted by volunteers.

While there are no other classes available for short-term visitors, the prominent

Ikenobō Society of Floral Art (☎ *231 4922, fax 255 3568)*, on Karasuma-dōri south of Oike-dori, can be helpful. The institution has a 500-year history in flower arranging, and students come from its branch schools around the world to further their studies. Periodically exhibits and events are held, and if you call in advance it may be possible to observe classes. There is also a **museum** (☎ *231 4922; free; open 9am-5pm Mon-Fri*) on the 3rd floor of the building displaying items such as scrolls, flower containers and teaching manuscripts.

Another worthwhile contact is the Kyoto chapter of **Ikebana International** (☎ *722 7882)*, which can provide information and introductions to local teachers.

Handwoven Textiles Orinasu-kan (Map 3) (☎ *431 0020; cost ¥5000, includes museum entry; open 10am-4pm, closed Mon*) in the Nishijin District offers traditional weaving workshops. The cost is for a three-hour course and you can take home your own handmade fabric. Reservations in Japanese are required one week in advance.

Metalwork *Kyō-zōgan* is a damascene technique of laying fine metals onto figures engraved on brass and can be tried at **Amita-honten (Map 6)** (☎ *761 7000; open 10am-6pm)*, just beside the Kyoto Handicraft Center on Marutamachi-dōri. The cost of making a small pendant is ¥3500 and it takes about an hour (it will be sent to you one week later).

Paper Fans You can learn to design your own *kyō-sensu* paper fan in about 90 minutes at **Kyōsen-dō (Map 10)** (☎ *371 0123; cost ¥2000; sessions 9am, 10.30am, 1pm & 3pm)*. Reservations in Japanese are necessary a few days in advance. Your fan will be sent to a Japanese address a month later (no overseas deliveries).

Paper Making Rakushi-kan (☎ *251 0078; open 10am-7pm, closed Mon*) offers paper-making workshops on Thursday, Friday and Saturday, with sessions at 1pm, 2pm, 3pm and 4pm. The one-hour course costs from ¥1000 for making sheets of washi, business cards or post cards. Reservations in Japanese should be made a week in advance and courses are only held for groups of five or more.

Motoshiro Washi (Map 13) (☎ 744 3388; open 9am-5pm), near Sanzen-in in Ōhara, is another good spot for making washi; the cost is ¥500 to make one sheet, and it takes about 30 minutes. You can pick up the dried paper after about an hour, so try to plan your visit before lunch or visiting the area temples. Reservations in Japanese are suggested at least one day in advance (minimum two people).

Pottery Near the Gojō-zaka slope at **Nishimura Koken (Map 7)** (☎ 561 3552; open 9am-6pm) you can throw a tea cup (¥3000) or tea ceremony bowl (¥5000). The process takes between one and two hours. Finished ceramics will be sent to you about two months later (postage costs are extra and pottery cannot be shipped abroad). Reservations should be made in Japanese a few days in advance (minimum two people).

Cultural Demonstrations & Classes

Kyoto International Community House (Map 6) (KICH; ☎ 752 3512; cost ¥1000 per class, ¥5000 per three-month semester) offers an intriguing variety of introductory courses in Japanese culture, which are open to all for observation (free) and participation. They also offer Japanese-language and calligraphy classes.

The basic demonstration schedule is as follows, but check to confirm the times and reserve a place:

The Way of Tea (tea ceremony)
Tues 2pm-4pm
Introduction to Nō (nō drama)
Thur 10am-noon
The Koto (a Japanese string instrument)
Wed 2pm-4pm
Introduction to Sencha (Chinese-style tea ceremony)
Thur 2pm-4pm

KICH is in eastern Kyoto, south-west of Nanzen-ji. Take the Tōzai line to the Keage stop and walk five minutes north-west (downhill) along the canal. Alternatively, you can walk there in about 15 minutes from Keihan Sanjō station.

Zen Meditation
Several of Kyoto's Zen temples offer public zazen (seated meditation) where you can discover for yourself the mystery of Zen.

Though these temples welcome visitors to participate, bear in mind that zazen is not held for the benefit of tourists and may not always live up to the perfect image of bald monks in robes. In fact, both physically and mentally it is much harder than you might imagine. Still, for many, a session of zazen can be an eye-opening encounter.

As there is very little English spoken at most temples, it helps if you speak a little Japanese, or go with someone who does. Enlightenment, unfortunately, does not always come for free; some temples require a donation. Reservations are generally not required, but you may want to call to confirm the schedule before setting your alarm clock. Most temples do not offer public zazen during the busy Obon season in August, or over the New Year holiday.

It's possible to practice Zen meditation at the following temples:

Daisen-in (☎ 491 8346) Map 3; cost ¥1000; on the 24th each month, 5pm-6pm Mar-Nov, 4.30pm-5.30pm Dec-Feb. In the Daitoku-ji complex.
Genkō-an (☎ 492 1858) Map 3; free; 7am-8.30am first & third Sun each month. In the Takagamine area (north-western Kyoto).
Ichiyō-in (☎ 491 7571) Registration fee ¥1500, then ¥2000 per day; 9am-5pm third Sun each month. Offers a day-long Zen experience: zazen, lectures, cooking and cleaning.
Kennin-ji (☎ 561-0190) Map 7; admission free; 8am-9am second Sun each month. In the Gion district.
Nanzen-in (771 0365) Map 6; admission free; 6am-7am second & fourth Sun each month. Within the grounds of Nanzen-ji.
Shōkoku-ji (☎ 231 0301) Map 3; admission ¥100; 9am-11am second & fourth Sun each month. North of Dōshisha University.

The Japanese Bath

The Japanese bath (o-furo) is a ritual that has to be learned at an early stage of your visit and, like so many other things in Japan, is initially confusing but quickly becomes second nature. The all-important rule for using a Japanese bath is that you wash *outside* the bath tub and use the bath itself purely for soaking. Getting into a bath unwashed, or equally dreadful, without rinsing all the soap off your body, would be a major error.

Bathing is done in the evening, before or after dinner; a pre-breakfast bath is thought of as distinctly strange. In a ryokan there's no possibility of missing bath-time – you will be clearly told when to bathe, which ensures that all guests or families can bathe in privacy. In a public bath (sentō), the facilities are segregated by sex (for more on this, see the Toilets & Public Baths section in the Facts for the Visitor chapter).

Once you arrive at the changing room, take off your yukata (dressing gown) or clothes and place them in the baskets provided. The bathroom has taps, plastic tubs (wooden ones in very traditional places) and stools along the wall. Draw up a stool to a set of taps and fill the tub from the taps or use the tub to scoop some water out of the bath itself. Sit on the stool and soap yourself. Rinse thoroughly so there's no soap or shampoo left on you, then you are ready to climb into the bath. Soak as long as you can stand the heat, then leave the bath, rinse yourself again, dry off and don your yukata or clothes.

For a more immersed experience, the **Hōsen-ji Zen Center** (☎/fax 81-0771-24 0378, 52 Naka-jō, Yamamoto Shinochō, Kameoka-shi, Kyoto 621-0825, W www.zazen.or.jp/, e zazen@zazen.or.jp; cost with meals & accommodation ¥3000/70,000 per day/month) in Kameoka on the western outskirts of Kyoto offers overnight lodging and intensive Zen training from one night to the rest of your life.

The retreat is an excellent place to learn about Zen and they are accustomed to foreign guests. The day begins at 5am and 'lights out' is at 10pm. The centre is a 15-minute walk from Umahori station on the JR San-in Main (Sagano) line. Apply by sending your name, address, date of arrival and length of stay by mail, fax or email. Then just show up; no confirmation will be sent to you. For more information, contact the centre.

Vipassana Meditation Retreat

If you're looking for some spiritual awakening and Zen is not your thing, consider learning the 'art of living' on a 10-day mental training course at the **Japan Vipassana Meditation Center** (e jvipa@mbox.kyoto-inet.or.jp, W www.dhamma.org, Aza Hatta, Mizucho-chō, Funai-gun, Kyoto 622-03). Originated in India and preserved in Myanmar (Burma), Vipassana means 'to see things as they really are'.

About 90 minutes by train in the mountains north-west of Kyoto, it is one of more than 50 such centres worldwide and conducts sessions in both Japanese and English.

Despite the prospect of spending nine full days in silence, the retreat comes recommended by many. There is no charge to take part, though donations are accepted.

Baths

After a day spent marching from temple to temple, nothing feels better than a good hot bath. Kyoto is full of sentō (public baths), ranging from small neighbourhood baths with one or two tubs to massive complexes offering saunas, mineral baths and even electric baths. The following baths are worth a visit and could even double as an evening's entertainment. It's best to bring your own bath supplies (soap, shampoo, a towel to dry yourself and another small one for washing); if you've forgotten, you can buy toiletries and rent towels at the front desk. Washing buckets are available for free inside the bathing area.

Funaoka Onsen (Map 3) Our favourite sentō in Kyoto, this old bath (☎ 441 3735; ¥340; open 3pm-1am, closed Tues) on Kuramaguchi-dōri boasts an outdoor bath and sauna, as well as some museum-quality woodcarvings in the changing room (apparently carved during Japan's invasion of Manchuria). To find it, head west from Horikawa-dōri on Kuramaguchi-dōri. It's on the left not far past the Lawson convenience store. Look for the large rocks out the front.

Gokō-yu (Map 7) This popular bath (☎ 841 7321; ¥340; open 2pm-midnight Mon-Sat, 7am-midnight Sun, 8am-midnight holidays) is another great spot to sample the joys of the sentō. It's a large two-storey bath with a wide variety of tubs. There's also a giant sauna with two rooms; one is merely hot, the other is incendiary! We also like the TV-fish tank in the entrance (you'll see what we mean).

Shomen-yu (Map 10) This place (☎ 561 3232; ¥340; open 1.30pm-1am, from 9am Sun; closed Tues) is perhaps the mother of all sentō. Three storeys high, with an outdoor bath on the roof, this is your chance to try riding an elevator naked (if you haven't already had the pleasure). Everything is on a grand scale here, including the sauna, which boasts a TV and room for 20. Men, don't be surprised if you spot some *yakuza* (gangsters) among the bathers (recognisable by their tattoos). It's a five-minute walk from Keihan Shichijō station.

Sports
Swimming Tosuikai (☎ 761 1275; open 10am-3pm Mon-Sat, noon-5pm Sun) allows non-members to use its pools for ¥1100 per visit. At the time of writing, the pools were being refurbished but are expected to be reopened by the time this book goes to press.

You can also swim in the **Kamo-gawa** in the summer. The best spot is about one kilometre north of Kamigamo-jinja (Map 3); just look for all the people. Keep in mind, however, that swimming here is not without hazard and people have drowned swimming in this river. Parents should keep a very close eye on their children.

See also the Kiyotaki-gawa Hike in this chapter for a few more summer swimming holes near Kyoto.

Outdoor Activities The mountains and rivers around Kyoto offer endless opportunities for the outdoor sports enthusiast. **Alpine River Guides** (☎ 0798-48 3750) offers river rafting tours on nearby rivers for ¥6800 per person. It also offers an excellent winter (Jan-Mar) snowshoe tour of Ashiū for ¥8800 (price includes snowshoe rental and transport from Katata station on the JR Kosei line). This is a great way to experience one of Kyoto-fu's most beautiful rural areas. From June to September, a river hiking course (¥8800) is offered in the same area. For more details on Ashiū, see the Miyama-chō section of the Excursions chapter.

Language Courses
Kyoto is a good place to study Japanese. **Kawara Juku (Map 9)** (☎ 231 1608) is a friendly little school that offers three-month part-time courses for ¥85,000. Courses start in April, September and January. They also offer a summer intensive course for the same price. Joining a class here is a great way to meet people when you're new in town.

Places to Stay

Kyoto has a wide range of accommodation to suit all budgets, from the finest *ryokan* (traditional inns) to youth hostels, guesthouses and *shukubō* (temple lodgings). Needless to say, there are also plenty of hotels, from cheap 'business hotels' to first-class luxury hotels, with a smattering of love hotels and capsule hotels thrown in for good measure.

Bear in mind that much of Kyoto's accommodation can be booked out during the high season (the early April cherry blossom season and the late October to late November fall foliage season). A few places also raise their rates during these busy periods. Whatever you do, try to reserve as early as possible if you plan to be in town during these times.

Credit cards (in particular Visa, Master-Card and American Express) are accepted at most hotels, but don't expect to pay with plastic at any of the budget places. At ryokan, the higher the price, the better the chances of being able to use a credit card.

Guesthouses

Most of Kyoto's guesthouses are casual affairs and, unlike youth hostels, are curfew-free. Shared bathrooms are common and there are usually cooking facilities. What many of these places lack in service they make up for in price.

For short stays expect to pay ¥1500 to ¥2000 per night for a dorm bed, or ¥2500 to ¥5000 for a private room. Most guesthouses offer reduced rates if you ask for weekly or monthly terms. Tax is usually included in the room price.

Ryokan

A night in a traditional Japanese inn is a highlight for many visitors to Kyoto. Most offer the chance to encounter Kyoto's classical wooden architecture and Japanese lifestyle, and to sample some fine *wa-shoku* (Japanese-style cuisine). In most cases the rates include one or two meals.

Lower-price ryokan typically charge ¥4000 to ¥6000 per person per night and in the mid-range you can expect to pay ¥8000 to ¥15,000. Higher-end ryokan rates go from around ¥16,000 to more than ¥50,000 per night. Reservations should always be made (well in advance for top-notch ryokan).

Hotels

Though less atmospheric than ryokan, hotels have the advantage of modern conveniences, services like dry-cleaning, and the better places usually have English-speakers on hand. They're also much easier to come and go from. Some offer both Japanese- and Western-style rooms, so you get the best of both worlds. Room rates at basic 'business hotels' average around ¥7000/12,000 for singles/doubles; regular hotels average about double these figures.

Shukubō

Shukubō, or temple lodgings, are usually in peaceful surroundings with spartan tatami rooms, optional attendance at early morning prayer sessions and an early evening curfew. Nightly rates hover at around ¥4000 per person (most with breakfast included), and guests usually use public baths near the temples.

A number of shukubō in Kyoto are hesitant to take foreigners who cannot speak Japanese, though those listed in this chapter have English-speakers on hand and are used to having non-Japanese guests. At the TIC you can also pick up a copy of a hand-out entitled *Shukubōs in Kyoto*, which has a comprehensive list of local temple lodgings.

Where to Stay

You can save time traversing the city if you organise your accommodation around the areas that interest you. While many prefer to be based in central Kyoto for easy access to sights in any direction, there are also advantages to staying in less populated parts of town (such as peace and quiet). The eastern

Staying at a Ryokan

On arrival at a better ryokan, you leave your shoes at the entrance, don a pair of slippers and are shown by a maid to your room, which has a *tatami* (reed mat) floor. Slippers are taken off before entering tatami rooms. Instead of using numbers, rooms are named after auspicious flowers, plants or trees.

The room will contain an alcove *(tokonoma)*, probably decorated with a flower display or a calligraphy scroll. One side of the room will have a cupboard with sliding doors for the bedding; the other side will have sliding screens covered with rice paper and may open onto a veranda with a garden view.

The room maid then serves tea with a sweet on a low table surrounded by cushions *(zabuton)* in the centre of the room. At the same time you are asked to sign the register. A tray is provided with a towel, gown *(yukata)* and belt *(obi)*, which you put on before taking your bath. Remember to wear the left side over the right – the reverse order is used for dressing the dead. In colder weather there will also be an outer jacket *(tanzen)*. Your clothes can be put in a closet or left on a hanger.

Dressed in your yukata you will be shown to the bath *(o-furo)*. At some ryokan there are rooms with private baths, but the communal ones are often designed with 'natural' pools or a window looking out onto a garden. Bathing is communal, but sexes are segregated. Make sure you can differentiate between the bathroom signs for men and women, though ryokan used to catering for foreigners will often have signs in English. Many inns will have family bathrooms for couples or families.

Dressed in your yukata after your bath, you return to your room where the maid will have laid out dinner – in some ryokan, dinner is provided in a separate room but you still wear your yukata for dining. Dinner usually includes standard dishes such as miso soup, pickles *(tsukemono)*, vegetables in vinegar *(sunomono)*, hors d'oeuvres *(zensai)*, fish either grilled or raw *(sashimi)*, and perhaps tempura and a stew. There will also be bowls for rice, dips and sauces. Depending on the price, these meals can be flamboyant displays of local cuisine or refined arrangements of *kaiseki* (a cuisine that obeys strict rules of form and etiquette for every detail of the meal and setting).

After dinner, while you are pottering around or strolling in the garden, the maid will clear the dishes and prepare your bedding. A mattress *(futon)* is placed on the tatami floor and a quilt put on top. In colder weather, you can also add a blanket *(mōfu)*.

FRANK CARTER

In the morning, the maid will knock to make sure you are awake and then come in to put away the bedding before serving breakfast – sometimes this is served in a separate room. Breakfast usually consists of pickles, dried seaweed *(nori)*, raw egg, dried fish, miso soup and rice. It can take a while for foreign stomachs to accept this novel fare early in the morning.

The Japanese tendency is to make the procedure at a ryokan seem rather rarefied for foreign comprehension and some ryokan are wary of accepting foreign guests. However, once you've grasped the basics, it really isn't that hard to fit in.

Keep in mind, also, that the procedure described herein applies to proper, high-class ryokan; many of the cheaper ryokan listed in this chapter dispense with the formalities and aren't nearly as grand as you might expect – they're really little more than small hotels with Japanese-style rooms. If you want a true ryokan experience you're going to have to pay at least mid-range prices.

PLACES TO STAY

Higashiyama area is popular, as it is near temples and the mountains yet also close enough to the city centre. As far as costs go, there is a wide range of choices throughout the city and in most areas you can find something to suit your budget.

The TIC (☎ 371 5649) **Map 10** offers advice, accommodation lists and can help with reservations at its Welcome Inn Reservation counter (open 9am-noon Mon-Fri). There's another Welcome Inn Reservation counter in the international arrivals lobby of Kansai airport (☎ 0724-56 6025).

To help with planning, the following listings have been sorted according to price, type and location.

In this section, we give transport directions from Kyoto station unless otherwise noted.

See the very end of this chapter for information on hotels at Kansai and Itami airports.

PLACES TO STAY – BUDGET
Camping
Though there is little in the way of facilities, it is possible to camp along the Kiyotaki-gawa between Kiyotaki and Hozukyō – see the boxed text 'Kiyotaki-gawa Hike' in the Things to See & Do chapter for transport details. You can camp by the river and use nearby trains or buses for the 30-minute trip into Kyoto. For bathing there is the river, or public baths in Kyoto. This is a realistic option from early April to late October. Keep in mind, though, that this is an 'unofficial' option and you may be asked to leave if you're discovered by local officials.

Hostels
Higashiyama Youth Hostel (☎ 761 8135, fax 761 8138) **Map 6** Transport: bus No 5 to the Higashiyama-Sanjō stop. Dorm beds ¥2650. Bicycle rental ¥1000 per day. Curfew 9.30pm. This spiffy hostel is an excellent base for the sights in eastern Kyoto. Unfortunately, it's also rather regimented and certainly not a good spot to stay if you want some nightlife. You can also walk here from the Sanjō Keihan area.

Utano Youth Hostel (☎ 462 2288, fax 462 2289) **Map 2** Transport: bus No 26 to the Yūsu-Hosuteru-mae stop. Dorm beds

¥2800. Curfew 10pm. The best hostel in Kyoto, Utano is friendly, well organised and makes a convenient base for the sights of north-western Kyoto. There's a meeting room with bilingual TV news, but for many travellers, fond memories are reserved for the heated toilet seats! If you want to skip the hostel food turn left along the main road to find several coffee shops offering cheap *teishoku* (set meals).

Kitayama Youth Hostel (☎ 492 5345) **Map 3** Transport: bus No 6 to the Genkō-anmae stop. Dorm beds ¥2800. This hostel is a superb place from which to visit the rural Takagamine area with its fine, secluded temples such as Kōetsu-ji, Jōshō-ji and Shōden-ji. To get here from the bus stop, walk west past a school, turn right and continue up the hill to the hostel (five minutes' walk).

Guesthouses
Kyoto Station Area & Central Kyoto
Tour Club (☎ 353 6968, e tourclub@ kyotojp.com, w www.kyotojp.com) **Map 10** Transport: 10-minute walk from Kyoto station. Dorm beds ¥2300, twins/triples ¥7400/8400. By far the best guesthouse in Kyoto, the clean new Tour Club is run by a charming and informative young couple. Facilities include Internet access, bicycle rentals, laundry, money exchange and free tea and coffee.

Uno House (☎ 231 7763) **Map 5** Transport: Karasuma line to Marutamachi station, walk east 10 minutes. Dorm beds ¥1650, private rooms from ¥2250 (tiny singles) to ¥5200 per room. A celebrated *gaijin* (foreigner's) house, Uno offers the dubious privilege of a really grungy accommodation experience. The attractions are the price and the absence of youth hostel regimentation.

Guest Inn Kyoto (☎ 341 1344) **Map 7** Transport: bus No 6 or 206 to the Shimbara-Guchi stop. Singles/doubles ¥3500/6800. This inexpensive choice gets mixed reviews from travellers. However, it's fairly conveniently located for exploration of sites around Kyoto station.

Tani House Annexe (☎ 211 5637) **Map 9** Transport: bus No 5 to the Kawaramachi-Sanjō stop or the Karasuma line to the

Karasuma-Oike stop. Doubles/triples with bath & air-con ¥6500/8000. The downtown branch of the popular Tani House (see the following Northern Kyoto section), this seems to be an on-again-off-again affair. Be sure to call well in advance.

Tōji-An Guest House (☎ 691 7017, fax 691 0304) **Map 7** Transport: 15-minute walk from Kyoto station. Dorm beds ¥2000, private rooms from ¥2300. No curfew. This cramped warren of tiny rooms is often full with long-termers. For those on a really tight budget it's a decent choice. Call for directions as it can be tricky to find.

Eastern Kyoto *ISE Dorm (☎ 771 0566)* **Map 6** Transport: bus No 206 to the Kumanojinja-mae stop. Rooms ¥2800 per day, ¥45,000-56,000 per month. This place is noisy and dirty but there is usually a room available and arrangements for a stay can be made very quickly. By all means, take a look at the place before you check in. Facilities include phone, fridge, air-con, shower and washing machine. The office is down a narrow alley, so ask for directions once you get into the general area.

Northern Kyoto *Aoi-Sō Inn (☎ 431 0788)* **Map 3** Transport: Karasuma line to Kuramaguchi station. Per-person from ¥2000. This is a quiet place with several small rooms and a quaint little garden. The inn is a five-minute walk north-west of Kuramaguchi station (exit No 2), between the Kyoto Hospital buildings.

Tani House (☎ 492 5489) **Map 3** Transport: bus No 206 to the Kenkunjinja-mae stop. Dorm beds ¥1700, doubles ¥4200-4600. No curfew. This place is an old favourite for both short-term and long-term visitors on a tight budget. There is a certain charm to this fine old house with its warren of rooms and quiet location next to Daitoku-ji. Ask at the police box near the temple for directions once you get into the area.

Greenpeace Inn Kyoto (☎ 791 9890) **Map 3** Transport: Karasuma line to Matsugasaki station. Dorm beds ¥4500/9400/26,000, singles ¥7000/15,000/42,000, doubles ¥8400/17,500/46,000 per three nights/week/month,

with a minimum stay of three nights. This archetypal gaijin house is popular with foreigners setting themselves up to live in Kyoto. It might do for a short stay, after which you'll definitely want something better and quieter. There is a common kitchen, and laundry facilities.

Takaya (☎ 431 5213) **Map 5** Transport: Karasuma line to Imadegawa station. Rooms ¥4000/50,000 per day/month. Near the Imperial Palace, this pleasant little gaijin house is usually full with long-termers but you might find a bed when someone's just moved out.

Hotels
Kyoto Station Area (Map 10) There are several cheap business hotels near Kyoto station, but don't expect much English to be spoken.

Kyoto White Hotel (☎ 351 5511) Transport: 5-minute walk from Kyoto station. Singles/doubles ¥4600/7300. This old hotel seems to specialise in housing Japanese businessmen travelling on tight budgets. It is just about the cheapest business hotel in town.

Pension Station Kyoto (☎ 882 6200) Transport: 10-minute walk from Kyoto station. Per-person ¥4400, ¥1600 extra for room with bath, ¥1000 higher on weekends. Breakfast ¥800 and dinner ¥2000. This simple pension has a convenient location near Kyoto station.

Eastern Kyoto *Amenity Capsule Hotel (☎ 525 3900)* **Map 8** Transport: bus No 206 to the Kiyomizu-michi stop. Single capsules ¥3600 (men only), twins ¥9000. If you've never tried one of Japan's unique capsule hotels, here's your chance. This place is no great shakes, but at this price, who can argue? It's conveniently close to Kiyomizu-dera.

PLACES TO STAY – MID-RANGE
Kyoto Station Area & Central Kyoto
Ryokan & Guesthouses *Ryokan Hinomoto (☎ 351 4563)* **Map 7** Transport: bus No 17 or 205 to the Kawaramachi-Matsubara stop. Singles ¥4000-5500, doubles

¥7500-8000. This small, simple place is a favourite with many frequent visitors to Kyoto. It's located near the centre of the city's nightlife action.

Ryokan Hiraiwa (☎ *351 6748*) **Map 10** Transport: 15-minute walk from Kyoto station or bus No 17 or 205 to the Kawaramachi-Shōmen stop. Per person ¥4000. This ryokan is used to foreigners and offers basic tatami rooms. It is close to both central and eastern Kyoto.

Matsubaya Ryokan (☎ *351 4268*) **Map 10** Transport: 10-minute walk from Kyoto station. Per-person ¥4500, triples ¥12,600. Close to Higashi Hongan-ji, this unpretentious little ryokan is another decent choice in the station area.

Ryokan Murakamiya (☎ *371 1260*) **Map 10** Transport: 10-minute walk from Kyoto station. Per person ¥4000. This homey little ryokan is conveniently located close to the station.

Riverside Takase (☎ *351 7925*) **Map 10** Transport: 15-minute walk from Kyoto station or bus No 17 or 205 to the Kawaramachi-Shōmen stop. Singles/doubles/triples ¥3300/6400/9600. There are five comfortable rooms in this long-time favourite of foreign travellers.

Yuhara Ryokan (☎ *371 9583*) **Map 10** Transport: 15-minute walk from Kyoto station or bus No 17 or 205 to the Kawaramachi-Shōmen stop. Per person ¥4000. With a riverside location and a family atmosphere, Yuhara is popular with foreigners.

Ryokan Kyōka (☎ *371 2709*) **Map 10** Transport: 10-minute walk from Kyoto station. Per person ¥4000. Getting a little long in the tooth, this ryokan has 10 fairly spacious rooms.

Hirota Guest House (☎ *221 2474*) **Map 5** Transport: Karasuma line to Karasuma-Oike or Tōzai-line to Shiyakusho-mae. Rooms from ¥5500 per person, suite rooms ¥7000 per person, private cottage ¥9000 per person. Japanese breakfasts ¥1000. Unassuming from the outside, the popular Hirota is a pleasant Japanese-style inn in an old *sake* brewery. Its cheerful English-speaking owner, Hirota-san, is a former tour guide and a valuable source of information.

Hotels In general, hotels are slightly more expensive than ryokan and have less character. However, they are generally a lot more flexible about the hours you keep and very convenient.

Sun Hotel Kyoto (☎ *241 3351, fax 241 0616*) **Map 9** Transport: bus No 5 to the Kawaramachi-Sanjō stop. Singles/doubles/twins ¥7000/12,200/12,200. This small but clean and hotel is one of the best in its class. Its central location can't be beaten.

APA Hotel (☎ *365 4111, fax 365 8720*) **Map 10** Transport: 5-minute walk from Kyoto station. Singles/twins from ¥7500/15,000. This brand-spanking new business hotel is located very close to Kyoto station. Good for those early morning departures.

Hotel Gimmond (☎ *221 4111, fax 221 8250*) **Map 9** Transport: Karasuma line to Karasuma-Oike station. Singles/doubles/twins from ¥8300/14,000/14,500. This is one of the cheapest hotels (as opposed to business hotels) in town with a convenient location and clean rooms.

Hotel New Hokke Kyoto (☎ *361 1251*) **Map 10** Transport: 1-minute walk from Kyoto station. Singles/twins from ¥5800/13,000. Just across from Kyoto station and recently refurbished, this is a good choice for those who want to be close to transport. Ask about their Welcome Plan which enables two people to stay for ¥9000.

Karasuma Kyoto Hotel (☎ *371 0111, fax 256 2351*) **Map 5** Transport: Karasuma line to Shijō station. Singles/doubles/twins ¥8800/20,000/16,000. With its downtown location and reasonably large rooms, this hotel is a good choice at the upper level of this price range.

Kyoto Central Inn (☎ *211 1666, fax 241 2765*) **Map 9** Transport: Hankyū Kyoto line to Kawaramachi station. Singles/doubles/twins ¥7000/11,000/11,000. This nondescript business hotel is right in the heart of Kyoto's nightlife and shopping district.

Kyoto Dai-Ichi Hotel (☎ *661 8800, fax 661 8110*) **Map 7** Transport: 10-minute walk from Kyoto station. Singles/doubles/twins ¥6800/12,000/13,500. There's not much to distinguish this standard business hotel on the south side of Kyoto station.

Kyoto Dai-San Tower Hotel (☎ *343 3111, fax 343 2054*) **Map 10** Transport: 5-minute walk from Kyoto station. Singles ¥6000-9000, doubles ¥15,000, twins ¥11,000-16,000. Try this business hotel if the other options around Kyoto station are full.

Eastern Kyoto

Ryokan *Three Sisters Inn* (*Rakutō-sō;* ☎ *761 6336, fax 761 6338*) **Map 6** Transport: bus No 5 to the Dōbutsu-en-mae stop. Singles/doubles/triples from ¥8900/13,000/19,500. Perfectly situated for exploration of eastern Kyoto, this long-time favourite of foreign travellers is our top pick in this class. The inn is very close to Heian-jingū.

Three Sisters Inn Annexe (*Rakutō-sō Bekkan;* ☎ *761 6333, fax 761 6335*) **Map 6** Transport: bus No 5 to the Dōbutsu-en-mae stop. Singles/doubles without bath ¥5635/11,270, singles/doubles with bath ¥10,810/18,170, triples with bath ¥23,805. The annexe of the aforementioned inn, this is another excellent choice. It has a pleasant breakfast nook that overlooks a wonderful Japanese garden. The bamboo-lined walkway is another highlight.

Ryokan Ōtō (☎ *541 7803*) **Map 10** Transport: bus No 206 or 208 to the Shichijō-Keihan-mae stop. Singles/doubles ¥4000/7600. A member of the Japanese Inn Group, the Ōtō is a decent choice but lacks the atmosphere of some of Kyoto's other ryokan. The location is pretty good for exploring the southern Higashiyama area.

Ryokan Seiki (☎ *682 0311*) **Map 7** Transport: bus No 206 to the Gojō-zaka stop. Singles/doubles/triples ¥3600/7500/11,000. Not far from Kiyomizu-dera, Seiki is yet another member of the Japanese Inn Group that is conveniently located for exploration of the southern Higashiyama area. Again, not much ryokan atmosphere, but the prices are competitive.

Ryokan Uemura (☎/*fax 561 0377*) **Map 8** Transport: bus No 206 to the Higashiyama-Yasui stop. Per-person ¥9000 including breakfast. Curfew10pm. A beautiful little ryokan near Kiyomizu-dera, the Uemura is at ease with foreign guests. It is located on Ishibei-kōji, a quaint cobblestone alley, just

down the hill from Kiyomizu-dera. You'll have to book well in advance as there are only three rooms. Note that the manager prefers bookings to be made by fax and asks that cancellations also be made by fax (with only three-rooms no-shows can be pretty damaging).

Iwanami Ryokan (☎ *561 7135*) **Map 6** Transport: bus No 206 to the Chioin-mae stop. Per person ¥9500 with breakfast. Iwanami is a pleasant, old-fashioned ryokan with a faithful following of foreign guests. It's right in the heart of Gion on a quiet side street. Book well in advance.

Gion Fukuzumi (☎ *541 5181*) **Map 6** Transport: bus No 206 to the Chioin-mae stop. Singles/doubles from ¥8000/12,000. A group-tour-oriented ryokan in a Western-style building, the Fukuzumi has clean, new rooms and a good Gion location.

Ryokan Mishima (*Mishima-jinja;* ☎ *551 0033*) **Map 8** Transport: bus No 206 to the Umamachi stop. Singles/doubles/triples ¥4000/7000/10,500. No curfew. This interesting option is a shrine that doubles as a place to stay. You'll be given keys and left to your own devices. It's simple but okay.

Hotels & Pensions (Map 6) *Kyoto Traveller's Inn* (☎ *771 0225*) Transport: bus No 5 to the Dōbutsu-en-mae stop. Singles/twins ¥5500/10,000. No curfew. This is a business hotel very close to Heian-jingū, offering both Western- and Japanese-style rooms. The *Green Box restaurant* on the 1st floor is open until 10pm.

Pension Higashiyama (☎ *882 1181, fax 862 0820*) Transport: bus No 206 to the Chioin-mae stop. Singles/doubles ¥4400/8800. A small pension by the Shira-kawa, it's conveniently located for the sights in Higashiyama. It's also a member of the Japanese Inn Group.

Sunflower Hotel (☎ *761 9111, fax 761 1333*) Transport: bus No 5 to the Higashi-Tennō-chō stop. Singles/doubles/twins ¥6000/10,000/10,000. This large, pleasant hotel is located close to the Higashiyama mountains. The rooftop beer garden is perfect for summer drinking.

PLACES TO STAY

Northern Kyoto

Ryokan Rakucho (☎ *721 2174, fax 791 7202*) **Map 3** Transport: Karasuma line to Kitaōji station, or bus No 205 to the Furitsu-Daigaku-mae stop. Singles/doubles from ¥4500/8000. This is a friendly little ryokan in the northern part of the city.

Western Kyoto

Minshuku Arashiyama (☎ *861 4398*) **Map 11** Transport: walk from Saga-Arashiyama on the JR San-in line or from the Sagaeki-mae station on the Keifuku Arashiyama line. Per-person ¥7000 with two meals, ¥5000 without. This little *minshuku* (Japanese B&B) is great for its convenient location and pleasant rooms. We suggest having a Japanese person call to reserve for you.

Pension Arashiyama (☎ *881 2294*) **Map 2** Transport: bus No 71, 72 or 73 to the Arisugawa-mae stop. Singles/doubles/triples ¥4200/8400/12,000. The rooms at Pension Arashiyama are mostly Western-style. It has a great location for exploring Arashiyama and Sagano.

Southern Kyoto

Teradaya (☎ *622 0243*) **Map 14** Transport: Keihan line to Chūshojima station. Per person ¥7000 with breakfast. Curfew 8pm. Despite the inconvenient location, Japanese history buffs may enjoy a night at the inn where Japan's revolutionary hero Sakamoto Ryōma stayed when visiting Kyoto.

Ōhara (Map 13)

Ōhara Sansō (☎ *744 2227*) Transport: Kyoto bus No 17 or 18 to the Ōhara stop. Per person ¥8000 with two meals. A pleasant inn, Ōhara Sansō is just down the road from Jakkō-in. There's a soothing outdoor bath.

Ryosō Chadani (☎ *744 2952*) Transport: Kyoto bus No 17 or 18 run to the Ōhara stop. Per person ¥6500 with meals. Not far from the Ōhara bus stop, Ryosō Chatani is part of the Welcome Inn Group (reservations can be made at the TIC).

PLACES TO STAY – TOP END

Top-end ryokan in Kyoto are very expensive. If a stay at one is within your means, you're guaranteed a memorable experience. Some of the ryokan that occasionally host foreign guests are listed here.

Central Kyoto

Ryokan Kinmata Ryokan (☎ *221 1039*) **Map 9** Transport: taxi from Kyoto station. Per person ¥25,000-35,000 with two meals. Kinmata commenced operations early in the 19th century and this is reflected in the original decor, interior gardens and *hinoki* (cypress) bathroom. The exquisite kaiseki meals alone are a good reason to stay here. It's in the centre of town, close to Nishiki Market.

Hiiragiya Ryokan (☎ *221 1136*) **Map 9** Transport: taxi from Kyoto station. Per person ¥30,000-100,000 with two meals. This elegant ryokan has long been favoured by celebrities from around the world.

Hiiragiya Ryokan Annexe (☎ *231 0151*) **Map 5** Transport: taxi from Kyoto station. Per-person from ¥15,000 with two meals. Close to the Hiiragiya, the annexe also offers top-notch ryokan service and surroundings at slightly more affordable rates.

Tawaraya Ryokan (☎ *211 5566*) **Map 9** Transport: taxi from Kyoto station. Per person from ¥35,000-75,000. Tawaraya has been operating for over three centuries and is classed as one of the finest places to stay in the world. Guests at this ryokan have included the imperial family and overseas royalty. It is a classic in every sense. Reservations are essential, preferably many months ahead.

Hotels The up-market ryokan experience is not for everyone, and if you want a hotel with full amenities, there are a number of good hotels in the central district.

Hotel Granvia Kyoto (☎ *344 8888, fax 344 4400*) **Map 10** Singles/doubles/twins ¥14,000/ 25,000/20,000. Located directly above Kyoto station, this is one of the finest hotels in Kyoto, with a wide range of excellent on-site restaurants and bars.

Kyoto Hotel (☎ *211 5111, fax 254 2529*) **Map 9** Transport: Tōzai line to Kyoto-Shiyakusho-mae station. Singles/doubles/twins from ¥16,000/28,000/22,000. This vast new hotel is considered by many to be the best hotel in Kyoto. Without a doubt it's got the widest range of on-site facilities, and is in a convenient downtown location.

Holiday Inn Kyoto (☎ 721 3131, fax 781 6178) **Map 4** Transport: free shuttle from Kyoto station (call ahead to arrange). Singles/doubles/twins ¥10,000/14,000/18,500. Although a little far from the city centre, the Holiday Inn gets good reviews for its large rooms and swimming pool.

Hotel Fujita Kyoto (☎ 222 1511, fax 222 1515) **Map 5** Transport: Tōzai line to Kyoto-Shiyakusho-mae station. Singles ¥9800-15,000, doubles ¥23,000-27,000, twins ¥16,000-28,000. This hotel is recommended for its riverside location, view of the mountains (ask for a room on the east side), summertime beer garden and great sunken garden/bar.

ANA Hotel Kyoto (☎ 231 1155, fax 231 5333) **Map 5** Transport: Tōzai line to Nijō-jō-mae. Singles/doubles/twins from ¥11,000/ 19,000/16,000. Just opposite Nijō-jō, this attractive hotel is a good choice for its on-site facilities (pool, restaurants, shopping etc).

International Hotel Kyoto (☎ 222 1111) **Map 5** Transport: Tōzai line to Nijō-jō-mae station. Singles ¥9000-13,000, doubles ¥23,000, twins ¥16,000-25,000. Directly across from Nijō-jō, this is a slightly less appealing choice than the ANA.

Kyoto Century Hotel (☎ 351 0111, fax 343 3721) **Map 10** Transport: 1-minute walk from Kyoto station. Singles/doubles/ twins ¥14,000/18,000/22,000. With clean and spacious rooms, this is a good choice for those who fancy being right near the station.

Kyoto New Hankyū Hotel (☎ 343 5300, fax 343 5324) **Map 10** Transport: 1-minute walk from Kyoto station. Singles ¥12,000-14,000, doubles ¥22,000, twins ¥17,000-33,000. A good range of on-site choices make this station-side hotel another decent choice in this bracket.

Kyoto Tokyū Hotel (☎ 341 2411, fax 341 2488) **Map 7** Transport: 15-minute walk from Kyoto station. Singles/doubles/twins from ¥12,000/24,000/20,000. This is a big, modern hotel with large rooms and good facilities.

Rihga Royal Hotel Kyoto (☎ 341 2311, fax 341 3037) **Map 10** Transport: 10-minute walk from Kyoto station. Singles ¥13,000-20,000, doubles ¥21,000-30,000, twins ¥18,000-30,000. Famous for its rooftop restaurant, this large hotel has a swimming pool and several good restaurants.

Eastern Kyoto

Hotels *Miyako Hotel (☎ 771 7111, fax 751 2490)* **Map 6** Transport: Tōzai line to Keage station. Singles/doubles/twins from ¥15,000/19,000/19,000, Japanese-style rooms from ¥28,000. The Miyako is a famous Western-style hotel perched on the hills and a classic choice for visiting foreign dignitaries. The hotel surroundings stretch over 6.4 hectares of wooded hillside and landscaped gardens.

Western Kyoto (Map 11)

Rankyō-kan Ryokan (☎ 871 0001) Transport: Keifuku Arashiyama line to Keifuku-Arashiyama station. Per person from ¥18,000 with two meals. Sitting in a secluded area on the south bank of the Oi-gawa in Arashiyama, this is a classic Japanese-style inn with manicured gardens, hot-spring baths and river views from most rooms. Walk five minutes up the riverside path or, better still, call ahead and be chauffeured by private boat from the Togetsu-kyō Bridge!

On the busier north side of Togetsu-kyō, there are several fine inns.

Arashiyama Benkei Ryokan (☎ 872 3355, fax 872 9310) Transport: Keifuku Arashiyama line to Keifuku-Arashiyama station. Per person from ¥20,000 with two meals. Like the aforementioned, this elegant ryokan has a pleasant riverside location and serves wonderful kaiseki cuisine.

Hotel Ran-tei (☎ 371 1119) Transport: Keifuku Arashiyama line to Keifuku-Arashiyama station. Per person ¥16,000-35,000. The excellent Ran-tei has spacious gardens and both Japanese- and Western-style rooms.

Kibune (Map 12)

The exquisite traditional inns in the small village of Kibune are famed for their riverside location and make a delightful escape from the city. They are renowned for fine seasonal cuisine, most notably *kawa-doko-ryōri* (above-river dining) – see the Places to Eat chapter for details. Kibune can be reached by taking the Eizan Dentetsu Eizan line to Kibune-guchi station.

Ryokan Ugenta (☎ 741 2146, fax 741 1068) Per person from ¥20,000 with two meals. The Ugenta is an attractive old inn with a wonderful stone bath tub.

Kibune Fujiya (☎ 741 2501, fax 741 1389) Per person from ¥20,000 with meals. This is another good ryokan with a lovely riverside location.

Hiroya Ryokan (☎ 741 2401, fax 741 3070) Per person from ¥30,000. A pleasant ryokan famous for its food. In winter they serve either a kaiseki or *botan-nabe* (wild boar) dinner, while in summer the fare is kawa-doko-ryōri.

Ōhara

Seryō Ryokan (☎ 744 2301) **Map 13** Transport: Kyoto bus No 17 or 18 to the Ōhara stop. Per person ¥13,000-20,000 with two meals. A stone's throw from Sanzen-in, this is a charming inn built in the *gasshō-zukuri* style (with a steeply pitched roof designed to keep snow from accumulating). The friendly owner can speak some English.

OTHER ACCOMMODATION
Shukubō

Myōren-ji (☎ 451 3527) **Map 3** Transport: bus No 9 to the Horikawa-Teranouchi stop. Per person ¥3500. No meals. This pleasant temple is used to dealing with foreign guests.

Shōhō-in (☎ 811 7768) **Map 7** Transport: Hankyū Kyoto line to Ōmiya station, or bus No 6 or 206 to the Ōmiya-Matsubara stop. Per person ¥5000 with breakfast. This temple also offers lessons in Japanese calligraphy. To inquire in English, call Ms Katō ☎ 090-3947-4520.

Hiden-in (☎ 561 8781) **Map 8** Transport: JR Nara line to Tōfukuji station, or bus No 208 to the Sennyuji-Michi stop. Per person ¥4500 with breakfast. This temple has a great location – it's near a lot of beautiful temples.

Women-Only Accommodation

Rokuō-in (☎ 861 1645) **Map 2** Transport: Keifuku Arashiyama line to Rokuōin station. Per person ¥4500 with breakfast. Close to Arashiyama, this is one of the few women-only shukubō in town.

There are several reasonable women-only hotels suitable for touring Kyoto's eastern Higashiyama area.

Lady's Hotel Chōraku-kan (☎ 561 0001) **Map 6** Transport: bus No 206 to the Higashiyama-Yasui stop. Per person ¥4500. Housed in a stately, late Meiji-era guesthouse, Lady's Hotel Chōraku-kan is central, near Maruyama-kōen.

Lady's Inn Sakata (☎ 541 2108) **Map 8** Transport: bus No 206 to the Higashiyama-yasui stop. Singles/doubles from ¥6500/11,000. Near the Ninen-zaka slope, this tiny place is good for those who want to hide away from the world.

Lady's Hotel Nishijin (☎ 415 1010) **Map 3** Transport: bus No 9 to the Horikawa-Teranouchi stop. Per person ¥4000. In the Nishijin garment district, this is a simple little hotel with a few years under its belt.

Arashiyama Lady's Hotel (☎ 882 0955, fax 882 1209) **Map 11** Transport: Keifuku Arashiyama line to Keifuku-Arashiyama station. Per person ¥3900. This decent hotel has Japanese- and Western-style rooms and is just beside the station.

Airport Hotels

Itami airport The best deal near Itami is *Hotel Crevette (☎ 06-6843 7201, fax 06-6843 0043)* Transport: free shuttle bus from airport. Singles/doubles/twins from ¥6500/15,000/12,000. Prices are discounted if you reserve through the main tourist information counter at the airport. The helpful folks at the information counter can also arrange for the hotel's shuttle bus to come and pick you up.

Kansai international airport The only hotel at the airport is the expensive *Hotel Nikkō Kansai Airport (☎ 0724-55 1111, fax 0724-55 1155)* Transport: walk from international arrivals hall. Singles/doubles/twins from ¥18,000/28,000/28,000. The rooms here are clean and new. You should definitely ask for a discount or promotional rate outside peak travel times.

LONG-TERM RENTALS

If you're planning on setting up shop in Kyoto, you can count on spending at least a month finding an acceptable place to live. We suggest booking a room in a place like the ISE Dorm or Greenpeace Inn Kyoto (see the earlier Budget section) while you look.

Once you're established in a decent guesthouse or 'gaijin house', you can start your search in earnest. The best places to look for houses and apartments are the message board of the KICH (see Useful Organisations in the Facts for the Visitor chapter) and the listings section of *Kansai Time Out*. There are additional listings in *Kansai Flea Market* and *Kansai Scene*. Word of mouth is also a great way to find a place, and the Pig & Whistle bar (see the Entertainment chapter) is where a lot of gaijin mouths congregate.

Another option is to approach a Japanese *fudōsan-yasan* (real estate agent). Unfortunately, this is where you're likely to find the worst form of anti-foreigner discrimination, for few fudōsan-yasan will rent to foreigners (unless you are married to a Japanese person). However, if you've got a work visa, some Japanese ability and a decent job, you just might find a fudōsan-yasan willing to deal with foreigners. You can easily locate them in any Kyoto neighbourhood by the lists of available apartments and houses that they post in their windows.

Kyoto rents average ¥40,000 per month for a room in a 'gaijin house' or around ¥65,000 for a whole house. Of course, as elsewhere in Japan, there are hidden fees like 'key money' and a damage deposit that may equal up to four month's rent. Some landlords do not require that you pay these fees (houses owned by these landlords are often passed down through the gaijin community by word of mouth).

Women might also consider the **YWCA** (☎ *431 0351*) **Map 5** Transport: Karasuma line to Marutamachi station. Room ¥27,000 per month, with kitchen & bathroom ¥35,000. Minimum three-month stay. This women-only dorm is a good place for longtermers *if* you can get a room – it's often full.

Places to Eat

Although it may not have the variety of New York or the reputation of Paris, we believe that Kyoto can hold its own with the world's great culinary capitals. Indeed, there are few cities in the world where you can eat as consistently well with so little effort.

Fans of Japanese food will, of course, find Kyoto a paradise – every type of Japanese cooking is well represented here. And fans of foreign food won't be disappointed – Kyoto boasts a wide array of Indian, Korean, Taiwanese, Italian and French restaurants.

Best of all, Kyoto provides an opportunity to experience the wonders of dining in a Japanese restaurant: attentive service, pleasant surroundings, careful preparation and exquisite presentation. Of course, it takes a bit of guts to charge into an unfamiliar restaurant, but the rewards awaiting you on the other side of the *noren* curtains are well worth the effort.

We present a wide selection of restaurants in this section, sorted according to location and price. Of course, the places listed here are only the tip of the iceberg; for an extended exploration of Kyoto's culinary delights, you can supplement the information here with the *Kyoto Visitor's Guide* (see Useful Publications in the Facts for the Visitor chapter) and Diane Durston's book *Old Kyoto: A Guide to Traditional Shops, Restaurants & Inns*. Both have listings of *kaiseki* and *kyō-ryōri* restaurants for those who feel like splashing out.

Also, keep in mind that all of Kyoto's department stores have *restauran-gai* (literally, 'restaurant towns') on their premises. Here, you'll find a wide variety of Japanese and foreign restaurants clustered together within the space of a few hundred metres. Most of these restaurants display daily specials outside and they're generally easier to enter than ordinary street-side restaurants.

For an explanation of Japanese dishes mentioned in this section, see the special section on Japanese cuisine in this chapter.

KYOTO STATION AREA (MAP 10)

The new Kyoto station building is chock-a-block with restaurants. For a quick cuppa while waiting for a train try *Café du Monde* on the second floor overlooking the central atrium. Or you might want to snag a few pieces of sushi off the conveyor belt at *Kaiten-zushi Iwamura*, on the ground floor at the east end of the station building.

For more substantial meals there are several food courts scattered about. On the 10th floor on the west side of the building the *Cootocco* food court has a variety of fast food restaurants, including *Bibimba Tai-ō*, which serves nice *bibimbap* (a Korean rice and vegetable dish) for ¥600.

Proper sit-down meals can be found in the two food courts on the 11th floor on the west side of the building: *The Cube* food court and Isetan department store's *Eat Paradise* food court (the latter is better for Japanese food).

You will also find a number of reasonable places in the basements of the buildings across from the station. Our favourite of these is *A Ri Shan* (☎ 344 1555) Dinner from ¥2500. Open 5pm-10.30pm. This Taiwanese *izakaya* serves a range of tasty little Chinese dishes like fried rice and dumplings.

Other choices near the station include: *Dai Ichi Asahi Rāmen* (☎ 351 6321) Rāmen from ¥600. Open 5am-2am, closed Thurs. The *rāmen* (noodles in broth with various toppings) is delicious at this unprepossessing rāmen joint that brings to mind the film *Tampopo*.

Shinpuku Saikan Rāmen (☎ 371 7648) Rāmen from ¥600. Open 7.30am-11pm, closed Wed. This classic rāmen joint is famous for its chicken-flavoured broth.

Iimura (☎ 351 8023) Set lunch ¥1000. Open noon-2pm. Try this classic little restaurant for its ever-changing set lunch. It's best to bring a Japanese speaker along to help interpret.

Suishin (☎ 365 0271) Dinner from ¥2000. Open 5pm-11.30pm. For a wide range of izakaya favourites, try this giant underground izakaya in front of Kyoto station. It's not much in terms of atmosphere or quality, but is convenient and cheap.

Second House (☎ *342 2555)* Coffee from ¥400. Open 10am-11pm. For a quick drink or a light meal near Nishi Hongan-ji, pop into this unusual coffee shop (it's built in an old bank).

KAWARAMACHI-KIYAMACHI AREA

The area between Oike-dōri and Shijō-dōri (north and south) and Kiyamachi-dōri and Karasuma-dōri (east and west) has the highest concentration of restaurants in the city. There's a wide range of both international and Japanese eateries in all price ranges. This is definitely the place for a night out in Kyoto.

Budget

Kyōhei (☎ *211 5700)* **Map 5** Rāmen from ¥600. Open 11am-7.45pm Mon-Fri, 11am-3pm Sun, closed Sat. People in the know have reported that this joint has the best rāmen in town – who are we to argue? It's near Kyoto City Hall.

Kōsendō-sumi (☎ *241 7377)* **Map 9** Lunch from ¥870. Open 11am-3pm, closed Sun & holidays. For a pleasant lunch while downtown, try this unpretentious little restaurant located in an old Japanese house. It serves a daily set lunch of simple Japanese fare. It's near the Museum of Kyoto.

Tagoto Honten (☎ *221 3030)* **Map 9** Noodle dishes from ¥700. Open 11am-9pm. This is one of Kyoto's oldest and most revered *soba* (thin, brown noodles) restaurants. It's in the Sanjō covered arcade.

Katsu Kura (☎ *212 3581)* **Map 9** Tonkatsu from ¥900. Open 11am-9pm. This restaurant in the Sanjō covered arcade is a good place to sample *tonkatsu* (deep fried breaded pork cutlets). It's not the best in Kyoto, but it's relatively cheap and casual.

Tenka-ippin **Map 4** Rāmen from ¥600. Open 4pm-5am. Try the *kotteri* (thick soup) rāmen with garlic at this brightly lit Kiyamachi rāmen house. Perfect for a snack after a night out in Kiyamachi.

Kane-yo (☎ *221 0669)* **Map 9** Unagi over rice ¥800. Open 11.30am-8.30pm. This is a good place to try *unagi* (eel). You can sit downstairs with a nice view of the waterfall or upstairs on the tatami. The *kane-yo donburi* set (¥800) is great value. Look for the barrels of live eels outside and the wooden facade.

A-Bar (☎ *213 2129)* **Map 9** Dishes from ¥500. Open 5pm-midnight. This student izakaya with a log-cabin interior is one of the best places in Kyoto for drinks and dinner. There's a big menu to choose from and everything's cheap. It's a little tough to find – look for the small black and white sign at the top of a flight of steps near a place called Reims.

Zappa (☎ *255 4437)* **Map 9** Dishes from ¥850. Open 6pm-midnight, closed Sun. Zappa is a cosy little place that is said to come recommended by David Bowie. The friendly owner, Hiroko-san, serves up savoury South-East Asian fare. Prices are reasonable and the music is groovy (but no Frank Zappa?). It's down a narrow alley between Kiyamachi-dōri and Kawaramachi-dōri; turn south at the wooden torii.

Musashi Sushi (☎ *222 0634)* **Map 9** All dishes ¥100. Open 11am-9.30pm. If you've never tried *kaiten-zushi*, don't miss this place. Look for the mini sushi conveyor belt in the window. It's just outside the entrance to the Sanjō covered arcade.

Biotei (☎ *255 0086)* **Map 9** Lunch ¥850. Open 11am-2pm, 5pm-midnight, closed Sun & Mon. Diagonally across from the Nakagyō post office, Biotei is a favourite of Kyoto vegetarians. Best for lunch, it serves a daily set of Japanese vegetarian food (the occasional bit of meat is offered as an option, but you'll be asked your preference).

Qu'il Fait Bon (☎ *254 8580)* **Map 9** Cakes from ¥500. Open 11am-8pm. For a quick cuppa or some tasty cakes, try this canal-side restaurant on Kiyamachi-dōri.

North of Oike-dōri are some more interesting choices.

Shin-shin-tei (☎ *221 6202)* **Map 5** Rāmen from ¥680. Open 10.30am-5pm, closed Sun & holidays. This place is famous for its *shiro* (white) miso rāmen. The building may not look like much, but the rāmen here is excellent.

Obanzai *(☎ 223 6623)* **Map 5** Lunch ¥840, dinner ¥2100. Open 11am-9pm. A little out of the way, but good value, Obanzai serves a fantastic buffet-style lunch/dinner of mostly organic food. It's north-west of the Karasuma-Oike crossing.

Okonomiyaki Mai *(☎ 223 2777)* **Map 5** Dinner from ¥600. Open 5pm-10.30pm, closed Sat. Pop into this homey little place behind the city hall for some good *okonomiyaki* (Japanese specialty involving a range of ingredients in batter).

Mid-Range

Kerala *(☎ 251 0141)* **Map 9** Lunch from ¥850, dinner from ¥3000. Open 11.30am-2pm, 5pm-9pm. The lunch sets at this reliable Kawaramachi-dōri Indian specialist are recommended. Dinners are a little overpriced.

Bistro de Paris *(☎ 256 1825)* **Map 5** Lunch from ¥1600, dinner from ¥2500. Open 11.30am-1.30pm, 5.30pm-9.30pm, closed Sun. We like this cramped little French spot for its authentic and carefully prepared fare. It's near the Shijō-Karasuma crossing.

Agatha *(☎ 223 2379)* **Map 9** Yakitori courses from ¥2000. Open 5pm-midnight. Creative twists on standard *yakitori* (skewers of grilled chicken) favourites are the draw at this foreigner-friendly restaurant on Kiyamachi-dōri.

Uontana *(☎ 221 2579)* **Map 9** Dinner from ¥3000. Open noon-3pm, 5pm-10pm, closed Wed. This slick upscale izakaya is a good spot to try a range of sake and elegantly presented Japanese fare. There is an English menu.

The 844 Store Café *(☎ 241 2120)* **Map 9** Dishes from ¥700. Open 5.30pm-11pm, closed Tues. Kyoto vegetarians like this offbeat cafe for specialties like veggie *gyōza* (Chinese dumplings). It's down a tiny alley near A-Bar (see the earlier Budget section).

Takasebune *(☎ 351 4032)* **Map 9** Lunch from ¥1000, dinner from ¥5000. Open 11am-3pm, 4.30pm-9.30pm, closed Mon. In a classic old Japanese house behind Hankyū department store, Takasebune serves fine

tempura sets for lunch or dinner. Prices depend on the amount of tempura you'd like. The sashimi is also good and there's a simple English menu.

Capricciosa *(☎ 221 7496)* **Map 9** Dinner from ¥1500. Open 11.30am-10.30pm. For heaping portions of acceptable Italian fare, you won't do much better than this longtime student favourite. It's near the Sanjō-Kawaramachi crossing.

Daniel's *(☎ 212 3268)* **Map 9** Mains ¥1500. Open 11.30am-3pm, 5.30pm-10pm. Behind Daimaru department store, this is the place to go for better Italian fare.

Merry Island Cafe *(☎ 213 0214)* **Map 9** Lunch ¥800. Open 11.30am-11pm, closed Mon. Behind the Kyoto Hotel, Merry Island is a good place for coffee or a light lunch. In warm weather the front doors are opened and the place takes on the air of a sidewalk cafe.

Zu Zu *(☎ 231 0736)* **Map 9** Dinner from ¥3000. Open 5pm-1am. This Ponto-chō izakaya is a fun place to eat and drink. The best bet is to ask the waiter for a recommendation. The fare is sort of nouveau-Japanese – things like shrimp and tōfu or chicken and plum sauce.

Tomi-zushi *(☎ 231 3628)* **Map 9** Dinner ¥3000. Open 5pm-midnight, closed third Thurs each month. For good sushi in lively surroundings try Tomi-zushi where you rub elbows with your neighbour, sit at a long marble counter and watch as some of the fastest sushi chefs in the land do their thing. Go early or wait in line. It's near the Shijō-Kawaramachi crossing.

Kappa Zushi *(☎ 213 4777)* **Map 9** Dinner ¥3000. Open 5pm-11pm. This is another popular sushi bar with fair prices and an English menu. It's on Pontochō-dōri.

Ganko Zushi *(☎ 255 1128)* **Map 9** Lunch ¥1000, dinner ¥3000. Open 11.30am-10.30pm. Near Sanjō-Ōhashi bridge, Ganko Zushi is a good place for sushi or just about anything else. Look for the large display of plastic food models in the window.

Ganko Nijō-en *(☎ 223 3456)* **Map 5** Lunch from ¥1500, dinner from ¥2500. Open 11.30am-9.30pm. This is an upscale branch of Ganko Zushi that serves sushi and kaiseki sets. There's a picture menu and you can also stroll in the stunning garden before or after your meal. It is near the Nijō-Kiyamachi crossing.

Ōiwa (☎ *231 7667*) **Map 5** Dinner ¥5000. Open 5pm-10pm, closed Wed. For excellent *kushi katsu* (skewered pork and vegetables fried) try Ōiwa, just south of the Fujita Hotel. Ordering is easy, just ask for the course (30 skewers) and say 'stop' when you're full (you'll only be charged for what you've eaten)

Sancho (☎ *211 0459*) **Map 9** Lunch/dinner from ¥1200. Open 11.30am-9pm. In a country where 'salad' usually means a mound of shredded cabbage, Sancho is a blessing; it serves up grilled chicken, meats and delicious salads on the side, or à la carte. It's near the Shijō-Kawaramachi crossing.

Shirukō (☎ *221 3250*) **Map 9** Lunch/dinner from ¥2600. Open 11.30am-8.30pm, closed Wed. For a light meal, Shirukō has been serving simple Kyoto *obanzai-ryōri* (home-style cooking) since 1932. The restaurant features more than 10 varieties of miso soup, and the rikyū bentō (¥2600) is a bona fide work of art. It's down a pedestrian street near Shijō-Kawaramachi crossing.

Misoka-an Kawamichi-ya (☎ *221 2525*) **Map 9** Dishes ¥700-3800. Open 11am-8pm, closed Thurs. For a taste of some of Kyoto's best soba noodles in traditional surroundings, head to Misoka-an Kawamichi-ya. They've been hand-making noodles here for 300 years. Try a simple bowl of *nishin* (topped with fish) soba, or the more elaborate *nabe* dishes (cooked in a special cast-iron pot).

Yamatomi (☎ *221 3268*) **Map 9** Dishes ¥150-2800. Open noon-2pm, 4pm-11pm, closed Mon. This is a fun spot on Pontochō-dōri where you can try your hand at the house special, *teppin-age*, frying up tasty tempura on skewers in a cast-iron pot (¥2800 per person).

Fujino-ya (☎ *221 2446*) **Map 9** Tempura set ¥2500. Open 5pm-10pm, closed Wed. Here you can feast on tempura, okonomiyaki, yaki-soba and kushi katsu in tatami rooms overlooking the Kamo-gawa. It's on Pontochō-dōri.

Top End

Uzuki (☎ *221 2358*) **Map 9** Dinner from ¥5000. Open 5pm-11pm, closed Wed. Uzuki is an elegant Ponto-chō kaiseki restaurant with a great platform for riverside dining in the summer.

Morita-ya (☎ *231 5118*) **Map 9** Dishes ¥8000. Open noon-11pm. This is Kyoto's most famous beef restaurant. It serves excellent *sukiyaki* and *shabu-shabu* in traditional tatami rooms, some overlooking the Kamo-gawa. It's on Kiyamachi-dōri.

Mishima-tei (☎ *221 0003*) **Map 9** Sukiyaki sets from ¥4400. Open 11.30am-11pm, closed Wed. In the Sanjō covered arcade, this is a cheaper place for sukiyaki. There is also an English menu.

Mukade-ya (☎ *256 7039*) **Map 5** Meals from ¥3000. Open 11am-2pm, 5pm-9pm, closed Wed. Mukade-ya is an atmospheric restaurant located in an exquisite kyō-machiya west of Karasuma-dōri. For lunch try the special bentō: two rounds (five small dishes each) of delectable *obanzai* fare (¥3000). Kaiseki courses start at ¥5000.

Yoshikawa (☎ *221 5544*) **Map 9** Lunch ¥2000-6000, dinner ¥6000-12,000. Open 11am-2pm, 5pm-8pm, closed Sun. For superb tempura head for Yoshikawa. It offers fancy table seating (¥6000/12,000 lunch/dinner), but it's much more interesting to sit and eat around the small counter (¥2000/6000) and observe the chefs at work. It's near Oike-dōri.

OTHER PARTS OF CENTRAL KYOTO (MAP 5)

Den Shichi (☎ *323 0700*) Lunch from ¥500, dinner from ¥4000. Open 11.30am-2pm, 5pm-10.30pm. This is our favourite sushi restaurant in Kyoto. It's a classic – long counter, bellowing sushi chefs and great fresh fish. The lunch sets are unbelievable value too. It's on Shijō-dōri in Saiin, about 100m west of Hankyū Saiin station.

Jūnidan-ya (☎ *211 5884*) Lunch/dinner from ¥1000. Open 11.30am-2.30pm, 5pm-8pm, closed Wed. This stylish Marutamachi-dōri restaurant is famous for its *ochazuke* (rice with Japanese tea poured over it – tastes better than it sounds).

PLACES TO EAT

Mankamerō (☎ 441 5020) Full meals ¥6000-30,000. Open noon-9pm. This place prepares traditional Kyoto cuisine and is well known for *cha-kaiseki* (a type of kaiseki cooking that accompanies the tea ceremony). It's located just west of Horikawa-dōri.

GION & KIYOMIZU-DERA AREA
Senmonten (☎ 531 2733) **Map 6** Ten dumplings for ¥460. Open 6pm-2am, closed Sun. This place serves only one thing: crisp fried *gyōza* (Chinese dumplings). They're the best in town.

Gonbei (☎ 791 4534) **Map 9** Noodle dishes from ¥630. Open 11.30am-10pm, closed Thurs. The English menu at this classic Gion noodle house makes ordering a breeze.

Imobō Hiranoya Honten (☎ 561 1603) **Map 6** Set meal ¥2400. Open 10.30am-8pm. Tucked inside the north gate of Maruyama-kōen, this traditional restaurant specialises in *imobō*, a dish consisting of a local type of sweet potato and dried fish. All meals are served in restful, private tatami rooms. There is an English menu.

Aunbo (☎ 525 2900) **Map 8** Lunch ¥2500, dinner ¥6000-10,000. Open noon-2pm, 5.30pm-11pm, closed Sun. Aunbo is an excellent establishment to sample creative Japanese cooking in traditional Gion surroundings. The delicious tasting menu is a feast for the eyes and the tastebuds. The lunch course is also praiseworthy. Aunbo takes reservations in the evening.

Minokō (☎ 561 0328) **Map 8** Lunch ¥4500, dinner ¥13,000. Open 11.30am-2.30pm, 5pm-8pm. This is another classic Gion restaurant serving lunch bentō and cha-kaiseki dinner.

NANZEN-JI AREA (MAP 6)
Hinode (☎ 751 9251) Noodle dishes from ¥400. Open 11am-7pm, closed Sun. Hinode serves filling noodle-and-rice dishes in a pleasant little shop with an English menu. Plain *udon* (thick white noodles) here is only ¥400, but we recommend you spring for the *nabeyaki udon* (pot-baked udon in broth) for ¥750.

Okutan (☎ 771 8709) Set meal ¥3000. Open 10.30am-6pm, closed Thurs. Just outside the precinct of Nanzen-ji you'll find Okutan, a restaurant inside the luxurious garden of Chōshō-in. This is a popular place that has specialised in vegetarian temple food for hundreds of years. Try a course of *yudōfu* (bean curd cooked in a pot) together with vegetable side dishes (¥3000).

Hyōtei (☎ 771 4116) Meals from ¥3500. This is one of Kyoto's oldest and most picturesque traditional restaurants. In the main building, you can sample exquisite kaiseki courses in private tearooms (¥18,000). The house speciality, *asa-gayu* (available 8am-10am, 1 Jul-31 Aug), is a variation on the traditional Japanese breakfast and features sumptuous rice porridge, seasonal vegetables, fresh fish and tōfu (¥4500); a similar *uzura-gayu* lunch special (available 11am-2pm, 12 Dec-15 Mar) features quail eggs in rice gruel (¥10,000). The restaurant has an annex in which both of these specials are served, as well as lovely bentō lunch and tōfu meals (¥3500). Stop by to pick up the restaurant's English brochure, which gives complete details.

KYOTO UNIVERSITY & GINKAKU-JI AREA
Budget travellers take heart: there *are* cheap places to eat in Kyoto. The neighbourhood around Kyoto University is crammed with good cheap restaurants, many of them along Imadegawa-dōri.

Eating House Hi-Lite (☎ 721 1997, **Map 6** Set meals from ¥500. Open 11am-10.30pm, closed Sun, second Sat each month & holidays. Kyoto University students cram into this popular *shokudō* (all-round restaurant) for filling set-course meals. Try the *cheezu chicken katsu teishoku* (fried chicken with cheese set meal) for ¥540; it's a little oily but how can you complain at these prices?

Tenka-ippin, Ginkaku-ji Branch (☎ 44. 1610) **Map 6** Rāmen from ¥600. Open 11am-3am, closed Sun. Try this tacky rāmen joint for filling sets of oily rāmen, dumplings and fried rice.

Café Carinho (☎ *752 3636*) **Map 6** Coffee from ¥400, lunch from ¥750. Open 9am-7.30pm, closed Mon. This tiny little cafe near Ginkaku-ji is great for strong coffee, good sandwiches and lovely pastries. The friendly owner speaks English.

Kuishinbō-no-Mise (☎ *712 0656*) **Map 6** Set meals from ¥500. Open noon-2pm, 6pm-11pm, closed Wed. Bring a large appetite to this cheap and filling shokudō near Ginkaku-ji. The daily lunch/dinner specials are a great value (ask for the *sabisu-teishoku*).

Yatai **Map 6** Dishes from ¥300. Open dusk to midnight. This little tent *(yatai)* pops up along Imadegawa-dōri every evening and serves a variety of foods to go, along with beer and sake. It's fun but don't expect any English to be spoken.

Matsuo (☎ *771 6345*) **Map 6** Rāmen ¥600. Open 11.30am-2.30pm, 5pm-9pm, closed Wed. This place specialises in *champon rāmen* (rāmen with a variety of meat and vegetables thrown in). It's a damn good bowl of noodles.

Tenka-ippin, Main Branch (☎ *722 0955*) **Map 9** Rāmen from ¥600. Open 11am-3pm, closed Thurs. This is the original store of Kyoto's most famous rāmen chain. We love the thick soup rāmen they serve here (but we didn't say it was healthy).

Gargantua (☎ *751 5335*) **Map 6** Lunch from ¥1500, dinner from ¥3000. Open noon-2pm, 5.30pm-10.30pm, closed Tues. This intimate French spot on Imadegawa-dōri has some creative takes on standard French dishes.

Kushi Hachi (☎ *751 6789*) **Map 6** Dinner from ¥2000. Open 5pm-11.30pm, closed Mon. This popular kushi katsu place has cheap prices and an English menu.

Kyoto University Student Cafeteria (*Kyōdai Shokudō*) **Map 6** Meals from ¥500. Open 8.20am-8pm Mon-Fri, 10am-2pm Sat, closed Sun & holidays, closed end of April to end of August. If you're on a tight budget, you can fill up here at this student cafeteria for a pittance. Technically it's for students only, but you won't be hassled. You might have to ask a student to point the way.

Hiragana-kan (☎ *701 4164*) **Map 4** Lunch/dinner from ¥800. Open 11.30am-9.30pm, closed Tues. This place, popular with Kyoto University students, dishes up creative variations on chicken, fish and meat. Most entrees come with rice, salad and miso soup for around ¥800. The menu is only in Japanese, but if you're at a loss for what to order try the tasty roll chicken katsu, a delectable and filling creation of chicken and vegetables.

Buttercups (☎ *751 9537*) **Map 6** Coffee from ¥300, meals from ¥580. Open 10am-11pm, closed Tues. Buttercups is a favourite of the local expat community and a great place for lunch, dinner or a cup of coffee. The menu is international. Look for the plants and whiteboard menu outside.

Omen (☎ *771 8994*) **Map 6** Noodles ¥900. Open 11am-10pm, closed Thurs. About five minutes' walk from Ginkaku-ji, Omen is a noodle shop that is named after the thick, white noodles served in a hot broth with a selection of seven fresh vegetables. Just say *'omen'* and you'll be given your choice of hot or cold noodles, a bowl of soup to dip them in and a plate of vegetables (you put these into the soup along with some sesame seeds). There is also an English menu.

MARUTAMACHI-DŌRI EAST OF THE KAMO-GAWA

Zac Baran (☎ *751 9748*) **Map 6** Dishes from ¥500. Open noon-4am. Near the Kyoto Handicraft Center, this is a good spot for a meal (try the dry curry special) or drink. It serves a variety of spaghetti dishes, as well as a good lunch special. Look for the picture of the Freak Brothers near the downstairs entrance. If you fancy dessert when you're done, step upstairs to the *Second House Cake Works*.

Earth Kitchen Company (☎ *771 1897*) **Map 5** Lunch ¥700. Open 10.30am-6.30pm, 10.30am-3.30pm Sat, closed Sun & holidays. Located on Marutamachi-dōri near the Kamo-gawa, the tiny Earth Kitchen Company seats just two people but does a bustling business serving tasty takeaway lunch bentō.

PLACES TO EAT

El Latino (☎ *751 0647*) **Map 6** Dinner from ¥2000. Open 6pm-midnight. El Latino is a fun little Mexican joint that serves good tacos, taqitos, guacamole and chips, and tasty frozen margaritas. It's located near the Higashiōji-Marutamachi crossing.

Ikarijō (☎ *751 7790*) **Map 6** Dinner ¥4000. Open 5pm-11pm, closed Sun. For an experience you won't soon forget, try Ikarijō, near the Sunflower Hotel. If it crawls, walks or swims, it's probably on the menu. The *inoshishi* (wild boar) barbecue is a good start. Non-meat eaters can try the fresh *ayu* (Japanese trout).

OTHER PARTS OF EASTERN KYOTO

Ichi-ban (☎ *751 1459*) **Map 9** Dinner from ¥3000. Open 5.30pm-midnight, closed Sun. This popular little yakitori joint on Sanjō-dōri has an English menu and a friendly young owner to help with ordering. Look for the yellow and red sign and the big lantern.

Dai-kitchi (☎ *771 3126*) **Map 6** Dishes ¥3000. Open 5pm-1am. The yakitori is good and the owner is friendly at this brightly-lit yakitori place on Sanjō-dōri. Look for the red lanterns outside.

Chishaku-in (☎ *531 0210*) **Map 8** Lunch ¥1500. Open 11am-6pm. Chishaku-in may be the cheapest place in town to sample shōjin-ryōri (Buddhist vegetarian cooking). It specialises in dishes made from konyaku (arum root). It's in the grounds of Chishaku-in, a few minutes walk east of the Kyoto National Museum.

Chabana (☎ *751 8691*) **Map 5** Okono-miyaki from ¥600. Open 5pm-4am. This is a classic okonomiyaki joint. If you don't have a favourite just ask for the mixed okonomiyaki (¥750). Good for a late-night snack. It's on Nijō-dōri. Look for the rotating light outside.

Mikō-an (☎ *751 5045*) **Map 5** Lunch ¥800, dinner ¥1000. Open 11am-11pm, 11am-10pm on Sun & holidays. Vegetarians should try this place for the daily set lunch or dinner set of mostly organic Japanese vegetarian fare. It's a catty spot (you'll see what we mean). It's on Kawabata-dōri north of Nijō-dōri.

NORTH-EASTERN KYOTO (MAP 4)

Speakeasy (☎ *781 2110*) Meals from ¥500. Open 9am-2am. Speakeasy is a foreigner's hangout in Shūgakuin, famous as the only place in town for a 'real' Western breakfast. It also serves good tuna melts, tacos and burgers. Look for the US flag outside.

Didi (☎ *791 8226*) Lunch from ¥750, dinner from ¥900. Open 11am-9.30pm, closed Wed. On Higashiōji-dōri, north of Mikage-dōri, you'll find this friendly little smoke-free restaurant serving passable Indian lunch/dinner sets.

Haruya (☎ *722 1782*) Lunch from ¥1000. Open noon-2.30pm and 5.30pm-8pm, noon-8pm on Sun & holidays, closed Thurs, Fri and lunchtime every second Sat each month. Up in the Kitayama-dōri area this place is one of Kyoto's gems. An all-natural eatery, it is run by a friendly young English-speaking couple. They serve up tasty international vegetarian food (great Indian curries) prepared with fresh seasonal vegetables. All ingredients are organic (even the wine!) and the woodsy, Japanese country-style decor is delightful.

Mago's (☎ *721 3443*) Lunch/dinner from ¥750. Open 11.30am-midnight, closed Mon. Mago's is a Western-style bistro that serves good sandwiches on fresh French bread or croissants.

NORTH-CENTRAL KYOTO

Honyaradō (☎ *222 1574*) **Map 5** Lunch ¥600. Open 10am-9pm. This woodsy place overlooking the Kyoto Imperial Palace Park is an institution, and has one of the best lunch deals in town (a daily stew set). It's a good place to relax over coffee and read a book.

NORTH-WESTERN KYOTO

A Ri Shan (☎ *465 7771*) **Map 5** Meals from ¥2000. Open 5pm-10pm. This is a fun Tai-wanese izakaya that serves a variety of small and tasty dishes. A picture menu is available. It's near the Imadegawa-Nishiōji crossing (Kitano Hakubaichō JR station).

Den Shichi (☎ *463 9991*) **Map 5** Sushi dinners from ¥3000. Open 11.30am-2pm,

5pm-10.30pm, closed Mon. This is near the Imadegawa-Nishiōji crossing (Kitano Hakubaichō), and is one of the better sushi restaurants in town (its sister restaurant is in Saiin).

Toyouke-jaya (☎ 462 3662) **Map 5** Meals from ¥650. Open 11am-3pm, closed Thurs. Locals line up for the tōfu lunch sets at this famous restaurant across from Kitano Tenman-gū.

Taco Tora (☎ 461 9292) **Map 5** Nine octopus balls ¥600. Open 5pm-2am, closed Mon. Try this spot for Kyoto's best *tako yaki* (fried octopus balls – no, not those balls). It's near Kitano-Tenman-gū.

Café Zinho (☎ 712 5477) **Map 3** Brazilian coffee ¥200, fejoada and rice ¥750. Open 9am-midnight. This tiny Brazilian-style restaurant is a good spot for a light meal or perhaps an evening drink when up north in Kyoto.

Saraca Nishijin (☎ 432 5075) **Map 3** Coffee from ¥400, lunch from ¥900. Open noon-10pm, closed Wed. It's well worth stopping in here just to see the unique interior – it's built inside an old *sentō* (public bathhouse) and the original tiles have been preserved. Check it out! It's near Funaoka Onsen.

Azekura (☎ 701 0161) **Map 3** Noodles from ¥800. Open 9am-5pm, closed Mon. Not far from Kamigamo-jinja, this place is an intriguing noodle shop/gallery in a converted Edo-period sake warehouse. The building features huge pine and cypress beams, earthen floors and an open hearth. Handmade soba noodles are the speciality.

Izusen (☎ 491 6665) **Map 3** Lunch ¥3000. Open 11am-4pm. Izusen, in the Daiji-in subtemple at Daitoku-ji, serves Zen vegetarian (*shōjin ryōri*) lunch. There are seven selections in vermilion-coloured lacquered bowls (*tepastu*) fashioned after monk's alms bowls.

Daitoku-ji Ikkyū (☎ 493 0019) **Map 3** Lunch from ¥3500. Open noon-6pm. In front of Daitoku-ji, this place boasts a 500-year history and is known for its special *natto* (fermented soybean) sauce. Try the basic lunch bentō for ¥3500.

Kanga-an (☎ 256 2480) **Map 3** Lunch ¥5000, dinner ¥8000. Open noon-3pm,

5pm-8pm. For Chinese-style banquet fare try Kanga-an, located in an atmospheric old building.

Kiyosu (☎ 231 5121) **Map 5** Dinner sets from ¥4000. Open 11.30am-1.30pm, 5pm-10pm, closed Mon. Kiyosu is a popular kaiseki-ryōri place. Try the courses (¥4000) or, for a light meal, the delightful vegetarian sushi à la carte (¥1000), which is made with *tsukemono* (Japanese pickles), including pickled eggplant, daikon and cucumber over vinegared rice.

ŌHARA (MAP 13)

Seryō-jaya (☎ 744 2301) Lunch sets from ¥1000. Open 11am-5pm. Just by the entry gate to Sanzen-in, Seryō-jaya serves wholesome *sansai ryōri* (mountain vegetable cooking), fresh river fish and soba noodles topped with grated yam.

Kumoi-jaya (☎ 744 2240) Meals from ¥800. Open 9am-5pm. Near Jakkō-in, Kumoi-jaya serves a delectable miso-based nabe (chicken stew; ¥2000) and has udon noodles (¥800).

Tamba-jaya (☎ 744 2527) Lunch from ¥1000. Open 10am-5pm. Also near Jakkō-in, this place dishes up great home-made udon – you can fill up on the *inaka-teishoku* (country cooking set; ¥1000).

KURAMA (MAP 12)

Near the gate to Kurama-dera are several places to grab lunch.

Yōshūji (☎ 741 2848) Meals from ¥1000. Open 10am-5.30pm, closed Tues. Yōshūji serves superb shōjin ryōri in a delightful old Japanese farmhouse with an *irori* (open hearth). The house special, a sumptuous selection of vegetarian dishes served in red lacquered bowls, is called *kurama-yama shōjin zen* (¥2500). Or if you just feel like a quick bite, try the *uzu-soba* (soba topped with mountain vegetables; ¥1000).

Aburaya-shokudō (☎ 741 2301) Meals from ¥800. Open 9.30am-5.30pm. Across the road from Yōshūji is another soba place specialising in local mountain vegetables. The *sansai teishoku* (¥1700) is a delightful selection of vegetables, rice and soba topped with grated yam.

Shōsai-an (☎ *741 3232)* Lunch ¥3500. Open 11.30am-2pm, closed Wed. Shōsai-an provides the chance to see the workings of an Edo-period townhouse. It serves a sumptuous yudōfu lunch course with vegetable tempura (¥3500).

KIBUNE (MAP 12)

Visitors to Kibune from June to September should not miss the chance to cool down by dining at one of the picturesque restaurants beside the Kibune-gawa. Known as *kawa-doko-ryōri,* meals are served on platforms suspended over the river as cool water flows just underneath. Most of the restaurants offer some kind of lunch special for around ¥3000. For a full kaiseki spread (¥5000-10,000) have a Japanese person call to reserve in advance. In the cold months you can dine indoors overlooking the river.

Nakayoshi (☎ *741 2000)* Lunch from ¥3500, dinner from ¥8500. Open 11am-9pm. One of the more reasonably priced restaurants is Nakayoshi, which serves a lunch bentō for ¥3500. Kaiseki dinners cost ¥8500.

Beniya (☎ *741 2041)* Meals from ¥6000. Open 11am-9pm. This elegant riverside restaurant serves kaiseki sets for ¥6000/8000/10,000 depending on size.

Tochigiku (☎ *741 5555)* Sukiyaki from ¥7000. Open 11.30am-9pm. Try this lovely riverside restaurant for sukiyaki and kaiseki sets.

Hirobun (☎ *741 2147)* Noodles ¥1200, kaiseki courses from ¥8000. Open 11am-7pm. If you don't feel like breaking the bank on a snazzy course lunch, head for this place. Here you can sample *nagashi-somen* (¥1200), thin white noodles that flow to you in globs down a split bamboo gutter; just pluck them out and slurp away.

ARASHIYAMA-SAGANO AREA (MAP 11)

Nakamuraya-no-Korokke Fried snacks from ¥60. Open 10am-5pm. For a quick snack before heading off temple-hopping, drop by Nakamuraya-no-Korokke, a tiny stand-and-eat stall across from the station. Grab a couple of tasty *korokke* (potato puffs; ¥60 each) or kushi katsu (¥100). Greasy but good.

Kushi-tei (☎ *861 0098)* Lunch from ¥2500, dinner from ¥3000. Open noon-10pm. Try the course of kushi katsu here for lunch or dinner.

Gyātei (☎ *862 2411)* Lunch ¥1500, dinner ¥2000. Open 11am-2.30pm, 5pm-9.50pm, closed Mon. Just beside the station, this place offers an all-you-can-eat lunch buffet of Japanese fare (over 30 dishes). In the evening, Gyātei turns into an izakaya, with à la carte choices (¥500) or a full-course tasting menu (¥3000).

Sunday's Sun (☎ *861 8836)* Lunch from ¥900 Open 7am-2am. If you fancy some Western food, then head into this casual 'family restaurant' for things like steak and chicken.

Seizansō-dō (☎ *861 1609)* Courses from ¥3000. Open 11.30am-5pm, closed Wed. For a sample of the area's acclaimed tōfu, try this place where the yudōfu teishoku is good value (¥3000). The seven-course meal includes a pot of fresh yudōfu and an array of tōfu-based dishes displaying the creative possibilities of the soya bean. As lunchtime hours can get packed here, take a number and be prepared to wait.

Togetsu-tei (☎ *871 1310)* Lunch from ¥2700. Open 11am-7pm. On the south side of Togetsu-kyō Bridge, Togetsu-tei has great riverside views. Try the delightful take-kago bentō basket with locally grown bamboo shoots (¥2700) or tōfu-ryōri courses (¥3500).

Rankyō-kan Ryokan (☎ *871 0001)* Lunch from ¥4000. Open 11am-3pm. Upriver from Togetsu-tei, Rankyō-kan has a fine lunchtime bentō (¥4000), and mini-kaiseki courses (¥5000). It even offers a soothing Japanese bath (¥300) to lunch guests, with a small towel supplied.

Bokuseki (☎ *862 2110)* Lunch from ¥1800. Open 10am-5pm, closed Wed. In the Sagano area, on the road up to Adashino Nembutsu-ji, Bokuseki serves a wholesome lunch set (¥1800).

Shigetsu (☎ *882-9725)* Lunch from ¥3000. Open 11am-2pm. To sample shōjin ryōri try Shigetsu in the precinct of Tenryū-ji. It has beautiful garden views.

continued on page 197

Cuisine

CUISINE

FRANK CARTER

FRANK CARTER

FRANK CARTER

Title Page: A neighbour-hood restaurant in Kyoto The *noren* (cloth banner) bears the name of the restaurant and indicates that the shop is open for business (Photograph by Stuart Wasserman).

Top: Selecting a meal from a conveyor belt at a rotary sushi bar.

Middle: Customers enjoy the restaurants' summer platforms overlooking the Kamo-gawa river.

Bottom: Plastic food on display in restaurants makes ordering a breeze.

STUART WASSERMAN

Those familiar with Japanese food *nihon ryōri* know that eating is half the fun of travelling in Japan. Even if you've already tried some of Japan's better-known specialities in Japanese restaurants in your own country, you're likely to be surprised by how delicious the original is when served on its home turf. More importantly, the adventurous eater will be delighted to find that Japanese food is far more than just sushi, tempura or sukiyaki. Indeed, it could be possible to spend a month in Japan and sample a different speciality restaurant every night.

Variety, though, is fairly new to Japan. Until the beginning of the 20th century, Japanese food was basic at best (at least among the farming masses); a typical meal consisted of a bowl of rice, some *miso-shiru* (miso soup), a few pickled vegetables and, if one was lucky, some preserved fish. As a Buddhist nation, meat was not eaten until the Meiji Restoration of 1868. Even then, it took some getting used to. Early accounts of Japan's first foreign residents are rife with horrified stories of the grotesque dietary practices of 'the barbarians' including the 'unthinkable' consumption of milk!

These days the Japanese have gone to the opposite extreme and have heartily embraced foreign cuisine. Unfortunately this often means a glut of fast-food restaurants in the downtown areas of cities. In fact, there are so many branches of McDonald's that the president of McDonald's Japan once remarked that it was only a matter of time before Japanese youth started growing blonde hair.

Those in search of a truly Japanese experience will probably want to avoid Western-style fast food, in favour of sampling authentic Japanese cuisine. Luckily this is quite easy to do, although some may baulk at charging into a restaurant where both the language and the menu are likely to be incomprehensible. The best way to get over this fear is to familiarise yourself with the main types of Japanese restaurants so that you have some idea of what's on offer and how to order it. Those timid of heart should take solace in the fact that the Japanese will go to extraordinary lengths to understand what you want and will help you to order.

GLENN BEANLAND

Right: Preparation and presentation are two essential concepts in Japanese cuisine.

CUISINE

With the exception of *shokudō* (all-round restaurants) and *izakaya* (pub-style restaurants), most Japanese restaurants concentrate on a speciality cuisine. This naturally makes for delicious eating, but does limit your choice. The following will introduce the main types of Japanese restaurants, along with a menu sample of some of the most common dishes served. With a little courage and effort you will soon discover that Japan is a gourmet paradise where good food is taken seriously.

Kyoto Specialities

Kyoto is justifiably famous for its cuisine. Kyoto specialities include *kyō-ryōri*, *shōjin-ryōri* and *tōfu-ryōri* (see the following sections for an explanation of these). Kyoto is also known for its wealth of *kaiseki* restaurants, some of which serve a type of kaiseki known as *cha-kaiseki*, which traditionally accompanied the tea ceremony but now often stands alone (see the Kaiseki section later). *Obanzai-ryōri* is another type of food common in Kyoto. It refers to a range of dishes typically served in Japanese homes. For advice on where to sample these cuisines, see the Places to Eat chapter.

Kyō-ryōri *Kyō-ryōri*, or Kyoto cuisine, is a style of cooking that evolved out of Kyoto's landlocked location and the age-old customs of the imperial court. The preparation of dishes makes ingenious use of fresh seasonal vegetables and emphasises subtlety, revealing the natural flavours of the ingredients. Kyō-ryōri is selected according to the mood and hues of the ever-changing seasons, and the presentation and atmosphere are as important as the flavour.

Shōjin-ryōri Another style of cooking for which Kyoto is renowned is *shōjin-ryōri*. This is a vegetarian cuisine (no meat, fish, eggs or dairy products are used), which was introduced from China along with Buddhism and is now available in special restaurants usually connected with temples. As it is a style of cooking that has its origins in Buddhist asceticism, don't expect a hearty affair – great attention is given to presentation and servings tend to be small.

Typically, the meal will include a variety of fresh vegetables such as boiled *daikon* (radish). Tōfu also plays a prominent role in the menu. For a meal of this type, several Kyoto temples offer lunch courses from around ¥3000. Most shōjin-ryōri restaurants require reservations a few days in advance and in some cases a minimum of four people.

Another variation on shōjin-ryōri is the Chinese-influenced *fucha-ryōri*, and there are a handful of places in Kyoto where you can sample this fare.

Tōfu-ryōri Kyoto is famed for its tōfu (soybean curd). There are numerous tōfu makers *(tōfu-ya-san)* scattered throughout the city and a legion of exquisite *yudōfu* (boiled tōfu) restaurants – many are concentrated along the road into Nanzen-ji and in the Arashiyama area. One typical Kyoto tōfu byproduct, *yuba*, is a sheet of the chewy thin film which settles on the surface of vats of simmering soy milk.

Eating Etiquette

When it comes to eating in Japan, there are a number of implicit rules but they're fairly easy to remember. If you're worried about putting your foot in it, relax – the Japanese almost expect foreigners to make fools of themselves in formal situations and are unlikely to be offended, as long as you follow the rules of politeness standard in your own country.

Among the more important eating 'rules' are those regarding chopsticks. Sticking them upright in your rice is very bad form – that's how rice is offered to the dead! It's also bad form to pass food from your chopsticks to someone else's – another Buddhist funeral rite which involves passing the remains of the cremated deceased among members of the family using chopsticks.

It's worth remembering that a lot of effort has gone into the preparation of the food so don't pour soy sauce all over it (especially the rice) and don't mix it up with your chopsticks. Also, if possible, eat everything you are given. And don't forget to slurp your noodles!

When eating with other people, especially when you're a guest, it is polite to say *'Itadakimasu'* (literally, 'I will receive') before digging in. This is as close as the Japanese come to saying grace. Similarly, at the end of the meal you should thank your host by saying *'Gochisō-sama deshita'*.

When drinking, it is impolite to fill your own glass; fill that of the person next to you and wait for them to reciprocate. Filling your own glass amounts to admitting to everyone at the table that you're an alcoholic. Raise your glass a little off the table while it is being filled. Once everyone's glass is full, the usual starting signal is a chorus of *'kampai'* which means 'cheers!'. Constant topping up means a bottomless glass – just put your hand over your glass if you've had enough.

There is also a definite etiquette to bill-paying. If someone invites you to eat or drink with them, they will be paying. Even among groups eating together it is unusual for bills to be split. The exception to this is found among young people and close friends and is called *warikan* (each person paying their own share). Generally, at the end of the meal something of a struggle will ensue to see who gets the privilege of paying. It is polite to at least make an effort to pay – it is extremely unlikely that your Japanese 'hosts' will acquiesce.

CC

Eating in a Japanese Restaurant

When you enter a restaurant in Japan, you'll be greeted with a hearty *'Irasshaimase!'* ('Welcome!'). In all but the most casual places the waiter will next ask you *'Nan-mei sama?'* ('How many people?'). Answer with your fingers, which is what the Japanese do. You will be led to a table, a place at the counter or a *tatami* (straw mat) room.

At this point you will be given an *oshibori* (hot towel), a cup of tea and a menu. The oshibori is for cleaning your hands (while actually considered bad form, many Japanese men wipe their faces as well). When you're done with it, just roll or fold it up and leave it next to your place. Now comes the hard part: ordering. If you don't read Japanese, you can use the romanised translations in this book to help you, or direct the waiter's attention to the Japanese script. If this doesn't work, there are two phrases that may help: *'O-susume wa nan desu ka?'* ('What do you recommend?') and *'O-makase shimasu'* ('Please decide for me').

When you've finished eating, ask for the bill by saying *'O-kanjō kudasai'*. Remember that there is no tipping in Japan and tea is provided free of charge. Usually you will be given a bill to take to the cashier at the front of the restaurant. At more upmarket places, the host of the party will discreetly pay before the group leaves. Unlike in the West, don't leave cash on the table. Only bigger and international places take credit cards.

When leaving, it is polite to say to the restaurant staff, *'Gochisō-sama deshita'* which means 'It was a real feast'.

Shokudō 食堂

A *shokudō* (eating place) is the most common type of restaurant, and is found near train stations, tourist spots and just about any other place where people congregate. Easily distinguished by the presence of plastic models of dishes in the window, these inexpensive places usually serve a variety of *washoku* (Japanese) and *yoshoku* (Western) foods.

At lunch, and sometimes dinner, the easiest way to order at a shokudō is to order a *teishoku* (set course meal), which is sometimes also called *ranchi setto* (lunch set), or *kōsu*. This usually includes a main dish of meat or fish, a bowl of rice, miso, shredded cabbage and a few Japanese pickles called *tsukemono*. In addition, most *shokudō* serve a fairly standard selection of *donburi-mono* (rice dishes) and *menrui* (noodle dishes). When you order noodles, you can choose between either *soba* or *udon*, both of which are served with a number of different toppings. If you're at a loss as to what to order, simply tell the waiter *'kyō-no-ranchi'* ('today's lunch') and they'll do the rest. You can expect to spend about ¥800 to ¥1000 for a meal at a shokudō.

Rice Dishes どんぶり

katsu-don	カツ丼	rice topped with a fried pork cutlet
oyako-don	親子丼	rice topped with egg and chicken
niku-don	肉丼	rice topped with thin slices of cooked beef
ten-don	天丼	rice topped with tempura shrimp and vegetables

Noodle Dishes 麺類

soba	そば	buckwheat noodles
udon	うどん	white wheat noodles
kake	かけ	plain noodles in broth
kitsune	きつね	noodles with fried tofu
tempura	天ぷら	noodles with tempura shrimp
tsukimi	月見	noodles with raw egg on top

Izakaya 居酒屋

An izakaya is the Japanese equivalent of a pub. It's a good place to visit when you want a casual meal, a wide selection of food, a hearty atmosphere and, of course, plenty of beer and sake. You are given the choice of sitting around the counter, at a table or on a tatami floor. You usually order a bit at a time, choosing from a selection of typical Japanese foods like *yakitori*, *sashimi* and grilled fish, as well as Japanese interpretations of Western foods like French fries and beef stew.

Izakaya can be identified by their rustic facades, and the red lanterns outside their doors bearing the kanji for izakaya. Since izakaya food is casual fare to go with drinking, it is usually fairly inexpensive. Depending on how much you drink, you can expect to get away with ¥2500 to ¥5000 per person. The following dishes (as well as others in the Yakitori and Sushi headings later) are available at an izakaya.

agedashi-dōfu	揚げだし豆腐	deep fried tofu in a fish stock soup
jaga-batā	ジャガバター	baked potatoes with butter
niku-jaga	肉じゃが	beef and potato stew
shio-yaki-zakana	塩焼魚	a whole fish grilled with salt
yaki-onigiri	焼きおにぎり	a triangle of grilled rice with yakitori sauce
poteto furai	ポテトフライ	French fries
chiizu-age	チーズ揚げ	deep fried cheese
hiya-yakko	冷奴	a cold block of tofu with soy sauce and scallions
tsuna sarada	ツナサラダ	tuna salad over cabbage
yaki-soba	焼きそば	fried noodles with meat and vegetables
kata yaki-soba	固焼きそば	hard fried noodles with meat and vegetables
sashimi mori-awase	刺身盛り合わせ	a selection of sliced sashimi

Robatayaki ろばた焼き

Similar to an izakaya; robatayaki means 'hearthside cooking' and every effort is made in these restaurants to re-create the atmosphere of an old country house – which was always centred around a large hearth or irori.

Eating at a robatayaki restaurant is a feast for the eyes as well as the taste buds; you sit around a counter with the food spread out in front of you on a layer of ice, behind which is a large charcoal grill. You don't need a word of Japanese to order. There are menus, but no-one uses them – just point and eat. The chef will grill your selection and pass it to you on a long wooden paddle – grab your food quickly before he snatches it back. Some of the best robatayaki chefs are real performers and make a show of cooking the food and serving customers. You'll wonder how no-one winds up getting injured by flying food.

The drink of choice is beer or sake. Expect to spend about ¥3000 per head. Not as common as izakaya, robatayaki usually have rustic wooden facades modelled on traditional Japanese farmhouses.

Okonomiyaki お好み焼き

The name means 'cook what you like', and an *okonomiyaki* restaurant provides you with an inexpensive opportunity to do just that. Sometimes described as Japanese pizza or pancake, the resemblance is in form only. At an okonomiyaki restaurant you sit around a *teppan* (an iron hotplate) armed with a spatula and chopsticks to cook your choice of meat, seafood and vegetables in a cabbage and vegetable batter.

Some places will do most of the cooking and bring the nearly finished product over to your hotplate for you to season with *katsuo bushi* (bonito flakes), *shōyu* (soy sauce), parsley, Japanese Worcestershire-style sauce (*sōso*) and mayonnaise. Cheaper places will simply hand you a bowl filled with the ingredients and expect you to cook it for yourself. If this happens, don't panic. First, mix the batter and filling thoroughly, then place it on the hot grill, flattening it into a pancake shape. After five minutes or so, use the spatulas to flip it and cook for another five minutes. Then dig in.

Most okonomiyaki places also serve *yaki-soba* (fried noodles) and *yasai-itame* (stir-fried vegetables). All of this is washed down with mugs of draft beer. Don't worry too much about preparation of the food – the waiter will keep an eye on you to make sure no disasters occur.

mikkusu okonomiyaki	ミックス焼き	mixed fillings of seafood, meat and vegetables
modan-yaki	モダン焼き	okonomiyaki with fried egg
ika okonomiyaki	いかお好み焼き	squid okonomiyaki
gyū okonomiyaki	牛お好み焼き	beef okonomiyaki
yasai okonomiyaki	野菜お好み焼き	vegetable okonomiyaki
negi okonomiyaki	ネギお好み焼き	thin okonomiyaki with scallions

Yakitori 焼き鳥

Yakitori means 'skewers of grilled chicken', a popular after-work meal. Yakitori is not so much a full meal as it is an accompaniment for beer and sake. At a *yakitori-ya* (yakitori restaurant) you sit around a counter with the other patrons and watch the chef grill your selections over charcoal. The best way to eat here is to order a few skewers of several varieties and then order seconds of the ones you really like. One serving often means two or three skewers (be careful – the price listed on the menu is usually that of a single skewer).

In summer, the beverage of choice at a yakitori restaurant is beer or cold sake, while in winter it's hot sake. A few drinks and enough skewers to fill you up should run from ¥3000 to ¥4000 per person. Yakitori restaurants are usually small places, often near train stations, and are best identified by a red lantern outside and the smell of grilling chicken.

yakitori	焼き鳥	plain, grilled white meat
hasami/negima	はさみ／ねぎま	pieces of white meat alternating with leek
sasami	ささみ	skinless chicken breast pieces
kawa	皮	chicken skin
tsukune	つくね	chicken meat balls
gyū-niku	牛肉	pieces of beef
rebā	レバー	chicken livers
tebasaki	手羽先	chicken wings
shiitake	しいたけ	Japanese mushrooms
piiman	ピーマン	small green peppers
tama-negi	たまねぎ	round, white onions

Right: *Yakitori* skewers grilled to perfection over hot coals, and *tsukune* meatballs, all usually washed down with a cold beer. Yakitori restaurants and stands are popular early-evening gathering places for office workers who stop for a quick snack before the train ride home.

GLENN BEANLAND

Sushi & Sashimi 寿司／刺身

Like yakitori, sushi is considered an accompaniment for beer and sake. Nonetheless, both the Japanese and foreigners often make a meal of it and it's one of the healthiest meals around. Although sushi is now popular in the West, few foreigners are prepared for the delicacy and taste of the real thing. Without a doubt, this is one dish that the visitor to Japan should sample at least once.

There are two main types of sushi: *nigiri-zushi* (served on a small handful of rice – the most common variety) and *maki-zushi* (served in a seaweed roll). Lesser known varieties include *chirashi-zushi* (a layer of rice covered in egg and fish toppings), *oshi-zushi* (fish pressed in a mould over rice) and *inari-zushi* (rice in a pocket of sweet, fried tōfu). Whatever kind of sushi you try, it will be served with lightly vinegared rice. In the case of nigiri-zushi and maki-zushi, it will contain a bit of *wasabi* (hot, green horseradish).

Sushi is not difficult to order. If you sit at the counter you can simply point at what you want, as most of the selections are in a refrigerated glass case between you and the sushi chef. You can also order a la carte from the menu. *Ichi-nin mae* (one portion) usually means two pieces of sushi but be careful – the price on the menu will be that of only one piece. If you like, you can take care of your whole order with an assort-ment plate of nigiri-zushi called a *mori-awase*. These usually come in three grades: *futsū nigiri* (regular nigiri), *jō nigiri* (special nigiri) and *toku-jō nigiri* (extra special nigiri). The difference is in the type of fish used. Most mori-awase contain six or seven pieces of sushi. Of course you can order fish without the rice, in which case it is called sashimi.

Be warned that a good sushi restaurant can cost upwards of ¥10,000, while an average place can run to ¥3000 to ¥5000 per person. One way to sample the joy of sushi on the cheap is to try an automatic sushi place, usually called *kaiten-zushi*, where the sushi is served on a conveyor belt which runs along a counter. Here you simply reach up and grab whatever looks good. You're charged for how many plates of sushi you eat. Plates are colour-coded according to price and the cost is written either on the plate itself or on a sign on the wall. You can usually fill yourself up in one of these places for ¥1000 to ¥2000 per person. Kaiten-zushi places are often distinguished by miniature conveyor belts in the window while regular sushi restaurants often have fish tanks in the window or a white lantern with the char-acters for sushi written in black letters.

Before popping the sushi into your mouth, dip it in *shōyu* (soy sauce) which you pour from a small decanter into a low dish specially provided for the purpose. If you're not good at using chopsticks, don't worry, sushi is one of the few foods in Japan that it is perfectly ac-ceptable to eat with your hands. Slices of *gari* (pickled ginger) will also be served to help refresh the palate. The beverage of choice with sushi is beer or sake (hot in the winter and cold in the summer), with a cup of green tea at the end of the meal.

ama-ebi	甘海老	sweet shrimp
awabi	あわび	abalone
ebi	海老	prawn or shrimp
hamachi	はまち	yellowtail
ika	いか	squid
ikura	イクラ	salmon roe
kai-bashira	貝柱	scallop
kani	かに	crab
katsuo	かつお	bonito
maguro	まぐろ	tuna
tai	鯛	sea bream
tamago	たまご	sweetened egg
toro	とろ	the choicest cut of fatty tuna belly, very expensive
unagi	うなぎ	eel with a sweet sauce
uni	うに	sea urchin roe

Sukiyaki & Shabu-shabu しゃぶしゃぶ

Restaurants usually specialise in both these dishes. Popular in the West, sukiyaki is a favourite of most foreign visitors to Japan. When made with high-quality beef, like Kōbe beef, it is a sublime experience. Sukiyaki consists of thin slices of beef cooked in a broth of soy sauce, sugar and sake and is accompanied by a variety of vegetables and tōfu. After cooking, all the ingredients are dipped in raw egg (the heat of the ingredients tends to lightly cook the egg) before being eaten.

Shabu-shabu consists of thin slices of beef and vegetables cooked by swirling the ingredients in a light broth and then dipping them in a variety of special sesame seed and citrus-based sauces. Both of these dishes are prepared in a pot over a fire at your private table – the waiter or waitress will usually help you get started and then keep a close watch as you proceed. The key is to take your time and add the ingredients a little at a time, savouring the flavours as you go.

Right: Freshly made *zaru-soba*, buckwheat noodles served cold on a bamboo screen and sprinkled with *nori* (seaweed), is a warm-weather favourite.

GLENN BEANLAND

Sukiyaki and shabu-shabu restaurants usually have a traditional Japanese decor and sometimes a picture of a cow to help you recognise them. Ordering is not difficult. Simply say sukiyaki or shabu-shabu and indicate how many people's worth of food is required. Expect to pay between ¥3000 to ¥10,000 per person.

Tempura 天ぷら

Tempura's origins aren't Japanese at all; in fact, the cooking style was borrowed from Portuguese traders and missionaries of the 16th century. Since then, the Japanese have refined the speciality into something uniquely their own. Good tempura is portions of fish, prawns and vegetables cooked in fluffy, non-greasy batter.

When you sit down at a tempura restaurant, you will be given a small bowl filled with *ten-tsuyu* (a light brown sauce) and a plate of grated *daikon* (white radish); you mix this into the sauce. Dip each piece of tempura into this sauce before eating it. Tempura is best when it's hot, so don't wait too long – use the sauce to cool each piece and dig in.

While it's possible to order a la carte, most diners choose to order a teishoku (full set), which includes rice, miso-shiru and Japanese pickles. Some tempura restaurants also offer courses which include different numbers of tempura pieces.

Expect to pay between ¥2000 and ¥10,000 for a full tempura meal. Finding these restaurants is tricky as they have no distinctive facade or decor. If you look through the window you'll see customers around the counter watching the chefs as they work over large woks filled with oil.

tempura moriawase	天ぷら盛り合わせ	a selection of tempura
shōjin age	精進揚げ	vegetarian tempura
kaki age	かき揚げ	tempura with shredded vegetables or fish

Rāmen ラーメン

The Japanese imported this dish from China and put their own spin on it to make what is one of the world's most delicious fast foods. *Rāmen* dishes are big bowls of noodles in a meat broth served with a variety of toppings, such as sliced pork, bean sprouts and leeks. You may be asked if you'd prefer *kotteri* (thick) or *assari* (thin) soup. Other than this, ordering is simple: just sidle up to the counter and say *'Rāmen'*, or ask for any of the other choices usually on offer. Expect to pay between ¥500 and ¥900 for a bowl. Since rāmen is originally Chinese food, some rāmen restaurants also serve *chāhan* or *yaki-meshi* (fried rice), *gyōza* (dumplings) and *kara-age* (deep-fried chicken pieces).

Rāmen restaurants are recognisable by their long counters lined with customers hunched over steaming bowls. You can sometimes hear a rāmen shop as you wander by – it's considered polite to slurp the noodles and aficionados claim that it brings out the full flavour of the broth.

rāmen	ラーメン	standard issue, the cheapest item on the menu – soup and noodles with a sprinkling of meat and vegetables
chāshū-men	チャーシューメン	rāmen topped with slices of roasted pork
wantan-men	ワンタンメン	rāmen with meat dumplings
miso-rāmen	味噌ラーメン	rāmen with miso-flavoured broth
chānpon-men	チャンポンメン	Nagasaki-style rāmen with assorted vegetables and meat in the broth

Soba & Udon そば／うどん

Soba and udon are the Japanese answer to Chinese-style rāmen. Soba noodles are thin, brown, buckwheat noodles; udon noodles are thick, white, wheat noodles. Most Japanese noodle shops serve both noodles prepared in a variety of ways. The noodles are usually served in a bowl containing a light, bonito-flavoured broth, but you can also order them served cold and piled on a bamboo screen with a cold broth for dipping.

By far the most popular type of cold noodles is *zaru soba*, which is served with bits of *nori* (seaweed) on top. If you order these you'll receive a small plate of wasabi and sliced scallions – put these into the cup of broth and eat the noodles by dipping them in this mixture. At the end of your meal, the waiter will give you some hot broth to mix with the leftover sauce which you drink like a kind of tea. As with rāmen, feel free to slurp as loudly as you please.

Soba and udon places are usually quite cheap (about ¥900), but some fancy places can be significantly more expensive (the decor is a good indication of the price). See under Shokudō for more soba and udon dishes.

| zaru soba | ざるそば | cold noodles with seaweed strips served on a bamboo tray |

Unagi うなぎ

Unagi, or eel, is an expensive and popular delicacy in Japan. Even if you can't stand the creature back home, you owe it to yourself to try unagi at least once while in Japan. It's cooked over hot coals and brushed with a rich mix of soy sauce and sake. Full unagi dinners can be expensive, but many unagi restaurants offer *unagi bentō* (boxed lunches) and lunch sets for around ¥1500. Most unagi restaurants display plastic models of their sets in their front windows and have barrels of live eels to entice passers-by.

unagi teishoku	うなぎ定食	full set meal with rice, grilled eel, eel-liver soup and pickles
unadon	うな丼	grilled eel over a bowl of rice
unajū	うな重	grilled eel over a flat tray of rice (larger than unadon)
kabayaki	蒲焼	skewers of grilled eel without rice

Nabemono 鍋物

A *nabe* is a large cast-iron cooking pot and *nabemono* refers to any of a variety of dishes cooked in these pots. Like sukiyaki and shabu-shabu, nabemono are cooked at your table on a small gas burner or a clay *hibachi*. Eating nabemono is a participatory experience, with each diner putting in ingredients from trays of prepared, raw food. The most famous nabemono is called *chanko-nabe*, the high-calorie stew eaten by sumo wrestlers during training. Chanko-nabe restaurants are often run by retired sumo wrestlers who festoon the walls with sumo arcana.

 Since nabemono are filling and hot, they are usually eaten during winter. They are also popular as banquet and party dishes since the eating of a nabe dish is a very communal experience. It is difficult to pick out a nabe restaurant – the best way is to ask a Japanese friend for a recommendation.

mizutaki	水炊き	clear soup stew with chicken, fish and vegetables. Served with vinegared sauce
sukiyaki	すき焼き	soy sauce based stew with thinly sliced beef and vegetables. Often dipped in raw egg.
chanko-nabe	ちゃんこ鍋	sumo wrestlers' stew of meat and vegetables
botan-nabe	ぼたん鍋	wild boar stew with vegetables
yose-nabe	寄せ鍋	seafood and chicken stew with vegetables

Fugu ふぐ

The deadly *fugu*, or globefish, is eaten more for the thrill than the taste. It's actually rather bland – most people liken the taste to chicken – but acclaimed for its fine texture. Nonetheless, if you have the money to lay out for a fugu dinner (around ¥10,000), it makes a good 'been there, done that' story back home.

 Although the danger of fugu poisoning is negligible, some Japanese joke that you should always let the other person try the first piece – if they are still talking after five minutes, consider it safe and have some yourself. If you need a shot of liquid courage to get started, try a glass of *hirezake* (toasted fugu tail in hot sake) – the traditional accompaniment to a fugu dinner.

 Fugu is a seasonal delicacy best eaten in winter. Fugu restaurants usually serve only fugu and can be identified by a picture of a fugu on the sign out the front.

fugu teishoku	ふぐ定食	a set course of fugu served several ways, plus rice and soup
fugu chiri	ふぐちり	a stew made from fugu and vegetables
fugu sashimi	ふぐ刺身	thinly sliced raw fugu
yaki fugu	焼きふぐ	fugu grilled on a hibachi at your table

Tonkatsu トンカツ

Tonkatsu is a deep-fried breaded pork cutlet served with a special sauce, usually as part of a set meal (tonkatsu teishoku). Tonkatsu is served both at speciality restaurants and at shokudō. Naturally, the best tonkatsu is to be found at the speciality places, where a full set will run from ¥1500 to ¥2500. When ordering, you can choose between *rōsu*, a fatter cut and *hire*, a leaner cut of pork.

tonkatsu teishoku	トンカツ定食	a full set meal of tonkatsu, rice, miso-shiru and shredded cabbage
minchi katsu	ミンチカツ	minced pork cutlet
hire katsu	ヒレカツ	tonkatsu fillet
kushikatsu	串カツ	deep-fried pork and vegetables on skewers

Kushiage & Kushikatsu 串揚げ／串カツ

Dieters beware, this is the fried food to beat all fried foods. *Kushiage* and *kushikatsu* are deep-fried skewers of meat, seafood and vegetables eaten as an accompaniment to beer. *Kushi* means 'skewer' and if food can be fitted on to one, it's probably on the menu. Cabbage is often eaten with the meal, a clever way to ease the guilt of eating all that grease.

You order kushiage and kushikatsu by the skewer (one skewer is *ippon*, but you can always use your fingers to indicate how many you want). Like yakitori, this food is popular with after-work salarymen and students and is therefore fairly inexpensive, though upmarket places exist. Expect to pay from ¥2000 to ¥5000 for a full meal and a couple of beers. Not particularly distinctive in appearance, the best way to find a kushiage and kushikatsu place is to ask a Japanese friend.

ebi	海老	shrimp
ika	いか	squid
renkon	レンコン	lotus root
tama-negi	たまねぎ	white onion
gyū-niku	牛肉	beef pieces
shiitake	しいたけ	Japanese mushrooms
ginnan	銀杏	ginkgo nuts
imo	いも	potato

Kaiseki 懐石

Kaiseki is the pinnacle of Japanese cuisine where ingredients, preparation, setting and presentation come together to create a dining experience quite unlike any other. Born as an adjunct to the tea ceremony, kaiseki is a largely vegetarian affair, and though fish is often served, meat never appears on the kaiseki menu. One usually eats kaiseki in the private room of a *ryōtei* (an especially elegant style of traditional restaurant), often overlooking a private, tranquil garden. The meal is served in several small courses, giving one the opportunity to admire the plates and bowls which are carefully chosen to complement the food and seasons. Rice is eaten last (usually with an assortment of pickles) and the drink of choice is sake or beer.

This all comes at a steep price – a good kaiseki dinner costs upwards of ¥10,000 per person. One way to sample the delights of kaiseki is to visit for lunch. Most places offer a boxed lunch *(bentō)* containing a sampling of their dinner fare for around ¥2500.

Unfortunately for foreigners, kaiseki restaurants can be intimidating places to enter. If possible, bring along a Japanese friend or ask a Japanese friend to call ahead and make arrangements. There is usually only one set course, but some places offer a choice of three courses – graded *ume* (regular), *take* (special) and *matsu* (extra special).

kaiseki ryōri	懐石料理	traditional, expensive Kyoto-style cuisine
ryōtei	料亭	a restaurant serving a variety of traditional Japanese dishes
bentō	弁当	boxed lunch
ume	梅	regular course
take	竹	special course
matsu	松	extra-special course

LPP

Left: Sold in tiny street takeaways, bustling department stores and on station platforms, the *bentō* (boxed lunch) serves as a handy, cheap and nutritious meal of rice, seafood, meat and vegetables.

Sweets お菓子

Although most restaurants don't serve dessert (plates of sliced fruit are sometimes served at the end of a meal) there is no lack of sweets in Japan. Most sweets (known generically as *wagashi*) are sold in speciality stores for you to eat at home. Many of the more delicate-looking ones are made to balance the strong, bitter taste of the special *matcha* tea served during the tea ceremony. For confectionery aficionados, Kyoto is undisputedly the place to be.

Although pleasant enough to look at, some Westerners may find Japanese sweets unappealing – perhaps because many of them contain the unfamiliar sweet, red adzuki-bean paste called *anko*. This unusual filling turns up in even the most innocuous looking pastries. But don't let anyone make up your mind for you; try a Japanese sweet for yourself.

With such a wide variety of sweets it's difficult to specify names. However, you'll probably find many variations on the anko-covered-by-glutinous rice *(mochi)* theme. Another sweet to look out for is the *yōkan* – a sweet, bean jelly slice.

Sweet shops are easy to spot; they usually have open fronts with their wares laid out in wooden trays to entice passers-by. Buying sweets is simple – just point at what you want and indicate how many you'd like.

wagashi	和菓子	Japanese-style sweets
anko	あんこ	sweet paste or jam made from adzuki beans
mochi	餅	pounded rice cakes made of glutinous rice
yōkan	ようかん	sweet red bean jelly

Eating on the Cheap

Japan can be an expensive place to eat; however, with a little effort you should be able to get away with a daily food budget of ¥1800, perhaps less.

Like anywhere else, the cheapest way to fill yourself up in Japan is to do your own cooking. Unfortunately, apart from some youth hostels, there are not many places where this is possible, although you can fix instant noodles just about anywhere. Failing that, you can purchase food from supermarkets and convenience stores which involves little or no preparation.

If you have to stick to restaurants, there are a variety of options. Fast food is an obvious contender, but most people haven't come to Japan to eat what they can get at home. Your best bet is probably the humble shokudō where noodle and rice dishes usually start at around ¥550. A good option is the lunch set *(ranchi setto)* served at shokudō, coffee shops and many other restaurants. They usually start at ¥600.

Another possible option is the cafeterias of major universities, many of which are open to all and serve government-subsidised meals for around ¥500.

DRINKING IN JAPAN

What you pay for your drink depends on where you drink and, in the case of a hostess bar, with whom you drink. As a rule, hostess bars are the most expensive (up to ¥10,000 per drink), followed by upmarket traditional Japanese bars, hotel bars, beer halls and casual pubs. If you are not sure, ask about prices and cover charges before sitting down.

As a rule, if you are served a small snack with your first round, you'll be paying a cover charge (usually a few hundred yen, but sometimes much more).

Izakaya and yakitori-ya are cheap places for beer, sake and food in a casual atmosphere resembling that of a pub. Informal bars are popular with young Japanese and resident gaijin, who usually refer to such places as 'gaijin bars'. In summer, many department stores open up beer gardens on the roof. They are a popular spot to cool off with an inexpensive beer. Many rooftop gardens offer all-you-can-eat/drink specials for around ¥3000 per person. Beer halls are affordable and popular places to swill your beer in a faux-German atmosphere.

The bars which are found in their hundreds, jammed into tiny rooms of large buildings in the entertainment districts of many cities, are often used by their customers as a type of club – if you drop in unexpectedly the reception may be cool or, more likely, you'll simply be told that they're full.

Hostess bars are inevitably expensive, often exorbitant and, without an introduction, best avoided. They cater mainly to those entertaining on business accounts. Hostesses pamper customers with compliments or lend a sympathetic ear to their problems. The best way to visit is in the company of a Japanese friend who knows the routine.

Japan, of course, is also where karaoke got its beginnings. If you've never sung in a karaoke bar, it's worth a try at least once. The uninitiated usually find that a few stiff drinks beforehand helps. Customers sing to the accompaniment of taped music and, as the evening wears on, voices get progressively more ragged. Sobbing, mournful *enka* (folk ballads) are the norm, although more and more Western hits are finding their way into karaoke 'menus'. If you visit a karaoke place with a Japanese friend, it's unlikely that you'll escape without singing at least one song – a version of *Yesterday* or *My Way* will usually satisfy the crowd.

izakaya	居酒屋	pub-style restaurant
yakitori-ya	焼き鳥屋	yakitori restaurant

Alcoholic Drinks

Drinking is the glue that holds Japanese society together. It is practised by almost every adult, and a good number of teenagers (alcohol is sold from vending machines and underage drinking is not as frowned upon as in some countries). Going out for a few rounds after work with co-workers is both the joy and bane of the Japanese worker's life. After a few drinks, Japanese workers feel secure enough to vent their frustrations and speak their minds, confident that all will be forgiven by the time they arrive at the office in the morning. Occasionally, Japanese drinking crosses the boundary between good-natured fun and ugly inebriation, as anyone who has been in a public park during cherry blossom season can attest; however, drunkenness rarely leads to violence in Japan.

Beer ビール

Introduced at the end of last century, *biiru* (beer) is now the favourite tipple of the Japanese. The quality is generally excellent and the most popular type is the light lager, although recently some breweries have been experimenting with darker brews. The major breweries are Kirin, Asahi, Sapporo and Suntory. Beer is dispensed everywhere, from vending machines to beer halls and even in some temple lodgings. A standard can of beer from a vending machine is about ¥250, although some of the monstrous cans cost over ¥1000. At bars, a beer goes up from ¥500, depending on the establishment. *Nama biiru* (draught beer) is widely available, as are imported beers.

biiru	ビール	beer
nama biiru	生ビール	draught beer

Sake 酒

Made from fermented rice wine, sake has been brewed for centuries in Japan. Once restricted to imperial brewers, it was later produced at temples and shrines across the country. In recent years, consumption of beer has overtaken that of sake, but it's still a standard item in homes, restaurants and drinking places. Large casks of sake are often seen piled up as offerings outside temples and shrines, and it plays an important part in most celebrations and festivals.

Most Westerners come to Japan with a bad image of sake; the result of having consumed low grade brands overseas. Although it won't appeal to all palates, some of the higher grades are actually very good and a trip to a restaurant specialising in sake is a great way to sample some of the better brews.

There are several major types of sake, including *nigori* (cloudy), *nama* (unrefined) and regular, clear sake. Of these, the clear sake is by far the most common. Clear sake is usually divided into three grades: *tokkyū* (premium), *ikkyū* (first grade) and *nikyū* (second grade). Nikyū is the routine choice. Sake can be further divided into *karakuchi* (dry) and *amakuchi* (sweet). Apart from the national brewing giants, there are thousands of provincial brewers producing local brews called *jizake*.

Sake is served *atsukan* (warm) and *reishu* (cold), with warm sake not surprisingly being more popular in the winter. It is usually served in a small flask called a *tokkuri*. These come in two sizes, so you should specify whether you want an *ichigō* (small) or a *nigō* (large). From these flasks you pour the sake into small ceramic cups called *o-choko* or *sakazuki*. Another way to sample sake is to drink it from a small wooden box called a *masu,* with a bit of salt on the rim.

STUART WASSERMAN

Left: You will often see casks of *sake* left as temple and shrine offerings. Sake has long been offered to the *kami* (gods) who watch over the rice harvest. After WWII, rice shortages required that pure alcohol be mixed with rice mash to increase yields of drink. Nearly all sake is produced this way today.

However you drink it, with a 17% alcohol content, sake is likely to go right to your head, particularly the warm stuff. After a few bouts you'll come to understand why the Japanese drink it in such small cups. Particularly memorable is a hangover born of too much cheap sake. The best advice is not to indulge the day before you have to get on a plane.

sake	酒	Japanese rice wine
nigori	にごり	cloudy sake
nama	生	regular clear sake
tokkyū	特級	premium grade sake
ikkyū	一級	first grade sake
nikkyū	二級	second grade sake
karakuchi	辛口	dry sake
amakuchi	甘口	sweet sake
jizake	地酒	local brew
atsukan	熱燗	warm sake
reishu	冷酒	cold sake
o-choko	お猪口	ceramic sake cup
sakazuki	杯	ceramic sake cup

Shōchū 焼酎

For those looking for a quick and cheap escape route from the world of sorrows, *shōchū* is the answer. It's a distilled spirit, with an alcohol content of about 30%, which has been resurrected from its previous low esteem (it was used as a disinfectant in the Edo period) to the status of a trendy drink. You can drink it as an *oyu-wari* (with hot water) or as a *chūhai* (a highball with soda and lemon). A 720ml bottle sells for about ¥600 which makes it a relatively cheap option compared to other spirits.

shōchū	焼酎	distilled grain liquor
oyu-wari	お湯割り	shōchū with hot water
chūhai	酎ハイ	shōchū with soda and lemon

Wine, Imported Drinks & Whisky

Japanese wines are available from areas such as Yamanashi, Nagano, Tōhoku and Hokkaidō. Standard wines are often blended with imports from South America or Eastern Europe. The major producers are Suntory, Mann's and Mercian. Prices are high – expect to pay at least ¥1000 for a bottle of something drinkable. Imported wines are often stocked by large liquor stores or department stores in the cities. Bargains are sometimes available at ¥600, but most of the quaffable imports are considerably more expensive.

Prices of imported spirits have been coming down and bargain liquor stores have been popping up. However, if you really like imported spirits, it is probably a good idea to pick up a duty-free bottle or two on your way through the airport. Whisky is available at most drinking establishments and is usually drunk *mizu-wari* (with water and ice) or *onzarokku* (on the rocks). Local brands, such as Suntory and Nikka, are sensibly priced and most measure up to foreign standards. Expensive foreign labels are popular as gifts.

Most other imported spirits can be had at drinking establishments in Japan. Bars with a large foreign clientele, including hotel bars, can usually mix anything at your request. If not, they will certainly tailor a drink to your specifications.

whisky	ウィスキー	whisky
mizu-wari	水割り	whisky and ice and water
onzarokku	オンザロック	whisky with ice

Nonalcoholic Drinks

Most of the drinks you're used to at home will be available in Japan, with a few colourfully named additions like Pocari Sweat and Calpis Water. One convenient aspect of Japan is the presence of drink machines on virtually every street corner – ¥120 refreshment is rarely more than a few steps away.

Coffee & Tea コーヒー／紅茶

Kōhii (coffee) served in a *kisaten* (coffee shop), tends to be pretty expensive, costing between ¥350 and ¥500 a cup, with some places charging up to ¥1000. However, there are some cheap alternatives with of the newer chains of coffee restaurants like Doutor or Pronto or donut shops like Mr Donut (which offers free refills). An even cheaper alternative is a can of coffee, hot or cold, from a vending machine. Although it is unpleasantly sweet, at ¥120 the price is hard to beat.

When ordering coffee at a coffee shop in Japan, you'll be asked whether you like it *hotto* (hot) or *aisu* (cold). Black tea also comes hot or cold, with *miruku* (milk) or *remon* (lemon). A good way to start a day of sightseeing in Japan is with a *mōningu setto* (morning set) of tea or coffee, toast and eggs, which costs around ¥400.

kōhii	コーヒー	regular coffee
burendo kōhii	ブレンドコーヒー	blended coffee, fairly strong
american kōhii	アメリカンコーヒー	weak coffee
kōcha	紅茶	black, British-style tea
kafe ōre	カフェオレ	café au lait, hot or cold
orenji jūsu	オレンジジュース	orange juice

Japanese Tea お茶

Unlike the black tea that Westerners are familiar with, Japanese tea is green and contains a lot of vitamin C and caffeine. The powdered form used in the tea ceremony is called *matcha* and is drunk after being whipped into a frothy consistency. The more common form is *o-cha* (a leafy green tea), which is drunk after being steeped in a pot. While *sencha* is one popular variety of green tea, most restaurants will serve a free cup of brownish tea called *bancha*. In summer a cold beverage called *mugicha* (roasted barley tea) is served in private homes.

Although not particularly popular in the West, Japanese tea is very healthy and refreshing and is said by some to prevent cancer. Most department stores carry a wide selection of Japanese teas.

o-cha	お茶	green tea
sencha	煎茶	medium grade green tea
matcha	抹茶	powdered green tea used in the tea ceremony
bancha	番茶	ordinary grade green tea, has a brownish colour
mugicha	麦茶	roasted barley tea

continued from page 176

FUSHIMI-INARI & FUSHIMI
Teuchiudon Kendonya (☎ 641 1330) **Map 2**
Daily lunch set ¥680. Open 11am-3pm,
5pm-9pm, closed Wed. For a quick lunch before or after visiting Fushimi-Inari-taisha,
pop into this shop that specialises in handmade udon noodles. To get there from Keihan Fushimi-Inari station, exit the station and
turn right, cross the street at the light and
look for it next to a yakitori restaurant.
Uosaburō (☎ 601 0061) **Map 14** Dinner
¥10,000. Open 11am-7pm. Another Fushimi
treat is the exquisite kaiseki haunt Uosaburō,
based since 1764 in a magnificent kyō-
machiya. It serves lovely *hanakago* bentō
lunch of seasonal dishes brilliantly presented
in flower-shaped baskets (¥4000).
Sancho (☎ 622 1458) **Map 14** Meals
from ¥900. Open 11.30am-9pm, closed
Wed. Not far from Uosaburō, more casual
fare is available at this tasty-salad restaurant.
Ōryū-kaku (☎ 0774-32 3900) Vegetarian
course ¥5000. Open 11am-1pm (bookings
necessary). This lovely spot at Mampuku-ji
(Map 1) serves vegetarian *fuchya-ryōri* (a
type of temple cuisine). It also has a lunch
bentō (¥3150) and full courses (¥5000).
There is a temple entry fee of ¥500.
Genya (☎ 602 1492) **Map 14** Rāmen from
¥600. Open 11.30am-7.30pm, closed Thurs.
For a great body warmer, try the *sake-kasu*
rāmen noodles (¥650) at this place; the central ingredient is the *kasu* (sediment) left behind in the sake brewing process.
Kizakura Kappa Country (☎ 611 9919)
Map 14 Meals from ¥800. Open 11.30am-
2pm, 5pm-10pm. This sake brewery restau-
rant/bar has full-course barbecue dinner
(¥2000), an all-you-can-eat lunch buffet
(¥800; Mon-Fri), and three shades of delicious microbrew beer on tap.

UJI (MAP 15)
If you're hungry while in Uji and can't wait
to get back to Kyoto, there are plenty of
places for a quick lunch, most of which are
located along the road leading to Byōdō-in.
Tsūen-jaya Annex (☎ 0774-24 3523)
Light meals from ¥700. Open 10am-5pm,

closed Thurs. Tsūen-jaya, the modern annex
of the old Tsūen tea shop, is on the road up
to Ujigami-jinja. It serves tasty soba and sansai, as well as tempting desserts made with
fresh green tea (try the *matcha* parfait).
Kawabun (☎ 0774-21 2556) Donburi
from ¥750. Open 11am-6pm. Try this simple shokudō for Uji sweets, tea and simple
meals. It's very near the temple.

COFFEE SHOPS
The Japanese are eager coffee drinkers and
Kyoto is packed with coffee shops. Some
are old Japanese-style places, others are
modern spots with cappuccino and trendy
décor. Several of the places we list below
are worth a special trip for their great ambience and tasty coffee.
Café Doji (☎ 491 3422) **Map 3** Coffee
from ¥500. Open noon-11pm, closed Thurs.
This Kitayama-dōri coffee shop might just
be the most atmospheric cafe in town. Light
meals are also served. The place is named
for its resident dog.
Inoda Coffee (☎ 221 0507) **Map 9** Coffee from ¥500. Open 7am-6pm. This chain
is a Kyoto institution with branches
throughout the city centre. Though slightly
overrated for the price, the old-Japan atmosphere at its main shop on Sakaimachi-
dōri, south of Sanjō-dōri, is worth a try.
Saracca (☎ 231 8797) **Map 9** Coffee
from ¥400, light meals from ¥700. Open
noon-midnight, closed Wed. You'll have to
look long and hard to find a coffee shop
more relaxing than this one. They serve a
variety of international food, some of it
vegetarian. It's in the centre of town.
*Shinshindō Notre Pain Quotidien (☎ 701
4121)* **Map 6** Coffee from ¥340. Open 8am-
6pm, closed Tues. This atmospheric old
Kyoto coffee shop is a favourite of Kyoto
University students for its curry and bread
lunch set (¥780) – it's kind of an acquired
taste. It's near Kyoto University.
Bazaar Café (☎ 411 2379) **Map 5** Coffee from ¥400. Open 11.30am-8pm, Thurs-
Sat. This coffee shop is almost never open,
but if you catch it when it is you're sure
to like its airy atmosphere. It's near the
Karasuma-Imadegawa crossing.

Amazon (☎ *561 8875*) **Map 10** Coffee from ¥400. Open 7.30am-6pm. This typical Japanese coffee shop near Sanjūsangen-dō turns out some surprisingly scrumptious sandwiches.

Mole (☎ *250 2038*) **Map 5** Coffee from ¥400. Open 11.30pm-6pm, closed Wed. We love the woodsy, plant-filled atmosphere at this hip new coffee shop near Kyoto City Hall.

Nishiki Market

If you're interested in viewing, or perhaps purchasing, all the weird and wonderful foods required for Kyoto-style cooking (*kyō-ryōri*), wander through Nishiki Market (Map 9). It began as a fish market in the early 1300s, and many of the shops today have been in business for centuries. Better known as 'Kyoto's Kitchen', Nishiki is a must-see, a remarkable remnant of old Kyoto smack in the centre of town.

About 150 speciality shops line the narrow 400m-long covered alley. Many specialise in the high-quality ingredients used in the elegant *kaiseki-ryōri*. The street bustles with customers shopping for fresh fish, vegetables and extremely colourful Japanese pickles (*tsukemono*).

Nishiki is an all-sensory experience and a great place to visit on a rainy day or as a break from temple-hopping. It is particularly lively in the morning when chefs from Kyoto's finest restaurants and inns come to hand-pick the makings for the day's special delicacy. Also in the late afternoon, Kyotoites come to see what's fresh for dinner. At year's end, the market becomes jam-packed with shoppers searching for the best ingredients to prepare *osechi-ryōri*, traditional New Year cuisine. Many Nishiki shops sell several types of ready-to-eat foods, like kushi-katsu skewers, tempura and sweet bean-filled rice cakes.

The market runs one block north of (and parallel to) Shijō-dōri, between the shopping arcade of Teramachi and Takakura-dōri (near the rear of Daimaru department store). Most shops are open from about 10am to 6pm.

Papa Jon's (☎ *415 2655*) Coffee ¥400, cheesecake ¥550. There are three branches of Papa Jon's; one is near the north-west corner of the Imperial Palace Park **Map 3**; another on Kitayama-dōri **Map 4**, just west of Kitashirakawa-dōri; and a third is in the city centre in the Shinkyōgoku covered arcade **Map 9**. All three are known for good coffee, cappuccino and cheesecake.

Starbucks **Map 3** This chain has made serious inroads in Kyoto. There are branches on Sanjō-dōri, Shijō-dōri and Karasuma-dōri, among others.

Doutor **Map 9** Coffee ¥180. For a cheap coffee fix you can't beat Doutor. There are branches all over Kyoto, including this one on Shijō-dōri.

TEA & SWEET SHOPS

While coffee shops have made serious inroads into Kyoto, for a more authentic Japanese experience we recommend stopping into a traditional tea shop or sweet shop (many places listed here serve both tea and sweets, a favourite Japanese combination).

Gion Koishi (☎ *531 0301*) **Map 6** Tea from ¥500. Open 11am-7pm, closed Wed. If it's a hot summer day and you need a cooling break, try this tea shop for some typical Japanese summer treats. The speciality here is *Uji kintoki* (¥700), a mountain of shaved ice flavoured with green tea, sweetened milk and sweat beans (it tastes a lot better than it sounds, trust us). This is only available in the summer months.

Momiji-an (☎ *561 2933*) **Map 8** Tea and sweet beans ¥600. Open 9am-5pm. Located in a rustic old Kyoto house overlooking Maruyama-kōen, this is a great spot for a rest while touring the Higashiyama area. Ask for the *usucha* (thin green tea).

Ōharameya (☎ *561 1905*) **Map 9** Sweet set for ¥2500. Open 11am-8pm, closed every second Tues each month. If you fancy a thorough education in Japanese sweets try the full course *amato kaiseki* (sweet set; ¥2500) at this famous Gion sweet shop.

Umezono (☎ *221 5017*) **Map 9** Mitarashi dangō set ¥500. Open 10.30am-7.30pm. Locals line up for the *dangō* (sweet rice gluten balls) at this downtown Kyoto institution.

Kagizen Yoshifusa (☎ *525 0011*) **Map 9**
Tea from ¥400. Open 9am-6pm, closed
Mon. This place in Gion is one of Kyoto's
oldest and best known *okashi-ya* (sweet
shops). It sells a variety of traditional sweets
and has a cosy tearoom upstairs where you
can sample cold *kuzukiri* (transparent ar-
rowroot noodles), served with a *kuro-mitsu*
(sweet black sugar) dipping sauce.

Kasagi-ya (☎ *561 9526*) **Map 8** Sweets
from ¥600. Open 11am-6pm, closed Tues.
At Kasagi-ya, on the Ninen-zaka slope near
Kiyomizu-dera, you can try o-hagi cakes
made from *azuki* (sweet red beans).

Kagiya Masaaki (☎ *761 5311*) **Map 6**
Sweets from ¥700. Open 9am-6pm, closed
Sun. Since 1682, Kagiya Masaaki has been
preparing a delightful Kyoto confection
called *tokiwagi*. It's near Kyoto University.

Kazariya (☎ *491 9402*) **Map 3** Sweets for
¥500. Open 10am-5pm, closed Wed. For
more than 300 years, Kazariya has been specialising in *aburi-mochi* (grilled rice cakes
coated with soybean flower) and served with
miso-dare (sweet bean paste). It's north of
Daitoku-ji.

Tsuruya Yoshinobu (☎ *441-0105*) **Map
5** Sweets from ¥600. Open 9am-6pm. This
is one of Kyoto's most esteemed sweet
makers. It's on Imadegawa-dōri west of
Horikawa-dōri.

SELF-CATERING

If you want a break from eating out, there
are plenty of options for self-catering in
Kyoto. You'll find supermarkets in every
neighbourhood in town. The city also has a
wide selection of fruit and vegetable shops
(yao-ya), fish shops *(sakana-ya)* and bak-
eries *(pan-ya)*.

To do all your food shopping under one
roof, try one of Kyoto's many *shōtengai*
(market streets). The best of these is
Demachiyanagi Shōtengai (Map 5), a humble shopping street in the northern part of
town. **Nishiki Market (Map 9)**, in the centre
of town, is a much more upscale version that
caters primarily to Kyoto restaurateurs. All
of Kyoto's department stores also have food
floors where you can buy just about any
food item, domestic or imported, but you'll
certainly have to pay for the convenience.

If you're looking specifically for imported foods, try one of the shops listed in
the Imported Food & Gourmet Items section of the shopping chapter.

Lastly, if all of the above options are
closed, say during the New Year holiday
period, you can put together an acceptable
meal at one of Kyoto's many convenience
stores – more than one starving Lonely
Planet writer has survived the holidays on a
steady diet of *conbeni-ryōri*

Entertainment

If you've still got some energy left after a day of temple-hopping, there's plenty to do in Kyoto after night falls. Indeed, the central Kawaramachi-Kiyamachi area fairly pulses with activity almost any night of the week. You can choose from *izakaya* (Japanese pubs), bars, clubs and karaoke boxes, many of which stay open almost until dawn. The fact is, Kyoto knows how to party – it's just a matter of whether you can keep up.

As for traditional Japanese culture, you're going to have to work a little harder. Most of Kyoto's cultural entertainment is of an occasional nature, and you'll need to check with the Tourist Information Centre (TIC), *Kansai Time Out* or *Kyoto Visitor's Guide* to find whether anything interesting is going on while you're in town. Regular events are generally geared toward the tourist market and tend to be expensive and, naturally, somewhat touristy.

PUBS & BARS (MAP 9)

Kyoto has an astounding variety of bars, from exclusive Gion clubs, where it's possible to spend ¥100,000 in a single evening, to grungy *gaijin* (foreigner) bars. Most bars are concentrated in the central Kawaramachi-Kiyamachi area. During the warmer months, rooftop beer gardens spring up throughout town and offer tempting all-you-can-eat/drink deals and great views of the surrounding mountains (see the boxed text 'Gardens of Beer'). For something a little more upscale than the bars and pubs listed in this section, try one of the bars in any of Kyoto's upscale hotels; both the Fujita and the Granvia have excellent bars (see the Places to Stay chapter).

Perhaps the best place to start a Kyoto evening is at *A-Bar* (☎ 213 2129) A raucous student izakaya with a log-cabin interior in the Kiyamachi area. There's a big menu to choose from and everything's cheap. The best part is when they add up the bill – you'll swear they've undercharged

you by half. It's a little tough to find – look for the small black-and-white sign at the top of a flight of concrete steps above a place called Reims.

Pig & Whistle (☎ 761 6022) The Pig is one of Kyoto's most popular gaijin hangouts. Like its counterparts in Osaka, it's a British-style pub with darts, pint glasses and fish & chips. The pub's two main drawcards are Guinness on tap and its friendly bilingual manager, Ginzo. It's on the second floor of the Shobi building near the Sanjō-Kawabata crossing.

Ing (☎ 255 5087) This bar/izakaya on Kiyamachi is one of our favourite spots for a drink in Kyoto. It's got cheap bar snacks and drinks, good music and a friendly staff. It's in the Royal building on the second floor; you'll know you're getting close when you see all the hostesses out trawling for customers on the streets nearby.

Sama Sama (☎ 213 1150) A groovy spot with cosy floor seating and a nice wooden bar; it might just take the honours as Kyoto's most atmospheric bar. Sama Sama is run by long-term Kyoto resident Teddy, an Indonesian who serves up spicy island food and cold Bintang beer. It's on one of the narrow east-west streets between Kiyamachi-dōri and Kawaramachi-dōri.

Pub Africa (☎ 221 6049) This long-time 'gaijin bar' is pretty much your standard issue dimly lit bar. It's not a good place to meet people because the video screens tend to dominate everyone's attention.

Hill of Tara (☎ 213 3330) Some Kyoto expats prefer this Irish-style pub to the Pig & Whistle, although we're not entirely sure why; it's more expensive and the food can be pretty uneven. One plus: it's less smoky than the Pig.

Bar, Isn't It? (☎ 221 5399) This basement bar/club is popular with young Japanese and foreign men desperately searching for local females. It's huge, loud and often very crowded. All drinks are ¥500 and there's a simple bar-food menu.

Rub-a-Dub (☎ 256 3122) At the northern end of Kiyamachi-dōri, Rub-a-Dub is a funky little reggae bar with a shabby tropical look. It's a good place for a quiet drink on weekdays, but on Friday and Saturday nights you'll have no choice but to bop along with the crowd. Look for the stairs heading down to the basement beside the popular (and delightfully 'fragrant') Nagahama rāmen shop.

Rai's House 6½ (☎ 212 1060) A short stumble south of Rub-a-Dub on Kiyamachi-dōri, 6½ (pronounced 'Roku Han' in Japanese) is a hip after-hours bar and one of the few places in town that can still be packed at 7am on a Sunday morning. All drinks are ¥600 and hip-hop music is the rule.

Teddy's (☎ 255 7717) This bar/club features faux tropical surroundings and a great view over the Kamo-gawa. On some nights there's dancing and on others it's a quiet spot with table seating. It's on the 7th floor of the Empire building on Kiyamachi, just south of Oike-dōri.

Cock-a-Hoop (☎ 221 4939) In the same building as Teddy's, this Latin-influenced bar/restaurant is an interesting spot for drinks and dinner (they serve such things as chorizo sausages and clams with basil).

Hachimonjiya (☎ 256 1731) Hachimonjiya is a popular haunt with local artists and takes the cake as the messiest bar in Kyoto: it's cluttered floor-to-ceiling with books, postcards and pictures by acclaimed street photographer (and bar owner) Kai-san. There is a ¥500 table charge, which includes a bit of food. Drinks are reasonably priced. It's on Kiyamachi-dōri; take the elevator to the 3rd floor.

Shizuka (☎ 221 5148) Tucked down a tiny little alley near the Shinkyōgoku covered arcade, this izakaya has a classic traditional Japanese atmosphere and cheap beer and sake. Food is also served here, but we advise you to eat before you come.

Backgammon (☎ 223 0416) On a little alley off Kiyamachi-dōri, one street north of Sanjō-dōri, Backgammon is popular with Kyoto's young malcontents. Check out the crow's nest drinking area at the top of the ladder – if you don't want to climb down for the next round, they'll send it up to you with a special drink elevator. A certain Lonely Planet writer was a regular here, until he realised that it was bad for his health.

Atlantis (☎ 241 1621) This bar is one of the few bars on Pontochō that foreigners can walk into without a Japanese friend. In summer you can sit outside on a platform looking over the Kamo-gawa. Drinks average ¥1000.

Gion Moss Kitchin Bar (☎ 532 5517) There aren't many spots that welcome foreigners in Gion; this is one of them. It's a casual, hip bar that also serves a variety of food, both Western and Japanese. There's a ¥500 table charge and drinks average ¥800.

Northern Kyoto

Post Coitus (☎ 781 4152) **Map 4** Near Kyoto University, Post Coitus is worth a visit. The interior decorations are an experiment in radical minimalism, intended to make you concentrate on the drink at hand. This place has plenty to choose from – a real connoisseur's haven. Funny about the name though – we always thought that drinking was a pre-coital thing.

The Flying Keg (☎ 701 0245) **Map 4** Off Higashiōji-dōri a few steps west on Mikage-dōri, the Flying Keg is an aptly named beer emporium with an enormous selection of brews from over 25 countries. It's quiet, casual, reasonably priced and has an impressive selection of wines; all-in-all a nice break from the fracas downtown.

Mekhong (☎ 495 9292) **Map 2** Mekhong is an appealing option, especially if you're lodging way up north. It's an atmospheric candle-lit bar done up in South East Asian decor. There is a ¥100 'candle charge' and ample Mekhong (Thai whisky) behind the bar. It's a 15-minute walk north-west of Kamigamo-jinja, across the Kamo-gawa.

CLUBS & DISCOS

Yes, you can dance the night away in the cultural heart of Japan and give the temples and shrines a miss the next day while you sleep off your hangover. Most clubs charge an admission fee of ¥2000, which usually includes a drink or two.

ENTERTAINMENT

Gardens of Beer

So you've strolled around wooded ponds, seen misty moss gardens and unravelled the meaning of dry rock-garden landscapes, all in Kyoto's sweltering summer heat; maybe it's time to soak up a bit of 'borrowed scenery' from the rooftop of a tall building at one of Kyoto's many beer gardens.

The beer garden season generally runs from mid-May to mid-September, but always check before you go. Each spot in town has a distinct view and a slightly different system; some serve beer and food à la carte, and others offer tempting all-you-can-eat and drink specials. One of the best places is the **Sunflower Hotel** (Map 6; ☎ 761 9111), which is right at the eastern end of Marutamachi-dōri. The view of the Higashiyama mountains from the roof is one of the finest in town.

Other beer gardens with great views include:

ANA Hotel (Map 5; ☎ 231 1155) just across from Nijō-jō Castle on Horikawa-dōri
Gion Hotel (Map 6; ☎ 551 2111) at the eastern end of Shijō-dōri, near Yasaka-jinja
Hotel Fujita Kyoto (Map 5; ☎ 222 1511) on Nijō-dōri, on the west bank of the Kamo-gawa
Kikusui Beer Garden (Map 9; ☎ 561 1001) across from the north-east end of the Shijō-Ōhashi Bridge
Kyoto Tower Hotel (Map 10; ☎ 361 3222) just across from Kyoto station

Metro **Map 5** Admission ¥2000 Sat & Sun, free Wed & Thur. Metro is part disco, part 'live house' and even hosts the occasional art exhibition. It attracts an eclectic mix of creative types and every night has a different theme, so check ahead in *Kansai Time Out* to see what's going on. Some of the best gigs are Latin night and the popular Non-Hetero-At-The-Metro night, which draws gays, lesbians and everyone in between. Metro is inside the No 2 exit of Keihan Marutamachi station.

CK Café **Map 6** Another hip spot is CK Cafe. This place is about as close to Tokyo nightlife as you'll get in Kyoto, right down to *chapatsu* (dyed brown hair) girls in criminally short miniskirts gyrating on the loudspeakers. The normal admission is ¥2500 (with two drinks), sometimes foreigners and women get reduced admission. It's opposite Yasaka-jinja on the 4th floor of the Gion Kaikan building.

See the following section for entries for additional places where dancing occurs.

ROCK/FOLK/ACOUSTIC MUSIC

There are several options for live music. Most venues vary the type of music they feature from night to night. Check the *Kansai Time Out* to see what's happening at the following 'live houses'.

Taku-Taku (☎ 351 1321) **Map 7** Admission ¥1500-3500. This is one of Kyoto's most atmospheric clubs, located in an old *saka-gura* (sake warehouse). It's central, on Tominokōji-dōri south of Shijō-dōri, and tends to present major acts (the Neville Brothers, Los Lobos and Dr John have all performed here).

Juttoku (☎ 841 1691) **Map 5** Admission ¥1000. Juttoku is also situated in an atmospheric saka-gura. It's north of Nijō-jō.

Toga-Toga (☎ 361 6900) **Map 9** On Teramachi-dōri south of Shijō-dōri, Toga-Toga is a basement-level joint hosting a wide variety of both amateur and professional artists.

Other Side (☎ 256 5259) **Map 5** Admission varies. South of Imadegawa-dōri on Kawaramachi-dōri, this is a good spot to hear amateur acoustic acts (it has an open-mike night 7pm till midnight on Wednesday).

Honky Tonk (☎ 701 8015) **Map 2** Admission varies. Open until 11pm. For the best in live country music it's well worth the trip up north to Honky Tonk near the Kyoto International Conference Hall. This place is a gas; an authentic Western saloon full of Japanese cowboys dressed in full garb – hats, boots and, occasionally, spurs. The friendly owner, Beau, speaks English well and is a regular performer. Call to confirm that there's a show on before making the haul out.

ENTERTAINMENT

JAZZ

Live jazz takes place irregularly at several clubs in town. The best of these is *Rag* (☎ *241 0446, 5th floor, Empire bldg on Kiyamachi-dōri)* **Map 9** Admission ¥1500-4000.

TRADITIONAL DANCE, THEATRE & MUSIC

Gion Corner (☎ 561 1119) **Map 8** Admission ¥2800. Presents shows every evening at 7.40pm & 8.40pm 1 Mar-29 Nov; closed 16 Aug. You should think carefully about whether tourist-oriented events of this kind are your cup of tea before forking out the entry charge. While you get a chance to see snippets of the tea ceremony, Koto music, flower arrangement, *gagaku* (court music), *kyōgen* (ancient comic plays), *Kyōmai* (Kyoto-style dance) and *bunraku* (puppet plays), you will be doing so with a couple of camera and video toting tour groups, and the presentation is a little on the tacky side. On top of this, 50 minutes of entertainment for ¥2800 is a little steep by anyone's standards.

Geisha Dances

Annually in autumn and spring, geisha and their maiko apprentices from Kyoto's five schools dress elaborately to perform traditional dances in praise of the seasons. The cheapest tickets cost about ¥1650 (unreserved on tatami mats), better seats cost ¥3000 to ¥3800, and spending an extra ¥500 includes participation in a quick tea ceremony. The dances are similar from place to place and are repeated several times a day. Dates and times vary, so check with the TIC.

Gion Odori 1–10 November; *Gion Kaikan Theatre (☎ 561 0160)* **Map 6** near Yasaka-jinja.

Kamogawa Odori 1–24 May and 15 October to 7 November; *Pontochō Kaburen-jō Theatre (☎ 221 2025)* **Map 9** in Pontochō.

Kitano Odori 15–25 April; *Kamishichiken Kaburen-jō Theatre (☎ 461 0148)* **Map 5** east of Kitano-Tenman-gū.

Kyō Odori From the first to the third Sunday in April; *Miyagawa-chō Kaburen-jō Theatre (☎ 561 1151)* **Map 7** east of the Kamo-gawa between Shijō-dōri and Gojō-dōri.

Miyako Odori Throughout April at the *Gion Kōbu Kaburen-jō Theatre (☎ 561 1115)* **Map 8** near Gion Corner (see earlier in this section).

Kabuki

Minami-za (☎ 561 0160) **Map 9** The oldest kabuki theatre in Japan is in Gion. The major event of the year is the Kao-mise Festival (1–26 December), which features Japan's finest kabuki actors. Other performances take place on an irregular basis. Those interested should check with the TIC. The most likely months for performances are May, June and September.

Nō

For performances of nō the main theatres are the *Kanze Kaikan Nō Theatre (☎ 771 6114)* **Map 6** and the *Kawamura Theatre (☎ 451 4513)* **Map 3**. Takigi-Nō is an especially picturesque form of nō performed in the light of blazing fires. In Kyoto, this takes place in the evenings of 1 and 2 June at Heian-jingū – tickets cost ¥2000 if you pay in advance (ask at the TIC for the location of ticket agencies) or you can pay ¥3300 at the entrance gate.

Musical Performances

Musical performances featuring the koto, *shamisen* and *shakuhachi* are held in Kyoto on an irregular basis. Performances of *bugaku* (court music and dance) are often held at Kyoto shrines during festival periods. Occasionally contemporary *butō* dance is also performed in Kyoto. Check with the TIC to see if any performances are scheduled to be held while you are in town.

CLASSICAL MUSIC

The *Kyoto Concert Hall (☎ 361 6629)* **Map 3** and *ALTI (Kyoto Fumin Hall; ☎ 441 1414)* **Map 5** both hold regular performances of classical music and dance (traditional and contemporary). Ticket prices average between ¥3000 and ¥5000. Kyoto Concert Hall holds regular performances of classical music and dance (traditional and contemporary). Again, check with the usual sources for current schedules.

CINEMAS

You'll find a large number of movie theatres in Kyoto's downtown Kawaramachi-Kiyamachi district. Like elsewhere, these

ENTERTAINMENT

theatres are dominated by Hollywood films, which arrive in Japan up to six months after their original release. Foreign films are screened in their original language, with Japanese subtitles. Unfortunately, tickets are expensive, averaging around ¥1800. The only exception to this is the first Tuesday of each month (Movie Day or *Eiga-no-Hi*), when tickets cost only ¥1000.

If you want to check out a Hollywood film, try *Sukara-za* **Map 9** just south of Sanjō-Kawaramachi crossing.

There are also a few places in town that feature both Japanese and foreign independent and art-house films:

Asahi Cinema (☎ 255 6760) **Map 9** This small cinema is a good spot to catch arty foreign films. It's just north of the Sanjō-Kawaramachi-dōri crossing.

Minami Kaikan (☎ 661 3993) **Map 7** Try this theatre for lesser-known imports and eclectic Japanese films, including Japanese *anime* (animation). It's on Kujō-dōri, not far from Kujō station on the Karasuma line.

Japan Foundation (☎ 211 1312) **Map 9** One of Kyoto's best deals is the free Wednesday (2pm) showing of classic Japanese films with English subtitles at the Japan Foundation – see Useful Organisations in the Facts for the Visitor chapter for more details.

KARAOKE

It would be crazy to come all the way to Japan and not sing karaoke! One of the cheapest places to indulge in this most Japanese of pastimes is *Jumbo Karaoke Hiroba* (☎ 761 3939) **Map 9** ¥480 per person per hour, ¥580 on Sat, Sun and holidays; price includes a free drink. Open 11am-6am. Kyoto expats love this place because it's in the same building as the city's most popular 'gaijin bar', the Pig & Whistle – more than one drunken evening has started at the Pig and moved on to this 'karaoke box'! The best thing about this place is that each group gets their own room (hence the name 'karaoke box'). Thus, no matter how bad your voice, you can sing with great gusto, knowing that only your closest friends will suffer for it.

Shopping

Kyoto offers ample opportunity to deplete your supply of yen. Whether you're hardcore souvenir hunting or simply window shopping, you'll run out of energy before you run out of shops to explore. You'll find everything from Japan's latest electronic products to traditional Kyoto handicrafts. And if you've got the chance, don't miss one of Kyoto's regular markets.

WHAT TO BUY

Some of the best purchases in town are crafts native to Kyoto such as *kyō-ningyō* (dolls), *kyō-shikki* (lacquerware), *kyō-sensu* (fans) and *kyō-yaki* (ceramics). *Nishijin-ori* is a special technique of silk textile weaving and *kyō-yūzen* is a local form of silk-dyeing. *Zōgan* is a damascene technique laying pure gold and silver onto figures engraved on brass.

Other good Kyoto souvenirs include *washi* (Japanese paper), Japanese tea, Japanese knives and cooking utensils, sake, Japanese sweets and woodblock prints.

WHERE TO SHOP

The heart of Kyoto's shopping district is the intersection of Shijō-dōri and Kawaramachi-dōri. The blocks running north and west of here are packed with all sorts of stores selling both traditional and modern goods. Several of Kyoto's largest department stores are here as well, including *Hankyū*, *Daimaru* and *Takashimaya*.

While you're in these department stores, be sure to check their basement food floors. It's difficult to believe the variety of food on display, as well as some of the prices (check out the ¥10,000 melons for example). Better still, head to *Nishiki Market* (Map 9) for a look at all the wondrous things that go into Japanese cuisine.

Teramachi-dōri, below Shijō-dōri, is Kyoto's electronics ghetto with the full range of the latest in computers, stereos and home appliances. The same street, north of Oike-dōri, is the place to look for a wide variety of traditional Japanese items. A stroll up this street to the Kyoto Imperial Palace Park is a great way to spend an afternoon, even if you don't plan on making any purchases.

The fashion-conscious should explore Kyoto's department stores or the chic boutiques on Kitayama-dōri. Unfortunately, you'll be hard pressed to find much of a selection of larger ('gaijin-sized') clothes and shoes. If you're living in Kyoto, we suggest doing your clothes shopping by mail order from back home.

Antiques hunters should head straight for Shinmonzen-dōri in the Gion District, the aforementioned Teramachi-dōri, or one of the city's lively monthly markets (see Markets in this chapter).

To supplement the information in this chapter, pick up a copy of *Old Kyoto: A Guide to Traditional Shops, Restaurants & Inns* by Diane Durston, available at *Maruzen* bookshop (Map 9). It's good for finding traditional items sold (and often produced) by ancient Kyoto shops. *Kyoto Visitors Guide* also has a listing of traditional shops and markets going on in town. Lastly, the TIC can help locate unusual or hard-to-find items.

Art & Craft Emporiums

If you want to do all your shopping under one roof, the following places offer a wide selection of Kyoto arts and crafts at reasonable prices.

Kyoto Handicraft Center (☎ 761 5080) **Map 6** Open 9.30am-6pm, 9.30-5.30pm Jan, Feb & Dec. This huge cooperative exhibits, sells and demonstrates crafts. We particularly like the woodblock prints here. It's near Heian-jingū.

Kyoto Craft Center (☎ 561 9660) **Map 6** Open 11am-6pm, closed Wed. This centre, near Maruyama-kōen, exhibits and sells a decent selection of handicrafts.

Kyūkyu-dō (☎ 231 0510) **Map 9** Open 10am-6pm, closed Mon. This old shop in

Kyoto Shopping at a Glance

Here's a quick shopping guide to help you make the most of your shopping time. Please bear in mind that this is by no means a definitive list, just a few picks for some common purchases. For details on the stores listed here, see the full entries in this chapter.

item	where to buy it
antiques	Shinmonzen-dōri (Gion) **Map 6**/Teramachi-dōri **Map 5**/markets
books/magazines	Maruzen bookshop **Map 9**
clothing	Kawaramachi-dōri **Map 7**/Kitayama-dōri **Map 3**/department stores
electronics	Teramachi-dōri **Map 5**
fans	Yamani **Map 7**/Kyōsen-dō **Map 10**
imported food	Meiji-ya **Map 9**/Maki **Map 4**
Japanese food	Nishiki Market **Map 9**/supermarkets
kimono	Kyō-kimono Plaza **Map 7**/Shikunshi **Map 5**/markets
kitchenware	Aritsugi **Map 9**/department stores
outdoor sporting equipment	Kōjitsu **Map 9**
pottery	Gojō-dōri **Map 7**/Kiyomizu-dera area **Map 8**/markets
souvenirs/crafts	Kyoto Handicraft Center **Map 6**/Kyoto Craft Center **Map 6**/markets
tea	Ippō-dō **Map 9**
washi (Japanese paper)	Morita Washi **Map 7**/Kakimoto **Map 5**
wood-block prints	Kyoto Handicraft Center **Map 6**

the Teramachi covered arcade sells a selection of incense, *shodō* (calligraphy) goods, tea ceremony supplies and washi. Prices are on the high side but the quality is good.

Shopping Centres & Arcades

If you want to see where the Kyoto kids are hanging out try one of the following shopping centres and arcades.

Qanat **Map 4** Open 10am-8pm. This huge new complex in Takano (northern Kyoto) has stores selling just about everything as well as a big food court with a Starbucks and a place that sells decent pizza (something of a rarity here).

Avanti **Map 10** Open 10am-8pm. On the south side of Kyoto station (take the underground passage from the station), this shopping centre has a decent bookshop and supermarket, among other things.

Zest Underground Shopping Arcade **Map 9** Open 10.30am-8.30pm, closed third Wed each month. This new mall under Oike-dōri in front of Kyoto City Hall has a variety of boutiques, restaurants and a small branch of Kinokuniya bookshop.

OPA **Map 10** Open 10am-8pm, closed Wed. This new youth emporium is the place to go to see swarms of *ko-gyaru* (brightly-clad Japanese girls) and their mates.

In addition to these, you might take a stroll through *Teramachi* and *Shinkyōgoku* **(Map 9)** covered shopping arcades. Lined with restaurants, cinemas and a mix of tacky souvenir shops and more traditional, upmarket stores, they're usually swarming with Japanese students on school excursions.

Markets

A visit to one of the monthly markets may very well be a highlight of your trip to Kyoto. It's also a good chance to pick up Japanese souvenirs at reasonable prices. Scores of dealers set up open-air stalls to display and sell their wares – this is one of the few occasions where bargaining is the norm. Wares on offer at these markets include antiques, pottery, food, used clothing, bric-a-brac and antique kimono. Most vendors can manage a bit of English but a smile will often go as far as fluent Japanese. If you're looking for antiques, arrive early and prepare to bargain. There is a better selection in the morning, but vendors loosen up with prices as the market winds down.

Tō-ji & Kitano Kōbō-san Market Map 7

On the 21st of each month this market is held at Tō-ji to commemorate the death of Kōbō Taishi (Kūkai), who in 823 was appointed abbot of the temple.

Tenjin-san Market Map 3 Another major market is held on the 25th of each month at Kitano Tenman-gū, marking the day of birth (and coincidentally the death) of the Heian-era statesman Sugawara Michizane (845–903).

If you aren't in Kyoto on the 21st, there is also a regular *antiques fair* at Tō-ji on the first Sunday of each month.

Other Markets

Other markets are held monthly at various temples around town, featuring household goods and handmade wares, among other things.

Myōren-ji (☎ 451 3527) Map 3 On the 12th of each month there is a bazaar at this temple, north-west of Imadegawa-Horikawa.

Chion-ji (☎ 781 9171) Map 6 On the 15th of each month, the Tezukuri-ichi is held at this temple. Wares include food and handmade clothes.

YWCA's thrift shop (☎ 431 0352) Map 5 Open 11am-2pm. On the first and third Saturday of each month there is a flea market and general get-together of foreigners there.

Kyoto International Community House (☎ 752 3010) Map 6 Open 11am-4pm. Twice a year, in spring and fall, recycled items, clothes and household goods are sold here. Call for dates as they vary each year.

Antique & Craft Fairs

The Antique Grand Fair is a major event, with over 100 dealers selling a wide range of Japanese and foreign curios. It is held thrice-yearly at *Pulse Plaza* (Map 2) in Fushimi (southern Kyoto). Ask at the TIC for more details as times vary each year.

There are also several annual pottery events that are great opportunities for finding deals on both local wares and ceramics from around Japan. These include:

Toki-ichi *(☎ 461 5973)* Map 3 Open 9-12 July. A large pottery fair is held at Senbon Shaka-dō with around 30 vendors selling various wares.

Toki Matsuri *(☎ 581 6188)* Map 8 Open 18-20 July. A famed ceramics bazaar held at Kiyomizu-danchi has some 60 vendors selling primarily Kiyomizu-yaki style pottery.

Toki Matsuri Map 8 Open 7-10 Aug. On Gojō-zaka, the sloping stretch of Gojō-dōri near Kiyomizu-dera, this is one of Japan's greatest pottery fairs, with around 450 vendors.

Arts & Handicrafts

Bamboo Crafts *Kagoshin (☎ 771 0209)* Map 6 Open 9am-6pm. This small shop sells a wide variety of inexpensive bamboo products like flower holders and baskets.

Onouechikuzaiten (☎ 751 0221) Map 6 Open 10am-7pm. Just a few doors from the above, it's almost a carbon copy.

Ceramics In eastern Kyoto, Ninen-zaka and Sannen-zaka slopes **(Map 8)**, close to Kiyomizu-dera, are famed for ceramics, in particular a distinctive type of pottery known as *Kiyomizu-yaki*. You'll find more pottery to the north of Gojō-dōri between Higashiōji-dōri and Kawabata-dōri. Of course, you'll get far better deals at the Tō-ji and Kitano markets listed earlier in this chapter.

Dolls *Matsuya (☎ 221 5902)* Map 9 Open 10am-6pm, closed Wed. Just north of Shijō-dōri, on the eastern side of Kawaramachi-dōri, Matsuya sells an impressive assortment of delicately painted kyō-ningyō.

Tanakaya (☎ 221 1959) Map 9 Open 10am-6pm, closed Wed. On Shijō-dōri, Tanakaya is another good option for dolls.

Fans *Yamani (☎ 351 2622)* Map 7 Open 9am-5pm, closed Sun & 2nd & 3rd Sat each month. A short walk south of Gojō-dōri, Yamani also boasts a wide selection of fans.

Kyōsen-dō (☎ 371 4151) Map 10 Open 9am-5pm, closed Sun, holidays & 2nd Sat each month. About a 10-minute walk northeast of Kyoto station, Kyōsen-dō sells a colourful variety of paper fans; here you can see the process of assembling the fans and even paint your own.

Japanese Paper *Morita Washi* (☎ *341 1419*) **Map 7** Open 9.30am-5.30pm. A short walk from the Shijō-Karasuma crossing, this place sells a fabulous variety of handmade washi for reasonable prices. It's one of our favourite shops in Kyoto for souvenirs.

Kakimoto (☎ *211 3481*) **Map 5** Open 9am-6pm, closed Sun. This shop is a close second to the above for exquisite washi (even some for use in computer printers!).

Rakushi-kan (☎ *251 0078*) **Map 9** Open 10am-7.30pm. On the 1st floor of the Museum of Kyoto, this shop sells a decent variety of washi goods.

Lacquerware *Asobe* (☎ *211 0803*) **Map 9** Open 9.30am-6pm, closed Wed. Across from Daimaru department store, Asobe specialises in exquisite kyō-shikki. It also has a small branch on the 6th floor of Takashimaya department store.

Metalwork *Amita-honten* (☎ *761 7000*) **Map 6** Open 10am-6pm. You'll find a small selection of traditional Japanese metalwork at this souvenir emporium.

Noren *Tanakaya* (☎ *221 3076*) **Map 9** Open 9am-5pm Mon-Fri, 10am-6pm Sat, Sun & holidays. This shop sells *noren* (curtains that hang in the entry of Japanese restaurants) and a wide variety of other fabric goods like placemats, *tenugui* (small hand towels), handkerchiefs, bedding etc. It's near Daimaru department store.

Textiles & Kimono There are several central kimono shops worth stopping at for a peek at the elegant fabrics and kimono.

Shikunshi (☎ *221 0456*) **Map 5** Open 10.30am-7pm. In a wonderful old kyō-machiya on Shijō-dōri, east of Nishinotōin-dōri, this shop sells a variety of kimono. Have a look at the small shop in the restored warehouse at the back.

Kyō-kimono Plaza (☎ *352 2323*) **Map 7** Open 10am-5pm. This is another possibility for kimono; it's near the corner of Karasuma-dōri and Takatsuji-dōri.

Nishijin Textile Center (☎ *451 9231*) **Map 5** If you're looking for Nishijin-ori fabrics, some of which are used in kimono, try the shop here.

Erizen (☎ *221 1618*) **Map 9** For kyō-yūzen fabrics, you should head for Erizen, near the Takashimaya department store on Shijō-dōri.

Wood-Block Prints We suggest the Kyoto Handicraft Center (see Art & Craft Emporiums in this chapter) for high-quality and inexpensive wood-block prints. Two other possibilities are:

Nishiharu (☎ *211 2849*) Open 1pm-6.30pm. This is an attractive shop dealing in wood-block prints *(han-ga* or *moku-han)*. All the prints are accompanied by English explanations and the owner is happy to take the time to find something you really like.

Tessai-dō (☎ *531 9566*) **Map 6** Open 10am-5pm. Just outside Kōdai-ji, this small shop deals in original wood-block prints. Prices average ¥10,000 per piece.

Woodwork *Enami* (☎ *361 2816*) **Map 7** Open 9am-5pm, closed Sun. About five minutes' walk south of the Gojō-dōri and Karasuma-dōri crossing, Enami deals in high-quality local kyō-sashimono wood wares *(mokkōhin)*, from small trays to delicate implements for tea ceremony.

Other Items
Imported Food & Gourmet Items
Sometimes you just can't do without a taste of home. Kyoto expats have long patronised the following stores for things you can't usually find in more general Japanese supermarkets.

Meiji-ya (☎ *221 7661*) **Map 9** Open 10am-8pm. This famous Sanjō-dōri gourmet supermarket has Kyoto's best selection of imported food and an excellent selection of wine. Prices are high.

Maki (☎ *781 3670*) **Map 4** Open 10am-10pm, closed Wed. North of Kyoto University, this small shop carries a decent selection of imports at prices a shade lower than the above.

Demachiyanagi Yunyū Shokuhin (☎ *231 1110*) **Map 5** Open 10am-7pm. Near

MARTIN MOOS

The Umeda Sky building in Osaka, with its twin towers joined at the top, as seen from below.

FRANK CARTER

The rebuilt Osaka-jō; the original 1583 castle was destroyed by the armies of Tokugawa Ieyasu.

FRANK CARTER

Sumo wrestlers in Osaka. Salt is thrown into the ring to purify it before a bout.

The spectacular 14th-century Himeji-jō. The castle survives in its original (nonconcrete) form.

MARTIN MOOS

MASON FLORENCE

A rice-farmer at work in Miyama-chō.

MASON FLORENCE

Kitamura is famous for its thatched-roof houses.

the Kawaramachi-Imadegawa crossing, this shop has good deals on coffee, cookies and chocolate.

Incense *Kungyoku-dō* (☎ *371 0162*) **Map 10** Open 9am-7pm, closed 1st & 3rd Sun each month. A haven for the olfactory sense, this place has sold incense and aromatic woods (for burning like incense) for four centuries. It's opposite the gate of Nishi Hongan-ji.

Japanese Knives & Kitchenware *Aritsugi* (☎ *221 1091*) **Map 9** Open 9am-5.30pm. While you're in the Nishiki Market have a look at this store where you can find some of the best kitchen knives in the world. They also carry a selection of excellent and unique Japanese kitchenware.

Japanese Tea *Ippō-dō* (☎ *211 3421*) **Map 9** Open 9am-7pm, closed Sun. This old-style tea shop sells the best Japanese tea in

Kyoto. Their *matcha* (powdered green tea used in the tea ceremony) makes an excellent and lightweight souvenir. Try a 40-gram container of *wa-no-mukashi* (Old Time Japan) for ¥1600, which makes 25 cups of excellent green tea. The tea shop is north of the city hall, near Teramachi-dōri.

Outdoor Sporting Goods *Kōjitsu* (☎ *257 7050*) **Map 9** Open 10.30am-8pm. If you plan to do some hiking or camping while in Japan, you can stock up on equipment at this excellent little shop on Kawaramachi. You'll find that Japanese outdoor sporting equipment is very high quality (with prices to match).

Umbrellas *Tsujikura* (☎ *221 4396*) **Map 9** Open 11am-8.30pm, closed Wed. A short walk north of the Shijō-Kawaramachi crossing, Tsujikura has a good selection of waxed-paper umbrellas and paper lanterns with traditional and modern designs.

Excursions

While Kyoto has enough wonders to keep you busy for weeks, it's worth heading out of the city at least once to sample some of Kansai's other attractions, most of which are less than an hour's train ride away. Nara, Japan's first permanent capital, boasts a collection of temples to rival Kyoto's, including Tōdai-ji, with its enormous Daibutsu (Great Buddha), and Hōryū-ji, which houses some of Japan's most important Buddhist treasures. Down-to-earth Osaka, Japan's second city, is a great place to see modern Japan without traipsing all the way to Tokyo. Kōbe, Japan's version of San Francisco, is a pleasant city with great cafes and restaurants. Smaller destinations include Himeji, home of Japan's finest surviving castle, and Miyama-chō, northern Kyoto's rustic hinterland filled with quaint villages and thatched-roof houses.

NARA 奈良

☎ 0742 • pop 363,000

Nara, Japan's capital from 710 to 785, is the number two tourist attraction in Kansai after Kyoto. Like Kyoto, Nara is uninspiring at first glance, but careful inspection will reveal the rich history and hidden beauty of the city. Indeed, with eight Unesco World Heritage sites, Nara is second only to Kyoto as a repository of Japan's cultural legacy.

Orientation

Nara's two main train stations, JR Nara station and Kintetsu Nara station, are roughly in the middle of the city and Nara-kōen, which contains most of the important sights, is on the east side against the bare flank of Wakakusa-yama. Most of the other sights are south-west of the city and are best reached by buses that leave from both train stations (or by train in the case of Hōryū-ji). It's easy to cover the city centre and the major attractions in nearby Nara-kōen on foot, though some may prefer to rent a bicycle (see the Getting Around section later).

Information

The best source of information is the Nara City Tourist Center (☎ 22 3900), which is open from 9am to 9pm daily. It's only a short walk from JR Nara or Kintetsu Nara stations.

The tourist centre can put you in touch with volunteer guides who speak English and other foreign languages but you will have to book in advance. Two of these services are the YMCA Goodwill Guides (☎ 45 5920 or 22 5595) and Nara Student Guides (☎ 26 4753). Remember that the guides are volunteers so you should offer to cover the day's expenses for your guide (although most temple and museum admissions are waived for registered guides).

There are three additional tourist information offices in Nara: the JR Nara station office (☎ 22 9821), the Kintetsu Nara station office (☎ 24 4858) and the Sarusawa information office (☎ 26 1991). All of these three offices are open from 9am to 5pm daily. The JR Nara station office may also be able to help you with *ryokan* and *minshuku* reservations.

Nara tourist information offices have two useful maps: the excellent *Strolling Around Nara* map, which is best for sightseeing within the city limits, and the *Japan: Nara Prefecture* map, which is best for outlying areas.

There is an ATM that accepts international cards on the ground floor of the building opposite Kintetsu Nara station. In the same building you can purchase tickets for highway buses (to Tokyo etc), airport buses (to Kansai airport) and tour buses (around Nara and surrounding areas).

For Internet services, try the CAN computer school (☎ 20 7188), which charges ¥200 for 30 minutes and is located inside Keirindō bookshop. At the time of writing, it was also possible to log on for free at the offices of Nara Dotto FM (☎ 24 8415) in Naramachi. The office is open from 10am to 5pm.

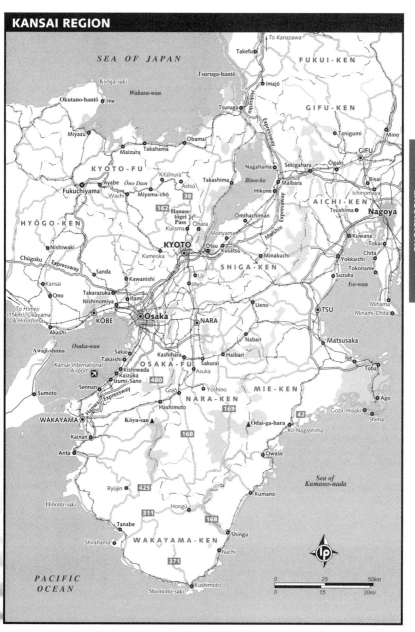

KANSAI REGION

EXCURSIONS

Nara-kōen

This park was created from wasteland in 1880 and covers a large area at the foot of Wakakusa-yama. The JNTO's leaflet called *Walking Tour Courses in Nara* (available at the Kyoto TIC) includes a map for this area. Although walking time is estimated at two hours, you'll need at least half a day to see a selection of the sights and a full day to see the lot.

The park is home to about 1200 deer, which in old times were considered to be messengers of the gods and today enjoy the status of national treasures. They roam the park and surrounding areas in search of handouts from tourists. You can buy special biscuits (*shika-sembei*, ¥150) from vendors to feed the deer (don't eat them yourself, as we saw one misguided foreign tourist doing).

Kōfuku-ji Kōfuku-ji (☎ *22 7755; grounds free, National Treasure Hall ¥500; grounds open dawn to dusk, National Treasure Hall open 9am-4.30pm)* was transferred here from Kyoto in 710 as the main temple for the Fujiwara family. Although the original temple complex had 175 buildings, fires and destruction through power struggles have left only a dozen still standing. There are two pagodas, a three-storey one and a five-storey one, dating from 1143 and 1426 respectively. The taller of the two pagodas is the second tallest in Japan, outclassed by the one at Kyoto's Tō-ji by only a few centimetres.

The **National Treasure Hall** (Kokuhō-kan) contains a variety of statues and art objects salvaged from previous structures.

Nara National Museum Devoted to Buddhist Art, the Nara National Museum (☎ *22 7771; general admission ¥420, special exhibit admission ¥830; open 9am-4.30pm)* is divided into two wings. The western gallery exhibits archaeological finds and the eastern gallery has displays of sculptures, paintings and calligraphy. The galleries are linked by an underground passage.

A special exhibition is held in May and the contents of the Shōsō-in hall, which holds the treasures of Tōdai-ji, are displayed here from around 21 October to 8 November (call the tourist centre to check as these dates vary slightly each year). The exhibits include priceless items from the cultures along the Silk Road.

Isui-en & Neiraku Bijutsukan Nara's most splendid garden, Isui-en (☎ *22 2173; admission ¥600; open 9.30am-4pm, closed Tues & 18 Dec-6 Jan)*, which dates from the Meiji era, is beautifully laid out with abundant greenery and a pond filled with ornamental carp. It's without a doubt the best garden in the city and is well worth a visit. For ¥450 you can enjoy a cup of tea on tatami mats overlooking the garden or have lunch in nearby Sanshū restaurant (see Places to Eat & Drink), which also shares the view.

The adjoining art museum, the **Neiraku Bijutsukan** (☎ *22 2173; admission included in garden admission; open 9.30am-4pm, closed Tues & 18 Dec-6 Jan)*, displays Chinese and Korean ceramics and bronzes. It's something of an anticlimax after the garden.

Tōdai-ji

Tōdai-ji (☎ *22 5511; Daibutsu-den ¥500, Kaidan-in ¥500, Sangatsu-dō ¥500; open 8am-4.30pm Nov-Feb, 8am-5pm Mar, 7.30am-5.30pm Apr-Sept, 7.30am-5pm Oct)*, with its vast Daibutsu-den hall and enormous bronze Buddha image, is Nara's star attraction. For this reason, it is often packed with groups of schoolchildren being herded around by microphone-wielding tour guides. Nonetheless, it is an awe-inspiring sight and should be high on any sightseeing itinerary.

On your way to the temple you'll pass through the **Nandai-mon**, a gate containing two fierce-looking Niō guardians. These recently restored wooden images, carved in the 13th century by the sculptor Unkei, are some of the finest wooden statues in all of Japan, if not the world. They are truly dramatic works of art and seem ready to spring to life at any moment.

Tōdai-ji's **Daibutsu-den** (Hall of the Great Buddha) is the largest wooden building in the world. Unbelievably, the present structure, rebuilt in 1709, is a mere two-thirds the size of the original! The Daibutsu (Great Buddha) contained within is one of the largest bronze figures in the world and was originally cast in 746. The present statue, recast in the Edo period, stands just over 16m high and consists of 437 tonnes of bronze and 130kg of gold.

As you circle the statue towards the back of the Buddha, you'll see a wooden column with a hole through its base. Popular belief maintains that those who can squeeze through the hole, which is exactly the same size as one of the Great Buddha's nostrils, are ensured of enlightenment. It's fun to watch the kids wiggle through nimbly and the adults get wedged in like champagne corks. A hint for determined adults: it's a lot easier to go through with both arms held above your head.

A short walk west of the entrance gate to the Daibutsu-den, the **Kaidan-in,** a hall that was used for ordination ceremonies, is famous for its clay images of the Shi Tennō (Four Heavenly Guardians).

Walk east from the entrance to the Daibutsu-den, climb up a flight of stone steps, and continue to your left to reach the following two halls.

Nigatsu-dō is a hall famed for its Omizutori Festival (see the later section on Nara Special Events for details) and a splendid view across Nara that makes the climb up the hill worthwhile – particularly at dusk.

A short walk south of Nigatsu-dō is **Sangatsu-dō,** which is the oldest building in the Tōdai-ji complex. This hall contains a small collection of fine statues from the Nara period.

Shōsō-in Treasure Repository A short walk north of Daibutsu-den you will find the Shōsō-in Treasure Repository *(☎ 26 2811; admission free; grounds open 10am-3pm, closed Sat, Sun & national holidays, building open only during special exhibitions).* If you discount the slight curve to the roof, the structure is reminiscent of a log cabin from North America. The building was used to house fabulous imperial treasures and its wooden construction allowed

precise regulation of humidity through natural expansion and contraction. The treasures have been removed and are shown in the autumn at the Nara National Museum (see earlier). The Shōsō-in building is open to the public at the same time.

Kasuga-taisha

Kasuga-taisha *(☎ 22 7788; admission free; open dawn-dusk),* Nara's most important shrine, was founded in the 8th century by the Fujiwara family and was completely rebuilt every 20 years according to Shintō tradition, until the end of the 19th century. It lies at the foot of the hill in a pleasant wooded setting with herds of sacred deer awaiting hand-outs.

The approaches to the shrine are lined with hundreds of lanterns and there are many more hundreds in the shrine itself. The lantern festivals held twice a year at the shrine are a major attraction. For details about these and other festivals held at the nearby Wakamiya-jinja, see the Special Events section later.

The **Hōmotsu-den** (Treasure Hall) *(☎ 22 7788; admission ¥420; open 9am-4pm)* is just north of the entrance torii for the shrine. The hall displays Shintō ceremonial regalia and equipment used in *bugaku*, *nō* and *gagaku* performances.

Naramachi 奈良町

South of Sanjō-dōri and Sarusawa-ike pond you will find the pleasant neighbourhood of Naramachi, with many well-preserved *machiya* (traditional city houses). It's a nice place for a stroll before or after hitting the big sights of Nara-kōen and there are several good restaurants in the area to entice hungry travellers (see the Places to Eat & Drink section later).

Highlights of Naramachi include the **Naramachi Shiryō-kan Museum** *(☎ 22 5509; admission free; open 10am-4pm, closed Mon),* which has a decent collection of bric-a-brac from the area, including a display of old Japanese coins and bills. A good place to check out a traditional Japanese house is the **Naramachi Koshi-no-Ie** *(☎ 22 4820; admission free; open 9am-5pm, closed Mon).*

EXCURSIONS

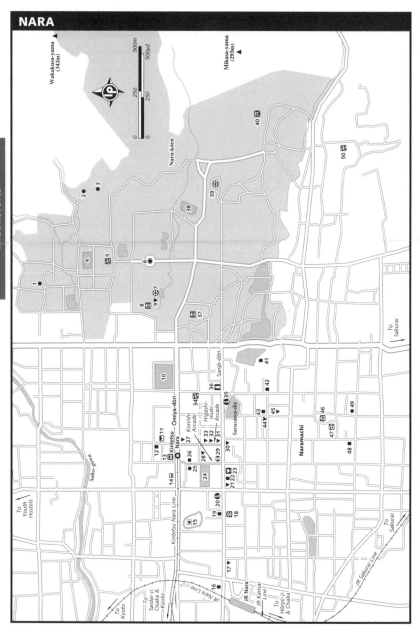

NARA

Wakakusa-yama
(342m)

Mikasa-yama
(293m)

500m
500yd

250
250

Nara-kōen

Saho-gawa

Sanjō-dōri

Konishi
Arcade

Higashi-
muki
Arcade

Omiya-dōri

Kintetsu Nara Line

Sarusawa-ike

Naramachi

JR Nara Line

JR Sakurai Line

JR Kansai
Line

Kintetsu
Nara

JR Nara

To
Kyoto

To
Youth
Hostels

To
Saidai-ji,
Osaka &
Kyoto

To
Kyoto

To
Hōryū-ji
& Osaka

To
Sakurai

To
Sakurai

NARA

PLACES TO STAY

12 Green Hotel Ashibi
    グリーンホテルあしび
16 Nara Kokusai Hotel
    奈良国際ホテル
19 Hotel Fujita Nara
    ホテルフジタ奈良
22 Ryokan Hakuhō
    旅館白鳳
41 Nara Hotel
    奈良ホテル
42 Hotel Sunroute Nara
    ホテルサンルート奈良
43 Ryokan Matsumae
    旅館松前
48 Ryokan Seikan-sō
    旅館静観荘

PLACES TO EAT & DRINK

9   Sanshū
    三秀
17 Maguro-tei
    まぐろ亭
21 Toku Toku
    得々
23 Rumours
    ルーマーズ
27 Tsukihi-tei
    月日亭
28 Hira-no-Ie
    平の家
30 Miyono
    三好野
31 Beni-e
    べに江
32 Okaro
    おかろ
33 Za Don
    ザ；どん
44 Hirasō
    平宗

45 Tempura Asuka
    天ぷら飛鳥

OTHER

1   Shōsō-in Treasure
    Repository
    正倉院
2   Nigatsu-dō Hall
    二月堂
3   Sangatsu-dō Hall
    三月堂
4   Tōdai-ji Daibutsu-den
    東大寺大仏殿
5   Tōdai-ji Chū-mon
    東大寺中門
6   Tōdai-ji Nandai-mon
    東大寺南大門
7   Isui-en
    依水園
8   Neiraku Art Museum
    寧楽美術館
10 Nara Prefectural Office
    奈良県庁
11 Post Office
    郵便局
13 Tour Bus Tickets;
    Highway Bus Tickets;
    Airport Bus Tickets;
    International ATM
    観光バス切符売り場；
    高速バス切符売り場；
    エアポートリムジン
    バス切符売り場；
    国際ATM
14 Local Bus Stop
    市バス停
15 Emperor Kaika's
    Tomb
    開化天皇陵
18 NTT Telecom Square;
    International Phones

    テレコムスク
    ウェアー；国際電話
20 Nara City Tourist Center
    奈良市観光センター
24 Vivre Department Store
    ビブレ
25 Kintetsu Sunflower
    Rent-a-Cycle
    近鉄サンフラワー
    レンタサイクル
26 CAN Computer School
    CAN
29 Sumitomo Bank
    住友銀行
34 Kōfuku-ji National
    Treasure Hall
    興福寺国宝館
35 Sarusawa Tourist
    Information Office
    猿沢観光案内所
36 Kōfuku-ji Five-Storey
    Pagoda
    興福寺五重塔
37 Nara National Museum
    奈良国立博物館
38 Nara Prefectural Public
    Hall
    奈良県民ホール
39 Kasuga Taisha-en
    春日大社庭園
40 Kasuga-taisha
    春日大社
46 Naramachi Shiryō-kan
    Museum
    奈良町資料館
47 Nara Dotto FM
    奈良ドットFM
49 Naramachi Koshi-no-Ie
    ならまち格子の家
50 Shin-Yakushi-ji
    新薬師寺

EXCURSIONS

Temples South-West of Nara

There are several temples located south-west of Nara, the most important of which are Hōryū-ji, Yakushi-ji and Tōshōdai-ji. These three can be visited in one afternoon. The best way to do this is to head straight to Hōryū-ji (the most distant from downtown Nara) and then continue by bus No 52, 97 or 98 (¥560, 30 minutes) up to Yakushi-ji and Tōshōdai-ji, which are a 10-minute walk apart.

Hōryū-ji This temple (☎ 75 2555; admission ¥1000; open 9am-4.45pm) was founded in 607 by Prince Shōtoku, considered by many to be the patron saint of Japanese Buddhism. Hōryū-ji is a veritable shrine to Shōtoku and is renowned not only as the oldest temple in Japan, but also as a repository for some of the country's rarest treasures. Several of the temple's wooden buildings have survived earthquakes and fires to become the oldest of their kind in the world. The layout of the temple is divided into two parts, **Sai-in** (West Temple) and **Tō-in** (East Temple).

The entrance ticket allows admission to the Sai-in, Tō-in and Great Treasure Hall. A detailed map is provided and a guidebook is available in English and several other languages. The JNTO leaflet called *Walking Tour Courses in Nara* includes a basic map for the area around Hōryū-ji.

The main approach to the temple proceeds from the south along a tree-lined avenue and continues through the Nandai-mon and Chū-mon, the temple's two main gates, before entering the Sai-in precinct. As you enter the Sai-in, you'll see the **Kondō** (Main Hall) on your right, and a pagoda on your left.

The Kondō houses several treasures, including the triad of the Buddha Sākyamuni with two attendant Bodhisattvas. The pagoda contains clay images depicting scenes from the life of Buddha.

On the eastern side of the Sai-in are the two concrete buildings of the **Daihōzō-den** (Great Treasure Hall), containing numerous treasures from Hōryū-ji's long history.

If you leave this hall and continue east through the Tōdai-mon you reach the Tō-in. The **Yumedono** (Hall of Dreams) in this temple is where Prince Shōtoku is believed to have meditated and been given help with problem sutras by a kindly, golden apparition.

To get to the Hōryū-ji, take the JR Kansai line from JR Nara station to Hōryūji station (¥210, 10 minutes). From there, a bus service shuttles the short distance between the station and Hōryū-ji (No 73, ¥170, 5 minutes) or you can walk there in 20 minutes. Alternatively, take bus No 52, 60, 97 or 98 from either JR Nara station or Kintetsu Nara station and get off at the Hōryūji-mae stop (¥760, 50 minutes).

Yakushi-ji This temple (*☎ 33 6001; admission ¥500; open 8.30am-5pm*) was established by Emperor Tenmu in 680. With the exception of the **East Pagoda**, which dates to 730, the present buildings either date from the 13th century or are very recent reconstructions.

The main hall was rebuilt in 1976 and houses several images, including the famous Yakushi Triad (the Buddha Yakushi flanked by the Bodhisattvas of the sun and moon), dating from the 8th century.

Behind the East Pagoda is the **Tōin-dō** (East Hall), which houses the famous Shō-Kannon image, dating from the 7th century.

To get to Yakushi-ji, take bus No 52, 63, 70, 97 or 98 from either JR Nara station or Kintetsu Nara station and get off at the Yakushiji Higashiguchi stop (¥240, 18 minutes).

Tōshōdai-ji This temple (*☎ 33 7900; admission ¥600; open 8.30am-4.30pm*) was established in 759 by the Chinese priest Ganjin (Jian Zhen), who had been recruited by Emperor Shōmu to reform Buddhism in Japan. Ganjin didn't have much luck with his travel arrangements from China to Japan: five attempts were thwarted by shipwreck, storms and bureaucracy. Despite being blinded by eye disease, he finally made it on the sixth attempt and spread his teachings to Japan. The lacquer sculpture in the **Miei-dō** hall is a moving tribute to Ganjin: blind and rock steady. It is shown only once a year on 6 June – the anniversary of Ganjin's death.

If you're not lucky enough to be in Nara on that day, it's still well worth visiting this temple to see the fantastic trinity of Buddhas in the **Kondō** hall of the temple. The centrepiece is a seated image of Rushana Buddha, which is flanked by two standing Buddha images, Yakushi-nyorai and Senjū-Kannon.

Tōshōdai-ji is a 10-minute walk north of Yakushi-ji's north gate; see the previous section for transport details from Nara.

Special Events

Nara has plenty of festivals throughout the year. The following is a brief list of the more interesting ones. More extensive information is readily available from Nara tourist offices or from the TIC in Kyoto.

Yamayaki (Grass Burning Festival; 15 January)
 To commemorate a feud many centuries ago between the monks of Tōdai-ji and Kōfuku-ji, Wakakusa-yama is set alight at 6pm with an accompanying display of fireworks.

Mantōrō (Lantern Festival; 2–4 February) Held at Kasuga-taisha at 6pm, this festival is renowned for its illumination with 3000 stone and bronze lanterns.

Omizutori (Water-Drawing Ceremony; 1–14 March) The monks of Tōdai-ji enter a special period of initiation during these days. On the evening of 12 March, they parade enormous flaming torches around the balcony of Nigatsu-dō (in the temple grounds) and rain down embers on the spectators to purify them. The water-drawing ceremony is performed after midnight.

Mantōrō (Lantern Festival; 14–15 August) The same as the February festival above.

Places to Stay

Youth Hostels *Nara-ken Seishōnen Kaikan Youth Hostel (☎/fax 22 5540)* Dorm beds/private rooms ¥2650/3350 per person. This is a nondescript, concrete place with a friendly staff. From JR Nara station or Kintetsu Nara station, take bus No 12, 13, 131 or 140 and get off at the Ikuei-gakuen bus stop, from which it's a five-minute walk.

Nara Youth Hostel (☎ 22 1334, fax 22 1335) Dorm beds ¥2300. This is a nicer hostel than the above. From either JR or Kintetsu Nara station, take bus No 108, 109, 111, 115 or 130 and get off at the Shieikyūjō-mae bus stop, from which it's a one-minute walk.

Ryokan *Ryokan Seikan-sō (☎/fax 22 2670)* From ¥4000 per person without bath. This friendly place with wooden architecture and a pleasant garden is probably the best-value ryokan in Nara.

Ryokan Matsumae (☎ 22 3686) From ¥4500 per person without bath. This ryokan lacks the atmosphere of the Seikan-sō, but it's got a very convenient location.

Ryokan Hakuhō (☎ 26 7891, fax 26 7893) From ¥6500 per person without bath. This ryokan is in the centre of town, just a five-minute walk from JR Nara station. It's starting to show its age and has less atmosphere than the Seikan-sō.

Hotels *Green Hotel Ashibi (☎ 26 7815, fax 24 2465)* Singles/doubles/twins from ¥6400/11,000/12,000. Close to Kintetsu Nara station, this small, serviceable hotel is one of the better value hotels in Nara.

Hotel Fujita Nara (☎ 23 8111) Singles/doubles/twins from ¥6500/12,000/ 10,000. A clean, new hotel with a convenient location. During off-peak times, you might get a reduced rate if you reserve through the Kintetsu Nara tourist information office.

Hotel Sunroute Nara (☎ 22 5151, fax 27 3759) Singles from ¥8000, doubles/twins from ¥15,000. This basic business hotel is near the south-west corner of Nara-kōen.

Nara Kokusai Hotel (☎ 26 6001, fax 23 1552) Singles/doubles/twins from ¥4300/ 7800/10,600. Right outside JR Nara station, this may be the cheapest hotel in town.

Nara Hotel (☎ 26 3300, fax 23 5252) Singles/doubles/twins from ¥14,000/23,000/ 22,000. Built near the turn of the century, Nara Hotel still ranks as the city's premier hotel. Rooms in the old wing have much more character than those in the new wing.

Places to Eat & Drink

Just outside Kintetsu Nara station, the Higashi-muki shopping arcade is a good place to hunt for reasonably priced restaurants. The restaurants in this section are open during usual business hours (11am to 2pm, 5pm to 10pm) unless otherwise noted.

Za Don (☎ 27 5314) Lunch/dinner from ¥400. The name is short for 'donburi' (rice bowl) and this place takes the honours in the cheapest eats category. It's healthy Japanese fast food and there's a picture menu to make ordering easier.

Okaro (☎ 24 3686) Okonomiyaki from ¥680. This is a casual spot to enjoy tasty okonomiyaki. Look for the food models in the window.

Hira-no-Ie (☎ 26 3918) Okonomiyaki from ¥680. Like Okaro, this is another good spot to try okonomiyaki.

Tsukihi-tei (☎ 23 5470) Lunch/dinner from ¥1000/1500. Tsukihi-tei serves simple *kaiseki* sets at reasonable prices. The *ten-shin bentō*, a good bet at ¥1500, includes sashimi, rice, vegetables, *chawan-mushi* and other tidbits.

Beni-e (☎ 22 9493) Lunch/dinner from ¥1500/2000. One of our favourites in Nara, Beni-e serves good tempura sets for ¥1500/2000/2500 (*hana*, *tsuki* and *yuki* sets

EXCURSIONS

respectively). It's located a little back from the street, behind a shoe store.

Miyono (☎ 22 5239) Lunch/dinner from ¥650. This simple place does good-value sets of typical Japanese fare. Stop by and check the daily lunch specials on display outside.

Toku Toku (☎ 35 3577) Lunch/dinner from ¥750. This *udon* specialist should satisfy even the biggest appetites – when you order you can ask for double or triple the normal amount of noodles for the same price!

Maguro-tei (☎ 20 5510) ¥1050 for women, ¥1575 for men. The all-you-can-eat sushi is only so-so, but the price can't be beat at this busy kaiten sushi hall.

Hirasō (☎ 22 0866) Lunch/dinner from ¥2100/4000. Closed Mon. This Naramachi restaurant does elegant kaiseki sets for that special night out.

Tempura Asuka (☎ 26 4308) Lunch/dinner from ¥1500/2000. Closed Mon. Tempura Asuka serves attractive sets of tempura and sashimi in a relatively casual atmosphere. At lunchtime try their nicely presented *yumei-dono bentō* for ¥1500.

Sanshū (☎ 22 2173) Lunch from ¥1200. Open 11.30am-2pm, closed Tues. Located alongside Isui-en, Sanshū serves *tororo*, a traditional dish made from grated yam, barley and rice. Guests sit on tatami mats enjoying the food while gazing out over the splendour of the garden. Ordering is simple due to the choice of either the *mugitoro gozen* (without eel) for ¥1200 or the *unatoro gozen* (with eel) for ¥2500.

Rumours (☎ 26 4327) This English-style pub is a decent spot for a few evening drinks and a good spot to meet local residents and other travellers.

Getting There & Away

Unless you have a Japan Rail Pass, the best option is the Kintetsu line (sometimes written in English as the Kinki Nippon railway), which links Kyoto (Kintetsu Kyoto station) and Nara (Kintetsu Nara station). There are direct limited express trains (¥1110, 35 minutes) and ordinary express trains (¥610, 45 minutes; may require a change at Saidai-ji). Kintetsu Kyoto station is on the south-west corner of the main Kyoto station building; go to the south side of the station (the *shinkansen* side) and follow the signs.

The JR Nara line also connects Kyoto station with JR Nara station. Your best bet is a *kaisoku* (rapid train; ¥690, 46 minutes), but departures are often few and far between.

Getting Around

Bus Most of the area around Nara-kōen is covered by two circular bus routes. Bus No 1 runs counter-clockwise and bus No 2 runs clockwise. There's a ¥180 flat fare. You can easily see the main sights in the park on foot and use the bus as an option if you are pressed for time or tired.

The most useful buses for western and south-western Nara (Tōshōdai-ji, Yakushi-ji and Hōryū-ji) are Nos 52, 97 and 98, which link all three destinations with the Kintetsu and JR stations. Buses run about every 30 minutes between 8am and 5pm, but are much less frequent outside these times.

Bicycle Bicycles are a good way to get around Nara. Kintetsu Sunflower Rent-a-Cycle (☎ 24 3528) is close to the Nara City Tourist Center. Weekday rates are ¥300 per hour and ¥900 per day; weekend rates are ¥350 per hour and ¥1000 per day.

OSAKA 大阪
☎ 06 • pop 2.48 million

Osaka is the working heart of Kansai. Famous for its down-to-earth citizens and hearty cuisine, Osaka combines a few historical and cultural attractions with all the delights of a modern Japanese city. Indeed, Osaka is surpassed only by Tokyo as a showcase of the Japanese urban phenomenon.

This isn't to say that Osaka is an attractive city; almost bombed flat in WWII, it appears as an endless expanse of concrete boxes punctuated by *pachinko* parlours and elevated highways. But the city somehow manages to rise above this and exert a peculiar charm. And by night, the city really comes into its own. This is when all those drab streets and alleys come alive with flashing neon, beckoning residents and travellers alike with promises of tasty food and good times.

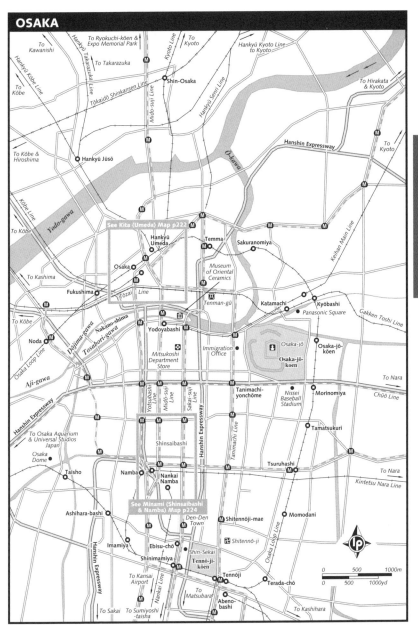

OSAKA

To Kawanishi

To Ryokuchi-kōen &
Expo Memorial Park

To Kyoto

Hankyū Kyoto Line
to Kyoto

To Takarazuka

Shin-Osaka

To Hirakata
& Kyoto

Tōkaidō Shinkansen Line

To Kōbe

Hanshin Expressway

To Kyoto

To Kōbe &
Hiroshima

Hankyū Jūsō

Ō-kawa

Yodo-gawa

To Kōbe

See Kita (Umeda) Map p222

Hankyū
Umeda

Temma

Sakuranomiya

Kehan Main Line

Gakken Toshi Line

To Kashima

Osaka

Museum
of Oriental
Ceramics

Fukushima

Tōzai Line

Tenman-gū

Katamachi

Kyōbashi

Panasonic Square

Noda

Dōjima-gawa

Nakano-shima

Tosabori-gawa

Yodoyabashi

Mitsukoshi
Department
Store

Immigration
Office

Osaka-jō

Osaka-jō-
kōen

To Kōbe

Osaka-jō-
koen

Aji-gawa

Osaka Loop Line

Hanshin Expressway

To Nara

Tanimachi-
yonchōme

Nissei
Baseball
Stadium

Morinomiya

Chūō Line

To Osaka Aquarium
& Universal Studios
Japan

Yotsubashi Line

Midō-suji Line

Sakai-suji Line

Hanshin Expressway

Tanimachi Line

Tamatsukuri

Osaka
Dome

Shinsaibashi

Taisho

Namba

Nankai
Namba

Tsuruhashi

To Nara

Kintetsu Nara Line

See Minami (Shinsaibashi
& Namba) Map p224

Ashihara-bashi

Den-Den
Town

Shitennō-ji-mae

Momodani

Osaka Loop Line

Imamiya

Ebisu-chō

Shin-Sekai

Shitennō-ji

Hanshin Expressway

Nankai Line

Shinimamiya

Tennō-ji-
kōen

Tennōji

Terada-chō

0   500   1000m

0   500   1000yd

To Kansai
Airport

To
Matsubara

Abeno-
bashi

To Kashihara

To Sakai

To Sumiyoshi
-taisha

Osaka's highlights include its famous castle Osaka-jō, Osaka Aquarium with its two resident whale sharks, and the sci-fi *Blade Runner* nightscapes of the Dōtombori area.

Orientation

Osaka is usually divided into two areas: Kita and Minami. Kita (Japanese for 'north') is the city's main business and administrative centre. Minami (Japanese for 'south') is the city's entertainment district and contains the bustling shopping and nightlife zones of Namba and Shinsaibashi.

The dividing line between Kita and Minami is formed by the Dōjima-gawa and the Tosabori-gawa, between which you'll find Nakano-shima, a peaceful green island which is home to the Museum of Oriental Ceramics. About one kilometre east of Nakano-shima you'll find Osaka-jō and its surrounding park, Osaka-jō-kōen.

To the south of the Minami area you'll find another group of sights clustered around Tennōji station. These include Shitennō-ji, Den-Den Town (the electronics neighbourhood) and the seriously low-rent entertainment district of Shin-Sekai.

Information

The Osaka Tourist Association has offices in Shin-Osaka (☎ 6305 3311), Osaka (☎ 6345 2189), Namba (☎ 6643 2125) and Tennōji (☎ 6774 3077) stations, the main office being the one in Osaka station. All are open from 8am to 8pm daily, and closed from 31 December to 3 January. Many travellers have problems finding the tourist office in Osaka station. To get there from JR trains, go out the Midō-suji exit, take a right, walk about 50 metres and look for it on your left, tucked into a corner. From the subway, go out exit No 9, take a left, walk past a cafe and look for it on your left.

The information offices have two excellent maps of the Osaka region, *Your Guide to Osaka* and *Osaka City Map*. Both have subway and transportation maps and detailed insets of the city's most important areas. Also worth picking up is *Meet Osaka*, a pocket-size reference guide to upcoming events and festivals, and *Osaka: How to Enjoy It*, a pamphlet with details on almost all of Osaka's tourist attractions.

In Kita, there's an international ATM in the Sumitomo Bank located on the B1 floor of Hankyū Umeda station (it's not far from subway exit No 1). Up on street level, you'll find another international ATM down the street from the Osaka Hilton Hotel (see the Kita map). In Minami, there's an international ATM at the Citibank in Shinsaibashi (see the Minami map).

For Internet access in Kita try Web House (☎ 6367 9555), open 11am to 8:30pm, with access for ¥500 per half hour. In Minami try Kinko's (☎ 6245 1922), open 24 hours and costing ¥500 per half hour; or the sometimes smoke-filled Mark's Cyberspace (☎ 4707 4611), open 11am to 11pm, at ¥250 per half hour.

Kita Area 北

By day, Osaka's centre of gravity is the Kita area. While Kita doesn't have any great attractions to detain the traveller, it does have a few good department stores, lots of good places to eat and the Umeda Sky Building.

Umeda Sky Building Just north-west of Osaka station, the Umeda Sky Building (☎ 6440 3855; admission ¥700; open 10am-10pm) is Osaka's most dramatic piece of architecture. The twin-tower complex looks like a space-age version of Paris' Arc de Triomphe.

There are two observation galleries, an outdoor one on the roof and an indoor one on the floor below. Getting to the top is half the fun as you take a glassed-in escalator for the final five storeys (definitely not for vertigo sufferers). Tickets for the observation decks can be purchased on the 3rd floor of the east tower.

Below the towers, you'll find **Takimi-kōji Alley**, a recreation of a Showa-era market street crammed with restaurants and *izakaya*.

The building is reached via an underground passage that starts just north of Osaka or Umeda stations (see the Kita map).

Central Osaka 大阪中心部

Osaka-jō Osaka's most popular attraction, Osaka-jō *(☎ 6941 3044; admission to grounds free, to castle keep ¥600; open 9am-5pm, until 8pm in summer)* is a 1931 concrete reconstruction of the original castle, which was completed in 1583 as a display of power on the part of Toyotomi Hideyoshi.

Refurbished at great cost in 1997, today's castle has a decidedly modern look (for a more authentic castle head west to Himeji-jō). The interior of the castle houses a museum of Toyotomi Hideyoshi memorabilia as well as displays relating the history of the castle.

Ōte-mon, the gate that serves as the main entrance to the park, is a 10-minute walk north-east of Tanimachi-yonchōme station on the Chūō and Tanimachi subway lines. You can also take the Osaka Loop Line, get off at Osaka-jō-kōen station and enter through the back of the castle.

Museum of Oriental Ceramics With more than 1300 exhibits, this museum *(☎ 6223 0055; admission ¥500; open 9.30am-5pm, closed Mon)* has one of the finest collections of Chinese and Korean ceramics in the world.

To get to the museum, go to Yodoyabashi station on either the Midō-suji line or the Keihan line (different stations). Walk north to the river and cross to Nakano-shima. Turn right, pass the city hall on your left, bear left with the road and the museum is on the left.

Minami Area 南

A few stops south of Kita on the Midō-suji subway line (get off at either Shinsaibashi or Namba stations), the Minami area is the place to spend the evening in Osaka. Its highlights include the Dōtombori Arcade, the National Bunraku Theatre, Dōgusuji-ya Arcade and Amerika-Mura.

Dōtombori This is Osaka's liveliest nightlife area. It's centred around **Dōtombori Canal** and **Dōtombori Arcade**. In the evening, head to **Ebisu-bashi**, the main footbridge over the canal, to sample the glittering nightscape, which calls to mind a scene from the science-fiction movie *Blade Runner*.

Only a short walk south of Dōtombori Arcade, you'll find **Hōzen-ji**, a tiny temple hidden down a narrow alley. The temple is built around a moss-covered **Fudō-myōō statue**. This statue is a favourite of people employed in the so-called 'water trade' or *mizu shōbai*. Nearby, you'll find the

EXCURSIONS

Business as Usual

First and foremost, Osaka is a working city and Osakans have business in their blood. Where else in the world do people commonly greet each other with the question, *'Mōkari makka?'* ('Are you making any money?'). Without question, Osaka is. In recent years the city has recorded a gross domestic product greater than all but eight countries in the world. This remarkable economic success has its roots deep in the history of the city, for Osaka was the merchant capital of Japan long before Tokyo was even incorporated as a city.

Aside from infinite legitimate enterprise, organised crime has long held a notorious presence here (romanticised in the West in the 1980s motion picture *Black Rain*). There have been countless Japanese TV shows and movies in which ominous *yakuza* (gangsters) visit Osaka 'bosses' and invariably end up blazing at each other in scathing *Osaka-ben* (Osaka dialect).

Unfortunately, Osaka is has been harder hit than Tokyo by Japan's seemingly interminable recession. The most visible sign of this is the army of homeless who live in Osaka's parks. Conservative estimates put their number at 10,000; others argue that the true number is double this. Efforts are underway to get the homeless off the street and into shelters. Cynics point out that this is merely because the city is trying to attract the 2008 summer Olympic Games. Whatever the case, Osaka is undergoing a vast transformation and it's an exciting time to be in the city.

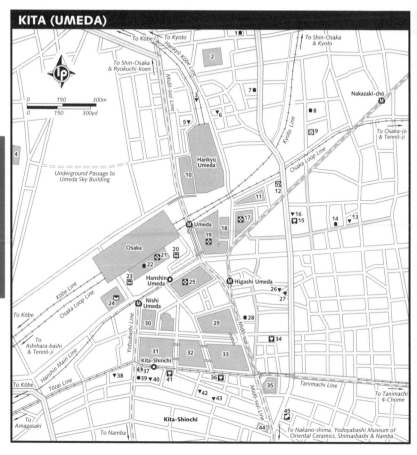

KITA (UMEDA)

atmospheric **Hōzen-ji Yokochō**, a tiny alley filled with traditional restaurants and bars.

Dōgusuji-ya Arcade If you desperately need a *tako-yaki* (octopus ball) fryer, a red lantern to hang outside your shop or plastic food models to lure the customers in, this shopping arcade is the place to go. You'll also find endless knives, pots and almost anything else that's even remotely related to the preparation and consumption of food.

Amerika-Mura Meaning 'America Village', Amerika-Mura is a compact enclave

of trendy shops and restaurants, with a few discreet love hotels thrown in for good measure. The best reason to come here is to view the hoards of colourful Japanese teens living out the myth of *Amerika*.

Amerika-Mura is located one or two blocks west of Midō-suji, bounded on the north by Suomachi-suji and the south by the Dōtombori-gawa.

Tennō-ji Area

Shitennō-ji Founded in 593, Shitennō-ji (☎ 6771 0066; admission free; open 9am-5pm) has the distinction of being one of

KITA (UMEDA)

the oldest Buddhist temples in Japan. However, none of the present buildings are originals: most are the usual concrete reproductions, with the exception of the big stone *torii* (entrance gate). The torii dates back to 1294, making it the oldest of its kind in Japan. Apart from the torii, there is little of real historical significance, and the absence of greenery in the raked-gravel grounds makes for a rather desolate atmosphere.

The temple is most easily reached from Shitennōji-mae station on the Tanimachi subway line. Take the southern exit, cross to the left side of the road and take the small road that goes off at an angle away from the subway station. The entrance to the temple is on the left.

Shin-Sekai For something completely different, take a walk through this retro entertainment district just west of Tennō-ji-kōen.

MINAMI (SHINSAIBASHI & NAMBA)

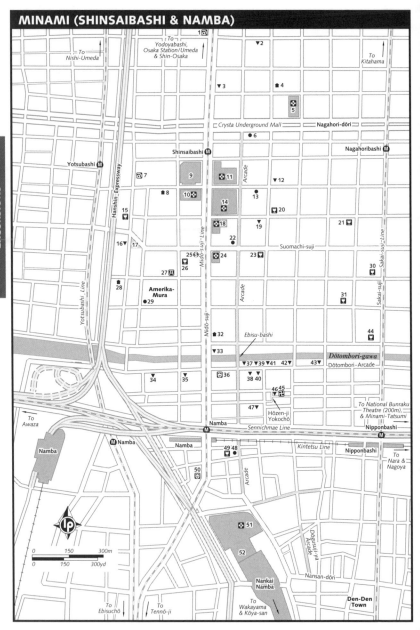

MINAMI (SHINSAIBASHI & NAMBA)

PLACES TO STAY
4 Hotel Do Sports Plaza
   ホテルドゥスポーツ
   プラザ
8 Hotel California
   ホテルカリフォルニア
9 Hotel Nikkō Osaka
   ホテル日航大阪
28 Asahi Plaza Hotel
   Amenity Shinsaibashi
   朝日プラザホテル
   アメニティー心斎橋
32 Holiday Inn Nankai
   Osaka
   ホリデーイン南海大阪
52 Nankai South Tower
   Hotel; Arc en Ciel;
   Namba City
   南海サウスタワー
   ホテル；アークアンシ
   エル；なんばシティ

PLACES TO EAT
2 Namaste
   ナマステ
3 Field of Farms
   フィールド；オブ；フ
   ァームス
12 Nishiya
   にし家
16 McDonald's
   マクドナルド
19 Capricciosa
   カプリチョーザ
33 Shabu-zen; Gin Sen
   しゃぶ禅；銀扇
34 La Bamba
   ラバーンバ
35 Santana
   サンタナ
37 Kani Dōraku Main
   Restaurant
   かに道楽本店

38 Ganko Sushi
   がんこ寿司
39 Krungtep
   クンテープ
40 Kuidaore
   くいだおれ
41 Zuboraya
   づぼらや
42 Kani Dōraku Annex
   かに道楽
43 Chibō
   千房
46 Tempura Maki
   天ぷら牧
47 Akiyoshi
   秋吉

OTHER
1 Kinko's
   キンコース
5 Tōkyū Hands
   Department Store
   東急ハンズ
6 Sony Tower
   ソニータワー
7 Mark's Cyberspace
   マークスサイバースペ
   ース
10 OPA Shopping Centre
   オーパ
11 Sogō Department
   Store
   そごう百貨店
13 Naniwa Camera
   カメラのナニワ
14 Daimaru Department
   Store
   大丸百貨店
15 Sunsplash
   サンスプラッシュ
17 Amerika Mura Triangle
   Park
   アメリカ村三角公園

18 Daimaru Department
   Store Annex
   大丸百貨店別館
20 Diva
   ディーバ
21 Murphy's
   マフィーズ
22 Athens Bookshop
   アテネ書店
23 Pig & Whistle
   ピッグアンドホイッスル
24 Vivre 21 Department
   Store
   ビブレ21
25 Citibank (International
   ATM)
   シティバンク
26 Uncle Steven's
   アンクルスティーブンス
27 Mitsugu-jinja
   御津八幡神社
29 Tower Records
   タワーレコード
30 Rakan
   羅漢
31 Nell's
   ネルズ
36 Shōchikuza
   Theatre
   松竹座
44 Dubliners'
   ダブリナーズ
45 Hōzen-ji
   法善寺
48 Discount Ticket Shop
   格安チケット売り場
49 Hub
   ハッブ
50 Shin-Kabukiza Theatre
   新歌舞伎座
51 Takashimaya
   Department Store
   高島屋百貨店

EXCURSIONS

At the heart of it all you'll find crusty old Tsūten-kaku tower, a 103m-high structure that dates back to 1912 (the present tower was rebuilt in 1969).

When the tower first went up it symbolised everything new and exciting about this once-happening neighbourhood ('Shin-Sekai' is Japanese for 'New World'). Now,

Shin-Sekai is a world that time forgot. You'll find ancient pachinko parlours, run-down theatres, dirt-cheap restaurants and all manner of raffish and suspicious characters.

Sumiyoshi-taisha Osaka's most important shrine, Sumiyoshi-taisha (*☎ 6672 0753; admission free; open 6am-6pm*) is dedicated to Shintō deities associated with the sea and sea travel, in commemoration of a safe passage to Korea by a 3rd-century empress.

Having survived the bombing of WWII, Sumiyoshi-taisha actually has a couple of buildings that date back to 1810. The shrine was founded in the early 3rd century and the buildings that can be seen today are faithful replicas of the originals.

Other interesting features are a collection of more than 700 stone lanterns donated by seafarers and businesspeople, a stone stage for performances of *bugaku* and court dancing and the attractive Taiko-bashi, an arched bridge surrounded by greenery.

The shrine is next to both Sumiyoshi-taisha station on the Nankai line and Sumiyoshi-torii-mae station on the Hankai line (the tram line that leaves from Tennō-ji station).

Other Attractions

Universal Studios Japan This funpark (☎ 4790 7000; adult/child ¥5500/3700; open 9am-7pm Mon-Fri & 9am-9pm Sat, Sun and holidays) is Osaka's answer to Tokyo Disneyland. Although it wasn't open while we were researching this guide, word has it that the park is a faithful reproduction of the American park, complete with all manner of movie-themed rides, stores and shops.

To get there, take the JR Loop Line to Nishi-kujō station, switch to one of the distinctively painted Universal Studio shuttle trains and get off at Universal City station. From Osaka station the trip costs ¥170 and takes about 20 minutes. There are also some direct trains from Osaka station (ask at the tourist office for times; the price is the same).

Osaka Aquarium 'Kaiyūkan' in Japanese, Osaka Aquarium (☎ 6576 5501; adult/child ¥2000/900; open 10am-8pm) is worth a visit, especially for those with children in tow. The aquarium is centred around the world's largest aquarium tank, which is home to the aquarium's star attractions, two enormous whale sharks, and a variety of smaller sharks, rays and other fish. A walkway winds its way around the main tank and past displays of life found on eight different ocean levels.

To get there, take the Chūō subway line to the last stop (Osaka-kō), and from here it's about a five-minute walk to the aquarium. Get there for opening time if you want to beat the crowds – on weekends and holidays long queues are the norm.

Special Events

The major festivals held in Osaka include the following:

Tōka Ebisu (9–11 January) Huge crowds of more than a million people flock to the Imamiya Ebisu Shrine to receive bamboo branches hung with auspicious tokens. The shrine is near Imamiya Ebisu station on the Nankai line.

Doya Doya (14 January) Billed as a 'huge naked festival', this event involves a competition between young men, clad in little more than headbands and loincloths, to obtain the 'amulet of the cow god'. This talisman is said to bring a good harvest to farmers. The festival takes place from 2pm at Shitennō-ji.

Tenjin Matsuri (24–25 July) This is one of Japan's three biggest festivals. Try to make the second day, when processions of portable shrines and people in traditional attire start at Temman-gū and end up in the O-kawa (in boats). As night falls the festival is marked with a huge fireworks display.

Kishiwada Danjiri Matsuri (14–15 September) Osaka's wildest festival, a kind of running of the bulls except with festival floats (*danjiri*), many weighing over 3000kg. The danjiri are hauled through the streets by hundreds of people using ropes, and in all the excitement there have been a couple of deaths – take care and stand back. Most of the action takes place on the second day. The best place to see it is west of Kishiwada station on the Nankai Honsen line (from Nankai Namba station).

Places to Stay

It makes little sense to stay in Osaka with Kyoto just over half an hour away. If you do want to stay in Osaka, however, there are lots of business hotels and regular hotels in both the Kita and Minami areas.

Kita Area *New Japan Sauna and Capsule Hotel* (☎ *6314 2100*) Capsules ¥2600, sauna ¥520. Located in one of Kita's busiest entertainment districts, this is the place to stay if you miss the last train.

Hotel Sunroute Umeda (☎ *6373 1111, fax 6374 0523*) Singles/doubles/twins from ¥7640/12,600/13,600. This is perhaps the best value business hotel in the area. It's located just north of Hankyū Umeda station.

Hotel Green Plaza Osaka (☎ *6374 1515, fax 6734 1089*) Singles/doubles/twins from ¥6800/9800/9800. This drab but economical business hotel is also fairly close to Osaka station.

Umeda OS Hotel (☎ *6312 1271, fax 6312 7283*) Singles/doubles/twins from ¥8300/14,800/11,800. About five minutes south of Osaka station, this clean modern hotel is more attractive than some of the other choices.

Osaka Tōkyū Hotel (☎ *6373 2411, fax 6376 0343*) Singles/doubles/twins from ¥10,000/16,000/18,000. Around the corner from Hankyū Umeda station, this is the cheapest hotel (as opposed to business hotel) in the area.

Hotel New Hankyū (☎ *6372 5101, fax 6374 6885*) Singles/doubles/twins from ¥12,000/24,000/19,000. Next to Hankyū Umeda station, this is a decent choice with fairly spacious rooms.

Granvia Hotel Osaka (☎ *6344 1235, fax 6344 1130*) Singles/doubles/twins from ¥13,500/21,000/21,000. You can't beat this hotel for convenience: it's located directly over Osaka station. Rooms and facilities are of a high standard.

Osaka Hilton Hotel (☎ *6347 7111, fax 6347 7001*) Singles/doubles/twins from ¥24,000/30,000/30,000. Just across from Osaka station, the Hilton is one of the city's most luxurious hotels with a swimming pool and business centre.

Hotel Hankyū International (☎ *6377 2100, fax 6377 3622*) Singles/doubles/twins from ¥27,000/40,000/42,000. This is Osaka's most luxurious hotel and almost all of the rooms have great views over the city.

Minami Area Considering the wealth of dining and entertainment options in the area, the Minami area is probably the best place in Osaka to be based.

Hotel California (☎ *6243 0333, fax 6243 0148*) Singles/doubles/twins from ¥7000/11,000/10,000. Though the hotel is starting to show its age, you might be interested in staying here in order to boast of having stayed at the Hotel California. Who says you can check out but you can never leave?

Asahi Plaza Hotel Amenity Shinsaibashi (☎ *6212 5111, fax 6212 5123*) Singles/doubles/twins from ¥7800/14,500/14,500. Located in the heart of Amerika-Mura, this standard business hotel is a good choice for those who plan a night of carousing in Minami.

Hotel Do Sports Plaza (☎ *6245 3311, fax 6245 5803*) Singles/doubles/twins from ¥9700/12,000/13,000. Another basic business hotel with slightly nicer rooms than the Asahi Plaza.

Holiday Inn Nankai Osaka (☎ *6213 8281, fax 6213 8640*) Singles/doubles/twins from ¥12,000/20,000/19,000. Located just a short walk from the Dōtombori area, this is the most reasonably priced hotel (as opposed to business hotel) in Minami.

Hotel Nikkō Osaka (☎ *6244 1111, fax 6245 2432*) Singles/doubles/twins from ¥18,500/28,5000/28,500. The Nikkō is one of Osaka's better hotels, with a great selection of restaurants and bars on the premises.

Nankai South Tower Hotel (☎ *6646 1119*) Singles/doubles/twins from ¥17,000/28,000/28,000. Located directly above Nankai Namba station, this clean, modern hotel has large rooms, most of which have great views.

Places to Eat
The restaurants in this section are open during usual business hours (11am to 2pm, 5pm to 10pm) unless otherwise noted.

Kita Japanese The Kita area is chock-a-block with good restaurants. For a wide selection of different cuisines under one roof, try the *Kappa Yokochō Arcade*, just north of Hankyū Umeda station.

Gataro (☎ *6373 1484)* Dinner around ¥3000. This cosy little spot does creative twists on standard izakaya themes. Look for the glass front on the left as you head north in the Kappa Yokochō Arcade.

Hatago (☎ *6373 3400)* All items ¥300. This restored farmhouse is a great spot to sample *robotayaki* (fireside) cooking. It's fun watching the chefs whirl the food around on paddles as they labour over the grill. Look for the low doorway and the wooden façade.

Isaribi (☎ *6373 2969)* Dinner from ¥2300. Down a flight of stairs outside Hankyū Umeda station, this is a slightly less appealing spot to sample robotayaki cooking.

Nawasushi (☎ *6312 9891)* Dinner from ¥3000. Located in the heart of Osaka's 'sushi ghetto', this is one of the more reasonable and popular spots in the Kita area for good sushi.

Kamesushi (☎ *6312 3862)* Dinner from ¥3000. Try this spacious sushi bar if Nawasushi is full.

Kani Dōraku (☎ *6344 5091)* Lunch from ¥1600, dinner from ¥3000. Crab done a hundred different ways is the draw at this popular crab specialist. Look for the giant crab waving its pincers above the entrance. There's a picture menu.

Maguro-tei (☎ *6452 5863)* ¥1000 for women, ¥1500 for men. This modern, noisy, automatic sushi place is famous for its all-you-can-eat sushi special.

Shabu-zen (☎ *6343 0250)* Dinner sets from ¥3300. On the 10th floor of the AX building, this is the place for delicious shabu-shabu sets in a pleasant setting.

International There are several cafes in Osaka station itself, the best of which is the **Kitchen Deli Bakery**. Otherwise, you might try the offerings in the nearby Osaka Hilton, which has a wide variety of restaurants on its two basement floors.

The In Place (☎ *6347 7111)* Curry buffet ¥1700. With six curries to choose from, this is the spot for ardent curry lovers. It's in the lobby of the Osaka Hilton.

Court Lodge Curry sets from ¥800. Try this tiny hole-in-the-wall spot for filling sets of Sri Lankan food. Look for the beer signs in the window.

Pina Khana (☎ *6375 5828)* Lunch/dinner from ¥850/3000. This crowded spot in the Kappa Yokochō Arcade is our favourite Indian restaurant in Kita.

Café Org (☎ *6312 0529)* Drinks from ¥250, meals from ¥700. This open, casual cafe is a good spot for a light meal or a quick pick-me-up while exploring Kita.

Herradura (☎ *6361 1011)* Dinner ¥2500. This intimate spot has all the usual Mexican favourites, including taco platters and frozen margaritas.

Minami Japanese The place to eat in Minami is the restaurant-packed Dōtombori Arcade. The restaurants in this area win no points for their refined atmosphere, but the prices are low and the portions large.

Kuidaore (☎ *6211 5300)* Meals from ¥600. The name means 'eat till you drop' and with eight floors serving every kind of Japanese food, it's easy to do just that. Look for the mechanical clown outside its doors.

Kani Dōraku (☎ *6211 8975)* Lunch/dinner from ¥1600/3000. Like its sister branch in Kita, this crab specialist does all kinds of imaginative things to the unfortunate crustaceans. If the main branch is full, there's an annex just down the road.

Zuboraya (☎ *6211 0181)* Fugu sashimi ¥1800, full dinners from ¥3000. This is the place to go when you've worked up the nerve to try *fugu* (Japanese puffer fish). Look for the giant fugu hanging out front.

Chibō (☎ *6212 2211)* Okonomiyaki from ¥800. This is a good spot to sample one of Osaka's most popular dishes, okonomiyaki. Chibō's *modan yaki* (a kind of okonomiyaki) is a good bet at ¥950.

Shabu-zen (☎ *6213 2953)* Shabu-shabu from ¥3000. On the 6th floor of the Gurukas building beside the Dÿtombori-gawa, this is an approachable place to sample shabu-shabu and sukiyaki.

Gin Sen (☎ *6213 7234)* All-you-can-eat kushi-katsu lunch/dinner ¥1980/2980. Gin Sen serves delicious *kushi katsu*, a greasy but tasty treat. It's on the 2nd floor of the Gurukas building.

Ganko Sushi (☎ *6212 1705*) Set meals from ¥1000. Part of Kansai's most popular sushi chain, this is a good place for ample sushi sets and a variety of other Japanese favourites.

Nishiya (☎ *6241 9221*) Meals from ¥1200. This rustic Osaka landmark serves udon noodles and a variety of hearty *nabe* (iron pot) dishes for reasonable prices.

Field of Farms (☎ *6253 0500*) Buffet lunch ¥900. This place is a favourite of Osaka vegetarians for its buffet lunch and extensive bilingual menu. It's in a basement but there's a sign on street level.

Tempura Maki (☎ *6211 8284*) Courses from ¥3900. In the atmospheric Hōzen-ji Yokochō, this is a good place to splash out on a tempura feast.

Akiyoshi (☎ *6212 0531*) Dinner from ¥2500. With a casual atmosphere and a picture menu, Akiyoshi is a good spot for *yakitori*.

International *Krungtep* (☎ *4708 0088*) Lunch buffet/dinner ¥980/2000. Dōtombori's most popular Thai place, Krungtep serves fairly authentic versions of the standard favourites like green curry and fried noodles.

Capricciosa (☎ *6243 6020*) Lunch/dinner from ¥800/2000. Giant portions of acceptable Japanese-style Italian food make this a popular spot for students and travellers.

Santana (☎ *6211 5181*) Lunch sets/dinner sets from ¥1000/2000. Santana is our favourite Indian place in Minami, with lots of veggie choices and delicious samosas.

La Bamba (☎ *6213 9612*) Dinner from ¥2000. Minami's most popular Mexican restaurant, La Bamba serves some mean guacamole and tasty fajitas.

Namaste (☎ *6241 6515*) Lunch sets/dinner from ¥750/2000. Up in the Shinsaibashi area, this friendly Indian restaurant serves filling set meals at reasonable prices.

Entertainment
Traditional Japanese Entertainment
The *National Bunraku Theatre* (☎ *6212 2531*) is Osaka's main *bunraku* (Japanese puppet) theatre. Although bunraku did not originate in Osaka, it was popularised here.

Performances are only held at certain times of the year; check with the tourist information offices. Tickets normally start at around ¥2300 and earphones and program guides in English are available.

Osaka Nō Hall (☎ *6373 1726*), a five-minute walk east of Osaka station, holds nō shows about four times a month, some of which are free.

Unfortunately, neither place has regularly scheduled shows. The best thing is to check with the tourist information offices about current shows, check the listings in the *Meet Osaka* guide or look in *Kansai Time Out*.

Bars & Clubs Osaka has a lively nightlife scene, with lots of bars and clubs that see mixed foreign and Japanese clientele. For up-to-date listings of upcoming club and music events check the *Kansai Time Out*.

Kita Although Minami is Osaka's real nightlife district, there are plenty of good bars and clubs in the neighbourhoods to the south and east of Osaka station.

Karma (☎ *6344 6181*) This very long-standing club is popular with Japanese and foreigners alike. On weekends they usually host techno events with cover charges averaging ¥2500.

Canopy This intimate cafe-style bar is a popular spot with expats for after-work snacks and drinks.

Pig & Whistle (☎ *6361 3198*) Part of Kansai's biggest British-style pub chain, this is the place for pints of Guinness and fish and chips.

Bar, Isn't It? (☎ *6363 4001*) On the 5th floor of the Kakusha building, this pick-up joint is one of Osaka's cheapest places to drink.

Windows on the World (☎ *6347 7111*) For drinks with a view, head to this bar on the 35th floor of the Osaka Hilton. Be warned that there's a ¥2500 per person table charge and drinks average ¥1000.

Minami Minami is the place for a wild night out in Osaka. You simply won't believe the number of bars, clubs and restaurants they've packed into the narrow streets and

EXCURSIONS

alleys of Dōtombori, Shinsaibashi, Namba and Amerika-Mura. Go on a weekend night and you'll be part of a colourful human parade of Osaka characters – this is one of Japan's best spots for people-watching.

Murphy's *(☎ 6282 0677)* One of the oldest Irish-style pubs in Japan, this is a good place to rub shoulders with local expats and young Japanese.

Diva *(☎ 6241 9733)* This karaoke box specialises in English songs (look for the English sign on street level, then take the elevator to the 6th floor).

Pig & Whistle *(☎ 6213 6911)* Like its sister branches in Kita and Kyoto, the Pig is the place to go for a pint and a plate of fish and chips.

Rakan *(☎ 6213 4000)* A new entry on the Minami scene, Rakan lures foreigners and Japanese alike with special theme nights and a stylish interior.

Dubliners' *(☎ 6212 7036)* Try to hit this Irish-style pub early for its 5pm to 8pm happy hour, when pints of Guinness and Kilkenny are ¥600.

Nell's *(☎ 6214 1783)* Nell's is an intimate little spot that is a favourite of Osaka's party set for late-night drinks.

Uncle Steven's *(☎ 6211 7574)* If you find yourself in Amerika-Mura, you might want to give this Tex-Mex bar a try for spicy food, music and beer.

Sunsplash *(☎ 6245 8486)* With a reggae soundtrack and an intimate atmosphere, Sunsplash is one of Amerika-Mura's more popular foreigner-friendly bars. From 8pm to 10pm, beers are only ¥300.

Hub *(☎ 6643 0900)* Hub is yet another pub-style bar with the usual pints and pub grub. It's close to Namba station.

Arc en Ciel *(☎ 6646 1119)* For something a little swanky, head up to this bar on the 36th floor of the Nankai South Tower Hotel. The view is fantastic and the prices are too: there's a ¥1500 per person table charge and drinks average ¥1200.

Tin's Hall *(☎ 6773 5955)* If you find yourself in the Tennō-ji area, try this long-running foreigner favourite. It's a casual spot with a good happy hour special: beers are only ¥300 from 6pm to 9pm. To get there,

leave Tennōji station by the north exit, go right and walk along the main road, turn right one block beyond the Tōei Hotel and look for it on the right.

Live Music For live blues and jazz, check the *Kansai Time Out* to see who's scheduled to play.

Blue Note Osaka *(☎ 6342 7722)* Tickets around ¥7000. This place draws some of the world's most famous jazz and blues performers (see the Kita map).

Shopping

For Osaka's local speciality, electronics, head to Den Den Town, an area of shops almost exclusively devoted to electronic goods. To avoid sales tax, check if the store has a 'Tax Free' sign outside and bring your passport. Most stores are closed Wednesday. Take the Sakaisuji subway line to Ebisu-chō station and exit at No 1 or No 2 exit. Alternatively, it's a 15-minute walk south of Nankai Namba station.

For anything related to cooking and eating, head to the Dōgusuji-ya Arcade (for more on this, see the Minami Area section earlier).

Getting There & Away

Other than the shinkansen, the fastest way between Kyoto station and Osaka is a JR *shinkaisoku* (special rapid train; ¥540, 29 minutes).

There is also the cheaper private Hankyū line, which runs between Kawaramachi, Karasuma and Ōmiya stations in Kyoto and Umeda station in Osaka (Kawaramachi-Umeda limited express ¥390, 40 minutes).

Alternatively, you can take the Keihan line between Demachiyanagi, Marutamachi, Sanjō, Shijō or Shichijō stations in Kyoto and Yodoyabashi station in Osaka (Sanjō-Yodoyabashi limited express ¥400, 45 minutes).

Getting Around

Like Tokyo, Osaka has a JR Loop Line (known in Japanese as the JR *kanjō-sen*) that circles the city area. There are also seven subway lines, the most useful of which is the Midō-suji line, which runs north-south stopping at Shin-Osaka, Umeda (next to Osaka station), Shinsaibashi, Namba and Tennōji stations.

If you're going to be using the rail system a lot on any day, it might be worth considering a 'one-day free ticket'. For ¥850 (¥650 on Fridays and the 20th of every month) you get unlimited travel on any subway, the New Tram line and all city buses (but not the JR line). Note that you'd really have to be moving around a lot to save any money with this ticket. These are available at the staffed ticket windows in most subway stations.

KŌBE 神戸

☎ 078 • pop 1.42 million

Perched on a hillside overlooking Osaka bay, Kōbe is one of Japan's most attractive cities. It's also one of the country's most famous, owing largely to the tragic earthquake of 17 January 1995, which levelled whole neighbourhoods and killed over 6000 people. Fortunately, the city has risen Phoenix-like from the ashes and is now more vibrant than ever.

One of Kōbe's best features is its relatively small size – most of the sights can be reached on foot from the main train stations. Keep in mind that none of these sights are really must-see attractions; most of what Kōbe has to offer is likely to appeal more to residents than to travellers. However, Kōbe does have some great restaurants, hip bars and happening clubs and is a good place for a night out in Kansai.

Orientation & Information

Kōbe's two main entry points are Sannomiya and Shin-Kōbe stations. Shin-Kōbe, in the north-east of town, is where the shinkansen pauses. A subway runs from here to the busier Sannomiya station, which has frequent rail connections with Osaka and Kyoto. It's possible to walk between the two stations in around 15 minutes. Sannomiya (not Kōbe) station marks the city centre. Before starting your exploration of Kōbe, pick up a copy of the *Kōbe Town Map*, at one of the two information centres.

The city's main tourist information office is outside Sannomiya station (☎ 322 0220), and opens 9am to 7pm. There's a smaller information counter on the second floor of Shin-Kōbe station.

There's an international ATM in the shopping arcade just south of Phoenix Plaza. Behind Kōbe city hall there's a Citibank with machines that also accept a variety of cards.

There's a branch of the Maruzen bookshop chain (☎ 391 6008) near Nankinmachi (Chinatown). For second-hand books, try Wantage Books (☎ 232 4517) near Shin-Kōbe station, open 10am to 5.30pm Monday to Friday.

Kitano 北野

Twenty minutes walk north of Sannomiya, this pleasant hillside neighbourhood is where local tourists come to enjoy the feeling of foreign travel without leaving Japanese soil. The European/American atmosphere is created by the winding streets and *ijinkan* (literally 'foreigners' houses') that housed some of Kōbe's early Western residents. Admission to some is free, others cost ¥300 to ¥700; most are open 9am to 5pm daily.

Phoenix Plaza

Phoenix Plaza (☎ *325 8558; admission free; open 10am-7pm*) is both an earthquake museum and a clearing house of information for Kōbe citizens who were affected by the disasterous 1995 quake. There are videos, dioramas, photos and explanations of the earthquake and its aftermath. Unfortunately, most of the information is in Japanese.

Kōbe City Museum

Kōbe City Museum (☎ *391 0035; admission ¥200; open 10am-4.30pm, closed Mon*) has a collection of Namban (literally 'southern barbarian') art and occasional special exhibits. Namban art is a school of painting that developed under the influence of early Jesuit missionaries in Japan, who taught Western painting techniques to Japanese students.

EXCURSIONS

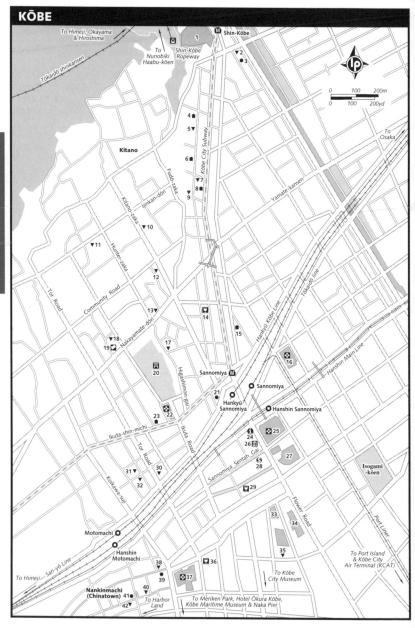

KŌBE

To Himeji, Okayama & Hiroshima

Tōkaidō shinkansen

To Nunobiki Haabu-kōen

Shin-Kōbe Ropeway

Shin-Kōbe

Kitano

Kōbe City Subway

Yamate-kansen

To Osaka

0   100   200m
0   100   200yd

Fudō-zaka

Jinkan-dōri

Kitano-zaka

Hunter-zaka

Tor Road

Community Road

Nakayamate-dōri

Higashimon-gai

Hankyū Kōbe Line

Tōkaidō Line

Hanshin Main Line

Sannomiya

Sannomiya

Hankyū Sannomiya

Hanshin Sannomiya

Ikuta-shin-michi

Tor Road

Ikuta Road

Koikawa-suji

Sannomiya Sentah Gai

Isogami -kōen

Port Liner

Flower Road

Motomachi

Hanshin Motomachi

San-yō Line

To Himeji

Nankinmachi (Chinatown)

To Harbor Land

To Meriken Park, Hotel Ōkura Kōbe, Kōbe Maritime Museum & Naka Pier

To Kōbe City Museum

To Port Island & Kōbe City Air Terminal (KCAT)

KŌBE

PLACES TO STAY
1   Shin-Kōbe Oriental
    Hotel; Shin-Kōbe
    Oriental City; OPA
    Shopping Centre
    新神戸オリエンタル
    ホテル；新神戸オリエ
    ンタルシティ；
    オーパ；
4   Green Hill Hotel Kōbe
    グリーンヒルホテル
    神戸
6   Kōbe YMCA Hotel
    神戸YMCAホテル
8   Green Hill Hotel
    Urban
    グリーンヒルホテル
    アーバン
15 Tomoe
    ともえ
23 Kōbe Washington
    Hotel Plaza
    神戸ワシントンホテル
    プラザ

PLACES TO EAT
2   Yoshinoya
    吉野屋
5   Nailey's
    ネイリーズ
7   Mikami
    みかみ
9   Real Thing
    リアルシング
10 Upwards
    アプワーズ

11 Tada
    多田
12 Court Lodge
    コートロッジ
13 Gaylord
    ゲイロード
17 Daruma
    達麿
18 Kōkaen
    鴻華園
30 Chai Pasal
    チャイパサル
31 Modernark Pharm
    モダンアークファーム
32 Tutto Benne; Tooth
    Tooth
    トゥートベーネ；
    トゥーストゥース
35 Fraises des Bois
    フレイズドゥヴォア
38 Kintoki
    金時
40 Minsei
    民性
42 Motomachi Gyōza-en
    元町ぎょうざ苑

OTHER
3   Wantage Books;
    Kansai Time Out Office
    ワンタージ書店；関西
    タイムアウト事務所
14 Oto-ya
    音屋
16 Daiei Department Store
    ダイエー百貨店

19 South Korea Consulate
    韓国領事館
20 Ikuta-jinja
    生田神社
21 Discount Ticket Shop
    格安切符売り場
22 Tōkyū Hands
    Department Store
    東急ハンズ
24 Tourist Information
    Office
    観光案内所
25 Sogō Department
    Store
    そごう百貨店
26 Phoenix Plaza
    フェニックスプラザ
27 Kōbe Kokusai Kaikan
    神戸国際会館
28 International ATM
    国際ATM
29 Polo Dog
    ポロドッグ
33 Citibank
    シティバンク
34 Kōbe City Hall
    神戸市役所
36 Dubliners
    ダブリナーズ
37 Daimaru Department
    Store
    大丸百貨店
39 Maruzen Books
    丸善書店
41 Nankinmachi Square
    南京町広場

EXCURSIONS

Nankinmachi 南京町 (Chinatown)

Nankinmachi, Kōbe's Chinatown, is not on a par with Chinatowns elsewhere in the world, but it is a good place for a stroll and a bite to eat. It's particularly attractive in the evening, when the lights of the area illuminate the gaudily painted facades of the shops. See the Places to Eat section later for details on some of the area's restaurants.

Kōbe Harbor Land & Meriken Park

Five minutes' walk south-east of Kōbe station, Kōbe Harbor Land is awash with new mega-mall shopping and dining developments. This may not appeal to foreign travellers the way it does to local youth, but it's still a nice place for a stroll in the afternoon.

Five minutes to the east of Harbor Land you'll find Meriken Park on a spit of reclaimed land jutting out into the bay. The main attraction here is the **Kōbe Maritime Museum** (☎ 391 6751; admission ¥500; open 10am-5pm, closed Mon). The museum has a good collection of ship models and displays with some English explanations. Nearby, the **Port Tower** (☎ 391 6751; admission ¥500; open 9am-7pm, later in *summer)* looks like a relic from an earlier age of tourism. It's probably not worth paying to ascend the tower when comparable views are available for free at some of the nearby shopping centres.

Special Events
The Luminarie festival, Kōbe's biggest yearly event, is held every evening from 13 to 26 December to celebrate the city's miraculous recovery from the '95 earthquake (check with the Kōbe tourist office to be sure of the dates as they change slightly every year). The streets south-west of Kōbe City Hall are decorated with countless illuminated metal archways and people flock from all over Kansai to stroll around and enjoy the usual festival food and drink.

Places to Stay
Places to Stay – Budget *Kōbe YMCA Hotel (☎ 241 7205, fax 231 1031)* Singles/ twins/triples from ¥5700/10,000/ 15,000. Check-in 4pm-10pm. Less than 10 minutes' walk from Shin-Kōbe station, this is the only decent bargain choice in town. Rooms are a little on the small side but are acceptable nonetheless.

Places to Stay – Mid-Range *Green Hill Hotel Urban (☎ 222 1221, fax 242 1194)* Singles/doubles/twins from ¥6500/11,500/ 11,500. This is probably the best-value business hotel in town.

Green Hill Hotel Kōbe (☎ 222 0909, fax 222 1139) Singles/twins from ¥7500/ 11,000. The rooms here are slightly better than at the Hotel Urban, making it another good business hotel choice.

Kōbe Washington Hotel Plaza (☎ 331 6111, fax 331 6651) Singles/doubles/twins from ¥7900/15,000/15,000. Close to Sannomiya station, this hotel has small but clean rooms.

Tomoe (☎ 221 1227, fax 221 0841) Singles/doubles ¥6600/11,800. This tiny ryokan/hotel has Japanese- and Western-style rooms. It's not as appealing as some of the other choices listed but it's very close to Sannomiya station.

Places to Stay – Top End *Shin-Kōbe Oriental Hotel (☎ 291 1121, fax 291 1154)* Singles/doubles from ¥13,000/23,000. Towering above Shin-Kōbe station, this hotel commands the best views of the city.

Hotel Ōkura Kōbe (☎ 333 0111, fax 333 6673) Singles/doubles from ¥16,000/19,000. On the waterfront behind Meriken Park, this is the most elegant hotel in town with fine rooms and spacious common areas.

Places to Eat
Japanese Although Kōbe is more famous for its international cuisine, there are plenty of good Japanese restaurants to be found. The restaurants in this section are open during usual business hours (11am to 2pm, 5pm to 10pm) unless otherwise noted.

Yoshinoya (☎ 265 6269) Gyū-don from ¥400. Close to Shin-Kōbe station, this fast food *gyū-don* (beef over rice) specialist is also good for a healthy breakfast.

Tada (☎ 222 1715) Lunch/dinner from ¥600. This casual okonomiyaki place in Kitano with counter seating also serves teppanyaki Kōbe beef from ¥1100 for a set.

Mikami (☎ 242 2500) Lunch/dinner from ¥400. Closed Sun. Try this friendly spot for good-value lunch and dinner sets of standard Japanese fare. Noodle dishes are available from ¥400 and teishoku sets from ¥600. There is also an English menu.

Kintoki (☎ 331 1037) Lunch/dinner from ¥500. For a taste of what Japan was like before it got rich, try this atmospheric old shokudō that serves the cheapest food in the city. You can order standard noodle and rice dishes from the menu (plain *soba* noodles are ¥250 and a small rice is ¥160) or choose from a variety of dishes laid out on the counter.

Daruma (☎ 331 2446) Dinner only; about ¥2500 per person. This izakaya specialises in the cuisine of the Hida Takayama region of Gifu-ken. Recommended is the *hoba yaki* (miso and vegetables cooked on a big leaf over a hibachi at your table).

Sazanka (☎ 333 0111) Dinner from ¥10,000. This teppanyaki restaurant on the first floor of Hotel Ōkura Kōbe is a good place to sample that most precious of meats: Kōbe beef.

International Kōbe is most famous for its Indian food and there are lots of places to choose from. There are also lots of trendy cafe-style spots in Kōbe, including a clutch of restaurants just north of Motomachi station in the fashionable Tor Road area. For Chinese food, the natural choice is Nankinmachi (Chinatown), just south of Motomachi station.

Chai Pasal (☎ *393 2775*) Lunch/dinner from ¥900/2000. This dimly lit Indian restaurant is a favourite of the locals.

Gaylord (☎ *251 4359*) Lunch/dinner from ¥900/3000. This long-standing Indian restaurant is the place to go for splashier meals and delicious curries.

Court Lodge (☎ *222 5504*) Lunch/dinner from ¥1000/2000. Right in the heart of Kitano, this Sri Lankan place serves tasty set meals and delicious Ceylon tea.

Tooth Tooth (☎ *334 1350*) Lunch/dinner from ¥900/2500. Near Motomachi station, this fashionable European-style cafe-restaurant does a variety of light meals.

Tutto Benne (☎ *230 3350*) Tea ¥400, lunch ¥900. Try this trendy little spot for a variety of cafe drinks and mouth-watering pastries.

Modernark Pharm (☎ *391 3060*) Lunch/dinner from ¥900/1500. An open spot popular with Kōbe's chic young things, Modernark Pharm serves tasty sets of Japanese and Western dishes, including burritos and rice dishes.

Nailey's (☎ *231 2008*) Coffee from ¥400, Lunch/dinner from ¥900/1200. A hip little cafe that serves espresso, light lunches and dinners. This is also a good spot for an evening drink.

Real Thing (☎ *242 7813*) Drinks from ¥400, Lunch/dinner from ¥900/1300. This chic spot draws Kōbe's beautiful people for European-influenced light meals and drinks. This is also a good spot for evening drinks.

Upwards (☎ *230 8551*) Lunch/dinner from ¥900/2000. This fashionable eatery in Kitano serves light Italian fare in an airy, open space. Another good spot for a drink in the evening.

Fraises des Bois (☎ *327 0740*) Lunch/dinner from ¥900/2000. Down by Kōbe City Hall, this new restaurant specialises in light European-style fare. The restaurant is divided into a casual cafe and a more serious dining room.

Motomachi Gyōza-en (☎ *331 4096*) Six dumplings ¥340. This is the best spot in Nankinmachi for Chinese dumplings (that's about all they serve). Try their wonderful fried dumplings *(yaki gyōza)* at lunch or dinner. At dinner they also make steamed gyōza *(sui gyōza)*. Use the vinegar, soy sauce and miso on the table to make a dipping sauce. The red sign is in Japanese only, so you may have to ask someone to point out the store.

Minsei (☎ *331 5435*) Lunch/dinner from ¥1500/2500. This is a popular Cantonese place in Nankinmachi. Look for the English writing on the yellow sign.

Kōkaen (☎ *231 7079*) Lunch/dinner from ¥1000/2000. Local cognoscenti favour this authentic little Chinese place for its good food and properly gruff owners.

Entertainment
Kōbe has a relatively large foreign community and a number of bars that see mixed Japanese and foreign crowds. For Japanese-style drinking establishments, try the izakaya in the neighbourhood between the JR tracks and Ikuta-jinja. Also bear in mind that a lot of Kōbe's nightlife is centred around the city's many cafes, most of which transform into bars come evening (see Places to Eat earlier).

Dubliners (☎ *334 3614*) A decent Irish-style pub that is also part of the Sapporo Lion House beer hall chain. They also serve lunch during the day.

Polo Dog (☎ *331 3944*) A short walk from Sannomiya station, this is a small casual bar at home with foreign customers.

Oto-ya (☎ *321 4880*) This is a live house that attracts some good local bands. Check *Kansai Time Out* to see what's happening while you're in town.

Getting There & Away
Sannomiya station is on the JR Tōkaidō/Sanyō line as well as the private Hankyū line, both of which connect it to Kyoto.

The fastest way between Kōbe and Kyoto is a JR shinkaisoku from Kyoto station (¥1050, 48 minutes).

The Hankyū line, which leaves from Kyoto's Kawaramachi, Karasuma and Ōmiya stations, is cheaper but less convenient (to/from Kawaramachi limited express ¥590, one hour; change at Osaka's Jūsō or Umeda stations).

JR Rail Pass holders should also note that Shin-Kōbe station is on the Tōkaidō/Sanyō shinkansen line.

Getting Around

Kōbe is small enough to travel around on foot. The JR, Hankyū and Hanshin railway lines run east to west across Kōbe, providing access to most of Kōbe's more distant sights. A subway line also connects Shin-Kōbe station with Sannomiya station (¥200). There is also a city loop bus service that makes a grand circle tour of most of the city's sightseeing spots (¥250 per ride, ¥650 for an all-day pass). The bus stops at both Sannomiya and Shin-Kōbe stations.

HIMEJI 姫路
☎ 0792 • pop 479,000

It's worth the long trip out to see Himeji-jō, unanimously acclaimed as the most splendid Japanese castle still standing.

Himeji can easily be visited as a day trip from Kyoto. A couple of hours at the castle plus the 10- to 15-minute walk from the station is all the time you really need. Other attractions include Himeji's history museum and Kōko-en, a fine garden next to the castle.

There's a tourist information counter (☎ 85 3792) at the station, on the ground floor to the right as you come off the escalator. Between 10am and 3pm English-speaking staff are on duty and can help with hotel/ryokan reservations.

Himeji-jō

Himeji-jō (☎ 85 1146; admission ¥600; open 9am-5pm, last admission 4pm, an hour later in summer) is the most magnificent of the handful of Japanese castles that survive in their original (nonconcrete)

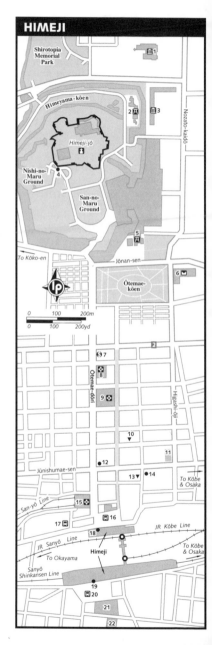

HIMEJI

PLACES TO STAY
11 Himeji Washington Hotel Plaza
姫路ワシントンホテル プラザ
21 Hotel Sun Garden Himeji
ホテルサンガーデン姫路
22 Hotel Himeji Plaza
ホテル姫路プラザ

PLACES TO EAT
10 Fukutei
ふく亭
13 Sekishin
赤心

OTHER
1 Hyōgo Prefectural Museum of History
兵庫県立歴史博物館

2 Himeji-jinja
姫路神社
3 Himeji City Museum of Art
姫路市立美術館
4 Castle Ticket Office
姫路城切符売り場
5 Gokoku-jinja
護国神社
6 Himeji Post Office
姫路郵便局
7 Sumitomo Bank
住友銀行
8 Daiei Department Store
ダイエー百貨店
9 Yamatoyashiki Department Store
ヤマトヤシキ百貨店

12 Seiden Electronics Shop
セイデンデンキ
14 Discount Ticket Shop
格安切符売り場
15 San-yō Department Store; San-yō Himeji
山陽百貨店；
山陽姫路駅
16 City Bus Terminal
市バスターミナル
17 Shinki Bus Terminal
神姫バスターミナル
18 North Exit
北口
19 South Exit
南口
20 City South Bus Terminal
市バス南ターミナル

EXCURSIONS

form. Although there have been fortifications in Himeji since 1333, today's castle was built in 1580 by Toyotomi Hideyoshi and enlarged some 30 years later by Ikeda Terumasa.

The castle has a five-storey main *donjon* (keep) and three smaller donjons, and the entire structure is surrounded by moats and defensive walls punctuated by rectangular, circular and triangular openings for firing guns and shooting arrows at attackers.

English-speaking guides are sometimes available and can really add a lot to your tour of the castle. Unfortunately, appointments aren't accepted and it's hit or miss whether any will be available on the day or your visit – ask at the ticket office of the castle and hope for the best. The guide service is free.

Kōko-en

Just across the moat on the west side of Himeji-jō, you'll find Kōko-en (☎ 89 4120; admission ¥300; open 9am-5pm), a reconstruction of the former samurai quarters of the castle in a garden setting. There are nine separate Edo-style gardens, two ponds, a stream, a tea arbor (¥500 for *matcha* tea) and the restaurant **Kassui-ken**

where you can enjoy lunch while gazing over the gardens. If you'd like to visit Kōko-en in conjunction with the castle, you can buy a combination ticket to both here for ¥720.

Hyōgo Prefectural Museum of History

This well-organised museum (☎ 88 9011; admission ¥200; open 10am-5pm, closed Mon) has good displays on Himeji-jō and other castles around Japan. In addition to the displays on castles, the museum covers the main periods of Japanese history with some English explanations. At 11am, 2pm and 3.30pm you can even try on a suit of samurai armour or a kimono.

The museum is a five-minute walk north of the castle.

Special Events

The Nada-no-Kenka Matsuri, held on 14 and 15 October, involves a conflict between three *mikoshi* (portable shrines) that are battered against each other until one smashes. The festival is held about five minutes' walk from Shirahamanomiya station (10 minutes from Himeji station on the Sanyō-Dentetsu line). Try to go on the second day when the festival reaches its peak (the action starts around noon).

Places to Stay

Himeji Washington Hotel Plaza (☎ 25 0111, fax 25 0133) Singles/doubles from ¥6754/13,508. The small clean rooms in this hotel make it about the best hotel option in Himeji.

Hotel Himeji Plaza (☎ 81 9000, fax 84 3549) Singles/doubles from ¥5900/12,300. Although cheaper than the Washington Plaza, this hotel is slightly less appealing.

Hotel Sun Garden Himeji (☎ 22 2231, fax 24 3731) Singles/doubles from ¥9000/17,500. This is the ritziest place in town with clean, newish rooms and a convenient location just outside the station.

Places to Eat

The *food court* in the underground mall at JR Himeji station has all the usual Western and Japanese dishes. It's just to the right as you exit the north ticket gate of the station.

Sekishin (☎ 22 3842) Tonkatsu ¥550, rice ¥200. The locals line up outside this hole-in-the-wall joint for tasty *tonkatsu* (pork cutlets). You might also try their special *tonjiru* (miso soup with bits of fatty pork). Look for the white curtains with red kanji.

Fukutei (☎ 23 0981). Lunch/dinner ¥1400/5000. Closed Thurs. If you want something a little nicer for lunch or dinner in Himeji, try this kaiseki specialist. From 11am to 2pm, try their mini-kaiseki course (¥1400).

Getting There & Away

The best way to get to Himeji from Kyoto is a shinkaisoku on the JR Tōkaidō line (¥2210, one hour and 20 minutes).

You can also reach Himeji from Kyoto via the Tōkaidō/Sanyō shinkansen line and this is a good option for JR Rail Pass holders.

On the way to Himeji, take a look out the train window at the new Akashi Kaikyō Bridge. Its 3910m span links the island of Honshū with Awaji-shima, making it the longest suspension bridge in the world. It comes into view on the south side of the train about 15km west of Kōbe.

BIWA-KO & SHIGA-KEN
琵琶湖／滋賀県

Just across the Higashiyama mountains from Kyoto is Shiga-ken, a small prefecture dominated by Biwa-ko, Japan's largest lake. The prefecture has a variety of attractions easily visited as day trips from Kyoto. Ōtsu and Hikone are the major sightseeing centres. Hiei-zan and Enryaku-ji are covered under Northern Kyoto in the Things To See & Do chapter of this book.

JNTO publishes a leaflet entitled *Lake Biwa, Ōtsu & Hikone*, which has useful mapping and concise information; it's available at the Kyoto TIC.

Ōtsu 大津
☎ 077 • pop 286,000

Ōtsu developed from a 7th-century imperial residence (the city was capital of Japan for a brief five years) into a lake port and major post station on the Tōkaidō highway between eastern and western Japan. It is now the capital of Shiga-ken.

The information office (☎ 522 3830) is inside JR Ōtsu station, and is open from 8.45am to 5.25pm. Some English is spoken and they have an excellent free map of the area entitled *Biwako Otsu Guide Map*.

Mii-dera Formally known as Onjō-ji, Mii-dera (☎ 522 2238; *admission ¥450; open 8am-5pm*) is a 10-minute walk from Hama-Ōtsu station. The temple, founded in the late 7th century, is the headquarters of the Jimon branch of the Tendai school of Buddhism. It started its days as a branch of Enryaku-ji on Hiei-zan, but later the two fell into conflict, and Mii-dera was repeatedly razed by Enryaku-ji's warrior monks.

Special Events The Ōtsu Dai Hanabi Taikai (Ōtsu Grand Fireworks Festival), takes place on 8 August at dusk. The best spots to watch from are along the waterfront near Hama-Ōtsu station. But be forewarned: trains to and from Kyoto are packed for hours before and after the event.

Getting There & Away From Kyoto you can either take the JR Tōkaidō line from

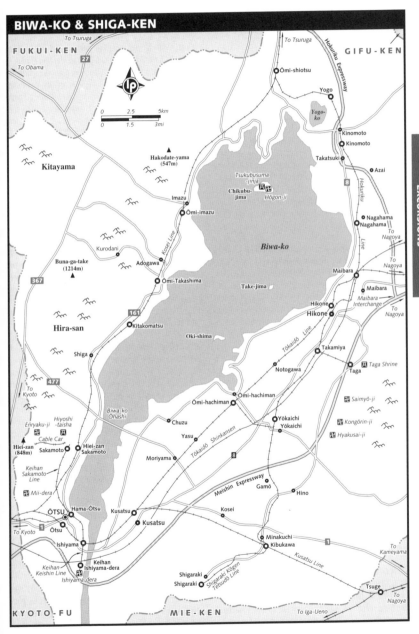

BIWA-KO & SHIGA-KEN

EXCURSIONS

FUKUI-KEN

To Tsuruga
To Obama
27

GIFU-KEN

To Tsuruga

Ōmi-shiotsu

Hokuriku Expressway

Yogo
Yogo-ko

Kinomoto
Kinomoto

Kitayama

Hakodate-yama
(547m)

Takatsuki

Azai

Hokuriku Line

0   2.5   5km
0   1.5   3mi

Imazu
Ōmi-imazu

Tsukubusuma
-jinja
Chikubu-
jima
Hōgon-ji

Nagahama
Nagahama
To Nagoya

Kosei Line

Kurodani

Biwa-ko

To Nagoya

Buna-ga-take
(1214m)

Adogawa

367

Ōmi-Takashima

Take-jima

Maibara

Maibara

161

Hira-san

Kitakomatsu

Hikone
Hikone

Maibara
Interchange

To Nagoya

Oki-shima

Tōkaidō Line

Shiga

Takamiya

Taga Shrine

477

Notogawa

Taga

To Kyoto

Saimyō-ji

Ōmi-hachiman
Ōmi-hachiman

Kongōrin-ji

Enryaku-ji   Hiyoshi
-taisha

Biwa-ko
Ōhashi

Chuzu

Yōkaichi
Yōkaichi

Hyakusai-ji

Hiei-zan
(848m)

Cable Car

Hiei-zan
Sakamoto

Yasu

Tōkaidō Shinkansen

Sakamoto

Moriyama

Keihan
Sakamoto
Line

Mii-dera

Meishin Expressway

Gamō

Hino

HAMA-ŌTSU
ŌTSU

Kusatsu

Kosei

8

Ōtsu

Kusatsu

To Kyoto

Ishiyama

Minakuchi
Kibukawa

1

To Kameyama

Keihan
Keishin Line

Keihan
Ishiyama-dera
Ishiyama-dera

Shigaraki
Shigaraki

Shigaraki Kōgen
Tetsudō Line

Kusatsu Line

Tsuge

To Nagoya

KYOTO-FU

MIE-KEN

To Iga-Ueno

Kyoto station to Ōtsu station (¥190, 10 minutes) or travel on the Kyoto Tōzai subway line from Sanjō Keihan station to Hama-Ōtsu station (¥390, 25 minutes).

Sakamoto

Sakamoto station is the main station for access from Shiga-ken to Enryaku-ji on Hiei-zan. It's best reached by taking the Kyoto Tōzai subway line from Keihan-Sanjō station in Kyoto to Hama-Ōtsu station and changing there to a Keihan line Sakamoto-bound local train. The total fare is ¥590 and with good connections the trip takes about 40 minutes. You can also take the JR line to Hiei-zan Sakamoto station – be careful to take the Kosei (west lake) line (¥320, 20 minutes).

Hiyoshi-taisha This shrine (☎ 578 0009; admission ¥300; open 9am-5pm) is a 15-minute walk from Sakamoto station. Dedicated to the deity of Hiei-zan, Hiyoshi-taisha is closely connected with Enryaku-ji. Displayed in a separate hall are the mikoshi that were carried into Kyoto by the monks of Hiei-zan whenever they wished to make demands of the emperor. During the Sannō Matsuri on 13 and 14 April, there are mikoshi fighting festivals and a procession of mikoshi on boats.

Ishiyama-dera This Shingon temple (☎ 537 0013; admission ¥400; open 8am-4.45pm) was founded in the 8th century. The room next to the temple's hondō (main hall) is famed as the place where Lady Murasaki wrote the Tale of the Genji.

The temple is a 10-minute walk from Keihan Ishiyama-dera station. Take the Kyoto Tōzai subway line from Sanjō Keihan station in Kyoto to Hama-Ōtsu and change there to a Keihan line Ishiyama-dera-bound local train (entire trip ¥520, 37 minutes).

Hikone 姫路

☎ 0749 • pop 106,000

Hikone is the second largest city in the prefecture and of special interest to visitors for its castle, which dominates the town.

There is a good tourist information office (☎ 22 2954) on your left as you leave the station, which has helpful maps and literature. The Street Map & Guide to Hikone has a map on one side and a suggested one-day bicycle tour of Hikone's sights on the reverse.

The castle is straight up the street from the station – about 10 minutes on foot.

Hikone-jō This castle (☎ 22 2742; admission ¥500; open 8.30am-5pm) was completed in 1622 by the Ii family who ruled as daimyō over Hikone. It is rightly considered one of the finest remaining castles in Japan – much of it is original – and there is a great view across the lake from the upper storeys. The castle is surrounded by more than 1000 cherry trees, making it a popular spot for spring-time hanami activities.

After visiting the castle, don't miss nearby **Genkyū-en** (☎ 22 2742; admission included in castle admission; open 8.30am-5pm), a lovely Chinese-influenced garden that was completed in 1677. Remember to hang on to your ticket when leaving the castle if you plan to visit the garden.

Getting There & Away You can reach Hikone from Kyoto on the JR Tōkaidō line (¥1110, 47 minutes). If you take the shinkansen, the best method is to ride from Kyoto to Maibara (Kodama shinkansen, ¥2060, 25 minutes) and then backtrack from there on the JR Tōkaidō line to Hikone (¥180, five minutes). Maibara is a major rail junction, the meeting place of the JR Tōkaidō, Hokuriku and Tōkaidō shinkansen lines. By special JR shinkaisoku, Maibara is 52 minutes from Kyoto on the JR Tōkaidō line (¥1110).

MIYAMA-CHŌ 見山町

☎ 0771 • pop 5000

If you yearn for a glimpse of old rural Japan, head to lovely Miyama-chō, a town nestled in the Kitayama mountains of northern Kyoto-fu.

The 'town' is composed of several village clusters spread over a large area. These picturesque hamlets are home to an abundance of traditional kayabuki-yane (thatched-roof)

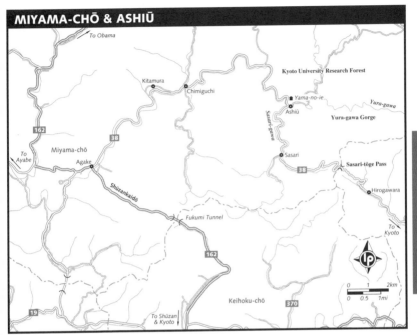

MIYAMA-CHŌ & ASHIŪ

farmhouses thatched with a thick roof of long *susuki* (pampas grass) reeds.

Miyama-chō has become a popular home for artists, and is also gaining attention from outdoor enthusiasts for its excellent hiking, camping and kayaking on the Yura-gawa. It is possible to travel to Miyama-chō as a day trip from Kyoto, but it makes a much nicer overnight trip.

The Japanese-language *Map Kyoto*, available at the Kyoto Tourism Federation above Kyoto station, covers the Miyama-chō area.

Kitamura 北村

Miyama-chō's star attraction is Kitamura (North Village) a small hamlet boasting a cluster of some 50 thatched-roof farmhouses. In 1994 the village was designated a national preservation site, and the local government has been generously subsidising the exorbitant cost of rethatching the roofs (at an average cost of ¥6 million – more than US$50,000!).

There's not much to do in the village except walk around and admire the wonderful old houses.

Ashiū 芦生

The quiet village of Ashiū sits on the far eastern edge of Miyama-chō. The main attraction of Ashiū is the 4200-hectare virgin forest that lies to the east of the village. Safeguarded under the administration of Kyoto University's Department of Agriculture, this is about the only remaining virgin forest in all of Kansai.

The best way to sample the beauty of Ashiū's forest is to hike up into the gorge of the Yura-gawa. Lonely Planet's new *Hiking in Japan* guide details a four-day hike up the river. Those with less time can do shorter day trips up the gorge. Hikers should get hold of Shōbunsha's Japanese-language *Kyoto Kitayama 2* map, part of their Yama-to-Kōgen Chizu series (available at bigger bookshops in Kyoto).

See also the Sports section at the end of the Things to See & Do chapter for information on snowshoe and river hiking tours of Ashiū, both of which come highly recommended.

In addition to the lodge in Ashiū (see Places to Stay), there are plenty of good, free camping spots along the Yura-gawa.

Places to Stay

There are a number of interesting places to stay in the Miyama-chō area. It's best to have a Japanese person call to make reservations at these places since few lodge owners speak English. Note that some of the owners will pick up guests in Hirogawara, the most convenient access point to Miyama-chō.

Matabe (☎ 77 0258) ¥7500 per person with 2 meals. This quaint *minshuku* (inn) in Kitamura is in a traditional thatched-roof house.

Kajika-sō (☎ 77 0014) ¥7000 per person with 2 meals. This is a large, outdoorsy complex about five minutes by car east of Kitamura (on the way to Ashiū).

Morishige (☎ 75 1086) ¥8000 per person with 2 meals. This is about seven minutes' driving time west from Kitamura. Guests dine by an open fire pit *(irori)* in a 130-year-old house.

Miyama Heimat Youth Hostel (☎ 75 0997) ¥4200 per person (¥5200 nonmembers). This simple youth hostel is the one of the cheaper options in the area. It's on the road to Ōno Dam.

Yama-no-Ie (☎ 77 0290) ¥1700 per person. This basic lodge is the only place to stay in Ashiū (other than camping). There are no meals served but there are simple cooking facilities. It's a few minutes on foot from the forest trailhead.

Getting There & Away

Miyama-chō is about 50km due north of Kyoto over a series of mountain passes.

There are no train lines to Miyama-chō, so you either have to rent a car, hitch, or take a series of buses from Kyoto.

To get to Kitamura by bus, take a JR from in front of Kyoto station to Shimonaka. At Shimonaka transfer to a Miyama-chō-ei bus to Agake. From Agake, take another Miyama-chō-ei bus bound for Chimiguchi and get off at Kitamura (entire trip ¥2320, 2½ hours).

From Kitamura, you can catch a Miyama-chō-ei bus onward to Chimiguchi, where you can catch another bus to Sasari (for Ashiū get off at Deai and walk the last kilometre into the village). Needless to say, the complexity and cost of this route makes either renting a car or hitching look awfully attractive.

The best road to Miyama-chō is Rte 162 (Shūzankaidō), though there is a lovely (but time-consuming) alternative route via Kurama in the north of Kyoto and over Hanase-tōgei Pass. Serious cyclists should be able to reach the area via either route by pedalling for about five arduous hours.

Another option is to take Kyoto bus No 32 from Kyoto's Demachiyanagi station to the last stop, Hirogawara (¥1050, 90 minutes), and hike over Sasari-tōge Pass. From Hirogawara follow the road to the pass and then take the hiking trail down into Ashiū (you'll probably need the hiking map mentioned earlier for this). The hike notwithstanding, this is probably the easiest route into Ashiū since it involves only one bus.

Those intent on seeing a lot of Miyama-chō without renting a car can combine the two bus routes described above to make one grand traverse of the area. Take the aforementioned buses all the way to Sasari from Kyoto station, hike over the pass and return to Kyoto by bus from Hirogawara (or vice-versa). Note that the road over the pass is closed in winter, when it makes a great snowshoe or cross-country ski route.

Language

Visitors to Kyoto shouldn't have too many language problems. Lots of people speak English, and there are quite a few English signs. The main issue is the writing system, which uses three different scripts. The most difficult of these are *kanji*, the ideographic script developed by the Chinese, of which approximately 2000 are in daily use.

If you're really ambitious or plan on living in Kyoto for a while, it would make sense to learn a little of the written language before arriving. You should first master the 48 *katakana* characters, which are used for writing imported words, including many items found on restaurant menus. Following this, you should learn the 48 *hiragana* characters, which are used for writing native words and word-endings. Maruzen bookshop (Map 10 has a wide selection of excellent Japanese-language textbooks.

The *romaji* used in this book follows the Hepburn system of romanisation/transliteration, with macrons (bars over vowels) used to indicate long vowels. Happily, Japanese is not tonal and pronunciation is fairly easy to master.

Traditionally, only close friends and children call each other by their first names, so a new Japanese acquaintance will normally just tell you their surname. Surnames come before given names, not after as in the West (although the names of famous Japanese are usually Westernised in English texts.) When addressing a person, follow their surname with *san*, equivalent to Mr, Mrs, Miss or Ms, eg, Ms Suzuki becomes *Suzuki-san*.

The following Japanese phrases should cover most everyday situations, but for a more comprehensive guide, get Lonely Planet's *Japanese phrasebook* or *Japanese audio pack*.

Pronunciation

Unlike Chinese, Vietnamese and Thai, among others, Japanese is not tonal and the pronunciation system is fairly easy to master.

The following examples reflect British pronunciation:

a	as in 'father'
e	as in 'get'
i	as in 'pin'
o	as in 'bone', but shorter
u	as in 'flu'

Vowels appearing in this book with a macron (or bar) over them (ā, ē, ō, ū) are pronounced in the same way as standard vowels except that the sound is held twice as long. You need to take care with this as vowel length can change the meaning of a word, eg, *yuki* means 'snow', while *yūki* means 'bravery'.

Consonants are generally pronounced as in English, with the following exceptions:

f	this sound is produced by pursing the lips and blowing lightly
g	as the 'g' in 'goal' at the start of word; and nasalised as the 'ng' in 'sing' in the middle of a word
r	more like an 'l' than an 'r'

Greetings & Civilities

Good morning.
ohayō gozaimasu
おはようございます。

Good afternoon.
konnichiwa
こんにちは。

Good evening.
kombanwa
こんばんは。

Goodbye.
sayōnara
さようなら。

See you later.
dewa mata
ではまた。

Please/Go ahead. (when offering)
dōzo
どうぞ。

Please. (when asking)
onegai shimasu
お願いします。

Thanks. (informal)
dōmo
どうも。

Kyoto Dialect

Kyoto's distinctive dialect, Kyoto-ben or Kyō-no-kotoba, is one of the city's most distinctive features. While the language overlaps in many areas with the Kansai dialect, Kansai-ben, which is spoken in Osaka, Kōbe, Nara and other parts of the region, Kyoto-ben has a personality and sound all its own.

In marked contrast to the grittier, straight-talking business jargon of Osaka, Kyoto-ben has a softer, melodic intonation. This, combined with the peculiar, cultured refinement of Kyotoites, produces a kind of speech comparable to that of a Louisiana southern belle.

Part of the mystery of Kyoto-ben lies in the indirect nature of the language and the elusive way in which Kyotoites interact with one another. Even when emotional, they are notorious among Japanese for concealing their true feelings. Kyotoites always seem to sound placid, and arguing in Kyoto-ben is considerably more difficult than in standard Japanese.

Though the Tokyo dialect *Kantō-ben* has become the national standard, this wasn't always the case. Kyoto was the capital for over 1000 years, during which time the precursor of today's Kyoto-ben was very much the standard of proper Japanese. Today's Kyoto-ben still has echoes of the almost baroque jargon of the ancient imperial court.

Today, though many elderly and people in traditional Kyoto industries, as well as *geisha* and *maiko* of the Gion entertainment district, still speak 'pure' Kyoto-ben, the old dialect has become significantly diluted with modern Japanese.

There are several Kyoto-ben phrases you are likely to hear, such as *oideyasu* for 'welcome' and *ōkini* for 'thank you' (you'll almost certainly hear these when entering and leaving a sento).

Anyone interested in general Kansai-ben should pick up a copy of Peter Tse's *Kansai Japanese*, or *Kinki Japanese* by Palter & Horiuchi. Both are good introductions to the local dialect. More specific to the Kyoto tongue, *Kyō no meisho to Kyō kotoba* by Kimura Kyōzō is an amusing presentation of Kyoto-ben, combining dialogues with short stories about famous sightseeing spots around the city.

Thank you.
dōmo arigatō
どうもありがとう。

Thank you very much.
dōmo arigatō gozaimasu
どうもありがとうございます。

Thanks for having me.
(when leaving)
o-sewa ni narimashita
お世話になりました。

You're welcome.
dō itashimasite
どういたしまして。

No, thank you.
iie, kekkō desu
いいえ、けっこうです。

Excuse me/Pardon.
sumimasen
すみません。

Excuse me. (when entering a room)
o-jama shimasu/shitsurei shimasu
おじゃまします。 / 失礼します。

I'm sorry.
gomen nasai
ごめんなさい。

What's your name?
o-namae wa nan desu ka?
お名前は何ですか？

My name is ...
watashi wa ... desu
私は...です。

This is Mr/Mrs/Ms (Smith).
kochira wa (Sumisu) san desu
こちらは（スミス）さんです。

Pleased to meet you.
dōzo yoroshiku
どうぞよろしく。

Pleased to meet you too.
hajimemashite, kochira koso dōzo yoroshiku
はじめまして、こちらこそどうぞ
よろしく。

Where are you from?
dochira no kata desu ka?
どちらのかたですか？

How are you?
o-genki desu ka?
お元気ですか？

Fine.
genki desu
元気です。

Is it OK to take a photo?
shashin o totte mo ii desu ka?
写真を撮ってもいいですか？

Cheers!
kampai!
乾杯！

Basics

Yes.
hai
はい。

No.
iie
いいえ。

No. (for indicating disagreement)
chigaimasu
違います。

No. (for indicating disagreement; less emphatic)
chotto chigaimasu
ちょっと違います。

OK.
daijōbu (desu)/ōke
だいじょうぶ（です）。／オーケー。

What?
nani? なに？

When?
itsu? いつ？

Where?
doko? どこ？

Who?
dare? だれ？

Requests

Please give me this/that.
kore/sore o kudasai
（これ／それ）をください。

Please give me a (cup of tea).
(o-cha) o kudasai
（お茶）をください。

Please wait (a while).
(shōshō) o-machi kudasai
（少々）お待ちください。

Please show me the (ticket).
(kippu) o misete kudasai
（切符）を見せてください。

Language Difficulties

Do you understand English/Japanese?
ei-go/nihon-go wa wakarimasu ka?
（英語／日本語）はわかりますか？

I don't understand
wakarimasen
わかりません。

Do you speak English?
eigo ga hanasemasu ka?
英語が話せますか？

I can't speak Japanese.
nihongo wa dekimasen
日本語はできません。

How do you say ... in Japanese?
nihongo de ... wa nan to iimasu ka?
日本語で...は何といいますか？

What does ... mean?
... wa donna imi desu ka?
...はどんな意味ですか？

What is this called?
kore wa nan to iimasu ka?
これは何といいますか？

Please write in Japanese/English.
nihongo/eigo de kaite kudasai
（日本語／英語）で書いてください。

Please speak more slowly.
mō chotto yukkuri itte kudasai
もうちょっとゆっくり言ってください。

Please say it again more slowly.
mō ichidō, yukkuri itte kudasai
もう一度、ゆっくり言ってください。

What is this called?
kore wa nan to iimasu ka?
これは何といいますか？

Getting Around

What time does the next ... leave?
tsugi no ... wa nanji ni demasu ka?
次の...は何時に出ますか？

What time does the next ... arrive?
tsugi no ... wa nanji ni tsukimasu ka?
次の...は何時に着きますか？

boat
bōto/fune ボート／船

bus (city)
shibasu 市バス

bus (intercity)
chōkyoribasu 長距離バス

bus stop
basutei バス停

Glossary of Useful Terms

Geography

-dake/take	岳	peak
-dani/tani	谷	valley
-gawa/kawa	川	river
-hama	浜	beach
-hantō	半島	peninsula
-jima/shima	島	island
-kaikyō	海峡	channel/strait
-ko	湖	lake
-kō	港	port
-kōen	公園	park
-kōgen	高原	plateau
kokutei kōen	国定公園	quasi-national park
kokuritsu kōen	国立公園	national park
-kyō	峡	gorge
-minato	港	harbour
-no-yu	…の湯	hot spring
-oka	丘	hill
onsen	温泉	hot spring
-san/zan	山	mountain
-shima/jima	島	island
shokubutsu-en	植物園	botanic garden
-shotō	諸島	archipelago
-take/dake	岳	peak
-taki	滝	waterfall
-tani/dani	谷	valley
-tō	島	island
-wan	湾	bay
-yama	山	mountain
-yu	湯	hot spring
-zaki/misaki	岬	cape
-zan/san	山	mountain

Regions

-shi	市	city
-chō	町	neighbourhood or village/s
-mura	村	village
-ken	県	prefecture
-gun	郡	county
-ku	区	ward

Sights

-dera/tera	寺	temple
-dō	堂	temple or hall of a temple
-en	園	garden
-in	院	temple or hall of a temple
-gū	宮	shrine
-ji	寺	temple
-jō	城	castle
-kōen	公園	park
-mon	門	gate
shokubutsu-en	植物園	botanical garden
-hori/bori	堀	moat
-jingū	神宮	shrine
-jinja	神社	shrine
-taisha	大社	shrine
-teien	庭園	garden
-tera/dera	寺	temple
-torii	鳥居	shrine gate

tram		
romen densha	路面電車	
train		
densha	電車	
subway		
chikatetsu	地下鉄	
station		
eki	駅	
ticket		
kippu	切符	
ticket office		
kippu uriba	切符売り場	
timetable		
jikokuhyō	時刻表	
taxi		
takushī	タクシー	
entrance		
iriguchi	入口	
exit		
deguchi	出口	
left-luggage office		
nimotsu azukarijo	荷物預かり所	
one way		
katamichi	片道	
return		
ōfuku	往復	
non-smoking seat		
kin'en seki	禁煙席	

Where is the ... ?
... wa doko desu ka?
…はどこですか？

How much is the fare to ...?
... made ikura desu ka?
…までいくらですか？

Does this (train, bus, etc) go to ...?
kore wa ... e ikimasu ka?
これは…へ行きますか？

Is the next station ...?
tsugi no eki wa ... desu ka?
次の駅は…ですか？

Please tell me when we get to ...
... ni tsuitara oshiete kudasai
…に着いたら教えてください。

Where is the ... exit?
... deguchi wa doko desu ka?
…出口はどこですか？

How far is it to walk?
aruite dono kurai kakarimasu ka?
歩いてどのくらいかかりますか？

I'd like to hire a ...
... o karitai no desu ga.
…を借りたいのですが。

I'd like to go to ...
... ni ikitai desu
…に行きたいです。

Please stop here.
koko de tomete kudasai
ここで停めてください。

How do I get to ...?
... e wa dono yō ni ikeba ii desu ka?
…へはどのように行けばいいですか？

Where is this address please?
kono jūsho wa doko desu ka?
この住所はどこですか？

Could you write down the address for me?
jūsho o kaite itadakemasen ka?
住所を書いていただけませんか？

Go straight ahead.
massugu itte まっすぐ行って。

Turn left/right.
hidari/migi e magatte
（左／右）へ曲がって。

near/far
chikai/tōi 近い／遠い

Around Town

bank
ginkō 銀行
embassy
taishi-kan 大使館
post office
yūbin kyoku 郵便局

Signs	
Information *annaijo*	案内所
Open *eigyōchū*	営業中
Closed *junbichū*	準備中
Toilets *o-tearai/toire*	お手洗い／トイレ
Men *otoko*	男
Women *onna*	女

market
ichiba 市場
a public telephone
kōshū denwa 公衆電話
toilet
o-tearai/toire お手洗い／トイレ
the tourist office
kankō annaijo 観光案内所

What time does it open/close?
nanji ni akimasu/shimarimasu ka
何時に（開きます／閉まります）か？

Accommodation

I'm looking for a ...
... o sagashite imasu
…を探しています。

hotel
hoteru ホテル
guesthouse
gesuto hausu ゲストハウス
inn
ryokan 旅館
youth hostel
yūsu hosuteru ユースホステル
camping ground
kyampu-jō キャンプ場
Japanese-style inn
ryokan 旅館
family-style inn
minshiku 民宿

Do you have any vacancies?
aki-beya wa arimasu ka?
空き部屋はありますか？

I don't have a reservation
yoyaku wa shiteimasen
予約はしていません。

single room
shinguru rūmu　シングルルーム
double room
daburu rūmu　ダブルルーム
twin room
tsuin rūmu　ツインルーム
Japanese-style room
washitsu　和室
Western-style room
yōshitsu　洋室
Japanese-style bath
o-furo　お風呂
room with a (Western-style) bath
basu tsuki no heya
バス付きの部屋

How much is it per night/per person?
ippaku/hitori ikura de suka?
（一泊 / 一人）いくらですか？
Does it include breakfast/a meal?
chōshoku/shokuji wa tsuite imasu ka?
（朝食 / 食事）は付いていますか？
I'm going to stay for one night/two nights.
hito-ban/futa-ban tomarimasu
（一晩 / 二晩）泊まります。
Can I leave my luggage here?
nimotsu o azukatte itadakemasen ka?
荷物を預かっていただけませんか？

Shopping

I'd like to buy ...
... o kaitai desu
…を買いたいです。
How much is it?
ikura desu ka?
いくらですか？
I'm just looking.
miteiru dake desu
見ているだけです。
It's cheap.
yasui desu
安いです。
It's too expensive.
taka-sugi masu
高すぎます。
I'll take this one.
kore o kudasai
これをください。
Can I have a receipt?
ryōshūsho o itadakemasen ka?
領収書をいただけませんか？

big
ōkii　大きい
small
chiisai　小さい
shop
mise　店
supermarket
sūpā　スーパー
bookshop
hon ya　本屋
camera shop
shashin ya　写真屋
department store
depāto　デパート

Food

breakfast
chōshoku/asa gohan　朝食 / 朝ご飯
lunch
ranchi/chūshoku/　ランチ / 昼食 /
hiru gohan　昼ご飯
dinner
yūshoku/ban gohan　夕食 / 晩ご飯

I'm a vegetarian.
watashi wa bejitarian desu
私はベジタリアンです。
Do you have any vegetarian meals?
bejitarian-ryōri wa arimasu ka?
ベジタリアン料理はありますか？
What do you recommend?
o-susume wa nan desu ka?
おすすめは何ですか？
Do you have an English menu?
eigo no menyū wa arimasu ka?
英語のメニューはありますか？
I'd like the set menu please.
setto menyū o o-negai shimasu
セットメニューをお願いします。
Please bring the bill.
o-kanjō o onegai shimasu
お勘定をお願いします。
This is delicious.
oishii desu
おいしいです。

Health

I need a doctor.
isha ga hitsuyō desu
医者が必要です。
How do you feel?
kibun wa ikaga desu ka?
気分はいかがですか？

I'm ill.
kibun ga warui desu
気分が悪いです。
It hurts here.
koko ga itai desu
ここが痛いです。
I have diarrhoea.
geri o shiteimasu
下痢をしています。
I have a toothache.
ha ga itamimasu
歯が痛みます。
I'm ...
watashi wa ...　　私は…
diabetic
tōnyōbyō desu　　糖尿病です。
epileptic
tenkan desu　　てんかんです。
asthmatic
zensoku desu　　喘息です。

I'm allergic to antibiotics/penicillin.
kōsei-busshitsu/penishirin ni arerugī ga arimasu
（抗生物質 / ペニシリン）に
アレルギーがあります。

antiseptic
shōdokuyaku　　消毒薬
aspirin
asupirin　　アスピリン
(a) cold
kaze　　風邪
condoms
kondōmu　　コンドーム
contraceptive
hinin yō piru　　避妊用ピル
dentist
ha-isha　　歯医者
diarrhoea
geri　　下痢
doctor
isha　　医者
fever
hatsunetsu　　発熱
food poisoning
shoku chūdoku　　食中毒
hospital
byōin　　病院
medicine
kusuri　　薬

Emergencies

Help!
tasukete!
助けて！
Call a doctor!
isha o yonde kudasai!
医者を呼んでください！
Call the police!
keisatsu o yonde kudasai!
警察を呼んでください！
I'm lost.
michi ni mayoi mashita
道に迷いました。
Go away!
hanarero!
離れろ！

migraine
henzutsū　　偏頭痛
pharmacy
yakkyoku　　薬局
tampons
tampon　　タンポン

Time, Days & Numbers

What time is it?
ima nan-ji desu ka?
今何時ですか？
today
kyō　　今日
tomorrow
ashita　　明日
yesterday
kinō　　きのう
morning/afternoon
asa/hiru　　朝 / 昼

Monday
getsuyōbi　　月曜日
Tuesday
kayōbi　　火曜日
Wednesday
suiyōbi　　水曜日
Thursday
mokuyōbi　　木曜日
Friday
kinyōbi　　金曜日
Saturday
doyōbi　　土曜日
Sunday
nichiyōbi　　日曜日

Numbers

0	*zero/rei*	ゼロ / 零
1	*ichi*	一
2	*ni*	二
3	*san*	三
4	*yon/shi*	四
5	*go*	五
6	*roku*	六
7	*nana/shichi*	七
8	*hachi*	八
9	*kyū/ku*	九
10	*jū*	十
11	*jūichi*	十一
12	*jūni*	十二
13	*jūsan*	十三

14	*jūyon/ jūshi*	十四
20	*nijū*	二十
21	*nijūichi*	二十一
30	*sanjū*	三十
100	*hyaku*	百
200	*nihyaku*	二百
1000	*sen*	千
5000	*gosen*	五千
10,000	*ichiman*	一万
20,000	*niman*	二万
100,000	*jūman*	十万

one million		
	hyakuman	百万

Glossary

ageya – traditional entertainment banquet halls which flourished during the Edo period
aka-chōchin – red-lantern bar; working man's pub with snack food like *yakitori*
Amida – Buddha of the Western Paradise

bashi – bridge (also *hashi*)
basho – *sumō* wrestling tournament
ben – dialect, as in *Kyoto-ben*
bentō – boxed lunch or dinner, usually of rice, fish or meat and vegetables
bijutsukan – art museum
biwa – Japanese version of a lute
bonkei – art of miniaturising whole landscapes
bonsai – art of cultivating miniature trees by careful pruning of the branches and roots
bonshō – temple bell
bosatsu – a bodhisattva, or Buddha attendant, assisting others attain enlightenment
bugaku – dance pieces played by court orchestras in ancient Japan
bunraku – classical puppet theatre using life-size puppets to enact dramas similar to those of *kabuki*
bushidō – way of the warrior; esoteric ethos of the *samurai* class
butsu – Buddha statue

carp – see *koi*
chadō – tea ceremony, or the way of tea (also pronounced *sadō*)
cha-kaiseki – a *kaiseki* meal that accompanies a tea ceremony
chanoyu – tea ceremony; see also *chadō*
chasen – bamboo whisk used for preparing powdered green tea
chashitsu – traditional tearoom
chizu – map
chō – city area (for large cities) between a *ku* (ward) and *chōme* in size
chōme – city area of a few blocks

dai – great; large
daimyō – regional lords under the *shōgun*
deguchi – exit, as at a train station
densha – train

depāto – department store
dōri – street (also *tōri*)

eki – railway station
ekiben – *bentō* lunch boxes sold at train stations
ema – small votive plaques that are hung in shrine sanctuaries as petitions to resident deities
en – garden (also niwa)
enka – often referred to as the Japanese equivalent of country & western music, these folk ballads about love and human suffering are popular among the older generation

fu – similar to prefecture (ken)
fugu – poisonous blowfish or pufferfish, elevated to haute cuisine with a bite
furo – bath
futon – cushion-like mattress that is rolled up and stored away during the day
futsū – literally, ordinary; a basic stopping-at-all-stations train

gagaku – music of the imperial court
gaijin – the usual term for a foreigner; the contracted form of gaikokujin (literally, outside country person)
gawa – river (also kawa)
geiko – Kyoto dialect for *geisha*
geisha – not a prostitute but a 'refined person'; a woman versed in the arts and other cultivated pursuits who entertains guests
genkan – foyer area where shoes are exchanged for slippers before entering the interior of a building
geta – traditional wooden sandals
goju-no-tō – a five-storey pagoda

haiden – hall of worship in a shrine
haiku – 17-syllable poem
hakubutsukan – museum
hanami – cherry blossom viewing
hanko – personal stamp or seal used to authenticate documents; carries the same weight as a signature in the West

251

hashi – chopsticks
higashi – east
hiragana – phonetic syllabary used to write Japanese words
honden – main building of a shrine
hondō – main building of a temple

ichiba – market
ike – pond
ikebana – art of flower arranging
irori – open hearth found in traditional Japanese houses
izakaya – Japanese version of a pub serving beer, sake and lots of snacks in a rustic, boisterous setting

ji – temple (see also *tera*)
jinja – shrine (also jingū or gū)
jitensha – bicycle
Jizō – guardian bosatsu of children and travellers
jō – castle (also shiro)

kabuki – form of Japanese theatre drawing on popular tales and characterised by elaborate costumes, stylised acting and the use of male actors for all roles
kaiseki – elegant, Buddhist-inspired meal, called *cha-kaiseki* when served as part of tea ceremony
kaisha – a company
kaisoku – rapid train
kaiten sushi – automatic, conveyor-belt sushi
kakejiku – painted or calligraphy scroll typically hung in the alcove of a *tatami* room
kami – *Shintō* gods or spirits associated with natural phenomena
kamikaze – literally, wind of the gods; originally the typhoon that sank Kublai Khan's 13th-century invasion fleet and the name adopted by Japanese suicide bombers in the waning days of WWII
kampai – cheers, as in a drinking toast
kan – building/hall
kana – the two Japanese syllabaries (*iragana* and *katakana*) used to supplement *kanji* in the Japanese writing system
kanji – literally, Chinese writing; Chinese ideographic script used for writing Japanese

Kannon – The Buddhist goddess of mercy (Guanyin in Chinese, Avalokiteshvara in Sanskrit)
kannushi – chief *Shintō* priest
karaoke – a now famous export where revellers sing along to taped music, minus the vocals
karesansui – dry-landscaped rock garden
kasa – umbrella
katakana – phonetic syllabary used to write foreign words, among other things
katamichi – one-way ticket
katana – Japanese sword
kayabuki-yane – traditional Japanese thatched-roof house (also kayabuki-ya)
keigo – honorific language used to show respect to elders and superiors
keitai denwa – mobile phone
ken – prefecture, as in Shiga-ken (Kyoto's eastern neighbour)
kendō – the way of the sword; fencing technique based on the two handed *samurai* sword
kimono – traditional outer garment similar to a robe
kin'en-sha – nonsmoking train carriage
kissaten – Japanese coffee shop
kita – north
ko – lake (also mizu-umi)
kōban – local police box; a common sight in urban Japan
kōen – park
koi – carp; considered a brave, tenacious fish; koinobori windsocks are flown in honour of sons whom it is hoped will inherit these virtues
koicha – thick green tea; as compared to the lighter usucha, thin green tea
kokuminshukusha – an inexpensive form of accommodation found in rural Japan; literally, peoples' lodges
kokutetsu – Japan Railways (JR); Japan's main train company
koma-inu – dog-like guardian stone statues found in pairs at the entrance to *Shintō* shrines
kondō – see *hondō*
kotatsu – heated table with quilt or cover to keep the lower body warm in the winter
koto – 13-stringed zither-like instrument
kura – traditional Japanese storehouses

kyōgen – drama performed as comic relief between *nō* plays, or as separate events
kyō-machiya – see *machiya*
kyō-ryōri – Kyoto cuisine
Kyoto-ben – distinctive dialect of Japanese spoken in Kyoto
kyūkō – ordinary express train (faster than *futsū*, stopping only at certain stations)

live house – nightclub or bar where live music is performed

machi – city area (for large cities) between a *ku* (ward) and *chōme* (area of a few blocks) in size
machiya – traditional wooden houses, in Kyoto called *kyō-machiya*
maiko – apprentice *geisha*
manga – Japanese comic books or magazines
matcha – powdered green tea used in tea ceremony
matsuri – festival
meishi – business card; very important in Japan
miko – shrine maidens
mikoshi – portable shrines carried during festivals; said to contain *kami*
minami – south
minshuku – Japanese equivalent of a B&B; family-run budget accommodation usually found in rural Japan
minyō – Japanese folk music
Miroku – the Buddha of the Future
mizu-shōbai – see *water trade*
momiji – Japanese maple trees; *momiji-gari* refers to the viewing of the changing autumn colours (*kōyō*) of trees
mon – temple gate
morning service – *mōningu sābisu*; a light breakfast served by coffee shops until around 10am; usually a thick slice of bread, a boiled egg, and jam and butter
mura – village

natsume – lacquerware container holding *matcha* powdered tea
Nihon or **Nippon** – the Japanese word for Japan; literally, source of the sun
ningyō – doll
niō – temple guardians
nishi – west

nō – classical Japanese mask drama performed on a bare stage
nomiya – traditional Japanese pub; similar but simpler than *izakaya*
noren – door curtain for restaurants, usually with the name of the establishment

o- – prefix used to show respect (usually applied to objects)
obanzai – Japanese home-style cooking, the Kyoto variant of this is sometimes called kyō-obanzai
obi – sash or belt worn with *kimono*
obon – mid-August festivals and ceremonies for deceased ancestors
o-bōsan – Buddhist priest
ofuku – return ticket
o-furo – traditional Japanese bath
o-jiisan – elderly man; grandfather
o-jisan – middle-aged man; uncle
okiya – old-style *geisha* quarters
OL – stands for Office Lady; female employee of a large firm; usually a clerical worker
o-mamori – good luck talismans sold at shrines
o-mikuji – paper fortunes drawn from a bamboo or metal stick and tied to tree branches at *Shintō* shrines
omiyage – souvenir; an obligatory purchase on any trip for Japanese
oni – a devil
onsen – mineral hot spring with bathing areas and accommodation
origami – art of paper folding
oshibori – hot towels given in restaurants

pachinko – vertical pinball game that is a Japanese craze (estimated to take in a mere ¥6 trillion a year) and a major source of tax evasion, *yakuza* funds and noise
pink salon – seedy hostess bars; pink is the Japanese equivalent of blue, as in pornography
puriipeido kādo – literally, prepaid card; a magnetically coded card for a sum of money for use on telephone calls, train tickets etc.

Raijin – god of thunder
rakugo – performances of stand-up comedy or long tales; a traditional art that is dying out

robotayaki – *yakitori* and the like, served in a boisterous, homey, rustic atmosphere

roji – stone walking path in a Japanese garden

romaji – roman script, as used in English

rotemburo – open-air baths

ryokan – traditional Japanese inn

ryōri – cooking, cuisine (Kyoto cuisine is known as *kyō-ryōri*)

ryōtei – traditional-style, high-class restaurants; *kaiseki* is typical fare

sabi – a poetic ideal finding beauty and pleasure in imperfection; often used in conjunction with *wabi*

sakura - cherry blossoms

salaryman – male employee of a large firm

sama – even more respectful than *san*

samurai – Japan's traditional warrior class

san – a respectful suffix applied to personal names; similar to Mr, Mrs or Ms but more widely used

sanshō – Japanese three-spice powder

seiza – formal sitting position (on knees with legs tucked under the body)

sembei – soy-flavoured crispy rice crackers often sold in tourist areas

sen – line, usually railway line

sencha – a variety of green tea

sensei – teacher, but also anyone worthy of respect

sensu – folding paper fan

sentō – public bath

setto – set meal; see also *teishoku*

Shaka – the historical Buddha (Sanskrit: Shakyamuni)

shakuhachi – wooden flute-like instrument

shamisen – a three-stringed, banjo-like instrument

shi – city (to distinguish cities with prefectures of the same name)

shibui – an aesthetic atmosphere of restrained elegance

shidare-zakura – a weeping cherry tree

shin – new

shinkaisoku – special rapid train

shinkansen – bullet train (literally, new trunk line)

Shintō – the indigenous Japanese religion

shodō – Japanese calligraphy; literally, the way of writing

shōgun – military ruler of pre-Meiji Japan

shojin-ryōri – Zen vegetarian cooking

shokudō – Japanese-style cafeteria/cheap restaurant

shukubō – temple lodging

soba – buckwheat noodles

sumi-e – black ink-brush paintings

sumō – Shintō-derived form of wrestling in which participants attempt to force each other out of a ring or to the ground

taiko – traditional Japanese drums

tako – traditional Japanese kite

tatami – tightly woven floor matting on which shoes should not be worn

tengu – long-nosed goblin

teishoku – a set meal in a restaurant

tera – temple (also *dera* or *ji*)

tokkyū – limited express train; faster than ordinary express (*kyūkō*)

torii – entrance gate to a Shintō shrine

tsukubai – stone water basin in gardens for washing hands before tea ceremony

ukiyo-e – wood-block prints; literally, pictures of the floating world

uranai – palm-reading

wabi – a Zen-inspired aesthetic of rustic simplicity

wagashi – traditional Japanese sweets that are served with tea

waka – 31-syllable poem

warikan – custom of sharing the bill (among good friends)

wasabi – spicy Japanese horseradish

washi – Japanese paper

water trade – the world of bars, entertainment and sex for sale

yakitori – grilled chicken etc on a stick

yakuza – Japanese mafia (also called bōryokudan)

yudōfu – tōfu cooked in hot water, common temple fare

yukata – like a dressing gown, worn for lounging after a bath; standard issue at *ryokan* and some budget business hotels

Zen – a form of Buddhism

zōgan – damascene ware

ACRONYMS

ANA – All Nippon Airways
IDC – International Digital Communication
ITJ – International Telecom Japan
JEE – Japan Environmental Exchange
JETRO – Japan External Trade Organization
JNTO – Japan National Tourist Organization
JR – Japan Railways
JTB – Japan Travel Bureau
KDD – Kokusai Denshin Denwa
KIX – Kansai International Airport

LDP – Liberal Democratic Party
MIPRO – Manufactured Imports Promotion Organization
MITI – Ministry of International Trade & Industry
NHK – Japan Broadcasting Corporation
NTT – Nippon Telegraph & Telephone Corporation
TIC – Tourist Information Center (usually referring to Kyoto Tourist Information Center)

Lonely Planet Guides by Region

Lonely Planet is known worldwide for publishing practical, reliable and no-nonsense travel information in our guides and on our Web site. The Lonely Planet list covers just about every accessible part of the world. Currently there are 16 series: Travel guides, Shoestring guides, Condensed guides, Phrasebooks, Read This First, Healthy Travel, Walking guides, Cycling guides, Watching Wildlife guides, Pisces Diving & Snorkeling guides, City Maps, Road Atlases, Out to Eat, World Food, Journeys travel literature and Pictorials.

AFRICA Africa on a shoestring • Botswana • Cairo • Cairo City Map • Cape Town • Cape Town City Map • East Africa • Egypt • Egyptian Arabic phrasebook • Ethiopia, Eritrea & Djibouti • Ethiopian Amharic phrasebook • The Gambia & Senegal • Healthy Travel Africa • Kenya • Malawi • Morocco • Moroccan Arabic phrasebook • Mozambique • Namibia • Read This First: Africa • South Africa, Lesotho & Swaziland • Southern Africa • Southern Africa Road Atlas • Swahili phrasebook • Tanzania, Zanzibar & Pemba • Trekking in East Africa • Tunisia • Watching Wildlife East Africa • Watching Wildlife Southern Africa • West Africa • World Food Morocco • Zambia • Zimbabwe, Botswana & Namibia
Travel Literature: Mali Blues: Traveling to an African Beat • The Rainbird: A Central African Journey • Songs to an African Sunset: A Zimbabwean Story

AUSTRALIA & THE PACIFIC Aboriginal Australia & the Torres Strait Islands •Auckland • Australia • Australian phrasebook • Australia Road Atlas • Cycling Australia • Cycling New Zealand • Fiji • Fijian phrasebook • Healthy Travel Australia, NZ & the Pacific • Islands of Australia's Great Barrier Reef • Melbourne • Melbourne City Map • Micronesia • New Caledonia • New South Wales • New Zealand • Northern Territory • Outback Australia • Out to Eat – Melbourne • Out to Eat – Sydney • Papua New Guinea • Pidgin phrasebook • Queensland • Rarotonga & the Cook Islands • Samoa • Solomon Islands • South Australia • South Pacific • South Pacific phrasebook • Sydney • Sydney City Map • Sydney Condensed • Tahiti & French Polynesia • Tasmania • Tonga • Tramping in New Zealand • Vanuatu • Victoria • Walking in Australia • Watching Wildlife Australia • Western Australia
Travel Literature: Islands in the Clouds: Travels in the Highlands of New Guinea • Kiwi Tracks: A New Zealand Journey • Sean & David's Long Drive

CENTRAL AMERICA & THE CARIBBEAN Bahamas, Turks & Caicos • Baja California • Belize, Guatemala & Yucatán • Bermuda • Central America on a shoestring • Costa Rica • Costa Rica Spanish phrasebook • Cuba • Cycling Cuba • Dominican Republic & Haiti • Eastern Caribbean • Guatemala • Havana • Healthy Travel Central & South America • Jamaica • Mexico • Mexico City • Panama • Puerto Rico • Read This First: Central & South America • Virgin Islands • World Food Caribbean • World Food Mexico • Yucatán
Travel Literature: Green Dreams: Travels in Central America

EUROPE Amsterdam • Amsterdam City Map • Amsterdam Condensed • Andalucía • Athens • Austria • Baltic States phrasebook • Barcelona • Barcelona City Map • Belgium & Luxembourg • Berlin • Berlin City Map • Britain • British phrasebook • Brussels, Bruges & Antwerp • Brussels City Map • Budapest • Budapest City Map • Canary Islands • Catalunya & the Costa Brava • Central Europe • Central Europe phrasebook • Copenhagen • Corfu & the Ionians • Corsica • Crete • Crete Condensed • Croatia • Cycling Britain • Cycling France • Cyprus • Czech & Slovak Republics • Czech phrasebook • Denmark • Dublin • Dublin City Map • Dublin Condensed • Eastern Europe • Eastern Europe phrasebook • Edinburgh • Edinburgh City Map • England • Estonia, Latvia & Lithuania • Europe on a shoestring • Europe phrasebook • Finland • Florence • Florence City Map • France • Frankfurt City Map • Frankfurt Condensed • French phrasebook • Georgia, Armenia & Azerbaijan • Germany • German phrasebook • Greece • Greek Islands • Greek phrasebook • Hungary • Iceland, Greenland & the Faroe Islands • Ireland • Italian phrasebook • Italy • Kraków • Lisbon • The Loire • London • London City Map • London Condensed • Madrid • Madrid City Map • Malta • Mediterranean Europe • Milan, Turin & Genoa • Moscow • Munich • Netherlands • Normandy • Norway • Out to Eat – London • Out to Eat – Paris • Paris • Paris City Map • Paris Condensed • Poland • Polish phrasebook • Portugal • Portuguese phrasebook • Prague • Prague City Map • Provence & the Côte d'Azur • Read This First: Europe • Rhodes & the Dodecanese • Romania & Moldova • Rome • Rome City Map • Rome Condensed • Russia, Ukraine & Belarus • Russian phrasebook • Scandinavian & Baltic Europe • Scandinavian phrasebook • Scotland • Sicily • Slovenia • South-West France • Spain • Spanish phrasebook • Stockholm • St Petersburg • St Petersburg City Map • Sweden • Switzerland • Tuscany • Ukrainian phrasebook • Venice • Vienna • Wales • Walking in Britain • Walking in France • Walking in Ireland • Walking in Italy • Walking in Scotland • Walking in Spain • Walking in Switzerland • Western Europe • World Food France • World Food Greece • World Food Ireland • World Food Italy • World Food Spain **Travel Literature:** After Yugoslavia • Love and War in the Apennines • The Olive Grove: Travels in Greece • On the Shores of the Mediterranean • Round Ireland in Low Gear • A Small Place in Italy

Lonely Planet Mail Order

onely Planet products are distributed worldwide. They are also available by mail order from Lonely Planet, so if you have difficulty finding a title please write to us. North and South American residents should write to 150 Linden St, Oakland, CA 94607, USA; European and African residents should write to 10a Spring Place, London NW5 3BH, UK; and residents of other countries to Locked Bag 1, Footscray, Victoria 3011, Australia.

INDIAN SUBCONTINENT & THE INDIAN OCEAN Bangladesh • Bengali phrasebook • Bhutan • Delhi • Goa • Healthy Travel Asia & India • Hindi & Urdu phrasebook • India • India & Bangladesh City Map • Indian Himalaya • Karakoram Highway • Kathmandu City Map • Kerala • Madagascar • Maldives • Mauritius, Réunion & Seychelles • Mumbai (Bombay) • Nepal • Nepali phrasebook • North India • Pakistan • Rajasthan • Read This First: Asia & India • South India • Sri Lanka • Sri Lanka phrasebook • Tibet • Tibetan phrasebook • Trekking in the Indian Himalaya • Trekking in the Karakoram & Hindukush • Trekking in the Nepal Himalaya • World Food India **Travel Literature:** The Age of Kali: Indian Travels and Encounters • Hello Goodnight: A Life of Goa • In Rajasthan • Maverick in Madagascar • A Season in Heaven: True Tales from the Road to Kathmandu • Shopping for Buddhas • A Short Walk in the Hindu Kush • Slowly Down the Ganges

MIDDLE EAST & CENTRAL ASIA Bahrain, Kuwait & Qatar • Central Asia • Central Asia phrasebook • Dubai • Farsi (Persian) phrasebook • Hebrew phrasebook • Iran • Israel & the Palestinian Territories • Istanbul • Istanbul City Map • Istanbul to Cairo • Istanbul to Kathmandu • Jerusalem • Jerusalem City Map • Jordan • Lebanon • Middle East • Oman & the United Arab Emirates • Syria • Turkey • Turkish phrasebook • World Food Turkey • Yemen **Travel Literature:** Black on Black: Iran Revisited • Breaking Ranks: Turbulent Travels in the Promised Land • The Gates of Damascus • Kingdom of the Film Stars: Journey into Jordan

NORTH AMERICA Alaska • Boston • Boston City Map • Boston Condensed • British Columbia • California & Nevada • California Condensed • Canada • Chicago • Chicago City Map • Chicago Condensed • Florida • Georgia & the Carolinas • Great Lakes • Hawaii • Hiking in Alaska • Hiking in the USA • Honolulu & Oahu City Map • Las Vegas • Los Angeles • Los Angeles City Map • Louisiana & the Deep South • Miami • Miami City Map • Montreal • New England • New Orleans • New Orleans City Map • New York City • New York City City Map • New York City Condensed • New York, New Jersey & Pennsylvania • Oahu • Out to Eat – San Francisco • Pacific Northwest • Rocky Mountains • San Diego & Tijuana • San Francisco • San Francisco City Map • Seattle • Seattle City Map • Southwest • Texas • Toronto • USA • USA phrasebook • Vancouver • Vancouver City Map • Virginia & the Capital Region • Washington, DC • Washington, DC City Map • World Food New Orleans **Travel Literature**: Caught Inside: A Surfer's Year on the California Coast • Drive Thru America

NORTH-EAST ASIA Beijing • Beijing City Map • Cantonese phrasebook • China • Hiking in Japan • Hong Kong & Macau • Hong Kong City Map • Hong Kong Condensed • Japan • Japanese phrasebook • Korea • Korean phrasebook • Kyoto • Mandarin phrasebook • Mongolia • Mongolian phrasebook • Seoul • Shanghai • South-West China • Taiwan • Tokyo • Tokyo Condensed • World Food Hong Kong • World Food Japan **Travel Literature:** In Xanadu: A Quest • Lost Japan

SOUTH AMERICA Argentina, Uruguay & Paraguay • Bolivia • Brazil • Brazilian phrasebook • Buenos Aires • Buenos Aires City Map • Chile & Easter Island • Colombia • Ecuador & the Galapagos Islands • Healthy Travel Central & South America • Latin American Spanish phrasebook • Peru • Quechua phrasebook • Read This First: Central & South America • Rio de Janeiro • Rio de Janeiro City Map • Santiago de Chile • South America on a shoestring • Trekking in the Patagonian Andes • Venezuela **Travel Literature**: Full Circle: A South American Journey

SOUTH-EAST ASIA Bali & Lombok • Bangkok • Bangkok City Map • Burmese phrasebook • Cambodia • Cycling Vietnam, Laos & Cambodia • East Timor phrasebook • Hanoi • Healthy Travel Asia & India • Hill Tribes phrasebook • Ho Chi Minh City (Saigon) • Indonesia • Indonesian phrasebook • Indonesia's Eastern Islands • Java • Lao phrasebook • Laos • Malay phrasebook • Malaysia, Singapore & Brunei • Myanmar (Burma) • Philippines • Pilipino (Tagalog) phrasebook • Read This First: Asia & India • Singapore • Singapore City Map • South-East Asia on a shoestring • South-East Asia phrasebook • Thailand • Thailand's Islands & Beaches • Thailand, Vietnam, Laos & Cambodia Road Atlas • Thai phrasebook • Vietnam • Vietnamese phrasebook • World Food Indonesia • World Food Thailand • World Food Vietnam

ALSO AVAILABLE: Antarctica • The Arctic • The Blue Man: Tales of Travel, Love and Coffee • Brief Encounters: Stories of Love, Sex & Travel • Buddhist Stupas in Asia: The Shape of Perfection • Chasing Rickshaws • The Last Grain Race • Lonely Planet ... On the Edge: Adventurous Escapades from Around the World • Lonely Planet Unpacked • Lonely Planet Unpacked Again • Not the Only Planet: Science Fiction Travel Stories • Ports of Call: A Journey by Sea • Sacred India • Travel Photography: A Guide to Taking Better Pictures • Travel with Children • Tuvalu: Portrait of an Island Nation

LONELY PLANET

You already know that Lonely Planet produces more than this one guidebook, but you might not be aware of the other products we have on this region. Here is a selection of titles that you may want to check out as well:

Japan
ISBN 0 86442 693 3
US$25.99 • UK£15.99

Hiking in Japan
ISBN 1 86450 039 5
US$19.99 • UK£12.99

Japanese phrasebook
ISBN 0 86442 616 X
US$6.95 • UK£4.50

Lost Japan
ISBN 0 86442 370 5
US$10.95 • UK£5.99

Tokyo
ISBN 0 86442 567 8
US$14.95 • UK£8.99

Healthy Travel Asia & India
ISBN 1 86450 051 4
US$5.95 • UK£3.99

Read this First: Asia & India
ISBN 1 86450 049 2
US$14.95 • UK£8.99

Chasing Rickshaws
ISBN 0 86442 640 2
US$34.95 • UK£19.99

World Food Japan
ISBN 1 74059 010 4
US$13.99 • UK£8.99

Available wherever books are sold

Index

Text

Places to Stay

Places to Eat

Boxed Text

Legend:
- Eizan Line
- Hankyū Line
- San-in Main Line (Sagano Line)
- Tōkaidō Main Line
- Karasuma Line (Subway)
- Keifuku Line
- Keifuku Cable Line
- Keihan Line
- Keihan Keishin Line
- Kintetsu Line
- Kosei Line
- Nara Line
- Tōkaidō Shinkansen Line
- Tōzai Line (Subway)

To Kurama/Kibune

Kyoto Seikadaimae 京都精華大前
Kino 木野
Iwakura 岩倉

Yaseyūen 八瀬遊園
Cable Yaseyūen ケーブル八瀬遊園
Cable Hiei ケーブル比叡
Ropeway Hiei ロープウェイ比叡
Ropeway Hiei Sanchō (Summit) ロープウェイ比叡山頂

Hachiman-mae 八幡前
Miyakehachiman 三宅八幡
Takagara-ike 宝ヶ池

Kokusai-kaikan 国際会館

Kitayama 北山
Matsugasaki 松ヶ崎
Shūgakuin 修学院

Kitaōji 北大路
Ichijōji 一乗寺
Chayama 茶山
Mototanaka 元田中

Kuramaguchi 鞍馬口
Imadegawa 今出川
Demachiyanagi (Eizan) 出町柳
Demachiyanagi (Keihan) 出町柳
Marutamachi 丸太町
Marutamachi 丸太町

Nijō 二条
Nijōjō-mae 二条城前
Karasuma-Oike 烏丸御池
Kyōto-Shiyakusho-mae 京都市役所前
Sanjō Keihan 三条京阪
Higashiyama 東山

Yamanouchi 山ノ内
Sanjō Guchi 三条口
Omiya 大宮
Sanjō 三条
Keage 蹴上
To Shiga

Arashiyama 嵐山
Saiin 西院
Karasuma 烏丸
Misasagi 御陵
To Ishiyama

Matsuo 松尾
Sai 西院
Shijō 四条
Shijō 四条
Kawaramachi 河原町

Kamikatsura 上桂
Tanbaguchi 丹波口
Shijō-Omiya 四条大宮
Gojō 五条
Gojō 五条

Nishikyōgoku 西京極
Nishiōji 西大路
KYOTO STATION 京都
Shichijō 七条

Yamashina 山科
Shinomiya 四宮
To Nagoya & Tokyo

Higashino 東野
Nagitsuji 椥辻

To Osaka (Umeda)
Higashi Muko 東向日
Katsura 桂
Mukōmachi 向日町

Tōji 東寺
Kujō 九条
Tōfukuji 東福寺
Tobakaidō 鳥羽街道

Nishi Muko 西向日
Jūjō 十条
Jūjō 十条
Fushimi-Inari 伏見稲荷
Inari 稲荷
Ono 小野

Nagaokakyo 長岡京
Kamitobaguchi 上鳥羽口
Kuinabashi くいな橋
Fukakusa 深草
Daigo 醍醐

Takeda 竹田
Sumizome 墨染
JR Fujinomori JR藤森
Fujinomori 藤森

Fushimi 伏見
Momoyama 桃山

Fushimi-Momoyama 伏見桃山
Tanbabashi 丹波橋
Chūshojima 中書島
Momoyama-Goryōmae 桃山御陵前
Rokujizō 六地蔵

To Osaka (Yodoyabashi)
Yodo 淀
Kangetsu-kyō 観月橋
Momoyama-Minamiguchi 桃山南口
Kohata 木幡
Kohata 木幡
Obaku 黄檗
Obaku 黄檗

Mukaijima 向島
To Nara
To Uji

To Hozukyō & Kameoka

Kitano-Hakubaichō 北野白梅町
Hanazono 花園

Saga Arashiyama 嵯峨嵐山
Uzumasa 太秦
Katabira-no-Tsuji 帷子の辻
Uzumasa 太秦
Kaikonoyashiro 蚕ノ社

Arashiyama 嵐山
Rokuōin 鹿王院
Arisugawa 有栖川

Sagaekimae 嵯峨駅前
Kurumazaki 車折

MAP 1 – AROUND KYOTO

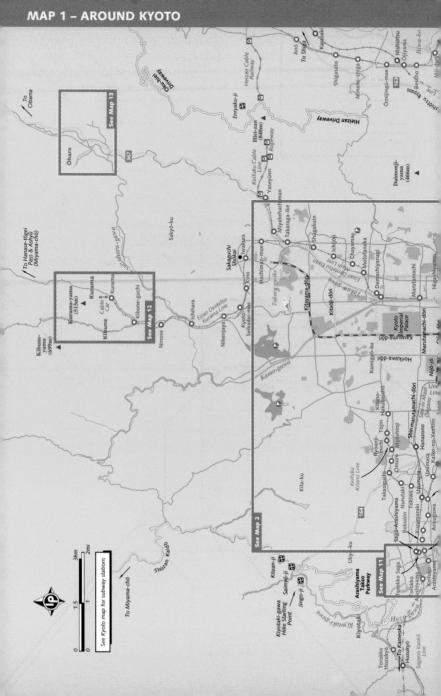

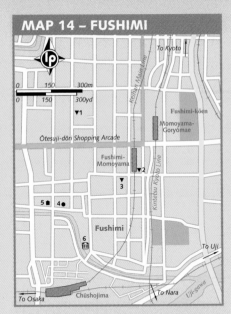

MAP 14 – FUSHIMI

PLACES TO EAT
1. Genya
   玄屋
2. Uosaburō
   魚三楼
3. Sancho
   サンチョ

OTHER
4. Kizakura Kappa
   Country
   カッパ天国黄桜酒
   場
5. Teradaya
   寺田屋
6. Gekkeikan Sake
   Ōkura Museum
   月桂冠大倉記念館

MAP 15 – UJI

PLACES TO EAT
1. Tsūen-jaya
   通圓茶屋
3. Kawamon
   川文
5. Taihō-an
   対鳳庵
6. Tsūen-jaya Annex
   通圓茶屋別館

OTHER
2. Uji Tourist
   Information Office
   宇治観光案内所
4. Byōdō-in
   平等院
7. Uji-jinja
   宇治神社
8. Ujigami-jinja
   宇治上神社

A collection of stone Buddhas at Kiyomizu-dera, a temple devoted to Jūichimen (11-headed Kannon).

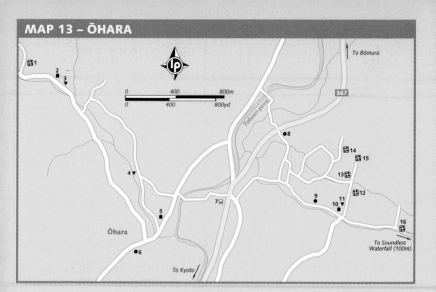

MAP 13 – ŌHARA

PLACES TO STAY
2 Ōhara Sansō
大原山荘
5 Ryosō Chadani
旅荘茶谷
10 Seryō Ryokan
芹生旅館

PLACES TO EAT
3 Kumoi-jaya
雲井茶屋
4 Tamba-jaya
たんば茶屋
11 Seryō-jaya
芹生茶屋

TEMPLES & SHRINES
1 Jakkō-in
寂光院
12 Sanzen-in
三千院
13 Jikkō-in
実光院
14 Hōsen-in
宝泉院
15 Shōrin-in
勝林院
16 Raigō-in
来迎院

OTHER
6 Ōhara Kōbō
大原工房
7 Ōhara Bus
Stop
大原バス停
8 Motoshiro
Washi
手すき和紙
もとしろ
9 Shibakyū
志ば久

A single red maple leaf provides a spot of colour on a steel man-hole cover.

FRANK CARTER

MAP 11 – ARASHIYAMA & SAGANO AREA

PLACES TO STAY
11 Rankyō-kan Ryokan
   旅館嵐峡館
16 Hotel Ran-tei
   ホテル嵐亭
17 Arashiyama Benkei
   Ryokan
   嵐山辨慶旅館
22 Arashiyama Lady's
   Hotel
   嵐山レディース
   ホテル
23 Minshuku Arashiyama
   民宿嵐山

PLACES TO EAT
2 Bokuseki
   木石
18 Kushi-tei
   串亭
19 Nakamuraya-no-
   Korokke
   中村屋のコロッケ

20 Seizansō-dō
   西山岫堂
21 Gyātei
   ぎゃあてい
24 Sunday's Sun
   サンデイズサン
26 Togetsu-tei
   渡月亭

TEMPLES & SHRINES
1 Adashino
   Nembutsu-ji
   化野念仏寺
3 Daikaku-ji
   大覚寺
4 Seiryō-ji
   清涼寺
5 Giō-ji
   祇王寺
6 Takiguchi-dera
   滝口寺
7 Nison-in
   二尊院

9 Jōjakkō-ji
   常寂光寺
10 Daihikaku Senkō-ji
   大悲閣千光寺
13 Nonomiya-jinja
   野宮神社
15 Tenryū-ji;
   Shigetsu
   天竜寺; 篩月
27 Hōrin-ji
   法輪寺

OTHER
8 Rakushisha
   落柿舎
12 Ōkōchi-sansō Villa
   大河内山荘
14 Tenryū-ji North
   Gate
   天竜寺北門
25 Convenience Store
   コンビニエンス
   ストア

MAP 12 – KURAMA & KIBUNE

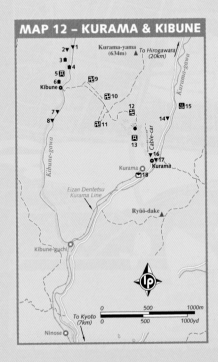

MAP 12 – KURAMA & KIBUNE

PLACES TO STAY
3 Ryokan Ugenta
   旅館右源太
4 Hiroya Ryokan
   京貴船ひろや
6 Kibune Fujiya
   貴船ふじや

PLACES TO EAT
1 Hirobun
   ひろ文
2 Nakayoshi
   仲よし
7 Tochigiku
   栃喜久
8 Beniya
   べにや
14 Shōsai-an
   匠済庵
16 Yōshūji
   雍州路
17 Aburaya
   -shokudō
   油屋食堂

TEMPLES & SHRINES
5 Kibune-jinja
   貴船神社
9 Okuno-in
   Maō-den
   奥ノ院魔王殿
10 Sōjō-ga-dani
   Fudō-dō
   僧正ガ谷不動堂
11 Ōsugi-gongen
   大杉権現
12 Kurama-dera
   鞍馬寺
13 Yuki-jinja
   由岐神社

OTHER
15 Kurama
   Onsen
   鞍馬温泉
18 Kurama Post
   Office
   鞍馬郵便局

1
2
3
Ishibei-kōji
4
5
6
7
8
Yasaka-dōri
9
10
11
Ninen-zaka
13
Higashiyama-ku
12
Kiyomizu-zaka
Sannen-zaka
Chawan-zaka
14
Gojō-dōri
Gojō-zaka
Start
15
16
1
Shibutani-dōri
Higashiyama Driveway
17
Tōkaidō Main Line (Biwako Line) & Kōsei Line
Tōkaidō Shinkansen Line
18
19
20
21

0   200   400m
0   200   400yd

········· Southern Higashiyama Walking Tour
------- Fushimi-Inari Hike

MAP 7 – AROUND KYOTO STATION

AROUND KYOTO STATION – MAP 7

Gion

Bukkōji-dōri

11

Takatsuji-dōri

13

Takakura-dōri

Sakaimachi-dōri

Yanaginobanba-dōri

Matsubara-dōri

Tominokōji-dōri

Fuyachō-dōri

Gokomachi-dōri

Kawaramachi-dōri

Takasegawa

Kiyamachi-dōri

Keihan Main Line

Kamogawa

Miyagawachō-dōri

14

15

16

1

18

...ji-dōri

...jō

Gojō

Gojō-dōri

Yamatoōji-dōri

19

Gojō
ōhashi

...kujō-dōri

Kawabata-dōri

Shōsei-en

21

Shichijō

22

Nara Line

Keihan Main Line

Higashiōji-dōri

...ji-dōri

Legend:
- 200 / 400m
- 200 / 400yd
- .... Fushimi-Inari Hike

Nishiōji

Tōfukuji

Finish

Kujō-dōri

Higashiyama-
bashi

Takeda Kaidō

Kawaramachi-dōri

Tobakaidō

A red Japanese umbrella in one of Kyoto's many gardens against a backdrop of blazing maple leaves.

MAP LEGEND

CITY ROUTES

Freeway .... Freeway	.... Unsealed Road
Highway .... Primary Road	.... One Way Street
Road .... Secondary Road	.... Pedestrian Street
Street .... Street	.... Stepped Street
Lane .... Lane	.... Tunnel
.... On/Off Ramp	.... Footbridge

REGIONAL ROUTES

.... Tollway, Freeway
.... Primary Road
.... Secondary Road
.... Minor Road

BOUNDARIES

.... International
.... Province
.... Disputed
.... Fortified Wall

HYDROGRAPHY

.... River, Creek	.... Dry Lake; Salt Lake
.... Canal	.... Spring; Rapids
.... Lake	.... Waterfalls

TRANSPORT ROUTES & STATIONS

.... JR Train	.... Cable Car, Chairlift
.... Shinkansen Train	.... Walking Trail
.... Private Train	.... Walking Tour
.... Underground Rail	.... Path
.... Metro	.... Pier or Jetty

AREA FEATURES

.... Building	.... Market	.... Beach
.... Park, Gardens	.... Sports Ground	.... Cemetery
		.... Campus
		.... Plaza

POPULATION SYMBOLS

CAPITAL .... National Capital	CITY .... City	Village .... Village
CAPITAL .... Provincial Capital	Town .... Town	.... Urban Area

MAP SYMBOLS

.... Place to Stay	.... Place to Eat	.... Point of Interest

.... Airport	.... Hospital	.... Pass	.... Swimming Pool
.... Bank	.... Internet Cafe	.... Police Station	.... Telephone
.... Bus Terminal	.... Lookout	.... Post Office	.... Temple
.... Castle	.... Monument	.... Pub or Bar	.... Theatre
.... Church	.... Mountain/Range	.... Shopping Centre	.... Toilet
.... Cinema	.... Museum	.... Shrine	.... Tourist Information
.... Golf Course	.... Onsen	.... Stately Home	.... Zoo

Note: not all symbols displayed above appear in this book

LONELY PLANET OFFICES

Australia
Locked Bag 1, Footscray, Victoria 3011
☎ 03 8379 8000 fax 03 8379 8111
email: talk2us@lonelyplanet.com.au

UK
10a Spring Place, London NW5 3BH
☎ 020 7428 4800 fax 020 7428 4828
email: go@lonelyplanet.co.uk

USA
150 Linden St, Oakland, CA 94607
☎ 510 893 8555 TOLL FREE: 800 275 8555
fax 510 893 8572
email: info@lonelyplanet.com

France
1 rue du Dahomey, 75011 Paris
☎ 01 55 25 33 00 fax 01 55 25 33 01
email: bip@lonelyplanet.fr
www.lonelyplanet.fr

World Wide Web: www.lonelyplanet.com *or* AOL keyword: lp
Lonely Planet Images: lpi@lonelyplanet.com.au